PRENTICE HALL

Health

SKILLS FOR WELLNESS

Third Edition

PRENTICE HALL
Glenview, Illinois • Needham, Massachusetts • Upper Saddle River, New Jersey

Program Components

Student Edition
Student Edition (soft cover)
Teacher's Edition
Teacher's Desk Reference
Teacher's Resource File
Health Update Newsletter
Human Sexuality
Human Sexuality, Teacher's Edition
English and Spanish Lesson
    Summaries

Skills for Physical Fitness
Classroom Manager
Student Activity Workbook
Product Testing Activities by *Consumer Reports*
Color Transparencies
Computer Test Bank with Dial-A-Test™
Self-Assessment Software
Videos
Web Site: www.phschool.com

**Prentice Hall dedicates this book to the good health of the youth of our world—
they are the future.**

Grateful acknowledgment is made to the following publishers for permission to reprint:

p. 6 "Illness-Wellness Continuum," adapted with permission from Travis and Ryan, *Wellness Workbook*, Berkeley, Ten Speed Press, 1977, 1981, 1988.

Credits continue on page 751.

ISBN 0-13-052126-4 (Student Edition, hardcover)
ISBN 0-13-052125-6 (Student Edition, softcover)
   3 4 5 6 7 8 9 10   03 02 01 00

Staff Credits

Editorial:

Natania Mlawer
Julia Fellows Osborne
Barbara Reber
Lois Teesdale

Marketing: Joel Gendler

Design: Linda D. Johnson
Paul Gagnon

Production: Barbara Albright
Janet Fauser
Elizabeth A. Good
David Graham
Robin L. Tiano
Kira Thaler
Pearl B. Weinstein

**On-line Services/
    Multimedia Department:** Gabriella Della Corte
Joanne Hudson
Cindy Noftel
Helen Young

Photo Research: Russell Lappa

Contributing Writers

Carol Bershad
Health Consultant
Natick, MA

Howard Portnoy
Health Writer
New York, NY

'Laine Gurley-Dilger
Biology Instructor
Rolling Meadows High School
Rolling Meadows, IL

Authors

B. E. (Buzz) Pruitt, Ed.D.
Professor of Health Education
Texas A&M University
College Station, Texas

Kathy Teer Crumpler, M.P.H.
Health and Safety Supervisor
Onslow County Schools
Jacksonville, North Carolina

Deborah Prothrow-Stith, M.D.
Associate Dean for Faculty
  Development
Harvard School of Public Health
Boston, Massachusetts

Buzz Pruitt began his career in health education as a high school teacher in Lewisville, Texas. A graduate of the University of Texas, he holds a master's degree in counseling and guidance and a doctorate in education. Buzz has served as executive director for the Association for the Advancement of Health Education, and has been the editor of the *Journal of Health Education*. He has published widely in the field of health education, especially in the areas of curriculum development and substance-abuse prevention. He has received numerous professional honors, including the National Professional Service Award from the Association for the Advancement of Health Education.

Kathy Crumpler supervises the health and safety programs for the Onslow County Schools in North Carolina, where she is responsible for the development of health curricula, staff development, and guidance services. She has also served as the project coordinator for adolescent pregnancy prevention for the Onslow County Schools. Kathy holds a master's degree in public health education from the University of North Carolina at Chapel Hill and is a graduate of the expanded program in immunization and epidemiology at Johns Hopkins University. She has also served as a technical trainer in health for the Peace Corps in Central African Republic.

Dr. Prothrow-Stith is a nationally recognized expert in the field of violence prevention. As Commissioner of Public Health in Massachusetts, she established the first state office of violence prevention and expanded treatment programs for AIDS, drug rehabilitation, and other urban issues. In addition to her work as Dean, she is currently Director and Professor of the Division of Public Health Practice at Harvard. For her work in community health, she has been given eight honorary doctorates, the World Health Day Award, the Secretary of Health and Human Service Award, and a position on the National Commission on Crime Control and Prevention.

Teacher Advisory Panel

Jeffrey D. Adams
Instructional Manager, Health
  Education
J.A. Craig Senior High School
Janesville, WI

Leslie G. Belcher
Health Teacher
Needham High School
Needham, MA

Cheryl A. Bower
Assistant Principal
District Health Education Facilitator
Newberg High School
Newberg, OR

Karen E. Cox
Coordinator, Health and Physical
  Education
Fulton County Board of Education
Atlanta, GA

John Grant, Jr.
Health Education Supervisor
Somerset School Department
Somerset, MA

Robert Gulardo
Health Coordinator
Haverhill Public Schools
Haverhill, MA

Fred G. Jacobson
Department Chair, Physical
  Education and Health
L'Anse Creuse Public Schools
Macomb, MI

Jim Jordan
Health Teacher/Coach
Edison High School
San Antonio, TX

Carol G. Music
Department Chairperson for
  Health and Physical Education
Morrow High School
Morrow, GA

William H. Stern, CSCS
Director of Health and Physical
  Education
Half Hollow Hills Central School
  District
Dix Hills, NY

B. Ruth Theile
Health Teacher/Family Life
  Educator
Bowen High School, Chicago Board
  of Education
Chicago, IL

Content Reviewers

Marc J. Ackerman, Ph.D.
Professor
Wisconsin School of
  Professional Psychology
Milwaukee, WI

M. J. Adams, Jr., M.D.
Division of Birth Defects and
  Developmental Disabilities
Centers for Disease Control and
  Prevention
Atlanta, GA

Charlene Agne-Traub, Ph.D., CHES
Historian
American Volkssport Association
Burke, VA

Franca B. Alphin, M.P.H., R.D.
Nutrition Director, Duke University
  Diet and Fitness Center
Durham, NC

Penny E. Borenstein, M.D., M.P.H.
Maryland Department of Health
  and Mental Hygiene
Baltimore, MD

John Brick, Ph.D.
Associate Professor of Biological
  Psychology
Rutgers University
Center of Alcohol Studies
Piscataway, NJ

Patti O. Britton, Ph.D
Deputy Director
Sex Information and Education
  Council of the U.S.
New York, NY

Kenneth G. Castro, M.D.
Assistant Director for TB and HIV
Office of the Associate Director
  for HIV/AIDS
Centers for Disease Control and
  Prevention
Atlanta, GA

Nancy Darling, Ph.D.
Psychology Department
Temple University
Philadelphia, PA

Claudia Feldman
Head, Public Affairs Cluster
National Institute on Aging, NIH
Bethesda, MD

Jay A. Fishman, M.D.
Assistant Professor of Medicine
Harvard Medical School
Massachusetts General Hospital
Boston, MA

Emogene Fox, Ed.D.
Associate Professor
Department of Health Education
University of Central Arkansas
Conway, AR

Dawn Graff-Haight, Ph.D., CHES
Assistant Professor
Department of Health Studies
Portland State University
Portland, OR

Suzanne M. Jaax, M.S., R.D.
Research Dietitian
Baylor College of Medicine
Houston, TX

Deborah Kafka, M.P.H., CHES
Health Education Specialist
University of California
  Medical Center
Los Angeles, CA

Kate Lajtha, Ph.D.
Assistant Professor
Department of Biology
Boston University
Boston, MA

Michael Marsh
Environmental Engineer, U.S.
  Environmental Protection Agency
Boston, MA

Angela D. Mickalide, Ph.D.
Program Director
National SAFE KIDS Campaign™
Washington, DC

Peter C. Scales, Ph.D.
Director of National Initiatives
Center for Early Adolescence
University of North Carolina at
  Chapel Hill
Carrboro, NC

Lynne W. Scott, M.A., R.D.
Assistant Professor
Director, Diet Modification Clinic
Baylor College of Medicine
Houston, TX

Laurence Steinberg, Ph.D.
Professor of Psychology
Temple University
Ardmore, PA

John L. Sullivan, M.D.
Professor of Pediatrics
Program in Molecular Medicine
University of Massachusetts
  Medical School
Worcester, MA

Janet H. VanNess, M.S.P.H.
Director of Health Education
Massachusetts Institute of
  Technology
Medical Department
Cambridge, MA

Mary Vernon, M.D., M.P.H.
Medical Officer
Centers for Disease Control and
  Prevention
Atlanta, GA

Elizabeth V. Wheeler, Ph.D.
Instructor of Medicine
Division of Preventive and
  Behavioral Medicine
University of Massachusetts
  Medical Center
Worcester, MA

Helene Raskin White, Ph.D.
Associate Professor
Center of Alcohol Studies
Rutgers University
Piscataway, NJ

S. Elizabeth White, M.Ed., ATC
Instructional Design Specialist
American Red Cross
Arlington, VA

David A. Whittaker, D.M.D.
Instructor
College of Dental Medicine
Medical University of South
  Carolina
Charleston, SC

Multicultural Advisors

Gail Nordmoe, Ed.D.
Assistant Superintendent
Danbury Public Schools
Danbury, CT

Bernardo Ortiz de Montellano, Ph.D.
Professor, Department of Anthropology
Wayne State University
Detroit, MI

CONTENTS

UNIT 2 Social Health

UNIT 3 Human Development

UNIT 4 Nutrition and Fitness

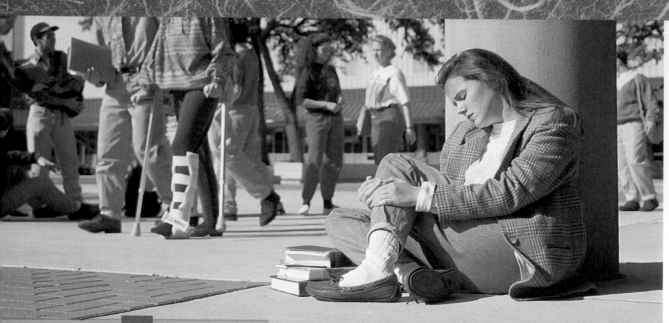

UNIT 5 Substance Abuse

UNIT **8** Safety and First Aid

FEATURES

BUILDING HEALTH SKILLS

Students can practice these skills with the Sharpen Your Skills features which appear frequently throughout the book.

DECIDE

MYTHS & FACTS

ACTIVITY

DIFFERENT VOICES SPEAKING

▶▶ BREAKTHROUGH ▶▶

Focus on Issues

CONNECTION

CAREERS

MAKING HEALTHY CHOICES

A day of skating with friends makes you feel alive with energy. More than anything else, the choices you make each day allow you to enjoy life to its fullest. In this chapter, you will find out how your lifestyle affects how you feel now and in the future. You will learn how you can choose a lifestyle that will keep you feeling fit, healthy, energetic, and happy.

CHAPTER PREVIEW

1-1 What Are Health and Wellness?

- Define the terms *health* and *wellness*.

1-2 Identifying Health Risks

- Identify risk factors that can affect a person's health.

1-3 Taking Responsibility for Your Health

- Explain the relationship between current decisions and future wellness.

BUILDING HEALTH SKILLS

- Identify a strategy for responsible decision-making.

CHECK YOUR WELLNESS

Your level of wellness is high if you can answer *yes* to the following questions.

- Do you eat a balanced diet and avoid saturated fats?
- Do you exercise at least three times a week?
- Do you like yourself?
- Do you set aside time each day to relax?
- Do you avoid alcohol, tobacco, and other harmful drugs?
- Do you get about eight hours of sleep each night?
- Are there people with whom you can talk about the things that matter to you?
- Can you express your feelings in healthy ways?
- Do you use a safety belt and avoid riding with a driver who is using alcohol or other drugs?
- Are your decisions based on your own values and goals, rather than on those of your friends?

KEEPING A JOURNAL

Imagine that you are 90 years old and have led a happy life. Write a letter to future generations letting them in on the secrets for living a satisfying, healthy life.

Take it to the Net
www.phschool.com

1

GUIDE FOR READING

Focus on these questions as you read this lesson.

- What are the three aspects of overall health?
- What is the Illness-Wellness continuum?

SKILLS

- Activity: Wellness in the Balance

What is health? How can I tell if I am healthy? Can I control my own health? How can I influence my future health? You may have just begun to ask yourself questions like these. At one time you might have said that a healthy person is anyone who does not have a cold or some other illness. Now that you are older, you may realize that this definition does not include all the things that cause you to feel well or to be healthy.

Health Today

Recently the term *health* has come to have a wider meaning than it used to. It no longer means just the absence of illness. Today—and in this book—**health** means the well-being of your body, your mind, and your relationships with other people. This new concept of health is closely related to another term you may have heard—*quality of life*. **Quality of life** is the degree of overall satisfaction that a person gets from life.

Why has the emphasis of health shifted from the absence of disease to a broader focus on the quality of a person's life? One reason for this shift has to do with the length and conditions of life that people can now expect. Medical advances and improvements in sanitation have made it possible for people today to live longer, healthier lives. Imagine for a moment that you were born in this country in the year 1900. You could have expected, on average, to live until about the age of 47. In contrast, if you were born in the year 1990, you could expect to live to the age of 75.

Until recently, disease and other physical hardships made surviving into one's 40s quite an accomplishment. This is still true in parts of the world today, particularly in areas experiencing food shortages or violence. People living in such conditions are too busy trying to stay alive to be concerned about quality of life. But for many people, day-to-day survival is no longer

Figure 1-1 *People who are healthy find that their lives are rewarding.*

a major concern. Instead, these people can think about the future—how they will feel and what they can accomplish during their added years of life. These people are concerned not only about feeling good in the present but also about planning for a long lifetime of health.

Characteristics of a Healthy Person

Take a moment to reread the definition of health on the previous page. Notice that the definition includes three different aspects of well-being. **The three aspects of well-being that are important for overall health are physical health, mental health, and social health.**

PHYSICAL HEALTH   Physical health refers to how well your body functions. When you are physically healthy, you are able to carry out everyday tasks without becoming overly tired. You have enough energy to go to school, enjoy your spare time, and take care of your responsibilities at home. A healthy diet, regular exercise, adequate sleep, and proper medical and dental care are all important for physical health.

MENTAL HEALTH   Mental health refers to how good you feel about yourself and how well you cope with the day-to-day demands of your life. When you are mentally healthy, you like yourself for who you are. You recognize your achievements and learn from your mistakes. Taking time to relax, sharing your feelings with others, and trying new experiences are all important for mental health.

SOCIAL HEALTH   Social health refers to how well you get along with others. When you are socially healthy, you have loving relationships, respect the rights of others, and give and accept help. Building healthy relationships with family members, making and keeping friends, and communicating your needs to others are all important for social health.

WELLNESS Have you ever gotten a headache or stomachache when you were nervous about something? Do you lose your temper more easily when you feel tired or ill? If these experiences sound familiar, then you already know that the three aspects of health are interrelated. Look at Figure 1-2. Like three pieces in a jigsaw puzzle, your physical health, mental health, and social health are linked together in everything you do.

This broader view of health, in which overall health is seen as a combination of physical, mental, and social well-being, is known as **wellness**. People with a wellness view of health know that all three aspects of their health are of equal importance to their overall well-being. They regard wellness as an important goal. A **goal** is a result that a person aims for and works hard to reach. To achieve the goal of wellness, a person must work hard to improve all three aspects of health, rather than concentrating on a single aspect.

Figure 1-2 *Do you have a wellness view of health? If you do, then you know that physical, mental, and social well-being are all equally important to health.*

WELLNESS IN THE BALANCE

In this activity you will create a mobile that balances the three aspects of wellness.

Materials

	magazines
cardboard	glue
scissors	string
pen or pencil	tape

Procedure

1. Using scissors, carefully cut out a cardboard triangle that is about 8 inches on each side. Label the sides of the triangle "Physical Health," "Mental Health," and "Social Health."

2. Using the tip of a pen or pencil, carefully punch a small hole through the center of the triangle. Thread a piece of string through the hole, and then tie a knot.

3. Cut out about ten pictures from magazines showing activities that contribute to each of the three aspects of wellness—physical, social, and mental.

4. Glue each picture onto cardboard. Then tape a piece of string to the top of each picture. Tape the other end of each string to the appropriate side of the triangle.

5. Hang the mobile from the center string to see how well it balances.

Discussion

1. Describe each of the activities in your mobile and explain how it contributes to physical, social, or mental health.

2. How well did your mobile balance? In your life, are your physical, social, and mental wellness in balance? Explain.

3. Describe some things you could do to improve each of the three aspects of your overall wellness.

The Illness-Wellness Continuum

Think for a moment about your overall level of health—the total of your physical, mental, and social health. Now suppose that someone asked you this question: "Would you say that you are in perfect health or in poor health?" How would you answer? Like most people, you might not feel comfortable choosing either of the two options. You might wish that you had been given some choices in between.

Of course, most people think of health as more than just the extremes of illness and wellness. Try to picture a solid line that is white at one end, then light gray, gray, dark gray, and finally black at the other end. What you have just pictured is one type of continuum. A **continuum** (kun TIN yoo um) is a gradual progression through many stages between one extreme and another. In the example of the colored line, the extremes are white and black and the stages are the many shades of gray in between.

Figure 1-3 shows another continuum, called the Illness-Wellness continuum. The **Illness-Wellness continuum** is a model that illustrates the full range of health between the extremes of illness and wellness. Because the continuum includes the full range of health, each person's health status

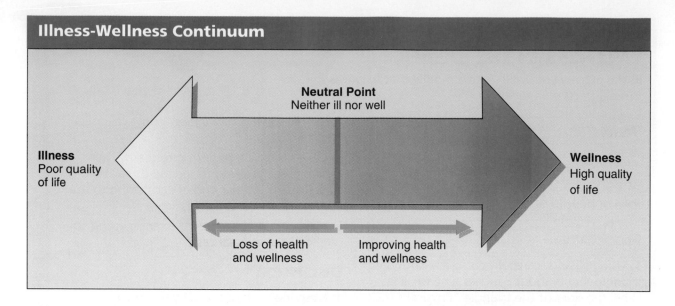

Illness-Wellness Continuum

Neutral Point
Neither ill nor well

Illness
Poor quality
of life

Wellness
High quality
of life

Loss of health
and wellness

Improving health
and wellness

Figure 1-3 *At what point along the continuum would you place yourself? How could you move closer to wellness?*

is marked by some point on the continuum. Which point on the continuum would you say best marks your current level of health?

Notice that on the Illness-Wellness continuum, shown above, you can move in either direction. As you move in one direction, you move toward illness; as you move the other way, you approach wellness. You can see also that there is a midpoint on the continuum. At this neutral point, you are not sick, but you are not enjoying the full benefits of overall health either.

At one time, many people in this country were satisfied just to be at the neutral point on the continuum. Then, people were much more concerned about avoiding illness and death than about improving the quality of their lives. Today, however, achieving a higher level of wellness and a better quality of life is possible for many people in this country. More than ever before, individual choices control where a person falls on the Illness-Wellness continuum.

LESSON **1** REVIEW

1. Name and briefly describe the three aspects of overall health.
2. Describe what is meant by a wellness view of health.
3. What is the Illness-Wellness continuum?

What Do You Think?

4. What are two ways you could improve your physical health? Your mental health? Your social health?

2 IDENTIFYING HEALTH RISKS

GUIDE FOR READING

Focus on these questions as you read this lesson.

- What types of risk factors can affect a person's health?
- Why is it important to weigh the risks of any action against its benefits?

SKILLS

- Analyzing Risks and Benefits

Suppose that a good friend came up to you and said, "A group of us are going swimming tonight at the lake after dark. Be ready at eight—I'll pick you up." What would you do? Would you go along without giving things a second thought? Or would you stop and think about the risks involved?

Most of the decisions you face each day involve risks. Like the risks involved in swimming at night, many risks are within your control. Other risks, like some you will read about, are not within your control. Both of these types of risks are important to your overall health. Perhaps more than anything else, the risks you face determine where on the Illness-Wellness continuum you fall.

What Is a Risk Factor?

When scientists talk about risks that people face, they use the term *risk factor*. A **risk factor** is any action or condition that increases the likelihood of injury, disease, or other negative outcome. Swimming after dark is a risk factor for injury because the chances are high that injury may result. Using tobacco is a risk factor for disease because the chemicals in tobacco can cause cancer as well as heart and respiratory diseases. Can you name some other common risk factors in teenagers' lives?

Figure 1-4 *Every activity involves a degree of risk. How can these people lessen their risks?*

For a moment, imagine a teenager who has many of the risk factors you just named. Then, look back at the Illness-Wellness continuum in Figure 1-3. Where on the continuum would that person be? Most probably the person would find himself or herself near the illness end of the continuum. A teen with few of the risk factors, on the other hand, might be closer to the wellness end of the continuum. Like chains that hold you back, risk factors can keep you from achieving wellness.

Many different risk factors can affect a person's health. **These risk factors fall into three categories—hereditary risk factors, environmental risk factors, and behavioral risk factors.** As you read about each type of risk factor, think about which factors can be avoided and which cannot.

Hereditary Risk Factors

To some extent, a person's level of health is already determined at the time he or she is born. This is because a person's **heredity,** all the traits that are passed biologically from parent to child, can affect health in many ways.

Inherited traits determine such things as a person's eye color, height, and build. Inherited traits also determine whether a person will be affected by certain disorders and disabilities. A **disability** is any physical or mental impairment that limits or reduces a person's ability to participate in normal activities. One example of an inherited condition that leads to a disability is muscular dystrophy–a disorder that causes a person's muscles to deteriorate gradually. Inherited conditions such as muscular dystrophy are unavoidable by the individuals who inherit them. Such conditions limit the level of wellness that a person can achieve.

Other hereditary risk factors, such as tendencies toward high blood pressure, breast cancer, diabetes, or other diseases, do not cause problems by themselves. In such cases the disease may never develop unless certain other risk factors are also present. For example, some people inherit a tendency toward high blood pressure, a condition that contributes to heart disease. If these people are aware of their condition, they can control their blood pressure by watching their diet, exercising, taking medication, and avoiding tobacco and alcohol. Their actions will allow them to lead long and healthy lives in spite of this inherited tendency. Most hereditary risk factors, then, need not prevent people from enjoying a high quality of life. The choices that people make every day may be more important than heredity in maintaining, harming, or improving their wellness.

Figure 1-5 *To stay healthy, a person who has inherited a tendency toward high blood pressure should exercise regularly.*

Figure 1-6 *Water pollution and cigarette smoke are two health threats in the outdoor and indoor environment.*

Environmental Risk Factors

Unlike hereditary risk factors, environmental risk factors originate in a person's environment, not in his or her body. **Environment** is all of the physical and social conditions surrounding a person and the influences they have on the person. Many environmental risk factors can be avoided. Others may be parts of a person's surroundings that are difficult or impossible to avoid.

PHYSICAL ENVIRONMENT Your physical environment includes both your outdoor and indoor surroundings. You can probably think of many ways that your outdoor surroundings affect your health. You know that the quality of the air you breathe and the water you drink is important to your health. Radiation from the sun and other sources, poisonous wastes, disease-causing organisms, and loud noise are other environmental risk factors of which you may be aware.

Recently, much attention has been given to risk factors that may be part of the indoor environment—homes, schools, factories, offices, and other places where people spend a lot of time. Suppose, for example, that you work after school in a smoke-filled restaurant. Repeated exposure to the chemicals in tobacco smoke can put you at risk for cancer and other diseases. Other substances such as radon, asbestos, lead, and carbon monoxide, when present indoors, can also have serious health effects.

If you are aware of the environmental risk factors you face, you can take steps to protect yourself from some of them. You can, for example, avoid swimming in polluted waters, wear sunscreen for protection against the sun's rays, and keep your radio's volume at less-than-harmful levels. You can stay informed of recent research findings about indoor and other environmental pollutants. Your own knowledge and behavior can help make your physical environment safer.

SOCIAL ENVIRONMENT Your environment is made up of more than just your physical surroundings. The people around you—your family, friends, classmates, and other people you spend time with—make up another part of your environment, your social environment.

When you were a child, your family was the major part of your social environment. Family members strongly influenced your feelings about yourself, your beliefs, and your ideas of how to get along with others. In addition, they taught you many health habits. Some health habits, such as washing your hands before eating, are so basic that you do not even think about them anymore. Other health habits, such as sharing your feelings with others or eating healthy meals, may still be goals you are working toward.

As you grew older, your social environment expanded to include friends, neighbors, schoolmates, teachers, and other people in your life. For most teenagers, friends can have a great influence on their level of wellness. Friends who practice dangerous or unhealthy behaviors can put a lot of pressure on you to do the same. It is sometimes difficult to stand up to that kind of pressure. Selecting friends who show concern for their own health and yours can make it easier for you to avoid health risks.

CULTURE One important part of a person's social environment is his or her culture. **Culture** is the beliefs and patterns of behavior that are shared by a group of people and passed from generation to generation. The group may be a nation, a region of a country, or an ethnic group. Culture includes language, food preferences, attitudes, traditions, religion, and more. Sometimes you are not even aware of the characteristics of your culture until you come in contact with

Figure 1-7 *The culture in which you live can influence your health in many ways.*

another culture. You may not be aware that you speak with an accent, for example, until you visit an area where people speak differently. In some cultures it is rude to take off your shoes when visiting someone else's house; in other cultures it is rude not to. In some cultures people eat little or no meat; in others meat is central to the diet. This last example illustrates that cultural practices can have an important influence on a person's health. Can you think of other examples?

As you read this book, you will encounter many health goals that are in agreement with the beliefs and traditions of your culture. You may also, however, encounter health goals that conflict with your cultural practices. Suppose, for example, that the typical foods of your culture are much higher in fat than is recommended by nutritionists. Or perhaps your culture frowns on taking time for rest and relaxation. You may feel torn between wanting to do what is good for your health and wanting to follow your culture's traditions. It can be difficult to know how to handle such conflicts. Talking about these issues with family members or community leaders may help you find solutions that are right for you.

Behavioral Risk Factors

While both hereditary and environmental risk factors are important to health, the decisions you make each day are often far more important. Should you go swimming with friends after dark? Should you start to smoke? Should you stay up all night to study? Depending on your answer to questions like these, you may or may not face some serious risk factors for health. These risk factors are called behavioral risk factors because they result from your actions and decisions. Unlike many other risk factors, you alone decide which behavioral risk factors you will face.

Figure 1-8 *Wearing a helmet while biking is one way to make a risky sport safer.*

Analyzing Risks and Benefits

Imagine that you are facing each of the decisions described below. List the possible risks and benefits associated with each situation, and then decide what you would do.

- Should you cheat on a final exam in a class that you are in danger of failing?
- Should you run for class president against a popular student?
- Should you go ice-skating with friends on a lake where the ice might be too thin?

Of course, most of the things you do each day involve some degree of risk. Without taking risks and trying new things, it would be impossible to grow as a person. How then can you decide which risks are worth taking and which are not? The key to making such important decisions is to take the time to weigh the risks against the possible benefits of the activity. Suppose, for example, that you are at your friend's house across town when you realize that your curfew is in five minutes. Should you drive fast to get home on time? Or, does the risk of serious injury outweigh the benefit of making it home on time? What would you do?

It is always worthwhile to think carefully about activities that involve risks before you do them. For some activities, there may be ways to make the activity safer and thus cut down on the risks. Mountain biking, for example, involves some risk of injury, but you can lessen your risks by wearing a helmet and by sticking to easy trails at first. By taking precautions like these, the benefits of this enjoyable and healthy activity may outweigh the risk.

Not all behavioral risk factors pose immediate threats to your physical safety. Instead, some health risks build over time. Suppose, for example, that you practically live on a fast-food diet. As you probably know, such foods are often high in fat, sugar, and salt. You may feel healthy and energetic now and pay little attention to people's concerns about your diet. Heart disease and other diet-related problems may seem too far in the future to worry about now. Suppose that you waited until you were older to care about your diet. Do you think it would be possible to undo the years of damage then? How difficult do you think it would be to change your eating patterns?

In thinking about behavioral risk factors, it is important not to overlook risk factors that can affect your mental and social health. Keeping anger and other strong feelings "bottled up" inside is one such risk factor. Not taking time to relax and have fun is another. By avoiding risk factors like these, you will be happier and healthier overall.

LESSON **2** REVIEW

1. What is meant by the term *risk factor*?
2. List the three types of risk factors that can affect a person's health. Give an example of each type.
3. Why is it important to weigh the risks of any action against its benefits?

What Do You Think?

4. Why do you think that teenagers face more behavioral risk factors than any other age group?

3 TAKING RESPONSIBILITY FOR YOUR HEALTH

GUIDE FOR READING

Focus on these questions as you read this lesson.

- Why is prevention the key to improving one's health?
- What steps are involved in the process of behavior change?

SKILLS

- Breaking a Bad Habit

Now is the time for you to start taking control of your own health. In the last few years, as you have become more physically and emotionally mature, you have begun to make many of the decisions that adults used to make for you. Who chooses your food or decides when you should go to bed? Who selects your friends and decides what to do with them? More and more often, the person making decisions for you is you.

Goals for the Years 2000 and 2010

Accepting responsibility for your health and making changes to improve it does not happen overnight. Perhaps, as you have been reading this chapter, you have recognized many of the positive ways you already safeguard your health. You may also have recognized some risk factors that you would like to change. How can you go about making healthy changes in your life? The United States has been facing this same question regarding the health of all our people.

HEALTHY PEOPLE 2000 For years, researchers for the United States Public Health Service have collected information about the health and health-related behavior of this nation's people. Figure 1-9 summarizes some of the statistics gathered for people aged 15 through 24. Examine the leading causes of death among this age group. Notice that none of the top causes of death are illness-related. Instead, they are tied to behavioral risk factors. Many of these deaths could be prevented if teenagers modified some of the risky behaviors that often cause death.

Figure 1-9 *More than illness, behavioral risk factors threaten the lives of young people today. What risk factors may be associated with the leading causes of death?*

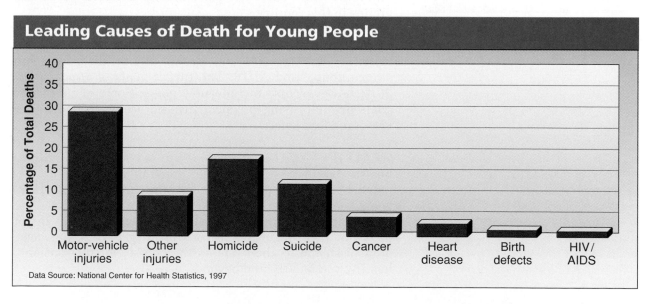

Leading Causes of Death for Young People

Percentage of Total Deaths

Motor-vehicle injuries · Other injuries · Homicide · Suicide · Cancer · Heart disease · Birth defects · HIV/AIDS

Data Source: National Center for Health Statistics, 1997

Some Target Goals of *Healthy People 2000*

Goal: Reduce by 48% the number of people who smoke cigarettes.
1995 Status: ⇑ There has been a 14% reduction in smoking.

Goal: Reduce by 12% the number of motor-vehicle deaths due to alcohol.
1995 Status: ⇑ There has been a 30% drop in alcohol-related motor-vehicle deaths.

Goal: Reduce by 30% the number of pregnancies among girls aged 17 and younger.
1995 Status: ⇓ There has been a 4.5% increase in the pregnancy rate among girls 17 and younger.

Goal: Reduce the homicide rate by 15%.
1995 Status: ⇓ The homicide rate has increased by 21%.

Goal: Double the number of people who use safety belts.
1995 Status: ⇑ There has been a 60% increase in the use of safety belts.

Goal: Reduce the number of deaths due to heart disease and stroke by 26% and 34%, respectively.
1995 Status: ⇑ The death rates have decreased by 15% and 13%, respectively.

Goal: Reduce the number of people infected by gonorrhea and syphilis by 25% and 45%, respectively.
1995 Status: ⇑ The infection rates for both gonorrhea and syphilis have decreased by 43%.

Key: ⇑ Right direction
     ⇓ Wrong direction

Figure 1-10 The Public Health Service tracked whether or not Americans were meeting the *Healthy People 2000* goals. The 1995 status report showed progress made at the halfway point.

Statistics collected from people of all ages showed the same trend: behavioral risk factors are at the root of many of this country's health problems. To confront these risky behaviors, the Public Health Service developed a plan called *Healthy People 2000*. The major goal of this plan was to prevent many of the deaths in this country by replacing risky behavior with healthy behavior. Within the overall plan, about 300 smaller target goals were identified. Notice that several of the *Healthy People 2000* target goals listed in Figure 1–10 show great improvement.

HEALTHY PEOPLE 2010   The success of *Healthy People 2000* was so encouraging that the Public Health Service started a new plan, *Healthy People 2010*. Hundreds of national and state health organizations worked together to develop this new plan. The focus on preventable health threats continues, but there is an additional goal: to reduce the health differences that currently exist among different population groups in this country.

Like the 2000 plan, *Healthy People 2010* includes small target goals that address familiar problems, such as tobacco use, violence, heart disease and stroke, mental disorders, substance abuse, and AIDS. The target goals of *Healthy People 2010*, however, also include new goals. Some of these new goals are improving physical fitness, access to health services, and food safety.

HEALTHY "YOU"   You, too, can set goals to eliminate health risk factors in your life. Some of your goals may be listed in the 2010 plan; some may be unique to you. Some goals, such as wearing a safety belt, can be put into effect immediately. Others, such as cutting down on the fat in you diet, may take longer. Whatever your target goals, your overall goal should be the same as the one set for this nation–a healthy you in 2010 and beyond.

Making Changes for Health

Have you ever tried to cut down on sweets, quit smoking, or make other healthy changes in your life? If so, then you know how difficult the process of changing a behavior can be. **Health professionals who have studied the process of behavior change point to four important steps— awareness, knowledge, decision-making, and applying skills.** This book is structured to help you through this step-by-step process of behavior change. The details are outlined below.

AWARENESS The process of behavior change always begins with awareness. A person must first recognize a potential health problem before anything can be done to change it.

Some health problems are easy to recognize. You know, for example, when you have twisted your ankle or are feeling run down. However, many other health problems, such as high blood pressure and depression, do not have such obvious signs. This is one reason why it is important to see a physician regularly. Physicians are trained to recognize early signs of illnesses of which you might not be aware. They are also trained to help you identify risk factors that might put your future health in jeopardy.

To help you increase your level of awareness about your health, each chapter in this book begins with a checklist called Check Your Wellness. Take some time to complete the checklist at the beginning of this chapter. How well did you do? Did the inventory help you recognize risk factors in your life? Did it also leave you wishing you knew more about some health topics?

KNOWLEDGE Once a person becomes aware of a health problem, the next step involves learning some of the facts about it. In the field of health, knowledge is growing every day. New discoveries and research studies appear in the news all the time. But are some sources of health information more reliable than others? How can you sort out the information that might be important to your life?

This book gives you a good foundation of health-related knowledge. It also suggests ways in which you can evaluate other health information you receive. It is up to you to stay informed about new findings that may affect your health. The process of updating your knowledge is one you will need to continue throughout your life.

Figure 1-11 *Your health class can give you a solid foundation of health information. You will need to update your knowledge throughout your life.*

DECISION-MAKING Even with awareness and knowledge, it is not always easy to decide on the best course of action. As you already know, most actions have both risks and benefits, and you must decide which one outweighs the other. Suppose, for example, that you were an inexperienced canoeist invited to go on a canoe trip down a difficult river. Your best friend, a great canoeist, would not be able to go on the trip if you did not go. Add some more complications, such as bad weather or an upcoming exam for which you need to study. How would you decide what to do?

Awareness of your own abilities is essential in this situation. Knowledge of the dangers of canoeing in bad weather is also important. But what about your friend or your exam? Here you must consider your **values**, the standards and beliefs that are most important to you. You may value friendship, but you may value your own and your friend's safety more. You may also value doing well in school, and know that your parents do too. Your decisions not only affect you, they affect other important people in your life.

The DECIDE process described in the Building Health Skills feature on page 18 provides a step-by-step procedure that can help you make difficult decisions. Look over the DECIDE process and review the steps. How could you apply these steps to the canoeing example?

APPLYING SKILLS What would you think of a baseball team that spent all its time thinking and learning about the game but never practiced? Do you think the team would win many games? Of course not. Many people think that knowing about healthy behaviors is enough to guarantee good health. This is not true. Like the baseball players, you have to practice. To have good health, you must be able to apply the healthy decisions you have made.

One quality a successful baseball player needs is skill. Awareness of natural talent, knowledge of the game, and a good choice of bat are not much good without the skill to hit a curve ball or lay down a bunt.

How do baseball players develop new skills? They usually begin by observing and analyzing their current behavior. Next they learn a new or better method of doing something. Then they practice and practice some more.

Just like the baseball player who works to change his or her swing, you may have some habits you wish to change. A **habit** is a pattern of behavior that has become automatic and is hard to change. Even though changing habits is difficult, however, you can break old habits by learning new skills. With practice, your new skills will become just as natural as the old habits were. The Building Health Skills features at the end of each chapter of this book can help you develop the skills you need to put healthy decisions into action. You will have many chances to practice your new skills, both in your own life and in the Sharpen Your Skills features like the one on this page.

Achieving Health Literacy

With your increasing awareness, growing knowledge, sound decision-making, and practiced skills, you will have all the tools you need to make healthy changes in your life. The term **health literacy** describes a person's ability to gather and understand health information and then use the information to improve his or her health. A health-literate person might, for example, read up on the latest research into the dangers of high-fat diets. He or she might then use this information to cut down on fried foods or alter other unhealthy eating habits. Because health literacy involves translating information into action, skills play as important a role as knowledge. Knowing both *what* you should do and *how* to do it will empower you to reduce health risks and move toward wellness.

Figure 1-12 *The only way to master a skill is through practice.*

Looking Beyond Yourself

Throughout this chapter, the focus has been on you—your health, your decisions, and your actions. It is important to remember, however, that your decisions and actions can affect others beyond yourself. Family members, friends, acquaintances, strangers, and even future generations can all be affected by the decisions you make.

Considering the effects of your behavior on others as well as on yourself is a sign of maturity. A mature person may advocate for the health of others by encouraging them to act responsibly. A health advocate also works to make his or her community a healthier place in which to live. You can make a big difference in the health of those around you. The best time to start is now.

LESSON 3 REVIEW

1. What are the three most common causes of death for young people today? Which type of risk factor is associated with all three?
2. Define the term *prevention*. Why is prevention an important goal of *Healthy People 2000*?
3. What are the four steps involved in the process of behavior change?
4. Define the term *values*. List three values that are important to you.

What Do You Think?

5. How would you try to convince a friend to take better care of his or her health?

Making a Decision

Suppose you had to make this decision: You've just found the perfect after-school job. It's near home, it's fun to do, and it will pay for the bicycle you need for your bicycling trip next summer. Then you make the basketball team that you've tried out for three times. Unfortunately, the team practices during the same hours as your job. How should you choose between the team and the job?

Although many of your decisions are not this complicated, you sometimes face even harder ones. Such decisions require much thought and soul-searching because they can make important differences in your life. Do you sometimes "hide from" tough choices because they make you feel anxious? Do you ever rush headlong into decisions without really thinking them through? There is a process, called DECIDE, that makes decision-making easier. This process is simple to remember because each letter in the word DECIDE stands for a step in the process.

The steps of the DECIDE process are described here. You will be given opportunities to practice DECIDE in many chapters throughout this book.

D efine the problem

Look carefully at the decision you are facing, and state the issue clearly. Is it important and complex enough to warrant using DECIDE? Some choices are so easy that you already know what to do. In other situations, your decision won't really make much difference—a flip of a coin would do.

E xplore the alternatives

Make a list of all possible alternatives for solving your problem. Be sure to include "doing nothing" if it is appropriate. If you need more information to fully understand the problem or any of the alternatives, do the research now. You may find that some of the choices are unrealistic. If so, do not include them.

C onsider the consequences

One by one, think through what might happen if you were to choose each alternative you listed. Include both the positive and negative results. Consider what probably would happen, not what you hope would happen. Ask yourself: How risky is

each alternative? What are its chances of success? How would it affect my future? Remember to consider the effects on other people as well.

Identify your values

Your values, the things you believe in strongly, affect how you live your life and how you feel about yourself. Sometimes your values influence your decisions even when you are not aware of them. At other times, you may overlook your values because you want something badly. When you do this, however, you may feel uncomfortable with your decision later.

In thinking about your values, consider your long-term goals as well as the beliefs of your family, religion, and community. Consider your own and others' health and safety, and your self-respect. Which choice is most in line with your values?

Decide and act

Use the information you have collected to compare each of the alternatives. Decide which one is best for you. Remember, sometimes there is more than one "right" choice.

Act on your decision by breaking it down into smaller steps and setting realistic deadlines for each step. Then follow through with your plan.

Evaluate the results

Sometime after you have put your decision into effect, take some time to review it. How did your decision work out? How has it affected your life? How has it affected others? What did you learn? If you could do it over again, what would you do differently? If you can still change some things for the better, do it now.

Apply the Skill

1. Imagine that you face the decision introduced at the beginning of this feature—to choose the job or the team. Follow the steps of DECIDE to determine what you would do in this situation. Be sure to consider all alternatives; there may be more than two. (For example, it may be possible to postpone a choice or to take another route to a goal.)

2. List other important decisions for which DECIDE might be useful. Do they fall into categories? What categories of decisions might not be suitable for DECIDE?

3. Write about a situation in which a person faces a complicated decision. Include enough information about the problem to show that it is a tough choice. Then use DECIDE to work through the decision-making process.

4. Think about a tough decision that you have made in the past or that you are facing now. Use DECIDE to determine what you should do (or should have done).

Did DECIDE help you focus on important values or choices you might otherwise have overlooked? Which ones? Did DECIDE make the decision-making process easier? Why or why not?

CHAPTER 1 REVIEW

KEY IDEAS

LESSON 1

- Health is the well-being of your body (physical health), mind (mental health), and relationships (social health).

- A person's level of wellness can be illustrated on the Illness-Wellness continuum. As you move in one direction, you move toward illness. In the other direction, you move toward overall wellness.

LESSON 2

- Hereditary risk factors include some disorders, disabilities, and tendencies toward illnesses. Environmental risk factors originate in a person's physical and social surroundings.

- Behavioral risk factors have the strongest influence on a person's level of wellness. It is important to analyze the risks and benefits of an activity before doing it.

LESSON 3

- The key to health is prevention—practicing behaviors that keep one free of health problems. People can set goals to eliminate the behavioral risk factors in their lives.

- The process of changing a poor health behavior involves increasing one's self-awareness, acquiring knowledge, making healthy decisions, and practicing and applying health skills.

KEY TERMS

LESSON 1	LESSON 2	LESSON 3
continuum	culture	habit
goal	disability	health literacy
health	environment	prevention
Illness-Wellness continuum	heredity	values
quality of life	risk factor	
wellness		

Listed above are some of the important terms in this chapter. Choose the term from the list that best matches each phrase below.

1. the practice of healthy behaviors that keep a person free of disease and other problems

2. all of the physical and social conditions surrounding a person and the influences they have on the person

3. the well-being of a person's body, mind, and relationships with other people

4. a model that illustrates the full range of health between illness and wellness

5. the standards and beliefs that are most important to a person

6. any action or condition that increases the likelihood of injury, disease, or other negative outcome

7. all the traits that are passed biologically from parent to child

8. a pattern of behavior that has become automatic and is hard to change

9. beliefs and patterns of behavior that are shared by a group of people and passed from generation to generation

10. a result that a person aims for and works hard to reach

11. the degree of overall satisfaction that a person gets from life

12. a physical or mental impairment that limits or reduces a person's ability to participate in normal activities

WHAT HAVE YOU LEARNED?

If the statement is true, write "true." If it is false, change the underlined word or words to make the statement true.

13. <u>Social</u> health refers to how well a person's body is functioning.

14. A <u>wellness</u> view of health recognizes that overall health is a combination of physical, mental, and social well-being.

15. <u>Environmental</u> risk factors are passed biologically from parent to child.

16. A person's <u>physical</u> environment includes both outdoor and indoor surroundings.

17. Deciding not to wear a safety belt is an example of a <u>behavioral</u> risk factor.

18. <u>Culture</u> includes traditions, language, food preferences, and religion.

19. It is important to weigh the risks of any activity against the <u>habits.</u>

20. In the decision-making process, a person must consider the important <u>values</u> that he or she holds.

Answer each of the following with complete sentences.

21. What is meant by the term *quality of life*?

22. Give an example of how the three aspects of well-being are interrelated.

23. What is the relationship between risk factors and the Illness-Wellness continuum?

24. How can hereditary risk factors affect your overall level of health?

25. List three possible health hazards in the physical environment. Explain how you can protect yourself from them.

26. List three behavioral risk factors that can result in death.

27. Describe a situation in which a risk is worth taking and explain why.

28. How can a physician help you increase your awareness about your health?

29. List two good sources and one poor source of health information.

30. Explain how values can affect a health-related decision.

WHAT DO YOU THINK?

31. Describe a problem you recently faced. Then explain how your physical, mental, and social health were affected by the problem.

32. Why do you think so many teenagers still smoke despite the health risks? What argument against smoking do you think would be effective for teens?

33. How does the saying, "an ounce of prevention is worth a pound of cure," apply to health?

34. Do you think that advertisements play a large part in influencing people to adopt unhealthy behaviors? Explain.

35. Give some thought to the term *quality of life*. What five elements do you think are most important to your quality of life? Why?

WHAT WOULD YOU DO?

36. You have a friend who lives on junk food and smokes cigarettes. He says he knows these behaviors are not harming him because he feels fine. What would you tell him?

37. What actions can you take now to promote your future well-being?

38. Your friends are drinking a liquid diet supplement instead of eating regular meals. When you ask about the diet, they give you the brochure that came with the supplement. How would you make a well-informed decision about this diet?

Getting Involved

39. Ask each person in your family to come up with his or her own definition of the term *health*. Together, list some ways you can help each other achieve health goals.

40. Find out about your school district's policy regarding smoking, drugs, physical education, or another health-related issue. Summarize your findings for your class. Discuss how the policy helps promote student health.

PERSONALITY AND SELF-ESTEEM

You've been looking forward to your party for weeks, but now you're feeling nervous. Glancing at yourself in the mirror, you relax when you see a confident person looking back. Feeling good about yourself is important for everything you do and for your overall health. In this chapter, you will explore how personality, self-esteem, and emotions affect your health.

CHAPTER PREVIEW

2-1 Personality and Mental Health

- Explain how personality contributes to mental health.

2-2 Theories of Personality

- Describe three theories that explain how personality forms.

2-3 Self-Esteem

- Identify ways to improve self-esteem.

2-4 Expressing Emotions

- Recognize emotions and express them in healthy ways.

BUILDING HEALTH SKILLS

- Practice expressing feelings in positive ways.

CHECK YOUR WELLNESS

How well do you know yourself? To find out, rate yourself on the personality traits below. (For example, if you fall midway between cautious and adventurous, give yourself a 4.) Then, ask 2 or 3 people who know you well to also rate you on these traits.

- Cautious   1 2 3 4 5 6 7   Adventurous
- Insensitive   1 2 3 4 5 6 7   Sensitive
- Calm   1 2 3 4 5 6 7   Anxious
- Excitable   1 2 3 4 5 6 7   Even-tempered
- Outgoing   1 2 3 4 5 6 7   Shy
- Suspicious   1 2 3 4 5 6 7   Trusting
- Imaginative   1 2 3 4 5 6 7   Practical
- Optimistic   1 2 3 4 5 6 7   Pessimistic

KEEPING A JOURNAL

Write about a situation in your past that demonstrated a personality trait of which you are proud.

Take it to the Net
www.phschool.com

GUIDE FOR READING

Focus on these questions as you read this lesson.

- What are the characteristics of a mentally healthy person?
- How does an individual's personality form?

SKILLS

- Being Assertive

Think about a party you have been to recently. Remember the different ways people were behaving. One person may have been the "life of the party." Perhaps some others enjoyed dancing, while yet another group of people held a quiet conversation. There might have been another person sitting quietly on the couch, watching the dancing and appearing not to have a care in the world.

Did you ever wonder why people act so differently in the same situation? It is because each person has a unique personality. Your **personality** consists of the unique combination of traits that make you an individual. These traits include behaviors, attitudes, feelings, and ways of thinking that are characteristic of you. For example, when you are introduced to new people, you may be characteristically outgoing or you may be shy. You may be easygoing and carefree, or you may worry a lot. You may get angry frequently or hardly ever. These traits are all part of your personality.

Describing Personality

How do you describe someone's personality? Here is how three teenagers described their own personalities:

Yoon: I have a lot of energy and make friends easily. I love sports and am very competitive. But if things don't go my way, I get upset and may lose my temper.

Richard: School doesn't interest me all that much, but I study enough to get by. Sometimes I don't feel like talking to people and prefer to be by myself. I like to stick to the things that I am used to doing.

Cory: I'm usually in a pretty good mood. Things don't bother me the way they do some people. If a problem comes up, I can usually figure out how to solve it. If not, I ask an adult or friend for help.

In describing their personalities, these teenagers chose the behaviors, feelings, and thoughts that best define the way they are. How would you describe your own personality? To answer this question think about the things you like to do and how you normally act.

- Would you say you are friendly and outgoing? This is called being an **extrovert** (EK struh vurt). Or are you more of an **introvert** (IN truh vurt), someone who is less outgoing and whose thoughts are directed inward?
- Are you an **optimist,** someone who focuses on the positive side of things? Or are you more of a **pessimist,** someone who looks at the negatives and expects the worst?

- Are you usually **assertive** (uh SUR tiv), able to stand up for yourself and express your feelings in a nonthreatening way? Or are you more **passive,** holding back your feelings and yielding to others, or **aggressive,** communicating your ideas and feelings in a forceful or threatening way?

What other personality traits would you use to describe yourself? Are you satisfied with the way you are? Which characteristics would you like to change?

The Healthy Personality

Look back at the descriptions of Yoon, Richard, and Cory. Which parts of their personalities would you consider healthy? Which parts would you consider unhealthy? Why?

When **psychologists** (sy KAHL uh jists), people who study the human mind and behavior, are asked to describe characteristics of a healthy personality, they often speak of mental health. **Mental health** is the state of being comfortable with yourself, with others, and with your surroundings. People who are mentally healthy are

- realistic about their strengths and weaknesses
- able to take on the responsibilities of daily living
- caring toward themselves and others
- able to handle disappointments and learn from them
- able to feel enjoyment and a sense of achievement

Psychologists like to think of mental health as a continuum, much like the Illness-Wellness continuum you read about in Chapter 1. Individuals can move toward the wellness end of the mental health continuum by developing the characteristics listed above. Psychologists have found some personality traits that are often associated with mental

Figure 2-1 *Your personality leads you to think and act in a way that is all your own.*

Figure 2-2 *Being happy and relaxed with yourself is a sign of mental health.*

health. **Mentally healthy people tend to be friendly, optimistic, and loving. They are also able to be assertive, laugh at themselves, try new experiences, and strive to do the best they can.** What other personality traits do you think are important for mental health?

How Is Personality Formed?

Some personality traits appear to be inborn. They are acquired by heredity, passing from parent to offspring just as hair color and eye color do. Other personality traits are shaped by a person's physical and social environment or surroundings. Most personality traits, however, are influenced by a combination of both heredity and environment.

HEREDITY   Why are some infants calm and cheerful while others tend to cry a lot? Why do some babies seem uncomfortable in new surroundings while others seem to thrive? These early differences are evidence that infants are born with distinct temperaments or tendencies to act in certain ways. In fact, even before birth some differences are evident. For example, some babies kick and move around a lot inside their mothers, while others are relatively quiet.

Psychologists are not sure how these early differences affect one's personality later in life. They are also not sure which personality traits are influenced by heredity and which are not. Some evidence indicates that traits such as shyness and aggressiveness may be inherited. It is also thought that talents, such as musical or artistic abilities, may be at least partly inherited. It is what you do with your inherited abilities, however, that determines how they will develop during your life.

ENVIRONMENT Although some early personality traits persist into adulthood, most are modified by a person's environment. Your friends, family members, school, and cultural group all affect your personality.

Experiences during childhood strongly influence the development of a healthy personality. A baby who is lovingly cared for learns to trust and love others. Children learn about feelings, attitudes, and appropriate ways of behaving from the people close to them. As children develop, they copy the behavior of others. This is called **modeling.** For example, a child may learn to be respectful of older adults by observing his or her parents' behavior toward the grandparents. Many family and cultural values are learned through modeling. Children also learn by being rewarded for desirable behaviors and punished for undesirable behaviors. A child who is repeatedly praised for trying to do new things for himself or herself is very likely to grow up self-reliant and willing to try new experiences.

Beginning with childhood and extending throughout the teenage years, friends, school, and community become increasingly important influences on personality. American teenagers spend more than half their time with other teens. These friends, who are about the same age and share similar interests, are known as a **peer group.** A peer group gives you a chance to learn about yourself and to get along with others. Being a part of a healthy peer group is likely to have a positive influence on your personality.

By young adulthood, your personality traits are fairly well established. This does not mean you cannot work to change personality traits with which you are dissatisfied. In fact, recognizing weaknesses and working to improve them is a sign of mental health. At the same time, it is important to recognize your strengths and achievements.

Figure 2-3 *Children learn family and cultural values by imitating their parents.*

LESSON 1 REVIEW

1. Define the term *personality*.
2. List five characteristics of mentally healthy people.
3. Explain how environment can influence personality.

What Do You Think?

4. Do you choose friends whose personality traits are similar to or different from yours? Why do you think that is so?

GUIDE FOR READING

Focus on this question as you read this lesson.

- How did Freud, Erikson, and Maslow believe that an individual's personality develops?

SKILLS

- Analyzing Advertising Appeal

People's personalities change as they grow and are exposed to new ideas, attitudes, and behaviors. Still, some basic personality traits stay the same throughout a person's life. Think back to when you were seven or eight. How has your personality changed since then? In what ways has it remained the same?

Psychologists have tried to explain how and why the human personality develops. These explanations are called theories. A **theory** (THEE uh ree) is an organized set of ideas used to explain something. **Three important theories of personality were proposed by Sigmund Freud, Erik Erikson, and Abraham Maslow.** As you read about these theories, keep in mind that their findings may not apply to all cultures of the world.

Figure 2-4 *According to Sigmund Freud, childhood experiences strongly influence personality.*

Freud

In the late 1800s, an Austrian physician named Sigmund Freud became interested in mental illness. From his work with the mentally ill, he concluded that each individual's personality is made up of three parts: the id, the ego, and the superego. The **id** consists of biological urges, such as hunger and thirst. The **ego** is the thoughtful, decision-making part of the personality. For example, if the id urged you to eat, the ego would help you find food. The **superego** is the part of the personality that judges right and wrong, or what you might refer to as your conscience. For example, the superego would direct you not to steal the food that your id urges you to eat.

According to Freud, people's minds operate at two levels of thought: conscious and unconscious. **Conscious** (KAHN shus) **thoughts** are those thoughts of which a person is aware. **Unconscious thoughts** are those of which a person is not aware. A forgotten childhood event is an example of an unconscious thought.

Freud believed that people often push unpleasant or frightening thoughts into their unconscious. These unconscious thoughts influence the individual's personality, even though he or she may not be aware of their effects. For example, a child who was unloved by a parent might, as an adult, be constantly searching for the approval of people in authority, people such as teachers or bosses. Such a person might seem overly obedient and anxious to please others.

To Freud's way of thinking, adult personalities are shaped mainly by early childhood experiences and conflicts. These memories are stored in the unconscious. Freud believed that by undergoing **psychoanalysis** (sy koh uh NAL ih sis), a treatment technique that brings memories into the conscious mind, the inner conflicts can be resolved.

Erikson

One follower of Freud, Erik Erikson, devised an eight-stage theory of personality development. Unlike Freud, Erikson believes that an individual's personality continues to be influenced by experiences beyond childhood. According to Erikson, people continue to develop socially and psychologically up until their death. Each phase of life has its own particular task to work on. If each task is accomplished in a satisfactory way, it has a positive effect on personality development. If, however, the task is not worked out in a satisfactory way, it has a negative effect on personality development.

Figure 2-5 outlines Erikson's theory of personality development. The first conflict that Erikson describes, that of trust versus mistrust, occurs during the first year of life. A

Figure 2-5 *In which of Erikson's stages is identity established? Independence?*

Erikson's Eight Stages of Development

Age	Stage	Important Task
Birth to 18 months	**Trust versus Mistrust** If cared for and loved, infant gains trust, views world as a safe place. Otherwise, mistrust and fear develop.	Feeding
18 months to 3 years	**Autonomy versus Shame/Doubt** Child learns bodily control—walking, talking, elimination. With encouragement, child gains confidence. Otherwise, inadequacy and doubt can result.	Toilet training
3 to 6 years	**Initiative versus Guilt** Child takes charge more, develops sense of right and wrong through play-acting. Self-worth grows, if encouraged. If not, low self-esteem and guilt can result.	Independence
6 to 12 years	**Industry versus Inferiority** Child accomplishes tasks and attempts new things. If encouraged, feels competent. If not praised, may feel like a failure.	School
12 to 19 years	**Identity versus Role Confusion** Teen seeks sense of self. Raises questions about sex, religion, role. If not resolved, confusion results.	Adolescence
Young Adulthood (20–40)	**Intimacy versus Isolation** Young adult develops close bonds with others, shares self. Otherwise suffers loneliness.	Love relationships
Middle Adulthood (41–64)	**Generativity versus Stagnation** Adult finds self-worth helping younger people. If self-absorbed, person lacks true satisfaction.	Parenting
Late Adulthood (65–death)	**Ego Integrity versus Despair** Older adult reflects on and accepts the life lived. Otherwise, approaches death with regret.	Reflections on life

Figure 2-6 *Learning about the things you value will help you establish your identity.*

SHARPEN YOUR SKILLS

Analyzing Advertising Appeal

Select an advertisement from a magazine aimed at teenagers. Why might the ad appeal to people involved in a search for identity?

young child who is cared for and loved learns to trust. The trusting child is likely to develop a secure personality.

The second conflict, that of self-control and independence versus lack of self-control and dependence, occurs during the second and third years of life. This is the time when children gain control over their own bodies. According to Erikson, children who are encouraged to become independent tend to develop confident personalities.

The third stage involves acquiring self-confidence. Between the ages of three and six, children explore who they are through fantasy play and imitating the behavior of others. They also develop a sense of right and wrong. Children who are encouraged to initiate activities on their own and to create fantasies tend to develop a sense of self-worth.

The fourth stage lasts until the teenage years; children learn how to accomplish real tasks. They learn how to help around the home, how to succeed at school, and how to get along with others. These skills make children feel competent. Without them, the child may feel like a failure.

The fifth stage is the one you are going through right now. According to Erikson, teenagers are concerned mainly with finding out who they are and what they want to do with their lives. Erikson calls this the search for **identity.** This search leads some teenagers to try new experiences and to behave in ways that differ from family teachings. Other teenagers focus on shaping their identities to go along with standards set by their families or communities. Often, the search for identity extends beyond the teenage years.

Look again at Figure 2-5. What is the next stage that you will be going through, according to Erikson? What conflict will you need to resolve during that stage?

Maslow

An American psychologist named Abraham Maslow theorized that everyone has a basic drive to achieve his or her fullest potential. Maslow used the term **self-actualization** to describe the process by which each person strives to be all that he or she can be. To define the characteristics of a self-actualized person, Maslow studied people who, in his view, had attained self-actualization. These people included Abraham Lincoln, Albert Einstein, Eleanor Roosevelt, and many others. Based on these studies, Maslow arrived at the list of ideal personality traits shown in Figure 2-7.

Maslow found that few people ever reach their full potential. He developed a theory to explain why. Maslow suggested that before people could achieve self-actualization, their basic needs had to be met. Maslow put these needs in an ascending order, called the **hierarchy of needs.** Notice that the hierarchy, shown in Figure 2–8, is a pyramid, with self-actualization at the top. At the base is what Maslow considered to be a person's most urgent needs: physical needs of the body. These include getting enough sleep, exercising, and satisfying hunger and thirst. If these basic needs are not met, a person has little or no energy to pursue higher needs.

Look again at Figure 2-8. The next need is safety. This includes the needs for adequate shelter, adequate income, and protection from danger. Once the need for safety is met, a person has the energy to pursue the next level of Maslow's hierarchy: social needs. Social needs include the need for friends, love, and acceptance.

Personality Traits of Self-Actualized People

- Realistic
- Accepting
- Independent, self-sufficient
- Appreciative of life
- Concerned about humankind
- Capable of loving others
- Fair, unprejudiced
- Creative
- Hardworking
- Not afraid to be different

Figure 2-7 *According to Maslow, self-actualized people show many of these personality traits. What other traits would you add to the list?*

Figure 2-8 *Which needs did Maslow feel must be satisfied before social needs can be met?*

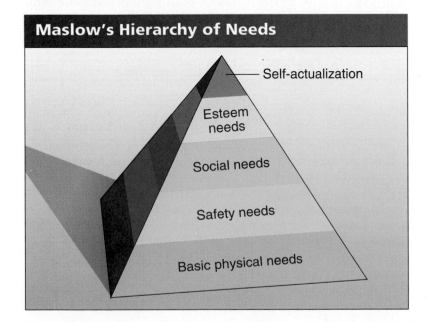

Maslow's Hierarchy of Needs

- Self-actualization
- Esteem needs
- Social needs
- Safety needs
- Basic physical needs

Figure 2-9 *Martin Luther King, Jr., is an example of a self-actualized person.*

Once social needs are met, people can direct their energies toward their esteem needs. Achieving success and gaining self-respect and the approval of others are all important esteem needs. Once these needs are satisfied, a person can go on to be creative, accepting, caring, unprejudiced, and to achieve all the other qualities of a self-actualized person.

Maslow's hierarchy provides a framework for thinking about human needs. It is possible to meet some of your basic needs only partially and still strive to meet higher needs. For example, many great artists, such as Mozart and van Gogh, were extremely creative even though some of their basic needs were not met. Nevertheless, a well-fed person who has adequate shelter is more likely to be friendly and self-confident and to perform tasks better than someone who lacks adequate food and shelter.

LESSON 2 REVIEW

1. What is psychoanalysis?
2. What is one major difference between Freud's view of personality development and Erikson's view?
3. According to Erikson, what three conflicts must adults resolve?
4. What are some of the characteristics of someone who has achieved self-actualization?

What Do You Think?

5. Look over Maslow's list of ideal personality traits in Figure 2-7. Which of these traits reflect American values that might not be shared by other cultures of the world?

DIFFERENT VOICES SPEAKING

Ivonne Medina moved from Mexico to Texas with her family when she was eight years old. Now 19, Ivonne is attending college, where she is studying biomedical engineering on a scholarship. After spending the past summer volunteering in the pediatric cancer ward of a Texas hospital, she is considering a career in medicine.

Q. Ivonne, what were some of the challenges you faced in adjusting to a new culture?

A. One of my first and greatest challenges was overcoming a language barrier. I spoke no English at all when my family arrived here. I remember well what it was like sitting in a classroom and not understanding a word of what was being said. It made me feel like a real outsider. Fortunately, I had a wonderful teacher who saw a lot of potential in me. She took me aside and worked patiently with me. Her belief in my abilities gave me confidence in myself. Within a year I was nearly fluent in English.

Q. Have you encountered other difficulties over the years?

A. Yes, mostly in the area of racial stereotypes. I've found that people tend to form and then believe misconceptions about cultures with which they are not familiar.

Q. How do you counter these misconceptions?

A. I tell people what it is really like to be a Mexican. If there is one thing I have retained, it is a strong sense of my cultural identity. My parents have always made a conscious effort to remain proud of their Mexican heritage and have seen to it that their children did the same. We still speak Spanish in our home, and my family celebrates all the Mexican holidays.

Ivonne Medina

Q. It sounds as though your family has had a real impact on your life.

A. They have. They have encouraged me to go out there and take advantage of the opportunities presented to me, and that is precisely what I have done. My older sister, who is an electrical engineer, is the same way. She is the sort of person who puts 100 percent into everything that she does. My sister has been a positive role model for me. I, in turn, see myself as a role model for my younger brother.

Q. Do you hope that your brother will follow in your footsteps?

A. I hope he'll be himself. I believe people have to know themselves and be who they are. That is the only way life can have meaning.

Journal Activity

Ivonne's self-confidence and positive outlook seem to be a product of both her family upbringing and her Mexican heritage. Choose a person who you know to have a positive, self-confident outlook on life. In your journal, write about the person and the events that shaped the development of his or her personality.

GUIDE FOR READING

Focus on these questions as you read this lesson.

- How does self-esteem affect health?
- What can you do to improve your self-esteem?

SKILLS

- Setting Goals

If you were to ask a psychologist to name the most important influence on mental health, the answer would be self-esteem. **Self-esteem** refers to how much you like yourself and feel good about yourself. You can think of self-esteem as a continuum, ranging from high self-esteem on one end to low self-esteem on the other. People with high self-esteem accept themselves for who they are. They have a realistic view of their strengths and weaknesses and maintain a positive attitude even when they fail at a task. They form close relationships with people who respect and value them. They show that they value themselves by taking care of their health and by avoiding risky behaviors.

People with low self-esteem have a negative opinion of themselves. They judge themselves harshly and worry too much about what others think of them. They may "put on an act" in public to impress others and hide their insecurities. Their fear of failure and looking bad may prevent them from trying new things. When they do try something new, their lack of self-confidence often causes them to fail. Negative thoughts such as "I can't do that" or "I'm not smart enough" make it difficult to succeed.

Figure 2-10 *Feeling good about yourself is the most important influence on your mental health.*

Self-Esteem and Your Health

Take a moment to think about some of the decisions you made today. What role did your sense of self-esteem play in each of your decisions? Most likely, how you felt about yourself influenced your decision about what to wear this morning. It also influenced your interactions with friends, teachers, and family members. In short, your sense of self-esteem affects almost everything you do.

More than any other factor, self-esteem has a direct effect on all aspects of your health—mental, social, and physical. Most psychologists agree that low self-esteem can contribute to many of the serious health problems affecting teenagers today. Teens with low self-esteem are more likely to use drugs, drop out of school, become pregnant, and suffer from eating disorders. They are also more likely to engage in violent or self-destructive behaviors.

High self-esteem, on the other hand, is an important influence on positive health behaviors. If you feel good about yourself, you will be more likely to eat well and to exercise regularly. You will also be more inclined to set goals for yourself, ask for help when you need it, and bounce back quickly from setbacks and disappointments.

How Self-Esteem Develops

Like your overall personality, your sense of self-esteem begins to develop when you are young. Young children need support and encouragement from family members to develop a sense of self-worth. They need chances to succeed at small tasks to become able and confident individuals.

As you grow older, teachers, friends, and others, as well as events in your life, influence your self-esteem. If you do well in school or excel at a sport, your achievements and the encouragement you receive can boost your self-esteem. Think about the people and events that influenced your self-esteem. How did they help you feel good about yourself?

Beyond your immediate world, your self-esteem is also influenced by the larger world around you. Every day, powerful messages from television, magazines, advertisements, and other sources bombard you—messages about your appearance, your sex, your cultural group, and more. Messages like "only thin people have fun" or "girls should not be loud or assertive" can make you feel that you are not as good as others. This can damage your self-esteem.

For most people, the teenage years are a critical time in the development of self-esteem. During these years, teens look critically at themselves—their appearances, their abilities, their interests, and their shortcomings. Teens also spend time comparing themselves to others. This is normal. Because the teen years are a time of rapid change, some teens are overly self-conscious and judge themselves too harshly. They may compare themselves only to the best athletes or to the most attractive celebrities. As a result, their self-esteem may suffer.

Can your self-esteem survive the teen years? Yes, it can. The key is to keep things in the proper perspective and to accept that you cannot be perfect. The next section outlines some concrete things you can do to build self-esteem.

Figure 2-11 *Being successful at things builds self-esteem. What accomplishments are you proud of?*

Setting Goals

List two things you hope to accomplish within the next year. Then, under each goal, list some steps you can take *now* to bring yourself closer to the goal. How does working toward a goal affect your self-esteem?

Improving Your Self-Esteem

What can you do if you are suffering from low self-esteem? While it may be difficult to improve your self-esteem, it can be done. Below are some tips for boosting self-esteem. Try to incorporate some of these suggestions into your daily life. You will gain confidence in your abilities and generally feel better about yourself.

- Take an inventory of your strengths and weaknesses. Learn to focus on your strengths and build on the things you do well.
- Select friends who will support you and encourage you to do your best.
- When you experience defeat, avoid dwelling on it. Try to learn something positive from the experience and then move on.
- Practice good health habits. A healthy diet, regular exercise, and good grooming habits will help you feel good about yourself.
- Avoid doing things just to "go along with the crowd." You will feel better about yourself when you do things that match your values.
- Set goals for yourself. Map out a plan to help you achieve your goals.
- Take some time each day to do something you really enjoy.
- Avoid negative thinking. Substitute positive thoughts like "I can do it if I try" for negative thoughts like "I'll never be able to do this."
- Develop a sense of humor. Learn to laugh at yourself, rather than taking everything seriously.
- Do something nice for others. Consider helping out more at home or doing volunteer work in your community.
- Reward yourself when you do something well. Learn to accept compliments when others give them.

LESSON 3 REVIEW

1. Define the term *self-esteem*.
2. Why is self-esteem important to health?
3. What are some important influences on a person's self-esteem?

What Do You Think?

4. Your best friend is struggling to overcome low self-esteem. What could you do to help?

4 EXPRESSING EMOTIONS

GUIDE FOR READING

Focus on these questions as you read this lesson.

- What are some common emotions that people experience?
- What are some positive ways to cope with strong emotions? What are some negative coping strategies?

SKILLS

- Activity: Drawing on Feelings

Read the following four descriptions and identify what each teenager might be feeling in the situation described.

- Patty just received a call from Bob, who asked her out. This is just what Patty had been hoping for. She cannot wait to tell her best friend.

- Clayton has flunked math and science. He dreads telling his parents about it. Worse still, he knows that he will have to give up being on the football team until he brings up his grades.

- Sarita is trying out for the lead in the class play. She has memorized her lines but is certain that she will forget them at the audition. Every time she thinks about getting on stage, her heart beats faster and she feels faint.

- Peter's dad has lost his job. Money is tight at home. Peter wants to help, but he has not been able to find an after-school job. Yesterday he spotted a twenty-dollar bill in his friend Bill's locker. When Bill looked away, Peter grabbed the money and stuffed it into his pocket.

Common Emotions

You and your classmates may disagree about exactly what Patty, Clayton, Sarita, or Peter is feeling. However, everyone probably would agree that each is experiencing some kind of **emotion,** or feeling. Psychologists define an emotion as a reaction to a situation that involves a person's mind, body, and behavior. **Some common emotions are love, anger, fear, guilt, happiness, and sadness.** The ability to recognize and appropriately express emotions is an important part of a healthy personality.

LOVE The word *love* might make you think of a romantic involvement between two people. While this certainly is one type of love, there are many other types as well. Love between family members, love in marriage, and love between friends are other common forms of love. What do these very different types of love have in common? All are marked by deep feelings of affection and concern. These feeling can be expressed in many ways—through caring words, loving touches, thoughtful actions, and more.

You can feel love toward places and things, as well as toward people. You may love your country. You may feel love and concern for your fellow humans. Love is one of the most positive emotions of which people are capable. The capacity to give and receive love is essential to mental health.

Figure 2-12 *You can express love by showing affection and concern for others.*

ANGER   Think about a time when you felt angry. Were your muscles tensed? Was your heart racing and your breathing rapid? This is how the body responds when you are angry.

Anger can be either a helpful or harmful emotion. Anger can provide you with the energy necessary to try to change things. Consider the case of Clayton, the teenager who flunked math and science. Clayton's first reaction to his poor grades might be anger toward his teachers. After thinking about his situation, however, Clayton may realize that he has to change his own behavior. He may have to give up some after-school activities and spend more time studying. Anger can also be a destructive emotion. Suppose Clayton continued to direct his anger at his teachers or turned his anger upon himself. He might give up on his schoolwork altogether or become aggressive or even violent. These reactions would worsen the situation instead of improve it.

What is the best way to deal with anger? First, it is important to accept your feelings rather than to ignore them. Second, find a healthful way of expressing your anger. For example, find a physical outlet such as jogging or hitting a punching bag. Third, after you have calmed down, think about exactly what made you angry. Writing down what happened or talking it over with a friend can help. Fourth, consider what constructive action you can take to improve the situation or to prevent another angry episode.

Figure 2-14 *Fear causes your body to prepare for action.*

FEAR   Everyone is afraid of something: a figure in the dark, spiders, or horror films. Fear can be a helpful emotion; it can lead you to run from life-threatening situations, such as a fire or a dangerous person. When you feel fear, your heart races and your breathing quickens. You are prepared to fight or flee the situation if necessary. Do you know people who enjoy scary films or frightening amusement park rides? These people like to feel the reaction brought on by fear.

Fear can also be a harmful emotion. A person who is afraid of something may choose to avoid the fearful situation rather than to confront it. Fear can lead to physical problems. You have probably experienced indigestion, loss of sleep, or headaches when you were afraid of something. If fears persist over a long period, serious health problems may result.

Admitting that you are afraid and talking about it with someone often make a fear more manageable. Sometimes it helps to picture your worst fears. For example, Sarita, who was nervous about auditioning for the school play, handled her fear by talking with her mother. Her mother asked Sarita to imagine the worst thing that could happen. Sarita said that she was terrified that she would forget her lines and everyone would laugh at her. To give Sarita more confidence in herself, her family acted as an audience for several nights. Although Sarita was nervous the day of her audition, she got the part.

GUILT   You feel guilty when you think you have done something wrong. Guilt can be a helpful emotion; it can stop you from doing something you know is wrong, or it can make you take action to correct something you've done. Feeling too much guilt, however, can make you doubt yourself and your actions.

The best way to deal with feelings of guilt is to correct the situation if possible and to talk about your feelings. Peter, the boy who stole money from his friend Bill, felt both anger and guilt. He was angry because his father was out of work. He felt guilty because he stole Bill's money. Peter tried to justify taking the money, but hc knew what he did was wrong. After a sleepless night, Peter decided to tell Bill about what he had done. Bill was understanding but said that he needed the money back. Together, the two boys worked out a plan by which Peter could pay back the money.

HAPPINESS   Like love, happiness is a strong, positive emotion. Think about a recent time when you felt happy. Were you happy about something you accomplished? Or was your happiness a result of a pleasant surprise? People feel happy for many different reasons and sometimes for no particular reason at all. Happiness is a normal response to pleasant events in one's life.

When a person feels happy, he or she also feels satisfied with life. Feeling happy makes you feel good about yourself. What makes you feel happy? Take some time to make a list of the things you enjoy. Then, try to "build" these happy times into your daily life. If you enjoy skating with your friends, for example, make plans with your friends to go skating. If

Figure 2-15 *When you are happy, you feel good and enjoy life.*

Figure 2-16 *Feeling sad is a normal response to a disappointing event in your life.*

you like to read books, set aside some time each day for reading. The good feelings that result from your activity will stay with you for the rest of the day.

SADNESS   Sadness is a feeling of sorrow or unhappiness that is a normal response to disappointing events in your life. A day when nothing goes right, a poor grade in school, family problems, or the death of a loved one can all leave you feeling sad and empty. You may cry, eat more or less than normal, feel tired and rundown, or withdraw from those around you.

In most cases, feelings of sadness pass quickly, and you move on with your life. If you feel sad for too long, however, this may be a sign that you are suffering from depression. **Depression** is an emotional state in which you feel hopeless and worthless. You will read more about depression in Chapter 4. People who remain in a depressed state for a long time may require the help of a counselor or psychologist.

If you are sad about the death of a loved one, you will probably experience a period of deep sorrow known as **grief.** Often, one's first reaction is to feel numb and deny the death. Then you may feel angry toward the person who has died. You may feel the person has abandoned you. You also may feel guilty about your angry feelings, because you know that the person could not help dying. Finally, you may feel depressed. All these feelings are normal reactions to the death of someone you love.

What can you do to overcome feelings of sadness? It is important to admit the emotion and to share your feelings with a close relative or friend. If you are sad about a failure, it might also help to make a list of your accomplishments or do something nice for yourself. If you are grieving, allow yourself to cry and to feel all of the emotions the loss brings on. It is important not to withdraw from other people or isolate yourself. If you do, the feeling can become overwhelming and may interfere with your ability to cope with everyday events.

Recognizing Your Emotions

Did you ever feel both happy and sad at the same time? Have you ever been overwhelmed by emotion without knowing what emotions you were feeling? If these experiences sound familiar, then you know how difficult it can sometimes be to understand what you are feeling. Yet, recognizing your emotions is the important first step toward dealing with them in healthful ways.

The next time you are experiencing a strong emotion, pause briefly to reflect on your feelings. During the pause, try to

- Put a name on the emotion you are feeling. Be aware, however, that some emotions, such as anger, can mask other emotions, such as fear or guilt.

DRAWING ON FEELINGS

In this activity you will express various feelings through artwork.

Materials

unlined paper, 2 sheets
pencil

Procedure

1. Choose one of the emotions discussed in this chapter—love, anger, fear, guilt, happiness, or sadness.

2. Think back to the last time you experienced the emotion.

3. As you relive the emotional experience, put the point of your pencil on a sheet of paper and make marks that feel like the emotion. Try not to think about what you are drawing. Instead, just allow the pencil to move on the page as you think about the emotional experience.

4. Repeat steps 1 through 3 for a different emotion.

5. Get together with a few of your classmates and see if they can identify the emotions you have drawn.

Discussion

1. Were there similarities in the way classmates drew certain emotions? If so, describe the similarities.

2. What did you learn about your emotions from this activity?

3. How could art and other forms of creative expression be used to help people understand themselves better?

- Determine what triggered the emotion. Try to pinpoint the exact source of your feeling without confusing the matter with surrounding events.

- Think back to past times that you felt the same way. What similarities do you notice? Are there any important differences?

By pausing to reflect on your feelings in this way, you will learn a lot about yourself and your emotions. With practice, recognizing your emotions will become more automatic. Over time, you will begin to see patterns in your reactions and emotional responses. Still, there will always be times when intense feelings cloud your ability to sort things out. When this occurs, pause and take the time to clarify your feelings. The end result will be a deeper understanding of the situation and of yourself.

Coping with Your Emotions

Sometimes emotions can become too much to handle. In such cases, people may use coping strategies. A **coping strategy** is a way of dealing with an uncomfortable or unbearable feeling or situation.

Common Defense Mechanisms

Compensation: making up for weaknesses in one area by excelling in another area	**Reaction Formation:** behaving in a way opposite to the way you're feeling
You do poorly in school, so you make up for it by becoming the lead saxophone player in the school band and starting up your own jazz band.	*You feel guilty smoking a cigarette. You cover up your feelings by bragging to friends about your smoking.*
Rationalization: making excuses for actions or feelings	**Projection:** putting your own faults onto another person
You work in a convenience store on weekends. When no one is watching, you take some candy and magazines. You figure it's a large store and they can afford it.	*At your after-school job you do not complete your tasks. When you get fired, you blame your boss, saying she did not take the time to explain the tasks to you.*
Denial: refusing to recognize the existence of an emotion or problem	**Regression:** returning to immature behaviors to express emotions
Your parents are getting divorced, but you act as though nothing is wrong. When concerned friends ask how you feel about it, you laugh and tell them it does not bother you.	*You are mad at your brother for using your bicycle. You scream at him and your parents, run into your room, and slam the door.*

Figure 2-17 *Which defense mechanisms have you used to cope with strong emotions?*

DEFENSE MECHANISMS   Some coping strategies occur on an unconscious level, that is, you are not aware of them. Freud called these unconscious coping strategies **defense mechanisms** because they are the ways people defend themselves against difficult feelings.

Figure 2-17 describes some common defense mechanisms. As you read through the descriptions, you will probably recognize some strategies that you use. You should also notice that all of the defense mechanisms involve a bit of fooling yourself. By twisting the reality of a situation a bit in your mind, it becomes easier to accept. Fooling yourself in this way allows you to put off dealing with the problem and the emotions it causes. You experience a feeling of temporary relief and can think through the problem with a clear mind.

If used in moderation, defense mechanisms can be helpful coping strategies. When overused, however, they can stunt emotional growth. If you become too dependent on defense mechanisms, you may not learn to express your true feelings. By using defense mechanisms to avoid problems, you may not develop skills that are important for mental health.

OTHER COPING STRATEGIES   Think back to the last time you experienced a strong, negative emotion. Perhaps you were angry at a friend or disappointed that you did not get the after-school job you wanted. How did you react?

Unconsciously, you probably used a defense mechanism, such as rationalization, to make the situation easier to accept. But how did you react outwardly, on the conscious level?

People react in many different ways to their own strong feelings. Some responses are helpful; that is, they improve the situation or help the person handle it better. Other responses are harmful—they worsen the situation and sometimes even create additional problems. Some helpful ways of coping are listed below. What other coping strategies have worked for you?

- Confront the situation head-on. If possible, take action to improve the situation.
- Release your built-up energy by exercising, cleaning your room, or being active in some other way.
- Take a break by reading a book, taking a walk, writing in your journal, or otherwise relaxing.
- Talk through your feelings with a family member, friend, counselor, or other trusted person.

HARMFUL WAYS OF COPING   Unfortunately, strong emotions sometimes cloud a person's sense of judgment. If this occurs, the person may turn to coping strategies that actually worsen his or her problems. Using alcohol or other drugs and acting out in violent ways are examples of negative coping strategies. Withdrawing from your friends and family is another harmful response.

Learning to express your emotions in positive ways is not an easy skill to master. Most people need help dealing with their emotions from time to time. If you find that you resort to harmful coping strategies, it may be time to ask for help. Try talking to a family member, friend, teacher, coach, or other trusted person. Sometimes, just talking about your feelings will help you see things more clearly. Other times, school counselors, members of the clergy, or mental health specialists may be available to help you learn to better cope with life situations.

LESSON 4 REVIEW

1. Define the term *emotion*.
2. Name five common emotions.
3. Why should you avoid using defense mechanisms too frequently?

What Do You Think?

4. Describe a situation in which you or a friend expressed an emotion in an unhealthy way. How could the emotion have been expressed in a healthy way?

EXPLORING

CAREERS

Art, Dance, and Music Therapists

Sometimes an effective way to help people understand themselves is through creative expression. Art, dance, and music therapists combine their artistic talents with therapy programs to improve a person's mental health.

An art therapist may help people express themselves by painting or creating things. A dance therapist may help people express themselves through movement. A music therapist may teach people to use music to express themselves.

Art, dance, and music therapists work with a wide range of people from the mentally ill to the physically disabled. They may also work with children at summer camps or with the elderly in nursing homes.

For these careers, you need a bachelor's degree in psychology or in art, dance, or music therapy. You also need a solid background in art, dance, or music.

Expressing Feelings in a Positive Way

Matthew had been going out with Joan for over a year, and he thought that things were great between them. Joan, however, felt differently. She wanted to start seeing other boys. When she told this to Matthew, he was so stunned that he couldn't even describe his feelings.

How would you react if you were in Matthew's situation? Yell? Cry? Act as if you didn't care? Pick a fight with your best friend? Talk to Joan? All of these behaviors are possible responses to strong feelings. They are ways of trying to cope with powerful emotions. While you cannot control what you feel, it *is* possible to control what you do—your behavior.

Some responses to strong feelings can improve the situation or at least make you feel better. Other responses can make a bad situation worse. The following guidelines will help you learn to express your feelings in constructive ways.

Remaining friends after a breakup is difficult. How can expressing your feelings help?

1. Accept your feelings

Strong emotions, even unpleasant ones, are normal. Denying them will not make them go away, and it may cause them to erupt later in destructive behaviors. It is important to identify and accept your feelings; then you can start to work on expressing them constructively.

2. Inventory how you typically react

Everyone experiences emotions such as love, fear, sadness, and anger. Are you aware of how you usually react to these feelings? On index cards, list your recent responses to each of these emotions. Briefly describe when and how you expressed each feeling in the recent past and how the situation was resolved. Circle those responses that you felt led to a positive outcome.

> ANGER
>
> 1. My sister wore my sweater. I yelled at her. She yelled back. Mom got mad. I was frustrated.
> 2. Argued with Dad about the car. Went for a bike ride. Cooled off. Then talked to Dad. Felt better.

3. Seek constructive alternatives

Your inventory will show what has worked well for you in the past. Here are some other tips to help you deal with your emotions in a positive way:

Communicate your feelings: Find someone you trust to talk to or to use as "a shoulder to cry on." Don't lash out at others and hurt people's feelings; that just adds to your—and their—problems. Try not to withdraw from those who care about you. They can be a big help if you let them.

Let off steam: Do something you enjoy that requires physical or creative energy. Run or do some other physical activity; paint or play an instrument. Even taking a walk to clear your head can help. Destructive behavior does *not* help. While you may feel better for a moment, you will have to deal with the damage later.

Confront the cause of the feeling: Once you have calmed down, talk to the person who caused the emotion. Make clear how you feel *without* blaming the other person. You may find that it was all a misunderstanding or that the person is now sorry. Even if the situation cannot be reversed by clearing the air, you may feel ready to move on after talking things out.

Avoid "drowning your sorrows": Do not turn to self-destructive behaviors. Although overeating or not eating, drinking, smoking, using drugs, or taking extreme physical risks

may help you forget your problems for a few moments, they can cause damage that lasts a lifetime.

4. Evaluate your progress

If the way you currently express your emotions works, keep it up. If not, try to stop and think for a moment before you act. Recall your own positive experiences (from your inventories) and the tips that you have just read. Remember always to consider the consequences of possible responses.

At first it may take a lot of self-control to change your responses to strong emotions, but the more you practice constructive behaviors, the more automatic they will become. If, however, persistence doesn't help, or if you often feel overwhelmed by your emotions, it is time to ask a trusted adult for some help.

Apply the Skill

1. Review Matthew's situation. What do you think he was feeling? List some positive and negative ways he could have expressed his emotions. For each, what might the results have been?

2. Make a response inventory for fear, love, sadness, and anger. Write each emotion at the top of an index card. Briefly describe three times in the past when you experienced that feeling, how you expressed it, and the outcome. What responses worked best? Worst? Why?

3. Look over your inventories. Make a new card for the emotion that gave you the most trouble. For a week, record each time you express that emotion. Try to improve your responses. If you are not happy with the progress you are making, consider asking someone for help.

CHAPTER  2 REVIEW

KEY IDEAS

LESSON 1

- Mentally healthy people tend to be friendly, optimistic, and loving. They are also able to be assertive, laugh at themselves, try new experiences, and strive to do the best they can.

- Most of an individual's personality traits are influenced by both heredity and his or her environment.

LESSON 2

- Sigmund Freud believed that personality is shaped by early childhood experiences. Erik Erikson believes that personality continues to develop throughout an individual's life.

- Abraham Maslow believed that every individual has a basic drive to achieve his or her full potential. This drive is blocked when the person's other, more basic, needs are not met.

LESSON 3

- More than any other factor, self-esteem has a direct affect on all aspects of health—mental, social, and physical.

LESSON 4

- The ability to recognize and appropriately express emotions is an important part of a healthy personality.

- People use coping strategies to deal with overwhelming feelings or situations.

KEY TERMS

LESSON 1
aggressive
assertive
extrovert
introvert
mental health
modeling
optimist
passive
peer group
personality

pessimist
psychologist

LESSON 2
conscious thought
ego
hierarchy of needs
id
identity
psychoanalysis
self-actualization
superego

theory
unconscious thought

LESSON 3
self-esteem

LESSON 4
coping strategy
defense mechanism
depression
emotion
grief

Listed above are some of the important terms in this chapter. Choose the term from the list that best matches each phrase below.

1. the unique combination of traits that makes each person an individual

2. an ordering of a person's needs from most basic to self-fulfillment

3. able to express one's feelings in a non-threatening way

4. the part of an individual's personality that distinguishes between right and wrong

5. a thought of which a person is not aware, but which affects a person's behavior

6. a friendly and outgoing person

7. the process of striving to reach one's full potential

8. how much one likes oneself or feels good about oneself

9. a reaction to a situation that involves a person's mind, body, and behavior

10. a way of dealing with an uncomfortable feeling or situation

WHAT HAVE YOU LEARNED?

If the statement is true, write "true." If it is false, change the underlined word or words to make the statement true.

11. An optimist focuses on the <u>negative</u> side of things.

12. A <u>psychologist</u> studies the human mind and behavior.

13. <u>Conscious</u> thoughts are thoughts of which a person is aware.

14. <u>Sigmund Freud</u> devised an eight-stage theory of personality development that covers a person's entire life span.

15. The <u>id</u> is the thoughtful, decision-making part of the personality

16. <u>Safety</u> needs include the need for friends, love, and acceptance.

17. People with <u>high</u> self-esteem accept themselves for who they are.

18. Compensation and regression are examples of <u>defense mechanisms</u>.

Answer each of the following with complete sentences.

19. Describe a mentally healthy person.

20. Explain how heredity and environment interact to shape personality.

21. What did Freud believe to be the most important influence on personality?

22. Compare and contrast the personality theories of Freud, Erikson, and Maslow.

23. According to Erikson, what conflict do teenagers face?

24. What factors affect self-esteem?

25. Explain why love is such a positive and important emotion.

26. How can guilt and fear be positive emotions? How can they be negative emotions?

27. Give an example of a situation in which using a defense mechanism is beneficial.

28. List two harmful coping strategies that people sometimes use to cope with strong emotions. Next to each, give a reason why it is a harmful response.

WHAT DO YOU THINK?

29. How do you think emotions add to the enjoyment of life?

30. Describe a person you know who you would say has achieved self-actualization.

31. How does school affect a person's self-esteem?

32. How does a loving home affect the development of an individual's personality?

33. Which do you think has a greater impact on personality: heredity or environment? Explain your answer.

WHAT WOULD YOU DO?

34. You are feeling angry because your friend broke one of your favorite tapes and refuses to pay for it. What would you do to work out your anger in a healthful way?

35. Describe what you are doing now or hope to do to develop a sense of who you are. How will these actions help you develop a secure identity?

36. Imagine that every time you fail at something, you rationalize your failure. How might this behavior be harmful? Think of a way that the habit of rationalizing could be broken.

37. If a good friend moved far away, what would you do to ease your sadness?

Getting Involved

38. Ask your family members to look over Maslow's list of ideal personality traits in Figure 2-7. Discuss how you would modify the list to reflect your family's values.

39. Create a poster to teach young children healthful ways to cope with anger.

MANAGING STRESS

The stresses of learning, living, growing, and changing are part of your everyday life. How does stress affect the body? Is all stress bad? Are there healthy ways to manage stress? The answers to these and other questions can be found in this chapter.

CHAPTER PREVIEW

3-1 What Causes Stress?

- Identify situations that cause stress.

3-2 How Stress Affects the Body

- Explain how the body responds when faced with stress.

3-3 Stress and Personality

- Describe the relationship between personality and stress.

3-4 Managing Stress

- Develop a plan for managing stress and maintaining health.

BUILDING HEALTH SKILLS

- Identify strategies for managing time effectively.

CHECK YOUR WELLNESS

If you can answer *yes* to the questions below, you show good stress management skills.

- Are you aware of the things that cause you stress?
- Do you plan your time to avoid last-minute rushes?
- Do you take time every day to relax and do things you enjoy?
- Do you get eight hours of sleep a night, eat a balanced diet, and get regular exercise?
- Do you avoid tobacco, alcohol, and other drugs?
- Can you laugh, cry, and express your emotions freely?
- Do you share your problems with close friends or family members?
- Do you know where to get help if the stresses in your life seem overwhelming?

KEEPING A JOURNAL

Imagine a day without stress. What would it be like? Choose one part of the day and write about your experiences in your journal.

Take it to the Net
www.phschool.com

1 WHAT CAUSES STRESS?

Imagine that it is early morning and you are fast asleep. Suddenly, your alarm clock sounds. You sit up quickly, open your eyes, and jump out of bed. As you react to the ringing alarm, you experience stress. **Stress** is a reaction of your body and mind to threatening or challenging events in your life. **You experience stress when situations, events, or people make demands on your body and mind.** These demands are often part of your daily routine.

The Many Causes of Stress

Many different situations, events, and people can cause stress. The causes of stress are called **stressors.** The alarm that wakes you is one example of a stressor. Other examples in your life may be upcoming tests or games or arguments with friends. These events make demands on your body and mind and cause you to react. Can you think of other stressors that you experience daily?

MAJOR LIFE CHANGES Figure 3-2 lists some significant stressors identified by high school students. Most of these stressors are major life changes, especially changes that affect one's family or school life. These changes are stressful because they threaten the person's sense of security or self-esteem. Each change is measured in "life-change units" and given a score. The number of life-change units you accumulate during a year is one way to measure the amount of stress you experience.

As you look over the stressors listed in Figure 3-2, notice that the list includes some positive changes as well as negative ones. While being accepted to the college of your choice is, indeed, a positive event, it can be just as stressful as a negative event. It is important to realize that change, both positive and negative, is in itself stressful. The Building Health Skills feature in Chapter 9 can help you learn to reduce the stress that accompanies change.

EVERYDAY PROBLEMS Some of the most common stressors are not listed in Figure 3-2. These common stressors are sometimes called "hassles"—minor, but frequent, everyday events that cause you stress. Hassles include misplacing or losing something, being concerned about how you look, or having too many things to do at once. While such problems seem minor, they contribute greatly to your overall feeling of stress. This is because hassles occur day in and day out. Can you remember a day in the past month that was free of hassles? Probably not.

Figure 3-1 *A surprise test is just one stressor you may encounter today.*

Ranking of Stressors by High School Students

Life-Change Units	Life Event	Life-Change Units	Life Event
101	Getting married	55	Experiencing the serious illness of a parent
92	Being pregnant and unwed	53	Breaking up with a boyfriend or girlfriend
87	Experiencing the death of a parent	53	Having a parent go to jail for 30 days or less
81	Acquiring a visible deformity	51	Beginning to date
77	Going through parents' divorce	50	Being suspended from school
77	Becoming an unwed father	50	Having a newborn brother or sister
76	Becoming involved with alcohol or other drugs	47	Having more arguments with parents
75	Having a parent jailed for a year or more	46	Having an outstanding personal achievement
69	Going through parents' separation	46	Observing an increase in the number of arguments between parents
68	Experiencing the death of a brother or sister		
67	Experiencing a change in acceptance by peers	46	Having a parent lose his or her job
64	Having an unwed, pregnant teenage sister	45	Experiencing a change in parents' financial status
64	Discovering that you are an adopted child	43	Being accepted at the college of your choice
63	Having a parent remarry	42	Being a senior in high school
62	Experiencing the death of a close friend	41	Experiencing a serious illness of a brother or sister
62	Having a visible congenital deformity	38	Experiencing a parent's increased absence from home due to a change in occupation
58	Having a serious illness requiring hospitalization		
		37	Experiencing the departure from home of a brother or sister
56	Moving to a new school district		
56	Failing a grade in school	36	Experiencing the death of a grandparent
55	Not making an extracurricular activity	34	Having a third adult added to the family

Figure 3-2 *Add the number of life-change units for each event you experienced last year. If your score is less than 150, you have experienced little life change; between 150 and 300, you have experienced moderate life change; over 300, your life has changed greatly.*

PHYSICAL SURROUNDINGS   Conditions in your immediate surroundings affect your level of stress each day. Suppose, for example, that you commute to school on an overcrowded subway or bus. Your level of stress might be quite high by the time you arrive at school.

A major stressor that occurs all around you but is often overlooked is noise. People who live near airports or in other noisy environments show signs of high stress levels. Living in unsafe, crowded, or polluted areas also tends to increase feelings of stress. Weather conditions, especially snowstorms, heat waves, and droughts, can also be contributing factors. Of course, earthquakes, fires, and other major catastrophes are highly stressful for those people who are affected by the disasters.

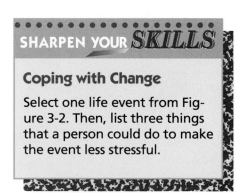

SHARPEN YOUR *SKILLS*

Coping with Change

Select one life event from Figure 3-2. Then, list three things that a person could do to make the event less stressful.

Figure 3-3 *Stress can be a positive or negative experience, depending on the results it brings.*

OTHER STRESSORS   Another major source of stress for teenagers is worrying about the future. As your high school years near an end, you face crucial decisions about your future. For many teenagers, this decision-making can be very stressful.

Conflict—disagreements with family members, friends, and others—is another source of stress for teens. Some teens experience more conflict than they did when they were young or disagree over different issues. These conflicts can be very stressful. Another source of stress is special events—dates, team tryouts, job interviews, and more. Think about special events that you have experienced over the past few months. Were these events stressful for you?

Positive Stress and Negative Stress

Although most people think of stress as a negative experience, it can be positive as well. Stress is positive when it promotes growth and accomplishment. Positive stress is sometimes called **eustress.** Negative stress, on the other hand, is sometimes called **distress.**

Think about something you have accomplished lately—perhaps you did well on a test or your team defeated a tough opponent in soccer. You may remember the feelings you experienced before and during the event. Do you think you performed better as a result of the stress?

Research has shown that, at moderate levels, stress can actually improve your ability to concentrate and perform at your best. Beyond that level, however, stress begins to take a negative toll on performance. Suppose, for example, that you were scheduled to take your driver's test next week. Feelings of stress might assure that you practice during the upcoming week. On the day of the test, your nervousness might make you more alert behind the wheel. But what if you experience overwhelming stress over the test? You might find it difficult to concentrate on your driving and make mistakes that cause you to fail the test.

LESSON *1* REVIEW

1. What is stress? When do people experience stress?
2. What is a stressor? Give some examples of stressors from your own life.
3. How can stress be either positive or negative?

What Do You Think?

4. List ten stressful experiences that you have faced in the past two weeks. Next to each, note whether it was a positive or a negative experience for you.

DIFFERENT VOICES SPEAKING

Seventeen-year-old Jeff Mentgen dreams of being an actor. Jeff, who lives in Texas, devotes a lot of his time to acting classes—about five hours a day, three to four days a week. He spent the past summer trying out for parts in TV shows, films, and commercials.

Q. Jeff, can you describe a typical audition?

A. It depends on the part, though most can be pretty nerve-racking. For me, feature films are the roughest. First, you get very little time to study the sides, or script—about a day if you're lucky—so you really have to cram the way you do when you study for a big exam in school. The real butterflies start when you sign in on the day of the call and find yourself surrounded by what seems like a million other kids trying out for the same part.

Jeff Mentgen

Q. What do you do in situations like that?

A. I find that deep breathing—in through the nose and out through the mouth—helps calm me down. So does face stretching—working out all the different facial muscles. This is a technique you learn in acting school. It's used mainly to prepare for comedy roles, where expressions have to be exaggerated, but I find it also helps me relax when the tension is high.

Q. Have you ever had stage fright?

A. You bet! Most auditions take place in a small room. The people you're auditioning for sit at a table, taking notes while you perform. It can really throw you for a loop and make you stutter and forget your lines. What I do is imagine that I'm in an empty room. That will get me through the audition.

Q. What do you do to help yourself handle the stress of your busy schedule?

A. An activity like riding the stationary bicycle helps me get rid of nervous energy. For example, I recently had a problem getting down a certain emotion for a role. So I went to the gym and pedaled for a while. I not only got rid of my frustration; I managed to get into the right mind-set for the role.

Q. How do you feel when you don't get a part for which you auditioned?

A. It's hard, I have to admit, especially when it's for something big and I feel that I did a better performance than the person who got the part. At times like those, I try to start thinking positively—that it's not the last audition of my life and that there will be others. That usually helps me get my life back on track.

Journal Activity

Think back to a time in the past when you had to perform or speak in front of other people. In your journal, explore how you felt before, during, and after your performance. What did you do to cope with the stress of the situation? What did you learn from the experience?

GUIDE FOR READING

Focus on these questions as you read this lesson.

- How does the body respond to stressful situations?
- What is the relationship between stress and illness?

SKILLS

- Recognizing Misleading Claims

Imagine that you are walking through a forest. Just as you are enjoying the sights, sounds, and smells of the forest, a huge black bear appears in front of you. How do you react?

Instantly, your mind sizes up the situation. You determine that the bear is a threat and that you do not have the resources to handle it. The result is stress.

Stages of Stress

As soon as you perceive something to be a stressor, your body springs into action. Your body's response is automatic—like your heartbeat, it is not under your control. All stressors—from serious ones like the bear to moderate ones like an upcoming test—trigger the same stress response in your body, although at different levels of intensity.

The body's response to stress occurs in three stages—the alarm stage, the resistance stage, and the exhaustion stage. The stages of the stress response are described below.

ALARM STAGE When your walk in the forest began, your body was in a state of balance. All your body's systems functioned smoothly, and your mind was at ease. This normal, balanced state is called **homeostasis** (hoh mee oh STAY sis). When you saw the bear, however, homeostasis was disturbed, and you entered the first stage of stress, the alarm stage.

In the alarm stage, your body releases a substance known as **adrenaline** (uh DREN uh lin) into your bloodstream. Adrenaline gives you a burst of energy and causes many other changes in your body. Your heart begins to beat faster, increasing the flow of blood to your muscles. Your breathing quickens, providing more oxygen for your body's activities. Your muscles tighten, making you ready to run. Less blood flows to your skin and digestive system, so that more is available for your arms and legs. Your pupils widen, allowing more light into your eyes. You feel a lump in your throat as your throat muscles contract to help open the airways to your lungs and make breathing easier.

As your body responds to the stressor, your mind also reacts. During the alarm stage, you become more alert. You take in information and become more aware of things going on around you.

All of these changes take only a few seconds, but once they have taken place, you are ready to react. You can react in one of two ways: you can stand and fight, or you can run away. This immediate reaction of the body to stress is called the

Figure 3-4 *When faced with a stressor, your body enters the alarm stage, just like this cat.*

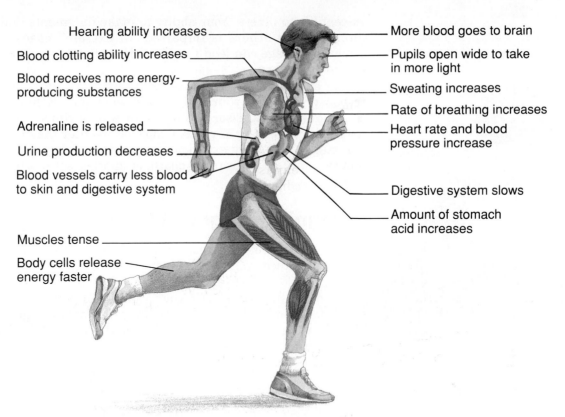

Hearing ability increases

Blood clotting ability increases

Blood receives more energy-producing substances

Adrenaline is released

Urine production decreases

Blood vessels carry less blood to skin and digestive system

Muscles tense

Body cells release energy faster

More blood goes to brain

Pupils open wide to take in more light

Sweating increases

Rate of breathing increases

Heart rate and blood pressure increase

Digestive system slows

Amount of stomach acid increases

fight or flight response, because the changes prepare you to either "fight" the stressor or "take flight" and escape.

Scientists believe that the fight or flight response was essential for primitive people who had to survive wild animals and other dangers. Today, the same reactions still occur with any stressor. When faced with a challenge, such as a difficult test or a theatrical performance, your body reacts with the same physical changes. These physical changes, which are shown in Figure 3-5, make it possible for you to choose between "fight" and "flight."

RESISTANCE STAGE   Of course, it is not always possible to either fight or take flight from a stressor. In such cases, if the stressor continues, you enter into the resistance stage of the stress response. During this stage the body tries to recover from the alarm of the first stage. Because the stressor still remains, the body cannot restore homeostasis. Instead, the body continues to function at a higher-than-normal level. Like a car in need of a tune-up, the body uses up a lot of energy in the resistance stage. As a result, you may become tired, irritable, and less able to handle any additional stress.

EXHAUSTION STAGE   If the stressor still continues, you may enter the exhaustion stage, the third stage of the stress response. In the exhaustion stage, the body is worn down and no longer has enough energy to fight off the stressor. As your body's balance remains disturbed, you become more

Figure 3-5 *In the alarm stage, your body and mind prepare you to fight or take flight.*

susceptible to illness. Your ability to make judgments and to interact with others is impaired. In extreme cases, the exhaustion stage can lead to unhealthy behavior, serious illness, or even death.

The exhaustion stage does not occur with each stress response. If it did, your body would wear out. Exhaustion occurs only if a stressor continues for a long time—usually weeks, months, or even years. People often enter the exhaustion stage when they experience stress that is beyond their control—such as a divorce, a death, or another serious family problem.

Recognizing Signs of Stress

How can you keep stress under control and prevent the resistance stage or the exhaustion stage from occurring? The first, and perhaps most important, step in controlling stress is recognizing when you are under stress. Some of the most common early warning signs are listed in Figure 3-7. As you look over the list, think about how you act and feel when under stress. From the list, select those reactions that apply to you. List them on a sheet of paper and title it "My Warning Signs of Stress." Add to your list any other reactions you have. The next time you experience some of your warning signs, you will know that you are under stress.

Recognizing when you are under stress will soon become automatic. You may begin to notice patterns—perhaps you always show signs of stress when you haven't had enough sleep, for example. You may be able to cut down on such avoidable stressors. By recognizing these signs early, you may also be able to prevent some of the more serious effects of stress. Some of these serious effects are described on the following pages.

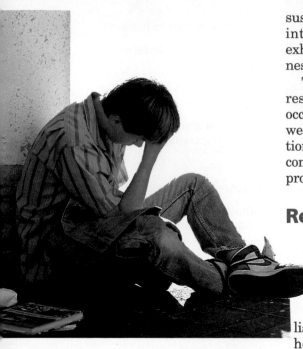

Figure 3-6 *If a stressor continues for a long time, your body enters the exhaustion stage, and illness can result.*

Figure 3-7 *Which of these common reactions do you experience during stressful situations?*

Early Warning Signs of Stress		
Physical Signs	**Emotional Signs**	**Behavioral Signs**
Muscle tension	Irritability, anger	Loss of appetite
Headache	Impatience	Overeating
Upset stomach	Nervousness	Drug abuse
Pounding heart	Forgetfulness	Sleep problems
Shortness of breath	Inability to concentrate	Restlessness
Increased sweating	Negative thinking	Hurrying, talking fast
Dry mouth	Excessive worrying	Withdrawing from relationships
Skin rash	Loss of interest	Criticizing others
Trembling or twitching	Self-criticism	Reckless behavior
Grinding teeth, nail biting	Increased crying	Fidgeting

Figure 3-8 *It is important not to let stress take your mind off what you are doing.*

Stress and Injuries

If you have ever tried to concentrate on a task after a stressful day, then you know how stress can interfere with your ability to focus and think clearly. Unfortunately, when people are distracted and preoccupied with other things, they are more likely to injure themselves and others.

Many stress-related injuries could be prevented if people were more aware of when they are under stress. Suppose, for example, that after arguing with a friend, you got on your bike to ride home. Without realizing it, you might be thinking more about the argument than about the traffic. To avoid such potentially dangerous situations, use the list of warning signs in Figure 3-7. Recognizing that you are under stress allows you to take extra care or to postpone activities until you are less distracted. When stress affects your ability to concentrate or think clearly, you need to be especially careful.

Stress and Illness

By itself, stress does not usually cause serious illness. Most people experience stress from time to time but regain homeostasis quickly. Severe or prolonged stress, however, can affect your health. It can lower your resistance to illness, and it can make some diseases harder to control.

You may have heard the term *psychosomatic illness* used to describe stress-related illnesses. *Psycho* means "of the mind," and *somatic* means "of the body." **Psychosomatic illnesses** (sy koh soh MAT ik) are physical disorders that result from stress or other emotional causes. These illnesses are evidence of the ways in which the mind affects the body. Some people think that psychosomatic illnesses are imagined, or that they are "all in your mind." This is not true. Psychosomatic illnesses are real physical disorders that are either brought on or made worse by stress.

LOWERED RESISTANCE The immune system protects the body from disease through a complicated process involving a number of specialized body cells. When you speak of

BIOLOGY
CONNECTION

How does stress contribute to headaches? For migraine sufferers, research has shown that stress triggers the nervous system to close down blood vessels in the brain. This reduces the brain's oxygen supply, which, in turn, triggers the blood vessels to open wider. As the blood vessels in the brain and scalp stretch, the painful throbbing of a migraine begins.

Recognizing Misleading Claims

You have been under a lot of stress lately and are feeling run down. While you are in a pharmacy one day, you come across a product called "Stress Vitamins." The product claims to "keep you healthy by replacing essential vitamins that are lost during times of stress." How would you decide whether or not to buy the vitamins?

fighting off the flu or a cold, the immune system does the fighting. When your immune system functions well, you are able to resist some illnesses to which you have been exposed.

Scientific research has shown that prolonged stress can prevent the immune system from functioning well. If your immune system is not working well, you may have minor illnesses, such as colds and flu, more often. For people with diseases such as cancer, a weakened immune system may worsen their condition.

Some researchers feel that a major stressful event, like divorce, lowers disease resistance for as long as a year.

ULCERS An **ulcer** is an open sore in the lining of the stomach or other part of the digestive tract. For some people, stress increases the amount of acid in the stomach, which worsens the ulcer and can prevent it from healing.

ASTHMA People with **asthma** (AZ muh), a disorder of the respiratory system that makes breathing difficult, may react to stress with an asthmatic attack. During an asthmatic attack, the person coughs, wheezes, and gasps for air. Although these symptoms usually can be controlled with medication, people with asthma need to recognize their bodies' reactions to stressors so that they can manage serious asthmatic attacks.

HIGH BLOOD PRESSURE AND HEART DISEASE As you already read, stress increases the blood flow in the body. Long periods of stress, then, can lead to high blood pressure. Because high blood pressure has no obvious symptoms and often goes undetected, it is sometimes called the "silent killer." If it is not controlled, high blood pressure can lead to heart disease and stroke.

Stress also contributes to heart disease in other ways. Because the heart must work harder when under stress, prolonged stress can damage the heart muscles. Over time, this can increase a person's risk of heart attacks.

LESSON 2 REVIEW

1. Name and describe the stages of the stress response.
2. What is meant by "fight or flight"?
3. Why is it important to recognize early signs of stress?
4. Describe three ways in which stress contributes to physical illness.

What Do You Think?

5. Many people think that stress affects them mentally, but not physically. Why do you think they believe this?

3 STRESS AND PERSONALITY

GUIDE FOR READING

Focus on these questions as you read this lesson.

- How does your personality affect the way you handle stress?
- How can controlling negative thoughts help reduce stress?

SKILLS

- DECIDE

Suppose your teacher walked into class one day and said, "Okay, everyone, put away your books. We are going to have a surprise quiz now." How would you react? Now look around the classroom and imagine your classmates' reactions. Would their reactions be the same as yours?

Your teacher's announcement might bring on a wide range of reactions—mild stress, extreme stress, confidence, and indifference are just some reactions you could predict. Why does one person remain calm when faced with a stressor while another becomes anxious and tense? The answer to this question points out an important fact about stress—it is a highly personal experience. How you react to a stressor depends on how you answer these two questions.

- Is this situation a threat to my well-being?
- Do I have the necessary resources (such as time, energy, skills, and experience) to meet the challenge?

Stress, then, is a personal response that depends on how you assess a situation. **Just as your personality is unique, so, too, is the way you react to potentially stressful situations.** In this lesson, you will explore the relationship between personality and stress.

Personality Type

One theory about the relationship between personality and stress was proposed by a group of researchers studying heart disease. The researchers saw a link between an individual's susceptibility to heart disease and his or her personality.

Figure 3-9 *The driven go-getter and the calm, unhurried person are two basic personality types.*

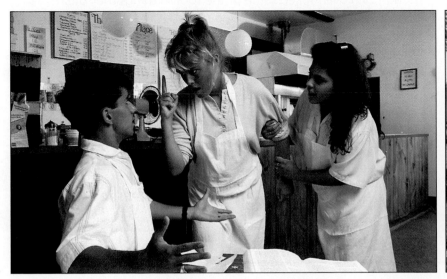

The researchers proposed that there are two basic personality types: type A and type B. **Type A personalities** tend to be rushed and competitive. These people try to accomplish as much as they can in the shortest time possible. Their desire to succeed drives them hard to accomplish their goals. Type A personalities have high standards for themselves. If they fail to meet these standards, they can become angry, frustrated, and even hostile.

Type B personalities are calmer, less competitive, and not as concerned about accomplishment. Type B personalities are less likely to feel stressed if they do not meet high standards for success. They are also less likely to develop stress-related illnesses. Some type B personalities, however, have difficulty facing challenges. They may cope with stressors by ignoring them. Doing this, they may miss opportunities for learning and achievement. These problems can create another kind of stress in which the person becomes bored and unchallenged.

In reality, few people are entirely type A or type B. Most people are really a combination of the two personality types. The differences between the types, however, can help you analyze your own personality in certain situations. Think about a time when you showed type A personality traits. Was your stress level high? Were you able to balance your type A behavior with some type B traits? Why is this balance important?

DEFINE
the problem

EXPLORE
alternatives

CONSIDER
the consequences

IDENTIFY
values

DECIDE
and act

EVALUATE
results

A Stressful Situation

Dan and his family recently moved to a new town. At school, Dan ate his lunch alone for weeks until three boys from his science class asked Dan to join them. Soon Dan was getting together with the boys after school, too. Thrilled to have new friends, Dan overlooked some of the foolish things they did.

One afternoon, Dan's friends said to him, "Here's your chance to prove your friendship. Tomorrow, when we visit you at the store where you work, you distract the other clerk while we pocket a few things." Stunned, Dan did not respond. After a sleepless night, he was still not sure what he should do.

1. Use the DECIDE process on page 18 to decide how you would handle this situation if you were Dan. Give your reasons for your decision.

2. How might your decision affect your stress level? Explain.

Perfectionism

Do you know a perfectionist? A **perfectionist** is a person who accepts nothing less than excellence of himself or herself. If you are a perfectionist about your appearance, for example, you may spend a lot of time choosing an outfit, preparing your hair, and otherwise getting yourself ready to go out. If you are a perfectionist about your work, you may spend weeks working on a term paper, rewriting each sentence many times.

While it is important to take pride in your work, perfectionists sometimes take things too far. One characteristic that perfectionists share is never being satisfied with what they have accomplished. This can lead to a vicious cycle of trying harder, not being satisfied, and trying harder still. Perfectionists often have trouble meeting deadlines and taking risks.

Because perfectionists put such pressure on themselves, it is no surprise that they suffer from high levels of stress. It is not easy to break the cycle of perfectionism. The first step is to accept that you cannot be perfect. Take pride in the things you do well, rather than focusing on your mistakes. The result will be a lower level of stress and an increased level of satisfaction.

Negative Thinking

Think back to the last time you were in a stressful situation. What thoughts were going through your mind? Were you thinking things like "I'll never be able to do this," or "Everyone will think I'm stupid," or "I'm not as good as the others"? For many people, negative thoughts like these accompany stressful situations. Of course, such negative thinking only

Figure 3-10 *People who put pressure on themselves to be perfect often suffer from high levels of stress.*

increases a person's stress level. With negative messages running through the person's mind, it becomes almost impossible to succeed.

How can you stop yourself from thinking negative thoughts when you are under stress? One way is to monitor your internal conversations closely and substitute positive or realistic thoughts when negative thoughts arise. For example, instead of thinking, "Everyone will think I'm stupid," you might think, more realistically, "No one is going to judge me on just this one small event." Another way to eliminate negative thinking is to "coach" yourself through an upcoming stressful event. To do this, go through the event in your mind, step by step, while giving yourself positive messages such as "You can do it." This will boost your self-confidence, which will help you during the actual event.

Hardiness

Some people experience a great deal of stress but do not become ill as a result. What protects these people from the negative effects of stress? Researchers have used the term **hardiness** to explain the remarkable resistance to stress that these people possess. Hardy individuals seem to share three characteristics.

- They view stressful events as challenges or opportunities rather than as threats.
- They are deeply involved in and committed to whatever they are doing.
- They have a sense of control over what they are doing. They feel that they can influence the outcome of the stressful event.

Of the three traits shared by hardy people, having a sense of control is perhaps of greatest importance. In the next lesson, you will explore some things you can do to control various stressors in your life.

LESSON 3 REVIEW

1. What is the difference between a type A personality and a type B personality?
2. In what ways does perfectionism contribute to stress?
3. How does negative thinking affect stress levels? Explain.
4. Define the term *hardiness*.

What Do You Think?

5. Imagine that your boyfriend or girlfriend just broke up with you. What negative thoughts might you have? How could you substitute more positive thoughts?

4 MANAGING STRESS

Although stress is a part of life, it does not have to control your life. You can do many things to keep stress under control. **Managing stress helps to restore balance in your life—it prevents the stressors from taking control and making you ill.**

In a sense, everything you do to maintain your health is a way to manage stress. Eating well, exercising regularly, expressing your feelings, and saying *no* to alcohol and other drugs—these are all ways in which a healthy person manages stress. But, you can do more. A variety of stress management techniques are presented below.

Confronting the Problem

Suppose that you were in danger of failing math. What could you do? You could ignore the problem and pretend not to be worried. Or you could confront the problem and devise a plan to improve your grade. Your plan might include asking a friend for help, cutting down on other activities to focus more on math, and paying closer attention in class.

Many people tend to think of all stress as being out of their control. This is not true. Like your poor performance in math, many stressors in your life are things that you can work to change. Suppose you constantly misplace things or feel self-conscious because you are out of shape. What could you do to reduce these sources of stress? What other stressors can you take action to change?

Of course, not all stressors are within your control. It is important to distinguish between stressors that can be controlled and those that cannot. Direct your energy toward those things that are within your power to change. You may be surprised to see what a difference you can make.

Time Management

Do you often wish there were more hours in the day? Do you tend to put things off until the last minute? If you answered *yes* to these questions, you may not be managing your time effectively. Poor time management is one of the biggest contributors to stress. The Building Health Skills feature at the end of this chapter can help you learn to use time more productively. Not only will you get more done each day, but you will also feel more in

GUIDE FOR READING

Focus on these questions as you read this lesson.

- Why is managing stress important for health?
- What techniques can you use to keep stress under control?

SKILLS

- Activity: Progressive Relaxation
- Supporting a Friend

Figure 3-11 *By studying hard for an upcoming test, you can turn a potentially stressful situation into a more relaxed one.*

Figure 3-12 *Being physically active when under stress helps to release the built-up tension in your muscles.*

control of your life. As a bonus, you might also end up with more time for fun and relaxation.

Physical Activity

Cleaning your room, shooting some baskets, taking a walk, fixing your bike—these are just some ways to release tension when you are under stress. By doing something physically active, you provide your body with a healthy outlet for built-up energy. At the same time, you take your mind off your problems and give yourself a chance to relax.

You do not have to be a star athlete to use physical activity to manage stress. The activities you choose do not have to be competitive sports, and you do not have to be the best or fastest at them. Instead, select activities that you enjoy and feel good doing. Try to incorporate physical activity into your daily routine. That way, you will always have a way to work off the day's tension.

Relaxation

Many special methods can help you achieve relaxation, a state in which your mind and body are resting. When you are relaxed, you may be awake and alert, but you are not responding actively to stressors.

You may relax your mind by reading a book, taking a nap, listening to music, or daydreaming. You may relax tense muscles by taking a hot shower or bath, stretching, or having someone massage your neck. Stretching the muscles in your neck, shoulders, and upper back is an especially useful way to relax because these muscles often become tense when you sit for long periods.

You can learn many specific exercises to help you relax. One method, called deep breathing, offers quick relief from stress. To do this exercise, take ten deep breaths, breathing in as much air as you can and making sure that your chest and abdomen expand. Deep breathing relaxes muscles throughout your body. By breathing this way, you take in more oxygen, which helps your body to function better.

Another method for relaxing tense muscles is called progressive relaxation. With this technique you relax by concentrating on each group of muscles in your body, one at a time. Progressive relaxation is described in the Activity below.

Mental Rehearsal

Suppose you have a big event coming up, such as an important speech. You might use a technique known as a mental rehearsal to help you prepare. In a mental rehearsal, you practice the entire event in your mind, imagining yourself performing at your best. You might rehearse every aspect of the event a few times over until you feel confident that you can perform it as you imagined.

PROGRESSIVE RELAXATION

In this activity you will release the tension that has built up in your muscles.

Procedure

1. Sit quietly in a comfortable chair and close your eyes. Make sure that your arms and legs are uncrossed.

2. Beginning with your forehead and working down to your toes, tighten each muscle group in your body, hold for 10 seconds, and relax. Try the following sequence:

• Forehead: Wrinkle your forehead—try to make your eyebrows touch your hairline.

• Eyes: Close your eyes as tightly as you can.

• Mouth: Form a frown with the corners of your mouth.

• Shoulders: Raise your shoulders up to your ears.

• Upper arms: Bend your elbows and tense your upper arms.

• Hands and forearms: Tightly clench your fists.

• Back: Gently arch your back.

• Stomach: Tighten your stomach muscles.

• Hips: Tighten your hip and buttock muscles.

• Thighs: Squeeze your legs together.

• Toes: Curl your toes under as tightly as you can.

3. Now tense all the muscles in your whole body. Hold for 10 seconds and relax.

Discussion

1. Compare how you felt before and after completing the progressive relaxation activity.

2. Think back to what you learned about "fight or flight" and the body's response to stress. Why do you think progressive relaxation is an effective stress-reduction technique?

3. List some times during a typical week when it would be useful to perform progressive relaxation.

Mental rehearsal is a popular technique with athletes in competitions such as the Olympics. This technique helps the athletes stay focused on their performances during highly stressful times. When you first try this technique, it may be difficult to keep your mind focused on your rehearsal. You might find that you are easily distracted by outside events. With practice, though, you will improve your ability to focus inward and put all distractions aside.

Biofeedback

Biofeedback is a special method of stress management in which a person learns to control a specific physical function by recognizing his or her body's signals. To learn biofeedback, special equipment is used that tells the person what is happening in the body. A trained health professional usually teaches this method.

The health professional might, for example, attach a special device to a patient's back muscles. The instrument lets the person know when he or she begins to tense those muscles. By identifying the thoughts that lead to muscle tensing, the person can learn to control the tensing by changing his or her thoughts.

With training and practice, people can master biofeedback. With practice, many people become able to recognize and control their tension without using the equipment. Biofeedback has proven useful for people who have stress-related symptoms or illnesses such as headaches, high blood pressure, or asthma.

Humor

Humor can be an effective way to deal with some stressful situations. Have you ever laughed at yourself after doing something that was not really funny, such as slipping on a wet floor or saying something embarrassing in front of a

Figure 3-13 *By running through the race in her mind, this athlete can keep stress under control.*

Figure 3-14 *Humor can be an effective way to ease tension and provide relief from stress.*

group of people? If so, you probably realized that your laughter helped to relieve your feelings of stress.

If used in moderation, humor can be an effective stress-management tool. It allows you to deal quickly with a stressor and keep it in the proper perspective. If, however, a person uses laughter to cover up his or her true feelings or if a person laughs inappropriately at a serious situation, humor may be an unhealthy way to cope.

Getting Help When You Need It

Learning ways to manage stress is important, but most people need extra help from time to time. Another skill that keeps you healthy is recognizing when the stresses in your life are becoming overwhelming. At those times, you may want to find someone to help you with your problems. Sometimes all you need is someone to talk to. Sharing your problems can help you see them more clearly. Just describing your concerns to someone else often helps you to understand the problem better.

Many people are willing to listen and lend support if you ask. You can try talking to a parent, teacher, sibling, friend, school counselor, coach, school nurse, or religious leader. If the person cannot help you with your specific concerns, he or she may be able to refer you to someone who can.

At some time in your life, you may want or need some kind of counseling. Many specialists are available to work with people who need help coping with stress. Some specialists are trained to treat mental illnesses, which you will learn about in Chapter 4. Others are trained to help you identify the stressors in your life and learn constructive strategies for coping with them.

LESSON 4 REVIEW

1. How can good stress management help keep you healthy?
2. Give an example of a time when confronting a problem (a) could lead to reduced stress, and (b) could lead to increased stress.
3. Why are physical activity and relaxation important stress-management tools?
4. Explain how the process of mental rehearsal can help you manage stress.

What Do You Think?

5. Suppose, after a particularly stressful day, you find yourself unable to fall asleep. How would you relax?

Time Management

John was late for school again. Last night, he stayed up late to write a report that was assigned two weeks ago. He planned to do his math homework in the morning, but then slept through his alarm. In his haste this morning, John left his gym clothes at home. Running toward the school as the bell rang, John felt anxious and tense.

Many people are like John. They rush from one activity to another with no clear goal or schedule. These people never seem to have enough time to do everything they want to do. John, for example, wants to get his driver's license. But he has no idea how he will fit driver's education classes into his life.

John and many other people could be more productive if they managed their time better. A good time manager is someone who completes daily tasks, works toward long-term goals, and still finds time to relax. The time management process outlined here will help you to plan your day-to-day schedule so you can accomplish the tasks that are important to you.

Time management skills can help you make better use of your time.

1. List your goals

Make a list of all the things you would like to accomplish in the next six months. Then rate each goal according to how important it is to you. Use this scale.

A = very important

B = somewhat important

C = not very important

My Six-Month Goals	
Get my driver's license	A
Buy a new bicycle	C
Make the baseball team	B
Pass Math	A
Get a part-time job	B

2. Outline your tasks

For each of the goals you rated "A," list all the activities you need to complete in order to accomplish the goal. If possible, break each activity down into smaller, more manageable tasks. This makes the activity easier to tackle.

You may also wish to outline the tasks for a few of your more important "B" goals, although these are of lower priority. Do not focus on your "C" goals unless you have extra time.

3. Outline an overall plan

For each task, assign a specific and realistic deadline. To do this, estimate how long the task will take and when you want it completed.

Top "A" Goal		
Activities	Time Needed	Deadline
1. Take driver's ed. course		
a. Find out schedule & fee	20 mins	today
b. Sign up for course	1/2 hr	tomorrow
2. Learn to drive		
a. Take permit test	2 hrs	next Fri.

4. Make a daily schedule

Each day, list the tasks from step 3 that you need to accomplish in order to stick to your overall plan. Also list the chores and other commitments you have that day.

Do not schedule too many tasks each day. Make a practice of allowing more time for a task than you think it will require. Allow some time for unplanned events.

Things to Do Today	
Find out driver's ed. schedule	A
Finish Math assignment	A
Take trash out	A
Help Matt rebuild bicycle	B
Watch TV	C
Clean room	B

5. Prioritize your tasks

Assign an "A," "B," or "C" rating to each task and chore for each day. Do "A" tasks and chores first each day, followed by "B" and "C" tasks, even if a "C" task is easier.

6. Monitor your progress

At different points during the day, ask yourself, "Is this the best use of my time?" If your answer is *no*, consider these questions.

- Is the task too overwhelming? If so, break it into smaller steps. Make a list of tasks that you can do in less than five minutes.

- Are you afraid you will fail or make mistakes? If so, list your fears. You may realize the task is not as difficult as you thought.

- What are you doing instead of your important tasks? Are these activities as important to you? Will they help you achieve your long-term goals?

Apply the Skill

1. Take ten minutes to list the goals you want to accomplish in the next six months.

2. Rate the goals using the A-B-C rating scale. Which goals will most benefit you in the long run? Assign an "A" rating to each of those goals.

3. Break down each "A" goal into simple activities, and then into even simpler tasks. Assign specific and realistic deadlines for these tasks.

4. Each day for a week, make a daily schedule and prioritize your tasks using the A-B-C scale. Do your "A" tasks first each day, followed by "B" and "C" tasks. If you find that you are putting things off, ask yourself the questions in step 6. At the end of the week, report to your class on how helpful the time management process has been for you.

CHAPTER **3** REVIEW

KEY IDEAS

LESSON 1

- You experience stress when situations, events, or people make demands on your body and mind.
- Stress is not always a negative experience. Positive stress leads to growth and accomplishment.

LESSON 2

- The body's response to stress occurs in three stages—the alarm stage, the resistance stage, and the exhaustion stage.
- Stress can lower the body's resistance to illness and can contribute to disorders such as ulcers, asthma, high blood pressure, and heart disease.

LESSON 3

- Personality affects how a person responds to potentially stressful situations. Type A personalities are more rushed and competitive than the calmer, less stress-prone type B personality.
- Perfectionism and negative thinking can lead to increased stress, while hardiness can decrease stress levels.

LESSON 4

- Methods for managing stress include confronting a problem, managing time well, being physically active, and making time for relaxation. Parents, teachers, and counselors are available to help people deal with stress.

KEY TERMS

LESSON 1
distress

eustress

stress

stressor

LESSON 2
adrenaline

asthma

fight or flight response

homeostasis

psychosomatic illness

ulcer

LESSON 3
hardiness

perfectionist

type A personality

type B personality

LESSON 4
biofeedback

Listed above are some of the important terms in this chapter. Choose the term from the list that best matches each phrase below.

1. immediate reaction to stress that prepares you to either confront or run away from a stressor

2. physical disorder that results from stress or other emotional causes

3. state in which the body's internal functions are in balance

4. substance that produces a burst of energy when released in the body

5. open sore in the lining of the stomach or other part of the digestive tract

6. method of stress management where a person controls physical functions by learning to recognize the body's signals

7. personality type that is competitive, driven to achieve, and likely to create stressors

8. negative stress

9. reaction of the body and mind to threatening or challenging events

10. characteristic of people who show remarkable resistance to stress

11. positive stress

12. a situation, event, or person that causes stress

13. personality type that is calm and noncompetitive

14. disorder of the respiratory system that makes breathing difficult

WHAT HAVE YOU LEARNED?

On a separate sheet of paper, write the word or words that best complete each statement.

15. Alarm clocks, tests, and arguments with friends are examples of _____.

16. Positive stress, or _____, promotes growth and accomplishment.

17. During the _____ stage of stress, reactions in the body prepare a person to fight or run away.

18. An ulcer is one example of a stress-related, or _____, illness.

19. _____ is a respiratory disorder that can be worsened by stress.

20. A _____ accepts nothing less than excellence of himself or herself.

21. An example of _____ is, "I'll never be able to do this."

22. Good _____ means using one's time productively to get the most done each day.

Answer each of the following with complete sentences.

23. What is stress? What is a stressor?

24. Explain how stress can be a positive experience.

25. What happens to your body during the fight or flight response?

26. Why does the body need to regain homeostasis soon after facing a stressor?

27. What two questions help a person assess whether a particular situation is stressful?

28. In what ways can stress lead to illness?

29. Why do type A personalities often experience high stress levels?

30. Explain how perfectionism and negative thinking affect a person's stress level.

31. Why is stress management essential for staying healthy?

32. List five things a person can do to prevent stress from becoming overwhelming.

WHAT DO YOU THINK?

33. Many people who experience serious stress do not seek help. Why do you think this is so?

34. What might life be like if there were no stress at all?

35. Why do you think stress is linked to changes in a person's life?

36. How would the fight or flight response help you if you were in a car accident?

37. What special stress management methods are most useful to you? Why?

38. Do you think that adolescence is an especially stressful time? Explain.

WHAT WOULD YOU DO?

39. Your best friend has been complaining of stiff, cramped muscles. The problem has become worse since her parents decided to separate. What things could you do to help her?

40. You have decided to run for class president and must make a speech in front of the entire student body. What can you do to help yourself relax so you can perform better during your speech?

41. You have a friend who is involved in so many activities that he no longer has time for you. Lately, he complains that he "can't think straight anymore." What advice would you give him?

42. You become anxious during a test and have difficulty concentrating. What can you do to calm yourself down?

Getting Involved

43. Ask students, teachers, and administrators at your school what can be done to reduce student stress. Choose the best suggestion and write a proposal for putting it into effect.

44. In one column, list things in your community that increase stress (for example, noise). In another column, list things that can lower stress (for example, bicycle paths).

MENTAL DISORDERS AND SUICIDE

It is important to have healthy outlets, such as painting, for expressing your feelings. Sometimes, however, a person's ability to cope with emotions and stressors breaks down. In this chapter you will explore the problems of mental disorders and suicide and learn where to find help.

CHAPTER PREVIEW

4-1 What Are Mental Disorders?

- Explain what mental disorders are and what may cause them.

4-2 Kinds of Mental Disorders

- Describe how mental disorders are classified.

4-3 Suicide

- Identify the warning signs of suicide

4-4 Treating Mental Disorders

- Identify ways to treat mental disorders.

BUILDING HEALTH SKILLS

- Create a directory of mental-health services in your community.

CHECK YOUR WELLNESS

To test how much you know about mental disorders, decide whether each statement is true or false.

- Some physical diseases, such as brain tumors, may lead to mental disorders.

- If feelings of depression are long-lasting and interfere with everyday activities, a person should seek help.

- Some mental disorders, such as clinical depression, tend to run in families.

- Eating disorders, such as anorexia nervosa and bulimia, are treated like mental disorders.

- Some warning signs of suicide are sudden personality change, inability to concentrate, and increased risk taking.

- Help for mental problems is available from family members, school counselors, hotlines, crisis centers, members of the clergy, local hospitals, and mental-health clinics.

KEEPING A JOURNAL

In your journal, explore why you think the teenage suicide rate has increased. What can people do to stop this trend?

Take it to **the Net**

www.phschool.com

1 WHAT ARE MENTAL DISORDERS?

Focus on these questions as you read this lesson.

- What are mental disorders?
- What are some of the causes of mental disorders?

SKILLS

- Finding the Facts

What behaviors are considered normal and appropriate? What behaviors are considered abnormal and inappropriate? As you read the descriptions of the teenagers below, decide whether or not you would consider their behaviors normal.

Linda: In the last six months, Linda has become more and more concerned about germs. She washes her hands at least 100 times a day, scrubs the doorknobs in her house, and insists that her knives, forks, and spoons be boiled before she uses them.

José: José is an avid skateboarder. Since his parents' divorce, he has used his skateboard in increasingly dangerous situations. Now, he regularly dodges cars and trucks as he skateboards across a four-lane highway near school.

Pat: Pat is 5 feet 6 inches tall and weighs 97 pounds. For the past three months, she has been on a strict diet of cottage cheese, lettuce, and water. She still considers herself heavy and wants to lose five pounds.

Arthur: Arthur enjoys collecting pictures and descriptions of past wars. Outside of school, he spends all of his spare time in his room organizing his collection. He has no time for friends or social activities.

Recognizing Mental Disorders

Most mental-health specialists would agree that each of these teenagers shows signs of a mental disorder. A **mental disorder** is an illness that affects the mind and prevents a person from being productive, adjusting to life situations, or getting along with others. **Most mental disorders are characterized by abnormal thoughts, feelings, or behaviors that make people uncomfortable with themselves or at odds with others.** The term **abnormal** is used to describe behaviors, feelings, or thoughts that are highly unusual and inappropriate in a given situation. Washing your hands before eating is considered normal behavior. Washing your hands 100 times a day, like Linda, is considered abnormal. When a mental disorder is present, its signs usually occur frequently and over a long period of time.

Labeling a person as mentally ill is difficult. It involves making a judgment. Unlike a cold or the flu, the signs of mental disorders are not always easy to identify. For example, it is sometimes hard to tell if someone is seriously depressed or just appropriately sad.

Figure 4-1 *People with mental disorders feel at odds with themselves and have trouble adjusting to life situations.*

Figure 4-2 *Some unusual behaviors may be considered normal in our culture.*

Since each person exists as part of a particular society and culture, each person's notion of mental illness is shaped by his or her culture, as well as by his or her family, community, and other experiences. A behavior or way of thinking that might be considered normal in one culture may be considered abnormal in another culture. Look at Figure 4-2. Do you think these behaviors would be considered abnormal in some cultures? Are these behaviors considered normal in our culture?

You may be surprised to find that not everyone in your class agrees on what is normal or abnormal behavior. Mental-health specialists also do not always agree. For this reason mental-health specialists meet every so often to discuss mental disorders. They define and describe mental disorders and group them according to similar symptoms, which are the signs or evidence of an illness.

Over the years the descriptions and classifications of mental disorders have changed. Today, over 230 types of mental disorders are recognized. Although many experts agree on the kinds of mental disorders, there are still many different opinions about the causes.

Causes of Mental Disorders

Some mental disorders can be traced to physical causes. When the cause of a mental disorder is physical, the mental disorder is classified as an **organic disorder.** One common type of organic disorder is **dementia** (dih MEN shuh), an irreversible loss of brain function. People with dementia suffer from memory loss, poor judgment, and mental confusion.

●●●●●●●●●●●●●●●●●●
SHARPEN YOUR *SKILLS*

Finding the Facts

At the library, find out about post-traumatic stress disorder, which has only recently been classified as a mental disorder. Who suffers from this disorder? How is it treated?

Should Criminals Be Allowed to Plead Insanity?

Americans were shocked when John Hinkley, Jr., shot President Reagan and two other men in 1981. Even more shocking, Hinkley was found *not guilty by reason of insanity. Insanity* is a legal term, not a psychological one. It means that a jury decided that a person who committed a crime was mentally ill and, thus, could not understand that the actions were wrong. The person is sent to a mental institution instead of to prison.

Some people feel the insanity defense protects citizens whose mental states prevent them from distinguishing right from wrong. These citizens are mentally ill, they argue, not criminals. They should be put in mental institutions, where they can get treatment.

Other people feel the insanity defense has been misused and should be eliminated. The key witnesses in these trials are psychiatrists, who base their testimonies on opinions, not facts. There have been cases where people who acted mentally ill during their trials were declared sane soon after they were institutionalized. Once released, some of these people repeated their crimes. In other cases people remained in mental institutions much longer than they would have stayed in prison.

☞ **Should we do away with the insanity defense? Why or why not?**

Dementia may occur when an individual has a growth, or tumor, in the brain. Prolonged drug or alcohol abuse can also lead to dementia. Alzheimer's disease, a disease that affects some adults and results in dementia, is discussed in Chapter 11.

Mental disorders that cannot be traced to physical causes are called **functional** (FUNGK shuh nul) **disorders.** The exact cause of most functional disorders is not understood. Often many factors are involved. These factors can include inborn causes, early experiences, current causes, or a combination of all three.

INBORN CAUSES   Some mental disorders may be inherited, or passed on to an individual before birth, just as physical characteristics, such as eye color, are. Sometimes an individual may inherit a tendency toward a disorder. The disorder may only become apparent when it is set off by events in the person's life, such as repeated physical abuse or other serious stressors.

EARLY EXPERIENCES   Other mental disorders may be the result of unpleasant experiences that occurred early in life. As you may recall from Chapter 2, Sigmund Freud believed that such early life experiences are pushed into the unconscious mind. Psychoanalysis, according to Freud, can help a person connect the symptoms of a mental disorder with his or her early experiences and conflicts.

CURRENT CAUSES   Some mental-health specialists think that recent experiences in a person's life are more important than early childhood experiences in bringing on a mental disorder. They consider significant events and people in the individual's current life when treating the disorder. Sometimes the specialist may involve the person's family or close friends in the treatment program.

LESSON 1 REVIEW

1. What is a mental disorder?
2. Why is it sometimes difficult for someone to recognize a mental disorder?
3. What is the difference between organic disorders and functional disorders?
4. List four possible causes of mental disorders.

What Do You Think?

5. Why do you think that some people seek a doctor's help for a physical disease, such as flu, but hesitate to seek professional help for a mental disorder?

2 KINDS OF MENTAL DISORDERS

GUIDE FOR READING

Focus on these questions as you read this lesson.

- How are mental disorders classified?
- What are the signs of clinical depression?

SKILLS
- DECIDE

If you have ever had the flu, you know the symptoms well—fever, muscle aches, runny nose, and more. For the flu and other physical disorders, symptoms do not differ much from person to person. With mental disorders, however, things are not so clearcut. Symptoms of mental disorders can vary greatly from one individual to the next. This makes it difficult to provide accurate descriptions of mental disorders.

One way to get a general picture of a mental disorder is to read a case history. A **case history** is a brief description of a person who suffers from a particular disorder. Although case histories focus on only a few symptoms of a disorder, those symptoms are usually the most common ones. As you read the case histories that follow, remember that only trained, mental-health professionals have the expertise to diagnose mental disorders.

Anxiety Disorders

Have you ever been afraid of a situation, person, or object that you knew could not really harm you? Have you been fearful without knowing why? If so, you have experienced anxiety. **Anxiety** (ang ZY ih tee) is fear that does not have an identifiable source or fear caused by a danger that no longer exists. Severe anxiety can cause people to flee from situations or objects that cannot really harm them.

Everyone experiences some anxiety at one time or another. For example, you may feel anxious before a final exam, a big date, or tryouts for the basketball team. These feelings are normal and usually short-lived. When anxiety persists and interferes with normal, everyday functioning, however, it is a sign of a mental illness known as an **anxiety disorder**. Some types of anxiety disorders are described below.

PHOBIC DISORDERS When anxiety is related to a specific situation or object, it is called a **phobia** (FOH bee uh).

> **Martin:** Martin was on his way to a job interview. As he walked toward the elevator, he began to feel dizzy and nauseous. His heart began to pound, and he had trouble catching his breath. He knew he could not face getting into the elevator, so he climbed three flights of stairs to get to his interview on time.

When Martin sought help in handling his severe anxiety, he was diagnosed as having claustrophobia—a fear of small, closed-in places. Figure 4-3 lists some common phobias. As you look over the list, think about how such fears might affect normal living.

Figure 4-3 *Which of these phobias might interfere with normal, everyday activities?*

Common Phobias	
Phobia	**Fear of:**
Acrophobia	high places
Agoraphobia	open or public places
Algophobia	pain
Astraphobia	lightning and thunder
Claustrophobia	small, closed-in places
Cynophobia	dogs
Hydrophobia	water
Monophobia	being alone
Mysophobia	dirt and germs
Nyctophobia	darkness
Ophidiophobia	snakes
Pyrophobia	fire
Thanatophobia	death and dying
Xenophobia	strangers
Zoophobia	animals

GENERAL ANXIETY AND PANIC DISORDERS   A person who feels anxious but cannot specify a cause for the anxiety has a general anxiety disorder. If a person experiences attacks of extreme anxiety that come and go for no apparent reason, he or she has a panic disorder. A person with a panic disorder can be anywhere when he or she suddenly starts to feel panicky or extremely anxious.

OBSESSIVE-COMPULSIVE DISORDER   Sometimes, a person responds to anxiety by letting an idea or thought take over his or her mind. An idea or thought that takes over the mind and cannot be forgotten is called an **obsession** (ub SESH un). An obsession sometimes leads to a **compulsion** (kum PUHL shun), an unreasonable need to behave in a certain way. A person who thinks and acts in such a rigid way is said to have an obsessive-compulsive disorder.

Think about the case history of Linda at the beginning of this chapter. Linda suffers from an obsessive-compulsive disorder. Because of some deep-seated anxiety, she is obsessed with germs. This causes her to behave in a compulsive way: washing her hands constantly, scrubbing doorknobs, and boiling her silverware.

Somatoform Disorders

A mental disorder in which a person complains of physical symptoms, such as pain, when no underlying physical cause can be found is known as a **somatoform** (soh MAT uh fawrm) **disorder.**

> **Juanita:** Juanita is convinced that she is about to become seriously ill. She takes her temperature every day and reads health magazines for the symptoms of major illnesses. At least once a week, she complains to the school nurse of chest pains, headaches, or stomach-aches. She blames her poor performance in school on her health. The school nurse and her physician tell Juanita that there is nothing wrong with her physically, but Juanita does not believe them.

Juanita is suffering from **hypochondria** (hy puh KAHN dree uh), a somatoform disorder characterized by a constant fear of disease and preoccupation with one's health. Sometimes, the underlying cause of hypochondria is anxiety or depression. In Juanita's case, the cause was anxiety. Juanita was extremely anxious about doing well in school because her older brother and sister had both excelled in school.

Many people confuse somatoform disorders such as hypochondria with the stress-related symptoms and psychosomatic illnesses discussed in Chapter 3. Stress-related conditions are characterized by real physical damage to the body. With somatoform disorders, a person complains of disease symptoms, but no physical damage can be found.

Eating Disorders

Sometimes, emotional problems reveal themselves through abnormal eating behaviors. Two serious eating disorders, anorexia nervosa and bulimia, affect a growing number of teenagers. Research on twins suggests a possible genetic link for anorexia nervosa, but most people feel that the disorder stems from today's emphasis on being thin.

ANOREXIA NERVOSA   Perhaps you recognized the symptoms of an eating disorder when you read the case history of Pat at the beginning of this chapter. Pat is suffering from **anorexia nervosa** (an uh REK see uh nur VOH suh), a serious eating disorder in which a person refuses to eat enough food to maintain a minimum normal body weight.

The main symptom of anorexia is an extreme loss of body weight. A person suffering from anorexia literally wastes away and can starve to death. Other symptoms include slowed heart and breathing rates, lowered body temperature, dry skin, growth of fine body hair, and loss of menstrual periods in females. In some cases, a lack of essential minerals causes the heart to stop suddenly, leading to death.

Typically, anorexia affects teenaged girls—as many as one out of every one hundred. Some boys also suffer from anorexia. Anorexics usually have low self-esteem and are overly concerned with pleasing others. They may feel that by becoming thin they can gain the respect and admiration of others. Anorexics also tend to be perfectionists, especially about their physical appearance. Although already underweight, anorexics often view themselves as fat and work even harder at losing weight.

Teams of physicians, nurses, mental-health specialists, and dietitians work together to treat people with anorexia. Because of their extreme weight loss, anorexics are often hospitalized at first to stabilize their weight and eating habits. Years of treatment, sometimes with family members, are often needed to resolve the underlying problems. With prompt attention from a mental-health professional and cooperation from the patient and family members, anorexia nervosa can be treated successfully.

Figure 4-5 *With counseling and strong family support, anorexics can overcome their disorder.*

D E C I D E

DEFINE
the problem

EXPLORE
alternatives

CONSIDER
the consequences

IDENTIFY
values

DECIDE
and act

EVALUATE
results

A Bulimic Friend?

Your girlfriend is a dancer. Most of her life revolves around dancing. She has always been thin, but lately is worried that she's becoming too fat to be a dancer.

Recently, you've noticed that she either eats very little or overeats and then forces herself to throw up. Although she doesn't seem to have lost much weight, you are worried about her. You have heard about the eating disorders anorexia nervosa and bulimia, and you are beginning to wonder if she could be developing one of them.

1. Use the DECIDE process on page 18 to decide what you would do in this situation. Explain your reasons for making this decision.

2. Suppose the action you decided to take did not bring satisfactory results. What would you do next? Explain.

BULIMIA Another eating disorder found primarily among teenaged girls is **bulimia** (byoo LIM ee uh). Individuals suffering from bulimia go on eating binges followed by purging, or getting rid of the food they have eaten. Bulimics get rid of their food by self-induced vomiting or using laxatives.

Although bulimia is much more prevalent than anorexia, it is difficult to know how many people suffer from this disorder. Bulimia is difficult to diagnose because the behavior is done in private and the person appears normal. Bulimia may begin in connection with a diet, but the person soon becomes unable to stop the binging and purging behavior.

While most bulimics do not become dangerously underweight, there are other serious health effects. Bulimics may suffer from dehydration and kidney damage. The enamel on their teeth may become eroded from the stomach acid introduced into the mouth when vomiting occurs. Some bulimics experience vitamin and mineral deficiencies as well as tearing and bleeding of the tongue and gums. Typically, bulimics become depressed and may consider suicide or abuse alcohol or other drugs. As with anorexia, bulimics should seek the immediate assistance of a mental-health professional.

Mood Disorders

A person whose moods or emotions become extreme and interfere with his or her daily life has a mental disorder known as a **mood disorder.**

Jason: Ever since Jason's girlfriend broke up with him, he has felt sad and hopeless. Jason used to love playing drums in the school band, but now he has quit. He cannot sleep and feels tired all the time. His grades have fallen from a B average to a D average.

Everyone feels depressed now and then. It is normal to feel depressed if you experience an important loss or a failure. For example, you would expect to feel depressed if a good friend had recently moved away or if you didn't make a team you tried out for. Usually, however, the feeling of depression lifts after a few days or weeks, and you get on with your life. In Jason's case, however, his feelings of hopelessness and depression have taken over his life, leaving him unable to cope with everyday activities.

CLINICAL DEPRESSION A person who is overwhelmed by sad feelings for months and stops being able to carry out everyday activities is suffering from a mental disorder known as **clinical depression,** or major depressive disorder. Clinical depression can be caused by stressors, or it can be a symptom of another disease, such as alcoholism. Depression tends to run in families. Negative attitudes learned early in life may also contribute to clinical depression.

Some of the early signs of clinical depression are listed in Figure 4-6. Some teenagers who develop clinical depression lose interest in most of their usual activities and become withdrawn like Jason. Other teenagers may become overly active or take unnecessary risks like José, whom you read about at the start of this chapter.

Signs of Clinical Depression

A person probably is suffering from clinical depression if the person feels sad and hopeless and has at least four of the following symptoms nearly every day for at least two weeks:

- Change in appetite: either poor appetite with significant weight loss or increased appetite with significant weight gain

- Change in sleep patterns: either difficulty sleeping or sleeping too much

- Change in activity level: either increased physical activity or slowed-down levels of activity

- Loss of interest or pleasure in usual activities

- Loss of energy, feeling tired all the time

- Feelings of worthlessness; excessive or inappropriate guilty feelings

- Difficulty thinking or concentrating

- Recurrent thoughts of death and suicide

Figure 4-6 *What would you do if a friend showed signs of clinical depression?*

SAD Patients See the Light

Do you suffer from the "winter blahs" as the days get shorter? Some people are not only sad in winter, they have SAD, seasonal affective disorder.

SAD is a deficiency disorder. Just as scurvy is caused by a lack of vitamin C, SAD is caused by a lack of the full range of light, which is not typically found indoors. As the supply of natural light decreases, people with SAD begin to show signs of depression. Unlike some depressed people, who have trouble eating and sleeping, SAD patients act more like hibernating animals. They sleep up to 18 hours a day, crave starchy foods, and gain weight.

Treatment for SAD sufferers involves phototherapy, exposure to a full range of bright lights, for two hours a day. For 80 percent of SAD sufferers, the light treatment seems to lower the level of certain chemicals in the body, which relieves the symptoms of SAD.

Phototherapy can help patients with SAD.

Anyone who shows signs of clinical depression should seek help from a parent, teacher, guidance counselor, physician, or mental-health professional. With help, clinical depression can be eased and will usually go away. Individuals suffering from clinical depression can learn new strategies for coping with problems. If a depressed person becomes extremely withdrawn, dangerous, or suicidal, it may be necessary for the person to enter a hospital.

BIPOLAR DISORDER Normally, people have moods that shift from happy and lively to sad and indifferent, depending on what is happening in their lives. People who suffer from bipolar, or manic-depressive, disorder shift from one emotional extreme to another for no apparent reason.

During a manic episode, manic-depressives usually become overly excited and restless. They may talk so rapidly that it is impossible to follow what they are trying to say. They may have difficulty concentrating for long on any one thing. They frequently show poor judgment. They may overspend during a shopping spree, for example, or they may drive recklessly. These manic episodes alternate with periods of deep depression. In between these periods of extreme moods, manic-depressives may behave normally.

Personality Disorders

Every person has a different way of dealing with life situations. You may like to have every minute of your day carefully planned, or you may love to do things on the spur of the moment. You may be neat, or you may be messy. You may

Figure 4-7 *Most people can get along with people whose personalities are different from theirs.*

crave time to yourself, or you may always like being with others. These patterns of behavior make up your personality.

A **personality disorder** is characterized by behavior that is inflexible and interferes with a person's pursuit of a happy, healthy life. Because personality traits are usually set by young adulthood, these disorders often require long-term treatment. Two types of personality disorders are described below.

PASSIVE-AGGRESSIVE PERSONALITY DISORDER
People with passive-aggressive personality disorders depend on others to direct them. At the same time, they resent being told what to do. Unable to be assertive and express their anger openly, they vent it indirectly.

> **Larry:** Larry hates his after-school job. Every day he arrives late and leaves early. His boss criticizes him for doing his work slowly and sloppily. Half the time, Larry "forgets" to do what his boss has told him.

Larry shows many of the signs of a passive-aggressive personality: chronic lateness, forgetfulness, slowness, and sloppiness. He expresses his resentment indirectly, through his failure to be reliable.

ANTISOCIAL PERSONALITY DISORDER
People with antisocial personality disorders perform cruel and violent acts without feeling any guilt. Because of their behavior, these people often have criminal records. Their crimes are random, impulsive, and often purposeless. Unfortunately, these dangerous people rarely seek professional help.

Dissociative Disorders

Suppose you read a newspaper article that began "Joan Smith was found wandering the snow-covered streets of the city. She was wearing summer clothing and did not know who she was." You might recognize that Joan shows signs of **amnesia** (am NEE zhuh), the sudden loss of memory. Amnesia is one type of **dissociative disorder,** a mental disorder in which a person becomes disconnected from his or her former identity. Amnesia may be brought on by a severe **trauma** (TROW muh), a painful physical or emotional experience. For example, a person who witnesses the death of a loved one may develop amnesia. Amnesia may last a short time or for the rest of a person's life.

Another dissociative disorder is called multiple personality disorder. People with this disorder switch between two or more separate personalities. Usually, they are not aware of the different personalities coexisting within their minds. They are also unable to control or predict their personality changes. Although multiple personality disorder is rare, you may have heard about it from books or movies.

Figure 4-8 *The movie* Sybil *portrayed a woman suffering from multiple personality disorder.*

Figure 4-9 *These self-portraits, done by a schizophrenic, reflect the artist's mental state before (left) and after (right) receiving treatment.*

Schizophrenia

One of the most serious mental disorders is **schizophrenia** (skit suh FREE nee uh), a disorder characterized by unpredictable disturbances in thinking, mood, awareness, and behavior. *Schizophrenia* means "split mind." People with this mental disorder have minds that are "split off" from reality.

Schizophrenics are rarely harmful to others. At times they may appear normal. At other times, schizophrenics may talk to themselves, exhibit inappropriate emotional responses, dress and act strangely, and withdraw from others. Some schizophrenics develop irrational fears that someone or something controls their thoughts or wants to harm them.

Figure 4-9 shows drawings done by a schizophrenic teenager. The drawing on the left shows a state of mental confusion. The drawing on the right shows that, with successful treatment, the artist's mental state has improved.

LESSON *2* REVIEW

1. What is an anxiety disorder?
2. What is a somatoform disorder? How does it differ from a psychosomatic illness?
3. List five signs of clinical depression.
4. What are the symptoms of schizophrenia?

What Do You Think?

5. How would you react if you found out that a friend was taking medication regularly for a mental disorder?

3 SUICIDE

A teenager named Vivienne wrote the poem below. Vivienne took her own life when she was 14. From the poem, would you have known that Vivienne was thinking of committing suicide?

> It takes tolerance
> Not to give in to death,
> To resist the temptation
> How easy just to die.
> To keep on living an empty life
> Takes patience from an empty person.

Suicide affects all kinds of people: young, old, bright, average, rich, poor, female, male. In this country, suicide is one of the leading causes of death among teenagers. Between 1950 and 1990, the teen suicide rate quadrupled. Then in the 1990s, it finally began to decline.

Because the topic of suicide is not openly discussed, many myths exist. Unfortunately, not knowing the facts about suicide can mean the difference between life and death. How much do you know about the problem of suicide? Read over the myths and facts about suicide on the next page. What new information about suicide did you learn?

The Warning Signs

Suicides often can be prevented if people know how to recognize and help potential victims. People who may be considering suicide often behave in telltale ways. **The crucial first step in helping a suicidal person is to recognize the problem as early as possible.**

Some of the warning signs to look for are the same as the signs of depression listed in Figure 4-6—withdrawal from usual activities, loss of energy, change in sleep patterns, and other deviations from normal behavior. Radical changes in personality—an outgoing person who suddenly withdraws or a shy person who becomes aggressive—are another sign of possible depression. Severe depression may cause a person to give up. Anyone who is suffering from a major depression should be watched carefully.

Sometimes, a person's actions are a warning sign. If a person has attempted suicide before, the risk is high that he or she will try again. A person who stops doing things that he or she enjoys or gives away favorite belongings may be in need of help. A decline in school performance or an increase in drug use may also be signs of trouble. Another sign, which is especially common among severely depressed teenagers, is a sudden increase in injuries or risk-taking behaviors. José's

GUIDE FOR READING

Focus on these questions as you read this lesson.

- How can you tell when someone is suicidal?
- What can you do to help a suicidal person?

SKILLS

- Intervening to Help a Friend

Figure 4-10 *If you are depressed, instead of being alone, it is better to talk to people you trust.*

MYTHS & FACTS

Suicide

1. **MYTH:** People who talk about suicide seldom attempt suicide.

   ● **FACT: Suicide victims often talk about suicide before they actually attempt it.**

2. **MYTH:** If you dare a suicidal person to go ahead and do it, the person is not likely to attempt suicide.

   ● **FACT: Daring a suicidal person to attempt suicide may only convince the person that nobody cares and may strengthen the person's resolve to commit suicide.**

3. **MYTH:** Suicidal persons are always tired, sad, and inactive.

   ● **FACT: Some suicidal persons, teenagers in particular, may become overly active and aggressive before attempting suicide.**

4. **MYTH:** If people try to take their own lives and do not succeed, they usually will not try to do it again.

   ● **FACT: Suicide victims often have a history of several suicide attempts.**

5. **MYTH:** If a suicidal person confides in you and makes you promise not to tell anyone of his or her plans to commit suicide, it is important to keep the secret, no matter what.

   ● **FACT: By sharing the secret with a parent, teacher, or other responsible adult, you may save the person's life.**

6. **MYTH:** If a depressed, suicidal person suddenly seems better, you do not need to worry.

   ● **FACT: A suicidal person's sudden shift in mood from depressed to happy may indicate that he or she has resolved to commit suicide and needs help.**

7. **MYTH:** Suicide attempts should be kept secret because the information could ruin a suicidal person's future.

   ● **FACT: The suicidal person may have no future unless the person seeks professional help.**

case history at the start of this chapter is a good example of this type of behavior. José risked his life each time he skateboarded across the highway.

A person may also reveal suicidal plans through the things he or she says. Comments like "I don't want to live anymore," or "They'll be sorry when I'm gone" should be taken seriously. Talk about death and dying or about an actual plan for committing suicide is also cause for concern.

If a person has suffered a major trauma recently, he or she may become suicidal. Changes such as moving to a new place, losing a boyfriend or girlfriend, getting a serious illness, having a family member or friend die, or going through a family divorce can lead to depression and, sometimes, to suicide.

Some of the warning signs of suicide can be deceptive. If a person you know has been severely depressed and suddenly becomes happy and carefree, you may conclude that the problem has passed. This is not necessarily so. A sudden change from depressed to happy may mean that the person has resolved to end his or her life. The person feels happy because the decision is made.

Prevention

Suicide is a tragic, but preventable act. You can do many things to help yourself or others who are considering suicide.

HELPING YOURSELF If you have been feeling depressed, remember that no matter how overwhelming the problems in your life may seem, suicide is never a solution. It is vital that you talk about your feelings to a trusted adult or professional counselor. Together, you will be able to find solutions that you may not have thought of on your own. No matter how isolated you may feel, you do not have to deal with your problems alone. No matter how hopeless you feel your situation is, there are positive steps that you can take.

In most communities, crisis centers and suicide-prevention hotlines provide support for suicidal and depressed people. Some communities have hotlines that are staffed by specially trained, concerned teenagers. You can obtain the telephone number of the crisis centers and hotlines in your area by calling the information operator.

HELPING OTHERS What should you do if someone you know seems suicidal? Figure 4-11 offers some do's and don't's for helping a potential suicide victim. An important thing to remember is that suicidal behavior is a cry for help in dealing with problems that seem impossible. Suicidal people often feel that they have looked to others for support and have received no response. It is vital that you show caring and concern for the person.

The best way to show you care about a suicidal person is to make sure the person gets professional help immediately. If you believe that a friend is thinking of suicide, or if you become aware of a suicide pact among a group of teenagers, you should report it immediately to an adult, such as a

Figure 4-11 *What is the most important thing a friend can do to help a suicidal person?*

How to Help a Suicidal Person

Do	Don't
• Trust your feelings if you believe the person may be suicidal.	• Do NOT dare the suicidal person to go ahead and make the suicide attempt.
• Take seriously a suicidal person's threats.	• Do NOT judge the suicidal person.
• Tell the suicidal person how concerned you are and how much you care about him or her.	• Do NOT analyze the suicidal person's motives.
• Listen carefully to the suicidal person.	• Do NOT argue or try to convince the suicidal person of reasons why he or she should not attempt suicide.
• Talk calmly with the suicidal person.	
• Find professional help for the suicidal person.	• Do NOT keep the suicidal person's self-destructive thoughts or actions a secret.
• Stay with the suicidal person until help arrives.	• Do NOT leave a suicidal person alone.

Figure 4-12 *Suicidal people need to know that friends care about them and want to help.*

<table>
</table>

SHARPEN YOUR *SKILLS*

Intervening to Help a Friend

Your friend Hilda has been very sad since her brother died last month. She is showing some of the signs of clinical depression listed in Figure 4-6. You are very worried about Hilda, but she refuses to talk to you about her feelings. What could you do to help Hilda?

parent, teacher, or physician. Sometimes a friend may make you promise not to tell anyone about a plan to commit suicide. Whether or not your friend realizes it, by confiding in you, your friend is asking you for help. To help your friend, you must break the promise and notify an adult that your friend is in danger.

Sometimes a suicide or an attempted suicide triggers a particularly tragic form of suicide known as cluster suicide. **Cluster suicides,** which are frequently associated with teenagers, occur when several people in the same school or social group attempt to kill themselves within a short period of time. To prevent cluster suicides, all the people in the school or social group where a suicide or an attempted suicide has occurred should receive immediate counseling.

Suicide is not a reasonable or useful solution to a problem. Suicidal people usually want to get rid of their pain or sense of helplessness, not their lives. You can help by listening to and providing support for friends or family members who are feeling depressed, hopeless, or overwhelmed by stress. When the support you offer is backed by professional intervention, a life may be saved.

LESSON 3 REVIEW

1. List four warning signs of suicide.
2. What should you do if someone is suicidal?
3. How can cluster suicides be prevented?

What Do You Think?

4. Why do you think cluster suicides occur most frequently among teenagers?

4 TREATING MENTAL DISORDERS

GUIDE FOR READING

Focus on these questions as you read this lesson.

- Where can people seek help for emotional problems?
- How are mental disorders treated?

SKILLS

- Activity: Help Wanted

About one out of every five adults in this country is likely to suffer from a mental disorder at some time during his or her life. The first step toward recovery is recognizing the need for help. Do not ignore the warning signs of mental disorders. Some of these warning signs include

- a sudden, radical change in personality
- self-destructive actions: overeating, undereating, drug abuse, and taking unnecessary risks
- violent, uncontrollable shifts in mood
- persistent feelings of worthlessness or hopelessness
- deepening sadness that interferes with functioning
- sleep disturbances
- inability to concentrate on anything
- trouble getting along with others
- paralyzing attacks of fear or anger
- frequent illness without a physical cause
- obsessive thoughts or compulsive actions
- delusions or hallucinations

Where to Find Help

In most communities, it is not difficult to find help for mental disorders. **Often, a parent, relative, teacher, school counselor, physician, or religious leader can tell you about mental health professionals and services in your community.**

In many communities, local hospitals have mental-health centers. Other communities have mental-health clinics or counseling centers. Some communities have drop-in centers for teens, where counselors provide help and guidance. The Building Health Skills feature found on page 93 at the end of this chapter will help you locate mental-health services in your community.

Types of Help

There are many types of mental-health professionals. These are people who are specially trained to recognize and treat mental disorders. The type of treatment they offer depends upon their training.

PSYCHIATRISTS A physician who specializes in diagnosing and treating mental disorders is called a **psychiatrist** (sy KY uh trist). Psychiatrists are M.D.'s (doctors of medicine)

Figure 4-13 *Mental-health centers and clinics exist in most communities. Where can you go for help with emotional problems?*

with advanced training in the treatment of mental illnesses. They look for physical, as well as nonphysical, reasons for mental illnesses. Psychiatrists talk with patients, and sometimes with family members, to identify symptoms of a mental disorder. They also examine patients for physical causes.

After diagnosing a disorder, a psychiatrist may treat the disorder in a variety of ways. Because psychiatrists are medical doctors, they can prescribe medications to treat mental disorders.

If a psychiatrist suspects that a patient's symptoms may have an organic cause, he or she may recommend testing by a neurologist. A **neurologist** (noo RAHL uh jist) is a physician who specializes in detecting and treating organic disorders of the brain and nervous system.

CLINICAL PSYCHOLOGISTS A **clinical psychologist** is a mental-health professional who specializes in recognizing and treating abnormal behavior. In addition to a doctoral degree in psychology, clinical psychologists have at least two years of practical training in clinics or hospitals. Because they are not medical doctors, clinical psychologists cannot prescribe medications.

Clinical psychologists use a variety of treatment methods. Often, psychologists work with psychiatrists. A psychologist may help a psychiatrist diagnose a mental disorder or give tests to determine the psychological condition of a patient.

SOCIAL WORKERS A **social worker** is a mental-health professional who counsels patients and provides a link between the patient and the treatment center. Many schools also have social workers available to counsel students. Social workers usually complete four years of college and two years of advanced study in social work.

Psychiatric social workers specialize in helping the mentally ill and their families accept and adjust to mental illness. Most psychiatric social workers work in hospitals, mental-health clinics, or family agencies.

Figure 4-14 *Social workers, occupational therapists, and hotline counselors are specially trained to help people with problems.*

HELP WANTED

In this activity you will create a "business card" to advertise your willingness to help out friends in need of support.

Materials

construction paper	markers or colored
scissors	pencils

Procedure

1. Use construction paper to design a "business card" to let friends know that you are available to support them in times of depression. List the qualities you possess that make you right for the job, your hours, and other information.

2. Decorate your card with drawings or other artwork to emphasize your message.

3. Make additional copies of your business card and distribute them to friends and family members.

Discussion

1. Why do you think people who are feeling depressed hesitate to ask others for help?

2. What qualities do you look for in a person in whom you confide your problems?

3. What is the best way to reach out to a friend who seems depressed?

4. How can having close relationships help you stay mentally healthy?

OTHER MENTAL-HEALTH SPECIALISTS Many other specialists help people with mental disorders. Psychiatric nurses specialize in the care and treatment of the mentally ill. **Occupational therapists** help the mentally ill become productive members of society by teaching them practical skills. **Pastoral counselors** are members of the religious community who have had practical training in counseling people with mental and social problems.

Some mental-health counselors work with specific problems or specific groups. Substance abuse counselors, for example, work with people who have drug problems. School counselors work with students who are having problems in school or at home. Youth counselors work with teenagers who are having problems.

Whatever the problem, there are people to help you. Parents or other adults in your family are a good place to start. Although it may be difficult, try to share your problems with a parent, guardian, or other responsible adult. Facing up to a problem is the first step to overcoming it.

Kinds of Treatments

After a mental disorder has been diagnosed, it may be treated in a number of ways. The particular **therapy,** or treatment technique, chosen depends upon the individual and the training of the mental-health professional. Treatments include psychotherapy, drug therapy, and hospitalization.

Figure 4-15 *Family therapy can be an effective means of solving some mental problems.*

PSYCHOTHERAPY   Most mental-health professionals use **psychotherapy** (sy koh THEHR uh pee), a treatment method that involves conversations with a trained professional who helps an individual understand and overcome a mental disorder. There are many types of psychotherapy. You are already familiar with one type—psychoanalysis. Other types are described below.

- Behavioral therapy helps a person change an abnormal behavior by substituting a new, more appropriate behavior in its place. Phobias and obsessive-compulsive disorders are often treated with behavioral therapy.
- Group therapy involves meeting with other people who suffer from similar disorders. A mental-health professional leads the group. Group members support each other and work together to develop coping skills.
- Family therapy focuses on family problems, such as divorce, and how they affect the family as a whole.
- Play therapy helps young patients act out problem situations and solutions using dolls and other toys.

DRUG THERAPY   Many mental disorders, such as anxiety disorders, affective disorders, manic-depressive disorder, and schizophrenia, can be treated effectively through medication. Although the medications may not cure the mental disorder, they do relieve the symptoms and allow patients to function normally. Unfortunately, some people experience negative side effects or develop a dependency on the medication.

HOSPITALIZATION   People with mental disorders who need constant attention or who are in danger of harming themselves or others may be hospitalized. In the hospital, patients receive psychotherapy, drug therapy, or both. The staff works with patients to prepare them for leaving the hospital. Occupational therapists teach patients practical skills to help them manage on their own. After patients leave the hospital, social workers help them readjust to everyday life.

LESSON **4** REVIEW

1. How can teens find out about mental-health services in their community?
2. Name three types of mental-health professionals and describe their training.
3. Describe three treatments for mental disorders.

What Do You Think?

4. Your friend has been acting strangely for a few weeks. You think he may need help. What would you do?

Locating Community Resources

Min has been feeling depressed since her parents told her they were getting a divorce. She hasn't been able to concentrate in school or fall asleep at night. Min just drags through each day feeling very tired and sad. She doesn't want to discuss her concerns with her parents because they both seem so upset already. But Min doesn't know who else to turn to for help.

Where can people like Min go for help with their problems? Below are some guidelines to help you find resources that are available in your community.

1. Talk to a trusted adult

When you have a problem or feel depressed, it helps to talk to an adult you know and trust—a parent, guardian, relative, teacher, school counselor, religious leader, school nurse, family doctor, or other adult. The person can

- help you clarify the problem
- provide moral support
- suggest resources in your community where you can go for help

2. Use your local telephone book

Telephone books vary from town to town, but they all contain vital information for helping you manage a mental or social health problem.

In some directories, you may find a "self help" or "health" guide at the front of the white or yellow pages. In addition to checking listings for specific problems, try looking under "Teen Concerns." In other directories, listings may be shown in the yellow pages under Community, Human, or Mental Health Services. Others may be listed under Counseling, Social Workers, or Psychologists.

If you still can't find help, try calling people who are likely to keep "help" numbers handy: 411, a library or church, or police and fire departments.

3. Call to find out what services are provided

Briefly discuss your problem to find out how the services can meet your needs. Ask about any fees, the hours, and the location. Write down this information so you can compare all the services. If the services do not meet your needs or are too costly, ask the person to suggest other places for you to call.

4. Select one resource and make an appointment to visit

You may wish to ask a trusted person to accompany you to your first visit. The person can wait outside so you can talk privately with the counselor.

If you are not satisfied with the place you have chosen, there may be other options. Discuss your concerns with the counselor or try a different organization.

Apply the Skill

With your classmates, list some common problems that young people face. Then make a class directory of resources for each problem. List each organization's name, address, phone number, hours, fees, and services.

CHAPTER 4 REVIEW

KEY IDEAS

LESSON 1

- Most mental disorders are characterized by abnormal thoughts, feelings, or behaviors that make people uncomfortable with themselves or at odds with others.

LESSON 2

- People with eating disorders, such as anorexia nervosa and bulimia, should seek prompt professional help.
- Mood disorders, such as clinical depression, result when moods or negative emotions interfere with normal activities.

LESSON 3

- Suicide can be prevented if people recognize the problem and know how to help.
- Warning signs of suicide include depression, change in personality, withdrawal, talk of death, and risk-taking behavior.

LESSON 4

- Psychiatrists, clinical psychologists, and social workers are trained to recognize and treat mental disorders.
- Mental disorders can be treated with drug therapy, psychotherapy, or hospitalization.

KEY TERMS

LESSON 1

abnormal

dementia

functional disorder

mental disorder

organic disorder

LESSON 2

anorexia nervosa

anxiety disorder

bulimia

case history

clinical depression

compulsion

dissociative disorder

hypochondria

mood disorder

obsession

phobia

schizophrenia

somatoform disorder

LESSON 3

cluster suicide

LESSON 4

clinical psychologist

occupational therapist

pastoral counselor

psychiatrist

psychotherapy

social worker

therapy

Listed above are some of the important terms in this chapter. Choose the term from the list that best matches each phrase below.

1. a brief description of a person who suffers from a particular disorder

2. a mental disorder with a physical cause

3. anxiety that is related to a specific situation or object

4. a physician who specializes in diagnosing and treating mental disorders

5. serious mental disorder characterized by unpredictable disturbances in thinking, mood, awareness, and behavior

6. a member of the religious community who has practical training in counseling

7. treatment involving conversations with a trained professional, who helps the patient understand and overcome a mental disorder

8. a mental disorder in which a person is overwhelmed by sad feelings and is unable to carry out everyday activities

9. a serious eating disorder in which a person refuses to eat enough food to maintain a minimum normal body weight

10. a mental disorder in which patients complain of physical symptoms, such as pain, that have no underlying physical cause

WHAT HAVE YOU LEARNED?

Choose the letter of the answer that best completes each statement.

11. Claustrophobia is a(n)
a. mood disorder   **c.** eating disorder
b. anxiety disorder   **d.** somatoform disorder

12. An unreasonable need to behave in a certain way is called a(n)
a. obsession   **c.** compulsion
b. organic disorder   **d.** trauma

13. An eating disorder marked by binging and purging is
a. hypochondria   **c.** bulimia
b. anorexia nervosa   **d.** amnesia

14. The sudden loss of memory is called
a. amnesia   **c.** schizophrenia
b. anxiety   **d.** bulimia

15. A physician who treats organic disorders of the brain and nervous system is a
a. clinical psychologist   **c.** neurologist
b. social worker   **d.** psychiatrist

16. If a person is suicidal, it is important to
a. seek professional help   **c.** show concern
b. take the person seriously   **d.** all of these

Answer each of the following with complete sentences.

17. Define *mental disorder.* Give an example.

18. What is an organic disorder?

19. Give an example of how a mental disorder might be caused by an experience in a person's life.

20. How are anorexia nervosa and bulimia similar? How do they differ?

21. Distinguish between passive-aggressive and antisocial personality disorders.

22. Why is schizophrenia one of the most severe of the mental disorders?

23. Why is depression linked to suicide?

24. List four common myths and then four facts about suicide.

WHAT DO YOU THINK?

25. People recovering from mental disorders sometimes live in "halfway houses," where they get treatment and readjust to life. How would you feel about having a halfway house in your neighborhood?

26. Families of the mentally ill frequently need support and counseling. Why do you think this is so? Do you think it is a good idea for families to seek help? Why or why not?

27. A child's family experiences influence his or her mental health. Give four examples of healthy family interactions that promote mental health.

28. Why do you think that eating disorders are classified as mental disorders? Do you agree or disagree with this classification? Explain.

WHAT WOULD YOU DO?

29. A friend of yours has dieted her weight down to 82 pounds from 120 pounds. You are very concerned about your friend's health. What would you do?

30. Your parents are getting a divorce, and you are having trouble sleeping, eating, and concentrating on your schoolwork. What steps could you take to help yourself?

31. Every time you have a big exam coming up, you feel really anxious. What could you do to help ease your anxiety?

32. When a friend seems depressed, what steps do you take to help him or her?

33. You feel down in the dumps sometimes, but always snap out of it quickly. Should you seek help? Why or why not?

Getting Involved

34. Discuss the increase in the rate of teen suicide with your family. Together, come up with a list of ways to reduce the number of teen suicides. Share your list with your class.

Chapter 5

YOU AND YOUR FAMILY

Sharing good times is important in every family, large and small. In this chapter you will learn about many kinds of families and the roles that people play in families. You also will read about how people cope with the daily stresses of family life and with the more serious problems that can occur.

CHAPTER PREVIEW

5-1 Families Today

- Identify similarities and differences among the variety of families that exist today.

5-2 Family Stress

- Describe some of the stressors that families face.

5-3 Keeping the Family Healthy

- Identify ways to strengthen family relationships.

BUILDING HEALTH SKILLS

- Demonstrate a method for resolving conflicts fairly.

CHECK YOUR WELLNESS

How healthy are your family relationships? See how many of these questions you can answer *yes* to.

- Do you make an effort to spend time with family members and enjoy their company?

- Are you able to express your feeling, including love, to members of your family?

- Do you recognize that there are things you can learn from other family members?

- Are you taking on responsibilities at home, such as doing chores and obeying family rules?

- When you disagree with your parent about something, do you discuss the problem respectfully?

- Do you avoid taking out your personal problems on family members?

- Do you know where you can go for help when you have family problems?

KEEPING A JOURNAL

"We may not be able to define what a family is, but we know one when we see it." In your journal, explore what you think the author meant by this quote.

Take it to the Net

1 FAMILIES TODAY

Focus on these questions as you read this lesson.
- Why is the family important for social health?
- What different family forms exist today?

SKILLS
- Coping with Change

$\mathbb{L}$ook closely at the pictures on these pages. If someone were to ask you to point out the differences among the pictures, you could easily find many. But what if you were asked to find the one similarity among the pictures? What would you say?

If you answered that all the pictures are of families, you are correct. While families exist in all different sizes and forms, they all have many things in common. The family is often called the "basic unit of society" because it is the structure within which children are raised and values and customs are passed from generation to generation. Whatever its size or form, perhaps nothing influences a person more than the family.

The Family and Social Health

More than just the basic unit of society, the family is also the basic unit of social health. A person's first **relationships,** or meaningful associations with others, are with members of his or her family. **Through relationships with family members, a child learns to love, respect, and get along with others and to function as part of a group**. The family also teaches a child about interdependence—that one person's actions affect the lives of all other family members. Interdependence teaches children that lasting relationships must be based on mutual caring, trust, and support.

The lessons that people learn about relationships from their families remain with them throughout their lives. Think about your current relationships with friends and other people outside of your family. The social skills that you use in these relationships—showing respect and caring, getting along with others, lending support, and more—were probably first learned and tested on members of your family.

The Changing Family

If you were to compare family life in the United States today to family life 40 years ago, you would find many differences. In the 1950s, a "typical" family consisted of a working father, a stay-at-home mother, and their children. Today, fewer than 10 percent of American families fit this form. What factors account for such a dramatic transformation in

Figure 5-1 *The "typical" American family of the 1950s is just one of many forms that exist today.*

American family life? Researchers point to three major forces of change, described below.

MORE WOMEN IN THE WORK FORCE

More than half of all mothers with preschool children are in the work force today. This is a dramatic increase from 1960, when the number was only 20 percent. Women work for many different reasons—to support their families, to further their careers, for personal fulfillment, or to bring in extra income.

When mothers work, children may spend much of their early life in the care of people other than their parents. Research has shown that, when child care programs are of high quality, children thrive and develop as they would at home. But, still, when parents work outside the home, families must adjust to spending less time together. Adjustments in household chores and schedules also may be needed.

HIGH DIVORCE RATE

Researchers estimate that 40 percent of women born in the 1970s will experience a **divorce,** a legal agreement to end a marriage. In 1990 alone, more than one million children under the age of 18 experienced their parents' divorce.

Divorce affects all aspects of the family—its structure, its finances, and its emotional health. Family members must adjust to new roles, relationships, and living arrrangements after a divorce. Because most people who divorce eventually remarry, families may face more readjustments later on.

POSTPONING MARRIAGE AND PARENTHOOD

Today an increasing number of young people delay marriage and parenthood until later in life. In fact, in a recent year, one third of all births were to women aged 30 or older. As a result, families tend to be smaller today. Most women have two children, and a growing number remain childless. In contrast, in the 1950s women had three or four children, on average.

Figure 5-2 *Today, families with working mothers and families with stepparents are common. What factors are responsible for these family forms?*

HISTORY CONNECTION

Until the mid-1800s, mothers and fathers both stayed home, farming or working at trades, and both shared in raising the children. The Industrial Revolution changed things—men went to work in factories and offices while women stayed home. Around 1900, an economic recession led many women to enter the work force. This trend has continued, except for a brief period after World War II, when many women returned to the home.

Some people feel the trend toward smaller families is a positive one. With fewer children, parents might be better able to provide for their families. Others worry that smaller families may not provide as strong a support network as do larger families.

Family Forms

More than ever before, the single word that best describes families today is *diversity*. Families reflect the diverse circumstances, needs, values, and cultures of the people in them. As you read about the diverse family forms below, think about the important qualities that all families share.

NUCLEAR FAMILY One basic family form is the nuclear family. A **nuclear family** consists of a mother and father and their child or children living together in one household. The children may be the parents' biological children, or they may have been adopted. **Adoption** is the legal process by which parents take another person's child into their family to be raised as their own.

SINGLE-PARENT FAMILY About half of all children today will live, at least for a time, in single-parent families. A **single-parent family** is a family in which only one parent lives with the child or children. Single-parent families are often the result of divorce. Other single-parent families form when one parent dies, when parents never marry, or when a single person adopts a child.

Mothers head about 90 percent of single-parent families, although a growing number of fathers are raising their children after divorce. Caring for the family alone can be difficult for single parents, who must earn a living, care for children, and perform all the other tasks needed to keep the family functioning. Financial worries are often a major problem in single-parent families.

EXTENDED FAMILY A nuclear family or single-parent family may be part of an **extended family,** or a network of close relatives living together or near each other. Extended families may include aunts, uncles, cousins, or grandparents living with parents and their children.

In extended families, family responsibilities are shared among all members. Children might be raised by their grandparents, aunts, and uncles as well as by their parents. Extended families provide a strong system of support for family members. For single parents, especially, this extra support helps strengthen the family.

Figure 5-3 *In extended families, children are cared for by relatives as well as by their parents.*

BLENDED FAMILY   When single parents remarry, they form a blended family. A **blended family** consists of a biological parent, a stepparent (a parent related by marriage), and the children of one or both parents. Today, seven million children under the age of 18 live in blended families.

When blended families form, the usual problems of families may become more complex. Sometimes, children may feel that a stepparent is an intruder and not really part of the family. Children also may have difficulties adjusting to new relationships with stepbrothers and stepsisters. Successful blended families say that it is important to make adjustments slowly and to be flexible. Over time, members of blended families can grow more comfortable with the new relationships and living arrangements.

FOSTER FAMILY   A **foster family** is a family in which an adult or couple provides care and a temporary home for children whose biological parents are unable to care for them. Foster family arrangements are usually made by government agencies. Some children remain in a foster family for an extended time. Sometimes foster parents are able to adopt the children in their care.

OTHER FAMILY FORMS   In addition to the families just described, other groups of people also are considered families. One example is a married couple without any children. Another is a group of unrelated people who do not have families of their own. These people may choose to live together and support and care for one another.

Responsibilities Within the Family

Whatever the family structure, family members must share responsibilities so that the family functions effectively. Some responsibilities belong to the adults, some to the children, and some are shared by all.

ADULTS' RESPONSIBILITIES   The heads of families are expected to provide for their children's basic needs. These needs include food, clothing, shelter, education, health care, security, and love. When children's basic needs are met, they feel loved and secure, and they gain self-esteem.

Another basic responsibility of heads of families is **socialization** (soh shuh lih ZAY shun), the process of teaching children to behave in a way that is acceptable to the family and to society. Through socialization, children develop into responsible adults. They learn to respect the rights of others and to give and receive love. They also absorb the values, beliefs, and customs that are important to their families.

Figure 5-4 *Through socialization, children learn behaviors and skills necessary for adulthood.*

- You must be home by 10 PM on weekdays and by midnight on weekends.
- No watching television before homework is done.
- You must keep your room clean, take out the trash, and help with the dishes.
- No friends in the house when we are not home without first checking with us.

Figure 5-5 *How would you negotiate to change one of these rules?*

Adult family members are also responsible for setting rules to protect the children's safety and to maintain order within the family. Figure 5-5 lists some typical rules that parents may set for their children.

CHILDREN'S RESPONSIBILITIES The responsibilities of children grow as children become older and more able. As a child, you may have been responsible for dressing yourself, tidying up your room, and doing your homework. Today, you may have other responsibilities as well, such as doing household chores, caring for younger brothers and sisters, or even adding to the family income with earnings from a part-time job. You are also responsible for following family rules and for showing respect for all family members.

At times, young people may disagree with some of the rules set by their parents. Disagreements may also arise between brothers and sisters. When such conflicts arise, family members need to discuss their problems in a calm, respectful manner. If each member recognizes the need for rules and limits that are satisfactory to all, it will be easier to work together to resolve the conflict.

SHARED RESPONSIBILITIES In most families, there never seems to be enough time for household chores. To get things done, many families divide the responsibilities among family members. For example, each person may prepare dinner one night a week. Children may take turns helping with laundry, grocery shopping, and other chores. All family members may help care for elderly or disabled family members.

Sharing household responsibilities not only gets more done in less time, but results in additional benefits as well. First, children master skills such as cooking that will be vital to them as adults. Second, because children are entrusted with important tasks, they develop a sense of responsibility and greater self-esteem. Most importantly, family members learn that the family is stronger when they work as a team and depend on each other to get things done.

LESSON *1* REVIEW

1. Why is the family the basic unit of social health?
2. How has the increase in the number of working women changed family life?
3. Describe three family forms that are common today.
4. What responsibilities do adults have in a family?

What Do You Think?

5. How do you think your family's rules are preparing you for adulthood?

DIFFERENT VOICES SPEAKING

Kent Allen, who is 16, lives with his parents, brother, and sister on a farm in Iowa. Kent is active in the 4-H Club and hopes someday to take over the family farm.

Q. Kent, can you describe a typical day for the Allen family?

A. We're all up pretty early in the morning. One of my jobs before heading to school is taking care of the cattle—we mainly raise cattle, though we also grow corn. My brother and sister help out with chores around the house, and sometimes my brother helps me feed the 20 hogs that I own. Often, the first time that we get together as a family is at dinner. Those are important times.

Q. Why are they important?

A. We do most of our talking around the dinner table. We catch each other up on events in our lives and discuss problems that have come up.

Q. What sorts of problems might arise?

A. I would guess they're the kinds of things most families have to deal with. My brother and I share a room, for example, and sometimes things get a little crowded in there. We end up having disputes over space. If we can't settle it, we'll take it up at dinner, though first we try to work it out between us.

Q. How do you work out problems like that?

A. We talk. One of us gets to say what's on his mind, then it's the other one's turn. Meanwhile, the one who's not talking has to listen. We're not always perfect at taking turns and listening—sometimes tempers and feelings get in the way—but we try our best.

Kent Allen

Q. Where did you learn to communicate that way?

A. From our parents—and not just by listening to them, but by watching them. I work a lot with my father taking care of the livestock and in the fields. I know I can express my opinion and that he'll respect it.

Q. Is respect important to your family's health?

A. Yes, especially at harvest and planting times. I'm out in the fields with my dad till midnight. He sometimes works till four in the morning and is back out at six. My mother, brother, and sister are busy around the house. Knowing that each one cares about the others comes in handy.

Q. What's the most important thing you children have learned from your parents?

A. We've learned to accept responsibility. There have been times when I wanted to hang out with friends rather than mix feed for my hogs. Still, I always did what I had to. Last year it paid off. My hogs won a "Grand Champion" ribbon. It helped me fetch a good price at market.

Journal Activity

Kent recognizes the importance of good communication for family health. In your journal, write a "charter" for your family. The charter should outline rules to ensure good communication during family discussions.

2 FAMILY STRESS

While families can be the greatest source of love and joy, they can, at times, be a source of stress. If you watch weekly television programs that depict family life, stressful situations are handled quickly and easily. Usually, within a half hour, television families are able to work out solutions to the problems they face—from simple misunderstandings to more serious crises.

In real-life families, stressful situations are not resolved so easily. **Divorce, drug abuse, financial problems, and family violence are some of the causes of family stress.** For a family to remain healthy, problems must be recognized, talked about, and dealt with by the whole family.

Separation and Divorce

Conflict and tension occur as a normal part of living together. When a husband and wife cannot resolve their difficulties, however, they may try a period of **separation,** an arrangement in which spouses live apart and try to work out their problems. A separation is often painful for children in the family. They may feel helpless because they are unable to solve their parents' problems. They may think that the separation is their fault. Children need to be reassured that they are not to blame for their parents' problems.

If a couple is not able to work out differences, a separation may lead to divorce. For many, divorce is a devastating experience. Often people who divorce believe that they are failures and suffer from grief and loss. Children may feel resentment, guilt, anger, sadness, or embarrassment over their parents' divorce.

If your parents are divorcing, it may help to concentrate on parts of your own life that you enjoy, such as school, friends, and activities. If you feel depressed, talk with a teacher, guidance counselor, or a member of the clergy. A brother or a sister can also be a good person to turn to for support. Reading articles and books or talking with others who have experienced a family breakup may also help. In some schools, teenagers have formed groups to help each other cope with divorce.

Figure 5-6 *When parents divorce, children need to deal with their anger and sadness.*

Drug Abuse

When a family member has a problem with alcohol or another drug, all family members are affected. Sometimes the effects are subtle—family members may be embarrassed or

worried about their loved one. Other times, the effects are more serious—family members may be afraid to go home or to bring friends home for fear that the person might behave violently.

In most communities, groups such as Al-Anon and Alateen can help with problems related to someone else's drinking or drug use. Al-Anon is an organization that helps people cope with an alcoholic family member. Alateen provides help for teenagers who have an alcoholic in the family. These groups hold meetings that are open to anyone who wants to share experiences about living with an alcoholic. You can find the telephone numbers of these organizations in your local telephone book. To find out about groups in your area that help family members of drug abusers, look under "Drug Abuse" in your telephone book.

Financial Problems

The loss of a job, a serious illness, a family breakup, or other family circumstances can lead to financial problems in the family. If money problems are serious or long-lasting, a family may be unable to afford such necessities as adequate food, health care, and a place to live. A growing number of families in the United States today have become homeless due to financial crises.

Financial problems can have serious emotional effects on all family members. Adults may feel guilty that they are unable to provide adequately for their families. Children may feel angry or embarrassed that they must go without things that friends may have. Both adults and children may have serious worries about the future.

SHARPEN YOUR *SKILLS*

Time Management

Because money is tight at home, you would like to help out by getting a part-time job. Your mother is worried that you will not have enough time for your schoolwork. Assuming that you will work 15 hours a week, come up with a schedule that accommodates both your job and your schoolwork.

Figure 5-8 *Some teenagers work part-time to help their families make ends meet.*

Financial problems can be less stressful if family members work together to improve the situation. Teenagers can try to find part-time work to help out. Younger children can find ways to cut back on their spending. Other relatives may offer help as well.

Family Violence

The problems associated with family violence may be the most disturbing and destructive problems in society today. Family violence strikes all kinds of families—rich or poor, uneducated or educated, urban or rural. People who resort to family violence often feel isolated and hopeless. They may believe they have no constructive way of dealing with their problems. In other cases, violence may be used to exert control over others.

PHYSICAL ABUSE   If punishment, even when it is given for a reason, leaves a mark that can be seen the next day, it is considered **physical abuse.** The mark could be a bruise, a burn, a scratch, or a welt, even a small one. Victims of physical abuse may be afraid to go home, or they may feel it is hopeless to try to avoid punishment. Victims can be children, spouses, or elderly relatives. Even when children are not themselves physically abused, they are emotionally damaged by family violence.

Many victims of abuse are afraid that if they tell someone, their family will be destroyed. Other victims believe that they somehow deserve the beatings. They worry that if they let someone know what is going on they will be told it is their own fault. As a result, their self-esteem drops.

Regardless of fears or feelings of guilt, it is far more damaging to keep silent than to seek help. A good place to seek help is the telephone book. There should be a listing for the

Child Abuse Hotline. Hotline numbers for battered women or elders are often listed as well. If children cannot find an appropriate group to call, they should talk with a teacher, a counselor, a trusted relative, a physician, or a member of the clergy. Speaking up about physical abuse is the first step toward putting an end to an intolerable, potentially dangerous situation. Victims are not responsible for abusive behavior, nor can they cure it by themselves.

SEXUAL ABUSE   When an adult uses a child or adolescent for sexual purposes, he or she commits a criminal offense known as **sexual abuse.** Sexual abuse ranges from unwanted kisses to inappropriate touching to sexual intercourse. Both boys and girls can be victims of sexual abuse. Typically, the adult is someone the child knows well—a parent, stepparent, sibling, another relative, or a family friend.

Even a single instance of sexual abuse can have a devastating effect on a child. The victim, through guilt and shame, assumes all the responsibility or blame in his or her own mind. It may be very difficult for the child to trust others and to develop caring relationships later in life.

Victims of any type of sexual abuse should seek the help of a trusted adult, such as a teacher, school counselor, physician, relative, or member of the clergy. Victims also can find help by calling the Child Abuse Hotline. Deciding to seek help can be extremely difficult. Victims risk angering, hurting, or betraying the family member who abused them. Sometimes other relatives may not want to believe what is going on and may accuse the victim of lying. Victims need to know they have the right not to be touched sexually by anyone. It is far more dangerous to believe the threats of the abuser than to report the abuse.

EMOTIONAL ABUSE   "You rotten, no-good, little punk, you never do anything right." "I wish you had never been born." A child who is constantly exposed to negative statements like these is likely to suffer from emotional abuse. **Emotional abuse**, the nonphysical mistreatment of a person, can destroy a person's sense of worth. When parents' attitudes are hostile and threatening much of the time, children do not receive the warmth and security they need.

Emotional neglect is the failure of parents to give their child love and emotional support. Although nothing harmful may be done or said to victims of emotional neglect, they suffer from the feeling that they do not belong. Victims also do not receive the emotional support necessary for the development of a healthy personality.

Even though most emotional abuse is invisible, it leaves victims feeling inadequate, helpless, or worthless. Children who are emotionally abused need to seek help as much as physically or sexually abused children. Emotionally abused children should talk with a trusted adult or call the Child Abuse Hotline.

Figure 5-9 *While emotional abuse leaves no physical scars, it can destroy a child's self-esteem.*

Figure 5-10 *Running away might seem to be a solution to problems. In reality, most runaways encounter serious problems while on their own.*

Runaways

Thousands of the nation's young people are runaways. Some leave home because of violence in their families. Others run away because of emotional problems or school failure. With no place to live or means to support themselves, runaways may become ill or turn to crime. People dealing in prostitution, pornography, and drugs often take advantage of runaways' circumstances.

Many communities have shelters for homeless youth and hotlines for runaways. Law-enforcement agencies, in cooperation with bus companies, conduct programs that offer free transportation to runaways who want to return home. Through these efforts, some runaways return home or get counseling for their problems.

If you are thinking of running away, you owe yourself a call to your local runaway hotline. Call the operator or look in the self-help pages at the front of your phone book. The counselors can advise you about where to get help for family or other problems.

LESSON **2** REVIEW

1. List some serious problems that occur in families.
2. Where can teenagers get help in dealing with a family member's drinking or drug problem?
3. Describe three kinds of family violence.
4. Why should emotional abuse not be ignored?

What Do You Think?

5. How do you think young people who experience divorce can help each other cope with family breakups?

3 KEEPING THE FAMILY HEALTHY

GUIDE FOR READING

Focus on these questions as you read this lesson.

- What skills are important for keeping families healthy?
- Where can families go for help with their problems?

SKILLS

- Expressing Feelings in a Positive Way
- Activity: Group Juggling

What factors determine whether or not a family is healthy? Members of healthy families say that caring and **communication,** the sharing of information, thoughts, and feelings, top the list. It is also important for members to cooperate with one another, share responsibilities, spend time together, and respect and appreciate each other.

Skills for Solving Family Problems

All families, even the most healthy ones, have problems from time to time. For a family to remain healthy, family members must develop skills to work through problems. **Family members must learn how to resolve conflicts, express emotions, and use decision-making techniques.**

RESOLVING CONFLICTS   Have you ever argued with your parent over household chores? What do you do if your parent dislikes your friends? Does your brother complain that you spend too much time on the phone?

In many conflict situations, family members struggle for power. Teenagers want control over their lives, while parents want family life to function in ways they believe are best. **Siblings**, brothers and sisters, compete with each other for their parent's attention, for possessions, and for recognition.

When trying to resolve conflicts, family members need to talk openly, honestly, and lovingly, with the idea of learning from one another. Good communication skills are the keys to conflict resolution. Saying what you mean, listening to others, and voicing disagreement respectfully are important for

Figure 5-11 *Enjoying activities together is essential to family health and happiness.*

Expressing Feelings in a Positive Way

Your younger sister has borrowed your bike without asking again. Now you have no way to get to your friend's house, where you were going to study for tomorrow's math test. "Just wait until she gets home," you think to yourself. How could you handle this situation in a positive manner?

good communication. Family members have to work at developing these skills. The Building Health Skills feature at the end of this chapter teaches a method for resolving conflicts in a way that benefits both people.

EXPRESSING EMOTIONS   Learning to express emotions constructively is important for communication and problem-solving. While everyone needs to express anger at times, angry outbursts that attack another person usually worsen problems and block communication. It is better to focus on your own feelings by saying things like "I get upset when people criticize me," than to attack another person's actions by saying "All you ever do is criticize me!"

Family members can help solve problems if they can express appreciation and show respect for one another's ideas. Being able to say "I love you" is also important for overcoming family difficulties. If family members understand that problem-solving is a loving process, not a time to judge and place blame, solutions may be achieved more easily and quickly.

USING DECISION-MAKING SKILLS   Families that are successful at resolving conflicts and finding solutions to problems frequently use decision-making skills. These skills involve choosing between two or more alternatives. For example, suppose you want to go to the movies Saturday night, but you promised your mother weeks ago that you would babysit your younger brother. What can you do?

By sitting down with your mother and going through the decision-making process together, you may be able to arrive at a solution that is mutually agreeable. Perhaps you can find another babysitter, or perhaps you can take your brother to the movies with you. By agreeing on a solution,

Figure 5-12 *Learning to express love toward family members can help strengthen family ties.*

GROUP JUGGLING

In this activity you will work with others to accomplish a difficult task.

Materials (per group)

3 lightweight balls, volleyball size

Procedure

1. Form a large circle with 10 other people. Everyone should stand and face the center.

2. Starting with one person and going clockwise, count off from 1 to 11, so that everyone has a number. Then decide how you will pass the ball around the circle—it is best to pass the ball across the circle to the opposite side (for example, 1 to 7, 7 to 2, 2 to 8, and so on).

3. Starting with person number 1, throw the ball across the circle to the next person according to the decided order. That person should then throw the ball to the next person, and on across the circle.

4. Continue passing the ball until it has gone around the circle five times. If the ball drops, just pick it up and continue passing it around.

5. Repeat steps 3 and 4, but with two balls instead of one. Start one ball with number 1 and the other with number 3.

6. When you have mastered "juggling" the two balls, add a third ball, starting it with number 5.

Discussion

1. How were cooperation and teamwork important in group juggling? How are those same skills important for living in a family?

2. How is group juggling easier than juggling by oneself? How is it more difficult? Relate this to living as part of a family.

3. Suppose that, while juggling three balls, the group suddenly reversed the direction of one of the balls. What do you think would happen? How is this similar to what happens when unexpected problems arise in families?

you can avoid an argument and show that you are a mature and responsible person.

Family decision-making can be a difficult process to follow. Each person may have different needs or opinions. Some may find it difficult to communicate their opinions in a respectful way. Sometimes family members or people outside the family may disrupt the decision-making process. In these cases, families may seek outside help to solve their problems.

Help for the Family

Where can families go for help in solving problems? Many families depend on relatives or trusted friends for help and support. Sometimes families seek advice from members of the clergy or mental-health professionals. If family members have no immediate source of help in a time of crisis, they may use a crisis hotline or contact a crisis center. People who work in crisis centers may serve as sympathetic listeners, or they may refer people to support groups, family-service agencies, or family therapists.

SUPPORT GROUPS Hundreds of thousands of support groups have been set up across the nation. A **support group** is a network of people who help each other cope with a particular problem. Group members learn from one another rather than from a group leader. They learn how to express their emotions in a positive way and how to deal effectively with their problems.

One well-known support group is Alcoholics Anonymous, which holds meetings in communities across the country for those who abuse alcohol. Other support groups help people cope with divorce, death, family violence, gambling, teenage delinquency, and serious illness.

FAMILY AGENCIES In many communities, families can get help through a variety of public and private service agencies. Local family-service agencies offer such services as counseling, education about family life and teen parenting, and pregnancy services. Mental-health agencies help meet the needs of the emotionally disturbed and mentally ill. Child-welfare agencies offer protective services for children, ranging from organizing foster care to dealing with abuse. Other agencies help families with financial aid, food, housing, employment, medical care, and other basic needs.

FAMILY THERAPY Some family agencies provide counseling or therapy for troubled families or refer families to outside therapists. Therapists work with family members to find better ways to solve problems. Family therapists usually encourage all family members to participate in order to resolve conflicts and improve family relationships.

Figure 5-13 *Most communities offer parenting courses or other services to help families deal with problems.*

Making the Most of Family Time

- Develop family traditions—celebrate holidays, birthdays, and other occasions in special ways; set aside time for regular family events.

- Make mealtimes special—try to eat together and share your day's events.

- Hold a family meeting—allow family members to discuss any important issues or problems, suggest some improvements, and make plans to do things together.

- Show caring—do a special household chore as a pleasant surprise; give a backrub; write a note of appreciation; call a family member on the phone just to chat; give a sincere compliment.

Figure 5-14 *What things can you do to bring your family members closer to each other?*

The Healthy Family

Recently, several major magazines polled thousands of families. These polls indicated that most Americans are satisfied with the way their families are functioning. Although many teenagers go through periods of insecurity and times when everything they do seems to drive their families crazy, these times are balanced by other times when teens feel loved and accepted.

The key to family health and happiness is to make the most of the time that families spend together. Many family members take their time together for granted. Figure 5-14 lists some simple ways that families can strengthen their relationships and improve the quality of their shared time. Maintaining family traditions and ties is an important characteristic of healthy families. When extended family members gather during holidays, birthdays, or other occasions, they often share a sense of belonging and security. When there are problems, extended family members can help each other with understanding, advice, and encouragement.

LESSON 3 REVIEW

1. What three skills can help solve family problems?
2. Why are the steps in decision-making sometimes hard for families to follow?
3. Where can families go for help with their problems?

What Do You Think?

4. If you were a parent of a teenager, how would you handle conflicts that arise between you?

Using "Win-Win" Negotiation

Dad, there's no good reason why I shouldn't be able to stay out late on weekends. I'm tired of being treated like a baby! You're only fifteen, Rosa. You can't just come and go as you please. Midnight is late enough.

Rosa and her father have been having this "discussion" for weeks. They just go around and around, getting more and more annoyed and stubborn. Conflicts like this are common between parents and children. Conflicts also occur between friends, neighbors, and even nations. Often at the heart of a disagreement is a breakdown in communication. When communication is poor, conflict can tear a relationship apart. But with good communication, conflict can lead not only to a solution but to greater understanding and growth as well.

The key to resolving conflicts is to find common goals that both parties share. The following steps can help you to turn a no-win situation into one where everyone comes out a winner.

By using "win-win" negotiation, you can resolve important conflicts in ways that satisfy both parties.

1. Describe the problem

When you are in a conflict with another person, take the time to really understand the problem. Write out answers to the following questions:

- What do you believe is happening in the situation?
- How does it make you feel?
- What don't you like about the situation?
- What do you want out of the situation?

Dad makes me come in so early. It makes me angry that he doesn't trust me, but I hate fighting with him. I'd like to have more freedom and to get along with him.

Rosa's not old enough to stay out late. I worry a lot about her safety. I don't want to fight with her, but I don't want her to get hurt either.

2. Explore the other point of view

Now describe the problem as you think the other person sees it. What do you think are the other person's beliefs, feelings, and interests?

Dad probably thinks he's protecting me. He worries when I'm out late, but he wants to get along with me and keep me out of trouble.

Rosa probably thinks I don't trust her. She's angry because she can't spend enough time with her friends. She wants me to trust her.

Obviously, it is best if both people go through the steps of win-win negotiation. Suggest and explain the process to the other person. Ask the other person to go through steps 1 and 2 on his or her own. If the person is not willing to try the process, you can still go through the steps yourself. Your willingness to see the other person's point of view may help the situation.

3. Share and discuss

Use the following guidelines to share your understanding of the situation with the other person involved in it.

• Listen closely to the other person and acknowledge that you understand his or her view. Understanding is not the same as agreeing with the person.

• Talk about and acknowledge each other's feelings. Unexpressed feelings often get in the way of resolving conflicts. Listen quietly without interrupting the other person.

• Attack the problem, not the person. Seek solutions, and do not blame.

• Look for shared goals. Avoid taking specific positions at first.

• Focus on what you want to happen in the future. Look forward, not back.

Dad, I understand that you worry when....

Rosa, I realize that time with your friends is important....

4. Invent solutions

Brainstorm a list of solutions that meet at least some of the needs that both of you have expressed. Invent solutions first; you can judge them later.

Dad, what if I call you if I'm out after 11 PM and have late hours twice a month?

Why don't you invite your friends over to our house sometimes, Rosa?

5. Agree on a solution

From your list, select the one solution that best meets the most important interests that you both have expressed. The two of you must agree on the solution.

So, Dad, I'll call you at 11 to let you know where I am and when I will be home.

OK, Rosa. That way I won't have to worry about where you are and whether you're all right.

Apply the Skill

1. Jack and Sam are having a disagreement. In writing, describe their problem and use win-win negotiation to find a solution.

Sam: "How could you go to a baseball game tonight, Jack? You promised to help me study for tomorrow's math test!"

Jack: "How could you expect me to turn down free tickets to the most important game of the season?"

2. List five common conflicts people your age may have with friends, family members, teachers, or others.

3. Think of a conflict you are now (or recently have been) involved in. Ask the other person to work through the win-win method with you. Then evaluate how successful the process was in resolving the conflict.

CHAPTER 5 REVIEW

KEY IDEAS

LESSON 1

- Three factors that have changed family life in the United States are the increase in the number of working women, the high divorce rate, and an increase in the number of people postponing marriage and parenthood.
- Today people live in a wide variety of family forms, including nuclear families, single-parent families, extended families, blended families, and foster families.

LESSON 2

- Divorce requires major adjustments for all members of the family. Children may feel guilty, angry, and embarrassed about divorce. It is important that they discuss their feelings with others.

- Acts of violence in families include physical abuse, sexual abuse, and emotional abuse. Drug abuse and financial problems also contribute to family stress. Many organizations exist to help family members deal with these types of problems.

LESSON 3

- Family members can learn skills to resolve conflicts, express their emotions, and make decisions to solve family problems. Families may seek help with problems through support groups, family agencies, or family therapy.
- Healthy families maintain family traditions and ties. Family members share good times together and enjoy each other's company.

KEY TERMS

LESSON 1
adoption
blended family
divorce
extended family
foster family
nuclear family

relationship
single-parent family
socialization

LESSON 2
emotional abuse
emotional neglect
physical abuse

separation
sexual abuse

LESSON 3
communication
sibling
support group

Listed above are some of the important terms in this chapter. Choose the term from the list that best matches each phrase below.

1. the sharing of information, thoughts, and feelings

2. the failure of a parent to give a child love and emotional support

3. network of people who help each other cope with a particular problem

4. a mother and father and their child or children living together in one household

5. the process of teaching children to behave in a way that is acceptable to the family and to society

6. a legal agreement to end a marriage

7. stepparents and their children and stepchildren

8. network of close relatives living together or near each other

9. family in which an adult or couple provides care and a temporary home for children whose biological parents are unable to care for them

10. a meaningful association with another person

WHAT HAVE YOU LEARNED?

On a separate sheet of paper, write the word or words that best complete each statement.

11. A person's first _____ are with members of his or her family.

12. An estimated 50 percent of all marriages since the 1970s will end in _____.

13. _____ is the legal process by which parents take another person's child into their family to be raised as their own.

14. A _____ family is a family in which only one parent lives with the children.

15. In a _____ family, a child may live with a biological parent, a stepparent, and the children of one or both parents.

16. When a couple cannot resolve their difficulties, they may try a period of _____.

17. _____ is punishment that leaves a mark that can be seen the next day.

18. The loss of a job or serious illness can lead to _____ problems in the family.

Answer each of the following with complete sentences.

19. What social skills do people first learn in their families?

20. List three factors that have changed family life in the United States.

21. What is an extended family? What are the benefits of living in an extended family?

22. Why does it take time to adjust to living in a blended family?

23. Why is it important that children be socialized?

24. What should a child abuse victim do?

25. List three stressful situations that affect some families.

26. How is witnessing family violence damaging to children?

27. How might support groups help children of divorce?

28. What kinds of communication skills can be useful to family members in resolving their conflicts?

29. What types of services do family agencies provide?

WHAT DO YOU THINK?

30. What factors do you think have contributed to this country's high divorce rate?

31. Do you think that companies should be required to grant parents a leave of absence upon the birth of a child? Should this benefit apply to fathers as well as mothers? Explain your reasons for your answer.

32. What kinds of family rules for teenagers do you think are fair and reasonable? Unfair and unreasonable?

33. Why do you think it is sometimes difficult for family members to communicate with one another?

WHAT WOULD YOU DO?

34. You suspect that your best friend's mother has an alcohol problem, although your friend has never said anything to you about it. What could you do to help your friend deal with this problem?

35. Several classmates want to start a support group for teens who have to cope with divorce or separation. They have asked you for advice on what to discuss at the first meeting. What would you tell them?

36. Your friend has confided that she is being sexually abused by her stepfather. How can you help her?

37. You would like to develop better communication with family members. How could you achieve this goal?

Getting Involved

38. With your family members, come up with a definition of the term *family*. Your definition should address the essential functions of the family as well as the diversity of family forms that exist today.

BUILDING HEALTHY RELATIONSHIPS

At work or at play—you spend most of your time with other people. In this chapter you will learn about communication and other skills that can help you get along with others. You'll also look at the types of relationships that are important during the teen years and beyond.

CHAPTER PREVIEW

6-1 Skills for Healthy Relationships

- Describe how the skills of communication, cooperation, and compromise are essential for healthy relationships.

6-2 Friendships

- Identify qualities that are important in close friends.

6-3 Intimate Relationships

- Explain why emotional intimacy is important in close relationships.

6-4 Thinking About Marriage

- List some characteristics of successful marriages.

BUILDING HEALTH SKILLS

- Identify strategies for choosing abstinence when faced with sexual pressures.

CHECK YOUR WELLNESS

Are your relationships healthy and satisfying? See if you can answer *yes* to the following questions.

- Are you friendly with a variety of people?
- Do you have close friends with whom you feel comfortable being yourself?
- Are you able to show your friends that you care about them? Can your friends show they care about you?
- Can you work out problems that arise between you and your friends?
- Are you able to express your emotions without feeling anxious or hurting others?
- Can you carry on conversations with people you would like to get to know?
- Do you stick to your limits for expressing affection on dates? Do you respect the limits set by others?

KEEPING A JOURNAL

Using drawings or pictures from magazines, create a page entitled "Friendship." Add words to identify the qualities that you feel are important in a friend.

Take it to the Net
www.phschool.com

Focus on these questions as you read this lesson.

- What skills are necessary for effective communication?
- Why are cooperation and compromise important in relationships?

SKILLS

- Working in Groups

1 SKILLS FOR HEALTHY RELATIONSHIPS

Imagine a large room filled with all the important people in your life. Walking around the room, you might see family members, friends, neighbors, teachers, and other special people. As you encounter each of these people, you might think back to the fun times you have shared or to other things that make your relationship special.

While each relationship you form is special in its own way, all relationships are built on similar skills. Three skills—communication, cooperation, and compromise—form the basis of all relationships.

Effective Communication

When you laugh at someone's joke, hug your younger sister or brother, ask a friend for advice, or write a letter, you are communicating. As you learned in Chapter 5, communication is the process of sharing information, thoughts, or feelings. It happens whenever you use words, sounds, gestures, or body movements to interact with other people.

Learning to communicate effectively is an acquired skill, much like learning to ride a bicycle. When you first started to ride a bicycle, you probably hesitated and fell. The more you practiced, however, the less you needed to think about what you were doing, and the better cyclist you became. The same is true of communication. **With practice, you can master the skills of effective communication—using "I" messages, active listening, assertiveness, and body language.**

Figure 6-1 *The skills of communication, cooperation, and compromise are important in all relationships.*

"I" MESSAGES   One of the most important steps in learning to communicate effectively is to take responsibility for your own feelings. Feelings can be difficult to communicate, especially feelings of anger or frustration. Think about the last time you were angry with someone. How did you let the person know you were upset?

To express your feelings accurately, you may want to use "I" messages. An **"I" message** is a statement of feelings and expectations that does not blame or judge the other person. Suppose you are upset with a friend who forgot to call you. When you speak to your friend the next day, you shout, "Can't you remember anything?" The question could put your friend on the defensive and cause a serious disagreement. Instead of putting the blame on your friend, it would be better to focus on yourself and on how the situation made you feel. By saying something like, "I'm upset because we didn't talk last night," you open the lines of communication between you and your friend.

Figure 6-2 *By using "I" messages, you can communicate your feelings without blaming or judging others.*

ACTIVE LISTENING   Many people think of communication as nothing more than talking. Actually, for communication to be effective, it must be a two-way process that involves a listener as well as a speaker. The listener must do more than simply hear what is said—he or she must be actively involved in the conversation.

Learning to be an active listener is one of the most useful communication skills you can acquire. **Active listening** is focusing your full attention on what the other person is saying and, at the same time, letting that person know you understand and care. Active listening is truly active. The listener makes the speaker feel comfortable about opening up and expressing personal feelings. To become an active listener, try the following:

- Show your interest by nodding your head and showing concern on your face.
- Encourage the speaker to begin by saying "Do you want to talk about it?" or "You seem upset about...."
- While the speaker is talking, offer comments such as "I know what you mean" or "Then what happened?"
- Avoid passing judgment on what the speaker says.
- Show you have been listening by summarizing the speaker's ideas with phrases such as "It sounds like you were angry when..." or "I heard you say...."
- Help the speaker explore things further with phrases such as "Tell me more about..." or "I guess you felt...."
- Do not steer the conversation away from the speaker's problem and onto your own.

BIOLOGY CONNECTION

Communication is crucial for survival in many species besides humans. Bees communicate the location of food by doing a complex dance on the walls of their hive. Elephants use low-pitched calls to communicate danger or the presence of potential mates. Even some species of plants communicate—they send chemical signals through the air that warn neighboring plants of an insect threat.

Building Healthy Relationships   **121**

ASSERTIVENESS   How do you express your opinions and feelings when they differ from those of another person? Are you **passive**, holding back your true feelings and going along with the other person? Are you **aggressive?** That is, do you communicate your opinions and feelings in a way that may seem threatening or disrespectful to other people? Or are you assertive? When you are **assertive** (uh SUR tiv), you express your true feelings in a way that does not threaten the other person or make you feel anxious.

Figure 6-3 compares assertive communication behaviors with passive and aggressive behaviors. Notice that assertiveness involves more than just what you say. How you say something, or the tone of your voice, also communicates your message. To understand how your tone of voice affects your message, try saying the sentence "Leave the package on the desk" three different ways—first in a loud, forceful voice, then in a whisper, and then in an assertive, direct tone. How does the meaning change each time?

People who are assertive tend to have healthier, more satisfying relationships than those who are either passive or aggressive. This is because assertive behavior communicates respect both for yourself and for the other person. What do you think passive and aggressive behaviors communicate?

BODY LANGUAGE   Communication is more than just speaking words; you communicate with your entire body. **Body language** is a way of communicating information or feelings nonverbally, through body movements, posture, gestures, and facial expressions. One way that people communicate with their faces is by making **eye contact,** or meeting someone's gaze. A failure to make eye contact may be interpreted by some people as shyness, embarrassment, indifference, or even sneakiness.

Figure 6-3 *Which of the assertive communication behaviors do you need to work at?*

Assertive, Passive, and Aggressive Communication

Assertive Behaviors	Passive Behaviors	Aggressive Behaviors
Using "I" messages to explain your feelings	Hoping the other person will guess your feelings	Using "you" messages to blame the other person
Actively listening to the person	Always listening; rarely talking	Interrupting; being sarcastic
Trying to understand the other person's feelings	Denying your own feelings; making excuses	Making fun of the other person's feelings; using name-calling
Expressing appreciation; being respectful	Criticizing yourself; always apologizing	Criticizing the other person; never giving a compliment
Seeking a compromise that does not go against either of your values	Always giving in to the other person	Always wanting your own way
Speaking clearly and confidently; making eye contact; appearing interested	Mumbling; looking away; fidgeting nervously	Yelling or refusing to talk; pointing your finger; glaring; using physical force

Figure 6-4 *Communication is more than spoken words. Are you aware of the messages sent by your body language?*

People are often unaware of the silent messages sent by their body language. Sometimes body language goes along with spoken words, as when a person gestures to emphasize a point. Other times, body language sends a silent message of its own, as when a student slouches down in his or her desk when unprepared for class. Still other times, body language may deliver a mixed message when it contradicts the spoken words. In fact, people who lie sometimes give themselves away through their body language. Their words may say one thing, but their body language—looking away, smiling, or keeping distant—says something different.

Like spoken language, body language varies greatly from culture to culture. For example, people from Latin American and Arab cultures generally stand closer together when they talk than do people from the United States. People from Japanese and Native American cultures consider it disrespectful to look a person in the eye in some situations. Hand gestures that mean one thing in one culture may mean something quite different in another culture. Even more than spoken language, body language can sometimes hinder communication between people from different cultures.

Cooperation

Have you ever worked with classmates to complete a project? If so, then you know the importance of **cooperation,** or working together for a common goal. Think about a successful sports team that you have watched play. Like teamwork, cooperation involves meeting your responsibilities and trusting others to meet theirs.

Cooperation is important in all relationships, especially those with family members and close friends. When family

Working in Groups

With four of your classmates, write a short skit that illustrates the importance of good communication. After you have completed the skit, discuss how well the members of your group worked together to get the task done.

Helping the Speech-Impaired

For some people, physical disabilities make communication difficult. But with the help of recent technology, this situation is changing.

A new computer system, called an Assistive Communication Device (ACD), is a welcome development for people who are not able to speak. ACDs enable these people to "speak" using the voice generated by a speech synthesizer that is part of the system.

The design of the ACD depends on the needs of the person using it. Some ACDs are equipped with a typical keyboard. The computer simply speaks the words typed in. Other ACDs have keyboards with pictures instead of letters. This simplifies typing, since each picture substitutes for an entire word. These systems are best for people who have limited use of their hands.

Despite their power and complexity, many ACDs are lap-sized and portable. ACD users can now take their "speech" wherever they go.

members work together to complete a household chore, things get done more easily than if one person had done it alone. When friends study together for an exam, each can help the others master difficult material. Cooperation builds strong relationships that are based on mutual trust, caring, and responsibility.

Compromise

Imagine that you and a friend are having a disagreement. You would like to go to a party tonight, but your friend would rather go bowling. How would you handle this problem?

Because disagreements arise from time to time in all close relationships, it is important to be willing to compromise. **Compromise** (KAHM pruh myz) is the willingness of each person to give up something in order to reach agreement. Compromising is a skill of give-and-take—both people must be willing to sacrifice something to get something in return. Both people also must feel comfortable with the solution reached.

In the situation above, you and your friend could compromise in a number of ways. You could agree to go to the party tonight and go bowling tomorrow. Or you could go bowling first and then go to the party. Or you could even decide to do a totally different activity. Whatever agreement you arrive at, the ability to compromise will strengthen your relationship. By compromising, you let your friend know how important the relationship is to you.

Of course, there are some situations in which it is important not to compromise. Suppose that a friend wanted to do something that was dangerous or that went against your values. Rather than compromising with your friend, it is best to use assertive communication. Let your friend know how you feel, and make it clear that there is no room for compromise on the issue.

LESSON 1 REVIEW

1. List three important communication skills.
2. Give an example of an "I" message.
3. How does active listening differ from just listening?
4. How can a willingness to compromise strengthen a relationship?

What Do You Think?

5. Do you think that a person's body language speaks louder than his or her words? Give an example to support your answer.

2 FRIENDSHIPS

GUIDE FOR READING

Focus on these questions as you read this lesson.

- Why do people need friends?
- What are some problems that can arise in friendships?

SKILLS

- Mediating a Conflict
- DECIDE

Do you have a close friend whom you have known since childhood? Perhaps, as preschoolers, you spent hours together building whole cities with wooden blocks. Later, you may have discussed sports or favorite television programs. Now, as teenagers, you may talk about problems you face at home and school and give each other advice and encouragement.

The bond that you and this person have established over the years is one kind of friendship. **Friendship** is a give-and-take relationship based on mutual trust, acceptance, and common interests or values. **People look to friends for honest reactions, for encouragement during bad times, and for understanding when they make mistakes.** Friends offer a sense of belonging and a handy way to remember an important fact: There are other people who understand and care about you.

The Importance of Friendships

Most teenagers consider it important to be part of one or more groups outside of their families. These may include school clubs, religious organizations, sports teams, or just a small group of friends. Interacting with others helps you to learn about yourself and to build self-esteem.

When you do things with friends, activities become more fun. All kinds of activities, such as studying for a test, going roller-skating, or washing a car, are more enjoyable to do with others. Something that might seem silly to do alone, like dressing up in a costume, can be fun to do with friends.

Friendships give you opportunities to develop your communication skills. Friendships allow you to try out a variety of roles: leader, helper, advice-seeker, or supporter. Experimenting with roles can help you learn how to relate with others. This knowledge will be important throughout your adult life—as you enter the work world, marry, start a family, or participate in community groups and decisions.

Types of Friendships

Friendships range from the casual acquaintances you greet in the halls at school to the friends who share your most intimate thoughts. Although some friendships are casual, and others are important enough to last a lifetime, each is valuable for different reasons.

CASUAL FRIENDSHIPS Casual friendships are often friendships of convenience. You and a neighbor may mow lawns together or go sledding after a snowstorm. You and a

Figure 6-5 *By sharing fun times with friends, you learn about yourself and others.*

classmate may be assigned to the same project in class. While doing volunteer work at the local hospital, you may meet a person who enjoys biking as much as you do.

Short-term, casual friendships offer the chance to have fun, to try new things, and to learn to get along with a variety of people. These friendships may remain casual, or they may develop into deeper, long-lasting friendships over time.

CLOSE FRIENDSHIPS   What determines whether a relationship will remain casual or become a close, lasting friendship? Researchers have found that people generally form close relationships with individuals who share similar goals, values, or interests. Other studies suggest that people get along better with individuals whose personalities complement their own. In other words, a friend may have some positive qualities that you lack, and you may have some positive qualities that your friend lacks. The two of you may get along well because you respect and admire each other's abilities.

No matter how close friendships form, most people agree on four qualities that are important in a close friend.

- Loyalty–A good friend sticks by you in both the good times and bad. Your friend likes you for who you are.

- Honesty–You can trust a good friend to be truthful with you, even when the truth is painful. You know that your friend is not trying to hurt your feelings.

- Empathy–A good friend is caring and sensitive to your feelings. A caring friend might say, "I know how much it hurts to be cut from the team." Words like these show **empathy** (EM puh thee), an ability to understand how another person feels.

- Reliability–A close friend can always be counted on. You know your friend will try hard not to let you down.

Figure 6-6 *What qualities do you look for in a close friend?*

Close friendships are important for many reasons. Close friendships provide emotional security, a sense of belonging, and the opportunity for people to see themselves as others see them. For teenagers, close friendships offer a way to grow outside of the family. By forming close friendships, teens can feel secure in a small group, much as they do within the family, but still have the chance to act independently.

FRIENDSHIPS WITH THE OPPOSITE SEX

When you were younger, you probably formed friendships with children of your own sex. Boys, for example, may have formed friendships with other boys with whom they could compete in sports or other activities. Girls, on the other hand, may have formed close one-to-one relationships with other girls.

Today, your friends may include both males and females. One reason that opposite-sex friendships develop more frequently today than in the past has to do with gender roles. **Gender roles** are the behaviors and attitudes that are socially accepted as either masculine or feminine. Gender roles vary from culture to culture. In the United States today, gender roles are less rigid than they have been in the past. Many people now participate in activities and behave in ways that traditionally were reserved for members of the other sex. Both males and females learn to express a variety of emotions, including tenderness, compassion, assertiveness, or whatever emotion a situation calls for.

In choosing friends today, people look for individuals of either sex with interests and goals similar to their own. Friendships between males and females can be satisfying and close but not involve romance. These friendships help you feel comfortable with members of the opposite sex and allow you to develop fully as a person. Some opposite-sex friendships may develop into romantic relationships as they progress. Many others simply remain friendships.

Figure 6-7 *Because gender roles are not as rigid today, it is common for friendships to develop between males and females.*

Making New Friends

Do you like to have many friends or just a few close friends? Whatever your friendship pattern, there are probably times when you would like to make new friends. But what do you look for in friends? How do you go about making friends?

Although there are no rules for choosing friends, it is best to look for people who share your interests and values. Also, look for people who demonstrate the qualities of loyalty, honesty, empathy, and reliability. Of course, it is difficult to judge someone before you get to know the person. With experience, you will become a better judge of the types of people you want as friends.

Making New Friends

To Meet New People	To Start a Conversation	To Keep Up a Conversation
• Go up to someone new and introduce yourself.	• Choose someone who is not in a rush and looks friendly.	• Use active listening techniques.
• Ask your friends to introduce you to someone you'd like to meet.	• Compliment the person and follow with a question.	• Ask questions that require more than a *yes* or *no* answer.
• Join a new club or team; do volunteer work in your community.	• Introduce yourself and talk about something that you like to do.	• Mention things you both have in common.
• Go to museums, libraries, sporting events, or parties.	• Ask the person about things he or she likes to do.	• Talk about something you've done that you think would interest the other person.

Figure 6-8 *Which of these tips can help you make new friends?*

Making new friends can sometimes be difficult. Many people feel shy or embarrassed introducing themselves to someone new. Figure 6-8 offers some tips for making new friends. The most important thing to remember is to be yourself. Putting on an act to win a friend will only make both of you feel uncomfortable.

Problems in Friendships

In all friendships, even strong ones, problems arise from time to time. For the relationship to be a lasting one, it is important that friends face any problems that do arise and work together to resolve them.

ENVY AND JEALOUSY   Feelings of envy and jealousy can arise in any friendship. A person may be envious of a friend's accomplishments, appearance, possessions, popularity, or something else. Jealousy may result when a friend wants to branch out of one group or best-friend relationship and develop other close relationships. This can cause feelings of anxiety about being left out.

While these feelings are normal at times, envy and jealousy can cause problems in a friendship. It is not easy to feel happy and proud for a friend when negative feelings get in the way. When envy or jealous feelings arise, use your communication skills to discuss the problem. First, use "I" messages to get your feelings out in the open. It is best to do this in person, but if this is too difficult, write a letter explaining your feelings. Be sure to listen to your friend's point of view and try to understand his or her feelings. By talking openly with your friend, you can gain a better understanding of your friendship and of ways to work things out.

TRANSFERRING ANGER   Occasionally, a friend may act cruelly toward you even though you have done nothing to anger him or her. The reason behind your friend's behavior may have nothing to do with you—your friend may be facing problems at home, school, or elsewhere.

Unfortunately people sometimes transfer the pain or anxiety they are feeling onto their close friends. If you are the victim of a friend's cruelty, you should confront your friend to find out what the real problem is. By confronting your friend, you communicate that you are not willing to be mistreated, and you also show your concern and desire to help your friend work things out.

CLIQUES AND GANGS Do you know a small, closed circle of friends that does not accept people who are different? If so, then you know a **clique** (KLEEK), a narrow, exclusive group of people with similar backgrounds or interests. Members of a clique often look down on people who are outside of their group.

While being a member of a clique can give a person a sense of belonging, it also can deprive a person of forming friendships with a variety of people. Cliques may hold members back from thinking and acting independently. Clique members may experience **peer pressure,** a need to conform to the expectations of friends. Peer pressure can be a positive force when friends encourage each other to study hard, avoid drugs, or work hard toward a goal. It can be a negative force when friends feel pressured to do things that go against their values.

Like cliques, gangs are made up of people with similar backgrounds, interests, and values who are unaccepting of anyone who is different. Gang members' dislike of others

---

D DEFINE
the problem

E EXPLORE
alternatives

C CONSIDER
the consequences

I IDENTIFY
values

D DECIDE
and act

E EVALUATE
results

Should You Tell a Friend that You Are Angry?

You and Cal have been friends for years, so it's hard to believe he didn't invite you to his party. All the other kids in your old group are going. That's how you found out about it—Ted asked you for a ride. Cal has also invited some people you don't know well but would like to meet. Maybe he doesn't think you're good enough for this crowd.

You're angry and hurt. It might feel good to tell Cal off, but what about your friendship? There are still three days left before the party, and Cal sits next to you in homeroom.

1. Use the DECIDE process on page 18 to decide what you would do in this situation. Explain your reasons for making this decision.

2. How might this situation become more difficult if you choose not to talk to Cal before the party?

Figure 6-9 *Members of a clique may feel pressured to dress and act in certain ways to go along with the group.*

may stem from **prejudices,** negative feelings about certain groups of people that are based on stereotypes. A **stereotype** is an exaggerated or overgeneralized belief about an entire group, such as an ethnic group, religious group, gender, or other group of people.

Like clique members, gang members are under intense pressure to go along with the group. Unlike cliques, though, gangs tend to be large and are sometimes involved in violent behaviors. You will learn more about gangs and violence in Chapter 7. Unfortunately, for some gang members, going along with the group means putting themselves and others at risk of physical harm.

LESSON **2** REVIEW

1. Why do you need friends?
2. Why are close and casual friendships important for personal growth?
3. How have changes in traditional gender roles affected friendship patterns?
4. In what ways are cliques and gangs similar? In what ways are they different?

What Do You Think?

5. What do you see as the most important problem that can arise within a friendship? How would you handle this problem?

3 DATING RELATIONSHIPS

GUIDE FOR READING

Focus on these questions as you read this lesson.

- Why is dating important for personal growth?
- How can emotional intimacy help a relationship grow?

SKILLS

- Expressing Feelings in a Positive Way

Developing as a person means also developing as a sexual being. As teenagers become aware of their sexuality, some tough questions arise: How can I show physical affection without things going too far? Are my sexual feelings normal? Are my partner and I emotionally ready for a sexual relationship?

There are no easy answers for these questions. The values you learn from your family, religious teachings, personal experiences, and friends influence your thinking about questions involving physical intimacy. It is important to spend time thinking about these questions and gathering as much information as you can before making decisions that can affect you for the rest of your life.

Physical Attraction and Dating

The teenage years are a time when most young people begin to experience feelings of physical attraction. Have you ever had a "crush" on a star performer, athlete, teacher, or other person you admire? Most teenagers have. These feelings of intense, sometimes overwhelming, attraction to another person are sometimes called **infatuation.** From these normal, healthy feelings of infatuation that you have as a teenager, you develop the ability to form close attachments later in your adult life.

Dating is typically the way that teenagers get to know people to whom they are attracted. Dating often grows out of group activities that include both boys and girls. A group of teens may enjoy skating together on a Saturday afternoon, for example, or going to school sports events and meeting for pizza afterward.

During mixed-group activities you may discover that you especially enjoy being with a certain friend. The person may be someone who shares your interests or has a similar sense of humor. You also may be physically attracted to this person. It is natural and healthy to feel physical attraction and to want to get to know the person better. This may lead to dating, either by yourselves or with other couples.

Dating gives you an opportunity to learn about members of the other sex. It may help you develop communication and decision-making skills and to learn how the other person views the gender roles that he or she learned as a child. You may even discover what qualities you want in a future marriage partner.

Dating practices vary with individuals and according to family and cultural guidelines. Some teenagers begin to date during high school, while others do not start dating until

Figure 6-10 *Questions about physical intimacy may arise during the teenage years.*

later. Still other teens may adhere to their cultural practices and not date at all. When teens date, some follow the traditional practice of the male initiating a date. Today, however, many young women make arrangements for dates and pay their share of expenses.

Steady Dating

At first, most teenagers date in a random, casual way. They may not focus on one special person or stick to a pattern of dating every Friday or Saturday night. After a few dates, however, a couple may decide not to date others and to see each other on a regular basis. Steady dating can be a form of security—partners are guaranteed a date whenever the need arises. For some couples, steady dating also can be a time of courtship that may lead to engagement and marriage.

Having a "steady" gives you a chance to get to know another person well, but steady dating also has some drawbacks. By dating the same person, you limit your chances of meeting other people with whom you might like to develop long-term relationships. You may also feel pressured to make decisions about physical intimacy before you are ready. If conflicts arise, and the relationship does not work out, it is sometimes difficult to break up with a steady boyfriend or girlfriend.

Physical Intimacy

It is natural for teenagers who have been dating to feel sexually attracted to one another. It is also natural to be confused and unsure of how to handle these feelings. Most teenagers try to think ahead and set limits for expressing their sexual feelings on dates. By setting limits before a situation arises, it is easier to stick to the standards you set.

SHARPEN YOUR SKILLS

Expressing Feelings in a Positive Way

You and Chris have been dating steadily for about six months. Although you still like Chris a lot, you would like to start dating other people. How could you communicate your feelings to Chris in a sensitive way?

In thinking about physical intimacy, there are some important issues to consider. These are discussed below.

EFFECT ON SELF-ESTEEM   Decisions about physical intimacy should be based on the values that you hold. Your values are shaped by many sources—family, friends, religious teachings, the media, and more. Sometimes these values can be contradictory, making it more difficult to sort out how you truly feel.

When a decision to become sexually involved goes against a person's values, the person may feel guilty and ashamed. The person may feel that he or she has let down parents, friends, and others as well as himself or herself. Lowered self-esteem often results when a person makes snap decisions about sexual intimacy or when sex is used to prove something to oneself and others.

EFFECT ON YOUR RELATIONSHIP   A decision to become physically intimate can affect all aspects of a relationship. It alters the way partners spend their time together and their relationships with other couples and friends. Sexual intimacy can also affect each partner's expectations of the relationship—one partner may expect to have sex whenever the couple is together, while the other partner may not. One partner may become more possessive of the other and put more demands on the other's time.

Often couples are unprepared for the additional complications that sexual intimacy adds to their relationship. Most couples find that the changes to their relationship are permanent. Although they may try, it is almost impossible to go back to the way things were before.

RISK OF PREGNANCY AND SEXUALLY TRANSMITTED DISEASES   Many teenagers who are thinking about becoming sexually involved do not believe that pregnancy can happen to them. But statistics show that one in six teenage girls who engage in sexual intercourse becomes pregnant. Many more sexually active teens become infected with the sexually transmitted diseases you will read about in Chapter 23.

Both teenage pregnancy and sexually transmitted diseases are serious health problems. Young mothers and their babies are more likely to face health, financial, and other problems than are older women. Many sexually transmitted diseases, if left untreated, can lead to a variety of problems including infertility and even death. AIDS, for example, kills tens of thousands of people each year and has now spread into the teen population. Because most teens want to avoid pregnancy, as well as any risk of a sexually transmitted disease, they should abstain from sex.

Figure 6-12 *It is important to think about how physical intimacy might affect you and your relationship.*

Figure 6-13 *Over time, couples can develop strong emotional bonds.*

Emotional Intimacy

On a television special that dealt with teenagers' sexual feelings, a young man said this about himself and his partner, "We're not ready for sexual intimacy, but we share lots of other intimate experiences."

Perhaps you are wondering how two people can share intimate experiences without being sexually involved. Partners share intimate experiences when they trust each other with personal feelings or dreams that they have not told anyone else. They may exchange "inside" jokes or do kind things for each other, and feel like best friends.

When young couples share experiences and show caring for each other without physical intimacy, their relationship can mature through emotional intimacy. The term **emotional intimacy** refers to the openness, sharing, affection, and trust that can develop in a close relationship. For emotional intimacy to develop, partners must communicate honestly and be accepting and supportive of each other.

Contrary to what you may think, not every teenager is sexually experienced. Millions of young people today are choosing to postpone sexual activity for a variety of good reasons. The Building Health Skills feature at the end of this chapter offers strategies for resisting the pressures to become sexually involved.

If you are sexually involved now and believe that building a relationship around emotional intimacy makes more sense, you can change. Try to talk honestly and sensitively with your partner about your decision. If your partner tries to make you feel guilty, then he or she may not be interested in respecting your feelings or getting to know you more deeply. Rather than staying in an unhealthy relationship, try to meet people who understand the importance of dealing responsibly with sexual feelings and of maintaining constructive, emotionally close relationships.

LESSON **3** REVIEW

1. What can people learn by dating?
2. What are some of the risks of physical intimacy?
3. How can emotional intimacy without physical intimacy help a relationship grow?

What Do You Think?

4. How do you think your friendships and dating relationships will help you identify important qualities in a future marriage partner?

4 THINKING ABOUT MARRIAGE

GUIDE FOR READING

Focus on these questions as you read this lesson.

- What qualities are important for a successful marriage?
- Why do teens who marry face more problems than older couples?

SKILLS

- Activity: On a Role

Ninety-five percent of all Americans marry at some time during their lives. Therefore it is highly likely that you will marry someday. If you do choose to marry, it will probably be one of the most important decisions you will make. It will affect you, your partner, your family, your friends, your acquaintances, and future generations.

What are your expectations about marriage? Do you hope to fulfill personal needs, including love, companionship, and emotional support? How will you divide the household responsibilities? Do you plan to have children?

Why People Marry

People marry for a variety of reasons. Some people marry because they desire another person's love and companionship. Others marry for financial or social reasons. Some couples marry in order to start a family of their own. Some marry simply because it is expected of them.

You probably feel, as most people do, that successful marriages are based on love. But what is love? Often young people mistake sexual attraction or short-lived infatuation for love. Real love is part of a long-lasting relationship in which people really know, like, and accept each other as they are. People who are truly in love appreciate the things they like about each other and accept the things they dislike. When you love someone, his or her well-being becomes as important to you as your own.

Figure 6-14 *Deciding to get married is one of the most important decisions you will make.*

Successful Marriages

Although love is a basic element in a successful marriage, it is not the only one. Some of the important factors to consider when thinking about marriage are listed in Figure 6-15 on the next page. It is important for partners to be compatible. **Compatibility** is the ability to exist in harmony with another person. Do you and your partner have similar interests and educational backgrounds? Do you share religious beliefs, ethnic heritage, and cultural values? Studies show that compatibility and shared interests and backgrounds increase the likelihood of a successful marriage. People who are quite different from each other also can have successful marriages, although they may have to work harder to overcome their differences.

Characteristics of a Successful Marriage

- Compatibility
- Love
- Friendship
- Similar interests, backgrounds, goals
- Strong commitment to each other and to the marriage
- Ability to communicate
- Shared responsibilities
- Physical attraction
- Mutual concern and respect
- Ability to compromise

Figure 6-15 *Which factors do you think are most important in a marriage?*

One quality that is important for a successful marriage is a couple's commitment to one another. The term **commitment** means the determination to develop a fulfilling relationship. In a fulfilling marital relationship, partners can share thoughts and feelings, have fun together, develop mutual respect, share responsibilities, satisfy sexual needs, and gain emotional security. Researchers have found that in successful marriages, spouses work at being a couple by setting aside time and energy for each other.

People usually set goals for what they want out of life and marriage. A marriage is more likely to succeed if partners can agree on some important goals. These goals may include buying a home, getting further education, pursuing a career, or having children.

Sometimes spouses have conflicting goals. A wife, for example, may want to pursue a career before having children, but her husband may not want to wait for children. A conflict may develop over whether money should be spent or saved for future needs. Communication and compromise help couples resolve conflicts and determine mutual goals.

Many happily married couples use the types of communication skills you read about earlier. Imagine, for example, that you are married and are having a conflict with your partner over a visit to your in-laws. You do not want to visit your spouse's parents every weekend even though you enjoy their company and know your partner looks forward to the weekly visits. How will you discuss this without hurting your partner's feelings? You could begin with an "I" message: "I enjoy seeing your parents, but I have other interests too...."

Some conflicts may require compromising. Suppose, for example, a wife wants to use the couple's savings for a new car while her husband wants to buy new furniture. The couple might agree to buy a used car, leaving enough money for some furniture as well.

Stresses in Marriage

Throughout all marriages, partners must be willing to make adjustments to meet each other's needs and wants. The changes in attitudes, expectations, and goals that these adjustments may require can produce stress.

One of the most difficult adjustments in marriage can be determining marital roles. **Marital roles** are the responsibilities that each partner assumes in a marriage. As you read in Chapter 5, not long ago most Americans accepted traditional marital roles—the husband earned money, and the wife took care of the home and children. Many married couples still follow this pattern. In many other marriages today, however, both partners work outside the home and share housework and child care.

Some couples decide early in their marriage how each person will contribute financially and who will do certain household tasks. Who will do the cooking? Who will pay the bills? By compromising and accepting tasks that fit their abilities, interests, and schedules, partners usually can develop a comfortable give-and-take relationship. When changes occur, such as the birth of a child or a new job, partners may need to renegotiate their marital roles.

Figure 6-16 *Many married couples share responsibilities both inside and outside the home.*

ON A ROLE

In this activity you and a "marriage partner" will decide on a fair way to share household responsibilities.

Materials (per pair)

paper	12–20 index cards
pen	

Procedure

1. Pair up with a partner of the opposite sex.

2. With your partner, list all the responsibilities that married couples commonly share (for example, cooking meals, earning a living).

3. Choose 12 responsibilities from your list. Write each on a separate index card.

4. Spread out the index cards on a desk. Together, determine which of you would be primarily responsible for each task if you were married. If a task would be shared equally, put the card aside. Replace the card by selecting another responsibility from your list, writing it on an index card, and adding it to the desk.

5. Continue negotiating with your partner until all the responsibilities have been assigned and both of you feel comfortable with the division.

Discussion

1. What difficulties did you and your partner encounter in trying to divide the responsibilities? Do you think that similar difficulties exist in real marriages?

2. Were any of your decisions about responsibilities based on gender roles or on your own family's division of responsibilities? Explain.

3. List some situations that might occur in a real marriage that would force partners to redistribute household responsibilities.

Couples also must determine how to manage the family income. Each partner may have a different idea or attitude about earning, spending, and managing money. Imagine, for example, that one spouse wants to spend any extra income on things such as restaurant dinners and vacations. The other spouse may be more cautious and insist on putting some of the earnings into savings. If partners cannot agree on money matters, there is likely to be conflict and stress. To resolve differences over finances, they may work together to come up with a budget that they both can accept.

Marriages can become strained when unexpected problems arise. The major wage earner may lose his or her job. A partner may become seriously ill. There may be an unplanned pregnancy. Effective communication can be an important tool in helping a couple get through a crisis. Sometimes a couple may need to seek help from community agencies that provide financial or counseling services. Turning to family and friends for emotional support is another way to get through hard times.

Teens and Marriage

When teenagers marry, they often face more stress than do those who marry later. The strains of adjusting to a new relationship, earning a living, and completing an education can feel overwhelming. If they have children, a young couple also may have difficulty adjusting to the emotional and financial responsibilities of parenthood.

Many married teenagers drop out of school. Without a high-school diploma, it can be difficult to find a good job. Even if both partners work, they may have difficulty earning enough money for rent and food. The couple may end up living with parents or other relatives. Such an arrangement can

Figure 6-18 *Teenagers who marry face many obstacles. Partners must be emotionally mature and committed to the marriage.*

limit a couple's opportunities to get to know each other, to make decisions, and to develop as a couple.

Another difficulty for married teenagers involves changes in their friendships. Unmarried friends may not have the same interests and goals as a married couple, especially if the couple has a baby. A married couple may be concerned about stretching a small income, while single friends may be more concerned about school or dating.

It is difficult to know when you are 17 or 18 just how you will feel when you are 25 or 30. People change a great deal during their teens and early twenties. For this reason, many teenagers choose to wait before making a long-term commitment. They want to find out more about themselves, to meet people, and to have other experiences. In spite of all the obstacles, some teenage marriages are successful. Partners must be willing to put in the effort needed to make their marriage work. They need to learn to communicate, to compromise, and to develop the qualities that are important for a fulfilling relationship.

LESSON 4 REVIEW

1. List five important factors for a successful marriage.
2. List three stresses that may challenge any marriage.
3. What obstacles might married teenagers face?

What Do You Think?

4. If you were married, what goals would you find it most difficult to compromise on? Why?

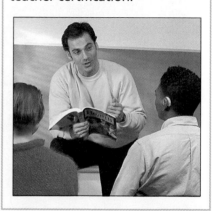

Choosing Abstinence

Ron and Tanya met in algebra class and became good friends. Soon, they started to date. As they spent more time together, Ron and Tanya began to express their feelings of affection physically—hugging, kissing, and holding hands. Each time they went out, however, Ron and Tanya felt the pressure to become more physically intimate growing stronger.

Both Ron and Tanya feel that abstinence (which means abstaining from, or not having, sex) is the best choice at this point in their lives. But how can they practice abstinence and still remain friends? How can they be physically affectionate without it leading too far? These questions are not easy ones to answer. The following guidelines can help people choose abstinence when faced with the pressure to become more physically intimate.

1. Set clear limits in your own mind

Take some time now to set limits that you feel comfortable with. It is important to know your limits before you go on a date so you can avoid making decisions "in the heat of the moment."

To help you set limits, be sure to consider the possible consequences of your actions and the important values that you hold. The DECIDE process on page 18 can help you make decisions with which you feel comfortable. Do not allow the expectations of friends, the media, and others to influence you to make decisions that may not be right for you.

2. Communicate your limits to your partner

Once you have decided on your limits, it is important to communicate your feelings to your partner. Of course, it is best to discuss things as early as possible in a relationship. Do not wait until a situation arises in which your partner's expectations may be different from yours. It may be difficult to have an open, constructive discussion if you wait until that point to talk to your partner.

Try to talk honestly to your partner about your feelings and values. You may be surprised at how relieved your partner is to hear how you feel. He or she may have been anxious about your expectations.

3. Avoid high-pressure situations

Sticking to the limits you have set can sometimes be difficult. You can make it easier for yourself by avoiding certain situations, such as unsupervised parties, where you might feel pressured to have sex. Instead, go to public places where the temptation to engage in sexual activities is not as great. It is also important to avoid alcohol and other drugs, as they can blur your ability to think clearly.

4. If you say *no,* say it as if you mean it

If you are in a situation where things have progressed too far for you, do not feel guilty about stopping them. Tell your partner clearly and directly that you want to stop. You may want to offer a reason, such as "I'm just not ready for sex yet," so that your partner won't feel hurt or rejected.

At times, however, saying *no* may not be effective. You may need to be firm and say something like "No! I said I don't want to do that." You may need to repeat yourself a few times to be believed. If necessary, get up and walk away.

Sometimes, a person may try to pressure a partner to change his or her mind. He or she may say that it is physically impossible to stop. This is not true—no physical harm will result from stopping. The person might also say things like "If you loved me, you wouldn't say *no,*" or "Everybody's doing it." Remember that you will respect yourself more for sticking to your limits than for giving in to this pressure. If your partner cannot respect the limits you set, the relationship may not be worth continuing.

Apply the Skill

1. Review Ron and Tanya's situation. If they were your friends, what advice would you offer them? How can they continue their relationship while sticking to their limits?

2. What response would you offer to these "pressure" lines?

If you loved me, you would have sex with me.

Everyone else is having sex. What's wrong with you?

You know you want to. Everyone wants to.

Everyone already thinks we're having sex. We might as well.

3. With three or four classmates (both male and female), develop a list of rules to follow in a dating relationship. Make sure your rules emphasize respect for yourself and others.

CHAPTER 6 REVIEW

KEY IDEAS

LESSON 1
- The skills of communication, cooperation, and compromise are important in all relationships.

LESSON 2
- Friendships give people a sense of belonging and feelings of emotional security. Some important qualities that are desirable in friends are loyalty, honesty, empathy, and reliability.

LESSON 3
- Dating provides an opportunity to understand others, develop communication and decision-making skills, and learn what qualities are important in a mate.

- When teenagers begin to date, they must make difficult decisions about sexual intimacy. Millions of teenagers maintain emotionally intimate relationships while postponing sexual activity.

LESSON 4
- Some qualities that are important for successful marriages are love, compatibility, an ability to compromise, and a commitment to the marriage.

- Changing marital roles, disagreements over money, and unexpected problems can create stress in a marriage. When teens marry, they often face more problems than do older couples.

KEY TERMS

LESSON 1
active listening
aggressive
assertive
body language
compromise
cooperation
eye contact
"I" message

passive

LESSON 2
clique
empathy
friendship
gender roles
peer pressure
prejudice
stereotype

LESSON 3
emotional intimacy
infatuation

LESSON 4
commitment
compatibility
marital roles

Listed above are some of the important terms in this chapter. Choose the term from the list that best matches each phrase below.

1. a narrow, exclusive group of people with similar backgrounds or interests

2. the ability to exist in harmony with another person

3. the willingness of people to give up something in order to reach agreement

4. the determination to develop a fulfilling relationship

5. communicating information or feelings nonverbally, through body movements, posture, gestures, and facial expressions

6. an exaggerated or overgeneralized belief about an entire group

7. expressing one's true feelings in a way that does not threaten others

8. a give-and-take relationship based on mutual trust, acceptance, and common interests or values

9. the ability to understand how another person feels

10. behaviors and attitudes that are socially accepted as either masculine or feminine

WHAT HAVE YOU LEARNED?

On a separate sheet of paper, write the word or words that best complete each statement.

11. A(n) _____ is a statement of your feelings that does not judge or blame the other person.

12. A(n) _____ person holds back true feelings and goes along with the other person.

13. Making _____ involves meeting another person's gaze.

14. _____ is a need to conform to the expectations of friends.

15. A(n) _____ is a negative feeling about a certain group based on a stereotype.

16. A(n) _____ is an intense or overwhelming feeling of attraction.

17. _____ is the openness, affection, and trust that can develop in a close relationship.

18. A husband doing the cooking and a wife doing yardwork are examples of _____.

Answer each of the following with complete sentences.

19. What is active listening? Why is it important in relationships?

20. What is assertive communication? How is the tone of a person's voice important in communication?

21. Give an example of how a person's body language might send a mixed message.

22. Describe the benefits that close friends can provide. How is a close friend different from other kinds of friends?

23. Why are friendships between members of the opposite sex more common today?

24. Why are communication skills important when problems arise within a friendship?

25. What are some drawbacks of being part of a clique or a gang?

26. What are the benefits of steady dating? What are the drawbacks?

27. What important issues do couples need to consider when they are thinking about physical intimacy?

28. How are the skills of communication and compromise important in a marriage?

29. How can teen marriages be successful?

WHAT DO YOU THINK?

30. How might communication skills help improve your relationships with others?

31. What are some common barriers to good communication between adults and teens?

32. Why do you think that some people find it difficult to make or to keep friends?

33. Do you think that mixed-group activities are important in the process of developing relationships with the other sex? Explain.

34. What do you think are the two most important factors in a successful marriage? Why are these factors important?

WHAT WOULD YOU DO?

35. You are visiting another country and are unable to speak the language. How can you communicate your needs?

36. You are at a party where you know only two people. How would you get acquainted with other people?

37. You are part of a close-knit group of friends at school. Members of your group sometimes tease a classmate who is mentally disabled. You think this behavior is not right. How would you handle the situation?

38. Your friends, a teenage couple who have dated for two years, plan to marry. Would you encourage or discourage them? Why?

Getting Involved

39. With a parent or another adult, select two letters about teenage relationships from an advice column in a newspaper. Separately, the two of you should write your own responses to the letters. Then compare your responses to each other's and to the actual advice offered in the newspaper.

Chapter 7

PREVENTING VIOLENCE

Every day, tragic acts of violence destroy individuals' lives, families, and even communities. Many people have begun to speak out and even demonstrate against the causes of violence in society. In this chapter, you will examine how fights start and learn to anticipate the things that make people angry. You will also explore some nonviolent alternatives to fighting.

CHAPTER PREVIEW

7-1 What Is Violence?

- Identify risk factors that are associated with violence.

7-2 How Fights Start

- Describe some situations that often lead to fights.

7-3 Preventing Fights

- Outline methods for resolving conflicts without fighting.

BUILDING HEALTH SKILLS

- Identify strategies for mediating conflicts.

CHECK YOUR WELLNESS

Do your actions help prevent fights? See if you agree with the following statements.

- I take time to think through a problem before I act.

- If I am upset with someone, I talk to the person in private rather than when friends are around.

- When someone has angered me, I state my concerns clearly, without insults or name-calling.

- I am able to apologize to someone if I said or did something to cause hurt feelings.

- When I feel angry, I can talk to a trusted adult.

- If two of my friends are upset with each other, I avoid carrying negative messages between them.

- If there is a fight brewing, I do not go watch, and I discourage friends from watching as well.

KEEPING A JOURNAL

"An eye for an eye and a tooth for a tooth." In your journal explore your reaction to this quote. Do you agree with its message? Why or why not?

Take it to the Net
www.phschool.com

Focus on these questions as you read this lesson.

- Who feels the effects of violence?
- What risk factors are associated with violent behavior?

SKILLS

- Activity: Logging Violence on Television

1 WHAT IS VIOLENCE?

Wars, riots, stabbings, shootings, rapes, spouse abuse, child beatings, street fights—it is impossible to watch the news without seeing reports of violence. **Violence,** the use of physical force with the intent to injure or kill, seems to be part of our culture.

The statistics in Figure 7-1 show the violence problem this country faces. **Homicide** (HAHM ih syd), the intentional killing of one person by another, is currently the second leading cause of death for people aged 15 to 24. Fortunately, teen violence may be starting to decline. In the past decade, the number of students who carried weapons dropped by 30 percent.

Myths About Violence

When most people think of violence, they think of a stranger surprising an unsuspecting victim. But statistics do not support this view. Instead, statistics show that in about half of all homicides the people involved knew each other. Many other myths exist about violence. Read over the myths and facts about violence on the next page. Which facts were you most surprised to learn?

The Many Costs of Violence

Imagine that a single act of violence has just been committed. Who will feel its effects? You may be surprised to see just how many people are affected by an act of violence.

COST TO THE VICTIM Of course, the first person who suffers from an act of violence is the **victim,** the person who is attacked and harmed physically. While death is the most serious outcome of a violent act, it is not the only possible result. Victims who survive their attacks may suffer serious permanent injuries that change their lives forever. Injuries to the head can lead to the permanent loss of brain function. Other injuries can cause permanent **paralysis** (puh RAL ih sis), the loss of feeling and movement in some part of the body. But even when injuries are less serious, they still may cause pain, require medical treatment, and take time to heal or leave permanent scars.

Beyond the physical injuries that victims suffer, there may also be emotional scars. Anger, fear, and sadness are some common feelings that victims experience. It is also common for victims to replay the actual event over and over in their minds. This may heighten the

Figure 7-1 *Acts of violence are all too common in the United States today. What can be done to stop the violence?*

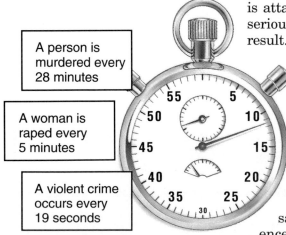

A person is murdered every 28 minutes

A woman is raped every 5 minutes

A violent crime occurs every 19 seconds

Source: Federal Bureau of Investigation

MYTHS & FACTS

Violence

1. **MYTH:** Most acts of violence are committed by strangers, often as part of robberies or other crimes.

   ● **FACT: About half of all homicides, most of rapes and assaults, and all acts of family violence are committed by people who know their victims.**

2. **MYTH:** Using violence can be an effective way to solve a problem.

   ● **FACT: Although violence might offer a temporary solution to a problem, it always creates more problems than it solves. Even when you win a fight, injuries, feelings of guilt, fear of revenge, and the threat of jail are some of the consequences you may face.**

3. **MYTH:** The best way to protect yourself from violence is to have a weapon.

   ● **FACT: Armed victims are twice as likely to be killed as are unarmed victims. In fact, a gun kept at home is 43 times more likely to kill a family member or friends than an intruder.**

4. **MYTH:** Most violence is racially motivated. Violent acts usually occur between people of different races.

   ● **FACT: About ninety percent of all homicide victims are of the same race as their killers.**

5. **MYTH:** Certain racial groups are more violent than others.

   ● **FACT: Although some racial groups are represented in higher numbers in violence statistics, the reasons have to do with poverty, not race. Comparisons of poor communities with very different racial makeups reveal that homicide rates are similarly high.**

6. **MYTH:** Youth gangs are responsible for the majority of homicides.

   ● **FACT: Only about 3 percent of all homicides are gang-related. In comparison, 12 percent of homicides are committed by family members. In many urban areas, however, gang violence is a serious and rapidly growing problem.**

---

victims' negative emotions and make it difficult to focus on the future rather than on the past.

A victim's family members and friends also feel the effects of violence. Feelings of loss and the burden of caring for an injured person are just some of the effects on these people. Fear, anger, and the desire for vengeance are common emotions that these people experience.

COST TO THE ASSAILANT   Another person whose life is changed by violence is the assailant. An **assailant** (uh SAY lunt) is a person who physically attacks another person. Like the victim, the assailant may suffer serious physical injuries in a fight. Emotionally, the assailant may feel sadness and guilt and may live in fear of an act of revenge. The assailant's family and friends may feel some of these same emotions. In addition, an assailant may face criminal charges, court costs, lawyer's fees, and possible jail time. Having a criminal record can seriously affect a person for the rest of his or her life. It can limit a person's chances of finding employment and housing and of pursuing other future goals.

COSTS TO SOCIETY   Suppose that you do not know either the victims or the assailants involved in violent acts. In what ways does the violence affect you? One way that you feel the effects is financially. The health-care costs alone for treating injuries that result from violence are estimated to be about 6 billion dollars a year. There are many other costs as well, including law-enforcement costs, legal costs, prison costs, insurance costs, and property damage costs. All of the taxpayers in this country pay dearly for violence.

There are also many emotional costs of violence. For some people, especially in communities where violence occurs regularly, a fear of violence controls many day-to-day decisions. Avoiding certain neighborhoods, not going out past a certain time of day, installing security locks and alarms—these are just some precautions that many people regard as routine.

Risk Factors for Violence

When scientists talk about preventing a disease such as cancer, they focus on eliminating those factors that put people at risk for the disease. The same reasoning has been applied to the study of violence. Violence-prevention experts have identified some specific risk factors for violence. **Poverty, exposure to media violence or to family violence, the availability of weapons, drug abuse, and membership in gangs are all important risk factors for violence.** As you read about these risk factors, think about the ways each one might increase the likelihood of violence.

POVERTY   Statistics show that violence rates are highest in poor urban communities where unemployment rates are high. The term **free-floating anger** is used to describe the frustration and hostility that sometimes result when people feel unable to improve their lives. A lack of jobs, money, adequate food, health care, and respect from others all contribute to feelings of hopelessness and anger. When free-floating anger is already high, a minor event may trigger a person to react more violently than normal. It is important to emphasize, however, that most people who are poor do not demonstrate violent behaviors. The anger and frustration of poverty is just one of many risk factors for violence.

MEDIA VIOLENCE   From your first cartoon to the latest movie, music video, or video/computer game, you have learned that violence, excitement and entertainment go together. You can probably recall lines or scenes from action movies that show violence as a reasonable response in many situations. What these scenes do not show, however, are the real results of violence—pain, tragedy, remorse, and more.

Studies suggest that people's attitudes, especially those of young children, can be shaped by

Figure 7-2 *The frustration and hopelessness that sometimes accompany poverty may lead to increased violence.*

LOGGING VIOLENCE ON TELEVISION

In this activity you will monitor the amount and types of violence that appear on television.

Procedure

1. Over the next week watch five hours of television. Include one hour of children's cartoons and one hour of a police or action show.

2. For each violent episode you see, record the type of violence, the number of people involved, the weapons used, and the outcome.

Discussion

1. How many violent episodes did you see in the five hours? How many weapons were used? How many people were injured? How many were killed?

2. Suppose that you watch ten hours of television a week. Estimate from your five hours of viewing how many violent episodes you would see in a week and in a year.

3. What messages about violence might the cartoon(s) that you watched send to viewers? What impact might these messages have on children's behaviors?

4. Review the myths and facts about violence on page 147. Which myths are reinforced by the portrayal of violence on television?

5. Do you think that violence on television should be regulated in any way? Defend your answer.

---

media violence. Because children have had little real-life experience, they may interpret what they see on television quite literally. Children who witness a lot of media violence may grow up with an exaggerated sense of the amount of violence in the world. They also may tend to overreact with violence when confronted with threatening situations in their own lives.

Recently much attention has been focused on the media's portrayal of violence towards women—especially in some kinds of music and music videos. The audience for these forms of entertainment is mostly teenagers and young adults. Some people suspect that these media portrayals are partly responsible for the rise in dating violence, rape, and other forms of violence towards women. Do you think this could be true?

FAMILY VIOLENCE   As you read in Chapter 2, children learn by imitating the behavior of parents and other important people in their lives. It is not surprising, then, that children who grow up in violent homes are more apt to use violence to solve their own problems. Violence may be the only problem-solving strategy that these children know.

How can children learn nonviolent methods for handling anger? The most effective way is to see such methods used by adults in solving their own problems and in disciplining their children. Second, parents need to discourage their children from fighting by suggesting alternative ways to resolve disagreements. Third, parents can impart antiviolence values by discouraging children from playing with certain toys or watching violent movies or television shows, and by sharing their own feelings about violence with their children.

AVAILABILITY OF WEAPONS

Do guns kill people, or do people kill people? This difficult question gets to the heart of a controversial issue—the relationship between weapons and violence.

Some people do not believe that the availability of weapons is an important risk factor for violence. They point to countries such as Switzerland, where guns are found in nearly every household. Still, homicide rates in Switzerland are very low. Other people, however, disagree. They point to comparisons like the one shown in Figure 7-3. This graph compares homicide rates in two cities that are similar in many respects except one—gun ownership is much more tightly regulated in Vancouver, British Columbia, than in Seattle, Washington. What does this graph suggest about the availability of guns?

Most people do agree that when weapons are used in fights, fights are more deadly. Yet the majority of people who purchase handguns in this country do so for protection. By having a gun, however, statistics show that these people are actually doubling their chances of being killed in a fight. What results is an unending cycle—high homicide rates lead to an increase in gun purchasing, which, in turn, leads to an increase in homicide rates. This then leads, once again, to more gun purchasing. Such a cycle may be difficult to break.

DRUG ABUSE

Would it surprise you to learn that 50 percent of all homicide victims have alcohol in their bloodstreams? Would you expect the statistics to be similarly high for assailants if they were known?

Figure 7-3 *Does the availability of guns lead to an increase in violence? One study suggests it may. Use the graph to compare the homicide rates by each weapon in the two cities. What difference do you note? How can you explain the difference?*

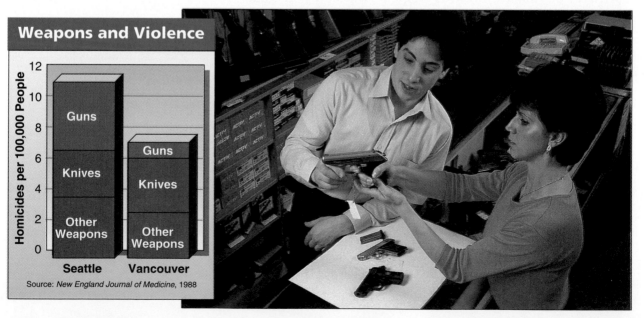

Weapons and Violence

Homicides per 100,000 People

Seattle
Guns
Knives
Other Weapons

Vancouver
Guns
Knives
Other Weapons

Source: *New England Journal of Medicine*, 1988

Although there is a correlation between violence and alcohol use, the reasons behind it are not entirely clear. As you will learn in Chapter 19, alcohol affects the brain, clouding a person's sense of judgment. A lack of judgment may lead a person to say or do things that he or she ordinarily would not. This behavior may lead to a fight. In other cases, however, alcohol is used more as an excuse or "to get up the nerve" to carry out preplanned acts of violence.

Drugs other than alcohol also are linked to violence. Like alcohol, illegal drugs such as crack cocaine can affect a person's judgment and behavior. In addition, people who are addicted to drugs may resort to robbery or other crimes to get money for drugs. Also, because many drugs are illegal and sold for a large profit, the people who sell drugs often carry weapons. Both of these facts add to the threat of violence.

MEMBERSHIP IN GANGS The term *gang* describes a variety of groups, from criminal organizations to loose bands of rowdy teens. Generally, *gang* refers to groups that are organized to control a specific neighborhood or "turf." Such gangs are called **territorial gangs** or "fighting" gangs because they will fight those who intrude on their turf. Most gangs sell drugs, and many have moved into the lucrative suburban and rural drug markets.

Although young people join gangs, about two-thirds of gang members are adults. They recruit poor students from troubled families. Often the recruits know of no other way, except gang membership, to gain a sense of belonging or community. Holding elaborate initiation ceremonies, wearing certain colors and jewelry, and using "secret" hand signs are some of the ways gang members identify themselves. To join a gang, new members may undergo a beating, or gang leaders may order them to commit a crime, such as robbery, kidnapping, rape, or murder. Quitting a gang can be much harder than joining one.

Small non-territorial gangs can form in any town. These groups may identify with a style of music or dress that sets them apart from their peers. Like all gangs, these groups isolate their members from the community.

LESSON 1 REVIEW

1. In what ways does violence affect all people?
2. Name six risk factors associated with violence.
3. What is meant by the phrase *free-floating anger?*
4. Describe the cycle of violence that weapons may cause.

What Do You Think?

5. How would you advise your child to deal with a bully?

GUIDE FOR READING

Focus on these questions as you read this lesson.

- Is a person's response to anger within his or her control?

- What are some conflict situations or factors that typically lead to violence?

SKILLS

- Supporting a Friend

Imagine that you had a special power to know when an act of violence was about to be committed. Suppose also that your powers enabled you to freeze the scene just moments before the violence began. What would you see? You might see two young men who have been drinking, and may be carrying weapons. This is a scene poised for violence.

Now suppose that you unfroze the scene to watch how the violence begins. What causes tempers to flare and things to get out of control? In this lesson you will take a close-up look at some situations that led to violence. As you read each of the scenarios, think about how the situation might have been prevented or resolved peacefully.

Arguments

Hey, what did you call me?

You heard what I said. What are you going to do about it?

Too often, a simple exchange like this one—on the basketball court, in the hallways at school, on the streets—leads to tragic results. What starts as a disagreement between friends, family members, or acquaintances ends in fighting, injury, and sometimes death. In fact, about 40 percent of all homicides stem directly from arguments.

At the root of most arguments, of course, is anger. When a person feels angry, the body reacts the same way it does to stress. As you may recall from Chapter 3, the body's reaction to stress is called the fight or flight response. This is because the changes that occur in the body—increased heart and breathing rates, tensed muscles, rise in blood pressure, and more—prepare a person to either fight or run away.

Although the body's reaction to anger is automatic, the way you choose to deal with the anger is within your control. Fighting or running away are not your only options for dealing with anger. In some situations you can use good communication skills to let the person who angered you know why. In other situations you can rechannel your anger into other activities such as lifting weights, painting, or playing an instrument.

If you resort to fighting when someone makes you angry, you give the other person control over you. The person knows that, by provoking you, he or she can force you to fight. This means that the person can cause you to be kicked out of a game, suspended from school, or suffer other negative consequences of fighting. By choosing not to fight, you do not give the other person this control. Some techniques for avoiding fights are presented later in the chapter.

Figure 7-4 *Fighting is not a constructive way to deal with anger. What other methods of handling anger work for you?*

Hurt Pride and Embarrassment

A fight broke out after yesterday's football game at South High School. Witnesses said that during the game a fan from North High School shouted insults at one of South's players. After North's decisive victory, the insults grew louder and punches were thrown. When police finally broke up the fight, five youths were rushed to the hospital with injuries.

Think about a time when your pride was hurt or when someone embarrassed you in front of others. Perhaps someone insulted your school or your family, or revealed a secret that you had shared in confidence. You may have been surprised at just how angry you felt. It is not surprising that hurt pride and embarrassment often lead to fighting.

You may know some people who seem to enjoy embarrassing others and starting fights. When you were younger, you probably called such people bullies. Bullies are often mean to others in an attempt to boost their own self-esteem. They take out their own frustrations and insecurities on others. Keeping this in mind may help you ignore a bully's behavior when it is directed toward you.

Peer Pressure

You're not going to let her get away with that, are you?

Girl, I wouldn't take that from anyone.

Why do you carry a knife if you're afraid to use it?

One aspect of fighting that is often overlooked is the role played by friends and onlookers. When you hear the term *peer pressure* in relation to violence, you may immediately think of the influence that gang members have on each other to fight. But peer pressure can be an important factor in non-gang violence as well.

Figure 7-5 *"Body language" can encourage or discourage a fight. Who do you think is more likely to fight, the boy on the left or the boy on the right?*

Ever since your friend missed the winning shot in last week's basketball game, another student at school has not let him forget it. Your friend is fed up with the person's continual insults and embarrassing comments. What could you say or do to discourage your friend from fighting?

Imagine that you just had a loud disagreement with someone and your friends made comments like the ones you just read. How might these comments affect you? Chances are they would increase your feelings of anger and embarrassment, and add to the pressure you might already feel to fight. You might feel trapped—you may not want to fight but you may think that your friends would lose respect for you if you walked away.

Friends who either knowingly or unknowingly urge you to fight act as instigators. **Instigators** (IN stih gay turz) are people who encourage fighting between others while staying out of the fights themselves. Some instigators, like the ones quoted on the previous page, may exaggerate a conflict or embarrass a person into fighting. Other instigators may spread rumors about one person to another to create a conflict between them.

Another form of instigation often occurs at the scene of a potential fight when a crowd gathers. The people who gather do so hoping to see a fight. They may yell things or in other ways urge the people to fight. It can be very difficult to settle a dispute peacefully once a crowd has gathered. If a fight does break out, the person who loses faces an additional problem—dealing with the embarrassment of having had so many people witness the defeat.

Prejudice

Last night, a 16-year-old boy was badly beaten by three youths. The violent act seemed to be racially motivated. According to the victim, the three boys shouted racial slurs as they repeatedly kicked and punched him.

Although 90 percent of all homicides involve people of the same race, prejudice is responsible for many acts of violence today. As you learned in Chapter 6, prejudice can be based on skin color, religious or political beliefs, nationality, or other differences among people. Prejudice leads to **intolerance,** a lack of acceptance of another's opinions, beliefs, or actions. Too often, people who are intolerant find reasons to start fights.

Intolerance can lead to violence in another way as well. People who are victims of intolerance may experience **discrimination,** the unfair mistreatment of a person or group based on prejudices. People may be discriminated against in unfair job hiring, housing rental, or other opportunities. Psychologists use the term **microinsults** to describe the small but frequent episodes of discrimination that some people experience. Microinsults include such things as being made to feel like an outsider, being treated impolitely, or having one's talents underestimated. The anger brought on by microinsults can build over time and may eventually lead to violence.

Figure 7-6 *Many acts of violence are rooted in prejudice and intolerance of others.*

White ⚡ Power

Many people believe that prejudice, intolerance, and discrimination are rooted in a fear of the unknown. This fear can result when a person lacks an understanding of behaviors that seem strange or threatening to him or her. Education, then, may be the key to reducing intolerance. By learning about other groups' customs and beliefs, and by getting to know individuals from other groups, people may become more tolerant of the differences.

Figure 7-7 *By working together and learning about different groups, tolerance can replace prejudice.*

Revenge

There's the guy who beat up your brother. What are you going to do?

He's going to pay for what he did. But this time I'll choose the time and place. He'll never know what hit him.

Some people mistakenly believe that fighting can settle an argument. More often, however, fighting starts a dangerous cycle of revenge. When a person loses a fight, his or her feelings of anger and embarrassment grow even stronger. The person may enlist the help of friends or family members to "even the score."

In many cases in which revenge is sought, the fighting can quickly **escalate,** or grow more intense. Where the first fight may have been a fistfight, the second fight may involve deadly weapons. Where the first fight may have involved only two people, the second fight may involve many more. And chances are good that the second fight will only lead to still more fighting.

Revenge is a common motive in gang fights. Gang members feel responsible for protecting one another. When one gang member is wronged, other members come to his or her aid. The result is a dangerous cycle of revenge that may last for years and years.

Control

Did you see her black eye and bruises?

Yes, and all because another guy gave her a ride home. How can a guy beat up on his girlfriend like that?

Girlfriend? He treats her more like a piece of property.

Violence toward women, especially toward wives and girl-friends, is a growing problem in this country. Often the motivation behind such violence is control. The man may think that, by using violence, the woman will be too afraid to leave him or to go against his wishes. Women who are in abusive relationships get caught in a trap of fear. They may be scared to stay with their husbands or boyfriends. They also may be too scared to leave or seek help.

Recently some states have passed laws to protect women in abusive relationships. Many organizations assist women with the legal, financial, emotional, and safety issues involved in ending their relationships. If someone you know is in an abusive relationship, encourage the person to seek help from a physician, counselor, member of the clergy, or support group for abused women. Victims of abuse need to know that there is a way out of their situations. Abusers also need help to learn to control their violent behavior.

LESSON **2** REVIEW

1. What choices does a person have for dealing with anger?
2. List four situations or factors that may lead to violence.
3. What role do instigators play in starting fights?

What Do You Think?

4. What can schools do to help eliminate prejudice?

DIFFERENT VOICES SPEAKING

Fredde Sanchez, 28, is a victim of violence. Two years ago he came to the United States hoping to go to architecture school. Three months later a bullet paralyzed him from the neck down. Fredde now lives in an extended-care hospital in New York.

Q. Can you describe what happened to you?

A. I was here three months from the Dominican Republic. The only people I knew were some guys I was friendly with ten years ago in my country. My sister warned me that they were selling drugs, but I didn't want to believe it. That night we went to a dance club. Two of my friends started arguing with two other guys. I went over to ask what was wrong. They told me to mind my own business, that it was their problem.

Q. So then what happened?

A. I finally convinced my friends to leave. One brought the car to the front of the club, and my friends got in. As I was about to get in, the guys they argued with began to fire at the car from a pretty short distance away. I was hit with a .38 caliber bullet that severed my spinal cord. My friends drove away and left me there. When I tried to get up, my legs would not respond. I could not move them at all.

Q. Do you speak to those friends anymore?

A. They visited me in the hospital a month after the shooting. My sister asked them, "Please, tell me who the guy is, so the police can capture him." They were too afraid to tell her, and they never visited again. One of them was murdered three months later. The other I never heard from again. So the person who shot me was never caught.

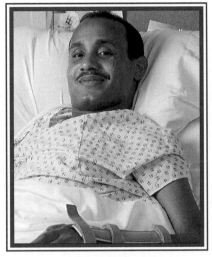

Fredde Sanchez

Q. What's your life like now?

A. I'm paralyzed from the neck down, but I have some use of my hands. I have to rely on people to do everything for me. I need to have people feed me, brush my teeth, and dress me.

Q. What message would you like to pass along?

A. You've got to be careful who your friends are and who you're hanging around with. Also, stay away from guns and drugs, because those situations always end up negative.

Q. How do you get this message out to young people?

A. I'm part of a group here at the hospital called "People Opening the World's Eyes to Reality." We go to schools and prisons to speak about the mistakes we've made and about the dangers of drugs, guns, and violence.

Q. What is the hardest thing for you now?

A. The hardest thing is when I lie in bed and think about how I used to be. How in a moment's time a bullet can change, can devastate, can ruin your life forever.

Journal Activity

In your journal, write a letter to Fredde. Tell him how you think he could best communicate his message to teens.

GUIDE FOR READING

Focus on these questions as you read this lesson.

- What should always be a person's first concern in any conflict?
- What strategies are important for resolving conflicts peacefully?

SKILLS

- Analyzing Risks and Benefits

Suppose that, after reading this chapter so far, you have concluded that fighting does not solve problems. You may now be wondering what peaceful alternatives exist. You also may be doubting whether it is really possible to pursue peaceful solutions if the other person wants to fight.

Although it is certainly not always easy to avoid fighting, it can be done. This lesson offers some strategies for seeking peaceful solutions to conflicts. As you read these strategies, you may come up with ways to adapt them to particular situations or personalities. You may also come up with strategies of your own that you can share with friends, siblings, and others that you care about.

Recognizing a Conflict Early

When people who know each other fight, there is usually a history of events that led to the fight. Events such as name-calling or rumor-spreading may go on for a day, a week, or more before a fight breaks out. By recognizing that a potential fight situation is building, you may be able to prevent it. The earlier you deal with things, the lower the levels of anger, and the easier it can be to resolve the problem.

Learning to Ignore Some Conflicts

Not all conflicts require that you respond. In some situations it may be smartest to walk away and do nothing at all. You may decide it is best to ignore a situation if

- it is unlikely you will ever see the person again
- the person or situation is not very important to you
- the conflict is based on rumors that may not be true
- the conflict is over something trivial or silly
- the person is just trying to make you angry so you will fight and get into trouble

Some people think that ignoring a conflict is a sign of cowardice. Actually it is a sign of maturity and self-control to walk away from some situations. Fighting out of pride or to "save face" may instead be an act of cowardice.

In deciding how to deal with any conflict, your safety should always be your first concern. If you think that a person might be more angered if you ignore the situation, you need to proceed carefully. It is important to trust your judgment and to be prepared to try a new tactic if your first choice does not diffuse the situation.

Figure 7-9 *When a conflict is over something unimportant, it may be best to simply walk away.*

Figure 7-10 *When confronting a person about a problem, what steps can you take to negotiate a peaceful solution?*

Confronting a Person Wisely

In some cases it may not be advisable or even possible to ignore a conflict. The person may be someone with whom you are in frequent contact, or the issue may be too important to ignore. In these cases you may decide to confront the person. The way in which you handle the confrontation, however, is critical to its success. The steps described here can help you resolve things peacefully.

CHOOSE THE TIME AND PLACE CAREFULLY   It is always best to confront a person when the two of you are alone. If friends are present, the person may think you are intentionally trying to embarrass him or her in front of them. The person may feel pressured to start a fight to avoid embarrassment. Choosing a time when the person is alone and when both of you are calm can help avoid a fight.

It is also important to avoid a confrontation when a person has been using alcohol or other drugs. As you have read, alcohol and other drugs impair judgment and may increase the likelihood of fighting. Never use alcohol or other drugs yourself. If you suspect the other person is under the influence of drugs, postpone your discussion until another time.

STAY CALM   Although it can be difficult to remain calm when you are upset, it is important for keeping peace. Try to keep your voice low and calm. By avoiding screaming or name-calling, you can remain in control of the situation.

Everybody has his or her own technique for keeping calm under pressure. Some people find it helpful to rehearse the confrontation beforehand with an uninvolved person. Other people use deep breathing or count to 20 when they feel their tempers beginning to rise. Despite all your efforts, however, you may find yourself unable to keep calm and control your temper. If that happens, it may be best to try to postpone your discussion until a later time.

SHARPEN YOUR SKILLS

Analyzing Risks and Benefits

You have just gotten a seat on a crowded subway when the person seated next to you lights up a cigarette. When you point out the *No Smoking* sign, the person replies, "Too bad. If you don't like it, move!" Make a list of the potential risks and benefits of confronting the person again. What would you do?

NEGOTIATE A SOLUTION Think back to the skills you learned in Chapters 5 and 6 for effective communication and negotiation. Skills such as using "I" messages, assertiveness, and seeing the other person's point of view are important for resolving conflicts peacefully. Saying things like "I get upset when..." or "I know this issue is important to both of us..." can open the lines of communication without putting the other person on the defensive. Showing an understanding of the other person's feelings can also help keep emotions under control. Some other strategies that may be useful in negotiating a peaceful solution are described below.

- **Do the unexpected.** If, instead of being hostile, you are friendly, confident, and caring, the other person may relax his or her guard. Try to make the situation seem as if it is not serious enough to fight about. The person may agree and decide to work with you to resolve things.

- **Provide the person with a way out.** Sometimes fighting breaks out simply because people see no other way to resolve things without losing pride. To avoid fighting, then, present the person with compromise solutions that you both can live with. By saying something like, "Let's try this for a week and see how it goes," you give the person an easy way out.

- **Be willing to apologize.** In some situations, be willing to say "I'm sorry" or "I didn't mean to embarrass you." Apologizing does not mean that you were wrong or that you are a coward. Instead, a sincere apology can be the quickest way to diffuse a fight.

Helping Others Avoid Fights

When you are not personally involved in a conflict, you can still play an important role in preventing fights. You have learned how friends and acquaintances can put pressure on people to fight. These same people, however, could instead play a key role in preventing fights.

MEDIATION A growing number of schools today are training students in the skill of mediation. **Mediation** (mee dee AY shun) is a process for resolving conflicts that involves a neutral third party. The Building Health Skills feature at the end of this chapter teaches the mediation process. As is true for all people involved in a conflict, mediators need to think about their own safety first. Mediators should never get involved in heated conflicts that have the potential for turning violent at any moment.

Figure 7-12 *Discouraging others from fighting is an important part of preventing violence. How do you show friends that you disapprove of fighting?*

YOUR ROLE AS AN ONLOOKER How can friends and acquaintances help reduce the pressure that others feel to fight? Friends can use their influence in many positive ways. A person can show disapproval of fighting by

- ignoring people when they talk badly about others
- refusing to spread rumors or to relay threats or insults to others
- staying away from potential fight scenes
- showing respect for people who can apologize to others, ignore insults, and otherwise avoid fights

People who advise friends to ignore someone's insults or not to hold grudges do their friends a very important service. They help keep their friends safe from the potential of deadly violence.

Getting Help When You Need It

Controlling anger and avoiding potentially violent situations are not skills that can be learned overnight. They are, however, skills that can be mastered.

If you are not satisfied with the way you now deal with anger, many people can help you. Parents, teachers, coaches, school counselors, and members of the clergy are just some of the people you can turn to for help. If these people cannot help you themselves, they may be able to refer you to trained counselors who can. By asking for help, you take an important first step toward gaining control over your behavior and your future.

Another time when it is important to ask for help is when a friend reveals plans of violence to you. Such plans should always be taken seriously, especially if your friend talks about using a weapon. Although it is never easy to break a friend's confidence, it is critical for you to share your friend's plans with a trusted adult. Doing so is a true act of caring. It shows that you care too much to let your friend be lost to violence.

LESSON **3** REVIEW

1. What should be a person's first concern in any conflict?
2. How can offering compromise solutions help resolve conflicts peacefully?
3. How can onlookers decrease the likelihood of a fight?

What Do You Think?

4. What could you say to a friend to discourage him or her from fighting?

Focus on Issues

How Can Schools Be Kept Safe?

Jonesboro, Paducah. . . Littleton, Conyers. . .

The list of schools that have experienced terror in their hallways seems to grow each year.

Surprisingly, however, school violence is actually declining. There are fewer homicides, fewer assaults, and fewer students carrying weapons into class. What has increased is a kind of random violence that seems more intent on the act of killing rather than a desire to injure a specific person. It may be the ultimate mark of isolation that these murderers cannot even identify an actual enemy.

The struggle against random violence has led to a variety of ideas:

- metal detectors, see-through backpacks, and security guards to reduce the number of weapons
- checklists and social workers to identify and help "at risk" teens
- school uniforms to help end the cliques and isolation that so many students feel
- more school activities to involve students
- a reduction in the violence of music, movies, and video and computer games

☞ **What do you think should be done to keep schools safe from violence? Explain.**

Mediating a Conflict

What makes you the big decision maker, Julia?

Because I'm the editor of this yearbook. And the editor chooses the cover photo.

Says who? I'm the photographer and I hate that photo. There's no way it's going on the cover.

Yes it is. And there's nothing you can do about it.

Oh yeah? We'll see about that.

Although Julia and Michael have been arguing for an hour, they are no closer to resolving their problem now than before. Instead, both have grown more stubborn and angry. If the argument gets more heated, one of them may throw something in frustration.

How can conflicts like this be resolved peacefully? One effective method, known as mediation, involves a third party in the negotiation process. The mediator explores the problem with the people to help them find a "win-win" solution—a solution that meets some of the important needs of both people. The guidelines that follow outline the process of mediation.

1. Emphasize your neutrality

Introduce the mediation session by establishing your neutrality. Make it clear to each party that you do not have a personal interest in the outcome. Say, *I am neutral. I will not take sides or decide who is right or wrong. My role is to help you find a solution that is acceptable to both of you.*

2. Establish guidelines

It is important to agree upon some rules that must be followed throughout the mediation session. Both parties must agree to

- keep everything that is said confidential
- be as honest as possible
- avoid name-calling and swearing
- refrain from interrupting the other person
- participate in proposing solutions that they can agree to
- follow through on any agreed-upon solution

3. Allow each person to state his or her views

Give each person a chance to state his or her view of the situation without interruption.

Listen carefully and ask questions to clarify anything that is unclear. To make sure you understood what was said, restate something and ask, *Is that what you mean?*

Do not go on to the next person until you really understand the first person's viewpoint. While you are listening and asking questions, try to get at the principle behind each person's position. That is, you should try to gain a deeper understanding of what each person truly cares about, not just what the person is saying.

● ● ● ● ● ● ● ● ● ● ● ● ● ● ● ● ●
4. Explore possible solutions

If participants seem relaxed, ask them to brainstorm a list of possible solutions together. Remind them that, during brainstorming, they should not judge the other person's proposed solution. Encourage the participants to invent new and different solutions and to use the other's suggestions to spark ideas in their minds.

If the participants are still tense or hostile, it may be best not to brainstorm. Instead, have them explore solutions one at a time. Start by asking one person to propose a solution. Then, get the other person's reaction and ask for a counterproposal. Continue until you find a solution that satisfies both people.

● ● ● ● ● ● ● ● ● ● ● ● ● ● ● ● ●
5. Don't give up

It is not always easy to find a win-win solution but it can be done. It is important to keep the focus on the common principle or goal that is behind the two different positions. Also, try to keep the participants actively involved in the process of proposing solutions. The more involved they are, the greater interest they will have in resolving the problem.

If, however, you are unable to find an agreeable solution, it may be necessary to ask for help. Enlist the help of an adult that both participants respect and trust. Together, you may be able to resolve the problem.

Apply the Skill

1. Review the disagreement that Julia and Michael are having. What questions would you ask Julia and Michael to get at the principle behind each person's position?

2. With two of your classmates, role-play the mediation session. Take turns playing the roles of mediator, Julia, and Michael. What solution, if any, did you reach in each of the role-plays? What difficulties did you encounter in mediating the conflict?

3. Think about a recent conflict that you had with a friend or family member. Do you think that a mediator would have been able to help you resolve the conflict? Why or why not?

4. Make a list of the types of conflicts that occur among teens. Which of the conflicts on your list would be appropriate for mediation? Which would not? Explain.

CHAPTER  REVIEW

KEY IDEAS

LESSON 1

- Homicide is the second leading cause of death for young people in this country. Almost half of all homicides involve people who knew each other.

- Violence affects more than just victims, assailants, and their families and friends. All people in this country feel the financial and emotional effects of violence.

- Risk factors for violence include poverty, exposure to media violence or to family violence, the availability of weapons, drug abuse, and membership in gangs.

LESSON 2

- Some reasons behind fights are arguments, hurt pride or embarrassment, peer pressure, prejudice, a desire for revenge, and control.

- The inability to control anger is the reason behind many fights. Communicating anger nonviolently and rechanneling anger in other directions are more constructive ways to handle anger.

LESSON 3

- In some conflicts it is best to ignore the problem and walk away. In other situations it is best to confront the person by using negotiation skills.

- People who are not directly involved in a conflict can act as mediators or use peer pressure to discourage their friends from fighting.

- People who have trouble handling anger can seek help from parents, teachers, coaches, school counselors, members of the clergy, and others.

KEY TERMS

LESSON 1
assailant
free-floating anger
homicide
paralysis
territorial gang
victim
violence

LESSON 2
discrimination
escalate
instigator

intolerance
microinsults

LESSON 3
mediation

Listed above are some of the important terms in this chapter. Choose the term from the list that best matches each phrase below.

1. a lack of acceptance of another's opinions, beliefs, or actions

2. to grow more intense

3. a process for resolving conflicts that involves a neutral third party

4. frustration and hostility that sometimes result when people feel unable to improve their lives

5. the unfair mistreatment of a person or group based on prejudice

6. a person who is attacked and harmed physically

7. the intentional killing of one person by another

8. a person who physically attacks another person

9. a person who encourages fighting between others but stays out of the fight

10. the use of physical force with the intent to injure or kill

11. small but frequent episodes of discrimination that some people experience

12. the loss of feeling and movement in some part of the body

WHAT HAVE YOU LEARNED?

If the statement is true, write "true." If it is false, change the underlined word or words to make the statement true.

13. Almost half of all <u>homicides</u> occur between people who knew each other.

14. For victims of violence, <u>physical</u> scars can include anger, fear, and sadness.

15. <u>Family</u> violence includes violence in cartoons, movies, and music videos.

16. <u>Territorial gangs</u> often fight to protect the boundaries of their "turf."

17. The body's automatic reaction to anger is called the <u>fight or flight response.</u>

18. Victims of <u>instigators</u> may experience discrimination in job hiring, housing rental, or other opportunities.

19. Doing the unexpected and being willing to apologize are important when trying to <u>negotiate</u> a solution to a conflict.

Answer each of the following with complete sentences.

20. Define the term *violence*.

21. What effect does violence have on victims? On assailants?

22. How may poverty contribute to violence?

23. How can parents help their children learn nonviolent methods for handling anger?

24. How do friends and acquaintances put pressure on people to fight? How could this pressure be used to discourage fighting?

25. How does a desire for revenge cause fights to escalate?

26. List three times when it may be best to ignore a conflict.

27. Why is it best to confront a person about a problem when the two of you are alone?

28. Why is it important to provide the other person with a way out of a conflict?

29. What is mediation?

WHAT DO YOU THINK?

30. What impact do you think violent movies and television shows have on teenagers? Give reasons to support your answer.

31. List three methods of discipline that parents could use with young children that teach a respect for nonviolent problem-solving.

32. Do you think that school courses in managing anger and conflict resolution could help students learn to handle anger better? Why or why not?

33. Why do you think that the homicide rate in the United States is much higher than it is in other industrialized nations? What could be done to lower the rate?

34. What do you think is the single biggest cause of fights among teens? What could be done to eliminate that cause?

WHAT WOULD YOU DO?

35. A fight is brewing between two students at school. You overheard someone say that one of the students has a knife and plans to use it to "take care of the guy." What would you do?

36. Your sister's boyfriend loves to watch violent movies and seems to enjoy getting into fights with others. Although he has never been violent with you or your sister, you are worried about her and your safety. What could you do?

37. Your friend has been spreading untrue rumors about a new student at school. The new student is getting very angry. How could you prevent this situation from escalating?

Getting Involved

38. Write a letter to your congressional representative offering your views on teen violence. Suggest ways to reduce violence among young people in your community.

Chapter 8

REPRODUCTION AND HEREDITY

Why do family members often look like—and even sound like—one another? Many of your physical characteristics and personality traits are inherited from your parents and through them, from your grandparents and so on. In this chapter, you'll find out how the human reproductive system works and how traits are passed from one generation to the next.

CHAPTER PREVIEW

8-1 The Endocrine System

* List the names and functions of the major endocrine glands and describe how they regulate many bodily functions.

8-2 The Male Reproductive System

* Explain how the male reproductive system functions.

8-3 The Female Reproductive System

* Explain how the female reproductive system functions.

8-4 Heredity

* Define the role heredity plays in determining physical traits and distinguish between dominant and recessive genes.

BUILDING HEALTH SKILLS

* Describe how to perform breast and testicular self-exams.

CHECK YOUR WELLNESS

Answer *true* or *false* to the following statements.

* Your reproductive system is controlled by glands in your brain.

* When a male reaches the teenage years, millions of sperm cells are produced in his body daily.

* From the teenage years until about the age of 50, a female releases a mature egg cell about once a month.

* Self-examination of the testes or breasts should be done once a month.

* Cleanliness is important to keep the reproductive system healthy.

* Children receive half of their genetic material from their father and half from their mother.

* The sperm, rather than the egg, determines the sex of a child.

KEEPING A JOURNAL

Find a picture of yourself as you looked five years ago and compare it with a recent one. In your journal, describe how you have changed in the last five years.

Take it to the Net
www.phschool.com

THE ENDOCRINE SYSTEM

GUIDE FOR READING

Focus on these questions as you read this lesson.

- How does the endocrine system work?
- What is the relationship between the endocrine system and reproduction?

SKILLS

- Finding the Facts

Every day, your body must perform many functions. Obtaining and using energy, responding to stress, growth, and sexual development are some of the many processes occurring inside your body right now. To control these and other important processes, some structures of the body work together as a giant communications system that carries chemical messages throughout the body. This system is known as the endocrine system. **The endocrine system not only controls many of your body's daily activities but also controls its overall development.**

How Your Endocrine System Works

Your endocrine system is made up of a group of organs, called **endocrine glands** (EN duh krin), that produce and release chemical substances. Some glands, such as sweat glands, have ducts that carry chemicals to the place where they will be used. An endocrine gland, on the other hand, is a gland that does not have a duct. Endocrine glands release substances directly into the bloodstream. Figure 8-2 shows the location of the major endocrine glands in the body.

The chemical substances produced by endocrine glands are known as **hormones.** Hormones act as chemical messengers in the body. Once released into the bloodstream, hormones travel to other parts of the body, where they stimulate a response. Some hormones affect only certain body cells, while others stimulate a response in many body cells. Some hormones are only produced at certain times in a person's life, while others are produced continually.

The endocrine system is a complicated system of checks and balances that works to keep the body healthy. When the endocrine system is working properly, hormones from one gland send chemical signals to another gland, which responds by regulating the chemicals of the first gland. Just as a thermostat may turn on when the temperature is below 68° and may turn off when the temperature is above 68°, so the endocrine system turns on and off in response to hormone levels. Each of the hormones of the endocrine system is kept in check by the production of another hormone or series of hormones. This control of hormones keeps the body's activities functioning smoothly. When the endocrine system is not functioning properly, your health, your physical appearance, your energy level, the balance of water in your body, and your ability to produce children may be affected.

Figure 8-1 *Your endocrine system works like a thermostat to regulate hormone levels in your body.*

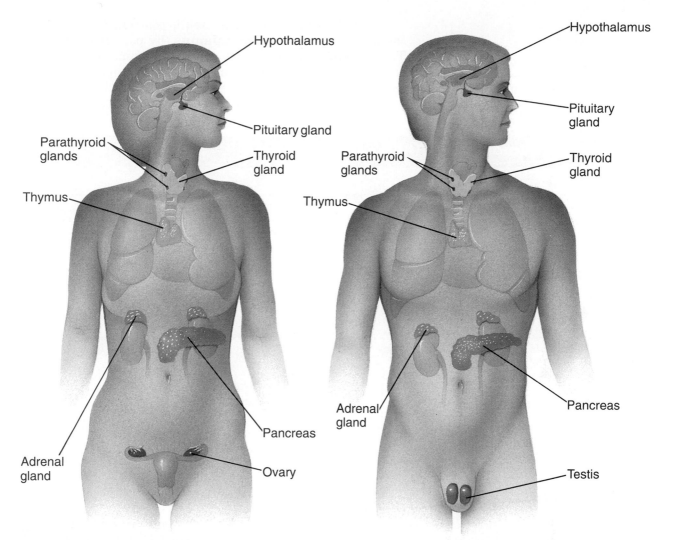

Labels on figure:

Hypothalamus

Pituitary gland

Parathyroid glands

Thyroid gland

Thymus

Adrenal gland

Pancreas

Ovary

Hypothalamus

Pituitary gland

Parathyroid glands

Thyroid gland

Thymus

Adrenal gland

Pancreas

Testis

Endocrine Glands

Each of your endocrine glands plays a specific, important role in your body. Figure 8-3 lists some of the hormones produced by the endocrine glands and their functions. To keep your body functioning properly, the endocrine glands interact in a complex but well-organized manner. In rare cases when the endocrine system fails to work properly, physical and mental disorders may result. In some of these cases of endocrine problems, doctors are able to identify and eventually correct the problem with specific hormone treatments.

THE PITUITARY GLAND AND HYPOTHALAMUS

Two of the body's endocrine glands are located in the brain. The **pituitary gland** (pih TOO ih tehr ee) is a small gland at the base of the brain. It controls many of the activities in your body, including growth rate, metabolism, and reproduction. The pituitary gland also regulates many of the other endocrine glands in the body. For this reason, the pituitary gland was once referred to as the "master gland."

Figure 8-2 *Each of the endocrine glands plays an important regulatory role in the body. Which endocrine glands are found only in females? In males?*

In fact, the pituitary gland itself is controlled by a part of the brain called the **hypothalamus** (hy poh THAL uh mus). The hypothalamus regulates your body temperature, use of water, and blood pressure, among other things. The hypothalamus is connected to the pituitary gland by blood vessels. In addition to its other functions, the hypothalamus oversees

Figure 8-3 *Which endocrine glands are in the brain?*

Endocrine Hormones and Their Functions

Gland	Hormone	Function
Adrenal glands	Adrenaline	Controls "fight or flight" response; increases heart rate and blood pressure; directs blood to muscles and brain; converts glycogen to glucose
	Aldosterone	Increases uptake of sodium and water by kidney
	Cortisol	Increases glucose, fat, protein metabolism; controls inflammation of connective body tissue
Thyroid gland	Thyroxine	Regulates body's overall metabolic rate
	Calcitonin	Controls calcium level in bloodstream
Parathyroid glands	Parathyroid hormone	Regulates level of calcium and phosphorus in bloodstream
Pancreas	Insulin	Regulates glucose level in bloodstream
	Glucagon	Stimulates liver to convert glycogen to glucose
Testes (males)	Testosterone	Regulates development of male sex organs in embryo and secondary sex characteristics at puberty; controls sex drive; works with FSH to control sperm production
Ovaries (females)	Estrogen	Regulates development of female secondary sex characteristics at puberty; controls sex drive; works with progesterone, FSH, and LH to produce egg cells
	Progesterone	Controls development of endometrium during menstrual cycle and maintenance of uterus during pregnancy; works with estrogen, FSH, and LH to produce egg cells
Hypothalamus	Releasing factors	Stimulates pituitary gland to secrete specific hormones
	Oxytocin	Controls muscle contractions of uterus and milk production in mammary glands
	Antidiuretic hormone (ADH)	Increases water uptake in kidney
Pituitary	Adrenocorticotropic hormone (ACTH)	Stimulates adrenal gland to secrete specific hormones
	Thyroid-stimulating hormone (TSH)	Stimulates thyroid gland to secrete specific hormones
	Growth hormone	Regulates growth of skeletal system
	Prolactin	Stimulates milk production in mammary glands
	Luteinizing hormone (LH)	In females: Stimulates ovulation, maturation of egg cell, and progesterone production In males: Stimulates sperm and testosterone production
	Follicle-stimulating hormone (FSH)	In females: Stimulates maturation of egg cell in ovary and estrogen production In males: Stimulates sperm production

many of the hormone levels in the body. When the level of a hormone is low, the hypothalamus sends a releasing hormone to the pituitary gland. The releasing hormone causes the pituitary gland, in turn, to release a specific hormone.

ADRENAL GLANDS   Under the control of the pituitary gland and the hypothalamus are a pair of glands known as the **adrenal glands** (uh DREE nul). The adrenal glands are found on both sides of your body, one above each kidney. Adrenal glands produce a number of hormones that affect the functioning of your kidneys, your metabolism, and your response to stressful situations. One hormone released by the adrenal glands is adrenaline. As you read in Chapter 3, **adrenaline** (uh DREN uh lin) is an important factor in the fight or flight response during which your heartbeat, breathing rate, and blood pressure increase, preparing you to either face or run away from a danger.

THYROID GLAND   The **thyroid gland** (THY royd) is a large gland shaped like a bow tie and located at the front of the neck. The thyroid gland, which is under the control of the pituitary gland, releases a hormone that regulates the rate of metabolism in the body. Another hormone released by the thyroid gland helps to regulate the amount of calcium in the blood.

OTHER ENDOCRINE GLANDS   Attached to the back of the thyroid gland are the four tiny **parathyroid glands**. These glands regulate the levels of two important minerals in the body, calcium and phosphorus. Calcium and phosphorus are necessary for proper bone and tooth formation and for muscle and nerve activity.

The **pancreas** (PANG kree us) is a large gland located behind the stomach. The pancreas is part of two systems—the digestive system and the endocrine system. Its function in the endocrine system involves controlling the level of sugar in the blood. An improperly functioning pancreas can cause several types of disorders. Diabetes can occur when the level of sugar in the blood is too high. **Hypoglycemia** (hy poh gly SEE mee uh) can occur when the level of sugar in the blood is too low. You will learn more about diabetes in Chapter 24 and hypoglycemia in Chapter 13.

The **thymus** is a gland located in the upper chest near the heart. The function of this gland is not thoroughly understood. The thymus gland appears to be most active early in life and plays a role in developing some of the body's defenses against infection.

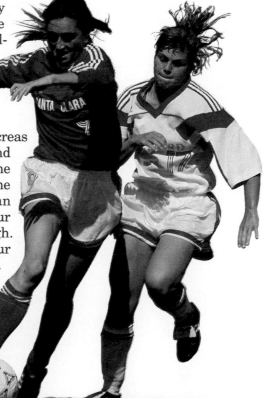

Figure 8-4 *Proper endocrine function is necessary to meet the high energy needs of active teenagers.*

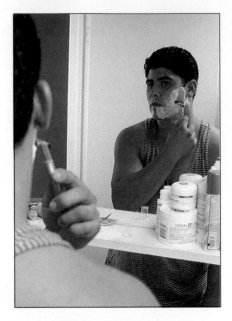

Figure 8-5 *In males, the growth of facial hair is controlled by the sex hormone testosterone.*

Reproduction and the Endocrine System

The reproductive glands are an important part of the endocrine system. They include the **ovaries** (OH vuh reez) in females and the **testes** (TES teez) in males. Like other glands in the endocrine system, the reproductive glands are controlled by the pituitary gland, which in turn is controlled by the hypothalamus. Until about the age of ten, the reproductive glands work at low levels in both girls and boys. After this age, hormone levels begin to increase, and physical changes occur. The hypothalamus releases substances that signal the pituitary gland to begin producing two hormones: **follicle-stimulating hormone** (FSH) and **luteinizing hormone** (LOO tee uh ny zing). These two hormones, which are important for reproduction, are produced in both males and females. They affect the testes in males and the ovaries in females.

In males, luteinizing hormone (LH) signals the testes to begin producing male sex hormones. The most important of these is **testosterone** (tes TAHS tuh rohn). Together testosterone and FSH control the production of **sperm**, the male sex cells. Testosterone is also responsible for developing and maintaining other traits that develop in males during the teenage years. These traits, which are not involved in reproduction, include deepening voice and the growth of body hair.

In females, the pituitary hormones LH and FSH stimulate the ovaries to produce the female sex hormones. There are two female sex hormones: **progesterone** (proh JES tuh rohn) and **estrogen** (ES truh jun). They are responsible for developing and maintaining other traits not directly connected with reproduction in females. These traits include breast development and widening of the hips. In addition, progesterone and estrogen work with FSH and LH to produce **ova** (singular: ovum), the female sex cells, also known as eggs.

LESSON 1 REVIEW

1. What is the function of the endocrine system?
2. Name two hormones and their functions.
3. Why has the pituitary gland been called the "master gland"? Which other gland controls the pituitary gland?

What Do You Think?

4. Suppose a friend began to lose weight and noticed that his appetite had increased greatly. Could this problem with his metabolism be caused by a malfunctioning endocrine gland? Explain your answer.

2 THE MALE REPRODUCTIVE SYSTEM

GUIDE FOR READING

Focus on these questions as you read this lesson.

- What are the structures of the male reproductive system?
- What should a male do to keep his reproductive system healthy?

SKILLS

- Finding the Facts

During the early- to mid-teen years, most boys notice many physical changes taking place in their bodies. Their voices may deepen, and hair growth may appear on their faces, underarms, legs, chests, and above the reproductive organs. These changes are signs that puberty has begun. **Puberty** is a period of sexual development during which males and females become sexually mature and able to produce children. At puberty, physical changes occur in a boy's body, and sperm production begins. Sperm development is controlled by the male hormone testosterone, which is produced by the testes.

Structure and Function

Figure 8-6 shows the male reproductive system. **The male reproductive system is made up of both internal and external organs.** The internal organs are a series of glands and ducts that store, nourish, and transport the sperm cells once they are produced. The external organs produce, store, and release the sperm. Once released, a sperm cell must unite with an egg from a female in order for reproduction to occur. The joining of a sperm cell with an egg cell, known as **fertilization,** begins the process of producing a baby.

TESTES The testes have two major functions: the production of the male hormone testosterone and the production of sperm. The testes are made up of coiled tubules in which the sperm are produced. The testes hang outside the body within a sac of skin called the **scrotum** (SKROH tum). The scrotum protects the sperm by keeping the temperature of the testes slightly lower than the normal body temperature. Sperm need this lower temperature in order to form and survive.

EPIDIDYMIS Sperm form in the testes and then move from the testes to the epididymis. The **epididymis** (ep ih DID uh mis) is a J-shaped tube located on the back of each testis. This tube is coiled and folded upon itself. While in the epididymis, the sperm mature and gain the ability to move. Sperm are then stored in the epididymis for several weeks.

PENIS The **penis** is the external sexual organ through which sperm leave the body. The tip of the penis, called the head, or **glans,** is covered with loose skin, called the foreskin. In some males the foreskin is removed shortly after birth. This surgical procedure is known as **circumcision** (sur kum SIZH un). In other males the foreskin is not removed. Over the years, circumcision has been performed for both religious and health reasons. Some physicians think that removing

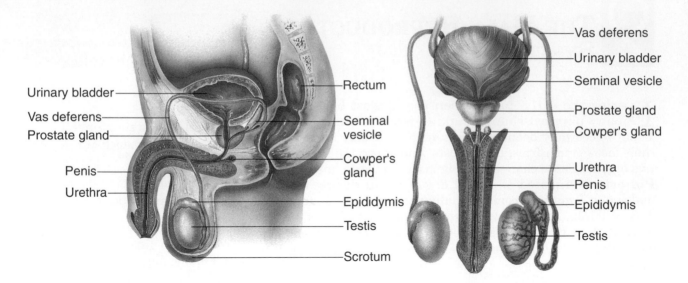

Figure 8-6 *Which structure of the male reproductive system is responsible for the production of sperm cells?*

the foreskin helps to keep the penis clean and free from possible infection. Others think regular daily cleanliness will prevent any possible problems. Each day, an uncircumcised male should pull the foreskin away from the glans and carefully wash the glans.

OTHER GLANDS AND DUCTS   Several other glands and ducts play an important role in storing and releasing sperm. Each **vas deferens** (vas DEF ur unz) is an 18-inch (45-cm) tube that receives sperm from the epididymis. The two vas deferens loop over the bladder and join at the **urethra** (yoo REE thruh), which is a tube that passes through the penis to the outside of the body. The urethra carries urine and sperm, but not at the same time. A valve within the urethra prevents the two fluids from mixing.

As the sperm travel through the vas deferens, they combine with fluids that are produced by other sex glands. These glands include the **seminal vesicles** (VES ih kulz), a pair of glands located near the bladder; the **Cowper's** (KOW purz) **glands,** a pair of glands located at the base of the penis; and the **prostate gland,** which is near the bladder at the midline of the body. Sperm mixes with the fluids from these glands to form a liquid known as **semen** (SEE mun). As you will learn in the next section, the fluids nourish the sperm and lubricate the passageways through which the sperm must travel.

Sperm Production

Once a male reaches puberty, millions of sperm are produced in his body each day. For most men, sperm production continues throughout adult life unless the reproductive system is altered in some way. Sperm production occurs when the hypothalamus signals the pituitary gland to release FSH and LH, which in turn stimulate the cells of the testes to produce

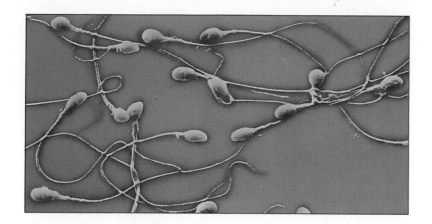

Figure 8-7 *The long tail of a mature sperm cell allows it to swim through the reproductive system.*

testosterone. These hormones—FSH, LH, and testosterone—work together to produce sperm within the testes and move them to the epididymis. Figure 8-7 shows the structure of mature sperm cells. As the sperm move through the vas deferens, fluids from the other glands are added to the sperm to form semen. The fluid from the seminal vesicles makes up 60 percent of the semen. It provides a source of energy for the active sperm. The clear fluid provided by the Cowper's glands makes up 5 percent of the semen. It lubricates the urethra. The milky white fluid produced by the prostate gland makes up 35 percent of the semen. It protects the sperm as it travels through the female reproductive tract.

The ejection of semen from the penis is called **ejaculation** (ih jak yuh LAY shun). Ejaculation occurs when muscles at the base of the bladder and in the prostate and seminal vesicles contract, forcing semen through the vas deferens and urethra. About 400 million sperm cells in about one tenth of an ounce (3.5 milliliters) of semen are released during one ejaculation. When the semen enters the female, the sperm "swim" upward through the female reproductive system by wiggling their tails. The semen contains nutrients that enable the sperm to survive for several days inside the female's body.

In its normal state, the penis is a soft, tubular organ that hangs from the front of the body. Ejaculation can occur when the penis is in an erect state. An erection is a condition in which the penis becomes larger and stiffer as blood chambers in the penis become filled with blood. An erection does not need to result in ejaculation; in fact, most do not. Erections can be caused by different factors, including sexual excitement or tight clothing. Sometimes an erection may occur for no reason at all. This is especially common during puberty. It is also common for a teenage male to experience a **nocturnal emission,** or "wet dream," which is erection and ejaculation during sleep. Nocturnal emissions occur for various reasons, including sexually arousing dreams. They are a normal occurrence and may happen frequently. It is also normal not to experience nocturnal emissions.

Disorders of the Male Reproductive System

A number of medical conditions involve the organs of the male reproductive system. Chapter 23 discusses some infections, known as sexually transmitted diseases, that also affect the reproductive system.

STERILITY   When a person is unable to reproduce, the condition is known as **sterility** (stuh RIL ih tee). Both males and females may be sterile. In males, sterility may be caused by a number of factors. Some males are unable to produce healthy sperm. Environmental factors, such as exposure to certain chemicals, may cause sterility. A sexually mature male who develops mumps, usually a childhood illness, may become sterile. Medical research is discovering more about the causes of sterility and how it can be prevented.

UNDESCENDED TESTES   Most men have two testes. In some males, a condition known as **undescended testes** results when one of the testes does not descend into the scrotum at birth. This condition does not necessarily cause any medical problems, but it is a risk factor for testicular cancer. In addition, sperm may not develop properly in an undescended testis because the temperature is too high. In most cases, undescended testes can be corrected by surgery or treatment with hormones.

INGUINAL HERNIA   A hernia occurs when an organ in the body pushes outward through the wall that normally contains it. Hernias can occur in various parts of the body. One of the most common hernias is called an **inguinal hernia** (ING gwuh nul HUR nee uh). An inguinal hernia occurs when part of the intestine pushes into the scrotum through a weak spot in the wall near the scrotum. Surgery is almost always necessary to correct this condition.

ENLARGED PROSTATE   Enlargement of the prostate gland is a common problem in men after middle age. Enlargement does not have to indicate either disease or illness, but it can cause some pain and discomfort. Since the prostate gland surrounds the urethra, an enlarged prostate may make urination painful or difficult. Surgery is required for an enlarged prostate.

CANCER OF THE PROSTATE AND TESTES   There are many kinds of cancer and many causes for it. Cancer is an area of uncontrolled cell growth that invades the surrounding tissue and destroys it. The most common form of cancer among men is cancer of the prostate. At this time, surgical removal of the prostate is the usual treatment for prostate cancer. Cancer of the testes occurs most commonly in men between the ages of 15 and 34. Hard lumps, enlargement of the testes, or an unusual thickening of tissue require medical

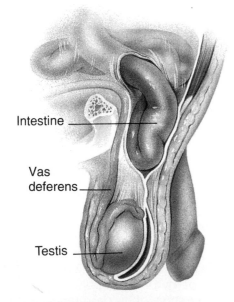

Intestine

Vas deferens

Testis

Figure 8-8 *An inguinal hernia occurs at the point where the vas deferens passes into the scrotum.*

Figure 8-9 *When playing a sport, males should wear a protector or supporter to prevent injury to the groin area.*

attention. Cancer of the testes can be treated in a variety of ways. As with all cancers, treatment is most effective when the cancer is in its early stages.

Keeping the Reproductive System Healthy

Healthy habits start with cleanliness. It is important to thoroughly clean the external organs—the penis and scrotum—daily, preferably during a shower or bath.

Good health also requires protection and prevention. During athletic activities, males should wear a protector or supporter. Tight clothing should be avoided, since tight trousers, jeans, or underwear can irritate or cause pain in the groin area. To prevent hernias, men should be careful when lifting heavy objects. Any signs of pain when urinating, unusual discharges, or sores on the genitals require a medical examination. Males should also examine their testes on a monthly basis for signs of cancer. If lumps or thickenings are discovered early, testicular cancer often can be treated successfully. Building Health Skills on pages 190–191 includes instructions on how to perform a testicular self-examination.

LESSON **2** REVIEW

1. Name the external male sexual organs.
2. What are the two major functions of the testes?
3. What is semen, and how is it formed?

What Do You Think?

4. What sexual changes would you tell your younger brother to expect as he reaches puberty?

3 THE FEMALE REPRODUCTIVE SYSTEM

Focus on these questions as you read this lesson.

- What are the structures of the female reproductive system?

- What should a female do to keep her reproductive system healthy?

SKILLS

- DECIDE

Just as boys experience physical changes during puberty, so do girls. When a girl enters puberty, the most obvious physical changes are breast development and widening of the hips. At this time, too, a girl's body begins to produce ova, mature egg cells. Many hormones in the endocrine system work together to produce a mature egg, which, if fertilized by a sperm cell, may develop into a baby.

Structure and Function

Figure 8-10 shows the internal organs of the female reproductive system. **The female reproductive system, like the male reproductive system, is made up of both external and internal structures.** In the female, the internal organs provide the environment in which a fertilized egg can develop into a baby.

OVARIES   The two ovaries are small organs, each about the size of an almond. They are located a few inches below the waist, one on each side of the body. The ovaries, as mentioned earlier, have two important functions: they release estrogen and progesterone, and they release mature egg cells. When a girl is born, each ovary contains hundreds of thousands of immature eggs. The eggs begin to mature, or ripen, when the female reaches puberty. Once puberty begins, the ovaries usually release one ripened egg every month in a process called **ovulation** (oh vyuh LAY shun). The tiny egg that is released is no larger than this period.

FALLOPIAN TUBES   The two **fallopian tubes** (fuh LOH pee un), or oviducts (ducts that carry eggs), are small tubes that carry the released eggs from the ovaries. The fallopian tubes lie on each side of the body. They are slightly curved so that one end of each tube lies close to an ovary. Each month, one of the ovaries releases a mature egg. The fingerlike ends of the fallopian tube draw the egg into the opening. Because eggs, unlike sperm, cannot swim, tiny hairs in the fallopian tubes sweep the egg through the tube. If sperm are present in the fallopian tubes, the egg may be fertilized. The fallopian tubes are where fertilization usually occurs.

UTERUS   Each of the fallopian tubes leads into the **uterus** (YOO tur us), a hollow, muscular, pear-shaped organ located between the two ovaries and behind the urinary bladder. It is here that a fertilized egg will develop and grow into a baby. The uterus has several layers of tissue and a rich supply of blood to protect and nourish a developing fetus. The narrow

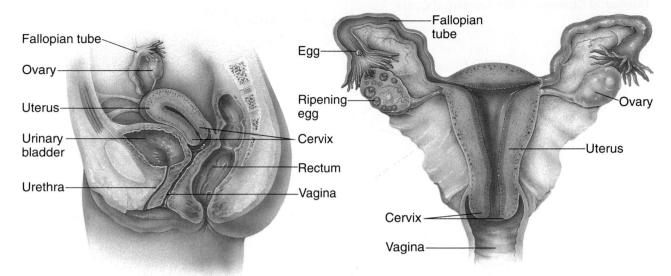

Fallopian tube
Ovary
Uterus
Urinary bladder
Urethra
Cervix
Rectum
Vagina

Fallopian tube
Egg
Ripening egg
Ovary
Uterus
Cervix
Vagina

Figure 8-10 *The female reproductive system provides the environment for a fertilized egg to develop.*

base of the uterus is called the **cervix**. When a baby is ready to be born, the cervix expands to allow the baby to pass through.

VAGINA   The **vagina** (vuh JY nuh), or birth canal, is a hollow, muscular passage leading from the uterus to the outside of the body. Sperm enter the female's body through the vagina. During childbirth, the baby passes out of the body through the vagina. The walls of the vagina are very elastic, which allows it to expand dramatically during childbirth.

The Menstrual Cycle

You may recall that males produce millions of sperm cells daily. Females, on the other hand, usually release only one mature egg cell each month. The process during which an egg matures and is released and the uterus prepares to receive it is known as the **menstrual cycle** (MEN stroo ul).

CHARACTERISTICS OF THE MENSTRUAL CYCLE   The menstrual cycle, which is shown in Figure 8-11, begins when an egg starts to mature in one of the ovaries. At the same time, the **endometrium** (en doh MEE tree um), the lining of the uterus, thickens. If the egg is not fertilized, the endometrium breaks down and is discharged from the body. This discharge of blood and tissue is known as **menstruation** (men stroo AY shun) or the menstrual period. As menstruation is taking place, another egg begins to mature in one of the ovaries. Thus menstruation marks the beginning of one cycle and the end of another.

STAGES OF THE MENSTRUAL CYCLE   On average, the menstrual cycle lasts 28 days, although cycles as short as 21 days or as long as 35 days are normal. The menstrual cycle is controlled by the endocrine system. During the first half of

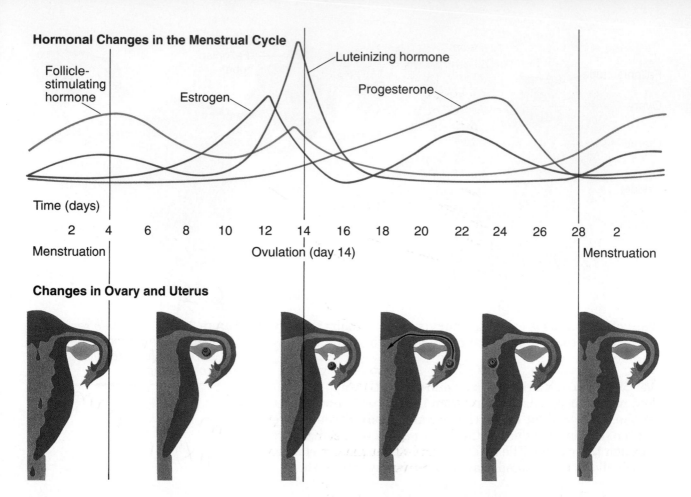

Hormonal Changes in the Menstrual Cycle

Follicle-stimulating hormone

Estrogen

Luteinizing hormone

Progesterone

Time (days)

2 4 6 8 10 12 14 16 18 20 22 24 26 28 2

Menstruation

Ovulation (day 14)

Menstruation

Changes in Ovary and Uterus

Figure 8-11 *The female endocrine system regulates the menstrual cycle. Which hormone level is highest when ovulation occurs?*

the cycle (days 1–14), the pituitary hormone FSH stimulates an egg to mature inside one of the ovaries. As the egg develops, estrogen is released, which causes the endometrium to thicken. At about the middle of the cycle (day 14), the level of LH begins to rise, and ovulation occurs. The mature egg is released by the ovary and travels into the fallopian tube. A woman is most fertile (able to become pregnant) around the time of ovulation.

It takes about seven days for the egg to travel through the fallopian tube into the uterus. During this time, the production of progesterone increases, which maintains the growth of the endometrium. If the egg has not been fertilized when it reaches the uterus, progesterone and estrogen levels drop. The endometrium breaks down and, along with the unfertilized egg, passes out of the body through the vagina. In general, a menstrual period lasts about 3 to 5 days. About 2 ounces (50–60 milliliters) of fluid is lost during menstruation. Most women wear either a sanitary pad or a tampon to absorb the menstrual flow.

FACTORS AFFECTING MENSTRUATION Although the endocrine system controls ovulation and menstruation, many other factors can influence the menstrual cycle. Diet, stress, illness, travel, exercise, and weight gain or loss can all affect the menstrual cycle. Every woman's menstrual cycle is different. The age when menstruation begins, the length of the menstrual cycle, and even the number of days it takes to discharge the menstrual flow varies from woman to woman. It is common for a woman's menstrual cycle to be irregular at times, especially for the first few years.

During the menstrual period, some women may experience cramps or other discomfort. Often a warm bath, the use of a heating pad, exercise, or a change in diet can relieve cramps. For severe cramps or for any other menstrual concerns, see a medical professional.

Some women experience discomfort some time before the menstrual period. This condition, known as **premenstrual syndrome** (PMS), is marked by nervous tension, mood swings, headaches, bloating, and irritability. Although PMS is not well understood, it is believed to be caused by a dramatic change in hormone levels. To treat PMS, some doctors recommend that women alter their diets to reduce their intake of salt, sugar, caffeine, and alcohol. Regular exercise and other stress-reduction techniques can also help to relieve PMS.

The menstrual cycle is a normal, natural sign of a healthy reproductive system. Except during pregnancy, menstruation occurs each month from puberty until about the age of 45 to 55. At that time of life, called **menopause** (MEN uh pawz), the ovaries slow down their hormone production and no longer release mature eggs. Gradually menstruation stops, and the woman is no longer fertile.

Figure 8-12 *Moderate exercise during the menstrual period may help relieve cramps.*

Disorders of the Female Reproductive System

Some diseases of the reproductive system are transmitted sexually and are discussed in Chapter 23. This section focuses on common medical conditions that affect the female reproductive system.

VAGINITIS   One common medical condition is **vaginitis** (vaj uh NY tis), a vaginal infection or irritation. There are several types of vaginitis, but the symptoms are similar—a thick discharge, odors, vaginal itching, and a burning sensation during urination. Only a doctor can diagnose the specific type of vaginitis and provide the correct medication for it.

ENDOMETRIOSIS   Occasionally tissue from the lining of the uterus grows outside the uterus, in the pelvic cavity. This condition, known as **endometriosis** (en doh mee tree OH sis), causes pain in the pelvic area, especially during menstrual periods. Often endometriosis can lead to sterility. This condition can sometimes be corrected with hormones or through surgical removal of the unwanted tissue.

Reproduction and Heredity   **181**

TOXIC SHOCK SYNDROME A bacterial infection can cause a rare disease known as **toxic shock syndrome**. Toxic shock syndrome is usually found in menstruating women who are using tampons. Although no one is certain about the connection between tampons and toxic shock syndrome, it is important to change tampons frequently to avoid infection. Some medical experts also recommend that women not use superabsorbent tampons.

The symptoms of toxic shock syndrome include a sudden high fever, a rash, vomiting, diarrhea, and dizziness. If a woman has these symptoms, it is important to contact a physician or get her to an emergency room immediately, since toxic shock syndrome can lead to death.

STERILITY Sterility can develop for a number of reasons. Some of the most common causes of female sterility include blocking of the fallopian tube, the failure of the ovaries to release eggs, and endometriosis. Some forms of sterility can be corrected through hormonal treatments or by surgery.

CYSTS AND CANCER An ovarian cyst is a growth on the inside of an ovary. Small cysts are common in women of all ages and often disappear on their own. Large cysts may be painful and must be surgically removed.

Cancer is a serious disease that can affect some of the organs of the female reproductive system. Of course, early detection and treatment are important. Cancer of the cervix

DECIDE

D DEFINE
the problem

E EXPLORE
alternatives

C CONSIDER
the consequences

I IDENTIFY
values

D DECIDE
and act

E EVALUATE
results

Choosing Abstinence

Brenda and Stan have been dating steadily for about a year. They are very much in love and think they would eventually like to marry and spend their lives together.

Recently a problem has developed in their relationship. Brenda has been pressuring Stan to have sex. She says that it will make them feel closer. Stan, on the other hand, feels that he's not ready for sex. He fears that sex will put too much pressure on their relationship. Also, he is afraid Brenda might get pregnant. He's not prepared to cope with fatherhood. He has decided not to have sex at this time.

1. Use the DECIDE process on page 18 to decide what you would do if you were Stan. Explain your reasons for making this decision.

2. What role might peer pressure play in influencing Stan's decision?

can be found by means of a **Pap test,** a medical procedure in which a sample of cells is taken from the cervix and examined under a microscope for signs of cancer. Most doctors recommend that once she begins menstruating, a female should have a Pap test done every year.

Breast cancer is another common cancer found in women. After lung cancer, it is the leading form of cancer among women, and the second leading cause of cancer death. Lumps or thickness in the breast tissue do not necessarily indicate cancer, but they do require medical attention.

Keeping the Reproductive System Healthy

It goes without saying that cleanliness is always important. During the menstrual period, cleanliness is especially important. Hormonal changes may cause the skin and hair to become more oily and the body to perspire more heavily. In addition, when the menstrual flow mixes with air outside the body, it can develop a slight odor. For this reason, it is important to change sanitary pads and tampons every few hours.

Female hygiene sprays, deodorants, douches, and deodorant tampons are not necessary. In fact, they may be harmful because they may cover up signs of an infection. If normal body odors are not eliminated through washing, or if any unusual discharge is noted, it is important to seek medical attention.

For the early detection of breast cancer, all women should perform a monthly breast self-examination, as described in Building Health Skills on page 190 at the end of this chapter. The **mammogram** (MAM uh gram), an X-ray of the breast, also detects breast cancer early. A yearly checkup of the reproductive system is recommended for all women who have reached puberty. Women should ask their doctor about their need for a mammogram and Pap test.

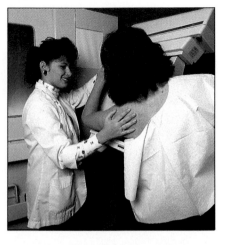

Figure 8-13 *A mammogram can detect cancer much earlier than a breast examination can.*

LESSON 3 REVIEW

1. Name two internal female reproductive structures and their functions.
2. What is ovulation, and how frequently does it occur?
3. What is the best way to assure early detection of breast cancer?

What Do You Think?

4. How could teenage women be convinced of the importance of regular breast self-exams?

- How are physical traits transmitted biologically from one generation to the next?
- What are some disorders that are inherited through genes?

SKILLS

- Activity: Observing Physical Genetic Traits

4 HEREDITY

When a baby is born, people often say, "She looks just like her father" or "He has his grandmother's eyes." Think about the ways in which children resemble their parents, grandparents, and any other relatives. The color of your eyes, the texture of your hair, your height—these are traits you inherit from your parents. **Heredity** is the passing on, or transmission, of biological characteristics from parent to child. **Because people inherit characteristics from two different parents, they are similar to both parents in some ways but different from both parents in other ways.**

Chromosomes and Genes

How are characteristics passed on from a mother and a father to their child? What determines the combination of characteristics that are passed on? To answer these questions, you must first understand the process that takes place in almost every cell in your body. This process involves **chromosomes** (KROH muh sohmz), tiny structures found within almost every cell. Your chromosomes carry the information about the characteristics you will inherit. Chromosomes are made up of a chemical substance known as **deoxyribonucleic acid** (dee ahk see ry boh noo KLEE ik), or DNA for short.

Figure 8-14 *Your looks are determined by the traits you inherit from your parents.*

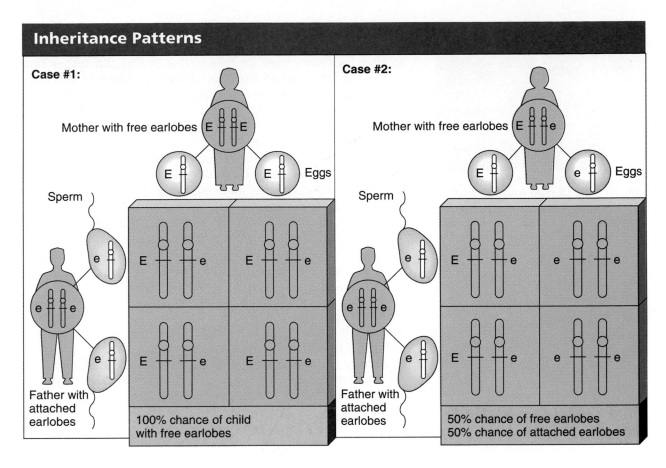

Case #1:

Mother with free earlobes E | | E

E Eggs
E

Sperm

E — e   E — e

e

E — e   E — e

Father with attached earlobes

e

e

100% chance of child with free earlobes

Case #2:

Mother with free earlobes E | | e

E Eggs
e

Sperm

E — e   e — e

e

E — e   e — e

Father with attached earlobes

e

E — e

50% chance of free earlobes
50% chance of attached earlobes

Most of the cells in your body contain 23 pairs of chromosomes—46 chromosomes in all. Each of your sex cells (the sperm or egg), however, contains half this number, or 23 chromosomes. When a sperm and egg unite, the fertilized egg ends up with 46 chromosomes—23 from each parent.

Each of the chromosomes in your body is made up of many genes. A **gene** is a section of a chromosome that determines a single trait, such as earlobe shape. Genes are considered the basic units of heredity. Like the chromosomes that contain them, genes come in pairs. Since a sex cell contains only one half of each chromosome pair, it also has only one half of each gene pair. Once the egg is fertilized, however, it contains two genes for each trait—one from the father and one from the mother. This is how hereditary information is passed from one generation to the next.

DOMINANT AND RECESSIVE GENES   Suppose a father has one trait and the mother has another. Which trait will their children have? The answer to that question depends on whether the trait is dominant or recessive. Dominant genes are expressed whenever they are present. Recessive genes are expressed only when the dominant gene is not present.

Consider a simple inherited trait such as earlobe shape. Earlobes can be either free or attached, as shown on page 186. The gene for free earlobes is dominant and the gene for

Figure 8-15 *A child with one dominant gene (E) and one recessive gene (e) will have free earlobes. A child with two recessive genes (ee) will have attached earlobes.*

BIOLOGY CONNECTION

The work of Gregor Mendel marked the beginning of modern genetics. In a monastery garden in the mid-1800s, Mendel began experimentation on the process of heredity. He was one of the first researchers to apply mathematics to the study of biology.

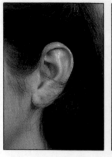

Figure 8-16 *A free earlobe (left) is a dominant trait; an attached earlobe (right) is a recessive trait.*

attached earlobes is recessive. Now consider the example of inheritance patterns shown in Figure 8-15. In Case #1, the mother has two genes for free earlobes and the father has two genes for attached earlobes. All the children of this couple will receive one dominant gene and one recessive gene. Because a recessive gene is not expressed when a dominant gene is present, all their children will have free earlobes.

There is a way that one parent with a dominant trait and one with a recessive trait can have a child with the recessive trait. As you can see in Case #2, the mother with free earlobes has one dominant gene and one recessive gene. Her eggs may carry either gene. If an egg with the gene for the recessive trait is fertilized by a sperm with a gene for the recessive trait, the baby will have the recessive trait.

Some other examples of dominant traits include a widow's peak and the ability to curl the tongue. A straight hairline and the inability to curl the tongue are recessive traits.

SEX DETERMINATION   Among the 23 pairs of chromosomes in each body cell is a single pair called the sex chromosomes. The genes on the sex chromosomes determine whether you are male or female and control most of your sexual characteristics. If you are a female, the two sex chromosomes in your cells are called X chromosomes. If you are a male, one of your sex chromosomes is an X chromosome and the other is called a Y chromosome.

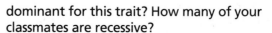

OBSERVING PHYSICAL GENETIC TRAITS

In this activity you will observe some dominant and recessive traits in your classmates.

Procedure

1. Figure 8-16 shows two general shapes of earlobes—free and attached. Examine your own ears and those of your classmates. How many people have attached earlobes? How many have free earlobes?

2. Try to curl your tongue. The ability to curl the tongue is a dominant trait. How many of your classmates can curl their tongues? How many cannot?

3. Examine the area on your fingers between the first and second knuckle behind the fingernail. Having hair growth in this area is a dominant trait. Are you dominant or recessive for this trait? How many of your classmates are

dominant for this trait? How many of your classmates are recessive?

4. Make a table to record your data. For each trait, record the number of students who are dominant for the trait and the number of students who are recessive for the trait. Then determine the percentage of students demonstrating each trait. Record this information in your table also.

Discussion

1. Which trait is the most common in your class? The least common?

2. What do you predict the results would be if you observed four other classes of students?

What happens to the sex chromosomes when egg and sperm cells form? As you read, only one chromosome of each pair is contained in the egg and sperm cells. Since females have only one type of sex chromosome, all eggs receive one X chromosome. In males, however, there are two different sex chromosomes. This means that half of a male's sperm cells have an X chromosome and half have a Y chromosome. When a sperm cell with an X chromosome fertilizes an egg, the fertilized egg will develop into a girl. When a sperm with a Y chromosome fertilizes an egg, the fertilized egg will develop into a boy. The sperm determines the sex of a child.

Genetic Disorders

Just like hair texture, eye color, and other inherited traits, genetic disorders can be passed from parent to child. A **genetic disorder** is an abnormal condition that a person inherits through genes or chromosomes. The genes that cause many genetic disorders are either dominant or recessive. Some examples of disorders caused by dominant genes include extra fingers on the hands and Huntington's disease (a disease of the nervous system). Because the genes for these disorders are dominant, the disorder shows up in people who receive one gene for the trait from either parent.

RECESSIVE DISORDERS   Many genetic disorders are recessive. With most recessive disorders, a child must receive two genes for the trait—one from each parent—in order for the disorder to show. People who receive one recessive gene and one dominant gene are called carriers. In carriers, the disorder is not expressed because it is masked by the dominant normal gene. Carriers can, however, pass the gene for the disorder to their children.

Sickle-cell disease is a genetic blood disorder that occurs most often among people of African descent. People who inherit two genes for this disease have a high number of red blood cells with an abnormal sickle shape. The sickle shape causes the red blood cells to clump and to block small blood vessels. The sickle-shaped red blood cells cannot carry as much oxygen as normally shaped red blood cells. A person

Figure 8-17 *Females have two X chromosomes (left), while males have one X and one Y chromosome (right).*

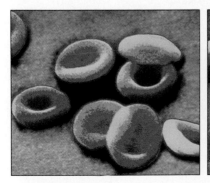 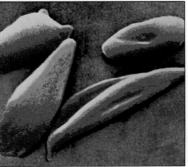

Figure 8-18 *How are normal red blood cells (left) different from sickle cells (right)?*

Cystic Fibrosis: Cure on the Way?

Coiled within almost every cell is a miniature code book built from strands of chromosomes, each strung with thousands of genes. Each gene is made of short bits of DNA—chemicals nicknamed A, G, C, and T. In all, your body contains about 3 billion bits of coded information that control everything from your eye color to the length of your earlobe.

If just one tiny bit of DNA is out of place—if an A is switched for a C, if there is just a bit too much T, if the G comes before the A instead of after it—the result can be a disease. Children born with sickle cell anemia have just one misplaced DNA "letter." Children with cystic fibrosis have one abnormal gene.

Scientists from all over the world have gotten together to identify and map genes of the human body. Their work— The Human Genome Project— will revolutionize medicine.

Cystic fibrosis is one of the more common fatal genetic diseases. As a result, researchers with the Human Genome Project have given it special attention. Already they have identified and mapped the gene that causes cystic fibrosis. Now patients all over the world are hoping that their work will lead to a cure.

with sickle-cell disease suffers from lack of oxygen in the blood and experiences pain and weakness. Carriers of the sickle-cell trait—people who have one sickle-cell gene—may show symptoms of the disease only under extreme circumstances, such as high altitude.

Another recessive genetic disorder, known as **Tay-Sachs disease,** is characterized by the lack of an important chemical in the brain. Tay-Sachs disease is found primarily among people of eastern European Jewish descent. Infants with two genes for Tay-Sachs disease appear healthy at first but soon show signs of brain damage. Unfortunately, there is no treatment for this disease.

Phenylketonuria (fen ul keet uh NOOR ee uh), or PKU, is a rare metabolic disorder that can cause severe mental retardation in infants. Babies who inherit two genes for this disease cannot break down phenylalanine, a chemical commonly found in food. As phenylalanine builds up in the body, the brain is affected. Although PKU is a serious disease, it can be treated successfully if the infant follows a special diet. Because PKU can be treated when it is recognized early in life, babies are routinely tested at birth for this disorder, even though it occurs only rarely.

Cystic fibrosis (SIS tik fy BROH sis) is a recessive disorder that occurs mainly among people of Caucasian descent. In children with two affected genes, the mucus that lines the lungs becomes thick and sticky. Normal mucus moves freely, carrying dirt and bacteria out of the lungs. The thick mucus associated with cystic fibrosis stays in the lungs, keeping bacteria with it. The presence of the bacteria leads to infections and eventually lung damage. The mucus also affects the pancreas and prevents it from releasing substances into the intestine to help digest food. Because of this, the body may not absorb enough nutrients. Treatment for cystic fibrosis includes physical therapy to dislodge the thick mucus from the lungs, antibiotics to treat lung infections, and medicated vapors to help keep the airways open.

Figure 8-19 *People with cystic fibrosis often have physical therapy to help keep the lungs clear of thick mucus.*

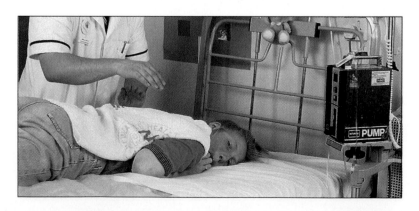

SEX-LINKED DISORDERS   A few genetic disorders are **sex-linked disorders**; that is, the gene for the disorder is found on a sex chromosome, usually the X chromosome. Sex-linked disorders are much more common in men than in women. This is because men have only one X chromosome and no corresponding genes on the Y chromosome. Since women have two X chromosomes, a recessive gene for a disorder on one X chromosome can be covered by a normal gene on the other X chromosome. The woman carrying the gene for the disorder, however, may pass it on to her children.

The most common sex-linked disorder is color blindness, the inability to distinguish certain colors. Other, more serious sex-linked disorders are Duchenne muscular dystrophy and hemophilia. **Duchenne muscular dystrophy** (DIS truh fee) is a condition in which the person lacks a protein needed for muscle function. As a result, muscle tissue begins to break down during childhood. A person with this disease eventually loses control of his muscles.

In **hemophilia** (hee muh FIL ee uh), a person's blood does not clot properly. In a person with hemophilia, physical activity can lead to internal bleeding that damages the person's joints. Blood plasma transfusions and injections of a blood-clotting substance are used to treat hemophilia.

DOWN SYNDROME   Some genetic disorders are the result of too few or too many chromosomes. One disorder, called **Down syndrome**, is the result of an extra chromosome (chromosome 21). An estimated 1 in 600 to 800 infants are born with Down syndrome. People with Down syndrome are mentally retarded and have a distinctive physical appearance. Mental retardation can range from mild to severe. Heart defects, which often can be treated successfully, are also common. Children with Down syndrome often lead full lives within their limitations. Many go to school and later enter the work force.

Figure 8-20 *Youngsters with Down syndrome can enjoy a full life in spite of their limitations.*

LESSON 4 REVIEW

1. What is a chromosome? What is a gene?
2. Explain the difference between dominant and recessive traits. Give examples of each.
3. Why do sex-linked genetic disorders most often affect males and not females?

What Do You Think?

4. List some physical traits exhibited by members of your family that you would say are controlled by dominant genes. Then list some you think are controlled by recessive genes. Explain your reasoning.

Breast and Testicular Self-Exams

Breast Self-Exam

Breast cancer is one of the most common forms of cancer among women. Although it is rare in young women, breast cancer becomes more common as women become older. Women with a history of breast cancer in their family are at higher risk for the disease.

Early detection is the best weapon women have against breast cancer. If signs of breast cancer are found early, the disease can be treated and often cured. That is why doctors and the American Cancer Society urge women to examine their breasts for lumps or other signs of cancer on a monthly basis. It is important to know how your breasts normally feel so that changes can be detected early. The teenage years are a good time to establish this important habit.

The steps for a breast self-examination are described below. The best time to do a breast self-exam is the week after a menstrual period, when the breasts are least swollen. For women who have reached menopause or have irregular periods, the exam should be done on the same day each month.

1. Do the shower check

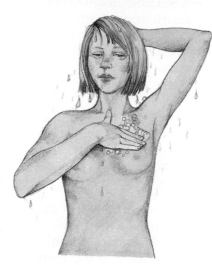

• Do the shower check while your hands are soapy and will glide easily over your skin. Lift your right arm up behind your head and feel your breast with the left hand. Touch every part of your breast firmly with the pads of your fingers to feel for lumps or thickening. (Your finger pads are the top third of your fingers.) Move your left

hand over your right breast in a small circle until you've gone over the entire breast. Notice that a firm ridge in the lower curve of the breast is normal.

• Now check your left breast with your right hand in the same way, with your left arm behind your head.

2. Check your breasts while lying down

• Lie down and put a pillow under your right shoulder. Place your right hand behind your head.

• Place the pads of your left fingers on the right breast and press firmly to feel for lumps or thickening. Begin at the outermost top point of the breast and move your fingers in a circular pattern around your breast, going over the entire breast and ending with the nipple.

• Repeat on the left breast.

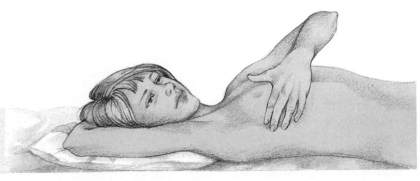

3. Look at your breasts while standing in front of the mirror

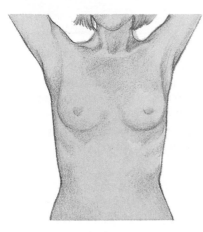

• Raise your arms high over your head and look for any change in breast shape (dimpling of skin, redness or swelling, or changes in the nipple). Then place your hands on your hips and check again.

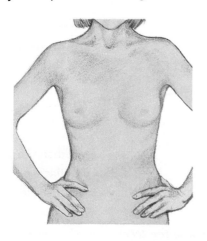

4. Report any abnormalities to your doctor right away

Many lumps are cysts or benign tumors that are not cancerous. But only a doctor can determine whether a growth is benign.

Testicular Self-Exam

Cancer of the testes, or testicular cancer, is one of the most common forms of cancer found in young men between 15 and 34 years of age.

Testicular cancer can be cured if it is found early enough and treated promptly. Most testicular cancers are noticed by men themselves, not their doctors. Men with an undescended or partially descended testicle are at much higher risk for developing testicular cancer than others. A simple procedure, performed by a doctor, can correct an undescended testis.

The steps for a testicular self-examination are described below. The best time to do a testicular self-exam is after a hot shower or bath when the scrotum is relaxed and the testes can be felt more easily.

1. Examine each testis separately with both hands

• Hold the underside of the testis with both hands and gently roll the testis between your thumb and finger, feeling for lumps or hard places about the size of a pea. Lumps are usually found in the front or sides of the testes.

• Learn to recognize what the epididymis feels like so you won't confuse it with a lump.

2. If you find any lumps, go to your doctor immediately

Lumps may not be malignant, but only a doctor can make a diagnosis. Other signs of testicular cancer are enlargement of the testis, dull aching in the genital area, or a feeling of heaviness in the scrotum.

Apply the Skill

Breast Self-Exam

1. Do the breast self-exam in the shower, lying down, and standing in front of the mirror one week after your next menstrual period.

2. Ask your mother if she does a monthly breast check. Describe the steps of the self-exam to her. Ask her if you have any history of breast cancer in your family.

Testicular Self-Exam

1. After a shower or hot bath, practice the testicular self-exam.

2. Ask your father if he does a monthly testicular self-exam. Describe the steps of the self-exam to him. Ask him if you have any history of testicular cancer in your family.

CHAPTER 8 REVIEW

KEY IDEAS

LESSON 1

- The endocrine system allows one part of the body to communicate with another. Endocrine glands control growth, metabolism, and reproduction.

- The endocrine glands that play a role in reproduction are testes, ovaries, pituitary gland, and hypothalamus.

LESSON 2

- In the male, the testes produce sperm cells and the male hormone testosterone.

- Fluids from seminal vesicles, prostate gland, and Cowper's glands form semen.

LESSON 3

- Internal female reproductive organs are ovaries, fallopian tubes, uterus, and vagina. The ovaries produce the female sex hormones estrogen and progesterone. Each month, the ovaries release a mature egg in a process called ovulation.

- Ovulation is part of a monthly process known as the menstrual cycle.

LESSON 4

- Heredity is the physical transmission of traits from parents to children. Chromosomes are the structures in cells that carry hereditary characteristics. A gene is a section of a chromosome that determines a single trait.

- Some genetic disorders are sickle cell disease, Tay-Sachs disease, phenylketonuria, cystic fibrosis, and Down syndrome.

KEY TERMS

LESSON 1
endocrine glands
estrogen
hormones
ovaries
pituitary gland
progesterone
testes

LESSON 2
ejaculation

epididymis
inguinal hernia
penis
puberty
scrotum
semen
vas deferens

LESSON 3
cervix
endometrium

fallopian tubes
menstruation
ovulation
toxic shock
   syndrome
uterus
vagina

LESSON 4
chromosomes
cystic fibrosis

Down syndrome
Duchenne muscular
   dystrophy
gene
hemophilia
phenylketonuria
   (PKU)
sex-linked disorders
sickle-cell disease
Tay-Sachs disease

Listed above are some of the important terms in this chapter. Choose the term from the list that best matches each phrase below.

1. the lining of the uterus

2. a genetic disorder of red blood cells

3. male reproductive structure in which sperm acquire the ability to move

4. male reproductive glands that produce testosterone and sperm

5. the process by which a mature egg is released from the ovary

6. hormone that causes the lining of the uterus to thicken

7. the birth canal

8. structures on which genes are located

9. genetic disorders in which the gene for the disorder is found on the X chromosome

10. endocrine gland that controls metabolism, growth, and reproduction

WHAT HAVE YOU LEARNED?

If the statement is true, write "true." If it is false, change the underlined word or words to make the statement true.

11. The endocrine glands produce chemical substances known as <u>hormones</u>.

12. The reproductive glands are controlled by the <u>thyroid gland</u>.

13. The testes hang outside the body in a sac known as the <u>epididymis</u>.

14. When a person is unable to reproduce, the condition is known as <u>sterility</u>.

15. The monthly cycle during which women release eggs is known as the <u>endometrial</u> cycle.

16. Cancer of the <u>cervix</u> can be found by means of a Pap test.

17. Females have two <u>X</u> chromosomes, while males have one X and one Y chromosome.

18. Sex-linked disorders are more common in <u>women</u> than in <u>men</u>.

Answer each of the following with complete sentences.

19. What is the endocrine system?

20. How are hormone levels regulated?

21. Name two hormones produced by the pituitary gland that are important for reproduction.

22. Describe the process by which sperm are formed.

23. What is the menstrual cycle? Which hormones play a role in this cycle?

24. List some causes of sterility in both males and females.

25. How often should breast or testicular self-examination be done?

26. How many chromosomes are contained in your body cells? Your sex cells?

27. Explain why the father, rather than the mother, determines the sex of their offspring.

28. What is Down syndrome?

WHAT DO YOU THINK?

29. If only one sperm is needed to fertilize an egg, why are so many sperm released during ejaculation?

30. Your 16-year-old sister does not menstruate regularly. Should she be concerned about this? Why or why not?

31. Because colorblindness is a sex-linked trait, it is more common in males than females. For a girl to be colorblind, what genes would she have to inherit from her parents? Would either of her parents be colorblind?

32. Some athletes misuse steroids, chemicals similar to testosterone, because of their effect on building muscles. Why do you think steroid misuse might have a harmful effect on the reproductive system?

WHAT WOULD YOU DO?

33. Your friend tells you that her younger sister has recently begun to menstruate but seems confused about the process. Your friend would like to help her sister feel more comfortable about her changing body. What should she say or do?

34. If you were worried that your body was not developing properly, what would you do?

35. A man with hemophilia is considering marriage. He is concerned that his children might be born with hemophilia. What questions should he ask his future wife? Explain.

36. Suppose that a friend of yours has confided in you that during a testicular self-examination, he detected a lump. Your friend is reluctant to see a doctor. What would you say to your friend?

Getting Involved

37. Invite parents with children who have a genetic disorder to talk to your class about their experience and how much they knew about the disorder before the child's birth.

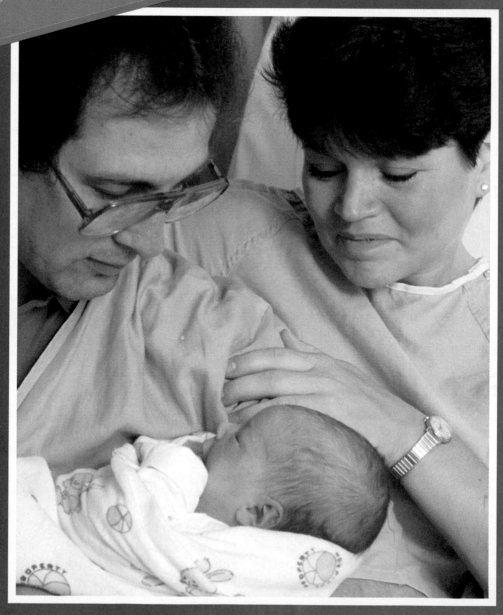

Chapter 9

PREGNANCY AND BIRTH

Being a parent is one of life's most rewarding—and most difficult—experiences. In this chapter, you'll learn what you should consider in deciding to become a parent. You'll also learn about pregnancy and fetal development, including ways to protect the health of both mother and baby.

CHAPTER PREVIEW

9-1 Deciding to Have Children

- List reasons why parents decide to have children.

9-2 Conception and Pregnancy

- Explain the events that lead to the conception and birth of a child.

9-3 Birth

- Describe the birth process.

BUILDING HEALTH SKILLS

- Describe mechanisms for coping with change.

CHECK YOUR WELLNESS

Decide whether each of the following statements is true or false.

- The decision to have a child involves considering the financial means, emotional maturity, and the time you have for a family.

- Fertilization occurs when an egg cell joins with a sperm cell.

- By the end of the second month of pregnancy, the embryo has recognizable features.

- A pregnant woman must eat nutritiously and avoid alcohol and drugs not prescribed by her doctor.

- Teenagers are more likely than older women to give birth to small, less healthy babies.

- Birth usually occurs after about 40 weeks of pregnancy.

KEEPING A JOURNAL

Describe what it would be like to be floating in a warm, safe environment with no sensations of hunger or pain and no light or loud noises. Then describe how you would feel if you were suddenly pushed out of this comfortable environment.

Take it to the **Net**

www.phschool.com

DECIDING TO HAVE CHILDREN

Focus on these questions as you read this lesson.

- What are some good reasons for having children?
- What are the steps involved in planning a family?

SKILLS

- DECIDE
- Working in Groups

Becoming a parent is the biggest commitment a person can make in his or her life. It is for keeps. There is no such thing as "undoing" parenthood if "it doesn't work out" or if you become bored with it. **Parents who have carefully thought through their reasons for having children have the best chance of raising a healthy family.**

Reasons for Having Children

Why do people have children? Usually there is a combination of reasons. If you were the baby-to-be, what would you think of the following reasons?

- The world needs more people like us!
- With our new jobs, we've finally saved enough money to have a family.
- We have lots of love to give to a child.
- My mother wants to be a grandma before she's 50.
- If I get pregnant, maybe he will marry me.
- All of our married friends are having babies. Maybe we should, too.
- Once I have a baby, the world will know I'm an adult.
- We really enjoy children.
- I need someone to love me.
- It's now or never. We're almost 40!

Figure 9-1 *The joys of parenthood are many, but so are the responsibilities.*

- If we have one more, maybe it will be a girl.
- I know our marriage will improve if we have a baby.

The baby-to-be might not care for some of these reasons. It needs parents who can focus on what they will give, not what they will get. The baby would want parents who

- are adults who like children and who really want to have a baby.
- love each other, are emotionally mature, and have a happy, stable marriage.
- have completed their educations and are financially able to support a child.
- know the responsibilities of parenthood and are committed to carrying them out.
- understand that their lives will change a great deal once the baby is born.
- are eager and able to give a child all the love, guidance, and attention it needs to be happy and healthy.
- are prepared to enter into a lifelong relationship with a new and unknown person.

Parenthood has many joys and satisfactions, but it is also stressful and involves a lot of hard work. The responsibilities of parenthood go far beyond most other occupations. Babies are demanding and totally helpless. Along with the loving feelings, smiles, and cuddles, new parents must face sleepless nights, times of worry about illness, and the loss of many freedoms and pleasures they used to enjoy. Couples with the qualifications listed above have the best chance of making decisions and practicing behaviors that will positively influence the development of their children.

Figure 9-2 *Caring for a young child is a full-time responsibility.*

MATHEMATICS
CONNECTION

Make a list of the items that are needed during a baby's first year. Then calculate how much it would cost to buy these items.

Planning a Family

At least one part of planning a family is purely practical. A couple has to review their budget to find out whether or not they can afford to provide food, clothing, shelter, and medical care for a child. They need to discuss who will care for the child if both of them must continue to work. They need to find out if their employers grant maternity or paternity leave, so that at least one of them can stay home with the baby for a few months and still return to the same job. They may also need to investigate the costs and availability of child care.

Even before a woman becomes pregnant, she has to start taking care of herself. She should be in good physical condition and eat a balanced diet. She should not use tobacco, drink alcohol, take any drugs that are not prescribed by her medical practitioner, or be exposed to any harmful substances or fumes in the environment.

It is also important to plan for **prenatal care** (pree NAYT ul), or medical care during pregnancy. Before becoming pregnant, the woman should visit her doctor. Good prenatal care is crucial to maintaining the health of the mother and having a healthy baby.

Finally, the couple has to stop using any method of preventing pregnancy. Preventing pregnancy is known as birth control, or **contraception** (kahn truh SEP shun). If pregnancy does not occur within one year after a couple has stopped using contraception, the couple may be **infertile** (in FUR tl), or unable to produce children. After a year, many infertile couples are tested to determine the cause of the infertility. Medical treatments are available to correct some forms of infertility in both men and women.

If pregnancy does not occur after treatment, or if the fertility problem cannot be corrected, a couple may consider a number of alternatives. One of the alternatives is adoption. **Adoption** is a legal procedure in which a child is taken into

Figure 9-3 *Good prenatal care includes regular medical checkups.*

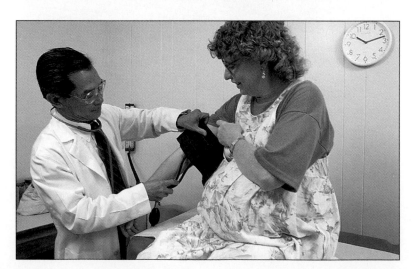

Should They Have Another Child?

Gil and Luisa are the parents of a five-year-old daughter, who will be entering kindergarten soon. They had always planned on having several children, but are now facing a difficult decision: Should they have another child now, wait a few more years, or perhaps not have any more children at all?

Gil feels that they should have more children while they are still young. He thinks that five years is a long time to wait to have another child, and he's not sure they should wait any longer. Also, Gil was an only child, and he always felt lonely. He wants his own daughter to have the experience of having brothers or sisters.

Luisa, on the other hand, is concerned about the additional expense of having another child. With their daughter entering kindergarten, she is considering going back to work to add to the family's income. Recently she has read some articles pointing out that being an only child can have some advantages for the child.

1. Using the DECIDE process on page 18, decide what you would do in this situation. Explain your reasons for making this decision.

2. Is there more than one decision that you could feel comfortable with?

a family to be raised in the same way as a child born to the parents. Adopted children are their parents' children in every respect except genetic inheritance. Another alternative involves becoming foster parents. **Foster parents** take care of children whose parents are unable to do so. The child may live with foster parents for a few weeks or several years, depending on the situation.

Teenage Pregnancy

Compared with teens of other industrialized nations, American adolescents have similar rates of sexual activity, but higher rates of pregnancy. Although our pregnancy rate finally began declining during the 1990s, it is still a huge problem: In the United States, a teen gives birth every minute of every day.

Teenage pregnancy is a serious health problem. Babies born to young mothers are often smaller and less healthy than those born to older women. Teenage mothers themselves are more likely to have health problems during pregnancy than older women. This is because pregnant teenagers do not always eat well or get adequate medical care during pregnancy, especially in the early months.

Aside from the health problems, how does having a baby affect the lives of a teenage couple? Parents are legally responsible for the care and well-being of their children. Teenage parents often report feeling overwhelmed and

Figure 9-4 *Teenage parents often have problems with finances.*

trapped by these responsibilities. Many teenage mothers drop out of school. Some fathers do not help support or care for the child; others drop out of school and work at low-paying jobs. As a result, many teenage parents never complete their educations, often live in poverty, and must depend on public assistance programs for survival.

Although many young people are aware of the health, economic, and social problems teenage parents face, they often do not believe pregnancy can happen to them. Few teenagers want to become pregnant. Statistics have shown, however, that one in six teenagers who engage in sexual intercourse becomes pregnant. Sexual intimacy is a high-risk behavior for anyone who is not ready to accept the lifelong responsibility of children.

LESSON 1 REVIEW

1. Name four responsibilities of parenthood.
2. Name two ways a woman can start taking care of herself and her planned baby before she becomes pregnant.
3. In what ways does having a baby change the lives of teenage parents?

What Do You Think?

4. Of the reasons for having children that are listed on pages 196–197, which ones do you think a baby-to-be would like the best?

2 CONCEPTION AND PREGNANCY

GUIDE FOR READING

Focus on these questions as you read this lesson.

- What are the stages of development of the embryo and fetus?
- What health care is important for a pregnant woman?

SKILLS

- Activity: Parent for a Day

Each person begins when two cells, one from the mother and one from the father, join. These cells are too small to be seen without a microscope, yet their union is the beginning of every human being.

Fertilization

Fertilization, also called conception, is the union of an egg (ovum) from the mother and a sperm from the father. As you learned in Chapter 8, an egg is released from one of the ovaries about once every 28 days. After its release, the egg enters the fallopian tube to begin its journey to the uterus. If sperm are deposited in the woman's vagina while the egg is on its way to the uterus, fertilization can occur. Fertilization is shown in Figure 9-5.

As many as half a billion sperm may be deposited in the vagina. However, only a few hundred survive the six-inch swim to the fallopian tubes. Most die along the way. Of the hundreds of sperm that do reach the egg, only one can fertilize it. Within seconds of fertilization, the surface of the egg changes so that no more sperm can enter the egg. At the moment of fertilization, the sex and genetic traits of the future individual are set.

THE ZYGOTE   The united egg and sperm are called a **zygote** (ZY goht). Within 36 hours, while the zygote is still traveling through the fallopian tube, it begins to divide. It divides into two cells, then into four, and so on, until it is made up of dozens of cells, as shown in Figure 9-6.

IMPLANTATION   Within four to five days after fertilization, the growing structure reaches the uterus, where it floats free for a few days. By this time, it is made up of about 500 cells. The structure is no longer a solid mass of cells. It has become a hollow sphere called a **blastocyst** (BLAS tuh sist). Once the blastocyst is formed, it begins to attach itself to the wall of the uterus. The process of attachment is called **implantation** (im plan TAY shun). After the blastocyst has been implanted, it is known as an **embryo** (EM bree oh). Over the next few weeks, the attachment holding the embryo in place will become more complex.

PREGNANCY TESTING   The most common sign of pregnancy is a missed menstrual period. Menstruation ceases during pregnancy because progesterone levels remain high. The wall of the uterus remains thick and is not discharged from the body.

Figure 9-5 *Fertilization occurs when a sperm unites with an egg.*

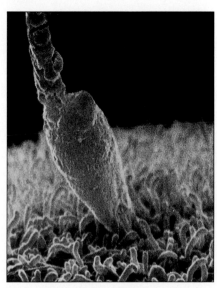

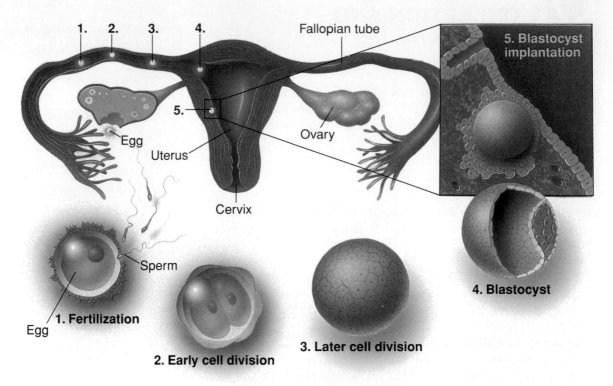

1. **2.** **3.** **4.** Fallopian tube

5. Blastocyst implantation

Egg

5.

Uterus

Ovary

Cervix

Sperm

Egg

1. Fertilization

2. Early cell division

3. Later cell division

4. Blastocyst

Figure 9-6 *The embryo becomes implanted in the wall of the uterus.*

Pregnancy can actually be determined as soon as implantation has occurred. This is possible because the embryo begins to produce a hormone called **human chorionic gonadotropin** (kawr ee AHN ik goh nad uh TROH pin), or HCG, at the time of implantation. HCG can be found in the blood of a pregnant woman within a few days after implantation. One week after menstruation should have begun, HCG can be found in a pregnant woman's urine. A pregnancy test is more reliable, however, if HCG is measured two weeks after menstruation should have begun.

The Embryo

The attachment that holds the embryo to the wall of the uterus develops into an organ called the **placenta** (pluh SEN tuh). About 25 days after fertilization, a cord develops between the embryo and the placenta. This cord, shown in Figure 9-7, is called the **umbilical cord** (um BIL ih kul). The umbilical cord is the embryo's lifeline. It contains blood vessels that carry nutrients and oxygen from the placenta to the embryo and wastes from the embryo to the placenta. The placenta acts as a filter between the mother's bloodstream and the embryo's bloodstream. However, the blood of the embryo and that of the mother do not mix. Many different substances can pass through this filter, including alcohol, drugs, the chemicals in tobacco smoke, and some microscopic organisms that cause disease. Any of those substances can seriously harm the developing embryo.

The developing embryo is enclosed in a bag of thin tissue called the **amniotic sac** (am nee AHT ik). The embryo floats within the sac in fluid called **amniotic fluid**. Amniotic fluid acts as a shock absorber and helps to keep the embryo's temperature constant.

By the end of the second month of pregnancy, the embryo is about 1.2 inches (3 centimeters) long and has recognizable features such as eyes, ears, hands, and feet. At this point and until birth, it is called a **fetus** (FEE tus).

The Fetus

Between the third and sixth months, the fetus grows until it is approximately 11 inches (28 centimeters) long and weighs about 1.5 pounds (680 grams). Hair grows on the head and body, and facial features and ears develop. Because the fetus has little fat under its skin, the skin is wrinkled. During this period, the fetus begins to move and kick, a sign that its skeleton and muscles are developing. As its nervous system continues to grow, the sense organs begin to function. The fetus becomes sensitive to light and sound and alternates periods of activity with periods of sleep. A fetus born at this stage probably will not survive. After 26 weeks, it has a good chance of surviving, although it may have significant medical problems.

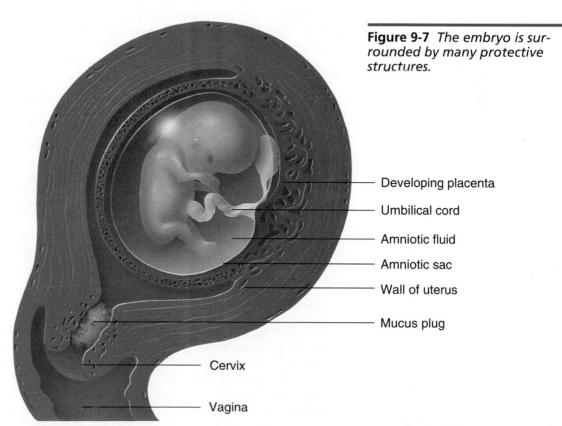

Figure 9-7 *The embryo is surrounded by many protective structures.*

Developing placenta

Umbilical cord

Amniotic fluid

Amniotic sac

Wall of uterus

Mucus plug

Cervix

Vagina

Figure 9-8 *The fetus has a recognizable human form and begins to make its presence felt.*

From the sixth to the ninth month, the fetus continues to grow and develop until it is ready to be born. The size of the body increases so that it is more in proportion to the size of the head. The eyelids open and close, and the skin becomes less wrinkled as body fat accumulates. By the end of the ninth month, the average fetus is 20 inches (51 centimeters) long and weighs 7.5 pounds (3.4 kilograms).

Expectant Parents

During the nine months that the baby is developing in the uterus, the expectant parents are preparing for its birth. The mother experiences the many physical changes of pregnancy. Both parents spend a lot of time thinking and talking about the baby to come. It is a time of excitement, expectation, and anxiety.

THE FIRST TRIMESTER The nine months of pregnancy are divided into three periods, known as **trimesters** (try MES turz). Each trimester is three months long. The mother experiences many physical changes during each trimester.

Early in the first trimester, while the embryo is developing into a fetus, the mother may experience morning sickness. **Morning sickness** consists of attacks of nausea and sometimes vomiting. It can occur in the morning or at any time of day. The cause is related to changes in the levels of certain hormones that occur as a result of the pregnancy. Morning sickness is the response of the mother's body as it adapts to these changes. Morning sickness usually disappears after a few weeks.

Other changes that occur during the first trimester are an increase in breast size and breast tenderness, the need to urinate frequently, and times of overwhelming sleepiness. Some of these changes last throughout pregnancy. Some may not occur at all. Every pregnancy is different. By the end of the first trimester, the mother's abdomen looks more rounded than usual, but the pregnancy is not obvious.

THE SECOND TRIMESTER During the second trimester, the mother's abdomen begins to swell, and she begins to feel the fetus moving. As the fetus and placenta grow, the enlarged uterus pushes against the mother's digestive tract. This can cause the mother to have constipation or indigestion (mostly "heartburn" and the need to burp). Toward the end of the second trimester, a thin fluid may begin to leak from the nipples. This fluid is the forerunner of breast milk.

THE THIRD TRIMESTER Most women gain between 25 and 35 pounds during pregnancy. By the third trimester, the mother is close to her maximum weight gain. As the fetus grows to its birth size and exercises its muscles, its movements can be seen and felt on the mother's abdomen. Indigestion and frequent urination continue and may even

PARENT FOR A DAY

In this activity you will experience some of the responsibilities of parenthood.

Materials

5-pound bag of flour   plastic bag with tie

Procedure

1. Place the bag of flour inside the plastic bag and fasten it shut. For the next 24 hours, you will be responsible for your bag of flour as if it were a real baby.

2. Choose a name for your "baby."

3. Follow these rules for taking care of your "baby."

• Every 5 hours, including during the night, set 20 minutes aside for feeding your "baby." During this time, you must remain seated in one place and devote your full attention to your "baby."

• Every 3 hours during the time that you are awake, allow 5 minutes for changing your "baby's" diaper.

• Spend 15 minutes in the evening talking or reading to your "baby."

• Never leave your "baby" alone. If necessary, arrange for someone to babysit.

Discussion

1. How did being a parent affect your life-style?

2. In what ways is a bag of flour an appropriate object to use to represent a baby?

3. When do you think is the best time for a person to become a parent?

increase as the fetus takes up more and more room in the abdomen. During the last few weeks of pregnancy, the mother may feel some irregular contractions. The uterus is preparing its muscles for the work of pushing the fetus out. Finally, at a time anywhere from two weeks to a few days before birth, the mother's lower abdomen hardens and protrudes as the fetus's head begins to move lower in the uterus.

EMOTIONAL CHANGES   What will our baby be like? Will it be a girl or a boy? Will it be healthy? Will we be good parents? These are only a few of the questions that parents ask themselves while they are waiting to welcome their child into the family.

During the first trimester of pregnancy, excitement and happiness are mixed with worries about responsibility and concerns about the physical discomfort of the mother. The bond between expectant parents can be especially strong during this time. In fact, some expectant fathers experience **sympathetic pregnancy,** a condition in which they share some of the mother's physical discomfort, such as morning sickness or frequent urination. Both parents worry about the health of the embryo or fetus and the possibility that something could go wrong in the course of its development.

These worries do not disappear entirely until the baby is born. However, by the second trimester, the parents are more confident. This is usually a pleasant time. The fetus begins to kick, and the parents begin to think of it as a person. As the time of birth approaches, they may choose a name for the baby and shop for things the baby will need. These activities help them to adjust to their role as parents. By the ninth month of pregnancy, both mother and father are eager to experience the birth of their child.

PRENATAL CARE   Prenatal care is extremely important. **The chances of having a healthy baby greatly increase if the mother practices good health habits and visits her doctor or clinic for regular checkups throughout pregnancy.** In addition to a well-balanced diet, most women require extra protein, iron, calcium, and B vitamins during pregnancy. Pregnant women require extra calories; the average pregnant woman needs between 2200 and 2400 calories per day. Exercise is another part of a healthy pregnancy. It helps to keep the heart fit so that it can meet the extra demands of providing for the developing fetus. Having muscles that are in good condition helps during childbirth.

As soon as she plans to become pregnant, a woman should abstain from alcohol, smoking, and any drugs not prescribed or approved by her doctor. These substances and others can cross into the baby's circulation and cause birth defects. Many learning disabilities can be linked to alcohol or other substance abuse during pregnancy. Women who drink alcohol during pregnancy risk having a baby with fetal alcohol syndrome. **Fetal alcohol syndrome** is mental retardation caused by alcohol, which damages the fetus's brain cells.

Other birth defects can be caused by viral infections during pregnancy or conditions that prevent the fetus from receiving enough oxygen. A woman who smokes during pregnancy exposes her fetus to many of the harmful chemicals

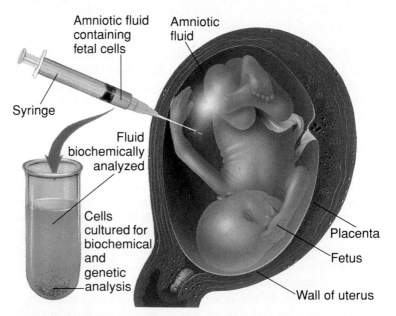

Figure 9-9 *In amniocentesis, a sample of amniotic fluid is used to detect certain disorders in the developing fetus.*

Amniotic fluid containing fetal cells

Amniotic fluid

Syringe

Fluid biochemically analyzed

Cells cultured for biochemical and genetic analysis

Placenta

Fetus

Wall of uterus

present in the smoke. Smoking also increases the chance that the fetus will be born prematurely. Smoking reduces the amount of oxygen obtained by the fetus, causing slow growth, low birth weight, or other problems.

Regular checkups during pregnancy allow the doctor to detect and deal with any problems as early as possible. If a fetal problem is suspected, the doctor can recommend a number of special tests. For example, more than 70 inherited disorders can be detected with either one of two methods. The older method, called **amniocentesis** (am nee oh sen TEE sis), involves the removal of a small amount of amniotic fluid from around the fetus.

Figure 9-9 illustrates how amniocentesis is carried out. The amniotic fluid is withdrawn around the fourteenth to sixteenth week of pregnancy. After a few weeks, this fluid is examined for the presence of substances that may indicate an inherited disorder.

The newer method, called **chorionic villus sampling**, allows results to be available by the eighth week of pregnancy. In this test, a small piece of the **chorion,** a part of the developing placenta, is removed for examination. Chorionic villus sampling is able to detect many of the same disorders as amniocentesis.

Sometimes high-frequency sound waves, or **ultrasound,** are used to make a "picture" of the developing fetus. Ultrasound can detect abnormal bone, muscle, and heart formation. It is also used to confirm the position of the fetus in the uterus or the presence of more than one fetus. Ultrasound can also be used to determine the age of the fetus.

Amniocentesis, chorionic villus sampling, and ultrasound are not used in every pregnancy. They are recommended if the woman is over 35 years of age or if the doctor or couple have reason to believe that something might be wrong with the fetus. Some of the disorders revealed by these tests can be treated before birth or during the newborn period.

LESSON 2 REVIEW

1. Name the two cells whose union causes fertilization.
2. Where does implantation occur?
3. How long is a trimester? How many trimesters are there in a pregnancy?
4. Name three health practices that are important for a pregnant woman.

What Do You Think?

5. If you were a woman used to swimming each day, would you give it up during pregnancy? Why or why not?

EXPLORING

CAREERS

Obstetrician and Nurse-Midwife

What kind of doctor cares for two patients at the same time? Answer: an **obstetrician,** who cares for pregnant women and their unborn babies.

Obstetricians know about the dietary needs, risks, and complications associated with pregnancy. They track the baby's progress while also watching the mother's health. When the time comes, obstetricians help the newborns come into the world.

To become an obstetrician, a person must attend college and four years of medical school. This is followed by several more years of study and training in obstetrics.

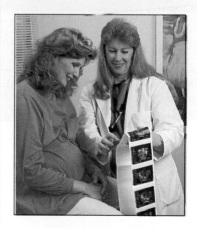

As an alternative, some women choose to be cared for by a **nurse-midwife.** A nurse-midwife must have a bachelor's degree in nursing and an additional year of study in obstetrics, with training in childbirth preparation.

Focus on these questions as you read this lesson.

- What are the three stages of labor?

- What are some complications that can arise during pregnancy and birth?

- What are some problems of adjustment for parents and the newborn during the postpartum period?

SKILLS

- Locating Community Resources

3 BIRTH

As pregnancy progresses, expectant parents begin to arrange for the birth of their baby. Most couples choose to have the baby in a hospital, sometimes in a **birthing room,** a hospital room that looks a lot like a bedroom. Hospital births are assisted by the doctor and specially trained nurses. Having a baby in a hospital is a good idea because doctors, nurses, and special equipment are available to help immediately should something go wrong. If the pregnancy has gone well and the mother is in good health, the parents may choose to have the baby at home with the help of a certified nurse-midwife, a person trained to assist in the birth process.

It is important for parents to know what to expect during pregnancy, birth, and the adjustment period after birth. Many expectant parents take childbirth classes during pregnancy. Childbirth classes teach the parents what to expect during the birth process and how they can make it easier. These classes may also provide information on how to care for the newborn.

The Stages of Birth

At the end of the ninth month of pregnancy, the fetus's head moves lower in the uterus. Birth begins when the muscular wall of the uterus begins a series of contractions that will push the fetus out of the mother. The work of pushing the fetus out is called **labor.**

Figure 9-10 *A hospital birthing room combines a homelike environment with modern medical facilities.*

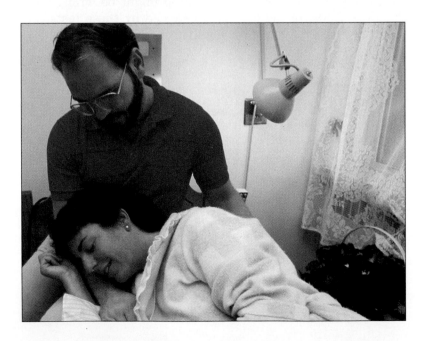

Labor has three stages. Refer to Figure 9-11 as each stage is described. The first stage usually lasts from 4 to 24 hours. During this time, strong contractions cause the cervix, the "neck" of the uterus, to dilate, or increase its width, from 1 inch to 4 inches (2.5 centimeters to 10 centimeters). Each contraction lasts 30 to 90 seconds. At first, the contractions may be minutes apart, but by the end of the first stage, they are usually only a few seconds apart. The sac containing the amniotic fluid breaks, and the cervix becomes softer to allow the fetus to pass through.

Stage two lasts from half an hour to two hours and involves the actual birth, or **delivery,** of the baby. Contractions of the uterus continue, and the baby is pushed out through the cervix and vagina. The baby usually enters the world head first.

Once the baby is out, the umbilical cord is clamped and cut. There are no nerve endings in the cord, so this does not hurt the baby or the mother. The baby's nose and mouth are suctioned to remove mucus and make breathing easier. Special eyedrops are put in the baby's eyes to prevent infection,

Figure 9-11 *The three stages of labor include delivery of the baby and the placenta.*

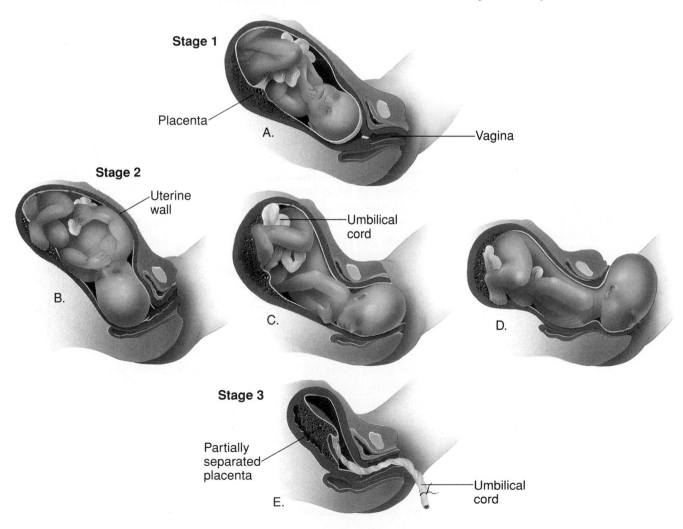

Stage 1

Placenta

A.

Vagina

Stage 2

Uterine wall

B.

Umbilical cord

C.

D.

Stage 3

Partially separated placenta

E.

Umbilical cord

and an injection of vitamin K is given to prevent excessive bleeding from the cut umbilical cord.

Within one minute of birth and then again five minutes later, the baby is examined and given an Apgar score. The **Apgar score** is a way to determine the baby's need for emergency care. The baby is rated from zero to two in each of five areas: heart rate, breathing, muscle tone, the ability to react to a stimulus by moving and crying, and skin color. A score of two in each area, for a total of ten, means the baby has come through the birth process in the best condition possible.

The third stage of birth consists of delivery of the placenta, which is sometimes called the **afterbirth.** This stage lasts from 15 to 30 minutes.

Complications of Pregnancy and Birth

Sometimes problems can develop during pregnancy and birth. Staying in good health; avoiding drugs, alcohol, and tobacco; and having regular checkups are the best ways of reducing the possibility of these problems.

PROBLEMS IN PREGNANCY Although most pregnancies go well, problems sometimes occur. Sometimes the zygote does not travel down the fallopian tube to the uterus. The blastocyst forms and becomes implanted in the fallopian tube or elsewhere in the abdomen. This condition, called **ectopic pregnancy** (ek TAHP ik), results in the death of the embryo. Surgery is necessary to remove the embryo and, if possible, repair the damaged fallopian tube.

Another event that ends a pregnancy is miscarriage. **Miscarriage** is the expulsion of a dead zygote, blastocyst, embryo, or fetus from the uterus. The usual cause of death is a serious genetic defect, but sometimes death is due to the mother's illness or a drug the mother has taken. In other cases, there is no apparent reason for a miscarriage. Miscarriage almost always occurs during the first trimester, and sometimes it occurs before a woman is even aware of pregnancy. It is a natural event that ends 15 to 20 percent of all pregnancies. **Stillbirth** is the birth of a dead, full-term fetus. There are a number of causes for a stillbirth, including physical injury to the fetus.

Some problems of pregnancy affect both the mother and the fetus. One of these is **toxemia** (tahk SEE mee uh). Toxemia is a serious condition characterized by high blood pressure, protein in the urine, and swelling, which is caused by fluid staying in the tissues. Toxemia requires hospital care. If toxemia is not treated, the mother can suffer convulsions, go into a coma, and die. Toxemia is most common in mothers for whom pregnancy is already a health risk: teenagers, women over the age of 40, women who had health problems before they became pregnant, and women who do not receive prenatal care.

Another problem that occurs in some pregnancies is caused by the Rh factor. Most people's blood contains a certain group of proteins. Their blood is said to be **Rh positive.** About 15 percent of the population has blood that lacks these proteins. Their blood is said to be **Rh negative.** As you learned in Chapter 8, a baby inherits many traits from its parents. If the father is Rh positive and the mother is Rh negative, the fetus may inherit the Rh positive trait from the father and be Rh positive. During delivery the mother's blood responds to the fetus's blood as if it is a foreign substance and builds up antibodies against it. This does not affect her first baby. If she becomes pregnant again, however, the antibodies will attack the red blood cells of an Rh-positive fetus. The baby will need a blood transfusion as soon as it is born. After the birth of her first baby, a woman can be given an injection to prevent antibodies from forming.

ENGLISH CONNECTION

The Rh factor was named for the rhesus monkey. It was first detected in the blood of this animal.

COMPLICATIONS AT BIRTH   Although the birth process usually proceeds smoothly, problems can occur. Sometimes delivery through the cervix and vagina is not possible because of the position of the fetus in the uterus or the narrowness of the mother's pelvis. Sometimes illness or other conditions may make labor and vaginal delivery dangerous for the mother or the fetus. For example, some sexually transmitted diseases can be transmitted to the fetus during a vaginal delivery. In these circumstances, the obstetrician will perform a cesarean section. A **cesarean section** (sih ZAIR ee un) is a surgical method of birth. The operation takes about one hour to complete, and the mother may be awake or asleep during the procedure. About 25 percent of all babies born in the United States are delivered by cesarean section.

Delivery of a live fetus before it is ready to be born is **premature birth.** Premature birth occurs early in the third trimester. At this time the fetus's lungs may not be fully

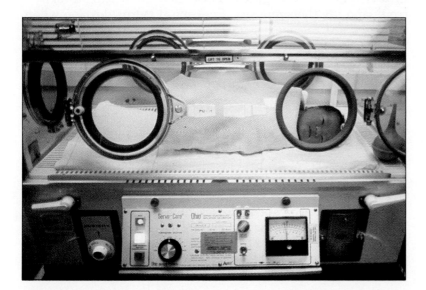

Figure 9-12 *A premature baby is usually cared for in an incubator until it becomes more fully developed.*

Figure 9-13 *Identical twins (left) inherit identical traits, whereas fraternal twins (right) do not.*

developed, so it cannot breathe by itself. Premature babies receive special care in **incubators**, special chambers designed to protect the baby until it is more developed.

MULTIPLE BIRTHS   The number of **multiple births**—the delivery of more than one baby—has increased dramatically in the United States. At century's end, the number of twins had increased 42 percent; the number of triplets had increased 272 percent. Doctors think that the increase is due to the number of older mothers and to the number of couples using fertility drugs.

What causes more than one fetus to develop? Consider the example of twins. There are two types of twins: identical twins and fraternal twins. **Identical twins** develop from the same fertilized egg, or zygote. Occasionally the zygote divides into two identical zygotes. They have identical inherited traits and are the same sex. **Fraternal twins** develop when two eggs are released from the ovary and are fertilized by two sperm. Fraternal twins are no more alike than any other siblings, and they may or may not be the same sex.

The Postpartum Period

The **postpartum period** begins with delivery and lasts about six weeks. It is a period of adjustment for the parents and their newborn.

CHANGES IN PARENTS   During the postpartum period, the mother's uterus shrinks back to its normal size, and the breasts produce milk for the baby. These changes are caused by hormones. **Prolactin** (proh LAK tin) causes milk to form in the breasts. **Oxytocin** (ahk sih TOH sin) causes the uterus to shrink. Oxytocin also helps the breast tissue to eject milk when the baby suckles. Other hormonal changes help the mother's body switch from the pregnant to the nonpregnant state. Hormonal adjustments and fatigue are likely to cause the mother to become depressed during the postpartum period.

Both parents are likely to feel happy but tired. Emotionally and mentally, they are getting used to being parents. Physically, they are taking care of a newborn baby, which is demanding work that goes on around the clock. Despite their joy and delight with their baby, the parents of a newborn sometimes feel exhausted and irritable. These feelings usually go away once the baby is sleeping for a few hours at a time and the mother and father are able to resume some sort of daily routine.

Figure 9-14 *The parent–child bond grows strong as the newborn baby adjusts to its new life.*

CHANGES IN THE NEWBORN   The newborn baby has just made the biggest physical adjustment of its life. It has been pushed from its cozy watery environment, where it automatically received everything it needed, into a place where it has to breathe, cry, and suckle to survive.

During the postpartum period, the newborn's lungs and digestive tract begin to function for the first time. Its circulatory system and heart undergo changes to send more blood to the lungs, where the baby now gets its oxygen. Its nervous system reacts to new sensations: light, air against the skin, the touch of its parents, hunger, and pain.

Even a healthy, full-term newborn with an Apgar score of ten has a lot of work to do during the postpartum period. While its body is adjusting to life outside the uterus, the newborn is learning to get what it needs by forming a strong bond with its mother and father. Once bonding has occurred, the parents and child have become a family.

LESSON 3 REVIEW

1. What organ pushes the fetus out of the mother?
2. What happens during the second stage of labor?
3. Why is a newborn baby given an Apgar score?
4. Name one problem of pregnancy.
5. Name two factors that can result in complications during birth.

What Do You Think?

6. Babies who form a close, loving bond with their parents grow faster and are healthier than babies who do not form this bond. Why do you think this is so?

Coping with Change

Dolores and Miguel brought their first baby home from the hospital last week. They had been planning and looking forward to the birth of their first child for months. They are happy and excited about being new parents.

Both Dolores and Miguel, however, are experiencing some feelings they didn't expect. Dolores is tired all the time. She never seems to get enough rest. She has been up every night during the past week, giving the baby a two o'clock feeding. Miguel is feeling a bit resentful of all the attention the baby is getting. He and Dolores used to enjoy talking about their shared interests. Now it seems that all they talk about is the baby. How can they cope with all these changes in their lives?

Dolores and Miguel's response to change is a common one. Many people feel overwhelmed or frightened by new experiences—even if the experience is one they had been looking forward to. The period between the old and new ways of life, called the transition time, can be difficult. The following guidelines will help you deal with transition periods in your life.

1. Accept change as normal

Change is a natural part of life. Some changes are a result of your decisions; others, such as the death of a loved one, are beyond your control. In either case, the transition is often stressful.

Think of some examples of changes from your past. List the positive and negative feelings you had about each one. Add to your list the strategies that you used to make the changes part of your life.

2. Expect mixed feelings

Because some fear and loss accompany even the most desirable new experience, change usually brings mixed feelings. Review the mix of feelings in the list you just made.

When you are faced with a significant change, make a chart of the advantages and disadvantages the change will bring into your life. This "change chart" will help you understand your mixed feelings.

3. Understand your resistance

Moving on to "unexplored territory" is stressful, and

resistance is common. Check your "change chart" to see which disadvantages are actually the short-term stresses of making the change. These will disappear if you integrate the new situation into your life. Now circle the disadvantages over which you have no control. Remind yourself often that you must "let go" of things you cannot control.

4. Build an inside support system

(a) You are already experienced at dealing with change. Review your list of past changes to see how you can build on former successes and learn from the times when coping was more difficult.

(b) Focus on the positive aspects of the change you are now facing. Jot down the most important benefits and add a reassuring message, such as "I can handle . . . and feel good!" Place your list where you will see it often.

5. Build an outside support system

List friends and family whose support was helpful to you in the past. Let them know you would appreciate their support again. Don't be discouraged if some of them are unable to help this time.

Seek new sources of support. You may want to try organized groups that are working on similar issues, new friends, or counselors.

6. Start with small steps

Decide on a goal and put it in words, such as "feeling more a part of my new school." Take a small, positive step toward that goal, such as attending one meeting of one after-school club. Even a small step allows you to demonstrate that you can handle change in your life. Tell yourself, "Great job!" Reward yourself for your new accomplishment.

7. Work through setbacks

It is not unusual to feel odd or scared, even as you are making progress. You may want to go back to what was safe and comfortable. Instead, remind yourself of your past successes and the steps you have already taken toward your goal. Tell yourself that you can do it . . . and you can!

Apply the Skill

1. List the positive and negative feelings Dolores and Miguel may be experiencing. Identify the factors they cannot control. How would "letting go" help them accept the changes?

2. List the positive and negative reactions you felt for at least two major changes in your life. Did you use any of the strategies above in coping with these changes? Explain.

3. Think about a change you are expecting. List its benefits and drawbacks, your mixed feelings, and your support system. Then decide on a first small step toward making the change a part of your life. Explain your choice.

CHAPTER  REVIEW

KEY IDEAS

LESSON 1

- In deciding to have children, couples must consider their emotional, mental, and financial readiness to become parents.
- Responsibilities of parenthood begin before pregnancy. They include the practice of good health habits by the woman, and prenatal care.

LESSON 2

- Fertilization takes place in the fallopian tube. Implantation takes place in the uterus.
- The embryo and fetus are protected within a fluid-filled sac and receive oxygen and nutrients from the mother's blood. These substances filter through the placenta.

- The nine months of pregnancy are divided into three trimesters, or three-month periods.

LESSON 3

- Labor has three stages: the amniotic sac breaks and the cervix begins to dilate and soften; the baby is born; and the placenta is delivered.
- Complications of pregnancy include ectopic pregnancy, miscarriage, toxemia, and Rh incompatibility. Complications of birth include cesarean section and premature birth.
- During the postpartum period, newborns' bodies change so they can breathe, digest food, and react to the environment.

KEY TERMS

LESSON 1

adoption

contraception

infertile

prenatal care

LESSON 2

amniocentesis

chorion

chorionic villus sampling

embryo

fertilization

fetal alcohol syndrome

fetus

human chorionic
  gonadotropin (HCG)

implantation

morning sickness

placenta

ultrasound

umbilical cord

zygote

LESSON 3

Apgar score

cesarean section

ectopic pregnancy

fraternal twins

identical twins

labor

miscarriage

oxytocin

postpartum period

premature birth

prolactin

Rh negative

Rh positive

toxemia

Listed above are some of the important terms in this chapter. Choose the term from the list that best matches each phrase below.

1. hormone that helps the uterus to shrink after birth

2. the work of pushing the fetus out

3. the six weeks following birth

4. surgical method of birth

5. the organ that holds the embryo to the wall of the uterus

6. nausea and vomiting during pregnancy

7. mental retardation caused by mother's use of alcohol during pregnancy

8. hormone that indicates pregnancy

9. fertilized egg

10. the structure that carries nutrients and oxygen to the embryo

WHAT HAVE YOU LEARNED?

On a separate sheet of paper, write the word or words that best complete each statement.

11. Pregnancy is divided into three periods known as _____.

12. Two siblings that develop from the same fertilized egg are called _____.

13. A "picture" of the developing fetus can be made using high-frequency sound waves, or _____.

14. The developing embryo or fetus is enclosed in a bag of thin tissue called the _____.

15. Another name for conception is _____.

16. The legal procedure in which a child is taken into a family is _____.

17. A term used to describe medical care during pregnancy is _____.

18. The actual birth of the baby is known as _____.

19. A pregnancy in which the blastocyst becomes implanted in the fallopian tube is called an _____.

20. A problem of pregnancy characterized by high blood pressure, protein in the urine, and swelling is _____.

Answer each of the following with complete sentences.

21. What expenses do new parents have?

22. What are two ways in which infertile couples can explore becoming parents?

23. What kinds of disorders are detected by amniocentesis and chorionic villus sampling?

24. How does smoking harm the fetus?

25. Besides prenatal care, how can expectant parents prepare for the experience of birth?

26. What stage of labor is the longest?

27. Why is premature birth dangerous?

28. Name two adjustments that parents face during the postpartum period.

WHAT DO YOU THINK?

29. Rate (from 1 to 5 in order of importance) the following needs of children:

- knowing what to expect
- being loved
- food, clothing, shelter, and medical care
- having two parents who love each other
- having parents who earn a lot of money

30. If you were the baby-to-be, what might bother you about the statement, "Once I have a baby, the world will treat me like an adult"?

31. Should a pregnant woman go on a starvation diet if she has already gained 25 pounds by the seventh month of pregnancy? Explain your answer.

32. Many expectant parents keep pregnancy a secret until after the first trimester. What do you think is the reason?

33. Why do you think newborn babies cry a lot?

WHAT WOULD YOU DO?

34. Your aunt is two months pregnant and experiencing severe morning sickness. Her doctor will not prescribe medication to help her overcome her nausea. What would you advise her? Should she try an over-the-counter medication? Why or why not?

35. Your best friend has a twin of the opposite sex. The twins look a lot alike, and they tell everyone that they are identical twins. You want to explain to them that they cannot be considered identical twins. What reasons would you give?

Getting Involved

36. Find out what kind of diet is recommended for a pregnant woman and plan a full week of menus. Include snacks and vitamin and mineral supplements, if appropriate. Be sure you have planned an appropriate number of calories per day.

chapter 10

CHILDHOOD AND ADOLESCENCE

Enjoying activities with friends of all ages is an important part of your teenage years. During this time, both boys and girls go through physical, mental, and emotional changes as they move from childhood to adulthood. In this chapter, you will learn about these changes and ways to deal with them.

CHAPTER PREVIEW

10-1 Infancy Through Childhood

- Identify the developmental stages of infancy and childhood.

10-2 Changes in Your Body

- Describe puberty and reproductive maturity.

10-3 Changing from Child to Adult

- Name the physical, mental, and emotional changes that happen during adolescence and state how these changes affect identity and interpersonal relationships.

10-4 Adolescence and Responsibility

- Identify and describe new responsibilities taken on at adolescence.

BUILDING HEALTH SKILLS

- List ways of supporting a friend.

CHECK YOUR WELLNESS

See how many of these questions you can answer *yes* to.

- Do you understand and feel comfortable with the changes now occurring in your body?
- Are you able to accept those things about yourself that you cannot change?
- Do you recognize your strengths and feel proud of your accomplishments?
- Are you accepting more responsibilities?
- Do you do what is best for you even if friends urge you to do otherwise?
- Are your decisions consistent with your values and those of your family, religion, and community?
- Do you accept responsibility for your actions?
- Do you think about your future and how your current choices will affect you years from now?

KEEPING A JOURNAL

As you grow up, you take on more responsibilities. In your journal, identify some of the responsibilities you have today. How do they compare with the responsibilities you had three years ago? Five years ago?

Take it to the **Net**

INFANCY THROUGH CHILDHOOD

Focus on these questions as you read this lesson.

- What physical and mental changes occur between birth and age 3?
- What physical and mental changes occur from ages 3 to 12?
- What is the role of the parents in caring for children of these ages?

SKILLS

- Working in Groups

Figure 10-1 *Toddlers and babies grow and develop rapidly.*

As you grow up, you go through different stages of development. You develop both physically and mentally. For example, if you have young brothers and sisters, you have probably noticed that they do not behave, feel, or think the way older children and adults do. Babies and young children are not miniature adults. At each stage, the child's physical and mental development determines how it will interact with the other people in its life and with its environment.

Birth to Eighteen Months

Have you ever seen or held a newborn baby? A newborn is born with some physical skills. It can suckle, cry, and look right at you and see you—or direct its gaze. However, it will not learn to smile until it is about one month old. At birth, many of the baby's organs and systems are not fully developed. Its bones are still soft and flexible.

By the time it is 3 or 4 months old, the baby's brain, nerves, and muscles are ready for more coordinated movement. It recognizes its parents and siblings and can get what it needs by crying or responding to attention with obvious delight. By the time it is 18 months old, the baby has grown a great deal. It has probably learned to sit, crawl, stand, and walk and may be able to say a few words. It has "baby" teeth and can chew solid food. If you have ever lived with an

18-month-old child, you know how active they are. Most children this age have completed a stage of growth and development that will not be equaled until they are ready to change from child to adult.

Parents of babies between birth and 18 months have one main responsibility: the physical care of their child. Babies need to be held and touched. Without hands-on, physical nurturing, the child will not survive.

Eighteen Months to Three Years

You probably learned to talk between 18 months and 3 years of age. This is also the age when children lose their babylike appearances. Appetite decreases as growth slows down. Baby fat is lost, the arms and legs get longer, and physical coordination improves.

During this time, most children are learning to assert themselves and to manipulate objects, such as toys. They may show off around family and friends but be shy around strangers. When they are with others their age, toddlers tend to play alongside, but not with, each other. They are not ready to share or to play interactively because they are busy learning how to do things for themselves. Most children between these ages learn to use the toilet.

Physical care continues to be an important parental responsibility, but it is slightly less intense. The child is no longer helpless. The main parental responsibility at this stage is to "keep an eye on" the child at all times. People who take care of toddlers have to be alert, because toddlers are too young to know when something can hurt them.

Three to Six Years

Between the ages of 3 and 6, most children lose all traces of babyhood. They become more independent and active. Muscles grow, energy is high, and the curious child is "into everything." Communication skills advance rapidly. You can understand what most 4-year-olds are saying. By the age of 5, most children begin to lose baby teeth.

During this stage, children learn to play interactively and to make friends. They begin school and learn how to behave in a group. Between 3 and 6, most children start spending less time with their parents and more time with their peers and teachers. This transition is sometimes difficult, unless they have a good sense of security and receive reassurance from their parents.

Parents of children between 3 and 6 find themselves in the role of teacher. The child still needs reassuring touches and hugs, but times of physical contact are less frequent. These tend to occur during specific activities, such as at bath time or while reading the child a story.

Figure 10-2 *Children between 3 and 6 are curious about everything that surrounds them.*

Figure 10-3 *Between the ages of 7 and 12, coordination improves.*

Seven to Twelve Years

Try to recall some of the changes that occurred when you were between the ages of 7 and 12. Many of them were physical. For example, between the ages of 6 and 8, a child's facial structure changes with the appearance of permanent teeth. Muscles and bones continue to grow, and coordination develops further. Children between the ages of 7 and 12 master all sorts of physical activities, from climbing trees to performing ballet. What kinds of activities appealed to you during that time? Toward the end of this stage, the bones begin to grow faster, mostly in the legs. Appetite increases, and the process of sexual maturation begins.

Mental development continues during this stage, as children learn higher-level thinking skills. The self-centeredness of early childhood lessens, and children learn values, such as honesty and fairness. You may have started having responsibilities at home, such as chores, during this stage.

The approval of peers and the desire to fit in with a social group become all-important at about the age of 10. While this can be a problem, it helps many children to work well in group situations. Noise and enthusiasm are part of most group activities at this age. Having a best friend of the same sex is also important and will remain so into the teen years.

Parents of children between 7 and 12 have new responsibilities. Children at this stage need loving guidance, encouragement, and respect. **The responsibility of providing food, clothing, medical care, and shelter continues until the child grows up and leaves home.** Love and concern for the child's well-being continue for life.

LESSON 1 REVIEW

1. What is the main responsibility of the parents of an infant? How does this responsibility change as the child grows older?
2. Of the four stages of childhood, which involves the fastest growth and development?
3. Why do 2-year-olds not play together readily?
4. At about what age does the approval of peers become more important to a child?

What Do You Think?

5. You have just arrived to take care of a 20-month-old child for the afternoon. When the parents start to leave, the child begins to cry. The parents try to comfort the child by explaining where they are going and when they will be back. Who gets the most comfort from the explanation, the child or its parents? Why?

2 CHANGES IN YOUR BODY

If you were to compare a current photograph of yourself to one taken three years ago, you would notice many changes. From about the ages of 12 to 19, you gradually change from a child into an adult. This period of gradual change is called **adolescence** (ad l ES uns). As photographs can reveal, adolescence is a period of rapid physical growth. Photographs, however, can detect only some of the changes taking place. Important physical changes are also occurring inside your body during this time. All of these physical changes are controlled by the hormones of your endocrine system.

Puberty

Even before you read Chapter 8, you were probably familiar with the term *puberty,* although you may have heard it used in many different ways. Some people think that puberty is another word for adolescence; this is not correct. **Puberty is the period of sexual development in which the body becomes physically able to produce children.** Usually puberty begins before you reach adolescence and ends during mid-adolescence or later.

As you also know, the changes that occur during puberty are controlled by the pituitary gland and the ovaries (in girls) or the testes (in boys). Between the ages of 9 and 14, the pituitary gland signals the ovaries or testes to begin producing sex hormones. Figure 10-4 lists the hormones that play a role in puberty. Early in puberty, the body does not produce sex hormones consistently. As the glands mature, hormone production becomes more regular. Girls start to ovulate and menstruate, while boys begin to produce sperm. Ovulation in girls and sperm production in boys signal **reproductive maturity,** the ability to produce children. It is important to realize that many girls begin to ovulate before their menstrual cycles become regular. In fact, in some girls, menstrual cycles do not become regular for many years.

The sex hormones also cause the development of **secondary sex characteristics,** physical changes that occur during puberty that are not directly related to reproduction. In girls, the breasts begin to enlarge, and the hips start to widen. In boys, the voice begins to deepen, and hair appears on the face, the arms, the legs, and sometimes on the chest. In both sexes, pubic hair begins to grow around the external sex organs, and underarm hair appears. In addition, the skin begins to secrete more oils, and body odor increases.

Some adolescents feel overwhelmed by all of the changes that accompany puberty. You may suddenly find that you

GUIDE FOR READING

Focus on these questions as you read this lesson.

- What is the difference between adolescence and puberty?
- What are some physical changes associated with puberty?
- Why does the timing of puberty and growth differ among individuals?

SKILLS

- Finding the Facts

Figure 10-4 *How do these hormones affect the body during puberty?*

Hormones Involved in Puberty
Pituitary Gland
Follicle-stimulating hormone (FSH)
Luteinizing hormone (LH)
Ovaries
Progesterone
Estrogen
Testes
Testosterone

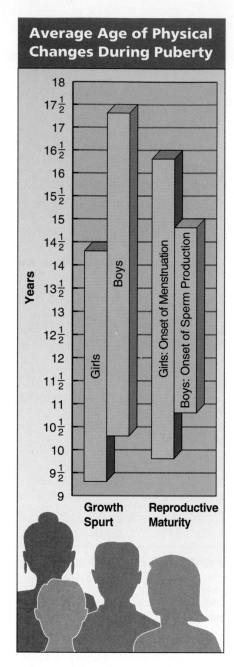

Average Age of Physical Changes During Puberty

Years

18
17½
17
16½
16
15½
15
14½
14
13½
13
12½
12
11½
11
10½
10
9½
9

Girls | Boys | Girls: Onset of Menstruation | Boys: Onset of Sperm Production

Growth Spurt | Reproductive Maturity

Figure 10-5 *The age range of normal physical development is wide.*

have acne, oily scalp and hair, and body odor. Regular bathing, shampooing, and deodorant use are important. Shaving may also become a regular part of adolescent boys' grooming habits. Girls may experience menstrual discomfort. Some adolescents have difficulty adjusting to their changing body shape. Some adolescents may be embarrassed or confused about the new sexual feelings they are experiencing. Having someone to talk to, especially a trusted older person, can help adolescents understand and accept their feelings.

Bone and Muscle Growth

Around the same time that puberty starts, the pituitary gland also increases its production of growth hormone, a chemical messenger that stimulates growth. You begin to get bigger. First your hands and feet grow, then your arms and legs. Growth does not occur in a regular fashion, but in spurts. Some months little growth hormone is produced, and you do not seem to grow at all. Other months there is a surge of growth hormone, and you seem to jump several shoe sizes in a very short time.

If you were to look at a group of young adolescents, you would notice that, for the most part, the girls are taller than the boys. The time line in Figure 10-5 shows why. As you can see, boys usually begin their growth spurt around the middle of their tenth year and may reach adult height during their seventeenth year. Girls, on the other hand, start to grow earlier than boys. On average, girls begin their growth spurt around the middle of their ninth year and may reach adult height during their fourteenth year. By the time adolescents reach the end of high school, the situation has reversed; for the most part, the boys have grown taller than the girls.

Changes in height are followed by changes in overall body structure. As puberty continues, boys generally develop wider shoulders and larger muscles than girls. Girls become more rounded as hips widen and breasts develop.

Many adolescents find it difficult to adjust to the changes in body proportion. Rapid lengthening of the bones in your arms and legs can be painful; some adolescents feel aches and cramps in their growing limbs. Most adolescents feel awkward at times. You may feel as if you are tripping over your own feet, or you may find you are no longer comfortable in your favorite chair. You may also find that you need to alter your posture and walking style to accommodate your new, adult proportions.

If you challenge your growing body with a variety of physical activities, you will adjust more rapidly to your new size and shape. Physical activity will also help to develop your muscles and coordination. As unlikely as it may seem, your feelings of discomfort and awkwardness will disappear soon.

You may notice one other effect that growth has on your body: it makes you hungry. Your family may remark that your stomach seems to be a "bottomless pit." This is normal during adolescence because you need extra energy to fuel your growing body. It is important, however, to eat nutritious meals and snacks to supply your body with energy it can use.

Figure 10-6 *Adolescence is a good time to learn to make some healthy snacks and meals for yourself.*

Early Bloomers and Late Bloomers

If you are like most adolescents, you have probably compared your own physical development to that of your peers. As you look around your classroom, you may wonder why your classmates are all at such different stages of physical development. Some of your classmates may already look like adults, while others may be just starting to show signs of puberty. Since they are all about the same age, what accounts for these differences?

The ages at which people mature sexually and grow to their adult height are determined by heredity. Chances are you are maturing at about the same age and speed as your parents did. Other factors that influence your unique timetable of development are nutrition and your overall state of health, including fitness.

Adolescents who develop at an early age, before most other adolescents, are sometimes called **early bloomers.** Those who develop at a late age, after most other adolescents, are called **late bloomers.** Most adolescents fall somewhere between these two extremes. Regardless of how you see yourself, sometimes you may feel envious of adolescents in the other groups.

Late bloomers may feel that early bloomers have an easier time than they do. This is not necessarily true. If a person is expecting the physical changes and is eager for them, being an early bloomer can be good. If the physical changes come

SHARPEN YOUR SKILLS

Finding the Facts

Use an outside source to find more specific information about hormones that control human growth and development. Summarize your findings in writing.

Childhood and Adolescence **225**

Figure 10-7 *Each of these girls is developing normally.*

as a surprise, however, being an early bloomer can be difficult. Early bloomers often feel the same self-consciousness and awkwardness that many adolescents experience. Since their friends have not yet experienced the same changes, it may be difficult for them to understand the early bloomer's feelings. Some early bloomers may even have to put up with some unsympathetic jokes and stares.

Since physically mature boys and girls look like adults, many people expect them to act like adults, too. Some early bloomers are mature enough to take on more responsibilities and handle these demands. Others do not have the emotional maturity to take on adult responsibilities. These demands, along with the physical changes, are too much for them to handle.

Late bloomers have a different set of problems to contend with. Because they look young, late bloomers may not be treated as adults by others, even if they are mentally and emotionally mature. Some late bloomers feel weak or inadequate when they compare themselves to their peers. Their peers may even make inconsiderate comments that worsen these feelings. Late bloomers may compensate in a number of ways. Some develop academic skills or become class clowns in an attempt to create a place for themselves among their peers.

Although they may not think so, most early bloomers and late bloomers are developing at a normal rate. If you turn back to Figure 10-5, you will see that "normal" includes early, average, and late physical development. Most adolescents worry that their development is not normal in some way. If you have these worries, you should tell them to your parents or your doctor. You are probably developing just as you should, but occasionally abnormal hormone production may cause accelerated or delayed puberty. In these cases, treatment usually can remedy the problem. Remember that these cases are rare. Everyone develops on his or her own schedule.

LESSON 2 REVIEW

1. What is puberty?
2. Name three ways that increased hormone production affects the body.
3. Explain why growth spurts can cause some adolescents to feel awkward.
4. Who is likely to begin puberty first, a boy or a girl?

What Do You Think?

5. In your opinion, is it more difficult to be an early bloomer or a late bloomer? Why?

3 CHANGING FROM CHILD TO ADULT

GUIDE FOR READING

Focus on these questions as you read this lesson.

- What are some of the positive and negative changes of adolescence?
- What are some mental and emotional changes that occur during adolescence?

SKILLS

- Analyzing Advertising Appeal

As you may have already realized, adolescence is a time of change. During adolescence, your entire body grows and changes until you look like an adult and you become able to produce children. In addition to these physical changes, you may also notice changes in the way you think, feel, and relate to others.

The News About Adolescence

Like most teenagers, you may be excited about some of the changes going on inside you. **Many positive and negative changes take place during adolescence.** The statements below capture some of the positive feelings. As you read the statements, see if any sound familiar to you.

"She thought I was in college!" The physical changes that occur during adolescence are exciting. As your body starts to look more like an adult's, you are expected to act more like an adult.

"I've got tickets to the concert!" Perhaps the most exciting thing about adolescence is your new independence. You are able to go places on your own, and you can decide for yourself how to spend your free time.

"I made the team!" Adolescence is also a time of discovery. You discover new talents and abilities that you did not know you had. These discoveries help you understand yourself and your abilities.

"I finally made up my mind." Learning to make choices is one of the most challenging tasks of adolescence. You realize that your decisions can have important consequences both now and in the future.

Unfortunately, not all of the changes that occur during adolescence are as positive and appealing as the ones you have just read. Some of the following complaints may also sound familiar to you. They show the not-so-positive side of adolescence.

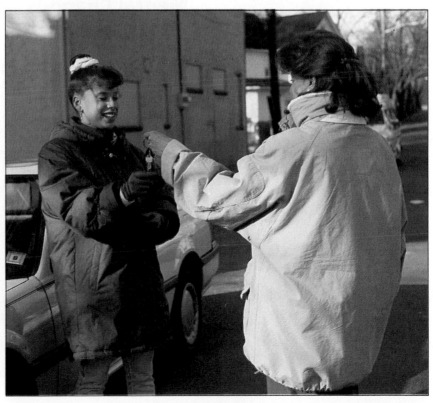

Figure 10-8 *Borrowing the family's car is one sign of an adolescent's growing independence.*

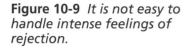
"Oh no! Not another pimple!" Some of the physical changes of adolescence are not exciting. Your face may break out. Your hair may become oily, and you may perspire more heavily. All of these changes may make you feel awkward and self-conscious.

"I'm in a really awful mood!" The physical and social changes you experience can make you feel "up" one minute and "down" the next. Your moods seem to change for no reason at all.

"I don't have a date for the prom." You may sometimes face rejection and disappointment. You may not be chosen for the team, or make the honor roll, or be accepted by the "in" crowd. Rejection happens to people of all ages, but it is especially difficult for adolescents.

"I don't know what to do." There are so many choices, and you have no idea which one is best for you. What should you do during your summer vacation? Should you take a job washing dishes at a restaurant, or should you volunteer as a camp counselor? Sometimes you face far more serious decisions. Should you do something you think is wrong just to go along with your friends? Will you lose your friends if you refuse? **Peer pressure,** a need to conform to the expectations of friends and classmates, can affect decision-making. Perhaps for the first time, you realize that decisions often involve giving up something. Making a choice is hard, especially if the thing you must give up is important to you.

Mental Changes

Did you know that between the ages of 13 and 15 the human brain reaches its full capacity to think and reason? If you are at this point right now, you are capable of thinking in ways that were not possible before. When you were a child, your thoughts and feelings were tied directly to your physical experiences at each moment. You thought about hunger

Figure 10-9 *It is not easy to handle intense feelings of rejection.*

Characteristics of Mature Thought

Thinking Skill	Definition	Example
Introspection	Looking inward; thinking about yourself and your own thoughts	I'm a good person, although I could be better in science if I studied.
Abstract thought	Thinking about ideas or objects that are not visible	Justice for all is difficult to achieve.
Ethical judgment	Making judgments based on your values and on others' intentions, rather than on how a situation affects you	He drove up on the curb and frightened me, but he did it to avoid hitting the dog.
Memory skill	Remembering details about objects and events	"Four score and seven years ago...."
Hypothesis testing	Approaching problem-solving by first predicting an outcome and then testing your prediction	If I ask about the dance when we're alone, I'll have a better chance.
Classification skill	Creating systems based on similar characteristics	Sharks and trout are fish, but whales are mammals.
Decentered thought	Understanding situations from someone else's point of view; considering the other person's intentions when you judge behavior	I would have been angry, too, if I thought he took my radio.
Use of symbols	Using one thing to stand for something else, such as an idea or object	X represents the unknown: 5 = 2 + X.
Deductive logic	Developing general ideas and then looking to the real, concrete world for specific examples	It is wrong to use people to satisfy one's own personal needs. That's why slavery was wrong.

when your stomach was empty and pain when you were hurt. Now, however, your thoughts and feelings are no longer tied only to your immediate experiences.

Your ways of thinking have begun to change. Now it is easier for you to predict consequences. You know, for example, that if you drop out of school, the action will change your life. Five years ago, you might not have been able to predict these changes.

Your ability to think is growing stronger. For example, your memory is improving. You also find it easier to use symbols to stand for something more complex. In math, you use x to represent an unknown quantity. Figure 10-10 lists other ways your ability to think is growing stronger. Can you think of times when you have used these thinking skills in school?

You use your new thinking abilities outside of school as well as in school. In fact, these skills affect your entire personal life. Your new mental skills may have changed some of the ways you have fun. You may become interested in more elaborate games, such as chess, that test your reasoning skills. You may start to enjoy participating in adult conversation on topics such as politics or world hunger. You

Figure 10-10 *Mature thought uses many different thinking skills. Which ones are your strengths?*

TV or History Paper?

Pros of watching TV:

I need to relax for a while.

My favorite show is on.

I want to watch TV

Cons of watching TV:

I won't get my paper done on time.

I will feel guilty about not writing my paper.

My grade in history will go down if the paper is late.

Pros of writing my history paper:

I will turn it in on time.

I will feel good about my decision.

My history grade might go up.

I will learn something.

Cons of writing my history paper:

I will not be able to relax for a while.

I will miss my favorite show.

I don't feel like writing it.

Figure 10-11 *Is this decision-making process familiar?*

may find that you enjoy fanciful discussions on topics such as "What if everyone in the world spoke the same language?" or "How are a fly and a tree alike?" If these kinds of questions interest you, it is because you now have the mental skills to think about them. You may find it fun to come up with your own questions and discuss them with friends.

Your new reasoning abilities will also affect the way you solve problems and make decisions. This is because you are now able to see more than one side of a question and to weigh the pros and cons of specific events. For example, if you were trying to decide whether to write your history paper or watch television, you might analyze the choices by making lists like the ones shown in Figure 10-11. You probably could not have made lists like these when you were a child.

Throughout adolescence, you will be trying out your new capacity for reasoning and decision-making. For example, in deciding whether to write your history paper or to watch television, you are deciding whether to enjoy an immediate pleasure or to do something that will be better for you in the long run. If you gain experience making wise choices in matters like this one, you will find it easier to choose correctly in more difficult situations later. For example, what if the person who drives you to a party gets drunk? Should you find another ride home for both of you, which may be difficult or embarrassing, or get into the car with a drunk driver, which may cost you your life?

Emotional Changes

As you grow physically and mentally, your emotional needs also become more like those of an adult. Adolescence is a time for questioning; you begin to question many things that you have simply accepted until now. You may also start to

Figure 10-12 *Adolescence is a time to look for meaning in life.*

question the values and actions of people around you, such as friends and family members. Most importantly, however, you may start to question yourself. Perhaps for the first time in your life you may wonder who you are, what you stand for, and what you will do with your life.

SEARCH FOR MEANING   It is not unusual during adolescence suddenly to question whether your friends are really true friends and whether happiness and love are possible to attain. These questions signal that you have begun to search for meaning in life. This search is important because in adolescence you are beginning to choose a way of life that is right for you. Some adolescents find answers to these questions by talking about them with parents or religious leaders. Other adolescents resolve these questions through their own experiences. Some adolescents volunteer their time to work in places such as hospitals, crisis centers, or runaway shelters. The experiences the adolescents have there often change the way they look at the world and help them decide what is important to them.

SEARCH FOR VALUES   Adolescents often begin to question the opinions and beliefs of others, especially those of their parents. This questioning helps adolescents discover their own **values,** those beliefs and ideals that are important to them and that help them clarify what they believe is right and wrong. Parents, teachers, clergy, and other adults can help you search for values. Although you may disagree with your parents at times, they can offer you guidance and serve as role models. For the most part, many of the values that adolescents eventually come to accept are similar to those of their parents.

SEARCH FOR SELF   Some of the most difficult questions that adolescents ask concern themselves and their place in the world. These questions are signs of a search for your **identity,** who you are. This search for identity may take many forms. At times you may sit and think about who you really are, comparing yourself to people you admire; or you may discuss the question with others. Sometimes you may try different personalities and behaviors in your daydreams. Other times you may actually try out new personalities by experimenting with new hairstyles, different clothing, and even new behaviors. Exploring your racial and ethnic traditions may be another important part of your search for identity.

Your search for identity is greatly influenced by your **self-esteem.** As you read in Chapter 2, self-esteem refers to how much you like yourself and feel good about yourself. How would you describe yourself? Do you feel good about yourself? Do you accept yourself for who you are? If you can answer *yes* to these questions, you have high self-esteem.

Figure 10-13 *Your identity can be expressed in unique ways.*

Figure 10-14 *During adolescence, it is important to feel good about yourself and the way you look.*

If you are like many adolescents, your self-esteem may not be as high today as it was a few years ago. Right now your feelings about yourself are strongly influenced by the opinions of others, particularly others of your age. You may worry about whether or not your peers approve of your clothing, your looks, your personality, and your interests. You may wonder whether or not members of the opposite sex find you attractive. You may worry about your looks.

It is not always easy to maintain a clear and consistent picture of yourself, even though you basically feel positive about who you are. Most adolescents, however, are able to recognize their strengths and achievements. Some teens find it useful to keep a private list of their accomplishments and talents. Then, when the question "Who am I?" comes up, this list supplies them with some good answers.

LESSON **3** REVIEW

1. Name three positive and three negative changes that may occur during adolescence.
2. How does decision-making in adolescence differ from that in childhood?
3. What are values? What factors influence the values developed during adolescence?

What Do You Think?

4. "Developing an identity is the most important task of adolescence." Do you agree with this statement? Why or why not?

DIFFERENT VOICES SPEAKING

Sixteen-year-old Milan Puente of New York City is a peer consultant for Madison Square Boys and Girls Club. Milan, who has swum competitively and enjoys volleyball, dreams of becoming a physical therapist.

Q. Milan, how did you first become involved with the club?

A. I started going there when I was six. I used to be shy, and my mother thought the club might bring me out of my shell. It's done that and more. It's helped me grow as a person and develop a sense of responsibility. Now, as a peer consultant, I get a chance to help other young people grow.

Q. What are some of your duties as a peer consultant?

A. One of my responsibilities is to bring other kids in from the community and beyond and make them aware of all the good things the club has to offer—there's a swimming pool, a gym, computers, people to discuss problems with. I also tutor kids in different school subjects and take part in the planning of special events and activities.

Q. What is an example of a special event run by the club?

A. I was recently part of a group effort among teens here to raise money for Hale House, a home in Harlem for abandoned babies with AIDS. What we decided to do was hold a carnival in the Madison Square gymnasium with all kinds of games and prizes. As an added bonus, we made the admission to the carnival three recyclable soda cans. That way, we were not only benefiting Mother Hale's babies but doing a little bit for the environment, too.

Milan Puente

Q. What prompted you to decide to raise money for AIDS babies?

A. AIDS is an important issue that too few people—young and adult—have opened their eyes to. The AIDS epidemic touches all of us. I recently read where the Surgeon General says there may not be a cure for a long, long time. It's pretty scary to think about.

Q. How did the carnival fundraiser turn out?

A. It was a great success: We raised a lot of money, and the kids had fun. The best part of all, though, was getting to visit Hale House and meet Mother Hale and see all the babies she cares for. They were so little and helpless. Many of them are born with drug addictions. It was an unforgettable experience.

Journal Activity

Milan's experiences at the club have helped her develop a sense of responsibility. Divide a page of your health journal into two columns. In the left column, identify some of the things for which Milan has been responsible (for example, planning a fundraiser). In the right column, identify a value of Milan's that each responsibility might reflect (for example, the importance of helping others).

4 ADOLESCENCE AND RESPONSIBILITY

GUIDE FOR READING

Focus on this question as you read this lesson.

- What are your responsibilities to yourself, your family, your friends, and your community?

SKILLS

- Activity: On Your Own
- Using "Win-Win" Negotiation

Adolescence brings increased privileges. You are treated more like an adult. Your opinion counts, and you make decisions that direct your life. However, the flip side of privilege is always responsibility. As an adult, you are expected to behave consistently and to assume responsibility for yourself and others. Often the move to this new status is not a smooth one. You may be anxious for the privileges but not so anxious for the responsibilities. Some days you may want to make all your own decisions; other days you may wish you could hide your head under your pillow and let someone older take charge. **Although the progress may sometimes seem uneven, your pathway to adulthood will be marked by your growing and expanding sense of responsibility.**

Responsibility to Yourself

During adolescence you become responsible for taking care of yourself. Eventually no one will tell you not to have those five candy bars. No one will force you to eat nutritious meals, exercise, or go to the dentist. You will have to decide when to wear your heavy jacket or whether to take your umbrella with you.

You will also become responsible for your own wardrobe, deciding not only what to take out of your closet every morning but also what to put in your closet when you go shopping. If you pay for some or all of your clothes, you will learn to manage your resources, including balancing your budget. You will also have to consider the "messages" particular styles send to others. Do you want your clothes to reflect your personal uniqueness or the identity of a group you belong to—or wish you belonged to?

While following the clothing styles of a particular "in-group" may be harmless fun, following all of their behaviors may have more serious consequences. Based on what you know is best for your own health and safety, you will have to make decisions about smoking, drinking, and drugs. Decisions about fad diets

Figure 10-15 *Learning to accept responsibility for yourself is a task of adolescence.*

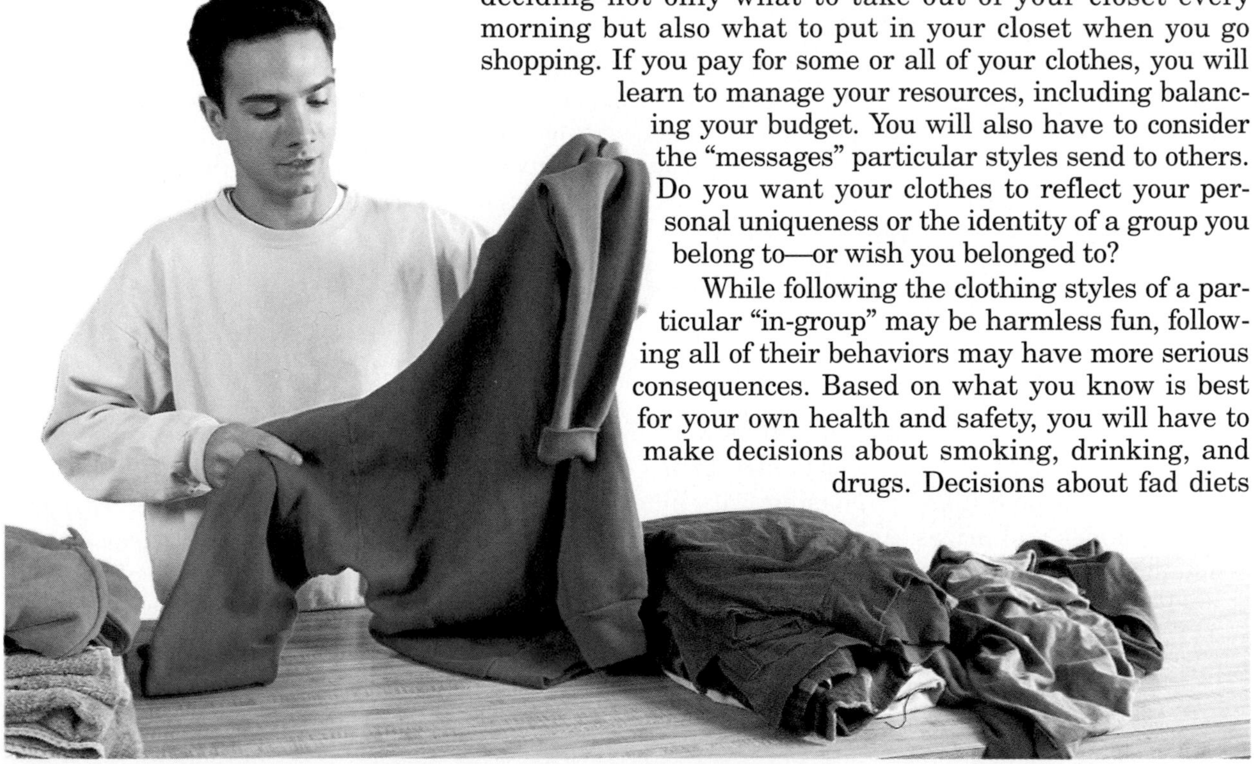

or after-school binges on junk food should also be based on your own health needs. You will also have to think about pressures to engage in sexual activity and the risks those behaviors involve. You will need to ask yourself, "What's most important for me right now?" You will also need to consider your family and community. Parents and other adults may make rules for you early in your teens, but eventually you will have to make these decisions on your own and take the responsibility for the results.

You will also be looking toward the future. Adolescence is a time to begin thinking seriously about career choices. During these years, you make many decisions that can affect your future career opportunities. You now know that you have to plan and work for what you want; these things do not just happen on their own. This means taking responsibility for your future in several ways. Your grades and course selection in high school are important for getting into college or other career-preparation programs. Being a high school graduate is essential to getting any good job. Volunteer work or part-time jobs can help you sample different kinds of careers or gain valuable experience.

ACTIVITY

ON YOUR OWN

In this activity, you will find out how much it would cost to leave home and live on your own.

Materials

employment ad section of newspaper

apartment ad section of newspaper

sample utility bills

advertising circulars from supermarkets

Procedure

1. Look through the employment ads, and find a job for which you think you are qualified. Write down the monthly salary, and then subtract 30 percent for taxes and other deductions. This amount is your spendable monthly income.

2. Look through the apartment ads to find out how much it costs to rent a one-bedroom apartment.

3. Use sample utility bills to estimate the monthly costs of electricity, gas, heat, and telephone.

4. Use the supermarket advertising circulars to estimate your total food costs for a month.

5. Estimate how much it costs to operate a car for a week, and multiply by four. Include gas, insurance, and repairs. Alternatively, calculate the cost of public transportation.

6. Estimate how often you like to go out for entertainment like movies and restaurants, and how much these would cost for a month.

7. Calculate how much you spend on clothing during a month.

Discussion

1. Total the amounts in items 2 through 7. Is it more or less than your monthly spendable income?

2. If your expenses are more than your income, what could you do to either increase your monthly income or decrease your monthly expenses?

Responsibility to Your Family

Your status in the family is changing. You may want and need more **autonomy** (aw TAHN uh mee), or independence. At the same time, your family is learning to treat you more like an adult. How does your new status affect your relationships within your family?

In many families, the family unit is valued more highly than individual autonomy. Teenagers in these families must find and fit into adequate roles within the family. This may lead to friction between generations, as parents expect adherence to the older ways and children are pulled the other way by their peers.

Despite the image of teenagers as angry, rude, and rebellious, most teenagers are happy, healthy people who value their families. Research shows that most families work out the conflicts that normally arise as teenagers strive for more independence. These conflicts are often visible in clothing styles. Most families work out these conflicts with some give and take. Showing respect for the feelings, tastes, and values of other family members in minor issues, such as hair and clothing styles, sets the stage for increased autonomy on other issues.

With increased autonomy comes increased responsibility. What are your responsibilities to your family? First, you may now be responsible for more of the physical work needed to maintain your household. You may need to learn new skills, such as house painting, grocery shopping, or laundering. You may be responsible for taking care of a younger brother or sister after school.

Figure 10-16 *Increased responsibility in family life is part of being treated like an adult. How do you help your family?*

Second, you are responsible for becoming more of a "giver" in your family relationships. You are mature enough to offer understanding and support to other family members. You participate more fully in the emotional life of your family. Is your sister's birthday next week? You can create or buy a present without being reminded.

Your third responsibility is to follow family guidelines about clothing, dating, and other activities. This does not mean that your parents make all of the rules all of the time. You can help your parents establish guidelines that are right for you. Look again at Figure 10-10. How many characteristics of mature thought will you need to use in negotiating guidelines with your parents? Just about every one of them!

Figure 10-17 *Taking care of younger brothers or sisters is one way that teenagers can contribute to their family's needs.*

Responsibility to Your Friends

In adolescence, you realize that friends are more than just people to have fun with. Friends are people who really listen when you talk and who are there for you when you have a problem. You have similar responsibilities to them. You should be willing to take time away from your other activities to help out a friend, to be a good listener, and to give comfort and encouragement when needed. You may also see some friends engaging in destructive or dangerous behaviors. When you have a real concern about a friend's health, safety, or well-being, you have a responsibility to intervene to try to help. Peer pressure—in spite of the way the term is usually used—is not always bad. You can use peer pressure to influence your friends in positive directions and to provide a network of concern and support in times of stress or crisis.

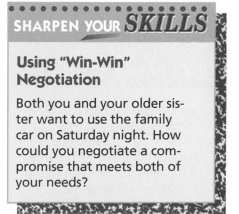

SHARPEN YOUR *SKILLS*

Using "Win-Win" Negotiation

Both you and your older sister want to use the family car on Saturday night. How could you negotiate a compromise that meets both of your needs?

Figure 10-18 *These two friends are testing water quality as part of a community project.*

Responsibility to Your Community

As you continue through your teen years, your interests will expand and so will your responsibilities. You will begin to see yourself as an important part of a larger community and recognize that your actions directly affect community life. For example, you appreciate clean streets and parks and buses that arrive on time. You like knowing that cars will stop at the red light when you are crossing the street. Now you are mature enough to see that these benefits depend on you and people like you. Littering, vandalism, disruptive horsing around on buses, or reckless driving endanger the quality of life that you want. Some of these irresponsible behaviors are also dangerous, and many of them are against the law. During your teens, you become responsible for knowing the laws of your community and for obeying them. You are expected to think about the effect that your actions will have not only on yourself and your friends but on the community as a whole. Acting responsibly is a way of showing your new maturity.

You may even want to go further in helping to improve your community. Participating in clean-up or fund-raising activities or giving more direct aid to less fortunate community members can be satisfying. During adolescence, many teens become more interested in public issues, and they find

ENGLISH CONNECTION

Read Judith Viorst's poem "If I Were in Charge of the World." What would you change if you were in charge of the world? How would the changes affect your life?

their actions can have a positive effect on their communities. You may start with school or neighborhood projects and organize petitions or write letters to local politicians or newspaper editors. Teenagers often become involved in political issues. They do volunteer work for candidates and causes they believe in. Involvement in community or political issues can be a positive, satisfying experience.

Eventually, you will have a say not only in local issues but in national elections, too. Your vote will mean as much as the vote of any other citizen, regardless of age. Becoming well-informed about candidates and issues and then exercising your right to vote will be a way of showing your sense of adult responsibility to your community.

LESSON 4 REVIEW

1. Why do adolescents have more responsibilities than children have?
2. To whom are you responsible in adolescence?
3. When you eat healthfully, exercise, and get enough sleep, to whom are you being responsible?

What Do You Think?

4. Sometimes you have to decide whether to be responsible to yourself or to your family. Describe a situation in which a teenager might have to choose between responsibility to self and responsibility to family.

Supporting a Friend

Ricardo has a part-time job after school. He just heard of an opening at work and immediately called his friend Luis to tell him about it. Ricardo told Luis the questions he was asked in his interview so that Luis could be prepared when he met the manager. Ricardo also talked to his boss to put in a good word for Luis. Ricardo knows that Luis really needs a job to help support his family because his father just lost his job.

What are all the ways you can support a friend? The guidelines that follow offer helpful suggestions.

1. Identify the ways you already support your friends

We offer many different kinds of support to friends—a phone call to see how they are, help fixing something, a ride to school, a sympathetic ear.

• Think of the important friends in your life. List the ways you think you support each of them.

• Ask yourself what else you could do to support them.

2. Offer support that empowers, not support that disempowers

Make sure that the kind of support you offer doesn't take power or responsibility away from your friend and make him or her feel helpless or incompetent. Support that empowers helps a friend to develop his or her own strengths and self-confidence.

• Offer help that builds your friend's strengths. Help him or her improve at a skill you may be good at. But also let your friend teach or help you with something in return. Empowering support is a two-way street.

• Encourage your friend when he or she tries something new. Compliment your friend on doing well.

- Be specific about what kind of support you want.

- Show your appreciation for what a friend does for you.

5. Encourage friends to ask you for support

- Ask your friends if you can help them. Offer suggestions for how you might help.

- Follow through on what you say you will do.

Apply the Skill

3. Listen carefully to your friend's needs

- Be an empathetic listener; don't be judgmental.

- If your friend asks for feedback, give it in a constructive way. First describe what your friend is doing well. Then offer suggestions for improving.

- If your friend is going through a difficult time, be especially sensitive. Make time to talk or spend time with him or her. Sometimes just being there can be helpful when people are doing something that is scary or hard for them.

- If your friend is doing something you think is dangerous or destructive, express your concern using "I" messages: "I feel … when you do.…" Offer specific help, and offer to go with your friend if you think he or she needs professional help.

4. Ask your friends for support

Friends are not mind readers. If you need or want support, ask for it. Show your friends that it is OK to ask for support. That will make it easier for them to ask you when they need it.

- Make a list of the ways you would like to be supported by your friends.

1. Make a chart showing all the ways you and your friends support each other. Review the chart. Are there any kinds of support you offer that take away power from your friend? How could you offer more empowering support?

2. For the next few days, do at least three things to support a friend. Also ask for support from one friend.

Friend	Ways I Support	Ways Friend Supports Me
Luis	• Tell him about job • Invite him to movies when he's having a hard time	• Practices soccer with me • Takes care of my younger brother when I want to go out
Carlos	• Work out with him • Help him with homework	• Gives me ride to school • Calls to see how I'm doing
Cristina	• Take her out to dinner • Teach her how to fix her bike	• Calls on phone and listens to my problems

CHAPTER 10 REVIEW

KEY IDEAS

LESSON 1

- Childhood is divided into four stages of development: birth to 18 months, 18 months to 3 years, 3 to 6 years, and 7 to 12 years.
- The responsibilities of parents change as a child grows older, but always include providing love and guidance as well as food, clothing, medical care, and shelter.

LESSON 2

- Puberty is the sexual development of the body that results in the ability to produce children. At the start of puberty, growth hormone stimulates bone growth in the hands, feet, arms, and legs. Growth continues in spurts until adult height is reached.
- Heredity, nutrition, and overall health and fitness affect the timetable of puberty, but the most important factor is heredity.

LESSON 3

- Mental abilities mature during adolescence. The ability to think and reason in new ways affects schoolwork, problem-solving and decision-making, and ways of having fun. Mental skills improve with use.
- During adolescence, teenagers often question values and opinions, search for meaning in life, and wonder about their identity. A teenager's identity is greatly influenced by the opinion of peers.

LESSON 4

- Along with increased privileges, adolescence brings increased responsibilities. The responsibilities of adolescence include responsibility to yourself, your family, your friends, and your community.

KEY TERMS

LESSON 2	LESSON 3	LESSON 4
adolescence	identity	autonomy
early bloomers	peer pressure	
late bloomers	self-esteem	
reproductive maturity	values	
secondary sex characteristics		

Listed above are some of the important terms in this chapter. Choose the term from the list that best matches each phrase below.

1. adolescents whose bodies develop at a later age than their peers

2. who you are

3. how much you like yourself and feel good about yourself

4. the time at which males and females have the ability to produce children

5. adolescents whose bodies develop at an earlier age than their peers

6. a need to conform to friends

7. independence from the influence or control of others

8. ideals, opinions, and beliefs that are important to you

9. the teenage years, which are marked by physical, mental, and emotional change

10. physical changes during puberty that are not directly related to reproduction

WHAT HAVE YOU LEARNED?

If the statement is true, write "true." If it is false, change the underlined word or words to make the statement true.

11. The process of sexual maturation begins between the ages of <u>3 and 6</u>.

12. The main responsibility of parents of babies between <u>birth and 18 months</u> is the physical care of their child.

13. Feeling independent is a <u>positive</u> aspect of adolescence.

14. The years during which you change from a child to an adult are your time of <u>infancy</u>.

15. The ages at which people mature sexually and grow to their adult height are determined by <u>heredity</u>.

16. The growth spurt starts when the <u>thyroid</u> gland increases its production of growth hormone.

17. The human brain reaches its full capacity to think and reason between the ages of <u>13 and 15</u>.

18. Ethical judgment is a thinking skill characteristic of <u>mature</u> thought.

19. As you gain independence during adolescence, your responsibility to your family and friends <u>decreases</u>.

Answer each of the following with complete sentences.

20. At what stage of development do children begin to share and make friends?

21. What changes occur in adolescence?

22. Why do growth spurts occur?

23. What physical change establishes reproductive maturity in girls? In boys?

24. By what ages do boys and girls usually reach adult height?

25. Define *introspection, hypothesis testing, decentered thought,* and *use of symbols.*

26. Why do adolescents go through many emotional changes?

27. Why is self-esteem important during adolescence?

28. Name two responsibilities you have to yourself, family, friends, and community.

WHAT DO YOU THINK?

29. In many cultures a special ceremony signals the end of childhood. What would be an appropriate ceremony in our society?

30. Name five physical activities you would encourage an adolescent to do as a way to challenge his or her new skills and strengths.

31. You are the parent of a teenager who "tries on" an identity you dislike. How could you show disapproval without destroying your child's self-confidence?

32. In your opinion, what is the most difficult thing about the adolescent years? Why? How could it be made less difficult?

33. What school assignments have you had that require mature thought?

WHAT WOULD YOU DO?

34. Your 1-year-old cousin is crawling around on the living room floor. The phone rings in the kitchen. What do you do? Why?

35. Your friend is short, and overall he still looks as he did in seventh grade. What advice would you give him?

36. You really want to play on the softball team, but you worry that your grades will suffer if you do. You can join the team and risk doing poorly, or not join and spend the time on your schoolwork. How would you decide?

Getting Involved

37. Find out what kinds of volunteer opportunities exist in your community. Sign up or make a commitment for one.

38. If your school has a peer help program, find out how you can become involved. If not, talk to interested teachers about the possibility of starting one.

Chapter 11

ADULTHOOD, AGING, AND DEATH

Adulthood is a time to work toward goals, to form and strengthen relationships, and to enjoy life. As you move through adulthood, you have a chance to think about and express new aspects of yourself. In this chapter, you'll learn about adulthood and the process of aging and about staying healthy and productive through all the stages of your life.

CHAPTER PREVIEW

11-1 Young Adulthood

- Discuss the tasks of young adulthood.

11-2 Middle Adulthood

- Identify the opportunities of the middle adult years.

11-3 Older Adulthood

- Describe ways to remain active during the older adult years.

11-4 Death and Dying

- Identify ways to cope with death.

BUILDING HEALTH SKILLS

- Name ways of identifying and setting goals.

CHECK YOUR WELLNESS

Are you beginning to prepare for your adult years? See if you can answer *yes* to these questions.

- Do you look forward to graduating from school and being on your own?

- Are you planning for an occupation that will use your interests and strengths?

- Have you chosen your school courses with your future goals in mind?

- Are you forming good habits now with your future health in mind?

- Are you developing hobbies and interests that you can enjoy for your entire life?

- Do you have positive goals for your life in 10 years? 25 years? 50 years?

KEEPING A JOURNAL

In your journal, write a description of your life at age 30. Include a discussion of your work, family life, and leisure activities. Then write similar descriptions of your life at ages 50 and 70.

Take it to the **Net**
www.phschool.com

GUIDE FOR READING

Focus on these questions as you read this lesson.

• What are some factors that affect physical aging?

• What is emotional maturity?

• What types of relationships are important in a young adult's life?

SKILLS

• Activity: Identifying Concerns

During the next few years, you will begin the transition from adolescence to adulthood. Some of you may have begun this change already. At what point do you become an adult? On a certain birthday? When you are financially independent? When you marry? When you finally become physically mature?

In general, Americans are considered to be adults legally at the age of 18 for some activities and 21 for others. From a physical and mental standpoint, it is difficult to say when adulthood begins. Change is an ongoing process from childhood to adolescence to young adulthood, and it continues throughout your life as an adult. In this chapter, young adulthood will be defined as the period between the ages of 20 and 40.

Physical Maturity

If you look up the term *adult* in the dictionary, you will find the definition "fully developed and mature." Certainly, most people reach **maturity** (muh TYOOR ih tee), the state of being full grown in the physical sense, by their late teens or early twenties. By this time, all of your body systems are fully developed, and you are as tall as you will ever be.

If you have been healthy and have had adequate nutrition and exercise, you are likely to reach your **physical peak** during young adulthood. Being at your physical peak means that your physical abilities are at their maximum levels. Measures of your physical abilities include strength, speed, and breathing and heart capacity.

Unfortunately, the image of a peak implies that all later changes will be downhill. Once you reach your maximum physical development, however, you can maintain your physical strengths for many years to come. You can do this by maintaining a healthy diet, getting adequate rest, exercising, having regular medical and dental checkups, and avoiding tobacco, alcohol, and other drugs.

Although you can remain at your physical peak for years, aging is a normal biological process. As your body ages, changes occur. **The rate at which physical aging occurs is influenced by many factors, including the factors listed in Figure 11-2.** For some people, physical aging may begin to be noticeable during young adulthood. As you age, your body gradually begins to slow and lose strength. Other early signs of aging include gray hair, balding, and wrinkles.

Figure 11-1 *Many people, such as pitcher Nolan Ryan, maintain their physical peak well beyond young adulthood.*

Emotional Maturity

What does acting like an emotionally mature adult mean? It means being independent, yet at the same time having close, loving relationships. It means expressing your feelings in a healthy way. It means being able to cope with stress or seeking help when you need it. It means enjoying life and continuing to change and learn new things. It means maintaining a positive image of yourself in spite of setbacks.

Your success in meeting all the tasks of adulthood depends on the physical and mental picture you have of yourself and your place in the world. If you have a strong, positive picture of yourself, you will be able to take your setbacks, as well as your successes, in stride. Knowing who you are—your skills, strengths, weaknesses, values, and beliefs—can help you to handle challenging situations. It can also aid you in seeking help when a problem is too much to handle alone.

No one acts in a mature, adult way all the time. Everyone has ups and downs, successes and defeats. Change is a basic element in every stage of life, including adulthood. How you adjust to the changes in your life is a major factor in determining how happy and healthy an adult you will be.

Vocation

One major concern of young adults is finding a vocation at which they are effective, productive, and satisfied. During adolescence, you think, plan, and prepare for your life's work. During young adulthood, you must make decisions and take actions. You must consider the income you need to earn to be

Factors That Affect Physical Aging

- Heredity
- Healthy behaviors
- Availability of good medical care
- Positive attitude
- Avoidance of diseases, injuries, and hazardous situations

Figure 11-2 *Which of these factors can you control?*

IDENTIFYING CONCERNS

In this activity you will role-play a conversation between a parent and a child who is leaving today for college.

Procedure

1. Choose a partner and decide who will role-play the part of the parent and who will role-play the child.

2. Prepare a list of concerns to bring up during your conversation. If you are the parent, what are your concerns about your child who is going away? If you are the child, what are your concerns?

3. Role-play the conversation, being careful to stick to the part you have chosen.

Discussion

1. Which of you found your part easier to play—the parent or the child? Why?

2. Who seemed to have the longest list of concerns? Did you both have some of the same concerns, but from different points of view?

3. Did you become aware of any concerns, as a result of the conversation, that hadn't occurred to you before?

self-supporting. You need to know what skills, education, and training are necessary to achieve your goal. If you are married and have children, you may need to juggle your work or school responsibilities with the needs of your family.

Although work can be rewarding, it also can be a source of stress. You may feel that you have no control over the kind of work you do; you may be fearful of being fired; you may worry that your business may fail; your work may prevent you from spending time with your family or friends. Using coping skills, such as those described in Chapter 3, can help you deal with the stress of work. An overly stressful job, however, may require a change of occupation.

Relationships

Young adulthood is characterized by several major psychological and social milestones. Perhaps one of the most important of these is the establishment of close, loving relationships with individuals outside your family. As you may remember from Chapter 2, the American psychologist Erik Erikson identified the search for intimacy versus a retreat into isolation as the central issue for young adults.

FAMILY RELATIONSHIPS   Young adults may live at home or away from home. Either way, parents and children must shift from a dependent child–parent relationship to a more independent adult–adult relationship. Young adults living away from home need to adjust to the separation from their families. Both young adults and their families may experience a sense of loss. Telephoning, writing, and getting together for special occasions can help ease the separation.

FRIENDSHIPS   You are more likely to form lasting friendships during young adulthood than during adolescence. Why? Because as a young adult you have a better sense of who you are. Young adults tend to choose friends with similar interests and values.

Friends provide you with companionship, entertainment, emotional support, and feedback about yourself. Friends are an important source of validation. Through **validation** (val ih DAY shun), you reassure a person that his or her feelings, ideas, or decisions are reasonable.

Suppose, for example, that a friend of yours has decided to enlist in the military. You might validate your friend's decision by telling him that his reasons make sense to you. In explaining why you agree with him, you may help your friend better understand the reasons behind his decision. If, however, you do not believe that his decision is best for him, you owe it to your friend to tell him so.

Figure 11-3 *Having a friend's support and reassurance is important during young adulthood.*

MARRIAGE AND PARENTHOOD Having a clear idea of who you are and trusting others are the basis for emotional intimacy. **Emotional intimacy** is the ability to share your innermost feelings with another person and have a caring, loving relationship. Being in a loving relationship means that you sometimes place another person's well-being and needs before your own. If you are in love with someone, you should be willing to compromise and make some adjustments and sacrifices for that person.

Nineteen out of twenty Americans marry at least once. Most of these marriages occur during young adulthood. People usually select marriage partners who are similar in age, education, and social background to themselves. Both men and women rate kindness, understanding, and intelligence as more important than physical attractiveness in selecting a mate.

You need to know yourself fairly well before you select a marriage partner. You need to know what your goals are and how you are going to achieve them. You need to know what is important to you. Some people continue their search for identity well into their 20s and 30s, and, for some, even beyond these years. These adults may not feel ready for marriage.

For other people, young adulthood is not only a time for marriage but also a time to become parents. The relationship between parent and child is critical to the development of a healthy child. In addition to food and shelter, children need loving care and attention. Young adults who become parents should be financially and emotionally ready to take on the responsibilities of parenthood.

Figure 11-4 *Before you marry, it is important to have a clear idea of who you are.*

LESSON 1 REVIEW

1. Name three factors affecting physical aging that you can control.
2. Describe two major issues that every young adult must resolve.
3. What is emotional intimacy?
4. Name three characteristics that are typical of emotionally mature adults.

What Do You Think?

5. Relate a recent conversation in which you gave or received validation.

GUIDE FOR READING

Focus on these questions as you read this lesson.

- What are some physical changes that occur during middle adulthood?
- What are some concerns of people in middle adulthood?

SKILLS

- Caring for Your Teeth

Middle adulthood is the period from about the age of 41 to the age of 64. Although you are years away from middle adulthood, you probably know people who are in this stage of life. What are your impressions of middle adulthood? Do you look forward to being middle-aged?

Physical Changes

By middle adulthood, physical signs of aging are more evident than they were in young adulthood. Graying and thinning hair and impaired vision and hearing are likely to affect all middle-aged people at some point. During these years, hormonal changes also occur within the body.

During middle adulthood, the production of sex hormones in both men and women gradually slows. This gradual change in hormone production, called the **climacteric** (kly MAK tur ik), takes place over a period of three to eight years. For women, the result of the climacteric is menopause, which is the end of menstruation. After menopause, women no longer release mature eggs and therefore cannot become pregnant. For some men, the climacteric is marked by reduced sexual activity, although men continue to produce sperm throughout their adult lives.

Concerns and Relationships

Middle adulthood is a time to share, apply, and benefit from the experiences you gained during young adulthood. For many people, middle adulthood is a time of peak professional ability and creativity.

Figure 11-5 *Although all of these people are in middle adulthood, they show varying degrees of aging.*

GENERATIVITY Erik Erikson identifies the central task of middle adulthood as **generativity** (jen ur uh TIV ih tee). Generativity means that people shift their concern from themselves in the present to the welfare of others in the future. Generativity is the ability to care for other generations, to direct your energy toward the welfare of others, while maintaining your own self-esteem and personal identity. During middle adulthood, you may be very busy taking care of children or aging parents, or both. By participating in community projects, you may work to improve your community. You may become politically active outside of your community. You may share your knowledge and experience with others. During this time, you find a balance between meeting your own needs and contributing to the welfare of others. The reward of generativity is the knowledge that you have done your best to make the world a better place.

SELF-EVALUATION It is common for people in middle adulthood to go through a period during which they evaluate their lives. This period of self-evaluation often occurs because adults realize that they are not going to live forever and they may not achieve all of their goals. During this period, people may compare the dreams they had during young adulthood with their actual accomplishments. They may ask themselves questions such as:

- Have I accomplished what I set out to do?
- Is my work satisfying?
- Is my marriage satisfying? Does my spouse really love and understand me?
- What do I want to do that I haven't already done?
- Have I done anything to make the world a better place?

Because questions like these can create anxiety, this period of self-evaluation is sometimes called the "mid-life crisis." It is through these types of questions, however, that people begin to evaluate their lives. For some, mid-life crises lead to change. A person may decide to take a new direction—change careers, return to school, or travel. For others, mid-life crises are times to appreciate what they have and to make their goals more realistic.

The likelihood of experiencing a mid-life crisis depends on your expectations, your sense of control, and your financial, social, and emotional resources. Do you expect your adulthood to be characterized by few changes, or do you understand that change is an element in all stages of life? Do you feel in control of your life, or do you think there is nothing you can do to direct your life? Are you able to overcome setbacks? Do you have family and friends on whom you can rely? If you realize that change is a part of life, and if you have the emotional resources to deal with change, you probably will experience only a healthy period of questioning and re-evaluation. Instead of a cause for crisis, the changes that

Figure 11-6 *Middle adulthood is a time when interests shift to the welfare of others.*

SHARPEN YOUR SKILLS

Caring for Your Teeth

Many people used to think that losing one's teeth during middle adulthood or old age was unavoidable. However, proper care of your teeth and gums can help your teeth last a lifetime. For information on care of the teeth, see Building Health Skills for Chapter 14.

Figure 11-7 *Many middle-aged couples experience a renewed interest in romance.*

occur during middle adulthood can be opportunities for growth and challenges that you can meet with optimism.

RELATIONSHIPS   The need for close relationships in middle adulthood is the same as it is in young adulthood. You do not outgrow your need for romance, close friends, or caring family relationships. Now, however, you may be concerned with your grandchildren and responsible for the care of your elderly parents.

One myth of middle adulthood is the "empty nest" feeling of sadness and worthlessness that occurs when children leave home. Most parents, of course, miss their children when they leave home. Many, however, view this time of life as an opportunity to participate in favorite activities, to spend time with friends, and to renew romantic love in their marriages. For some parents, the "empty nest" is delayed; more than half of all young adults aged 18 to 24 live at home with their parents.

LESSON 2 REVIEW

1. What external and internal physical changes occur during middle adulthood?
2. What is generativity?
3. Explain how self-evaluation during middle adulthood can affect people in a positive or negative way.

What Do You Think?

4. How can you help a parent or other close adult who is going through a mid-life crisis?

DIFFERENT VOICES SPEAKING

After retiring in 1974 from his position as Executive Director of the Urban League of Boston, Edward L. Cooper wanted to remain active in his later adult years. Now 89, Mr. Cooper is involved full time as director of Boston Urban Gardens, the inner-city garden project he founded.

Q. Mr. Cooper, please describe Boston Urban Gardens.

A. I like to think of the garden as an oasis in the heart of a low-income community. It occupies 20,000 acres and includes flower gardens and vegetable gardens. We're in the process of developing a canning facility. The project has come a long way from the debris-covered vacant lot I started out with.

Q. How did the project get its start?

A. When I retired at the age of 71, my initial thought was to bring together senior citizens

Edward L. Cooper

from the Highland Park section of Boston, where I had lived much of my adult life. I figured I would need some kind of gimmick to get people interested in coming to meetings. Since most people in Highland Park are African Americans from either the Deep South or West Indies, a garden seemed to be just the ticket.

Q. What significance does gardening hold for people from these areas?

A. Down South and in the islands, gardening is almost a way of life. I myself grew up in North Carolina, in a family with ten children. We had to get up at five o'clock every morning to pick string beans. Ironically, I remember at the time swearing that I would never tend a garden when I got older. After my retirement, however, when I had time to think, I became nostalgic; I wanted to get involved with the

good earth again. I will tell you, it sometimes amazes me just how little city children know about raising a tomato when they first get involved in Boston Urban Gardens.

Q. There are young people involved in your program, then?

A. Oh my, yes—hundreds of them! They come to see our gardens and greenhouses. Many of them stay to work with us. They learn a lot spending time with us.

Q. What do you think is the most important thing that young people learn?

A. I would like to think it's that senior citizens can make a difference. I believe that if more young people worked side by side with older people, the combination of wisdom and energy would make the world a great place.

Journal Activity

Edward Cooper's "oasis" demonstrates what people in older adulthood can accomplish. In your health journal, write a proposal to the officials in your city or town for a project in which senior citizens can work side by side with young people. Focus on something that will beautify or in some other way improve the quality of life in your town.

Focus on these questions as you read this lesson.

- What are some stereotypes about aging?
- What are some physical changes that occur during older adulthood?
- What are some concerns of people in older adulthood?

SKILLS

- Locating Community Resources

Figure 11-8 *Regular exercise can benefit people of any age.*

3 OLDER ADULTHOOD

Older adulthood, the period from age 65 on, now lasts longer than ever before. In your great-grandparents' time, life expectancy was only about 47 years. People born today can expect to live about 75 years. You also can look forward to being healthier and more active than older adults in the past.

In recent years, many of the stereotypes about aging have been shown to be false. Study the myths and facts about older adults listed on the next page. Which facts are new to you?

Physical Changes

Physical changes continue in older adulthood. These changes include increased wrinkling and the loss of skin elasticity. **Elasticity** (ih las TIS ih tee) refers to how well your skin molds to your body or snaps back into place when pulled. New signs of aging, such as age spots (darkened areas of the skin), may appear on the hands, face, and scalp. For men, a receding hairline and thinning hair may occur. For both men and women, the hair turns gray or white and loses some of its luster. As blood vessels weaken, older adults may bruise more easily and heal more slowly. As hormone production decreases, height and weight may decline. The senses of sight, taste, hearing, and touch gradually become less acute.

Aging also occurs inside the body. Many of the body systems slow down and become less efficient. Nevertheless, most older adults retain the ability to meet the demands of everyday life. Recent research has shown that exercise prolongs life and keeps older people healthy. Many older adults continue to work, travel, and pursue active sports, such as swimming or bicycling. Older adults can receive benefits from starting an exercise program, no matter what their age.

PHYSICAL DISEASES The most common diseases among older adults are heart disease, cancer, stroke, and lung disease. Many of these diseases are related to the health behaviors you choose now. Most of them can be treated in people of any age.

One of the body systems weakened by the aging process is the **immune system,** the human body's disease-fighting system. As a result, common infectious diseases, such as pneumonia and flu, are more threatening to an older adult. Older adults should take preventive measures, such as getting flu shots, to reduce their risk of death from infectious diseases.

Older Adults

1. **MYTH:** Old people complain a lot about their physical ailments.

   ● **FACT: Most elderly people report that they feel well and healthy most of the time.**

2. **MYTH:** Most older adults live in nursing homes and cannot get around by themselves.

   ● **FACT: Only about 5 percent of elderly people live in nursing homes, and fewer than 20 percent of elderly people are unable to get around by themselves.**

3. **MYTH:** Older adults do little more than sit around, watch television, and sleep.

   ● **FACT: Senior citizens have many interests and sleep fewer hours per day than most younger adults.**

4. **MYTH:** A large majority of people over the age of 65 regret being retired.

   ● **FACT: Most people over 65 say they are enjoying their retirement years.**

5. **MYTH:** Older adults who continue to work are inefficient and miss many work days due to illness.

   ● **FACT: Senior citizens are extremely productive workers and seldom are late to or absent from work.**

6. **MYTH:** Older people are forgetful, and they have trouble learning new things.

   ● **FACT: Aging has little effect on people's mental capabilities; older people are not unusually forgetful nor do they have trouble learning new things.**

7. **MYTH:** Old people tend to be lonely and often feel depressed.

   ● **FACT: Most older adults are content with their lives and are not lonely.**

8. **MYTH:** Most people over 65 have a physical disease or disorder that limits their freedom to do what they wish.

   ● **FACT: Most elderly people are healthy and physically active.**

9. **MYTH:** Older adults normally have no interest in members of the opposite sex.

   ● **FACT: The need for intimacy and loving relationships with members of the opposite sex does not diminish with age.**

10. **MYTH:** Older people are obsessed with dying and fear death more than people in any other age group.

    ● **FACT: Although older adults know that they will not live forever, the majority fear death less than any other age group.**

Parkinson's disease strikes one out of every 100 people over age 60. This serious illness is characterized by a progressive loss of normal muscle function. The muscles become stiff, causing shaky movements. People with Parkinson's have a low level of the brain chemical dopamine. Some cases seem to be related to environmental factors, such as toxic chemicals; others may result from a mutated gene.

Another major disabler of older adults is **arthritis.** Arthritis attacks the body's joints, making simple tasks, such as holding a pencil or climbing stairs, extremely painful.

About 10 percent of older adults suffer from **dementia** (dih MEN shuh), a group of symptoms characterized by loss of mental abilities, abnormal behavior, and personality changes. Dementia seems to have a variety of causes, including a lack of important nutrients, a physical injury to the brain, a stroke, and several drug interactions. Many of the

Many people continue or even begin to demonstrate their creativity during old age. For example, the Italian painter Titian (1488?–1576) painted into his nineties. Michelangelo (1475–1564) was working on a sculpture less than a week before his death at age 89. And the American painter Anna Mary Robertson Moses (Grandma Moses) had her first one-woman show in 1940, when she was 80 years old.

disorders that cause dementia can be treated. Therefore, thorough testing and diagnosis are necessary.

Alzheimer's disease (AHLTS hy murz) is a form of dementia that involves the degeneration of brain cells. Probable causes seem to be vascular disease, several small strokes, bacterial infections, or a buildup of protein in the brain. There is no cure, but some drugs seem to slow the progress of the disease. Alzheimer's is uncommon in middle adulthood, but the risk of the disease rises with age. About 17 percent of people above age 85 suffer from Alzheimer's.

An accurate diagnosis of Alzheimer's cannot be made on a living patient. However, the usual first symptom is forgetting things that occurred very recently. Later, mental confusion, frustration, and helplessness may become a problem as the person gradually loses their ability to function both mentally and physically. At this stage, the person may need as much care and attention as an infant. The survival rate for Alzheimer's varies from a few years to 10 or more years.

OSTEOPOROSIS   The bones of older people tend to break easily and heal slowly. This is due to **osteoporosis** (ahs tee oh puh ROH sis), a condition in which bones become weak and brittle. Osteoporosis is caused by a loss of bone calcium, the substance that makes bones strong and hard. Exercise and a diet high in calcium-rich foods help prevent osteoporosis. Teens can reduce their risk of osteopo-rosis by drinking an extra glass of milk each day. Once osteopo-rosis occurs, preventive measures, such as installing railings along stairs and bathtubs, can reduce the chance of falls.

Concerns and Relationships

Older adulthood is Erikson's eighth and final stage of psychological and social development. According to Erikson, this is a time for people to pause and reflect upon their lives. What have they accomplished? What do they still wish to do? Have

Figure 11-9 *Most adults remain active and alert throughout their lives.*

they had a positive effect on other people in their lives? What wisdom have they acquired? A positive outcome of this self-evaluation leads to a sense of wholeness, acceptance, and optimism. A negative outcome leads to a sense of despair and hopelessness.

INTEGRITY   Erikson says that the chief task of older adults is the achievement of **integrity,** the stage of feeling complete. This means reviewing your life and accepting the good and the bad without regrets. In short, achieving integrity means you feel content.

Older adults are likely to achieve integrity if they continue to be psychologically intimate with others and committed to something, such as family, friends, religion, or career, that gives meaning to their lives. Being part of a family or group and feeling confident and optimistic about their lives are other measures of integrity for older adults. Adults who achieve integrity are not only able to accept death, they are also able to enjoy the time they have left.

INTELLECTUAL SKILLS   Although there are some changes in mental functioning during older adulthood, these changes usually have little effect on thinking, learning, or long-term memory storage. The brain remains open to change and to learning. In fact, evidence suggests that the aging process can be slowed by keeping the mind active and challenged. Most older adults are fully capable of continuing stimulating intellectual work. Some choose to continue working; others decide to develop new interests or extend their educations.

SHARPEN YOUR SKILLS

Locating Community Resources

Many communities offer special services and programs for older adults. Find out what groups or agencies serve the older adults in your community and what programs they offer. Report your findings to your class.

Figure 11-10 *Older adulthood can be a time to develop new interests.*

Figure 11-11 *Retirement gives older adults an opportunity to spend more time with loved ones.*

RETIREMENT Although some people continue to work after the age of 65, many people retire. For most people, retirement is a time to try new activities and reexamine their life goals. Many retired people use the time to start new careers, expand their schooling, learn new hobbies, or spend more time with family and friends.

RELATIONSHIPS Like all adults, older adults need close and loving relationships with family members and friends. It may require additional effort and adaptability on the part of older adults, however, to meet these needs.

Because women tend to live longer than men in this country, it is likely that a woman will be widowed before a man. Either way, the loss of a mate is a major setback. The older adult must prepare for this by making an effort to maintain close relationships with others. It is not uncommon for a widowed person to start a new relationship with someone of the opposite sex. Loving relationships do not stop with the onset of old age.

To maintain loving family ties, both older adults and their children and grandchildren need to make an effort to see one another and to share experiences. The rewards of this effort can be great. Grandparents may have the time to take special outings with grandchildren or teach them skills they enjoy such as fishing or cooking. For older people who lack grandchildren, programs such as the Foster Grandparents program put older people in touch with younger people.

There are many other opportunities for social contact for the older person. Some communities have clubs to bring together older adults. A shared hobby can be a source of new friends. Some colleges and universities provide reduced tuition programs for people over 65. The Elderhostel program arranges travel at low rates. Many schools and cultural institutions encourage older adults to work as volunteers. In fact, older adulthood can be a most rewarding time of life.

LESSON **3** REVIEW

1. List three health problems that older adults may face.
2. What is meant by achieving integrity?
3. Name four stereotypes about aging and explain why they are false.
4. Describe three ways older adults can make the last stage of the life cycle challenging and rewarding.

What Do You Think?

5. Think of two ways that you could make the time you spend with an older person, such as a grandparent, more enjoyable and memorable.

4 DEATH AND DYING

Death is part of the normal cycle of all living things, including humans. No amount of fame, money, or love prevents death. While death marks the end of life, dying is a part of living.

Death with Dignity

As strange as it sounds, the process of dying has changed since the time of your great-grandparents. Until recently, most people died in their homes, surrounded by family and friends. The medical advances that have lengthened the average life span have also given doctors the ability to prolong the life of a dying person. This has created new concerns about death. Should a dying person's life be prolonged indefinitely, even when the person's mental and social life has ceased? Because of questions like this, many adults find that they fear the process of dying more than they fear death itself.

A program that provides physical, emotional, and spiritual care for dying people and support for their families is called **hospice** (HAHS pis). To make hospice affordable, most of the workers, except for medical personnel, are trained volunteers. Hospice workers visit the dying in hospitals, nursing homes, or at home. Some hospice programs have their own facilities where dying patients can be given round-the-clock care by hospice workers. Hospice workers help patients and their families to accept death and to enjoy the time that is left as much as possible.

GUIDE FOR READING

Focus on these questions as you read this lesson.

- What are the five stages of dying?
- What are some ways to cope with a dying loved one?

SKILLS

- Supporting a Friend

Figure 11-12 *Hospice workers encourage terminally ill patients to enjoy the time they have left.*

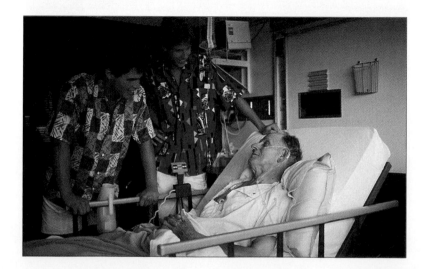
The Stages of Dying

A **terminal illness** is one that results in death. The way people cope with terminal illness depends on their expectations, their psychological strengths, and the reactions of loved ones. Elisabeth Kübler-Ross, a psychiatrist, studied the reactions of terminally ill people and their families to dying and death. **Dr. Kübler-Ross found that people experience five stages of dying: denial, anger, bargaining, depression, and acceptance.**

1. First, denial: "Oh, no, not me."
2. Second, anger and envy of healthy people: "Why me? Why not someone else?"
3. Third, a tendency to bargain or try to postpone death: "If I am good and give up drinking and cigarettes, I'll get better and live."
4. Fourth, depression or a sense of loss: "I can't work, I can't care for my children, I hurt all the time. I feel worthless. What's the use?"
5. Fifth, acceptance: "Soon this will be over. I'm ready. I've said all my goodbyes."

Other research has shown that not everyone reacts to death in the same way. Some people do not experience all five stages; others may experience them in a different order.

Coping with a Dying Loved One

Suppose your grandparent, parent, or friend is dying. You may find yourself going through some of the same emotional stages that the dying person experiences: "Oh, no, it can't be her turn to die! It's all a mistake." "Why him? Why couldn't it be someone else?" "If I am really good, maybe I can prevent her from dying." "Oh, I can't stand to see him suffer so much. Maybe it will be better when death finally comes."

Figure 11-13 *Visiting and talking openly with a dying person is a good way to show how much you care.*

Most people are uncomfortable with death and dying. Some may try to cover up their grief by false cheer. Others may keep away. Silence or absence helps neither the family nor the dying person. What should you do if a person close to you is dying? Focus your energies on the dying loved one. Visit the person as often as you can. Talk about your plans and hopes, even though that person will not be there to share the future with you. Listen to what the dying person has to say. Let him or her talk about the past.

Most dying people want to talk about what is happening to them. Do not be shy about discussion of death. If death frightens you, think of the dying person as someone who is about to set out on a long journey. You want to share your feelings of loss before a loved one goes. You may want to ask about the journey.

What if the dying person is in a coma, a state of deep unconsciousness? Does it matter whether you visit? Some people who have survived comas say they remember some events that occurred while they were in the coma. Touching and talking can help you, and perhaps the person can feel your touch and hear the words you speak.

Dealing with your own grief is not easy. There is no quick solution. You must not become so overwhelmed that you forget to take care of yourself, but at the same time, you should not deny how you feel. Talk about your loss with family and friends. Describe how you will miss the dying person. Think of how you would like to remember the person. Continue your usual routine as much as possible and include visits with the dying person. Also allow yourself some time to let go and grieve.

Your love for another person is a great tribute to that person. When a person is dying, your time to express your love is limited; you should use it well. Say all the loving, sad, and funny things you can think to say while you still have the opportunity. Make dying a time for loving and sharing, not loneliness and despair.

LESSON 4 REVIEW

1. What is a terminal illness?
2. What are the advantages of a hospice program?
3. Briefly describe the five stages that people may experience after they find out that their illness is terminal.

What Do You Think?

4. Suppose you have been told that you have only six months to live. Describe how you would like your family and friends to treat you.

Focus on Issues

Should People Have a Right to Die?

Most people prepare for death by writing a will, which tells how their belongings should be distributed. Now some people are also writing a second will known as a living will. A living will is highly controversial because it directs a person's family and health-care professionals not to use extreme medical means to prolong life if he or she becomes terminally ill.

Some people feel that individuals should have the right to die if they choose. They say that keeping a terminally ill person alive is just prolonging death, not life. They feel that this is cruel to both patients and their families. It is also extremely costly.

Other people feel that all individuals must be given every possible chance for life. Some of these people fear that financial considerations may influence a person's decision not to want to be kept alive. The fear that family savings will be used up may cause a person to decide to refuse expensive treatment. Living wills also do not cover cases of terminally ill infants or adults who have not made their feelings known.

☞ Do you think people should have the right to refuse medical procedures that would prolong their lives?

BUILDING HEALTH *SKILLS*

· ·

Setting Goals

Now that Mario is a senior in high school, everyone is asking him about his goals. When his uncle tells him to consider "where he'll be in ten years," his father complains that Mario doesn't know where he'll be next week. At school, Mario's advisor wants him to choose his courses in light of his college goals, and his girlfriend is concerned about whether or not he's going away to school. His best friend Joe keeps saying this year is their last chance to party before they have to act like adults.

Mario knows he should start looking ahead, but how far ahead? He's always said he wants to be an architect, but he's never done anything about it. His attention and energies seem to skip from one thing to another.

The following guidelines could help Mario focus his energies on achievable goals. You can use them, too, to help set your own realistic and reachable goals.

Discussing your goals with friends can help you determine what is most important to you.

1. Know yourself

Before deciding on specific goals, jot down what you know about yourself. What are your long-term interests? What activities do you enjoy? What are your abilities? What are the most important things in your life? Goals that correspond to your interests and values will be more desirable. Goals tied to your abilities will be easier to reach.

2. Make goals clear, specific, and positive

A clear, specific, positive goal accurately describes what you want to be doing when you achieve it. It describes an observable, measurable behavior. "I want to get all Bs this term" is clearer than "I want to do better in school." It allows you to measure your success by counting the number of Bs you receive. How do you measure "doing better"?

Getting all Bs is also more specific than the negative "I don't want any Fs this term." It is future-oriented, giving you something to strive for. Positive goals are like signposts ahead. You are able to measure your progress toward them, and each one is an achievement when you finally reach it.

3. Include deadlines

Set a reasonable time limit for your goals. Deadlines make goals more specific, add a sense of urgency, and provide a good way to measure success. If you cannot meet the deadline, you may need to consider a more realistic time limit. For example, if you were able to raise four out of five grades to B this term, this would be good progress, not failure. The goal of earning all Bs should be rescheduled for next term.

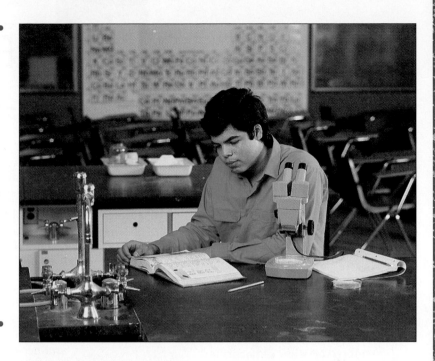

4. Break long-term goals into small steps

Long-term goals, such as running the marathon, should be broken into smaller, more manageable, measurable steps. Future marathoners begin their training with short distances. Only when they have built the speed and endurance necessary for long distances do they go on to run the full marathon course.

5. Keep written goals visible

Write your goals down. Then tape them to your closet door, mirror, notebook, or other place you look at frequently. This repeated reinforcement of a goal will keep you focused on achieving it.

6. Evaluate your progress

At times, stop and ask yourself if you are making progress toward your goal. If so, good. If not, how can you get on track?

Apply the Skill

1. Review Mario's situation. How could he use the steps given here to help set some long-term and short-term goals? How could he use a career goal to focus his energies during his senior year?

2. What is wrong with each of the goals below? Rewrite each example as one (or several) clear, specific, positive goals. Include realistic deadlines.

(a) I don't want to gain any more weight.

(b) I want to be a professional tennis player.

(c) I want to stop fighting with my parents so much.

(d) I want to eat better.

(e) I want to be happy.

3. Think about a time when you set a goal and tried to reach it.

Did you use any of the steps described above? Explain. Did you reach your goal? Why or why not?

4. Get to know yourself better by listing your interests, abilities, and values.

Keeping that list in mind, write two clear, specific, positive goals you want to achieve by

(a) the end of the school year

(b) the end of high school

(c) the end of ten years

Then break your goal down into manageable subgoals.

5. Review the list of your personal qualities from question 4. Using the guidelines above, set a goal with a realistic deadline of two weeks or less. Use subgoals if necessary. After two weeks, evaluate your success. How did the guidelines help make your goal achievable?

CHAPTER **11** REVIEW

KEY IDEAS

LESSON 1

- A strong personal identity helps adults of all ages cope successfully with the changes they face.

- A person reaches his or her physical peak during young adulthood.

- Forming close, loving relationships and finding productive work are the two major concerns of young adults.

LESSON 2

- The central task of middle adulthood is generativity, which is the concern for the welfare of other generations.

- The likelihood of a person experiencing a mid-life crisis during middle adulthood depends on the person's expectations, sense of control, and financial, social, and psychological resources.

LESSON 3

- Most older adults are healthy, mentally alert, and capable of productive work.

- The development of integrity is the chief task of older adulthood. If older adults feel content with the life they have lived, they will be able to accept death and enjoy the time remaining.

LESSON 4

- People with terminal illnesses often go through a specific pattern of reactions: denial, anger, bargaining, depression, and acceptance.

- Dying should be a time for loving and sharing, not loneliness and despair. It is best to spend the time you have with a dying loved one talking about the feelings the two of you have.

KEY TERMS

LESSON 1
emotional intimacy
maturity
physical peak
validation

LESSON 2
climacteric

generativity

LESSON 3
Alzheimer's disease
arthritis
dementia
elasticity
immune system

integrity
osteoporosis
Parkinson's disease

LESSON 4
hospice
terminal illness

Listed above are some of the important terms in this chapter. Choose the term from the list that best matches each phrase below.

1. reassuring a person that his or her feelings, ideas, or decisions are reasonable

2. the ability to share innermost feelings with someone else and to engage in a caring, loving relationship

3. the gradual reduction in the production of certain hormones in men and women during middle adulthood

4. a program that provides care and support for dying people and their families

5. an illness that results in death

6. an illness characterized by a progressive loss of normal muscle function

7. the loss of calcium from the bones during older adulthood

8. the loss of mental abilities, combined with abnormal behavior and personality changes

9. the shift of concern from oneself to the welfare of other generations

10. the time during which a person's physical abilities are at a maximum

WHAT HAVE YOU LEARNED?

Choose the letter of the answer that best completes each statement.

11. If you are full grown in the physical sense, you have reached
a. integrity **c.** maturity
b. generativity **d.** validation

12. A disease that cripples people by attacking the joints of the body is
a. arthritis **c.** Alzheimer's disease
b. Parkinson's disease **d.** osteoporosis

13. A disease caused by degeneration of brain cells is
a. osteoporosis **c.** stroke
b. arthritis **d.** Alzheimer's disease

14. As people become older, their skin loses
a. calcium **c.** elasticity
b. integrity **d.** brittleness

15. According to Erikson, the chief task of older adults is the achievement of
a. emotional intimacy **c.** generativity
b. integrity **d.** validation

16. For women, the result of the climacteric is
a. menopause **c.** pregnancy
b. menstruation **d.** validation

17. Older adults may be threatened by infectious diseases because of a weakened
a. skin elasticity **c.** intellectual function
b. bone structure **d.** immune system

18. According to Elisabeth Kübler-Ross, the fourth stage of dying is
a. acceptance **c.** bargaining
b. denial **d.** depression

Answer each of the following with complete sentences.

19. Why does age not necessarily reflect physical, emotional, and social maturity?

20. During what stage of the life cycle do you reach your physical peak?

21. List three ways a person might express generativity during middle adulthood.

22. Why do some middle-aged people never experience a mid-life crisis?

23. List five habits an older adult can follow to prolong life and good health.

24. How are the concerns of older adults like those of young and middle-aged adults?

25. Why are some people more afraid of the process of dying than they are of death itself?

26. Describe three behaviors that help you handle the terminal illness of a loved one.

WHAT DO YOU THINK?

27. What steps can you take to ensure a smooth transition into adulthood?

28. Emotionally and socially, what do you think parents need from their children during a mid-life crisis?

29. Why is a strong identity necessary for achieving intimacy in young adulthood and integrity in older adulthood?

30. Why is it helpful to think of a dying person as someone about to take a journey?

31. Suppose identical twins lose track of each other at age 20 and are reunited at age 40. Is it likely that their adult lives have been as similar as their childhoods?

WHAT WOULD YOU DO?

32. List four behaviors that will help you remain at your physical peak in adulthood.

33. How would you maintain a strong relationship with a grandparent in a nursing home?

34. A friend is terribly depressed about her father's death. How would you comfort her and help bring her out of her depression?

Getting Involved

35. Interview several adults, making sure to include one from each of the three age groups. Ask them what advice they would offer to teenagers. Compare the responses of the people you interviewed. What did you learn about adulthood from the interviews?

FOOD AND NUTRITION

Have you ever eaten food that you have grown in your own garden? Freshly picked fruits and vegetables taste delicious—but flavor is not their most important benefit. Vegetables, fruits, and other nutritious foods contain the materials that you need to grow and stay healthy. In this chapter, you will learn about the nutrients you need for a healthy diet.

CHAPTER PREVIEW

12-1 Your Nutritional Needs

- Identify the six classes of nutrients and describe their functions in your body.

12-2 Meeting Your Nutritional Needs

- Describe and explain the organization of the Food Guide Pyramid.

12-3 Hunger and Malnutrition

- Define malnutrition and explain its effects on health.

BUILDING HEALTH SKILLS

- Devise and implement a strategy for breaking a bad habit.

CHECK YOUR WELLNESS

How healthy are your eating habits? See if you can answer *yes* to these questions.

- Do you eat three nutritious meals, including breakfast, each day?
- Do you follow the Food Guide Pyramid and Daily Values as you choose foods to eat?
- Do you eat a variety of grains, vegetables, and fruits?
- Do you choose fresh foods whenever possible?
- Do you usually avoid foods that are high in saturated fats and cholesterol?
- Do you use salt and sweets only in moderation?
- Do you drink water throughout the day?

KEEPING A JOURNAL

Think of a special celebration, holiday, or festival in which food is important in your family or culture. Describe the foods that you associate with this occasion, and explain why they are important. Write about any traditions associated with these foods.

Take it to the Net
www.phschool.com

1 YOUR NUTRITIONAL NEEDS

Focus on these questions as you read this lesson.

- Which nutrients can be used as sources of energy?

- What are some important functions of specific vitamins and minerals?

SKILLS

- Activity: Those Hidden Fats

- Finding the Facts

What do you think of when you hear the word *food?* You probably recall your favorite foods. Maybe you imagine the smell of fresh-baked bread or the spicy taste of curry. You might also think of occasions when food is especially important, such as family celebrations and meals with friends. Food is more than something that satisfies your hunger. It is a source of enjoyment, and it is an important aspect of your social life as well.

Your body needs food, and the food that you eat affects your health in many ways—how you look and feel, how well you resist disease, and even how well you perform mentally and physically. It does all those things by providing your body with **nutrients** (NOO tree unts), which are the substances that the body needs to regulate bodily functions, promote growth, repair body tissues, and obtain energy. Your body requires over 40 different nutrients for these tasks. The process by which the body takes in and uses these nutrients is called **nutrition.**

Food and Energy

Food provides your body with energy. You use that energy for everything you do—running, playing a musical instrument, and even sleeping. Energy is needed to maintain your body temperature, to keep your heart beating, and to enable you to understand what you read.

When your body uses the nutrients in foods, a series of chemical reactions occurs inside your cells. As a result, energy is released. **Metabolism** (mih TAB uh liz um) is the chemical processes by which your body breaks down food to

Figure 12-1 *Of the foods shown below, which two have the most calories? Which have the fewest calories?*

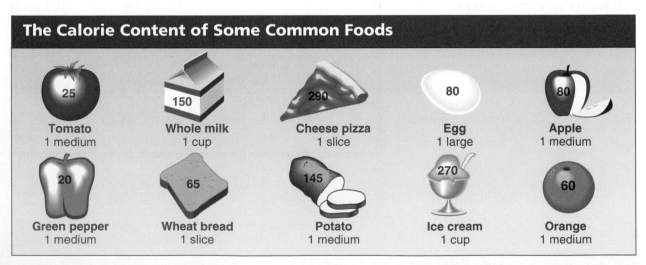

The Calorie Content of Some Common Foods

25	**150**	**290**	**80**	**80**
Tomato 1 medium	Whole milk 1 cup	Cheese pizza 1 slice	Egg 1 large	Apple 1 medium
20	**65**	**145**	**270**	**60**
Green pepper 1 medium	Wheat bread 1 slice	Potato 1 medium	Ice cream 1 cup	Orange 1 medium

release this energy. Metabolism also involves the use of energy and material from food for growth and repair of body tissues.

The amount of energy released when nutrients are burned is measured in units called **calories.** The more calories a food has, the more energy it contains. As you can see in Figure 12-1, the calorie content of different foods varies greatly. How would you compare the energy that you get from a slice of pizza with the energy that you get from an apple?

Before you reach for the pizza, though, you need to think of more than the energy it will give you. For good health, the number of calories in the food that you eat should match the caloric needs of your body. The relationship between calories and body fat will be discussed in the next chapter.

The Six Basic Nutrients

There are six classes of nutrients: carbohydrates, fats, proteins, vitamins, minerals, and water. **Carbohydrates, fats, and proteins can all be used by the body as sources of energy; vitamins, minerals, and water perform other essential functions.** Each type of nutrient is necessary for good health.

CARBOHYDRATES   Sugars and starches belong to the group known as carbohydrates. **Carbohydrates** (kahr boh HY drayts) are nutrients made of carbon, hydrogen, and oxygen, and they are an excellent source of energy.

There are two general types of carbohydrates—simple and complex. Simple carbohydrates consist of sugars. There are several types of sugars, but **glucose** (GLOO kohs) is the most important, because it is the major provider of energy for your body's cells. All other types of sugar are converted to glucose once they are inside your body. Sugars occur naturally in fruits, vegetables, and milk. They are added to many manufactured foods, such as cookies, candy, and soft drinks.

Complex carbohydrates are made up of sugars that are linked together chemically to form long chains, something like beads in a necklace. Starch, one of the main types of complex carbohydrates, is found in many plant foods, such as potatoes. Grains and grain products—for example, rice, cereals, and breads—are excellent sources of starch. Every time

Figure 12-2 *Your body needs energy from the carbohydrates found in these foods.*

you eat a tortilla, or a whole-wheat roll, or a Chinese moo shu pancake, you are helping to satisfy your need for starch. When you eat foods containing starch, your digestive system breaks the starch into simple sugars that can be absorbed into your bloodstream.

At a meal, you usually eat more carbohydrates than your body can immediately use. The extra glucose is converted into a type of starch called **glycogen** (GLY kuh jun), which is stored in the body. Then, when more glucose is needed, the glycogen is converted back to glucose. If you eat so many carbohydrates that the excess cannot be stored as glycogen, it is stored as fat instead.

Most nutrition experts believe that about 50 to 60 percent of a person's calories should come from carbohydrates. The carbohydrates they recommend are starches rather than sugars. One reason is that while sugars give quick bursts of energy, starches are better providers of long-term, sustained energy. In addition, foods that are high in starch, such as bread and pasta, usually contain a variety of nutrients. In contrast, foods high in sugar, such as candy and soft drinks, usually have few valuable nutrients. If you have a craving for sweets, eat naturally sweet foods, such as fruits and fruit juices. Those foods provide vitamins and trace amounts of some of the minerals you need.

Fiber is a type of complex carbohydrate that is found in plants. Strictly speaking, fiber is not really a nutrient, because it cannot be broken down and then absorbed into your bloodstream. Instead, fiber passes out of your body without being digested. However, it is still necessary for the proper functioning of your digestive system. It plays an important role in preventing constipation. In addition, a diet high in fiber may reduce the risk of lower bowel cancer and may play a role in preventing heart disease. Whole-grain breads and cereals, vegetables, fruits, and seeds provide fiber in your diet.

Figure 12-3 *Breads are excellent sources of starch.*

THOSE HIDDEN FATS

In this activity, you will test some foods to see whether or not they contain fat.

Materials

brown paper bag	milk chocolate
scissors	carrot
marker	whole milk
dropper	skim milk
potato chip	apple juice
	ground beef

Procedure

1. Cut a brown paper bag into squares about 3 inches (8 centimeters) on each side.

2. Write the name of each food on a square.

3. Rub some of each food on the square with its name. If the food is a liquid, place a few drops on the square.

4. Let the squares dry. Then hold each square up to a light.

Discussion

1. Which squares appeared spotted when you held them up to the light? Those foods contain fat. Which squares were not spotted?

2. Does your daily diet include many foods that are high in fat? (To be sure, try testing some foods that you commonly eat.) How could you reduce the amount of fat that you consume each day?

FATS Ounce for ounce, fats have more than twice as many calories as carbohydrates. Like carbohydrates, fats are made of carbon, hydrogen, and oxygen, but in different proportions. They supply your body with energy, form part of the structure of your cells, maintain body temperature, and protect the nerves and tissues. They are essential for growth and development as well as for healthy hair and skin.

Fats are made up of fatty acids, which come in two forms. **Unsaturated fats** have at least one bond where hydrogen can be added to the molecule. They are usually liquid at room temperature. Unsaturated fats are classified as either monounsaturated fats, which may turn cloudy as they cool, or polyunsaturated fats, which stay clear as they cool. Examples of monounsaturated fats include olive oil, peanuts, avocado, and canola oil; monounsaturated fats include safflower, sunflower, corn, and soybean oil plus seafood. Most vegetable oils, nuts, and seeds contain unsaturated fats.

Saturated fats have all the hydrogen the carbon atoms can hold. They are usually solid at room temperature. Most of the foods in Figure 12-4 contain saturated fats. Most Americans consume too many saturated fats. Nutritionists recommend that no more than 30 percent of your calories come from fat. One way to reduce your intake of saturated fat is to substitute low-fat foods, such as reduced-fat milk and cheeses, for the meats and dairy products that are high in saturated fats. Plant-based foods, such as grain products, vegetables, and fruits, are also excellent substitutes for high fat foods.

Figure 12-4 *Of the fatty foods shown below, only the olive oil is low in saturated fats.*

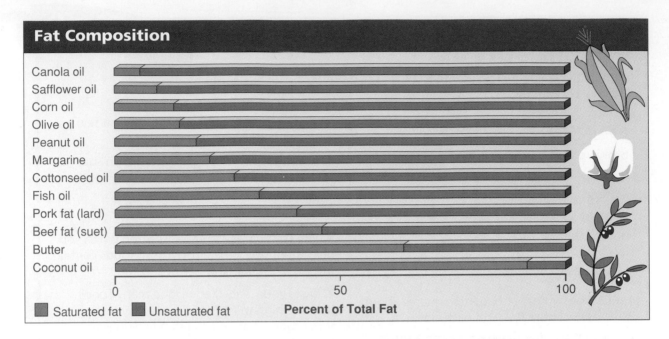

Fat Composition

Canola oil
Safflower oil
Corn oil
Olive oil
Peanut oil
Margarine
Cottonseed oil
Fish oil
Pork fat (lard)
Beef fat (suet)
Butter
Coconut oil

0   50   100

Percent of Total Fat

■ Saturated fat   ■ Unsaturated fat

Figure 12-5 *Which of the fat sources in the graph above is lowest in saturated fat?*

As you can see in Figure 12-5, many foods contain a combination of saturated and unsaturated fats. To improve our diets, some food manufacturers have replaced the saturated fats in their products with unsaturated fats. In many cases, however, the unsaturated fats are hydrogenated—a process that adds hydrogen to the fat molecule. Unfortunately, the hydrogenated fat—called a trans fat—seems to have few of the benefits of unsaturated fat and many of the negatives of saturated fat. Trans fats are found in baked goods, fried foods, and margarine. The stick forms of margarine tend to contain more trans fats than the softer, liquid margarines.

Avoiding saturated and trans fats has a bonus: lower cholesterol. **Cholesterol** (kuh LES tuh rawl) is a waxy, fat-like substance that is found in the cells of all animals. It is not present in plants. Like all animals, your body contains some cholesterol. Adding more cholesterol may raise the cholesterol in your blood to unsafe levels. High cholesterol levels are associated with heart disease because cholesterol can collect in blood vessels and clog them.

Most nutritionists recommend lowering cholesterol levels by reducing the amount of dietary fat that comes from meat and dairy products.

PROTEINS   Nutrients that contain nitrogen as well as carbon, hydrogen, and oxygen are called **proteins**. Like carbohydrates and fats, proteins can serve as a source of energy. The really important function of proteins, however, is their role in the growth and repair of your body's tissues. A good portion of your body is made up of protein.

Like carbohydrates, proteins are long chains of smaller "links" that are bound together chemically. These smaller substances are known as **amino acids** (uh MEE noh). When you eat protein, your digestive system breaks it down into individual amino acids. These amino acids are then absorbed into your bloodstream and reassembled by the cells to form the kinds of proteins you need. High-protein foods include meats, eggs, poultry, milk, and milk products, such as yogurt and some cheeses. Nuts, dried beans, dried peas, and lentils also contain a lot of protein.

The proteins in your body are made up of about 20 different amino acids. Your diet has to supply nine of these amino acids; your body can manufacture the rest. The nine amino acids that the body cannot manufacture are called **essential amino acids.** You can remember this by thinking of them as an *essential* part of your diet. Protein from animal sources—meats, fish, and so forth—is said to be complete protein because it contains all nine essential amino acids in the proportions needed to make human proteins. In contrast, most protein from plant sources, such as beans, is incomplete, because it lacks one or more essential amino acids.

To obtain all the essential amino acids from plant protein alone, you can combine two or more plant protein sources that, taken together, provide all the essential amino acids. Suppose, for example, you prepare a casserole that contains both rice and beans. The protein found in the rice and beans individually is incomplete. When they are combined, however, the rice and beans together supply all the essential amino acids needed by your body. When you combine incomplete protein foods in such a way that you obtain all nine essential amino acids, you form a complementary protein combination.

VITAMINS   Nutrients that are made by living things, are required only in small amounts, and assist many chemical reactions in the body are **vitamins.** Unlike carbohydrates, fats, and proteins, vitamins do not directly provide you with energy or the raw materials of which your cells are made. Instead, vitamins help the body with various processes, including the use of other nutrients. Your body is able to make some vitamins. For example, your skin manufactures vitamin D when it is exposed to sunlight. However, most

Figure 12-6 *Since rice and beans contain complementary proteins, when you eat both together, you obtain all the essential amino acids.*

Essential Vitamins

Vitamin		Good Sources	Main Functions	Effects of Deficiency	Some Effects of Overdose*
Fat Soluble	A	Liver; eggs; cheese; milk; yellow, orange, and dark green vegetables and fruit	Maintains healthy skin, bones, teeth, and hair; aids vision in dim light	Night blindness; rough skin; dry eyes; poor growth of bones and teeth	Blurred vision; headaches; fatigue; liver and nerve damage; dry skin
	D	Milk; eggs; liver; exposure of skin to sunlight	Maintains the bones and teeth; helps in the use of calcium and phosphorus	Rickets in children (bones and teeth do not develop properly)	Calcium deposits in body; hearing loss; muscle weakness; bone pain; anorexia
	E	Margarine; vegetable oils; wheat germ; whole grains; legumes; green, leafy vegetables	Aids in maintenance of red blood cells, vitamin A, and fats	Rupture of red blood cells	Bruising; bleeding
	K	Green, leafy vegetables; potatoes; liver; made by intestinal bacteria	Aids in blood clotting	Hemorrhage; slow clotting of blood	Jaundice in infants
Water Soluble	B_1 (Thiamin)	Pork products; liver; whole-grain foods; legumes	Aids in carbohydrate use and nervous system function	Beriberi (damage to nervous system, heart, and muscles)	Yellow/orange urine
	B_2 (Riboflavin)	Milk; eggs; meat; whole grains; dark green vegetables	Aids in metabolism of carbohydrates, proteins, and fats	Skin disorders; sensitive eyes	Yellow/orange urine
	B_3 (Niacin)	Poultry; meat; fish; whole grains; nuts	Aids in energy metabolism	Pellagra (diarrhea, skin disorders, depression)	Ulcers; abnormal liver function; wheezing
	B_6 (Pyroxidine)	Meats; poultry; fish; whole-grain foods; green vegetables	Aids in protein, fat, and carbohydrate metabolism	Skin disorders; anemia	Dependency; depression; irritability; paralysis; burning pain
	B_{12} (Cobalamin)	Meat; fish; poultry; eggs; milk; cheese	Maintains healthy nervous system and red blood cells	Anemia; fatigue	Yellow/orange urine
	Folate (Folic acid)	Green, leafy vegetables; legumes	Aids in formation of red blood cells and protein	Anemia; diarrhea	Yellow/orange urine
	Pantothenic acid	Organ meats; poultry; fish; eggs; grains	Aids in energy metabolism	Vomiting; insomnia; fatigue	Unknown
	Biotin	Organ meats; poultry; fish; eggs; peas; bananas; melons	Aids in energy metabolism	Abnormal heart function; skin disorders; loss of appetite	Unknown
	C (Ascorbic acid)	Citrus fruits; green vegetables; melons; potatoes; tomatoes	Aids in bone, teeth, and skin formation; resistance to infection; iron uptake	Scurvy (bleeding gums, loose teeth, wounds that do not heal)	Dependence; rectal bleeding; increased estrogen levels

*Common symptoms are nausea, vomiting, diarrhea, and rash

vitamins must be supplied in the food you eat. Figure 12-7 outlines the functions and food sources of each vitamin.

There are two classes of vitamins: fat-soluble vitamins, which dissolve in fatty materials, and water-soluble vitamins, which dissolve in water. Fat-soluble vitamins—A, D, E, and K—occur in vegetable oils, liver, eggs, and certain vegetables. The body can store fat-soluble vitamins.

Water soluble vitamins—C and all of the B vitamins—are found in fruits, vegetables, and other sources listed in Figure 12-7. Because the body cannot store water-soluble vitamins, it is important to eat foods that supply them every day.

Antioxidants are vitamins that help protect healthy cells from the damage caused by the normal aging process as well as certain types of cancer. Vitamins C and E are two of the most powerful antioxidants. Sources of C include citrus fruits, strawberries, broccoli, and potatoes. Sources of E include vegetable oils, whole grains, seeds, nuts, and peanut butter.

A **deficiency** (dih FISH un see) occurs when a person does not get enough of a specific nutrient. Figure 1-7 describes some problems that result from vitamin deficiencies. People who eat a variety of healthy foods seldom suffer from any nutrient deficiency. Vitamin supplements, therefore, are not necessary if your diet is nutritious. In fact, an excess of vitamins may damage your health. Common symptoms of vitamin overdose include nausea, vomiting, diarrhea, and rash.

MINERALS   Your body requires only small amounts of **minerals,** which are nutrients that occur naturally in rocks and soil. Plants absorb minerals from rocks and soil through their roots; animals obtain nutrients by either eating the plants or eating animals that have eaten the plants.

Figure 12-7 *(Opposite) Use the vitamin chart to identify a food that is a good source of both vitamin D and vitamin B₂.*

Figure 12-8 *Citrus fruits, melons, papayas, tomatoes, and peppers are all high in vitamin C.*

Essential Minerals

Mineral	Good Sources	Main Functions	Effects of Deficiency	Possible Effects of Overdose
Calcium	Milk and milk products; dark green, leafy vegetables; tofu; legumes	Helps build and maintain bones and teeth; nerve and muscle function; blood clotting	Rickets in children; osteoporosis in adults	Mineral imbalance of magnesium, iron and zinc
Phosphorus	Meat; eggs; poultry; fish; legumes; milk and milk products	Helps build and maintain bones and teeth; energy metabolism	Weakness; pain	Can create calcium deficiency
Magnesium	Leafy green vegetables; legumes; nuts; whole-grain foods	Helps build bones and protein; energy metabolism; muscle contraction	Weakness; mental disorders	Unclear
Sodium	Table salt; processed food; soy sauce	Helps maintain water balance; nerve function	Muscle cramps	Associated with high blood pressure
Chloride	Table salt; soy sauce; processed foods	Helps maintain water balance; digestion	Growth failure; loss of appetite	Vomiting
Potassium	Vegetables, fruits, meat, poultry, fish	Helps maintain water balance and make protein; functioning of heart and nervous system	Muscular weakness; confusion; abnormal heart function	Muscular weakness; vomiting
Sulfur	Milk and milk products; meat; poultry; fish; legumes; nuts	Forms part of some amino acids and B vitamins	Unclear	Unclear
Iodine	Seafood; iodized salt	Helps in metabolism as part of thyroid hormone	Goiter (enlargement of thyroid); mental and physical retardation in infants	Abnormal thyroid function
Iron	Red meats; seafood; legumes; green, leafy vegetables; fortified cereals; dried fruits	Part of red blood cells; helps in energy metabolism	Anemia (weakness, paleness, shortness of breath)	Damage to liver and heart; common cause of poisoning in young children
Selenium	Seafoods; meats; organ meats	Helps break down harmful substances	Muscle weakness and pain; heart damage	Nausea; nerve damage; fatigue; skin lesions
Zinc	Meats; poultry; seafood; milk; whole-grain foods	Part of many substances that help carry out body processes	Slow growth rate in children; slow healing	Nausea; diarrhea
Fluoride	Fish; fluoridated water; animal foods	Helps form strong teeth and bones	Tooth decay	Discoloration of teeth

Figure 12-9 *What minerals can you obtain by eating legumes?*

Twenty-four different minerals have been shown to be essential for good health. You need six of these minerals—calcium, magnesium, phosphorus, sodium, potassium, and chlorine—in significant amounts. You need only trace amounts of others, such as fluorine, iodine, iron, sulfur, copper, and zinc. Minerals perform a wide variety of functions in the body. Figure 12-9 summarizes important information about minerals.

Some minerals are of special nutritional concern. For example, many people's diets do not include enough calcium. Calcium is important in blood clotting and the functioning of your nervous system. It is an essential ingredient in the formation and maintenance of bones and teeth. A lack of calcium can sometimes lead to osteoporosis, a condition in which the bones gradually weaken. Osteoporosis will be further discussed in Chapter 15. Milk and dairy products are good sources of calcium, but many people cannot digest dairy products. Beet greens, collard greens, broccoli, and tofu are also good sources of calcium.

Iron is necessary for healthy red blood cells. These cells have an iron-containing substance called **hemoglobin** (HEE muh gloh bin), which carries oxygen from your lungs to all parts of your body. Adolescent girls and adult women need a lot of iron, because they lose iron during menstruation. Adolescent boys need a lot of iron too, since this mineral is involved with building muscle mass.

As Figure 12-11 indicates, there are many good sources of iron. During one day, for example, you might fulfill your iron requirements by eating an iron-fortified breakfast cereal, a salad containing garbanzo beans, a serving of cooked spinach, several dried apricots, and a serving of lean beef. If a person's diet does not include enough iron, he or she may develop **anemia** (uh NEE mee uh), a condition in which the red blood cells do not contain enough hemoglobin. People suffering from anemia are usually weak and tired, and they become sick easily.

Figure 12-10 *Yogurt provides plenty of calcium. It is also a good source of protein, carbohydrates, and vitamins.*

Figure 12-11 *These foods are rich in iron. Why is iron such an important mineral?*

Figure 12-12 *When you exercise vigorously, you need to replace the water that you lose through perspiration.*

In contrast to iron and calcium, most people consume far more sodium than they need. Table salt, or sodium chloride, is a major source of this mineral. So are some processed, or manufactured, foods, such as canned soups and frozen pizza. Salty snack foods, including chips and salted nuts, are also high in this mineral. Sodium is important in several body processes, including the functioning of the nervous system and heart. However, people who have high blood pressure should reduce their salt intake because an excess of sodium will raise their blood pressure levels.

WATER   About 65 percent of your body weight is water. You do not get energy from this nutrient directly; nevertheless, water is essential for all life processes, including energy production. Nearly all of the body's chemical reactions, including those that produce energy and build new tissues, take place in a water solution. Water is the primary component of blood and tissue fluids. It carries dissolved waste products out of the body and helps digest food.

Since perspiration helps your body cool down, water also helps regulate body temperature. Water contains dissolved substances called **electrolytes** that regulate many processes in cells. By helping to adjust body temperature and electrolyte balance, water plays an important role in homeostasis. **Homeostasis** (ho mee oh STAY sis) is the process of maintaining a steady state inside your body.

Every day, you need at least 8 cups (2 liters) of water or their equivalent in foods that contain a lot of water, such as fruit and vegetable juices. Very heavy perspiring or severe diarrhea can result in **dehydration** (dee hy DRAY shun), a serious reduction in the body's water content. When the body becomes dehydrated, it loses important electrolytes along with the water. The symptoms of dehydration can include weakness, rapid breathing, and weak heartbeat. Whenever your body loses a lot of water, you need to be careful to increase your water intake to prevent dehydration.

LESSON 1 REVIEW

1. Name three functions nutrients perform in your body.
2. Which nutrients supply your body with energy?
3. How does saturated fat in the diet affect the level of cholesterol in the blood?
4. Which of the two categories of vitamins should be supplied every day in the foods that you eat?

What Do You Think?

5. Is your present diet high in sugar or fat? If so, what practical changes could improve this situation?

2 MEETING YOUR NUTRITIONAL NEEDS

GUIDE FOR READING

Focus on these questions as you read this lesson.

- How is the structure of the Food Guide Pyramid related to its recommendations about diet?
- What are Daily Values?

SKILLS

- DECIDE
- Reading a Food Label

Good nutrition requires serious planning. You can use the Food Guide Pyramid and Daily Values for nutrients to develop good eating habits and to keep your body functioning at its best.

The Food Guide Pyramid

You know now that you need to obtain several types of nutrients from the food you eat. You probably realize, too, that you need to eat a variety of foods. But how should you choose the foods that you eat? To help people plan their meals and snacks, the United States Department of Agriculture has designed the Food Guide Pyramid, which is shown in Figure 12-13. The **Food Guide Pyramid** is a graph that groups foods according to types and indicates how many servings of each type should be eaten daily.

Notice in Figure 12-13 that there are six different groups of food in the pyramid. These groups are grain foods; vegetables; fruits; milk products; meat, poultry, fish, eggs, beans, and nuts; and finally, fats, oils, and sweets. **The structure of the Food Guide Pyramid conveys the idea that the bulk of people's diets should consist of grains, vegetables, and fruits; it also emphasizes a diet low in fats and sugar.** To communicate these recommendations, the pyramid arranges these six groups in four levels. The width

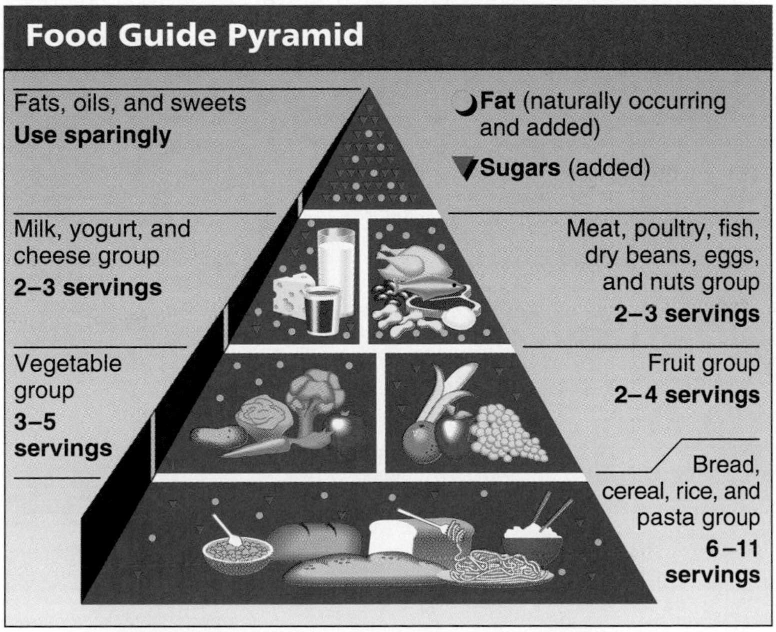

Food Guide Pyramid

Fats, oils, and sweets
Use sparingly

◗Fat (naturally occurring and added)

▼Sugars (added)

Milk, yogurt, and cheese group
2–3 servings

Meat, poultry, fish, dry beans, eggs, and nuts group
2–3 servings

Vegetable group
3–5 servings

Fruit group
2–4 servings

Bread, cereal, rice, and pasta group
6–11 servings

Figure 12-13 *The Food Guide Pyramid divides foods into groups and indicates how many servings you should eat from each group every day.*

Figure 12-14 *Noodles are made from grains. How many servings of grain foods should you eat each day?*

of each level roughly indicates the proportion of food you should eat from that level. In other words, since the bottom level—the grains group—is the widest, you should be choosing many more foods from that level than from the fats, oils, and sweets group at the narrow peak of the pyramid.

Notice the little triangles and circles scattered throughout the pyramid. The triangles represent sugar, and the circles represent fat. These symbols roughly indicate how much fat and sugar can be found in different levels.

As you read about each level of the pyramid, note the number of servings that you should be eating each day. If you follow the pyramid's serving recommendations, you will be eating a nutritious, balanced diet.

GRAINS   The base of the Food Guide Pyramid—and its widest level—consists of grains and foods made from grains. Some of these include different types of bread, such as pita bread, whole-wheat bread, rye bread, rolls, and tortillas. Pasta, such as macaroni, spaghetti, and rice noodles, is also in this group. Rice, crackers, couscous, bulghur, and breakfast cereals are other grain foods. You should eat six to eleven servings of grain products every day. One slice of bread is one serving; so is half a cup (120 milliliters) of rice. Observe that more servings are recommended from this level than any other level of the pyramid. That is because grain foods are generally high in complex carbohydrates and low in fat and sugar. When you eat grain products, you also obtain iron, B vitamins, and some protein.

Figure 12-15 *Every day, people should eat at least two servings of fruit and three servings of vegetables.*

VEGETABLES AND FRUITS   The second widest level, like the first, consists solely of foods that come from plants. It is made up of two groups, vegetables and fruits. A variety of vegetables, such as spinach, bok choy, carrots, plantains, and potatoes, is available in stores and produce markets. You can also choose an abundance of fruits, including bananas, mangoes, oranges, papayas, and grapes.

Both of these groups give you carbohydrates, vitamins, and minerals. All of your vitamin C and much of your vitamin A come from foods in these groups. Refer back to Figures 12-7 and 12-9 to see which additional vitamins and minerals are supplied by fruits and vegetables. Fruits and vegetables are also rich in fiber. You should choose three to five servings of vegetables and two to four servings of fruit every day. A typical serving size for a vegetable such as carrots consists of one half cup (120 milliliters). One medium-sized pear is a typical serving of fruit.

MILK, MEAT, AND OTHER HIGH-PROTEIN FOODS

The third level from the bottom, unlike the two levels beneath it, consists mainly of foods that come from animals. Notice that this level is made up of two groups. The first of these is the milk group. Besides milk itself, the milk group includes yogurt and cheese. It does not, however, include cream or butter, even though those foods are dairy products. That is because cream and butter are composed primarily of fat rather than other, more desirable nutrients.

Milk-group foods are an especially good source of calcium. They are also rich in protein and vitamins B_2 and B_{12}. Fortified milk is also a good source of vitamin D. The Food Guide Pyramid suggests two to three daily servings of milk-group foods. A serving might consist of one cup (240 milliliters) of milk or yogurt, or about 2 ounces (56 grams) of cheese. However, some people are unable to digest most milk products. The nutrients provided by milk-group foods can be obtained from other sources.

The second group in this level of the Food Guide Pyramid consists of an assortment of foods. Among these are meats, poultry, eggs, fish, and nuts. This group also includes legumes—seeds that are produced in pods. Kidney beans, garbanzos, fava beans, peanuts, navy beans, and lentils are

Figure 12-16 *Besides milk itself, milk-group foods include yogurt and a variety of cheeses.*

Figure 12-17 *Meats, poultry, fish, eggs, legumes, and nuts all contain a lot of protein. Which of these high-protein foods would a vegetarian choose?*

all legumes. Meats, legumes, and the other foods in this group all contain a lot of protein. Some members of this group also supply vitamins B_6 and B_{12} and the minerals iron, zinc, and magnesium. The Food Guide Pyramid recommends two to three servings from this group daily. Three ounces (84 grams) of meat, poultry, or fish is equal to a serving. So is a cup (240 milliliters) of cooked legumes.

FATS, OILS, AND SWEETS   The narrow peak of the Food Guide Pyramid consists of fats and sweets. Foods at this level include such things as soft drinks, ice cream, butter and margarine, cream, and candy bars. From the triangles and circles shown in this level of the pyramid, you can see that these foods are high in sugar or fat—or both.

Most of the foods in this level are low in **nutrient density**—the proportion of nutrients in a food compared to the number of calories. For example, one cup (240 milliliters) of low-fat milk has a high nutrient density, since it supplies protein, carbohydrates, vitamins, and minerals along with about 100 calories. The same volume of cola soft drink also has about 100 calories, but because it supplies few nutrients besides sugar, it has a low nutrient density.

In planning your meals and snacks, try to restrict fats and sweets. This does not mean that you cannot have margarine on your toast, or that you can never have that favorite chocolate bar. Just use the margarine sparingly and save the candy bar for an occasional treat.

D E C I D E

DEFINE
the problem

EXPLORE
alternatives

CONSIDER
the consequences

IDENTIFY
values

DECIDE
and act

EVALUATE
results

A Better Diet for the Family?

Rachel has become concerned about the food her family is eating. It tastes good, but she wonders whether it is too high in fat and too low in complex carbohydrates. Her family eats a lot of fried foods, but not too many vegetables or grain products. Rachel doesn't want to hurt her parents' feelings. Also, she knows that her mother and father are both very busy, and that it takes time to plan and shop for nutritious food.

1. Use the DECIDE process on page 18 to decide what you would do in this situation. Explain your reasons for making this decision.

2. What sources of information could you consult to help you make your decision?

3. What might be some positive effects of your decision? Some negative effects?

Figure 12-18 *A doughnut, which contains over 200 calories, is high in fat and contains practically no valuable nutrients. In contrast, a 60-calorie orange has practically no fat and supplies a lot of vitamin C. Which food is the more nutrient-dense snack?*

Daily Values

The Food Guide Pyramid helps you plan your food choices, but it does not tell you the amounts of specific nutrients that you need. Nutrition experts in the United States government have developed recommendations, called **Daily Values**, for the amounts of specific nutrients that the average person should obtain each day.

Daily Values specify amounts of vitamins and minerals that should be in the daily diet. They also indicate amounts of total fat, saturated fat, and cholesterol, as well as carbohydrates and fiber. When you buy food, the label on the food package indicates the percentage of the Daily Value for each nutrient in that food. For example, a label might indicate that a cereal provides 15 percent of the fiber that the average person needs each day. Food labels will be discussed further in the next chapter.

Daily Values are only a general guide, because they apply to the average person, and not everyone is average. Nutrient needs are affected by factors such as age, sex, heredity, and lifestyle. Rapidly growing adolescents, pregnant women, and nursing mothers may need more nutrients than the Daily Values indicate.

SHARPEN YOUR SKILLS

Reading a Food Label

Make a chart in which you compare the labels for several different types and brands of yogurt—for example, plain regular yogurt, plain low-fat yogurt, yogurt with fruit, and frozen yogurt. How do they compare for total fat, saturated fat, and cholesterol? Of which vitamins and minerals are they good sources?

LESSON 2 REVIEW

1. What is indicated by the different widths of the levels in the Food Guide Pyramid?
2. What is meant by nutrient density?
3. To whom do Daily Values for nutrients apply?

What Do You Think?

4. How can you use both the Food Guide Pyramid and the Daily Values listed on food labels to determine whether or not your diet meets your nutritional needs?

GUIDE FOR READING

Focus on these questions as you read this lesson.

- What are some effects of malnutrition?
- What groups of people in the United States are at risk for malnutrition?

SKILLS

- Locating Community Resources

As long as people can easily obtain an abundant and varied diet, it is not difficult for them to meet their nutritional needs. When such fortunate people become hungry, they can usually satisfy their need for food. However, many people in the world cannot obtain enough of the right foods—and in some cases cannot get much food at all. For them, hunger is a way of life—an ongoing, painful condition over which they have little control. Poor nutrition is a serious, worldwide problem.

Malnutrition

Technically, **malnutrition** (mal noo TRISH un) is any condition in which a person's nutrient consumption is inadequate or unbalanced. However, most cases are the result of consuming too little of one or more nutrients. **Malnutrition harms every system of the body and also damages emotional well-being.**

When people are malnourished, they do not have the energy to perform well in school or at work. Malnourished people are also more susceptible to disease than those who eat a healthy diet. Malnourished children usually grow much more slowly than children whose diet is adequate. If malnutrition occurs during pregnancy, the baby may weigh less than normal and have serious health problems.

There are various types of malnutrition, including the vitamin and mineral deficiencies discussed earlier in the chapter. In one especially serious condition known as **protein-energy malnutrition,** the diet does not contain

Figure 12-19 *Famine victims, such as this Somalian woman, search in vain to try to find food.*

adequate protein, nor does it supply enough calories to meet the body's energy needs. The effects of this condition are especially severe on children, since their bodies need protein and calories for growth. Severe cases can cause death, either directly through starvation or indirectly through the diseases to which its victims become susceptible. Protein-energy malnutrition is the most serious nutrition problem affecting people in developing countries today.

Malnutrition has various causes. In some cases, people may be undernourished because they are unaware of the foods that they need for good health. Also, diseases and other conditions may prevent the digestive system from absorbing nutrients. But indirectly, poverty is by far the most common cause of malnutrition. Victims of severe poverty cannot afford to buy or grow the food they need.

A World Problem

Hunger and malnutrition are an especially severe problem in many of the world's poorer nations. Severe famines, for example, have devastated countries like Somalia and Bangladesh. However, hunger is also a problem in more prosperous countries, including the United States. While few people starve in the United States, many are not receiving adequate nutrition. Hungry people in the United States are those who have little or no income, such as homeless people, teenage runaways, families dealing with unemployment, and some elderly people.

Various programs and organizations are trying to solve the problem of malnutrition and provide food for those who need it. For example, the Food and Agriculture Organization of the United Nations combats hunger by helping people improve methods of agriculture and food distribution. The United States government sponsors the Food Stamp Program, which enables low-income people to purchase the food that they need. Volunteers also work hard to help those who are hungry. For example, soup kitchens, which are often staffed by volunteers, provide meals for those in need.

SHARPEN YOUR SKILLS

Locating Community Resources

Many programs need volunteers to work on the problem of hunger. In Massachusetts, for example, Project Bread holds a "Walk for Hunger" in which volunteers raise money for food. Make a list of the programs in your community or state that are trying to help hungry people. Perhaps you can help, too.

LESSON 3 REVIEW

1. What are the effects of malnutrition?
2. List three causes of malnutrition.
3. Name two groups of people who are at risk for malnutrition in the United States.

What Do You Think?

4. Propose some possible solutions to the problem of worldwide hunger.

Breaking a Bad Habit

The teenager below has developed a poor nutritional habit—snacking on high-fat foods, such as potato chips and doughnuts. Although he may wish to cut down on the amount of these foods that he eats each day, he may not think that he has the willpower to do so. We all can develop habits that are not good for us. Yet, because they are habits, we continue to do them. Did you ever try to break a bad habit? Did you decide you didn't have the willpower?

It may surprise you to learn that breaking a habit does not depend on willpower. Instead, what you need more than anything else is "skillpower." You need to learn and practice the skill of behavior change.

The key to breaking a bad habit is to replace it with a new, positive habit. The process works best if it is done in small steps and if everything is put in writing in a behavior contract. The steps given here will help you break almost any bad habit.

1. Define your bad habit

Be sure to describe your bad habit in a specific manner. For example, instead of saying "I don't eat very well," describe a specific behavior that demonstrates the problem: "I eat too many potato chips."

2. Set your goal

A goal describes the behavior you would like to substitute for your bad habit. Your goal should be specific and clear and should have a realistic deadline. The goal should emphasize *doing* something rather than *not* doing something— "For snacks, I will choose foods low in fat, such as fruits and low-fat cheeses." If a goal is broad, break it into subgoals.

3. Design an action plan

(a) Monitor Your Bad Habit: Spend a week carefully observing and recording your bad habit. You might use a chart such as the one shown here.

Bad Habit Record			
BEFOREHAND		BEHAVIOR	AFTERWARDS
Scene	Feelings	Details	Results
Monday 12 noon lunch at school	tired and bored	1 oz. bag of potato chips	more energetic

Your record will help you understand the things that trigger and reinforce the habit.

(b) Write Your Plan: Describe in detail the specific day-to-day changes you will make to reach your goal. Your plan should be a gradual, step-wise process.

(c) Keep a Log: Log your new behavior daily, including any setbacks.

Behavior Log							
Action Plan	M	T	W	Th	F	Sa	Su
	← substitute fruit or cheese for chips →						
Behavior	✓	ate potato chips	✓	ate corn chips	✓	✓	✓

4. Build a supportive environment

You will need help from many sources. Plan to reward yourself for accomplishments along the way to your goal. Ask family and friends to keep an eye on your progress, and keep a list handy of the benefits of your new behavior. Structure your surroundings to support your efforts. For example, if you are trying to break a potato-chip habit, try not to keep any potato chips in your house.

Apply the Skill

1. Choose three habits that you would like to break. Look back over the "Check Your Wellness" inventories you have taken to help you identify your poor habits.

2. Out of the three habits, choose the one you would most like to change and clearly define it. Then set a specific goal of eliminating the habit.

Write this goal on a behavior contract, similar to the one shown here.

3. Monitor your bad habit for one week. Every time you exhibit the habit, record where and when it occurred, along with your thoughts and feelings both before and after. Can you detect any patterns in your behavior?

4. Devise a plan for breaking your habit, using your knowledge of your behavior. Record your plan in detail on your contract. Also, fill in ways that you can build a supportive environment.

5. Log your behavior for a three-week period.

6. After three weeks, evaluate your performance. Did you stick to your plan? If not, what made it hard for you? What aspects of your plan worked for you?

Behavior Contract

Bad habit: <u>eating too many chips</u>
I <u>Sam Brown</u>
plan to <u>substitute fruit or low-fat cheese</u> by <u>May 4th</u>.
I will reach this goal by doing the following target behavior:
<u>substituting fruit/cheese once a day at first and gradually increasing to three times a day</u>
To create a supportive change environment, I will get help from the following role models: <u>Mom and Loretta</u>, reward myself by <u>going to the movies with friends after successful weeks</u> along the way, and by <u>buying myself a new baseball glove</u> when I reach my goal.

Signed <u>Sam Brown</u> Date <u>March 6th</u>

CHAPTER 12 REVIEW

KEY IDEAS

LESSON 1

- Nutrients are the substances in food that the body needs to regulate bodily functions, promote growth, repair body tissues, and obtain energy.

- Carbohydrates, fats, and proteins can all be used by the body as sources of energy; vitamins, minerals, and water perform other essential functions.

LESSON 2

- The structure of the Food Guide Pyramid conveys the idea that the bulk of people's diet should consist of grains, vegetables, and fruits; it also emphasizes a diet low in fats and sugar.

- Daily Values indicate the amounts of specific nutrients that the average person should obtain daily from his or her diet.

LESSON 3

- Malnutrition harms the body and also damages emotional well-being.

- Hunger is a world problem that government organizations and volunteer efforts are trying to address.

KEY TERMS

LESSON 1

amino acids
anemia
calories
carbohydrates
cholesterol
deficiency
dehydration
essential amino acids
fats

fiber
glucose
glycogen
hemoglobin
homeostasis
metabolism
minerals
nutrients
nutrition
proteins

saturated fats
unsaturated fats
vitamins

LESSON 2

Daily Values
Food Guide Pyramid
nutrient density

LESSON 3

malnutrition
protein-energy malnutrition

Listed above are some of the important terms in this chapter. Choose the term from the list that best matches each phrase below.

1. the process by which the body takes in and uses the substances that it needs to regulate body functions, promote growth, and obtain energy

2. units for measuring the amount of energy contained in food

3. a type of complex carbohydrate that passes through the digestive system without being broken down and absorbed

4. a waxy, fatlike substance found in animal cells

5. long-chain nutrients that contain nitrogen, carbon, hydrogen, and oxygen

6. a condition in which a person does not obtain enough of one specific nutrient

7. substance in red blood cells that carries oxygen

8. the process in which the body maintains a steady internal state

9. recommendations for the amounts of specific nutrients that the average person should be obtaining each day

10. any condition in which a person's nutrient consumption is inadequate or unbalanced

11. the class of nutrients that includes calcium, iron, phosphorus, iodine, and sodium

WHAT HAVE YOU LEARNED?

Choose the letter of the answer that best completes each statement.

12. Which of these nutrients is associated with high blood pressure?

a. sodium   **c.** iron
b. calcium   **d.** carbohydrate

13. Complex carbohydrates are

a. composed of sugars linked together
b. found in grain products
c. good sources of energy
d. all of these

14. Which of the following foods is high in protein?

a. an apple   **c.** candy
b. lettuce   **d.** chicken

15. Loss of water through heavy perspiring can result in

a. homeostasis   **c.** anemia
b. dehydration   **d.** all of these

16. The base of the Food Guide Pyramid consists of foods made from

a. grains   **c.** sugar
b. meats   **d.** dairy products

17. Indirectly, the most common cause of malnutrition is

a. disease   **c.** poverty
b. ignorance   **d.** crop damage

Answer each of the following with complete sentences.

18. Why should you try to limit your intake of fats and cholesterol?

19. Why is fiber necessary for the proper functioning of the digestive system?

20. Name a mineral that helps build strong bones and teeth.

21. Why is it a good idea to choose foods with high nutrient densities?

22. Give three reasons why water is such an important nutrient.

23. List the major nutrients supplied by foods in each group in the Food Guide Pyramid.

24. If a person's diet does not contain enough iron, his or her tissues may not be getting all the oxygen they need. Explain why this is so.

WHAT DO YOU THINK?

25. Many American teenagers do not have good diets. Why do you think this is so?

26. In many cultures, people get very little protein from animal sources. How might these people obtain the protein they need?

27. In your opinion, which is a better solution to the world hunger problem: giving food to needy people directly, or reducing poverty and thus enabling people to take care of their own food needs? Explain.

28. Several friends are planning a week-long backpacking trip in the mountains. They must carry all of their food in backpacks, so amounts must be limited. What kind of foods could they take to meet their nutritional needs?

WHAT WOULD YOU DO?

29. Laurie dislikes dairy products. Plan three meals for her that include calcium-rich foods that are not dairy products.

30. Recently, your sister has been skipping lunch to work on a school project. She is not worried about her diet because she takes a vitamin supplement each day. What would you tell her?

Getting Involved

31. Research the eating habits of people in another country. What are the most popular foods? What nutritional strengths does the diet have? Are there any nutritional weaknesses, such as deficiencies or excessive fat? Prepare some foods that are typical of that country and share them with your classmates.

MAKING HEALTHY FOOD CHOICES

Grocery stores are often busy places, as customers choose from a variety of colorful, fresh, and appetizing foods. What should customers consider when they are selecting food? The nutrients in the food are important, but so are freshness and price—and, of course, flavor. In this chapter you will learn how to consider all these factors in choosing foods.

CHAPTER PREVIEW

13-1 Planning a Balanced Diet

- Identify several things you can do to have a healthy diet.

13-2 Managing Your Weight

- Explain how a person's weight is related to both calories in food and calories used in daily activities.

13-3 Special Diets

- Describe special diets for physical conditions such as diabetes and hypoglycemia.

13-4 Buying Food Wisely

- Identify the kinds of information provided on a food label.

BUILDING HEALTH SKILLS

- Interpret the information contained on a food label.

CHECK YOUR WELLNESS

Do you choose food wisely? To each of the following questions, answer *usually, sometimes,* or *never*.

- When you eat out, do you select nutritious foods?

- Do you choose nutritious snacks, such as fresh fruit, raw vegetables, popcorn, and nuts?

- Do you eat only when you are hungry and stop before you are full?

- Do you avoid either overeating or undereating when you are bored or unhappy?

- Do you balance food and exercise to maintain a healthy weight?

- Do you read food labels in order to decide which foods to buy?

KEEPING A JOURNAL

Think of a recent situation in which you chose food for yourself—a meal or a snack. Identify the foods that you ate and then analyze why you chose those particular foods.

Take it to **the Net**

1 PLANNING A BALANCED DIET

Focus on these questions as you read this lesson.

- What factors should you consider when planning meals and snacks?
- What do the Dietary Guidelines for Americans recommend?

SKILLS

- Activity: Sugar in Your Food

Up and down Elm Street, families begin the day with healthy breakfasts. The Gilmores eat bran muffins, orange juice, and shredded-wheat cereal with milk. Across the street, the Lins sit down to a traditional Korean breakfast of soybean soup with chunks of bean curd and rice.

People's food choices are influenced by many factors, one of which is their culture. The term *culture* refers to the way of life of a group of people, including their customs and beliefs. Food is one important aspect of culture. As the two breakfasts demonstrate, different groups consume different foods.

Both culture and personal preferences affect the types of food that are served in your household. Some families may dislike fish, for example, while others may choose not to eat red meat. In addition, most people respond to peer pressure when selecting food—when you eat a meal with friends, you may choose different foods than when you are by yourself or with your family. Your economic situation also plays a role in what you decide to eat. People with low incomes cannot afford to buy certain foods.

When you are making decisions about what to eat, consider the nutrition content of foods. There are many ways of meeting your nutritional needs, no matter what your preferences are. With a little imagination, you can have a variety of well-balanced meals and snacks.

Figure 13-1 *Breakfasts can be as varied as you want them to be. Which of these breakfasts would you choose? Why?*

Nontraditional Breakfast Foods

Breakfast Menu	Vegetable Group	Fruit Group	Dairy Group	Meat-Poultry-Fish-Dry Beans-Eggs-Nuts Group	Grain Group
Yogurt and fruit; whole-wheat toast		✔	✔		✔
Peanut butter on bread; orange juice; milk		✔	✔	✔	✔
Tortilla with beans and cheese; vegetable juice	✔		✔	✔	✔
Cream of tomato soup; crackers and cheese	✔		✔		✔

Figure 13-2 *You are in control of the foods you select in the school cafeteria. Be sure to consider the nutrient value of your lunch selections.*

Meals

What is your favorite meal of the day? Whether it is breakfast, lunch, or supper, it and your other meals should provide you with a balance of healthy nutrients.

BREAKFAST   Even if you are rushed in the morning, do not neglect breakfast, because many nutritionists believe that breakfast is the most important meal. After a night without food, your stomach is empty, and your body needs fuel for the day's activities. A good, balanced breakfast should provide as much as one-third of your daily food needs. If your breakfast is inadequate, you may be tempted later to eat snacks that are low in nutrient density. Your breakfast should reflect the recommendations of the Food Guide Pyramid that you read about in Chapter 12.

LUNCH   School cafeterias provide nutritionally balanced meals planned by dietitians. Some school cafeterias even offer nutritious snacks, salad bars, and special diet foods. Since lunch makes up another third of your food needs for the day, make sure that you choose nutrient-dense foods. You might, for example, eat a turkey sandwich on whole-wheat bread, a salad, a carton of milk, and an orange.

SUPPER   In many cultures around the world, lunch is the major meal of the day. In the United States, the biggest meal is generally the evening meal. Since you may be less physically active after this meal, supper should not account for more than the final third of your daily calorie needs. The evening meal can be an opportunity to fill in gaps in the day's Food Guide Pyramid selections. Suppose, for example, you have not eaten foods from the vegetable group at breakfast and lunch. You might volunteer to prepare a fresh green salad for dinner that includes several vegetables, such as spinach, carrots, and celery.

ART CONNECTION

Many works of art, both ancient and modern, portray people eating, preparing, or serving meals. A wall painting in the tomb of the ancient Egyptian pharaoh Seti I, for example, shows the pharaoh carrying a tray laden with a meal of roast fowl, bread, and fruit. The painting "Luncheon on the Grass," by Claude Monet, shows a group of people enjoying an elaborate picnic. In "The Harvesters," Pieter Bruegel the Elder depicts farm workers eating a simple meal while they take a break from cutting hay.

Snacks

Snacks can contribute significantly to your nutritional needs if you choose them wisely. However, many snack foods, such as those frequently sold in movie theaters, vending machines, and the snack-food sections of supermarkets, are high in fats and sugar, and low in nutrient density. If you fill up on chips, soft drinks, and candy bars, you may have no appetite for the nutrient-dense foods that you need. Moreover, since snack foods are often high in calories, frequent snacking may result in unwanted weight gain. Finally, many snack foods, such as soft drinks and chocolate, contain caffeine, which can cause nervousness and sleeplessness.

For snacks, choose foods with a high nutrient density. Instead of an evening snack of cookies, try satisfying your craving for sweets with some fruit. Make a bagel, not a doughnut, your after-school treat. When you go to the movies, choose unbuttered popcorn instead of chips or candy.

Fast Foods

Tom and his friend Jamal drop by their favorite fast-food restaurant several times a week for a meal of double cheeseburgers, fries, and shakes. Figure 13-3 shows a nutritional breakdown of Tom and Jamal's favorite fast-food meal. Like this one, many fast-food meals are high in fat and calories. When you eat in fast-food restaurants, follow these guidelines:

- Substitute low-fat or nonfat milk or orange juice for shakes and soft drinks.
- Select the salad bar in place of fries and onion rings.
- Choose a grilled chicken sandwich instead of a hamburger or cheeseburger.
- Sauces and dressings can add a lot of fat. Use them sparingly.
- Taste food before adding extra salt to it.

Figure 13-3 *Nutrition experts recommend that no more than 30 percent of your calories come from fat. Is this fast-food meal in line with that recommendation?*

Calories and Fat in a Typical Fast-Food Meal

Food	Total Calories	Calories from Fat	Percent Calories from Fat
Double cheeseburger	490	245	50%
French fries	330	160	49%
Chocolate shake	290	14	5%
Totals for whole meal	1,110	419	38%

SUGAR IN YOUR FOOD

In this activity, you will test foods for the presence of glucose, a simple sugar.

Materials

glucose test strips

foods prepared for testing (fruits, vegetables, soft drinks, breakfast cereals)

watch or clock with second hand

Procedure

1. Obtain food samples from your teacher. If the foods are not liquids, they will be crushed and mixed with water.

2. Dip your test strip into a food sample. After 10 seconds, remove the test strip and note the color change. Do not leave the test strip in the food any longer than 10 seconds.

3. Use the test strip color indicator chart to determine the glucose content of the food. Record this information.

4. Repeat the testing procedure for other food samples.

Discussion

1. In general, how does the glucose content of fruits compare to that of vegetables?

2. Which of the foods you tested had the greatest glucose content?

3. Did any results surprise you? Why?

Improving Your Diet

The Food Guide Pyramid's recommendations can help you select specific kinds and amounts of food. In addition, nutrition experts have identified some general ways in which the American diet can be improved. **Their recommendations, called the Dietary Guidelines for Americans, can help you plan a healthy diet.**

- **Eat a variety of foods.** To obtain all the different nutrients you need, choose a wide selection of foods.

- **Balance the food you eat with physical activity—maintain or improve your weight.** Health problems can develop if you are too fat or too thin. Lesson 2 gives recommendations for balancing food intake with exercise.

- **Choose a diet with plenty of grain products, vegetables, and fruits.** These foods are especially rich in starch and fiber.

- **Choose a diet low in fat, saturated fat, and cholesterol.** Choose lean meats, fish, poultry, and legumes instead of fatty meat. Cut away all visible fat on meats, and remove the skin from poultry. Limit fried foods, including potato chips, French fries, and doughnuts.

- **Choose a diet moderate in sugars.** Foods high in sugar are high in calories but often low in more useful nutrients. Limit your intake of sweet snacks and soft drinks.

Figure 13-4 *Good nutrition can help older people stay active and healthy.*

- **Choose a diet moderate in salt and sodium.** Recall from Chapter 12 that sodium, which is found in table salt and salty foods, has been linked to high blood pressure. Avoid eating too many salty snacks, pickled foods, luncheon meats, and canned soups. Do not add salt to foods at the table.

- **Adults who use alcohol should do so in moderation.** Alcoholic beverages are very low in nutrient density. In addition, as you will learn in Chapter 19, alcohol can damage every system in your body. Many adults choose not to drink at all, but those who do drink alcohol should strictly limit their intake.

Changing Nutritional Needs

Just as your body changes throughout life, so do your nutritional needs. During infancy, childhood, and adolescence, the body needs great amounts of all the nutrients necessary for physical growth. Teenagers need ample protein in their diets to support their physical growth. Adolescents also need significant amounts of iron; girls lose iron during menstruation, and boys need additional iron to support the development of muscle mass. The need for calcium also reaches its peak during the teenage years. Adolescent girls, in particular, are advised to eat calcium-rich foods as a means of preventing the weakening of bone that can occur later in life.

Once adolescents become adults, their activity levels generally decrease, and continue to go down as they grow older. As activity decreases, so do energy needs. For this reason, adults need to watch their caloric intake carefully. Older adults, moreover, may need to increase the fiber in their diet as an aid to digestion. With proper attention to their nutritional needs, older people can live healthy and vigorous lives.

LESSON 1 REVIEW

1. Name four factors that affect your food choices.
2. Why do nutritionists consider breakfast the most important meal of the day?
3. Name three guidelines Americans should use to improve the quality of their diets.
4. When you are an older adult, how will your calorie needs probably be different from now?

What Do You Think?

5. What are some of the advantages and disadvantages of obtaining meals at fast-food restaurants?

DIFFERENT VOICES SPEAKING

Aliyenur Ozeroglu, 15, who enjoys sports, has long understood the importance of eating healthfully. Ali, as she is known to her friends, lives in Oklahoma with her family.

Q. Where did you learn about nutrition, Ali?

A. Some of what I know—about eating disorders, for instance, and the importance of a diet low in fat and cholesterol—I learned in health and family living classes at school. Those are topics that I find interesting. A lot of my knowledge, though, I "inherited" from my family and culture.

Q. Can you explain the role your family and culture have played in your outlook on food?

A. Yes. My parents came here from Turkey 18 years ago, but they never lost touch with Turkish ways of eating. Turkish meals are built around vegetables—leeks and spinach, for example—plus rice or spaghetti and small amounts of grilled chicken or fish. That's the way my mother and I prepare food in our home, and that's the way the family likes to eat. We would never dream of sitting down to a big piece of red meat or of pouring heavy dressing on a salad. We do eat salads, but dressed only with olive oil and lemon juice.

Q. You mention that you do some cooking. What sorts of foods do you like to prepare?

A. One of my favorite dishes—not just to cook but to eat—is *pilav.* This is rice simmered in chicken broth and then mixed with shreds of chicken and small beans. The rice absorbs the broth, which makes it taste wonderful. I get hungry just thinking about it!

Aliyenur Ozeroglu

Q. What else might you eat on a typical day?

A. For breakfast, I usually have a cheese called *tenek,* which is similar to feta, with black or green olives and home-baked bread. For lunch, I might have *dolma,* which is bell pepper or grape leaves stuffed with rice, onion, a little meat, and parsley in tomato sauce.

Q. When you don't eat with your family, do you ignore good nutrition?

A. Not really. When I'm out with friends, for example, I might have frozen yogurt. I'm not a big fan of the sorts of things my friends like to eat. I will confess that I have a sweet tooth, but I try to watch the Middle Eastern pastries.

Q. What do you advise teenagers about eating?

A. Mainly I would encourage all of them to try new foods. Some of my American friends have sampled Turkish food, and now they're "believers." Sometimes new tastes can surprise you.

Journal Activity

When someone asks you to try a food that you have not eaten before, how do you react? Write about such an experience. Indicate whether you tried the food, and if you did so, how it tasted.

MANAGING YOUR WEIGHT

GUIDE FOR READING

Focus on these questions as you read this lesson.

- What are some factors that determine a person's appropriate weight?
- What are some safe ways that people can change their weight?

SKILLS

- Being Assertive

Are you content with your weight, or would you like to change it in some way? If you are comparing yourself to athletes, film stars, and friends whose appearance you admire, you may be trying to achieve a weight that is unrealistic for you—and even unhealthy. When people have unrealistic expectations about their weight, they sometimes develop eating disorders such as anorexia nervosa and bulimia. These disorders are discussed in Chapter 4. However, some people do have good reasons for wanting to lose or gain weight. Those reasons relate to health, and not to some idealized concept of beauty or handsomeness.

Assessing Your Weight

Cassie and her best friend Thuy are the same height. Cassie weighs 10 pounds more than Thuy, but both girls have a weight that is appropriate for them. Thuy is small-boned, while Cassie has a larger bone structure. In addition, Cassie is very athletic, and some of her extra weight is in the form of muscle mass, not body fat. **A person's appropriate weight depends on various factors, including body structure and level of activity.** Your appropriate weight is one that you feel comfortable with—and one that does not present any health risks. A physician or nutrition expert can help you determine your appropriate weight.

The amount of body fat, rather than weight, should be your concern. Various tests measure body fat. In one test, for example, an instrument called a skin-fold caliper is used to measure the fat deposits that accumulate under the skin.

Figure 13-5 *Measurements with a skin-fold caliper can help determine whether body fat is within the limits of good health.*

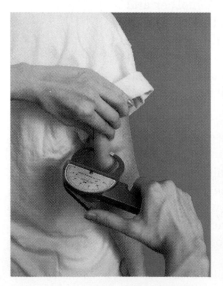
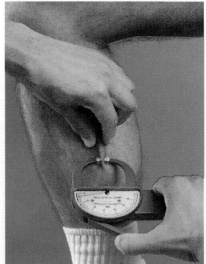

Even though you do not have skin-fold calipers, you can get a rough idea of whether or not you have too much body fat. Pinch a fold of skin on your upper arm and estimate its thickness. If the fold of skin is more than one inch (2.5 centimeters) thick, you may have excess fat. However, remember that your estimate is not as accurate as a test done by a professional who is trained in evaluating weight problems.

Figure 13-6 *People's basal metabolic rate tends to decrease as they age. Children use energy at a faster rate than older people.*

Appetite, Hunger, and Metabolism

If an appropriate test has determined that you should change your weight, you will probably need to modify your eating habits. Once you have achieved a healthy weight, you will want to maintain it. To maintain a healthy weight, the number of calories that you eat each day should match the daily calorie needs of your body. Recall from Chapter 12 that calories are units of energy. If you eat more calories than your body can use, it will store the excess energy as fat, causing you to gain weight. A diet that contains fewer calories than you need can make you lose weight.

Your calorie needs are partly determined by your activity level—the more active you are, the more calories you need. In addition, your **basal metabolic rate**—the rate at which you use energy when your body is completely at rest—affects your calorie needs. The higher your basal metabolic rate, the more calories you will burn. Various factors affect basal metabolic rate. For example, older people tend to have a lower basal metabolic rate than do younger ones. Children and pregnant women tend to have higher basal metabolic rates than the rest of the population. Regular exercise may help increase a person's basal metabolic rate.

If you are trying to change your eating habits, your task will be easier if you understand the physical and emotional factors that make you crave food. **Hunger** is a feeling of physical discomfort that is caused by your body's need for nutrients. **Appetite,** in contrast, is a desire for food that is based on emotional factors rather than nutritional need. Unlike hunger, which is an inborn response, appetite is learned. For example, suppose you smell chicken roasting. Your appetite may make you want to eat the chicken, because you have learned to associate that particular aroma with a delicious taste. Your appetite may sometimes make you eat even when you are not hungry.

Appetite and hunger are not the only factors that affect people's eating behavior. Emotional stress, for example, can influence eating. Some people crave more food when they experience stress, while others lose their appetite. People may eat because they are bored or because they are with others who are eating.

Dangers of Obesity

If you frequently eat more calories than you need, you risk becoming overweight. People are overweight if they weigh more than 10 percent above their appropriate weight. The condition known as **obesity** (oh BEE sih tee) occurs when a person's weight is 20 percent or more above an appropriate weight. Obesity can create many serious health problems and risks. Obese people may suffer from high blood pressure and experience difficulty breathing. Being obese also increases a person's risk of heart attack, stroke, diabetes, arthritis, and certain forms of cancer. People who are significantly overweight should make every effort to reduce to a healthier weight.

Figure 13-7 *Overeating can lead to obesity. People who are obese have an increased risk of developing many health problems.*

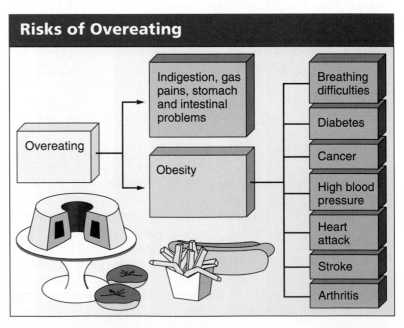

Risks of Overeating

Overeating → Indigestion, gas pains, stomach and intestinal problems

Overeating → Obesity → Breathing difficulties, Diabetes, Cancer, High blood pressure, Heart attack, Stroke, Arthritis

Dieting

1. **MYTH:** Eating starchy foods, such as bread and pasta, will make you gain weight.

   ● **FACT: Starchy foods, or complex-carbohydrate foods, have fewer calories per ounce than fats.**

2. **MYTH:** You can lose a lot of weight just by exercising.

   ● **FACT: To lose a pound by exercising alone, you would need to run for four-and-a-half hours or do aerobics for more than six hours.**

3. **MYTH:** You can lose weight if you don't eat breakfast.

   ● **FACT: Omitting any meal is likely to make you overeat at the next meal. If you skip breakfast, you will probably eat an extra-large lunch.**

4. **MYTH:** You can lose weight by eating only one food, such as grapefruit, bananas, rice, or celery.

   ● **FACT: Because one-food diets are monotonous and nutritionally inadequate, dieters return to previous eating patterns and regain weight.**

5. **MYTH:** Drinking caffeine always makes your appetite decrease.

   ● **FACT: Caffeine can make the level of sugar in your blood drop. This can make you hungry.**

6. **MYTH:** Once you lose weight, you can then resume your former eating habits.

   ● **FACT: Maintaining weight loss means changing eating and exercise patterns for the rest of your life.**

Reducing Weight and Fat Safely

A sensible program of weight loss involves choosing nutritionally balanced meals and snacks. Even though you want to reduce the number of calories that you consume, you still need to make sure that you are obtaining the nutrients necessary for good health. Choose low-calorie foods that are high in nutrient density.

RECOGNIZING EATING PATTERNS Before you plan your diet, keep a diary of what you presently eat. Record the foods that you consume, when you eat them, and how you feel at these times. Use calorie guides to count the approximate number of calories you consume each day.

As you review your diary, you may discover eating patterns or behaviors you were not aware of. You may even find out what triggers your overeating. Some people overeat when they are disappointed, depressed, excited, or tired.

PLANNING HELPFUL STRATEGIES The following are some strategies that will help you eat sensibly:

- Do not try to lose weight too fast. If you change your eating habits gradually rather than suddenly, your weight-loss program will be more successful in the long run.

- Take small portions of food and eat your food slowly, so that you enjoy its taste.

SHARPEN YOUR **SKILLS**

Being Assertive

Rick, who is trying very hard to lose weight, is at a party. His friend Paul keeps trying to get him to eat high-calorie party foods, saying things like "It won't hurt you to eat fattening foods this one time," and "These cookies are great!" How can Rick deal with Paul's behavior? Make a list with some suggestions.

Figure 13-8 *Regular exercise, such as swimming, should be part of any weight-loss plan.*

- If you tend to overeat when you are unhappy or bored, think of an enjoyable behavior that you might substitute for eating—taking a walk, for example.
- To avoid between-meal hunger, save some food from regular meals, such as bread, and later eat it as a snack.
- If you occasionally overeat, do not become upset. Just go back to your sensible eating habits.

EXERCISING   Your weight reduction program should involve regular exercise, such as walking, dancing, or swimming. Changing your eating habits alone is far less effective than eating changes combined with exercise. When you decrease your calorie intake but do not exercise, your basal metabolic rate goes down. Thus your body does not burn calories as rapidly as it did before you began reducing your calorie consumption, and your weight loss slows or stops.

Fad Diets, Diet Aids, and Fasting

Many people want to lose weight very quickly, and so they rely on strategies such as fad diets, pills, or fasting. These approaches are unrealistic and unsafe.

FAD DIETS   A **fad diet** is a popular diet that may help a person lose weight but without proper regard for nutrition and other matters of health. Fad diets range from high protein, low carbohydrate diets to diets with special ingredients that are supposed to help you burn fat. These diets often exclude some important nutrients.

The weight loss achieved with a fad diet is usually only temporary. Frequently, fad diets restrict food choices too much. People become so bored with the diet's limitations that they stop dieting and begin to overeat again.

DIET PILLS   Diet aids, such as pills and candies, are supposed to suppress the appetite. However, they are usually ineffective and can be habit-forming. The major ingredient in most diet pills is caffeine, which may cause nervousness, sleeplessness, and high blood pressure. Diet aids do not provide long-term weight control. If you want to lose weight and keep it off, you need to change your eating behavior rather than rely on medication.

FASTING   When people refrain from eating all foods, they are **fasting.** Fasting is not a healthy way to lose weight, because muscle tissue as well as fat is lost. Long-term fasting may stunt your growth. It may also put a strain on your kidneys and cause hair loss. It has even been linked with irregular menstrual periods in girls and women.

Gaining Body Weight Wisely

Being too thin can be as emotionally painful as being too heavy. Underweight people weigh at least 10 percent less than is appropriate for them. If you are underweight, remember that teenagers as a rule need a large number of calories for growing. Eventually, your growth rate will become slower and then stop. You may put on weight when you are in your early twenties. In addition, some people are naturally thinner than others, and thinness is not a health problem unless it is excessive. However, since underweight can be an indication of health problems, underweight people should be checked by a physician.

The goal of gaining weight can best be achieved by changing any habits that keep you too thin. Eliminate snacks right before mealtimes, because they may spoil your appetite. When you do snack, choose nutrient-dense foods that are high in calories. Never skip a meal. At mealtimes, take bigger helpings of food than usual. While you are increasing your caloric intake, do not neglect exercise. Exercising will help you gain healthy muscle tissue as well as fat.

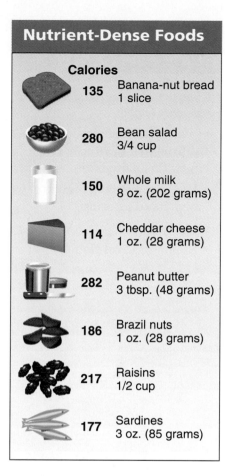

Nutrient-Dense Foods

Calories

135	Banana-nut bread	1 slice
280	Bean salad	3/4 cup
150	Whole milk	8 oz. (202 grams)
114	Cheddar cheese	1 oz. (28 grams)
282	Peanut butter	3 tbsp. (48 grams)
186	Brazil nuts	1 oz. (28 grams)
217	Raisins	1/2 cup
177	Sardines	3 oz. (85 grams)

Figure 13-9 *If you are trying to gain weight, snack on nutrient-dense foods such as these.*

LESSON 2 REVIEW

1. What are two factors that help determine how much you should weigh?
2. Explain why exercise is important in losing weight.
3. Describe two problems associated with fad diets.

What Do You Think?

4. Many people have an unrealistic expectation of what they should weigh. What factors might contribute to this misconception?

Focus on these questions as you read this lesson.

- What are some physical conditions that have special nutritional needs?

- How can diet help to control high blood pressure?

SKILLS

- Breaking a Bad Habit

SPECIAL DIETS

People's circumstances may call for special diets. **Certain physical conditions, such as diabetes and hypoglycemia, have special nutritional requirements.** Lifestyle choices, such as the decision not to eat meat, may also affect how people meet their dietary requirements.

Diet and High Blood Pressure

As blood flows through your body, it exerts a force called blood pressure that pushes against the walls of your blood vessels. High blood pressure, or hypertension, is a condition in which this force becomes too strong. Sodium, found in table salt and many other foods, is thought to be a factor in high blood pressure. People with high blood pressure need to limit their sodium intake. They can do this by using herbs and spices instead of table salt to add flavor to foods. They also need to avoid salty snack foods, such as potato chips. Many processed foods, such as soup mixes and canned vegetables, contain large amounts of sodium. Therefore, people with high blood pressure need to read food labels carefully to avoid high-sodium foods.

Diets for Diabetics

Glucose is the principal carbohydrate that circulates in your blood and is used by your cells for energy. A substance called **insulin** (IN suh lin) enables glucose to pass from the blood into the body's cells. **Diabetes mellitus** (dy uh BEE tis muh LY tus) is a disorder in which the body does not produce or properly use insulin, resulting in high levels of glucose in the blood. Symptoms may include sudden excessive thirst, an increase in appetite combined with a loss in weight, and frequent urination. Some people also feel fatigued, irritable, and confused. If you have a combination of any of these symptoms, you should see a physician.

Diabetes usually can be controlled. Diabetics may need to take daily insulin injections. They also need to eat balanced meals on a regular schedule. Frequently people with diabetes carry a snack that they can eat to regulate their blood glucose levels if they are unable to eat a regular meal.

Diabetics' diets should help to control blood glucose levels by leaving out foods high in sugar and focusing on complex carbohydrates. The American Diabetes Association also emphasizes the importance of foods high in fiber and low in fat. Obesity is a factor in one type of diabetes, and those diabetics need to control their weight.

Figure 13-10 *Herbs such as these can be used instead of salt to make food taste delicious.*

HERB GARDEN

Figure 13-11 *Protein sources such as seaweed and tofu can add variety to vegetarian meals.*

Diet and Hypoglycemia

If the body produces too much insulin, the level of glucose in the blood may fall dramatically. The result is a condition known as **hypoglycemia** (hy poh gly SEE mee uh), or low blood sugar. People with hypoglycemia may experience hunger, weakness, severe headaches, and shakiness as their blood glucose levels fall. Hypoglycemics need to eat several small meals per day instead of three big ones, with foods rich in complex carbohydrates and low in fat. Concentrated sweets, such as candy, should be avoided altogether.

Vegetarianism

A person who does not eat meat is called a **vegetarian** (vej ih TAIR ee un). Some vegetarians eat no foods that come from animal sources. Others, however, include eggs and dairy products. Milk, eggs, cheese, and yogurt contain complete proteins, while plant proteins are incomplete. Recall from Chapter 12 that complete proteins contain all the essential amino acids, but incomplete proteins do not. Vegetarians who eat no food from animal sources must make sure that their diets contain all the essential amino acids.

Vegetarians are less likely than others to suffer from heart disease, a problem that can result from eating too much animal fat. In addition to protein, however, vegetarians must make sure that they are obtaining adequate supplies of the vitamins and minerals they need. Variety is therefore especially important in a vegetarian diet.

Nutrition and Pregnancy

A woman's diet during pregnancy must provide for her needs as well as the needs of the developing baby. When a mother's diet is inadequate, she may give birth to a premature baby or a baby who weighs less than normal. A baby with a low birthweight may be susceptible to disease and slow to develop mentally and physically.

SHARPEN YOUR SKILLS

Breaking a Bad Habit
Meredith has just learned that she has hypoglycemia and must therefore avoid sweets. Unfortunately, Meredith is in the habit of eating a candy bar every afternoon as a snack. Devise a plan that could help Meredith break this habit.

Figure 13-12 *During pregnancy, a woman needs to provide nutrients for herself and her developing baby.*

Most pregnant women should gain between 25 and 35 pounds (about 11 to 16 kilograms) during the pregnancy. To do this, they need to consume more calories than they did before pregnancy—about 300 extra calories per day. A pregnant woman also needs extra amounts of protein and the vitamin folate, since both of these nutrients are essential for the formation of the baby's cells. The minerals calcium, phosphorus, and magnesium are needed for building the baby's teeth and bones. Iron is especially important—without it, the baby might not get enough oxygen from its mother's blood. For this reason, extra iron is often prescribed during pregnancy.

Pregnant teenagers have higher nutrient needs than any other group in the population. Since pregnant adolescents themselves are still growing, their diets need to supply both them and their babies with nutrients needed for growth. Young pregnant teenagers—those between the ages of 13 and 16—are encouraged to gain about 35 pounds (16 kilograms).

Diets for Athletes

Athletes should eat a basic well-balanced diet, but with added calories to accommodate a higher level of physical activity. Most of these calories should come from an increase in complex carbohydrates. High-fat and sugar-rich foods should be avoided. During competition, athletes should drink plenty of fluids to replace water lost in perspiration.

You have probably heard of runners practicing carbohydrate loading before a long race. **Carbohydrate loading** consists of greatly increased carbohydrate intake, accompanied by decreased levels of exercise, in the days immediately before a competition. This practice is an attempt to make extra carbohydrates available to supply energy for the muscles. Carbohydrate loading may benefit highly conditioned athletes who participate in long-lasting sports such as marathon running. However, for most athletes, the best policy is just to eat their normal diet.

LESSON 3 REVIEW

1. Name three physical conditions requiring special diets.
2. Why is it important for diabetics to be careful about the amount of sugar in their diets?
3. What substance should people with high blood pressure restrict?

What Do You Think?

4. Suppose a pregnant teenager decides to limit her caloric intake because she is afraid of becoming overweight. What do you think of her decision? Explain.

4 BUYING FOOD WISELY

T o choose nutrient-dense foods, you need knowledge and practice. When you buy food, do not be swayed by attractive packaging. Instead, use food labels and other information to evaluate foods.

Food Labels

The United States Food and Drug Administration (FDA) requires manufacturers of foods to list certain information on a food's label. Labels must provide the name and address of the manufacturer, the weight of the food, and a list of ingredients in descending order of weight. It must also indicate the number of servings per container, based on a standard serving size for that type of food.

NUTRITION INFORMATION   Food labels must also provide facts about the nutrient content of the product. **The nutrition information on food labels is especially important for consumers to read and evaluate.** The label indicates the following for each serving:

- the total number of calories per serving
- the number of those calories that come from fat
- the weight, in grams or milligrams, of nutrients such as saturated fat, total fat, cholesterol, sugar, dietary fiber, total carbohydrates, protein, and certain minerals
- the percentage of the Daily Values for different nutrients that are supplied by the food

Manufacturers are free to volunteer additional information. Any claims relating to nutrition or health, however, must meet FDA standards.

Focus on these questions as you read this lesson.

- What information on a food label is especially important?
- When buying food, what things should consumers consider?

SKILLS

- Evaluating Health Information
- Analyzing Advertising Appeal

Figure 13-13 *When you examine a food label, you should check the fat and calorie content of the product. What are some other things you might look for?*

Figure 13-14 *During processing, nutrients are added to fortified and enriched foods such as those shown here.*

FOOD ADDITIVES When you have read a food label, have you ever noticed a series of long chemical names in the ingredients list? These are food additives. **Additives** are chemicals that are added to a food to prevent spoiling, to control and improve color and texture, to replace or add nutrients, or to improve flavor. While some people may be allergic to specific additives, such as artificial colors, food additives are safe for most people.

Additives that are used to prevent spoilage or to keep foods from losing their natural color or texture are called **preservatives.** For example, the preservative calcium propionate prevents mold from growing on baked goods. Other preservatives keep peeled and cut fruits from becoming brown. Many preservatives prevent food poisoning and increase the length of time that a food is safe to eat.

Often when food is canned or processed in some other way, some of its vitamins and minerals may be lost. When nutrients are added to replace those that have been lost, the food has been **enriched.** Some breads and cereals are enriched with the vitamins thiamin, riboflavin, and niacin, and the mineral iron. If vitamins, minerals, and even proteins are added to a food that does not normally contain them, the food is **fortified.** Milk, for example, is fortified with vitamin D. The types of foods shown in Figure 13-14 are frequently enriched or fortified.

Sometimes manufacturers use additives to improve the texture or taste of foods. A **leavening agent** makes baked goods rise. An **emulsifier** (ih MUHL suh fy ur) is used to keep fats from separating from the other ingredients in a food. Emulsifiers in salad dressing, for example, keep the fat from floating to the top.

Evaluating Foods

Wise shoppers check the nutrient content of foods. Price and freshness are other characteristics to consider.

NUTRIENTS   Carefully read the label on a packaged food. Check the number of calories and whether the food contains large amounts of fat or sugar. Compare similar foods to determine which are more nutritious. If you are choosing breakfast cereals, for example, look at the amount of dietary fiber, vitamins, minerals, and protein in different products.

FRESHNESS   Many foods, such as meat and baked goods, have a date on their packages. This **product date** is an estimate of how long the product is usable. Reduced-price foods may not be a bargain if the product date has already passed.

PRICE   To find out which of two competing products is the better buy, compare the **unit price,** or cost per unit of measurement. The unit price is usually expressed in ounces or pounds. Suppose, for example, a 20-ounce loaf of bread and a 16-ounce loaf of bread both cost $1.50. The 20-ounce loaf has a unit price of about 8 cents per ounce, while the 16-ounce loaf costs about 9 cents per ounce. If both these loaves have approximately the same nutrients, which is the better buy?

Advertising and Food Choices

Advertising can have a strong influence on food choices. Often advertisers use special techniques, such as humor and lively music, to make products appealing. A TV commercial for frozen waffles, for instance, may show a smiling, healthy-looking family. Yet the waffles' label may reveal that the product is not particularly nutritious. As a smart food consumer, be aware that advertisements can mislead you. Some approaches commonly used in advertisements are analyzed in Building Health Skills for Chapters 18 and 20.

LESSON 4 REVIEW

1. Identify four kinds of information about nutrients that manufacturers must provide on food labels.
2. Why are preservatives added to food?
3. When you shop for foods, what are three factors you should consider?

What Do You Think?

4. Suppose you are comparing the labels for two frozen turkey dinners. What are some things that you might want to learn from the labels?

Reading a Food Label

Every time you go into a supermarket, you see thousands of different food products—cereals in brightly colored boxes, snack foods in shiny foil bags, frozen dinners in packages that can be used in a microwave oven. Attractive and convenient packaging is designed to make you want to purchase the product. In addition, before you even enter a store, advertisements in magazines, newspapers, and television try to convince you to buy certain foods.

To judge the nutritional value of a food, do not rely on advertisements or nice looking packages. Instead, read the food label carefully. The U.S. Food and Drug Administration (FDA) requires packaged foods to be labeled with a list of ingredients and nutrition information.

To use food labels to make healthy food choices, follow the steps that follow. As you read these steps, look at the sample food label for a macaroni and cheese mix.

1. Read the ingredients

Be aware of the ingredients that a food contains.

- Become familiar with terms for different kinds of ingredients. For example, even if the word *sugar* does not appear on the label, the product may contain sugar, since words ending in *-ose* are generally the names of different sugars.

- Notice that ingredients are listed in order by weight from most to least.

- If you have specific dietary restrictions, it is especially important to check the ingredients list first. For example, people who have an allergy for a particular food need to make sure that the product does not contain that ingredient.

2. Notice the number of servings per container

Serving sizes are standardized for over 100 different food categories, so you can compare similar food products for the number of servings they provide. For example, if you need enough lasagna to feed four people, a brand that provides four servings in one container may be a better purchase than one that provides only three servings per container.

3. Note the calories in one serving

Keep in mind that recommended daily caloric intake levels vary depending on a person's age, sex, weight, basal metabolism, and activity level. Active teenagers usually need more calories than do older people.

- If the number of calories is high and you are trying to lose weight, you might want to choose a different food.

- If you are trying to gain weight, a high-calorie food may be a good choice, as long as it provides useful nutrients.

4. Look at the percentages of the Daily Values

The food label indicates what percentages of the Daily Values for different nutrients are supplied by that product. For example, if the label says "Vitamin C—20%," that food supplies 20 percent of the vitamin C that the average person should obtain each day. Notice that the Daily Values are based on a diet of 2,000 calories per day.

- Check the percentages of valuable nutrients, such as dietary fiber, iron, calcium, and vitamins. Is this food a good source of many nutrients that you need?

- Also note the percentage of nutrients that you should limit, such as saturated fat and cholesterol. If a food is high in those nutrients, you may want to avoid it.

5. Read any health-related descriptions or claims

The FDA sets standards for the use of descriptions such as "high fiber" and "low fat." You can use those descriptions for guidance. Also notice any health claims on the package. For example, a label can indicate that high-calcium foods may help prevent osteoporosis.

Apply the Skill

1. Read the information on the label for the macaroni and cheese dinner. Use it to answer the following questions.

(a) What ingredients are contained in the macaroni part of the mix? Which of those ingredients is present in the largest amount?

(b) How many calories does one serving contain?

(c) What percentage of the Daily Values for saturated fat does one serving contain? If you wanted to eat this macaroni and cheese as part of a nutritionally balanced meal, could the other foods be relatively high in fat? Explain.

(d) Do you think that this food would be a good choice for someone on a low-sodium diet? Why or why not?

(e) Is this food a good source of vitamin A?

2. Go to a grocery store or look in your own cupboard and read labels to find three packaged foods that provide a lot of iron.

Then evaluate other nutritional aspects of the food. For example, is it high in sugar? If so, do you think that it still might be a good choice for people who want to increase their intake of iron? Explain.

3. Compare the ingredients list for several different types of cereals. How many different sugars are listed in each? How does the amount of sugar compare to the amounts of other ingredients in the product?

Mac-N-Cheddar

Nutrition Facts

Serving Size 1/2 cup (114 g)
Servings Per Container 4

Amount Per Serving

Calories 260   Calories from Fat 120

	%Daily Values*
Total Fat 13 g	**20%**
Saturated Fat 5 g	**25%**
Cholesterol 30 mg	**10%**
Sodium 660 mg	**28%**
Total Carbohydrate 31 g	**11%**
Sugars 5 g	
Dietary Fiber 0 g	**0%**
Protein 5 g	

Vitamin A 4%   Vitamin C 2%   Calcium 15%   Iron 4%

*Percents (%) of a Daily Value are based on a 2,000 calorie diet. Your Daily Values may vary higher or lower depending on your calorie needs:

	Calories	2,000	2,500
Total Fat	Less than	65 g	80 g
Sat Fat	Less than	20 g	25 g
Cholesterol	Less than	300 mg	300 mg
Sodium	Less than	2,400 mg	2,400 mg
Total Carbohydrate		300 g	375 g
Fiber		25 g	30 g

Calories per gram:
Fat 9 • Carbohydrate 4 • Protein 4

Ingredients: Enriched macaroni (flour, ferrous sulfate, niacin, riboflavin); cheese sauce mix (whey, dehydrated cheese, milk solids, salt); sodium tripolyphosphate, sodium phosphate, citric acid; yellow 5 (color)

CHAPTER 13 REVIEW

KEY IDEAS

LESSON 1

- Each of the main meals of the day should be nutritionally balanced. Taken together, meals and snacks should follow the Food Guide Pyramid's recommendations for servings of different types of foods.
- The recommendations in the Dietary Guidelines for Americans can help people plan a healthy diet.

LESSON 2

- A person's appropriate weight depends on factors such as body structure and level of activity.
- To be effective, a weight-management program should combine sensible eating with regular exercise.

LESSON 3

- Diabetes, hypoglycemia, and high blood pressure are diseases that can be managed, at least in part, through modifications in diet.
- To ensure the health of her baby, a pregnant woman must be sure that she obtains adequate nutrients from the food she eats.

LESSON 4

- Labels on all prepackaged foods must provide specific types of information regulated by the FDA. The wise consumer will consult such labels for information on nutrition when making food purchases.

KEY TERMS

LESSON 2	LESSON 3	emulsifier
appetite	carbohydrate loading	enriched
basal metabolic rate	diabetes mellitus	fortified
fad diet	hypoglycemia	leavening agent
fasting	insulin	preservatives
hunger	LESSON 4	product date
obesity	additives	unit price

Listed above are some of the important terms in this chapter. Choose the term from the list that best matches each phrase below.

1. speed at which the body uses calories when it is at rest

2. practice in which athletes increase their intake of starchy foods before a competition

3. a condition in which a person is 20 percent or more above a reasonable weight

4. a disorder in which the body does not produce or properly use insulin

5. a chemical used to prevent the separation of ingredients in a food

6. chemicals added to foods in order to prevent the foods from spoiling

7. a condition in which the level of sugar in the blood is low

8. cost per unit measure of a product

9. feeling of physical discomfort that is the body's response to its need for nutrients

10. term applied to food whose natural nutrients were lost during processing and then were later restored

11. a desire for food that is based on emotional factors rather than on physical need

12. chemical that enables sugar to pass from the blood into body cells

WHAT HAVE YOU LEARNED?

On a separate sheet of paper, write the word or words that best complete each statement.

13. Many nutritionists think that _____ is the most important meal of the day.

14. People with high blood pressure should limit their intake of _____.

15. It is especially important for pregnant women to obtain enough _____, since new cells cannot be made without this vitamin.

16. To obtain the extra energy that they need, athletes should increase their consumption of foods high in _____.

17. In determining whether a person needs to gain or lose weight, body _____ is a more reliable indicator than body weight.

18. A weight-loss program needs to include _____ as well as changes in diet.

19. Baked goods rise because _____ agents have been added to them.

20. Food labels list the percentage of the _____ Values supplied by different nutrients in the product.

Answer each of the following with complete sentences.

21. What are some practical ways of limiting cholesterol and saturated fats in your diet?

22. Why is it wise to avoid snacks like candy bars or sweet rolls?

23. Describe some measures you can take to improve the nutritional content of meals in fast-food restaurants.

24. Why should a person use a diet diary when attempting to gain or lose weight?

25. Why is fasting a poor way to lose weight?

26. How could a diabetic benefit from the information on a food label?

27. Why do fad diets not work for long?

28. Why do pregnant teenagers need to be especially concerned about their diets?

29. How do adults' nutritional needs change as they become older?

WHAT DO YOU THINK?

30. Esteban, who is very careful about the foods he eats, dislikes the choices at the restaurant where his friends prefer to eat. What can he do?

31. Explain why skipping meals in order to reduce caloric intake is not an effective way to lose weight.

32. When you buy food, why is it important to consider other things besides price?

33. If you are choosing a snack from a vending machine, what might be a good choice? Why?

34. Ruth wants to lose ten pounds in the two weeks before the big dance. She is thinking of using diet pills. Is this wise? Explain.

WHAT WOULD YOU DO?

35. Tim, who is thin, has started eating a lot of potato chips and other high-fat foods in an attempt to gain weight. What advice would you give him?

36. Plan menus for meals and snacks for one day. Your menus should follow the recommendations in the Food Guide Pyramid. Be sure to consider factors that might affect the availability of certain foods.

37. Rory insists that a cereal must be nutritious, because a famous football player advertises it on television. How would you respond to him?

Getting Involved

38. Collect the nutrition information that is now provided by many fast-food restaurants. Use this information to analyze the nutrient density, fat content, and calorie content of the different items. Plan a fast-food meal that is nutrient dense and relatively low in fat.

DIGESTION AND EXCRETION

Every time you take a bite of food, your digestive system begins to work. Eventually, the nutrients that the food contains will be broken down and used by your body. If you choose healthy foods, including those that are low in fat and sugar and high in complex carbohydrates, you will be helping your digestive system function well.

CHAPTER PREVIEW

14-1 Your Teeth and Gums

- Describe the structure of teeth and identify some ways of keeping teeth healthy.

14-2 Your Digestive System

- Trace the path of food through the digestive system and name some digestive system disorders.

14-3 Your Excretory System

- Explain the process by which the kidneys filter waste products from blood and describe some excretory system disorders.

BUILDING HEALTH SKILLS

- Apply proper techniques for brushing and flossing your teeth.

CHECK YOUR WELLNESS

Read each question below and answer *usually*, *sometimes*, or *never*.

- Do you brush your teeth at least twice a day?
- Do you floss your teeth daily?
- Do you see a dentist regularly?
- Do you limit your intake of sugary foods?
- Do you eat a lot of fresh vegetables, fresh fruits, and foods made from grains?
- Do you prepare and store food carefully to avoid contamination with bacteria and spoilage?
- Do you drink six to eight glasses of water each day?

KEEPING A JOURNAL

For one week, keep a record of when you eat meals and whether those meals are rushed or relaxed. At the end of the week, evaluate this record. If many of your meals are rushed, is there anything you can do to change this situation?

Take it to the Net

Focus on these questions as you read this lesson.

- What is the role of the teeth in digestion?
- What can you do to prevent tooth decay?

SKILLS

- Activity: Soft Drinks and Your Teeth

1 YOUR TEETH AND GUMS

What happens when you chew a crisp, juicy piece of carrot? As you learned in Chapter 12, the carrot contains various nutrients. Before your body can use those nutrients, however, they must be broken down into simpler forms and then absorbed by your bloodstream. **Digestion** is the process of breaking down the nutrients in foods into a form your body can absorb and use.

Digestion actually involves two different "breaking down" processes—mechanical digestion and chemical digestion. Chemical digestion breaks food down by chemical reactions—for example, the chemical reactions that change the carrot's starches into sugars. Chemical digestion generally follows mechanical digestion, in which food is broken down physically and mixed with other materials. Mechanical digestion is similar to chopping vegetables and then stirring them into a soup broth. **Chewing is a form of mechanical digestion, and your teeth are a very important part of your digestive system.**

Structure of Teeth

You have four types of teeth: incisors, canines, premolars, and molars. Figure 14-1 shows where these types of teeth are located in your jaws. Although your teeth vary in size and shape, they all have the same basic parts. The part of the tooth that can be seen above the gum is the **crown.** This is the part that comes in contact with the food you eat. Just below the gumline is the neck, and below the neck are the roots.

Each tooth is made of several layers of material. **Enamel,** the hard outer layer that covers the crown, is the hardest material in your body. Most of a tooth consists of **dentin**, a yellowish bonelike material. The root's dentin is covered by a layer of **cementum** (sih MEN tum), another bonelike material. A soft tissue called pulp fills the center of each tooth. The pulp contains nerves and blood vessels, which pass through a channel called the **root canal**. The gum, or **gingiva** (JIN juh vuh), is the tissue that surrounds the teeth and covers the bone around the teeth. Healthy gums fit tightly around the neck of each tooth, holding it firmly in place.

By the age of three, children usually have all 20 of their first set of teeth, called primary teeth. Around the age of 5 or 6, the primary teeth begin to fall out. They are eventually replaced by 32 permanent teeth. Most people acquire their last four permanent teeth, which are called wisdom teeth, between the ages of 17 and 21. Some people never develop wisdom teeth, or have fewer than four.

CHEMISTRY
CONNECTION

A physical change is a change in which the physical characteristics of a substance are altered, but the substance remains the same kind of matter. Mechanical digestion is a type of physical change. In a chemical change, however, a substance is changed into a different kind of substance. Chemical digestion is an example of chemical change.

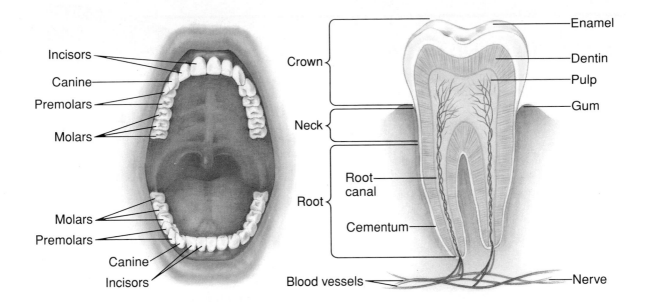

Tooth and Gum Problems

If your teeth are in poor condition, you cannot chew your food well. You also may not be able to speak clearly, since your teeth help you form certain sounds. Tooth and gum problems can also cause **halitosis** (hal ih TOH sis), or bad breath. With proper dental care, however, tooth and gum problems can be prevented.

TOOTH DECAY   Tooth decay occurs because of the action of bacteria. **Plaque** (PLAK) is a sticky, invisible, bacteria-filled film that covers the teeth. If plaque is not removed by regular brushing, the bacteria grow and multiply, breaking down the sugars and starches in food to produce an acid that eats away at tooth enamel. Figure 14-2 shows that when the enamel is broken down, a tiny hole, or cavity, forms. If the cavity is not treated by a dentist, it becomes larger and deeper. To treat the cavity, a dentist uses a drill to remove the decay and bacteria that are present and then fills the hole. Dentists often use an **amalgam** (uh MAL gum), a silver-colored mixture of several metals, to fill teeth.

If tooth decay is not treated, it will eventually spread to the pulp and roots of the tooth. When this happens, the dentist must use a treatment known as root canal therapy to remove the infected pulp from the tooth and replace it with a special material. Root canal therapy may also be necessary if a tooth is severely damaged or broken.

When a tooth is lost because of disease or an injury, it is often replaced with a false tooth, called a fixed bridge. If several neighboring teeth are lost, a removable denture, consisting of several false teeth, may be needed. Unlike a fixed bridge, a removable denture can be taken out of the mouth for cleaning.

Figure 14-1 *All of your teeth, no matter what type, are covered with a hard substance called enamel. The crown is the part of the tooth that you can see.*

Figure 14-2 *Tooth decay begins on the tooth's surface and spreads to the inner tissues.*

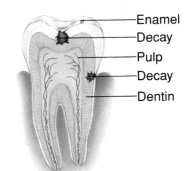

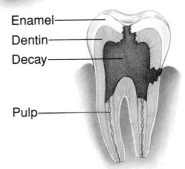

SOFT DRINKS AND YOUR TEETH

In this activity, you will determine the effects of soft drinks on eggshells, which are composed of some of the same materials as your teeth.

Materials

three cups	regular soft drink
tape for labeling	diet soft drink
three large pieces of eggshell	water

Procedure

1. Label one cup "regular soft drink"; label the second cup "diet soft drink"; and label the third cup "water." Put a piece of eggshell in each cup.

2. Pour some regular soft drink over the first piece of eggshell. Pour diet soft drink over the second piece and water over the third.

3. Leave the eggshell pieces in the fluids for three days. Then discard the fluids and examine each eggshell piece carefully.

Discussion

1. What happened to each of the three eggshells?

2. Which fluid had the least effect on the eggshell?

3. Compare the effects of regular soft drink and diet soft drink on the eggshells. Was there any difference?

4. If teeth are composed of materials similar to those in eggshells, which liquid—water, regular soft drink, or diet soft drink—will affect teeth the least?

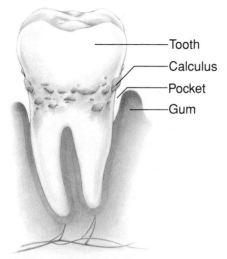

Figure 14-3 *If calculus builds up, it can cause periodontitis, and the teeth can become loose.*

Tooth
Calculus
Pocket
Gum

GUM PROBLEMS In addition to promoting tooth decay, plaque can damage the gums. If plaque forms and is not removed within 48 hours, it begins to harden into a material called tartar, or **calculus** (KAL kyuh lus), which irritates the gums. If calculus is not removed from the teeth, it eventually causes **gingivitis** (jin juh VY tis), a condition in which the gums become red and swollen and bleed easily.

Untreated gingivitis can develop into **periodontitis** (pehr ee uh dahn TY tis), a more advanced stage of gum disease. In periodontitis, the buildup of plaque and calculus causes the gums to pull away from the teeth and form pockets, as shown in Figure 14-3. Plaque, calculus, and food collect in the pockets, and the gums may become infected. If this infection is not treated, the teeth become loose and eventually fall out. Periodontitis can be treated surgically by dentists who specialize in gum disease.

MALOCCLUSION When the upper and lower teeth do not meet properly, the condition is known as a **malocclusion** (mal uh KLOO zhun), or improper bite. When the upper teeth stick out too far, the condition is called an overbite. In contrast, when the lower teeth stick out beyond the upper teeth, the condition is called an underbite.

A severe malocclusion can make chewing difficult or cause the teeth to wear down unevenly. People with malocclusions need the help of an **orthodontist** (awr thuh DAHN tist), a dentist who specializes in correcting the position of teeth. Orthodontists use brackets and wires—known as braces—to help move teeth to their proper positions. Once the teeth have been moved, an orthodontist may use other mechanical aids, such as a retainer, to keep the teeth in place until they become fixed in their new positions.

Dental Care

You can follow a few simple steps for healthy teeth and gums. You should eat a well-balanced diet that is low in sugar. Brush your teeth at least twice a day, and preferably after every meal. If you cannot brush immediately after eating, try to rinse your mouth with water.

Brushing and rinsing your teeth help to remove the food and some of the plaque that can cause cavities, gum disease, and halitosis. Use a soft-bristled toothbrush and fluoride toothpaste. Fluoride is a tasteless, odorless chemical that combines with tooth enamel, making it stronger and more resistant to decay.

Dental floss is nylon string that removes food and plaque from areas that a toothbrush cannot reach. You should floss your teeth once a day, preferably at bedtime. Building Health Skills on page 333 describes the proper way to brush and floss your teeth.

If you think you have a dental problem, see a dentist right away. Even if you do not have problems, you should see a dentist twice a year for checkups. Regular dental checkups can stop problems before they become painful or hard to treat. Because of dental checkups and preventive care, young people today generally have fewer cavities than their parents did when they were growing up. The use of fluoride—in toothpaste, drinking water, and special dental treatments—has greatly reduced tooth decay.

LESSON 1 REVIEW

1. Which is chewing—mechanical digestion or chemical digestion? Explain.
2. What material covers the crown of a tooth?
3. How is tooth decay related to plaque?
4. What does flossing accomplish?

What Do You Think?

5. People with gingivitis sometimes stop brushing their teeth because their gums hurt too much. Do you think this will solve the problem of painful gums? Explain.

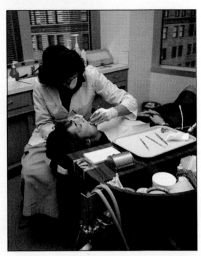

Focus on these questions as you read this lesson.

- What happens to nutrients in the process of digestion?
- What factors affect the functioning of your digestive system?

SKILLS

- Reading a Food Label

Figure 14-4 *As food travels through the digestive system, it is broken down and absorbed.*

2 YOUR DIGESTIVE SYSTEM

Your body is made up of billions of cells. A **cell** is the smallest living unit of the body. Your cells are so small that they cannot be seen without the help of a microscope. Each cell in your body needs a supply of nutrients for energy, growth, and repair. The process of digestion is the first step in transferring the nutrients in food to the cells of the body.

How the Digestive System Works

Digestion takes place in a series of steps as the food you eat moves through several organs. The organs of the digestive system are shown in Figure 14-4. As you read about digestion, refer to this illustration.

Recall that both mechanical and chemical processes are involved in the breakdown of food. When you chew your food, the teeth begin mechanical digestion by cutting, tearing, and grinding food. Mechanical and chemical digestion both take

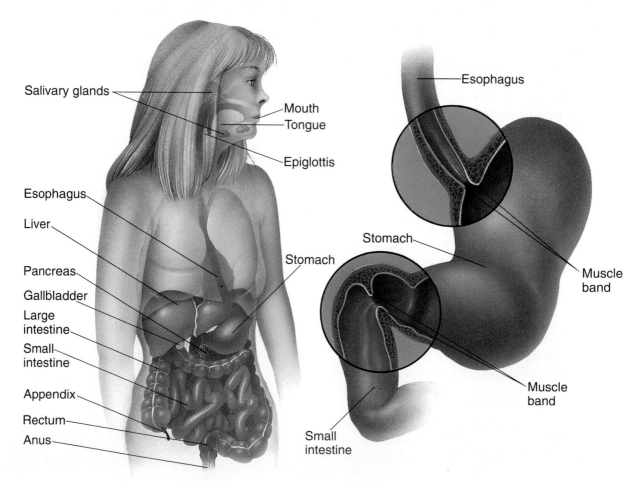

place as food travels through the digestive system. **After nutrients are broken down, they pass into the bloodstream and are taken to the body cells for use in metabolism and growth.**

THE MOUTH   Imagine that a pizza has just been removed from the oven. It smells wonderful, and you can feel your mouth water. Your mouth is producing **saliva,** a liquid that aids in digestion. Saliva consists mostly of water, which moistens the food, making it easier to chew and swallow.

Saliva also contains an enzyme that helps break starches down into sugars. **Enzymes** are substances that help carry out chemical reactions in the body. Digestive enzymes are essential for chemical digestion. Each enzyme acts on only one kind of nutrient. For example, an enzyme that breaks down starches has no effect on fats or proteins.

Mechanical digestion helps prepare food for chemical digestion, because after food has been broken into small pieces, it has a greater surface area on which digestive enzymes can act. You can compare this process to a sugar cube dissolving in a hot cup of tea. If you crush the cube first, the sugar will dissolve faster, because it has been broken down into tiny grains. It is important to chew your food well, because chewing breaks food into pieces and therefore helps speed chemical digestion.

After food is chewed and mixed with saliva, the tongue helps form it into a small ball and moves it to the back of the mouth so it can be swallowed. As you swallow, a small flap of tissue called the **epiglottis** (ep ih GLAHT is) automatically covers the opening to your windpipe. This action prevents food from entering your air passage.

Have you ever had food "go down the wrong pipe"? This sometimes happens if you talk or laugh with food in your mouth. When you talk, the epiglottis opens, and food can slip into the windpipe.

THE ESOPHAGUS   When you swallow food, it moves into your **esophagus** (ih SAHF uh gus), which is a muscular tube

Figure 14-5 *Notice how the epiglottis closes the opening to the windpipe and prevents food from entering the air passages.*

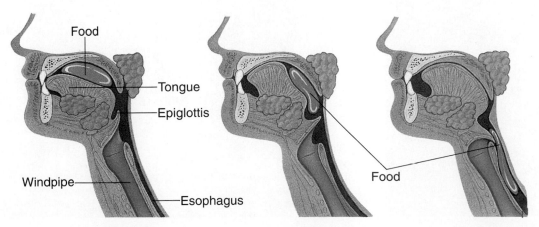

Food — Tongue — Epiglottis — Windpipe — Esophagus — Food

Digestion and Excretion   **321**

that connects the mouth and the stomach. The esophagus is about 12 inches (30 centimeters) long. The muscles of the wall of the esophagus push food downward toward the stomach. The wavelike muscular action that pushes food through the esophagus and the rest of the digestive system is called **peristalsis** (pehr ih STAWL sis). Peristalsis is similar to the way you push toothpaste through the tube. As you squeeze the tube, the toothpaste is pushed ahead of the place where you squeeze. As the muscles squeeze, they push the food downward.

THE STOMACH
The **stomach** is a muscular, saclike organ with a circular band of muscle at each end. These circular bands keep the contents of the stomach from leaking back into the esophagus or forward into the intestine. Layers of muscles in the stomach wall contract and relax, churning and mixing the food. This mixing is a form of mechanical digestion. If you have ever been hungry and heard your stomach rumble, what you heard was the sound of your empty stomach as these muscles contracted.

The stomach produces gastric juice, which is a mixture of hydrochloric acid and enzymes. The enzymes begin the chemical digestion of proteins, such as those in the cheese on your slice of pizza. Hydrochloric acid helps the enzymes function and also kills bacteria present in food. The stomach lining is coated with mucus, which protects the stomach from the strong acid. After food has mixed with gastric juice, the result is a thick liquid called **chyme** (kym). When the chyme is ready to leave the stomach, the lower band of muscle opens, releasing chyme into the small intestine bit by bit.

THE SMALL INTESTINE
The **small intestine** is a long, tubelike organ in which chemical digestion and the absorption of nutrients are completed. It gets its name from its small diameter—only about 1 inch (2.5 centimeters). As chyme moves through the small intestine, many enzymes are

Figure 14-6 *Tiny fingerlike villi, shown in the photograph and the diagram, provide a large surface area for the absorption of food in the small intestine.*

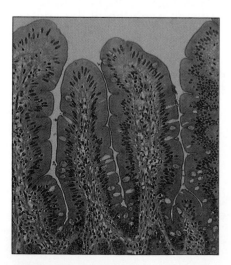

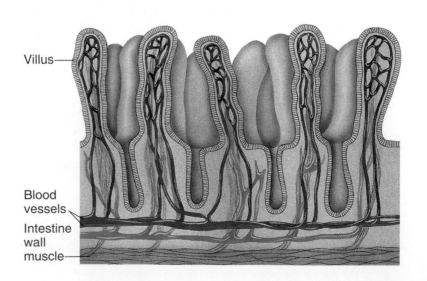

Villus

Blood vessels

Intestine wall muscle

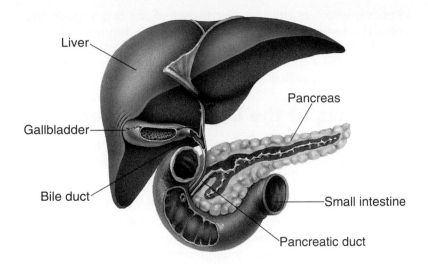

Figure 14-7 *Food does not pass through the liver and pancreas, but these two organs supply substances that help break down food.*

Liver

Pancreas

Gallbladder

Bile duct

Small intestine

Pancreatic duct

added to it. As a result, complex nutrients are broken down into simple sugars, amino acids, and simple forms of fats.

The wall of the small intestine is lined with millions of tiny, fingerlike projections called **villi** (VIL eye). As shown in Figure 14-6, each villus contains tiny blood vessels. When digestion is complete, the simple nutrients, along with some water, are absorbed through the villi and then pass into the blood. Once in the bloodstream, nutrients are carried to all the cells of the body.

THE LIVER AND PANCREAS   Although food never enters the liver and pancreas, these organs are part of the digestive system. Each produces substances that flow through tubes into the small intestine, where they help the digestive processes.

The **liver** is a large organ that removes harmful materials from the body and also produces a digestive juice called bile. **Bile** aids in the digestion of fats by breaking large droplets of fat into smaller ones. Bile is stored in the **gallbladder,** a sac attached to the liver. From the gallbladder, bile flows through a tube into the small intestine. The **pancreas** (PANG kree us) is an organ that produces hormones and several digestive enzymes. One enzyme breaks down carbohydrates, another breaks down fats, and a third breaks down proteins.

THE LARGE INTESTINE   Some materials in food, such as fiber, cannot be broken down and absorbed by your body. These indigestible materials, along with water, pass into the **large intestine,** a tubelike organ that absorbs water and gets rid of waste. Although it is much shorter than the small intestine, the large intestine is larger in diameter—about 2.5 inches (6 centimeters). Part of the large intestine is sometimes called the colon.

As wastes move through the large intestine, much water is absorbed through the intestinal wall. The watery chyme then becomes a solid material called **feces** (FEE seez). The

Reading a Food Label

People with lactose intolerance usually try to avoid foods containing dairy products. Examine the labels on different types of prepared foods, such as frozen dinners, rice mixes, pasta mixes, and frozen desserts. List the foods that contain dairy products. If you were trying to avoid dairy products, what foods could you substitute?

rectum, which is the last few inches of the large intestine, holds the feces until they are released from the body. At the end of the rectum is a circular band of muscle that controls the **anus,** the opening of the rectum. The release of wastes from the body is called elimination.

Disorders of the Digestive System

Some disorders of the digestive system, such as indigestion, are fairly common. Mild digestive problems can often be corrected or controlled by changes in eating habits.

INDIGESTION Most people suffer occasionally from indigestion, which is an inability to break down certain foods properly. Soon after eating, they may experience sharp chest pains, abdominal cramps, gas, or nausea. For many people, particular foods may trigger indigestion, and avoiding those foods will prevent the problem. Stress can also contribute to indigestion. Therefore, eating in a calm, relaxed environment may help.

Many people suffer serious indigestion when they eat dairy products. Milk and other dairy products contain the sugar lactose. The enzyme lactase is needed for the digestion of the sugar. **Lactose intolerance** is an inability to digest lactose because the digestive system does not produce enough lactase.

Cheese and yogurt have less lactose than milk, and some people with lactose intolerance are able to eat those dairy products, particularly if they only have small amounts at a time. In addition, dairy products can be pretreated with the enzyme, and people can take capsules of the enzyme when they eat dairy products. However, the nutrients in dairy products can be obtained from other sources, and many people with lactose intolerance choose to avoid dairy products.

Figure 14-8 *If you cannot eat dairy products, you can obtain calcium from foods such as legumes, sardines, broccoli, almonds, and tofu.*

DIARRHEA AND CONSTIPATION   Food that moves too quickly through your digestive system may result in frequent, watery bowel movements, or diarrhea. Mild cases of diarrhea usually do not need medical attention. However, prolonged diarrhea can lead to dehydration, which is a severe loss of water and minerals. If diarrhea lasts longer than 48 hours, or if you notice the signs of dehydration, such as dry lips or a lack of tears or urination, seek medical help.

Constipation occurs when the large intestine removes too much water. Elimination becomes difficult and bowel movements are infrequent. Constipation tends to happen if foods move through the digestive system too slowly. To prevent constipation, drink plenty of water. Also eat foods with a lot of fiber, since high-fiber foods pass through your digestive system quickly. Limit your intake of high-fat foods, which pass slowly through the digestive system, and get plenty of exercise.

Figure 14-9 *By eating high-fiber foods such as these, you will help maintain the health of your digestive system.*

FOOD POISONING   Most food poisoning stems from eating undercooked animal foods, such as meat, milk, eggs, or fish. However, the bacteria that cause these illnesses may change.

Salmonella and *shigella* are common causes of food poisoning. *Salmonella* spreads when contaminated food, such as meat, poultry, or eggs, is undercooked or when raw food touches cooked food. *Shigella* spreads when someone who has not washed his or her hands touches food that is not cooked again.

Recently, *E. coli* and listeria poisonings have been increasing. Undercooked contaminated meat is the main cause of *E. coli*; you should avoid rare or "pink" ground beef. Listeria is less common, but it causes about half of our food poisoning deaths. It is spread in raw animal products, such as unpasteurized milk and cheese. Contaminated drinking water is a source of both *E. coli* bacteria and listeria disease.

Boulism is caused by particularly lethal bacteria that grow in improperly processed foods. To avoid botulism, do not eat from swollen, creased, or badly dented cans, and avoid cracked jars as well as containers with loose or dented lids.

Figure 14-10 *What measures can you take to prevent perishable food from spoiling at a picnic?*

Food poisoning can usually be prevented if food is prepared, handled, and stored carefully.

- Wash your hands before and after you work with food.
- Thoroughly clean utensils, cutting boards, and counters each time you use them.
- Alway cook meats, poultry, and eggs thoroughly.
- Cooked food should be eaten immediately and leftovers refrigerated quickly.
- If a can of food is creased or bulging, discard it.

ULCERS A **peptic ulcer** is a sore that forms when stomach acid damages the lining of the digestive tract. The result is a burning pain felt just below the breastbone. An ulcer in the stomach is called a gastric ulcer; an ulcer in the small intestine (the duodenum) is known as a duodenal ulcer. Many peptic ulcers are caused by the bacterium *H. pylori* and can be cured in just a few weeks with antibiotics.

Stress is also believed to play a role in ulcers. Some researchers suggest that stress may make the body more susceptible to an *H. pylori* infection. Others note that stress, smoking, alcohol abuse, and a lack of sleep make it more difficult for the ulcer to heal. In any case, ulcers should be treated promptly by a physician.

HEMORRHOIDS Enlarged veins in the anal area are called **hemorrhoids** (HEM uh roydz). They cause pain, itching, and bleeding. They may be caused by straining during bowel movements, lifting heavy weights, and by chronic constipation. Hemorrhoids are common in people who are overweight, inactive, or pregnant. Regular, daily exercise and a diet of whole grains, fresh fruit, and vegetables can help to relieve the symptoms of hemorrhoids.

APPENDICITIS   A small pouch called the appendix is located near the place where the small and large intestines meet. **Appendicitis** (uh pen dih SY tis) is an infection of the appendix; its symptoms are pain in the lower right side of the abdomen, fever, nausea, and vomiting. The treatment for appendicitis is surgery to remove the appendix. If surgery is not performed quickly, the appendix may burst, releasing the infection into the abdomen.

CROHN'S DISEASE   Abdominal pain and diarrhea are symptoms of many disorders of the digestive system. If they occur repeatedly, they may indicate **Crohn's disease,** which is an ongoing inflammation of the lower part of the small intestine. It is more common in young people than in people over 40. In severe cases, the inflammation interferes with the absorption of nutrients. Physicians treat Crohn's disease by prescribing medication and a special diet. Severe cases may need surgery to remove part of the small intestine.

Figure 14-11 *Meals should be relaxing, pleasant times. Try not to rush or overeat.*

Keeping the Digestive System Healthy

Obviously, what you eat is important to maintaining a healthy digestive system. Avoid foods that are high in fat. A well-balanced diet that includes plenty of fresh vegetables, fresh fruit, and grain products helps keep food moving smoothly through the intestines. Eat moderately, because overeating can strain the digestive tract.

How you eat is important, too. You should try to plan meals for a time when you can relax and enjoy them. Chew your food slowly and thoroughly. Also drink water during your meal and at other times throughout the day. In addition, exercise is important for a healthy digestive system, since it helps to prevent constipation.

LESSON **2** REVIEW

1. What happens to nutrients after they are broken down by the digestive system?
2. Trace the path of food through the digestive system.
3. What part of the digestive system is lined with structures that absorb nutrients?
4. List three eating habits that help keep the digestive system healthy.

What Do You Think?

5. Suppose you brought tuna salad to a picnic. By the end of the day, the tuna salad has been at room temperature for several hours. What should you do with the leftovers?

DIFFERENT VOICES SPEAKING

Until he received a kidney at age 17, Corey McManus spent much of his time in hospitals. Today, Corey leads a relatively normal life and plans a career in hotel and restaurant management.

Q. Corey, when did your health problems begin?

A. They started when I was 18 months old. I was diagnosed as having diabetes. When I was 13 years old, the disease caused kidney failure. My life really went downhill.

Q. What do you mean by that?

A. I had to go live in a hospital. It was a special hospital with a school program for chronically ill kids. It's the only one like it in the country. I stayed there for four years.

Corey McManus

Q. Were there any happy times during those years?

A. There were a few. I made some new friends at the hospital—other kids who were sick, plus a couple of funny nurses. My mother and grandmother also came to visit me a lot, and that helped. The real happy times for me came when the doctors told me they had found a kidney match and that I would be going to Philadelphia for an operation.

Q. How has your life been since the transplant?

A. It's been better. Before the kidney came, I had to be on dialysis—medical treatments to take waste out of my blood. That was four times a day over a four-hour period. Now I can do a lot of things I couldn't do before. I like to bowl—I'm in a bowling league—and I play tennis. I like swimming, too, though I'm sensitive about body scars from all the medical work done to me, so I wear a T-shirt.

Q. It sounds as though you're interested in physical fitness.

A. I know how far I can push my body and get away with it. I'll push myself to that limit, so I guess you might say I'm into physical fitness. I'm not physically fit, though. I have trouble breathing and get winded often.

Q. Do you have any advice for people waiting for a kidney transplant?

A. I would tell them to hang in there and not to give up—that even though things look bad, life is precious. I know because, at one point back when I was on dialysis, I needed surgery. There were complications, and I was in a coma for three weeks. They tell me I almost died. Now I notice things most people don't, like how the air smells different on different days. When you realize how precious life is, you learn to appreciate every single second.

Journal Activity

Write a paragraph in which you identify what you believe to be the most difficult part of Corey's struggle. Explain why you think that this part was especially difficult. Then explore the attitudes, character traits, and support from others that can help people cope with difficulties such as this.

3 YOUR EXCRETORY SYSTEM

Like a fire, your cells use fuel—nutrients—as a source of energy. Just as a fire leaves ashes, the chemical reactions in your cells leave waste products. The gas carbon dioxide is one such waste product. **Urea** (yoo REE uh) is another—it contains nitrogen and is the major waste produced from the breakdown of protein. These wastes would poison you if they were not removed from your body.

Excretion is the process by which the body collects and removes wastes produced by its cells. **Waste removal is carried out by the excretory system, whose main organs are the kidneys, ureters, bladder, and urethra.** The skin, lungs, and liver also are involved in excretion.

The Kidneys

Waste products pass out of your body cells and into your bloodstream. The **kidneys** are the organs that filter wastes—particularly urea—from the blood. As you can see in Figure 14-12, you have two kidneys, each about the size of a fist. The kidneys are located on either side of your spine at the level of your elbows.

Focus on these questions as you read this lesson.

Focus on these questions as you read this lesson.

- What is the function of each of the main organs of the excretory system?
- What are some disorders of the excretory system?

SKILLS

- Finding the Facts

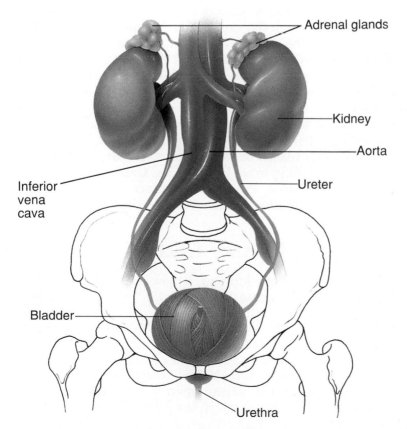

Figure 14-12 *In the diagram of the human excretory system, the blood vessels shown in red carry blood to the kidneys, and the blue blood vessels carry filtered blood away from the kidneys.*

Adrenal glands

Kidney

Aorta

Ureter

Inferior vena cava

Bladder

Urethra

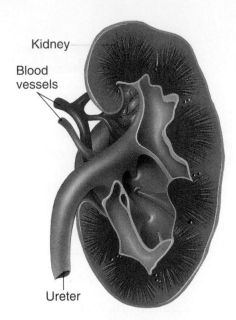

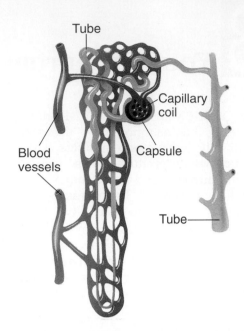

Figure 14-13 *Each kidney (left) contains over a million nephrons (right). Trace the path of the tube that begins with the capsule.*

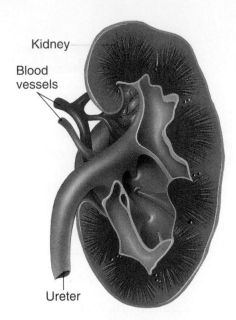
Blood reaches the kidneys through large blood vessels. Inside the kidneys, these vessels branch into smaller and smaller vessels, the smallest of which are the capillaries. Each capillary eventually forms a tight coil. This capillary coil is part of the **nephron** (NEF rahn), the filtering unit of the kidney. Each kidney contains over a million nephrons, like the one shown in Figure 14-13.

The capillary coil is surrounded by a cuplike capsule. As blood flows through the capillary coil, some of the liquid part moves out of the capillary and into the capsule, while the blood cells stay behind. The liquid that moves into the capsule consists of water with materials dissolved in it.

The watery solution that flows into the capsule contains the waste product urea, but it also contains many substances that are not wastes—substances that your body needs. As the solution flows from the capsule through a long, twisted tube, the body reabsorbs the "good" materials, leaving waste products, including urea, in the tube. **Urine,** which is composed of water, urea, and other substances, is the liquid that is left in the tube after this reabsorption process.

The Lower Urinary Tract

After urine leaves the kidneys, it flows through the remaining structures shown in Figure 14-12. These structures do not filter or change the urine in any way. They carry the urine away from the kidney and out of the body. A long tube, called a **ureter** (yoo REE tur), carries urine away from the kidney. One ureter from each kidney leads into the **bladder,** a muscular sac that stores urine. When the bladder is full, muscles squeeze the urine down the **urethra** (yoo REE thruh), the tube through which urine leaves the body.

Other Excretory Organs

Your lungs, skin, and liver all play a role in removing waste products from your body. Recall that one of the waste products that is formed when cells release energy from food is carbon dioxide. This waste enters the blood, but is not filtered by the kidneys. Instead, carbon dioxide leaves the body through the lungs. The lungs release carbon dioxide and some water, which pass out of the body as you exhale, or breathe out.

By producing perspiration, your skin also functions as an excretory organ. Perspiration, or sweat, consists of water and dissolved waste materials. When you perspire, these wastes are released from your body.

Your liver plays a complex role in excretion. It chemically changes wastes, impurities, poisons, alcohol, and drugs to less harmful substances. Some of these substances then travel through the bloodstream to the kidneys, where they are removed. Other substances become part of the bile and pass into the small intestine, to be eliminated with the feces.

Figure 14-14 *To help keep your kidneys healthy, drink a lot of water.*

Disorders of the Excretory System

Infections of the bladder and urethra, which are caused by bacteria, are the most common excretory disorders. People with these infections have to urinate frequently, and they usually experience a burning, painful feeling during urination. Bladder and urethra infections should be treated promptly, because the infection can spread to the kidneys. Infections are the most common cause of **nephritis** (nuh FRY tis), an inflammation, or swelling, of the nephrons.

Kidney stones are pebblelike masses of salts in the kidneys or urinary tract. When kidney stones become stuck in the urinary tract, they are very painful. While many of these stones eventually pass out of the urinary tract by themselves, some must be removed by medical procedures.

Figure 14-15 *When you exhale, you get rid of carbon dioxide and some water. You can "see your breath" in cold weather because some of this water freezes into tiny ice crystals.*

Lasers Shatter Kidney Stones

Approximately 350,000 people in the United States are admitted to hospitals each year for kidney stone treatment. To get rid of the stones, physicians may prescribe medication or use a device called a lithotripter, which generates sound waves that shatter the stones. Until recently, large stones and stones that are shielded from sound waves by the hip bones had to be removed by surgery. Now a new technique that uses laser light provides an alternative to surgery.

To treat kidney stones with laser light, a physician threads an optic fiber of the instrument up through the bladder and places it in contact with a stone. A pulse of light is sent through the fiber. When the light hits the stone, it produces a sparklike flash, which shatters the stone. Shattered stones can generally be passed out of the body in the urine. In addition to reaching areas the lithotripter cannot reach, laser light is less expensive and less cumbersome to use.

Until recently, surgery was necessary to remove such kidney stones. Now an ultrasound machine can be used to smash the stones by bombarding them with sound waves. Lasers are also used to destroy kidney stones.

Another serious disorder is **uremia** (yoo REE mee uh), poisoning of the body caused by the failure of the kidneys to remove wastes from the bloodstream. If uremia results from a kidney infection, antibiotics can be used to treat the condition. If the kidneys stop working completely, the condition is known as kidney failure.

Victims of kidney failure must undergo **kidney dialysis** (dy AL ih sis), a process in which a machine is used to filter blood in place of the kidneys. This treatment takes a few hours every week. Blood is removed from the body by tubes that then carry it through the dialysis machine. There the blood is filtered of wastes and then returned to the body. Sometimes the only means of survival in cases of kidney failure is a kidney transplant, in which the patient's diseased kidney is replaced with a healthy one from another person.

Keeping the Excretory System Healthy

The waste products that are filtered by the kidneys are poisons. The most important way to keep your kidneys healthy is to dilute these poisons as much as possible. You should try to drink six to eight glasses of water a day, and more if you are exercising or perspiring heavily. If you have a fever or some other infection, your kidneys must work even harder to remove impurities. At these times, it is especially important to drink lots of water.

LESSON **3** REVIEW

1. List the main organs in the excretory system and describe the function of each.
2. What waste product is produced when proteins are broken down?
3. What are kidney stones, and how are they treated?
4. What is the most important thing you can do to keep your kidneys healthy?

What Do You Think?

5. A person with a bladder infection is usually given antibiotics to kill the bacteria and told to drink extra amounts of water. Why is extra water so important in treating the infection?

Caring for Your Teeth

1. Brushing

You need to brush all surfaces of your teeth. The illustrations show the proper way to do this.

• Brush the outer surfaces with short, side-to-side strokes. Gently brush the gums too.

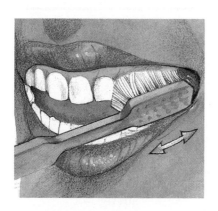

• Hold the brush flat and move it back and forth over the chewing surfaces of your molars, as shown in the illustration below. Use a scrubbing motion.

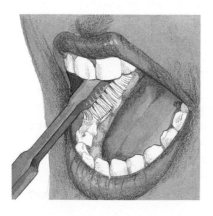

• To brush the inside of your front teeth, hold the brush upright and use up-and-down strokes.

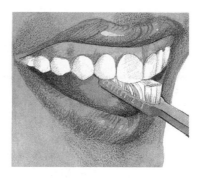

• Use short, angled strokes for the inside of your back teeth.

2. Flossing

Use about 18 inches (45 centimeters) of either waxed or unwaxed dental floss—whichever you prefer.

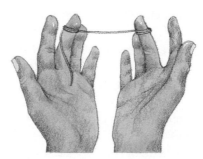

• Wrap the ends of the floss around your middle fingers. Then carefully guide the floss between your teeth. Do not jerk it or pull it hard.

• Gently move the floss up and down between your teeth.

• Unwind and use a clean section of floss as you repeat the procedure with each tooth.

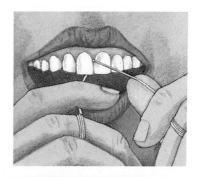

Apply the Skill

1. Brush your teeth after every meal. If you cannot do that, brush at least twice a day. Use the procedures described and illustrated on this page.

2. Floss your teeth once every day following the procedure shown here.

3. When you have finished brushing and flossing, rinse your mouth with water.

CHAPTER 14 REVIEW

KEY IDEAS

LESSON 1

- Chewing is a form of mechanical digestion.
- Most tooth and gum problems can be prevented by using proper brushing and flossing techniques.

LESSON 2

- Nutrients pass into the bloodstream after they have been broken down by the digestive system.

- Many disorders of the digestive system, such as indigestion and constipation, respond to modifications in diet.

LESSON 3

- The kidneys, ureters, bladder, and urethra filter waste products from the blood and then remove them from the body.
- Disorders of the excretory system include infections, kidney stones, uremia, and kidney failure.

KEY TERMS

LESSON 1
amalgam
calculus
cementum
crown
dentin
enamel
gingiva
gingivitis
malocclusion
orthodontist

periodontitis
plaque
root canal

LESSON 2
bile
cell
chyme
Crohn's disease
enzyme
epiglottis
esophagus

gall bladder
lactose intolerance
large intestine
liver
pancreas
peptic ulcer
peristalsis
saliva
stomach
small intestine
villi

LESSON 3
bladder
kidney dialysis
kidney stones
nephritis
nephron
urea
uremia
ureter
urethra

Listed above are some of the important terms in this chapter. Chose the term from the list that best matches each phrase below.

1. substance that helps carry out chemical reactions in the body

2. a condition in which the upper and lower teeth do not meet properly

3. a long, tubelike organ in which chemical digestion is completed

4. a large organ that produces bile and also removes harmful materials from the body

5. a condition in which there is too little of the enzyme that digests milk

6. dentist who specializes in correcting the position of teeth

7. hard material that covers the visible part of the tooth

8. a muscular storage sac that holds urine until it is released from the body

9. part of the kidney in which wastes are filtered from the blood

10. flap of tissue that prevents food from entering the windpipe

11. advanced form of gum disease in which gums pull away from the teeth

12. tiny projections that absorb digested food in the small intestine

13. pebblelike masses of salts in the kidneys or urinary tract

14. tube that carries urine from the kidney

WHAT HAVE YOU LEARNED?

On a separate sheet of paper, write the word or words that best complete each statement.

15. _____ is an ongoing inflammation of the lower part of the small intestine.

16. The breakdown of proteins produces the waste product called _____.

17. Eating in a(n) _____ atmosphere may help you avoid indigestion.

18. Prolonged diarrhea can lead to _____, a condition in which the body loses a lot of water.

19. Chewing, churning, and mixing are all forms of _____ digestion.

20. A tooth is made mostly of _____, a bone-like material.

21. The bacteria that cause _____ food poisoning are found in raw poultry, eggs, and meats.

22. An open sore in the stomach or small intestine is called a(n) _____.

23. The _____ produces both hormones and digestive enzymes.

24. Bile is stored in the _____.

Answer each of the following with complete sentences.

25. What is the smallest living unit of the body?

26. Name two organs of the digestive system through which food does not pass.

27. Name and describe the process by which food is moved through the digestive system.

28. Describe the process of kidney dialysis.

29. What role does the liver play in digestion? What role does the liver play in excretion?

30. List three factors that are believed to contribute to the formation of peptic ulcers.

31. How do the lungs and skin function in excretion?

32. Explain how tooth decay is caused. How does removing plaque help to prevent tooth decay?

33. What is halitosis and what can you do to help prevent it?

WHAT DO YOU THINK?

34. Some sugarless gums contain starches. Why could this be a problem for your teeth?

35. A burst, or ruptured, appendix is an extremely dangerous condition. Why do you think this is the case?

36. Why should you see a physician if you have recurring abdominal pain and diarrhea?

37. Explain why malocclusion can interfere with the digestive process.

38. To prepare dinner, a cook first cuts up a raw chicken on a cutting board. Then, without washing the cutting board, the cook uses it for slicing salad vegetables. Is this a safe practice? Explain.

WHAT WOULD YOU DO?

39. Wayne rushes through lunch. About an hour later, he complains that his stomach hurts. What would you tell him?

40. You are planning a pizza party. One of the friends you want to invite has lactose intolerance. What would you do?

41. It is a hot summer day. You have finished two hours of yard work and are perspiring heavily. What should you do and why?

Getting Involved

42. Organize a panel discussion on the subject of organ transplants and organ donation. Use library resources to learn the laws and procedures that regulate organ donation in your state. Also read about ethical issues—for example, those relating to the donation of organs from accident victims.

MOVEMENT AND COORDINATION

Springing gracefully from the high board, the diver arcs smoothly through the air. To accomplish this feat of coordination, her bones, muscles, and nerves must all work together. In this chapter you will discover how your skeletal, muscular, and nervous system enable you to perform both simple and complicated movements.

CHAPTER PREVIEW

15-1 Your Skeletal System

- Describe the function and formation of bone and some disorders of the skeletal system.

15-2 Your Muscular System

- Identify the three types of muscles and describe some disorders of the muscular system.

15-3 Your Nervous System

- Name the three types of nerves and list some safety measures that protect the brain and spinal cord.

BUILDING HEALTH SKILLS

- Evaluate the strength, endurance, and flexibility of muscles.

CHECK YOUR WELLNESS

Read each statement below and answer *usually, sometimes,* or *never*.

- Do you eat well-balanced meals to obtain nutrients necessary for bone and muscle growth?

- Can you do light exercise or household chores without feeling sore afterwards?

- Do you exercise on a regular basis?

- Do you warm up before exercising?

- When you exercise or play sports, are you careful not to put too much stress on your bones and muscles?

- Do you wear a helmet when you bike, skate, or play contact sports?

- Do you fasten your safety belt when you are in a car?

KEEPING A JOURNAL

Drop a penny on the floor and then pick it up. Write a description of all the movements that you made while you accomplished this seemingly simple activity. Be as detailed as you can.

Take it to the **Net**
www.phschool.com

1 YOUR SKELETAL SYSTEM

Focus on these questions as you read this lesson.

- What are the main functions of your bones?
- What can you do to ensure a healthy skeletal system?

SKILLS

- Intervening to Help a Friend

Whenever you run, your feet hit the ground again and again. Each time, the bones of your legs absorb a force of thousands of pounds. Bones are incredibly, amazingly strong. They are harder to break than some kinds of iron bars. **The bones of your skeletal system support your body and give it shape, and they work with your muscles to enable you to move.** Your skeletal system also protects delicate internal organs and produces blood cells. Finally, your bones store important minerals, such as phosphorus and calcium, and release them when other parts of the body need them. Bones may seem solid and unchanging, but they actually are part of a dynamic, living system.

The Skeleton

To make your study of the human skeleton easier, you can look at it in two parts—the axial skeleton and the appendicular skeleton. The **axial skeleton** (AK see ul) includes the bones in your head, your breastbone, your ribs, and the bones in your backbone. All the other bones in your body make up the **appendicular skeleton** (ap un DIK yuh lur). Figure 15-2 illustrates the bones in the skeleton.

THE AXIAL SKELETON Did you know that your skull actually consists of many small bones that are joined tightly together? Some of these bones make up the **cranium** (KRAY nee um), which is the thick, hard part of the skull that encloses the brain and protects it. Most of the remaining skull bones give your face its form. Still another bone, your jawbone, is the only bone in your skull that can move.

Your backbone, or spinal column, consists of 33 bones called **vertebrae** (VUR tuh bray). Together the vertebrae support your head and give flexibility to your neck and back. Like the cranium, the backbone also has a protective function—it helps shield the spinal cord from injury. The delicate spinal cord runs down from the brain through holes in the vertebrae. Disks of **cartilage** (KAHR tl ij), which is a tough, supportive tissue that is softer and more flexible than bone, separate individual vertebrae from each other. The cartilage makes the backbone flexible and also absorbs shocks. The bones of your chest, which include the ribs and breastbone, form a protective cage around the heart and lungs.

Figure 15-1 *Strong bones support the players' bodies and enable them to jump, run, twist, and throw.*

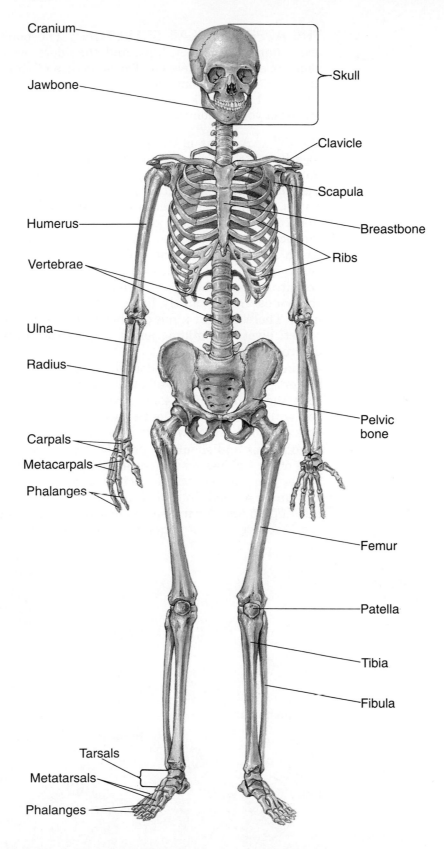

Figure 15-2 *Which is the longest bone in the human skeleton?*

THE APPENDICULAR SKELETON The bones in your arms, hands, legs, feet, hips, and shoulders are all part of your appendicular skeleton. The structure of your leg bones and pelvis, or hip bone, supports your upper body and lets you stand and walk upright. The pelvis also protects the organs of your abdomen.

JOINTS A **joint** is the point at which two bones come together. Strong, fibrous bands called **ligaments** (LIG uh munts) hold bones together at movable joints and prevent them from popping apart. A smooth layer of tough cartilage covers, cushions, and protects the ends of the bones where they come together in a joint. Membranes around the joint produce a secretion called **synovial fluid** (sih NOH vee ul), which lubricates the joint and reduces wear on the bones. Joints are classified according to the type of movement they permit. In immovable joints, such as those in the cranium, the bones are so tightly fitted together that they cannot move. There are four kinds of movable joints: hinge, ball-and-socket, pivot, and gliding joints. Figure 15-3 illustrates the different kinds of joints.

Hinge joints work like a door hinge to allow back-and-forth movement. Your knees, elbows, and the outer knuckles of your fingers have hinge joints. When you move your fingers, you will notice that the outer two knuckles will only bend back and forth—they won't twist or rotate.

Your hips and shoulders have ball-and-socket joints. This type of joint allows movement in all directions. The ball-and-socket joint in the shoulder lets a baseball player wind up and throw a pitch. In a pivot joint, bones move from side to side and up and down. You can nod your head *yes* and shake it *no* because of pivot joints between vertebrae in your neck.

Figure 15-3 *Which type of joint permits the widest range of movement?*

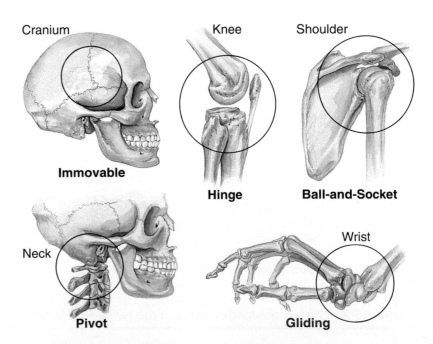

Cranium

Immovable

Knee

Hinge

Shoulder

Ball-and-Socket

Neck

Pivot

Wrist

Gliding

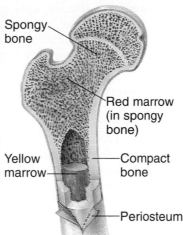

Spongy bone

Red marrow (in spongy bone)

Yellow marrow

Compact bone

Periosteum

Figure 15-4 *In the photograph of the cross section of a thigh bone (left), notice the cavities that contain blood vessels. The diagram of the internal structure of bone (right) shows how spongy bone differs from compact bone.*

Your wrists and ankles are flexible because the bones there have gliding joints. A gliding joint allows bones to slide over one another.

Bones

You have more than 200 bones in your skeletal system. Bones are complex organs that remain active even after they stop growing.

STRUCTURE OF BONES   All of your bones are covered with a tough membrane called the **periosteum** (pehr ee AHS tee um), which you can see in Figure 15-4. The periosteum contains cells that form new bone during growth and repair. Blood vessels run through the periosteum and branch into the bone. The blood that flows through these vessels carries nutrients to the bone cells and takes away wastes.

Directly beneath the periosteum is a layer of tissue called compact bone, which is very hard and dense. Beneath compact bone is spongy bone. In contrast to compact bone, spongy bone is light in weight, because it is filled with spaces. These spaces enable spongy bone to act as a shock absorber. In the long part, or shaft, of long bones such as those in your arms and legs, spongy bone is a thin layer. The rounded ends of bones are made up mostly of spongy bone.

The spaces inside bones are filled with a soft tissue known as **marrow.** There are two types of marrow—red and yellow. Red marrow fills the spaces in spongy bones. Most of your blood cells are manufactured in red marrow. Yellow marrow is located in the center of long bones and is made mostly of fat. Yellow marrow also produces some blood cells, but not many in comparison to red marrow.

DEVELOPMENT OF BONE   The skeleton begins developing long before birth. A newborn baby's skeleton is made mostly of cartilage. Eventually most of this cartilage is replaced by bone in the process of **ossification** (ahs uh fih

KAY shun). During this process, minerals, such as calcium and phosphorus, are deposited within the cartilage, making it hard. Ossification began before you were born and will continue until you are 20 to 25 years old.

Skeletal System Disorders

Because your bones and joints get constant use, they sometimes develop problems. A few conditions are the result of disease or poor nutrition. Many skeletal problems, however, occur because people push their skeletal systems beyond endurance or have not properly warmed up for exercise.

FRACTURES   A **fracture** is a break in a bone. In a complete fracture, the bone is broken all the way across, into two or more pieces. An incomplete fracture, in contrast, is a break that does not go all the way across the bone, and the pieces of bone do not separate. When the broken bone does not pierce the skin, the break is called a closed fracture. An open fracture is one in which the bone pierces the skin. Because the skin is broken, germs can get inside the body and infect body tissues, including the broken bone.

Fractures are treated by putting the broken ends of the bone back together and then preventing them from moving until the bone tissue can repair itself. Splints or casts are often used to hold broken bones in place, but sometimes a surgeon will insert a metal pin to stabilize a bone. In the case of open fractures, a physician will also give antibiotics to kill germs that may have entered the body.

JOINT DISORDERS   Many joint disorders are caused by injury involving excessive force, such as a fall or a severe twist. In a **dislocation,** the ends of the bones are forced out of their normal positions in a joint. Dislocations are treated in a manner similar to that of fractures—the bones are put

Figure 15-5 *X-ray photographs reveal fractures and other bone conditions. Find the location of the fracture in the forearm.*

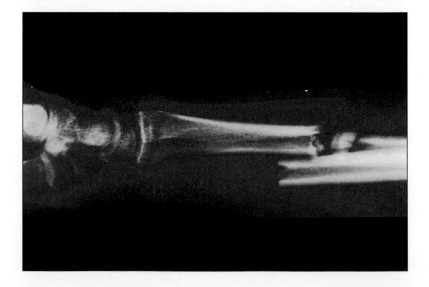

Figure 15-6 *The stress on football players' joints can be tremendous.*

back into their proper positions and then held in place, usually by a bandage or cast, until healing takes place.

Chances are good that you or someone you know has sprained an ankle, knee, or some other joint. A **sprain** consists of overstretched or torn ligaments or tendons. Sprains occur more frequently than any other joint injury. If a sprain is mild, it will heal by itself if you allow the joint to rest and try to avoid using it. If the pain is severe, however, you need medical care. Sometimes an injury that appears to be a sprain is actually a fracture—particularly if there is difficulty moving the joint.

Torn cartilage is serious damage to the cartilage that covers the ends of bones in a joint. The knees are particularly susceptible to this injury. Therefore it occurs most often among athletes who participate in sports such as football that involve severe stress on the knees. Surgery is necessary to repair torn cartilage.

Two painful conditions of the joints are bursitis and arthritis. A bursa is a fluid-filled sac that cushions certain joints and tendons. **Bursitis** (bur SY tis), which is a painful irritation of this sac, may be caused by injury or repeated strenuous activity. The elbow and shoulder joints are common locations for bursitis. The usual treatment consists of resting the joint, although medication may also be used. In **arthritis** (ahr THRY tis), the joints become painful and swollen. Arthritis is discussed in detail in Chapter 24.

SCOLIOSIS   If you have a yearly physical examination, the nurse or physician probably checks you for **scoliosis** (skoh lee OH sis), an abnormal curvature of the spine. In this condition, which is more common in girls than in boys, the vertebrae in the backbone line up in such a way that the backbone twists to one side. Scoliosis usually begins to develop during childhood, but it may not be detected until adolescence.

PHYSICS CONNECTION

Physicians use X-ray photographs as tools for diagnosing fractures, dislocations, and other skeletal problems. X-rays are one type of electromagnetic radiation; some other types include visible light, ultraviolet light, microwaves, and radio waves. Unlike light rays, X-rays penetrate the body's soft tissues, producing a clear image of bones on photographic film.

Although this condition can be inherited, it can also result from certain diseases, including polio, rheumatoid arthritis, and cerebral palsy. Early symptoms of scoliosis include shoulders that are not level, uneven hips, and an uneven waistline. Sometimes exercises will improve mild scoliosis. Severe scoliosis may require braces or even surgery.

OSTEOPOROSIS   As people become older, their bones begin to lose some of their calcium. This loss can lead to **osteoporosis** (ahs tee oh puh ROH sis), a condition in which bones become weak and break easily. Elderly women are more likely to develop osteoporosis than are elderly men. Evidence indicates that regular exercise can help prevent osteoporosis. In addition, it is important for people to obtain enough calcium from the food that they eat. Your calcium intake now, during adolescence, can help you avoid osteoporosis later in life.

Keeping the Skeletal System Healthy

You can take steps to make sure that your bones develop well and remain strong. Certain nutrients, including calcium and vitamins D, A, and C, are essential for the formation of healthy bones. In addition, by getting enough exercise, young people can help ensure that their bones are developing properly. Walking, running, and dancing are all good exercises, as are most sports, such as basketball and soccer. To prevent injury, always warm up before exercising.

If you eat well and exercise during childhood, adolescence, and young adulthood, you will help ensure that your bones remain healthy as you become older. Evidence indicates that if you build strong bones now, you can help prevent osteoporosis from developing later in life. In addition, if you establish good nutrition and exercise habits when you are young, you will be more likely to continue to make these efforts as you grow older.

LESSON *1* REVIEW

1. Identify three functions of bones.
2. What are the parts of the axial skeleton?
3. Compare and contrast spongy and compact bone.
4. Why should a severe sprain be checked by a physician?

What Do You Think?
5. What negative health habits may contribute to the loss of bone strength as you age?

2 YOUR MUSCULAR SYSTEM

GUIDE FOR READING

Focus on these questions as you read this lesson.

- What are the three types of muscles, and what is the function of each type?
- How can you keep your muscular system healthy?

SKILLS

- Activity: Tired Muscles

To open this book and turn its pages, you use muscles in your arms and hands. Muscles move your eyes as you read the printed words. Muscles in your chest make you breathe, and muscles in your heart pump blood. Every time your body moves, muscles are at work.

How Muscles Work

Many of your muscles do their work by making bones move. Others control the movements of internal organs, such as your stomach.

TYPES OF MUSCLES Different kinds of muscles perform different functions. **You have three types of muscles in your body—skeletal, smooth, and cardiac.** The first type, **skeletal muscle,** is voluntary muscle—you control its movement deliberately. As the name indicates, skeletal muscles are attached to the bones of your skeleton. These are the muscles that enable you to do such things as run, throw a basketball, and play a guitar. All of these actions are voluntary—you choose to do them.

Skeletal muscles are attached to bones by thick strands of connective tissue called **tendons.** Most skeletal muscles work in pairs—one muscle in the pair moves the bone in one direction, while the other moves the bone in the opposite direction. Figure 15-7 illustrates one such muscle pair.

You deliberately direct the actions of your skeletal muscles. In contrast, **smooth muscle** is not under voluntary control. Instead, smooth muscle works automatically to control movements inside your body, such as those involved in digestion. Smooth muscles in the walls of your esophagus

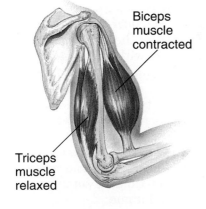
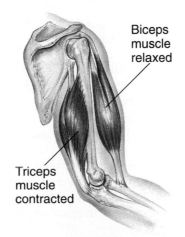

Biceps muscle contracted

Triceps muscle relaxed

Bent

Biceps muscle relaxed

Triceps muscle contracted

Extended

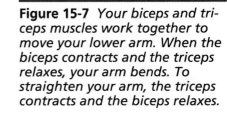

Figure 15-7 *Your biceps and triceps muscles work together to move your lower arm. When the biceps contracts and the triceps relaxes, your arm bends. To straighten your arm, the triceps contracts and the biceps relaxes.*

and intestine push food through your digestive system. Other smooth muscles in your blood vessels help circulate your blood and control blood pressure.

The third type of muscle, **cardiac muscle,** is found only in the heart. Like smooth muscle, it is involuntary. All your life, cardiac muscle contracts automatically, over and over, enabling your heart to pump blood to all parts of your body.

MUSCLE CONTRACTION   All muscles do their work by contracting, or becoming shorter and thicker. Muscles contract because their cells have the ability to become shorter. Muscle cells, which are often called fibers, contract when they are stimulated by impulses from the nervous system.

Even when muscles are not moving, some of their fibers are contracting. **Muscle tone** is the slight, constant contraction of a muscle that is due to the contraction of some of its fibers. Muscle tone enables you to maintain your posture. The muscles in your neck, for example, may not contract enough to move your head, but they contract enough to keep your head upright.

ENERGY AND MUSCLE CONTRACTION   Muscles use energy when they contract. The energy comes from chemical reactions within muscle cells. These chemical reactions use the sugar glucose, which you obtain from the food that you eat. Usually glucose combines chemically with oxygen to produce energy. Blood carries both oxygen and glucose to your muscle cells.

If muscles are active at a high intensity, oxygen cannot be supplied to many muscle fibers fast enough. When that happens, your muscles still obtain their energy from a chemical reaction—but one that does not use oxygen. This chemical reaction produces a substance called **lactic acid** as a waste product. After very intense exercise, lactic acid sometimes accumulates in muscles, causing muscle fatigue.

TIRED MUSCLES

In this activity, you will work with a partner to determine how your arm muscles perform after a period of exercise.

Materials

book

clock or watch with second hand

Procedure

1. Stand up and hold a book in your right hand. Your right arm should hang straight down at your side.

2. While your partner watches the clock, you will count the number of times you can lift the book in 30 seconds. When your partner says "go," lift the book to shoulder height, keeping your arm straight and extended out to your side. Then lower it. Repeat this procedure as many times as you can, until, after 30 seconds, your partner tells you to stop. Record the number of times you lifted the book.

3. Rest for a minute and then repeat step 2.

4. Repeat steps 2 and 3, but this time use your left arm.

Discussion

1. For each hand, how did your performance on the second trial compare with your performance on the first trial? How can you account for these results?

2. Which muscles are stronger, those of your right arm or your left?

Disorders of the Muscular System

Your muscles, like your bones, are remarkably strong, especially when you consider that you use them over and over, day after day. Sometimes, however, muscles can become injured or develop other problems.

MUSCLE INJURIES   A muscle strain, or a pulled muscle, is a painful injury that may happen when muscles are overworked or stretched too far or too quickly. Sometimes muscle fibers rip, resulting in a torn muscle. The condition known as tennis elbow, which consists of pain in the forearm, is one type of **tendinitis** (ten duh NY tis), a painful irritation of a tendon. Like other muscle injuries, tendinitis is usually caused by strain or overuse.

Generally all these muscle injuries are treated by allowing the affected muscle or tendon to rest as much as possible. Pain medication such as aspirin can often reduce the discomfort. If the soreness does not go away after a few days, the injury should be checked by a physician.

Runners sometimes experience shin splints, or severe pain in the lower leg. This type of injury happens when tendons of muscles in the lower leg pull away from the bone. Shin splints can often be prevented if runners warm up properly before they start to run.

Figure 15-9 *To help avoid muscle injuries, warm up before you exercise.*

MUSCLE CRAMPS   Have you ever felt a sudden, sharp pain in your leg or arm? If so, you may have been having a muscle cramp, which is a strong, uncontrolled contraction of a muscle. Muscle cramps may result from dehydration, poor circulation of blood, exercise that is too strenuous, or an imbalance of certain minerals, such as potassium. To relieve a cramp, try massaging the affected area and exercising the limb gently.

MUSCULAR DYSTROPHY   In the condition known as **muscular dystrophy** (DIS truh fee), the muscles gradually become weaker and weaker because the muscle fibers are slowly destroyed. There are several types of muscular dystrophy, and all are inherited. The most serious type causes paralysis and eventually death, because heart muscles and the muscles involved in breathing can no longer function. Presently no cure exists for muscular dystrophy. However, scientists have identified the gene that causes the most serious type, and this breakthrough may eventually lead to an effective treatment.

Keeping the Muscular System Healthy

Exercise is important in maintaining muscular strength and flexibility. Exercise makes individual fibers grow, which, in turn, causes the entire muscle to become thicker. Exercise also helps ensure good muscle tone.

Some athletes are tempted to use anabolic steroids to increase their muscle mass. However, these drugs are dangerous and should be avoided because they can damage various body systems. Anabolic steroids are discussed further in Chapter 21.

To prevent injury, avoid putting too much stress on your muscles. In addition, warm up before vigorous exercise, and afterwards allow a cooling-down period of mild exercise. Safe warm-up exercises are described in Chapter 17.

LESSON 2 REVIEW

1. Identify the three types of muscles and describe the function of each.
2. What substance combines chemically with oxygen to provide the energy for muscle contraction?
3. What can you do to prevent muscle injuries?

What Do You Think?

4. You do not have voluntary control over some of your muscles. Why is this an advantage?

3 YOUR NERVOUS SYSTEM

Have you ever stopped to think about the hundreds of actions you perform each day and the thousands of thoughts you have in one hour? Your nervous system coordinates all these thoughts and actions. First it receives information about your environment and the other parts of your body. Then it interprets this information. Finally it causes the body to respond to the information.

Suppose you are playing soccer, and the ball speeds toward you. Your nervous system receives this information through your eyes and sends it to your brain. Your brain interprets what you have seen and sends a signal to nerves in your leg. The nerve impulses make your leg muscles contract, and you aim a hard kick at the swiftly moving ball. All of these events occur in less than a second.

Nerves and Nerve Cells

The **neuron** (NOOR ahn) is the basic cell of the nervous system. **Neurons carry nerve messages, or impulses, from one part of your body to another.** A neuron's structure enables it to perform this function.

STRUCTURE OF A NERVE CELL A neuron, as shown in Figure 15-10, has three parts—a cell body, an axon, and dendrites. The central cell body controls the cell's growth. The **dendrites** (DEN dryts) are short, branching fibers that carry nerve impulses toward the cell body. Notice the long, thin fiber called an **axon** (AK sahn), which carries impulses away from the cell body. Many axons are coated with a fatty material called **myelin** (MY uh lin), which insulates the axon and increases the speed at which an impulse travels.

A nerve impulse begins when dendrites are stimulated. The impulse travels along the dendrites to the cell body, and

GUIDE FOR READING

Focus on these questions as you read this lesson.

- What is the function of neurons?
- What functions are performed by each part of the brain?
- What are some ways to prevent brain and spinal cord injuries?

SKILLS

- DECIDE

Figure 15-10 *In this diagram of a neuron, observe that the myelin on the axon is not continuous.*

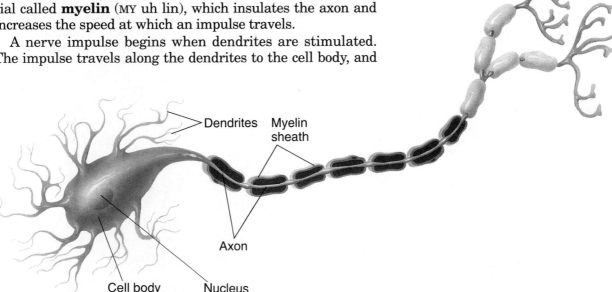

Dendrites Myelin sheath

Axon

Cell body Nucleus

then away from the cell body on the axon. When it reaches the end of the axon, the impulse must cross a **synapse** (SIN aps), which is the space between an axon and the structure with which the neuron communicates. That structure may be a muscle or another neuron.

TYPES OF NERVE CELLS   There are three different types of neurons. Each type of neuron performs a different function. **Sensory neurons** pick up information about your external and internal environment from your sense organs and your body. **Motor neurons** send impulses to your muscles and glands, causing them to react. **Interneurons,** which are located only in the brain and spinal cord, pass impulses from one neuron to another.

The Central Nervous System

The nervous system consists of two parts. Your brain and spinal cord make up one part, the **central nervous system.** The **peripheral nervous system** (puh RIF ur ul), which is the other part, is made up of all the nerves that connect the brain and spinal cord to other parts of your body.

THE BRAIN   The **brain**, a moist, spongy organ weighing about three pounds (1.4 kilograms) is made up of billions of neurons that control almost everything you do and experience. Your brain controls your sense experiences, actions, thoughts, and memory.

Recall that the skull protects the brain. Beneath the skull are the **meninges** (muh NIN jeez), which are three layers of membranes that cover the brain and give it further protection. **Cerebrospinal fluid,** a liquid found between the middle and inner meninges and in certain spaces within the brain, helps to cushion and protect the brain and spinal cord.

Figure 15-11 *The illustration shows the parts of the human brain. Notice how the cerebrum is divided into two halves.*

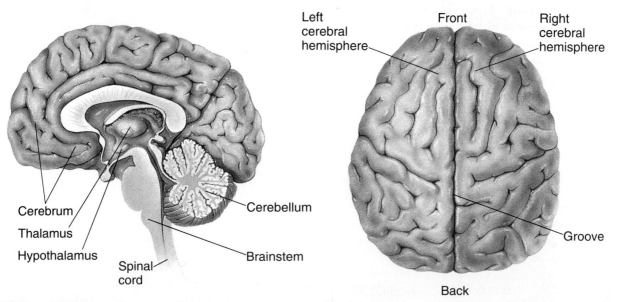

The brain is divided into three areas—the cerebrum, the cerebellum, and the brainstem—shown in Figure 15-11. The **cerebrum** (suh REE brum) is the large upper region. Its surface is folded into many ridges and depressions like the meat of a walnut. The cerebrum consists of a number of different, specialized regions. Some regions control the movement of skeletal muscles; others control memory and reasoning. Still other regions receive messages from the sense organs. These areas of the cerebrum interpret the messages as smells, tastes, sounds, sights, and touch sensations.

A deep groove divides the cerebrum into left and right sides, known as the left hemisphere and the right hemisphere. The right hemisphere controls the muscles on the left side of your body, and the left hemisphere controls the muscles on the right side. If a person receives an injury to the left side of the cerebrum, which side of the body is affected?

The **cerebellum** (sehr uh BEL um), just beneath the back part of the cerebrum, coordinates the contraction of your muscles. While the cerebrum, and not the cerebellum, sends messages to your muscles, the cerebellum processes these nerve impulses, adjusting and reducing some of them. Without the cerebellum's work, seemingly simple movements, such as picking up a glass of water without spilling it or walking without staggering, would be impossible for you. The **brainstem,** located below the cerebellum at the base of the skull, acts as the body's life-support system. It controls heartbeat, breathing, and blood pressure.

In Figure 15-11, observe the two smaller parts of the brain, the thalamus and the hypothalamus, that extend out from the brainstem. The **thalamus** (THAL uh mus) is a relay station for the senses, receiving impulses from sense organs and modifying them before they reach the cerebrum. The

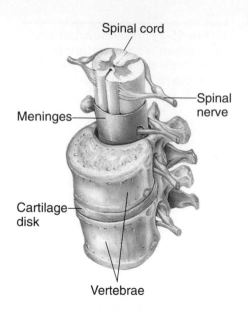

Spinal cord

Meninges

Spinal nerve

Cartilage disk

Vertebrae

Figure 15-13 *In the diagram of the spinal cord, observe how spinal nerves emerge from holes in the vertebrae.*

hypothalamus (hy poh THAL uh mus) regulates body temperature, sleep, water balance, and blood pressure. It also regulates the hormones of the endocrine system, which are discussed in Chapter 8.

THE SPINAL CORD   The other part of the central nervous system is the **spinal cord,** nerve tissue that extends from the brain down the back to just below the ribs. As you look at Figure 15-13, you will notice that, like the brain, the spinal cord is covered with meninges; it is also bathed in cerebrospinal fluid. Nerve impulses travel from the brain, down the spinal cord, and then out to the body. In the reverse of this process, impulses travel from parts of your body to the spinal cord, and then to the brain.

The Peripheral Nervous System

The peripheral nervous system includes all parts of the nervous system except the brain and spinal cord. The cranial and spinal nerves are included in this division of the nervous system. The **cranial nerves** are 12 pairs of nerves that emerge from the brain. Most of these nerves connect with areas in your head, such as your eyes, ears, nose, and face. Thirty-one pairs of **spinal nerves** branch off from the spinal cord, passing through openings in the vertebrae. Each pair serves a particular part of your body. One pair, for example, speeds up the heartbeat, while other pairs make the muscles in your arms and legs move.

Like the central nervous system, the peripheral nervous system consists of two parts. The **somatic nervous system** (soh MAT ik) is responsible for actions that you can control. The **autonomic nervous system** (aw tuh NAHM ik), in contrast, regulates actions that happen automatically, without your thinking about them, such as your heartbeat, breathing rate, and digestion.

Control of Movement

When you move, your muscles are at work. However, your nervous system controls movement by sending impulses to muscles that direct them to contract. Various factors can affect the way your nervous system does this.

COORDINATION   Walking across a room is not as simple as it seems. You need information from your eyes; otherwise, you wouldn't be able to direct your legs where to go, and you might trip over things. You need to coordinate the movement of your right and left legs, because it would not work to step forward with both feet at the same time. Also, you have to maintain your balance as your legs move your body forward. Finally, you must adjust the speed of the movement. Your nervous system coordinates those and other movements of your body, enabling different muscles to work together.

Practice helps you improve the skill of many kinds of movements, such as those involved in holding a pencil and riding a bike. This happens because your brain stores memories of these movements. Each time you perform the action, your brain adds new information to this stored memory, enabling your performance to improve over time.

REFLEXES   When you have accidentally touched something very hot, such as a burning candle, have you noticed that your hand quickly and automatically jerks away? Such an automatic response of the nervous system to the environment is called a **reflex.** Many reflex actions, such as the arm movement just described, involve nerves and muscles that are usually under voluntary control. When these muscles act voluntarily, they are directed by nerve impulses that originate in the cerebrum. When those same muscles perform a reflex action, the cerebrum is not involved. Figure 15-14 diagrams the arm-reflex pathway, in which impulses travel from the skin to the spinal cord, and then from the spinal cord out to the arm muscles. While this is happening, messages of pain are traveling to the brain. Shortly after your arm moves, you feel pain. Many reflexes help protect your body from harm. If you did not pull your hand away from a hot object quickly, what might happen to your skin?

Disorders of the Nervous System

Problems associated with the nervous system range from relatively mild conditions to serious illnesses and injuries. These conditions have various causes and treatments.

INJURIES   The brain and spinal cord are delicate organs that can be injured. A **concussion,** for example, is a short loss of consciousness following a severe bump to the head, during which the soft brain tissue comes into contact with

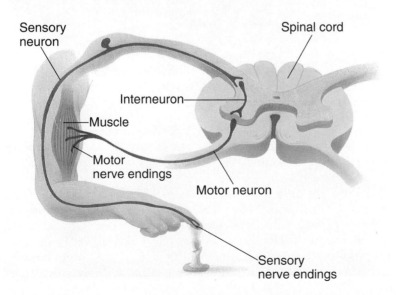

Figure 15-14 *If you touch a flame, an impulse travels on sensory neurons to your spinal cord. Interneurons pass these impulses to motor neurons in your arm. The motor neurons then make your arm muscles contract and quickly pull your hand away from the flame.*

the skull. While a concussion generally heals by itself, you should seek medical attention if, following a blow to the head, you are unconscious for even a brief time, or if you vomit or feel drowsy or confused. These symptoms can indicate a serious head injury, such as a cracked skull or bleeding within the brain. A severe brain injury sometimes results in a **coma,** which is a prolonged period of deep unconsciousness. Comas are also caused by some diseases and overdoses of certain drugs.

Spinal cord injuries can result in **paralysis,** or the loss of the ability to move some part of the body. Paralysis occurs when some nerves are so damaged that they can no longer signal the muscles they control. The extent of the paralysis is often related to the location of the spinal cord injury. Severe damage to the spinal cord in the neck area may result in **quadriplegia** (kwahd ruh PLEE jee uh), or paralysis of the body from the neck down, including the arms as well as the legs. **Paraplegia** (pa ruh PLEE jee uh), which is paralysis of the lower body and legs, is usually the effect of an injury to a lower part of the spinal cord.

INFECTIONS Nervous system infections are rare, since germs cannot easily gain access to these tissues. When they do occur, however, infections of the nervous system are generally serious conditions. **Meningitis** (men in JY tis) is an inflammation of the meninges of the brain and spinal cord. It generally follows an infection in some other part of the body, such as the lungs or heart, and children are the most common victims. The symptoms of meningitis are fever, severe headache, stiff neck, and vomiting. Severe cases can cause permanent brain damage and even death. Physicians prescribe antibiotics to treat meningitis caused by bacteria.

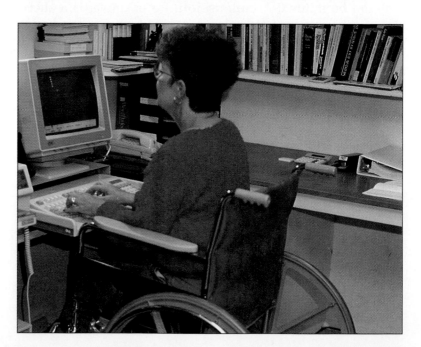

Figure 15-15 *As this computer operator demonstrates, paraplegics can hold jobs and lead full lives.*

Too Few Safety Belts

It is Saturday afternoon, and you and your friends are at George's house. George, who has his driver's license, suggests that he drive you all to a nearby movie theater. Unfortunately, however, George's parents' car—the one he would use—has only five safety belts, and there are six of you altogether. George suggests that you not worry about safety belts—just all squeeze into the car. You know that it is unsafe to travel anywhere in a car without using a safety belt, because you risk injury to your nervous system and other parts of your body.

1. Use the DECIDE process on page 18 to decide what you would do in this situation. Explain the reasons for your decision.

2. What might happen if everyone else in the group opposed your decision? Explain how peer pressure might influence the group's behavior in a situation like this.

A bite from an infected animal can transmit **rabies,** an infection of the central nervous system that, if left untreated, is almost always fatal. Wild animals, such as raccoons and bats, can carry rabies—but so can domestic cats and dogs. Avoid contact with wild animals, or with domestic animals that act sick or behave strangely. If you are ever bitten by an animal, you should get medical attention.

OTHER CONDITIONS　Tension headaches, which result from tightness in the muscles of the neck and head, may be caused by either physical or emotional stress. **Migraine headaches** (MY grayn) are especially severe headaches that usually last a long time. The cause of migraines is uncertain, but they may be associated with changes in the diameter of the brain's blood vessels. A person with a migraine headache is usually sensitive to light and noise and may experience nausea and blurring of vision.

Nervous system damage that occurs before, during, or shortly after birth is called **cerebral palsy** (SEHR uh brul PAWL zee). The damage results in a lack of full control of body movement. The causes range from a lack of oxygen at birth to head injury and meningitis.

Occasionally, the impulses produced by the brain become disturbed, causing a condition known as **epilepsy** (EP uh lep see). The sudden storm of brain activity results in an epileptic attack, or **seizure** (SEE zhur). During a severe seizure, the individual may lose consciousness, the arms and legs may

Figure 15-16 *Wear protective headgear in situations where there is risk of head injury.*

jerk, and the teeth may lock together. A milder form of epilepsy causes only one or two seconds of unconsciousness. Epilepsy can usually be controlled with medication, and most people with this condition can function normally.

Recall that the axons of some nerve cells are covered by a fatty substance called myelin. In **multiple sclerosis** (skluh ROH sis), patches of myelin are slowly destroyed. People with this condition may have difficulty with muscular control and experience problems with vision and speech. While multiple sclerosis may eventually cause paralysis, the disease usually progresses slowly, with periods in which symptoms diminish or disappear. The cause of multiple sclerosis is not known.

Keeping the Nervous System Healthy

Rest, sleep, good nutrition, and daily exercise help keep your nervous system in good condition. Avoid substances such as drugs and alcohol that can cause permanent damage to your nervous system. Injuries are the most common cause of brain and spinal cord damage. Many of these injuries occur when people are under the influence of alcohol or drugs. You can help avoid injuries by following a few basic safety rules:

- Do not use drugs or alcohol. Never ride in a motor vehicle whose driver is under the influence of drugs or alcohol.
- Fasten your safety belt every time you ride in a car.
- Before diving into water, be certain that it is deep enough and that there are no underwater hazards.
- Be sure to wear a protective helmet when you work on mechanical equipment, play contact sports, or ride a bicycle or motorcycle.

By following these safety guidelines, you will be helping to maintain the health of your nervous system.

LESSON 3 REVIEW

1. What function do neurons perform?
2. Name the three types of neurons and describe the function of each.
3. List the three main areas of the brain and describe the function of each part.
4. How are migraine headaches different from tension headaches?

What Do You Think?

5. Explain why people should wear a helmet every time they ride a bike, not just during races.

Assessing Muscular Strength, Endurance, and Flexibility

To be physically fit, you must have muscles that perform well. The three main components of muscular fitness are strength, endurance, and flexibility. Muscular strength is the ability of a muscle to exert or resist a force. When you push, pull, or lift an object, your muscles are exerting a force. Muscular endurance is the ability of a muscle or a group of muscles to apply force over a period of time. When you rake leaves, shovel snow, or do sit-ups, you are performing acts of muscular endurance.

Flexibility is the ability to use a muscle throughout the entire range of motion. If your muscles are flexible, you can bend, stretch, and twist easily, and you are unlikely to get stiff when you exercise.

Knowing how you rate in the areas of muscular strength, muscular endurance, and flexibility is an important step in setting up a fitness program to meet your needs. Follow the guidelines below to assess your fitness in these three areas. Work with a partner who can observe your performance. For some of the tests, your partner will need a watch or clock with a second hand. Although the tests below do not evaluate all your muscles, they are usually good indicators of the fitness of the muscles of the body as a whole.

Before you perform any of these tests, get a medical checkup by a physician or other health-care professional. Do not perform these tests unless you have the physician's approval.

1. Assess your abdominal muscular strength and endurance

To test the muscular strength and endurance of your abdominal muscles, you can do the modified sit-up exercise that is described below.

(a) Lie on your back with your feet flat on the floor, your knees bent, and your heels between 1 and 1.5 feet from your buttocks.

(b) After crossing your arms over your chest, place your hands on your shoulders as shown in the illustration below.

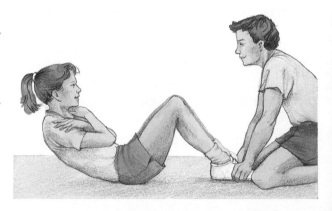

(c) Have your partner hold your feet down, or secure them under a chair or couch.

(d) Then tuck your chin to your chest and curl to a sitting position so that your elbows touch your thighs.

(e) Lower your back by uncurling it. Do not go all the way down—uncurl only until the middle of your back touches the floor, to the position shown in the illustration.

(f) Repeat as many sit-ups as possible in 60 seconds. Count one sit-up each time your elbows touch your thighs. To be within the optimal level of fitness, you need to achieve the minimum scores in the table on page 359.

2. Assess your upper body muscular strength and endurance

To test your upper body strength and endurance, you can do the pull-up exercise.

(a) Hang by your hands from a bar using an overhand grip. The backs of your hands—not the tips of your fingers—should be facing you. Your legs and arms should hang down so that they are fully extended. Your feet should not touch the floor. A spotter should be nearby to catch you if you lose your grip.

(b) From this hanging position, try to pull your body up until your chin is over the bar.

(c) Return to the fully extended position.

(d) Repeat the pull-up as many times as you can. There is no time limit. See the table on page 359 for fitness standards in this category.

3. Assess your flexibility

No single test measures the flexibility of all joints. The sit-and-reach test evaluates the flexibility of the lower back and posterior thighs. Before doing this test, slowly stretch the muscles of your lower back and legs. Use any of the back, hip, and upper-leg stretching exercises in Building Health Skills, Chapter 17, pages 412–413. Then follow the steps below.

(a) Take off your shoes and sit on the floor with your feet flat against a sturdy box, as shown in the illustration below. The box should be about one foot high, and ideally its top should extend out over your feet.

(b) With your knees and back straight, reach as far forward as you can with your fingertips fully extended in front of you and one hand on top of the other. Hold this position for a count of three. Do not bounce.

(c) Have a partner hold a ruler on the top of the box to measure the distance (in inches) your fingers reach in reference to your toes. If your hands just reach your toes, your measurement will be "0." If your hands do not reach as far as your toes, your score will be a negative number. If your hands stretch beyond your toes, your score will be a positive number. Have your partner record this distance and note whether it is a positive or negative number.

(d) Allow yourself four trials, and take the measurement from the last trial. The table on page 359 shows how far you should be able to reach.

Fitness Standards for Muscular Strength, Endurance, and Flexibility

Age	Girls	Boys
Sit-up Strength-Endurance Test		
14	35	40
15	35	42
16	35	44
17	35	44
18	35	44
Pull-up Strength-Endurance Test		
14	1	4
15	1	5
16	1	5
17	1	5
18	1	5
Sit-and-Reach Flexibility Test		
14–18	1 inch past toes	1 inch past toes

Activities for Developing Strength, Endurance, and Flexibility

Muscular Strength	Muscular Endurance
Weight training Archery Backpacking Calisthenics Gymnastics Judo/karate Rowing Skiing (cross country and downhill)	All activities listed for muscular strength plus Basketball Bicycling Canoeing Dance (aerobic) Football (tag/touch) Golf (walking) Handball/paddleball/racquetball Jogging Rope jumping Skating (ice/roller) Skiing (cross country) Soccer Swimming Surfing Walking

Moderate Flexibility	High Flexibility
Backpacking/hiking Badminton Baseball/softball Canoeing (rowing) Handball/paddleball/racquetball Sailing Skiing Soccer Surfing Tennis Volleyball Walking	Calisthenics Dance (aerobic) Gymnastics Judo/karate Swimming Wrestling

Apply the Skill

1. Pair off with a partner and perform the sit-up strength and endurance test. Ask your partner to count aloud the number of sit-ups as you complete them. Record and compare your results with the optimal fitness level.

2. Perform the pull-up strength and endurance test. Compare your results with the fitness level recommended in the table.

3. Evaluate your results for the two strength and endurance tests. If your scores did not meet the standards, you need to engage in activities that help build your strength and endurance. The table lists some activities that can help you do this.

4. Pair off with a partner and perform the flexibility sit-and-reach test. Be sure to warm up before performing this test. Ask your partner to record the results.

5. Evaluate your flexibility test results. If you need to improve your flexibility, consult the table for activities that will help with this.

6. After looking at the recommended activities in the tables, design an exercise program to maintain or improve your muscular strength, endurance, and flexibility. Discuss your proposed plan with your physician.

CHAPTER 15 REVIEW

KEY IDEAS

LESSON 1

- Bones support your body, give it shape, and work with muscles to enable it to move. In addition, bones store minerals and produce blood cells.

- Diet and exercise are important in ensuring strong, healthy bones and in preventing osteoporosis.

LESSON 2

- Skeletal muscles are attached to bones and control voluntary movements. Smooth muscle, which is involuntary, controls body processes that happen automatically. Cardiac muscle, which is also involuntary, is found only in the heart.

LESSON 3

- Neurons, which are the cells that make up the nervous system, carry impulses from one part of your body to another. There are three types—sensory neurons, motor neurons, and interneurons.

- Injuries are the most common cause of brain and spinal cord damage.

KEY TERMS

LESSON 1	muscular dystrophy	concussion
arthritis	skeletal muscle	dendrites
bursitis	smooth muscle	interneuron
cartilage	tendinitis	meninges
dislocation	tendons	meningitis
fracture	LESSON 3	motor neuron
osteoporosis	axon	multiple sclerosis
scoliosis	brainstem	neuron
sprain	central nervous system	peripheral nervous system
vertebrae	cerebellum	reflex
LESSON 2	cerebral palsy	sensory neuron
cardiac muscle	cerebrum	spinal cord

Listed above are some of the important terms in this chapter. Choose the term from the list that best matches each phrase below.

1. part of the nervous system that includes the brain and spinal cord

2. part of a neuron that carries messages away from the cell body

3. abnormal curvature of the spine

4. tough, supportive tissue that is more flexible than bone

5. type of muscle that controls voluntary movement

6. weakening of the bones due to calcium loss

7. thick strands of tissue attaching muscles to bones

8. inflammation of the membranes that cover the brain and spinal cord

9. type of nerve cell that sends impulses to your muscles and glands

10. part of the brain that coordinates the contraction of muscles

11. a condition in which the muscle fibers gradually become weaker and weaker

WHAT HAVE YOU LEARNED?

Choose the letter of the answer that best completes each statement.

12. Nerve cells that pass impulses from one neuron to another are called

a. motor neurons   **c.** spinal nerves
b. synapses   **d.** interneurons

13. Which of the following structures are found in the peripheral nervous system?

a. cerebrum   **c.** meninges
b. cranial nerves   **d.** all of these

14. Your backbone consists of 33

a. vertebrae   **c.** tendons
b. dendrites   **d.** cells

15. Which of the following encloses the brain?

a. cerebrum   **c.** neuron
b. cranium   **d.** bursa

16. Tennis elbow is an example of

a. bursitis   **c.** arthritis
b. tendinitis   **d.** none of these

17. Movement in all directions is allowed by which type of joint?

a. ball-and-socket joint   **c.** pivot joint
b. hinge joint   **d.** all of these

18. Cardiac muscle is found in your

a. digestive system   **c.** heart
b. arms and legs   **d.** lungs

19. The part of your brain that controls memory and reasoning is the

a. cerebrum   **c.** meninges
b. cerebellum   **d.** brainstem

Answer each of the following with complete sentences.

20. Describe the two major divisions of the human skeleton.

21. What is ossification and when during a person's lifetime does it occur?

22. Describe the structure of a typical bone.

23. Explain the difference between a tendon and a ligament.

24. Describe the condition known as multiple sclerosis.

25. What is the difference between a complete and an incomplete fracture?

26. What is the treatment for muscle strain?

27. Why does practice improve the performance of actions such as typing and dancing?

WHAT DO YOU THINK?

28. Which injury is more serious—an open fracture or a closed fracture? Explain.

29. Why is good muscle tone important?

30. Symptoms of osteoporosis are not usually present in younger people. Does that mean that you do not need to do anything now to prevent osteoporosis? Explain.

31. One reflex action consists of blinking your eye whenever something touches your eyelash. Explain how this reflex has a protective function.

32. Explain how the nervous, skeletal, and muscular systems are all involved when a person rides a bike.

WHAT WOULD YOU DO?

33. Every night you notice a raccoon in your backyard. Your brother wants to trap it and keep it as a pet. What would you advise?

34. After falling and hitting her head, your sister is unconscious for a few seconds, but she quickly recovers consciousness. Would you urge her to see a doctor? Why or why not?

35. Suppose a friend of yours has bursitis in her shoulder. She decides to play tennis, and she takes extra pain medication so that her shoulder will not hurt during the game.

Would you encourage her to do this? Explain.

Getting Involved

36. Create a poster that explains safety measures that can help prevent brain and spinal cord injuries. Display the poster in some public place.

CARDIOVASCULAR AND RESPIRATORY HEALTH

When you kick a ball, the cells in your leg and foot muscles need oxygen to function. Your respiratory and cardiovascular systems work together to supply that oxygen. In this chapter, you will learn more about the close relationship between these two systems—and how the health of one depends on the health of the other.

CHAPTER PREVIEW

16-1 Your Respiratory System

- Explain the function of the respiratory system.

16-2 Your Cardiovascular System

- Explain how the heart, blood vessels, and blood bring materials to your body cells and carry waste products away.

16-3 Cardiovascular Disorders

- Identify a heart disorder that is a major cause of death in the United States.

16-4 Healthy Heart and Lungs

- Identify some lifestyle choices that reduce a person's risk of developing circulatory and respiratory problems.

BUILDING HEALTH SKILLS

- Practice a strategy for assessing cardiovascular fitness.

CHECK YOUR WELLNESS

Are your circulatory and respiratory systems in good condition? To find out, see how many *yes* answers you can give.

- Do you breathe easily after climbing a flight of stairs?

- Do you exercise regularly?

- Do you usually have enough energy to do the things you want to do?

- Do you avoid smoking and smoke-filled areas?

- Do you avoid foods that are high in cholesterol and saturated fat?

- Can you participate in a vigorous activity, such as running, biking, walking, or swimming, for at least 20 minutes?

KEEPING A JOURNAL

What do you think when you hear the words *heart attack?* Write your ideas in your journal. Then, as you read the chapter, note whether your ideas change.

Take it to **the Net**
www.phschool.com

GUIDE FOR READING

Focus on these questions as you read this lesson.

- What is the primary function of your respiratory system?
- What are three disorders of the respiratory system that are related to smoking?

SKILLS

- Activity: Breath Volume

All of your cells use oxygen and produce carbon dioxide as a waste product. Blood carries oxygen to your cells and carries carbon dioxide from them. **In the process of respiration, your respiratory system gets oxygen into your bloodstream and removes carbon dioxide from it.**

The Pathway of Air

Before the oxygen in air can get into your bloodstream, air must reach your lungs. As you read about the passage of air from the external environment to the lungs, refer to Figure 16-2, which shows the structure of the respiratory system.

THE NOSE, MOUTH, AND THROAT When you breathe in, or inhale, air passing through your nose is warmed and cleaned. The nostrils and other air passages are lined with mucous membranes. **Mucous membranes** produce mucus, which moistens the air and traps bacteria and dust particles before they reach the lungs. Your air passages are also lined with **cilia** (SIL ee uh), which are tiny hairlike structures that are in constant motion. The movement of the cilia helps trap dust and bacteria. It also helps remove mucus; otherwise, mucus would build up in your air passages. Above the nasal cavity are several hollow spaces, or **sinuses.** Like the nasal cavity, the sinuses are lined with mucous membranes. When you have a cold, mucus may clog your sinuses, causing pain below your eyes and on either side of your nose.

At the back of the nasal cavity, air enters the **pharynx** (FAR ingks), or throat. The **trachea** (TRAY kee uh), which is

Figure 16-1 *Singers need healthy respiratory systems. The larynx, or voice box, is the respiratory organ that produces sounds.*

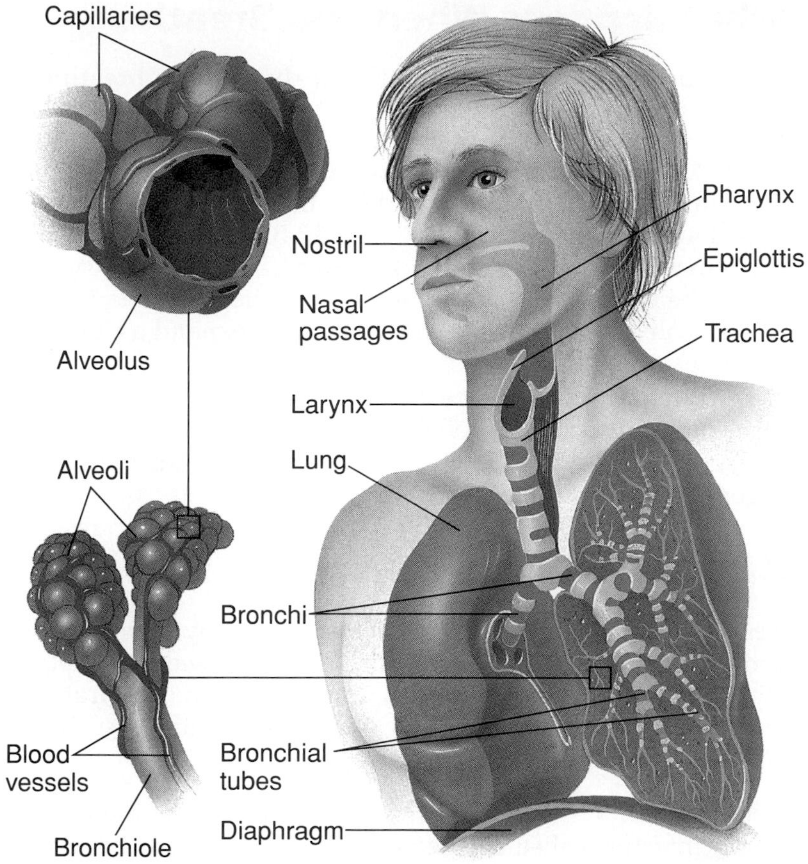

Figure 16-2 *In this diagram of the respiratory system, trace the path of air as it travels from the nostrils to alveoli in the lungs.*

Capillaries

Alveolus

Alveoli

Blood vessels

Bronchiole

Nostril

Nasal passages

Larynx

Lung

Bronchi

Bronchial tubes

Diaphragm

Pharynx

Epiglottis

Trachea

also called the windpipe, is the pathway through which air moves from the pharynx into the chest. The epiglottis blocks off the opening of the trachea when you swallow, preventing food from entering the trachea. Rings of cartilage support the trachea and keep it from collapsing as you inhale. Notice in Figure 16-2 that the **larynx** (LAR ingks), or voice box, is found at the top of the trachea. The larynx is also made of cartilage. When you talk or sing, the vocal cords in the larynx create vibrations that produce sound.

THE LUNG In the chest cavity, the trachea divides to form two **bronchi** (BRAHNG ky), cartilage-ringed tubes that go to each lung. The **lungs** are the elastic, spongy organs through which the body absorbs oxygen. After the bronchi enter the lungs, they divide, like the branches of a tree, into smaller and smaller tubes. The smallest are called **bronchioles** (BRAHNG kee ohlz). Tiny sacs called **alveoli** (al VEE uh ly) are located at the end of bronchioles.

The alveoli are surrounded by capillaries. Oxygen in the air passes through the thin wall of the alveoli into the bloodstream. Carbon dioxide moves in the reverse direction—it passes out of the bloodstream and into the air in the alveoli. When you breathe out, or exhale, you get rid of this carbon dioxide.

What Happens When You Breathe

Your lungs have no muscles. Instead, the work of breathing is done by muscles located in your chest and abdomen. The **diaphragm** (DY uh fram), a dome-shaped muscle that lies just below the lungs, is the main muscle involved in breathing. During inhalation, or breathing in, the diaphragm flattens downward as shown in Figure 16-3. At the same time, rib muscles pull the ribs up and out. These two motions make the chest cavity larger, and air rushes into the lungs. The alveoli are somewhat elastic, and they expand as air fills the lungs.

During exhalation, or breathing out, the diaphragm moves upward and the ribs drop. These movements make the chest cavity smaller. At the same time, the alveoli contract slightly. Together, all these actions squeeze air from the lungs.

Disorders of the Respiratory System

Respiratory infections are problems caused by microorganisms. Colds and tuberculosis, which are discussed in Chapter 22, are both infections of the respiratory system. Respiratory problems can also be caused by harmful substances such as smoke and polluted air.

RESPIRATORY INFECTIONS   The symptoms of the respiratory infection called **influenza** (in floo EN zuh), or flu, commonly include fever, headache, muscle aches, sore throat, and a cough. The treatment for influenza is basically the same as that for a cold—staying at home, resting, and drinking a lot of liquids. Influenza can occasionally lead to more severe diseases, such as pneumonia. Therefore, if flu is especially severe or does not go away after a few days, it should receive medical attention.

Two infectious diseases that affect the lungs are pneumonia and tuberculosis. **Pneumonia** (noo MOHN yuh) is an

Figure 16-3 *When you breathe in, rib muscles make the rib cage larger, and the diaphragm moves downward. The opposite happens when you breathe out—the rib cage becomes smaller and the diaphragm moves upward.*

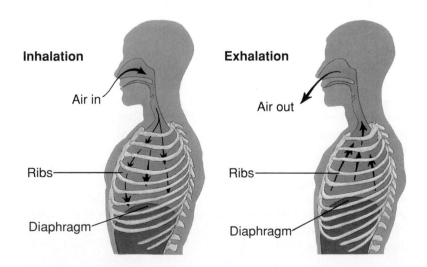

Inhalation

Air in

Ribs

Diaphragm

Exhalation

Air out

Ribs

Diaphragm

BREATH VOLUME

In this activity you will indirectly measure the volume of air that you can exhale during one breath.

Materials

round balloon	metric tape measure

Procedure

1. Stretch the balloon several times by inflating it and then allowing the air to escape.

2. Inhale normally. Then exhale as much as you can into the balloon. Then hold the balloon opening tightly so that no air can escape.

3. Have your partner measure the circumference of the balloon where it is the biggest. Record this measurement.

4. Repeat steps 1 and 2 two more times.

5. Compute the average circumference for the three trials. Then compute the average diameter by dividing the circumference by 3.14.

6. Use the graph to determine the average volume of the air you exhaled.

Discussion

1. How does the average volume of your breath compare with that of your classmates?

2. What factors might affect the volume of air that a person normally inhales and exhales?

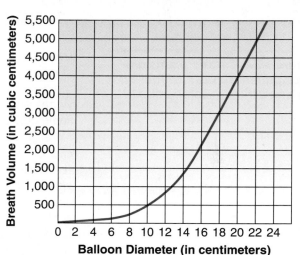

infection in which fluids accumulate in the alveoli, decreasing the lungs' ability to take in oxygen and eliminate carbon dioxide. People with pneumonia generally have a cough and a fever, and in severe cases they may also have difficulty breathing. When pneumonia is caused by bacteria, physicians generally prescribe antibiotics to treat it.

Tuberculosis (too bur kyuh LOH sis) is a chronic, or long-term, bacterial disease that affects the lungs and other parts of the body. Symptoms of tuberculosis—or TB, as it is also called—usually include fever, tiredness, weight loss, and an ongoing cough. These symptoms usually do not begin until months—and sometimes even years—after the bacteria have infected the body. Due to AIDS, tuberculosis increased in the 1970s and 1980s. In the 1990s, it decreased again.

ASTHMA Some respiratory conditions, such as asthma, are not caused by infections. **Asthma** (AZ muh) is a disorder in which the air passages become narrower than normal. This narrowing of the air passages causes wheezing, coughing, and difficulty in breathing. Some cases of asthma are caused by an **allergy,** which is a reaction of the body to an

Figure 16-4 *Certain plants produce pollen that can trigger an asthma attack in some people.*

irritating substance. Pollen, dust, and mold are all substances that can trigger asthma in certain people. Asthma tends to be a chronic problem. It may be aggravated by emotional stress. More children than adults have asthma, and some children outgrow the condition.

Asthma attacks are not usually dangerous, although they can become so if the flow of air into the lungs is severely restricted. There is no cure for asthma, but people who have asthma can sometimes control the condition. If the attacks are caused by an allergy, a series of tests can identify what substances cause the problem. Medications are sometimes used to relieve the symptoms of asthma. Often, these medications are taken in the form of mist from an inhaler.

BRONCHITIS Recall that the bronchi are lined with mucous membranes. **Bronchitis** (brahn KY tis) is an inflammation and swelling of these membranes. The inflamed membranes secrete a large amount of thick, sticky mucus. Hoarseness and coughing are two symptoms of this respiratory condition. The coughing is the body's attempt to clear out the thick mucus.

Bronchitis has different causes. It can result from a respiratory infection that spreads from the nose and throat to the bronchi. Rest, fluids, and cough medicines are the usual treatments for this condition. If the infection is caused by bacteria, antibiotics may be prescribed. Bronchitis can also be caused by smoking and air pollution—and in that case it is usually a chronic and serious condition that cannot be cured. "Smoker's cough" and shortness of breath are symptoms of this type of bronchitis.

EMPHYSEMA People with advanced emphysema are short of breath after the slightest exertion. **Emphysema** (em fih SEE muh) is a respiratory disorder in which the alveoli lose their ability to expand and contract. As the disease progresses, the walls of the alveoli stretch and sometimes break. This damage to the alveoli interferes with the processes of inhalation and exhalation, and the lungs become less efficient at absorbing oxygen and eliminating carbon dioxide. This reduction in oxygen intake, along with the overexertion involved in gasping for breath, eventually damages the cardiovascular system. Emphysema cannot be cured.

People who smoke are much more likely to develop emphysema than are nonsmokers. The treatment for emphysema is to quit smoking and avoid being near smoke. Losing weight can also reduce the strain on both the respiratory and circulatory systems. People with severe emphysema must sometimes be given extra oxygen, which they inhale through tubes inserted into the nose or trachea.

Figure 16-5 *The pollutants pouring out of these smokestacks can damage the delicate tissues of your respiratory system.*

EFFECTS OF AIR POLLUTION AND SMOKING When you inhale, everything that is in the air enters your respiratory passages and lungs. Tobacco smoke and air pollutants are two types of materials that can harm delicate respiratory tissues. If you only inhale harmful materials occasionally, they will probably not damage your respiratory system permanently. However, long-term exposure to cigarette smoke and other air pollutants can seriously and permanently harm your respiratory health.

Tobacco smoke and harmful materials in polluted air can damage your respiratory system in several ways. They may irritate the mucous membranes of the nasal cavity, making your nose run. Smoke and other pollutants can damage the cilia in the air passages. The cilia are then no longer able to trap microorganisms and other harmful particles, nor are they able to remove mucus. As a result of cilia damage, mucus builds up in the air passages, causing coughing.

If the particles and chemicals from tobacco smoke accumulate in your lungs, they can seriously damage the alveoli, reducing their ability to absorb oxygen and eliminate carbon dioxide. In addition, long-term cigarette smokers are more likely to develop lung cancer than are nonsmokers.

LESSON 1 REVIEW

1. What function does your respiratory system perform?
2. Contrast the movement of oxygen and carbon dioxide in the alveoli.
3. Explain what happens when you inhale.
4. Why is it important to seek medical attention for a case of influenza that does not go away after a few days?

What Do You Think?

5. Bronchitis that is the result of long-term smoking is generally a more serious condition than the bronchitis caused by microorganisms. Why do you think this is true?

YOUR CARDIOVASCULAR SYSTEM

GUIDE FOR READING

Focus on these questions as you read this lesson.

- What are the main functions of blood?

- What pathway does blood follow through the heart and the rest of the circulatory system?

SKILLS

- Finding the Facts

Night and day, in a process that never stops, blood flows through your blood vessels. **Blood brings oxygen, nutrients, and other necessary materials to your body cells and carries waste products away.** The circulatory system, which is also called the **cardiovascular system,** provides a pathway through which blood can carry materials throughout your body. Blood also helps regulate body temperature and water balance.

The Heart

The **heart,** shown in Figure 16-6, is a muscular organ that pumps blood throughout the body. Your heart is about the size of your fist and is located near the middle of your chest. Each minute, the average adult's heart pumps approximately 5 quarts (about 5 liters) of blood through the blood vessels.

STRUCTURE OF THE HEART   Your heart has a left and a right side, separated by a thick wall. Each side has two chambers: an atrium and a ventricle. The **atrium** (AY tree um) receives blood entering the heart. Blood flows from each atrium into a **ventricle,** which is the chamber that pumps blood from the heart to the rest of the body.

Figure 16-6 *In the diagram below, the arrows show the pathway of blood through the heart. Notice the valves that prevent blood from flowing backward.*

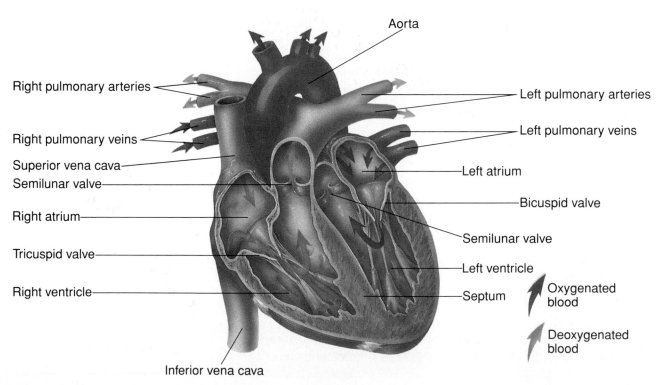

Aorta

Right pulmonary arteries

Right pulmonary veins

Superior vena cava

Semilunar valve

Right atrium

Tricuspid valve

Right ventricle

Left pulmonary arteries

Left pulmonary veins

Left atrium

Bicuspid valve

Semilunar valve

Left ventricle

Septum

Oxygenated blood

Deoxygenated blood

Inferior vena cava

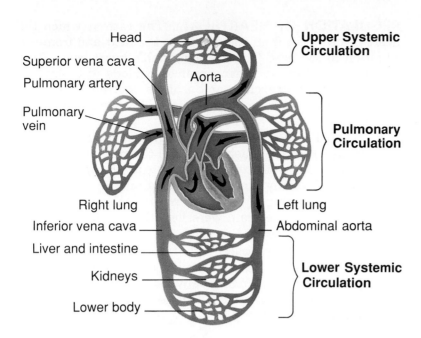

Head — Upper Systemic Circulation

Superior vena cava

Pulmonary artery

Aorta

Pulmonary vein

Pulmonary Circulation

Right lung

Left lung

Inferior vena cava

Abdominal aorta

Liver and intestine

Kidneys

Lower Systemic Circulation

Lower body

Figure 16-7 *The arrows show the path of blood through the pulmonary and systemic circulations. The blood vessels transporting blood that is rich in oxygen are shown in red, and those carrying blood with little oxygen are colored blue.*

Notice the flaplike valves between the atria and the ventricles. These valves keep blood from moving back into the atria when the ventricles contract. The closing of the valves is responsible for the sound of your heartbeat. Also observe that the walls of the ventricles are much thicker than those of the atria. The thick, muscular walls enable the ventricles to contract with enough force to propel blood to all parts of the body.

PULMONARY AND SYSTEMIC CIRCULATIONS The heart is actually a double pump. The right side of the heart pumps blood to the lungs, and the left side pumps it to the rest of the body. The pathway that blood follows from the heart to the lungs is called the **pulmonary circulation** (POOL muh nehr ee). The **systemic circulation** (sih STEM ik) is the route that blood travels from the heart to most of the body and then back to the heart.

Blood from most of the body flows into the right atrium. This blood has little oxygen, but it contains a lot of carbon dioxide, which is a waste product produced by the body's cells. The blood passes from the right atrium into the right ventricle, which pumps it to the lungs. As the blood passes through the lungs, it gains oxygen from the air. At the same time, carbon dioxide leaves the blood and passes into the air in the lungs.

From the lungs, oxygen-rich blood returns to the left side of the heart. The left ventricle then pumps blood to the farthest points of the body. As blood flows through the body, oxygen passes from the blood to the body tissues, and carbon dioxide moves from the tissues into the blood. Oxygen-poor blood then returns to the right side of the heart, and the cycle begins over again.

ENGLISH CONNECTION

In Edgar Allan Poe's short story "The Tell-Tale Heart," the insane narrator describes the sound that a heart makes as it beats: "It was a low, dull, quick sound—much the sound a watch makes when enveloped in cotton."

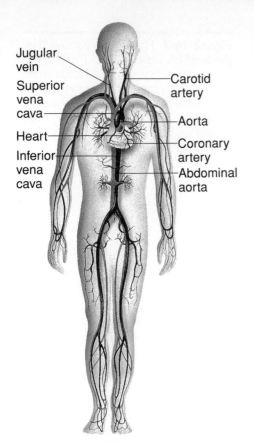

Jugular vein
Superior vena cava
Heart
Inferior vena cava
Carotid artery
Aorta
Coronary artery
Abdominal aorta

Figure 16-8 *The diagram shows the major blood vessels in the human body. Blood vessels that carry oxygen-rich blood are shown here in red, and the blue ones are those that carry blood that has released its oxygen to body tissues.*

REGULATION OF HEARTBEAT The rate at which the heart beats varies from one person to the next and from one situation to the next. The average adult's heart beats 70 to 80 times per minute during rest or periods of inactivity. When a person exercises or becomes excited, the heart speeds up in response to the body's need for more oxygen and nutrients.

In the wall of the right atrium is a group of cells called the **pacemaker** because it helps regulate the rate at which the heart beats, or contracts. The brain can change the rate of the heartbeat by making the pacemaker increase or decrease the number of beats per minute. However, even if the connection to the brain were lost, the pacemaker would continue to stimulate the heart to beat.

If the heart's natural pacemaker begins to malfunction, an artificial one can be surgically placed inside the person's body. The artificial pacemaker delivers an electric impulse to the heart at regular intervals. This series of impulses keeps the heart beating regularly.

Blood Vessels

The heart pumps blood through an extensive network of blood vessels. If your blood vessels were all connected, they would extend over 100,000 miles (161,000 kilometers).

KINDS OF BLOOD VESSELS The thick-walled, elastic vessels that carry blood away from the heart are called **arteries.** Blood travels from the right ventricle to the lungs through the pulmonary arteries, which form part of the pulmonary circulation. The largest artery in the body is the **aorta** (ay AWR tuh), which is part of the systemic circulation. Blood leaves the left ventricle through the aorta, which then branches into many smaller arteries. Some of these arteries carry blood to organs such as the brain, stomach, or kidneys. Other arteries carry blood to bones and muscles in the legs and arms. The **coronary arteries** carry blood to the heart muscle itself.

As an artery enters an organ or tissue, it branches to form smaller blood vessels called **arterioles** (ahr TIHR ee ohlz). Branching off the arterioles are many **capillaries,** the smallest blood vessels in your body. Capillaries are so tiny that blood cells can only pass through them single file. Oxygen and dissolved nutrients pass to body cells from the blood as it flows through capillaries. At the same time, wastes such as carbon dioxide pass from the cells to the blood.

From the capillaries, blood flows into **venules** (VEN yoolz), small blood vessels that join together to form veins. **Veins** are large, thin-walled, slightly elastic vessels that carry blood to the heart. Valves inside the veins prevent blood from flowing backward.

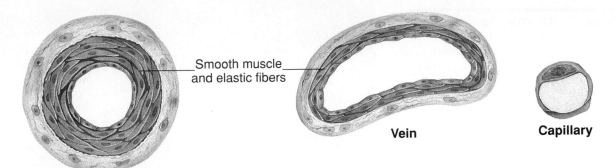

Smooth muscle and elastic fibers

Artery

Vein

Capillary

BLOOD PRESSURE

Each time the ventricles of the heart contract, blood surges out of the heart and through the body's blood vessels. **Blood pressure** is the force with which blood pushes against the walls of the blood vessels.

When your blood pressure is measured, two readings are taken. These two measurements are expressed as a fraction—for example, 140/85. The first, and higher, number is the **systolic pressure** (sih STAHL ik), which is the force caused by the surge of blood that moves as a result of the contraction of the ventricles. The second, and lower, number is the **diastolic pressure** (dy uh STAHL ik), or the force recorded when the ventricles are relaxed.

Like your heart rate, your blood pressure varies depending on your level of activity. Blood pressure increases as you exercise, and then decreases as you relax after the exercise. An average blood pressure reading for healthy young adults at rest is about 120/80.

Blood

Blood is a complex tissue that consists of different types of cells suspended in a watery solution. The average adult has about 4 to 6 quarts (4 to 6 liters) of blood circulating through the blood vessels in his or her body.

PLASMA The liquid part of blood is called **plasma.** This straw-colored liquid makes up about 55 percent of the blood volume. Plasma is mostly water, with various substances dissolved in it. The dissolved materials include nutrients such as glucose and other substances that are necessary for various processes that occur in living cells. Plasma also contains waste products such as urea.

BLOOD CELLS The cells that carry oxygen from the lungs to all the parts of your body are **red blood cells,** which are more numerous than any other type of blood cell. Red blood cells contain hemoglobin, which is the iron-containing substance that gives the blood cells their red color. Oxygen in the lungs combines with hemoglobin, making it bright red. When

Figure 16-9 *Compare these cross-sections of an artery, a vein, and a capillary. Which type of blood vessel has the thinnest wall?*

Figure 16-10 *Whatever your age, you should have your blood pressure checked regularly. Do you know your own blood pressure?*

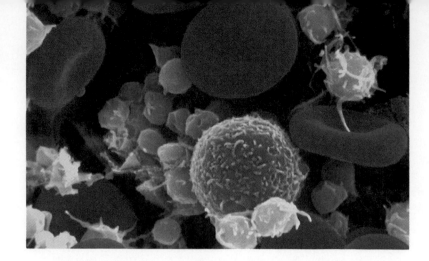

Figure 16-11 *This photograph of blood cells was taken with an electron microscope and then enhanced by a computer. Notice that the white blood cell has a rougher surface than the red blood cells. Also observe the platelets, which are much smaller than the white blood cells and red blood cells.*

the red blood cells reach tissues and organs in the body, the oxygen is released from the hemoglobin. Without oxygen, the hemoglobin is a dull, dark red color.

White blood cells help protect the body against diseases and foreign substances. They are much larger than red blood cells, but far less numerous. There are several kinds of white blood cells. Some make chemicals that help your body resist diseases. Other white blood cells destroy bacteria and other invading microorganisms by surrounding and consuming them. White blood cells are part of the immune system, which is described in Chapter 22.

Blood contains a third type of solid structure—the platelets. **Platelets** (PLAYT lits) are pieces of cells that start the process of blood clotting. When you get a cut and start to bleed, platelets stick to the edges of the cut and release proteins called clotting factors. The clotting factors combine with other proteins in the plasma. Together these proteins form a net of fibers across the cut. The fibers trap more platelets, as well as blood cells. Gradually a plug forms, and the cut is closed. When the plug dries, it forms a scab.

TRANSFUSIONS AND BLOOD GROUPS The procedure in which blood is taken from one person and then transferred to someone else's bloodstream is called a **blood transfusion.** A person may need a transfusion after losing a lot of blood in an injury or certain kinds of surgery. People with some diseases and physical conditions may also need blood transfusions. A blood donor is an individual who gives blood that will be used for a transfusion.

Before someone can receive a blood transfusion, his or her blood group must be determined. A **blood group,** or blood type, is a classification based on whether certain proteins are present on the surface of the red blood cells. Depending on what proteins are present, your blood is classified into one of these groups—O, A, B, or AB. When a transfusion is performed, the donor's blood group must generally be the same as that of the person receiving the transfusion. For example, a person whose blood group is A cannot donate blood to a

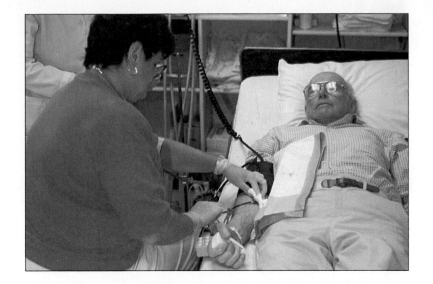

Figure 16-12 *The American Red Cross conducts blood drives that encourage people to donate blood.*

person whose blood group is B. If different blood types are mixed, the red blood cells will usually clump together.

One set of proteins determines whether a person's blood belongs to group O, A, B, or AB. An entirely different protein, called the **Rh factor,** determines a blood group called the Rh group. If your red blood cells have the Rh factor, your blood is said to be Rh positive. If your red blood cells lack the Rh factor, your blood is Rh negative. About 85 percent of people are Rh positive.

Because of the damage that could result from a mismatched transfusion, donated blood is carefully tested to determine its blood groups. In addition, donated blood is checked for the presence of microorganisms that cause several diseases, including hepatitis and AIDS. Since disposable needles are used when blood is taken, a blood donor runs no risk whatever of contracting a disease. By donating blood, people can help others in a safe and important way.

LESSON 2 REVIEW

1. Name two main functions of blood.
2. Explain the difference between the pulmonary and systemic circulations.
3. In which kind of blood vessel does the exchange of materials between the blood and body cells take place?
4. Describe the role of platelets.

What Do You Think?

5. A man's blood belongs to group O and is Rh negative. Should he receive a transfusion of blood that is group O and Rh positive? Explain.

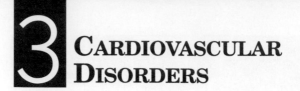

3 CARDIOVASCULAR DISORDERS

GUIDE FOR READING

Focus on these questions as you read this lesson.

- How does the buildup of cholesterol in arteries affect the heart?
- What are some risk factors for high blood pressure?

SKILLS

- Locating Community Resources
- DECIDE

Most cardiovascular disorders are at least partly related to choices that a person makes—choices about such things as nutrition, exercise, and smoking.

Heart Disorders

When most people hear the term *heart disease*, they immediately think of heart attacks. While heart attacks are serious, they are not the only kind of heart problem. For example, structural problems, or malformations, may interfere with the heart's functioning.

CORONARY HEART DISEASE Figure 16-13 shows a cross section of a normal artery and one that is clogged with cholesterol. **Atherosclerosis** (ath uh roh skluh ROH sis) is a buildup of cholesterol and other fatty materials on artery walls, which restricts the flow of blood. Atherosclerosis can occur in the coronary arteries, which are the blood vessels that provide heart muscle with its own blood supply. When the coronary arteries become clogged as a result of atherosclerosis, **coronary heart disease** results. Coronary heart disease is a major cause of death in the United States.

As cholesterol collects in the coronary arteries, less blood—and therefore less oxygen—is able to reach the heart muscle. This lack of oxygen causes a type of pain called **angina pectoris** (an JY nuh PEK tur is). Angina pectoris is not a heart attack, but it can be a sign that a person is at risk of having a heart attack.

A **heart attack** occurs when blood flow to part of the heart muscle is blocked. The blockage may result from atherosclerosis alone, or it may be caused by a blood clot that becomes trapped in an artery narrowed by atherosclerosis. Cells in the part of the heart that is not receiving blood may

Figure 16-13 *Contrast the normal artery (left) with the one that is almost totally blocked because of atherosclerosis (right).*

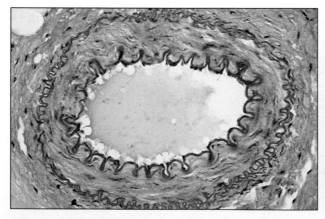
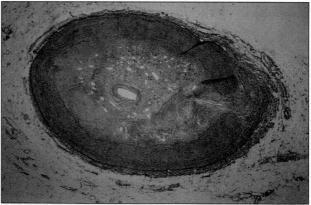

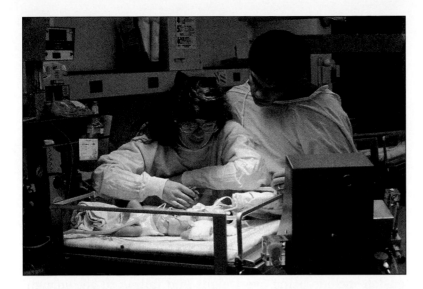

Figure 16-14 *Today, treatment is available for many babies born with heart defects and other serious health problems.*

die, resulting in permanent damage. A severe heart attack can cause death. In about 25 percent of heart attack victims, there were no previous symptoms of coronary heart disease.

The development of atherosclerosis—and therefore coronary heart disease—is closely related to levels of cholesterol in the blood. Cholesterol travels in tiny protein-containing packets called lipoproteins. There are two types of these— low-density lipoproteins (LDL) and high-density lipoproteins (HDL). The relative amounts of LDL and HDL help determine whether atherosclerosis occurs.

You can compare these cholesterol carriers to two kinds of trucks. LDL is like a freight truck that carries cholesterol to the walls of arteries, while HDL is like a garbage truck that transports cholesterol to a place where it can be disposed. Therefore, high levels of LDL are likely to lead to atherosclerosis, but high levels of HDL help eliminate cholesterol from the body. You can keep your LDL level low by limiting the amount of saturated fat and cholesterol in your diet. Exercising regularly can help raise your HDL level.

Cholesterol is not the only risk factor for developing coronary heart disease. Smokers are far more likely to have heart attacks than are nonsmokers. In addition, any excess body weight puts a strain on the heart.

STRUCTURAL PROBLEMS When structural problems of the heart are present at birth, they are called **congenital heart disorders.** In one type, there is an opening between the left and right side of the heart. Faulty heart valves are another type of congenital heart disorder—they produce an unusual heartbeat sound called a heart murmur. A heart with a defective valve does not pump blood well. Mild congenital heart disorders may correct themselves as the child grows. In some severe cases, surgery can repair the problem.

Rheumatic fever is a disease caused by streptococcus bacteria. It can result in **rheumatic heart disease** (roo MAT ik),

SHARPEN YOUR *SKILLS*

Locating Community Resources

Contact local hospitals, medical centers, and physicians' offices to find out where people can have their blood pressure checked in your community. Ask about free or low-cost blood-pressure screening programs. Ask a local newspaper to print a list of these programs for the benefit of its readers.

which damages the valves of the heart. Most victims of rheumatic fever are children or adolescents. Because rheumatic fever can develop from an untreated strep throat, any sore throat that is especially severe or that lasts for a long time should receive medical attention.

Hypertension

Blood pressure that is consistently higher than normal is called **hypertension** (hy pur TEN shun). A person whose resting blood pressure is more than 140 over 90 has hypertension. Some people with hypertension experience dizziness, headaches, or nervousness, but about half of the people who have hypertension experience no symptoms. The only way to tell if your blood pressure is high is to have it measured.

Risk factors that increase your chances of having hypertension include being overweight and failing to get enough exercise. Emotional stress and heredity may also contribute. Hypertension can sometimes be controlled through weight loss and low-sodium diets, but some patients must take medication to lower their blood pressure to normal levels. If not treated, hypertension can lead to other disorders, including atherosclerosis and kidney damage. Hypertension is one cause of **stroke,** in which the blood flow to a part of the brain is suddenly cut off. Strokes can cause severe brain damage and even death.

D DEFINE
the problem

E EXPLORE
alternatives

C CONSIDER
the consequences

I IDENTIFY
values

D DECIDE
and act

E EVALUATE
results

Keeping Fit?

After weeks of looking for a part-time job, you've been hired by the local ice cream parlor to work after school and on weekends. Since the job will take a lot of time, you are concerned about getting exercise. Until now, you have always gotten a lot of exercise, through taking walks and playing on some school sports teams. You have heard that exercise helps keep your circulatory system fit. But how will you be able to keep fit while working?

1. Use the DECIDE process on page 18 to decide what you would do in this situation. Explain your reasons for making this decision.

2. What does your decision say about you—your values, goals, strengths, and weaknesses?

3. What steps would you need to take in order to implement your decision? Explain.

Blood Disorders

Some blood disorders involve plasma. Hemophilia, for example, is an inherited disorder in which the plasma lacks certain substances necessary for normal blood clotting. When hemophiliacs are cut or injured, their blood does not clot normally. Most disorders of the blood, however, involve blood cells. Leukemia is a cancer of the bone-marrow tissues that form white blood cells. Leukemia produces large numbers of abnormal white blood cells, which interfere with the way in which the body fights disease. Anemia and sickle-cell disease are two other conditions involving blood cells.

ANEMIA   The most common blood disorder is **anemia,** a condition in which there are too few red blood cells or too little hemoglobin in the blood. As a result, the blood cannot carry as much oxygen as the body needs. People with anemia are usually weak, pale, and tired. Iron-deficiency anemia is a condition that may develop if people's diets do not contain enough iron. Women are susceptible to iron-deficiency anemia, since they lose blood during menstruation. Anemia can also be caused by vitamin deficiencies and conditions in which red blood cells are destroyed.

SICKLE-CELL DISEASE   Some people have an adequate supply of hemoglobin in their cells, but the hemoglobin itself is not formed correctly. **Sickle-cell disease** is a condition in which red blood cells curve into a sickle shape because of a flaw in the hemoglobin. The curved cells do not pass through capillaries easily, so they sometimes block the flow of blood. This tends to happen during physical exertion, when the body's use of oxygen is greatest. The blockage causes pain, especially in the limbs. If the blockage is severe, the tissues that do not receive enough blood may be damaged. As you learned in Chapter 8, sickle-cell disease is hereditary, and it is most common among people of African descent.

LESSON 3 REVIEW

1. What is atherosclerosis, and how is it related to coronary heart disease?
2. What is hypertension, and how can it be controlled?
3. Contrast the effects of HDL and LDL on cholesterol.
4. What causes a heart murmur?

What Do You Think?

5. A blood count is a test in which the blood cells in a measured sample of blood are counted. How could a blood count be useful in diagnosing anemia?

GUIDE FOR READING

Focus on these questions as you read this lesson.

- What are some ways that you can decrease your risk of developing cardiovascular and respiratory disorders?
- How does excessive body weight affect the respiratory and cardiovascular systems?

SKILLS

- Supporting a Friend

The cardiovascular and respiratory systems work closely together. Both systems are necessary for supplying cells with oxygen and removing carbon dioxide. The lungs are the organs through which oxygen enters the body and carbon dioxide leaves. Without blood, however, those substances could not be transported to and from the tissues.

Because of this linkage, the health of the cardiovascular and respiratory systems are closely related to each other. If one of those systems is damaged, chances are good that the other will also be harmed. A majority of cardiovascular and respiratory conditions are significantly affected by people's choices about their behavior. **Some of the most important ways to protect your cardiovascular and respiratory systems are to avoid smoking, control your weight, and exercise regularly.**

The Air You Breathe

Harmful materials in air can damage your air passages and lungs. As much as you can, try to control the quality of the air you inhale. For example, wear a mask when you do work that generates dust or fumes, such as sanding wood or sweeping out a dusty garage. If you are painting or using other chemicals that produce fumes, try to work in an open, well-ventilated area rather than a closed room.

Figure 16-15 *When you are working in a dusty environment, wear a mask to protect your respiratory system.*

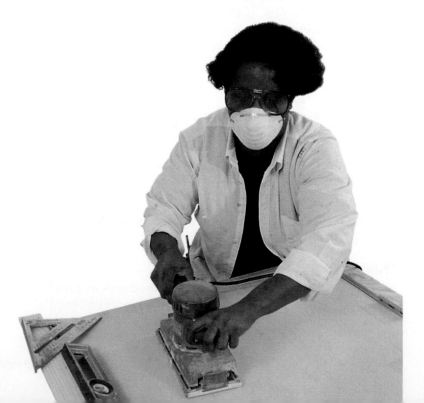

One of the most important choices you can make is not to smoke. Smoking damages the respiratory system and also greatly increases the risk of developing cardiovascular disease. If you do smoke, quit now. Some of the smoke-related damage to mucous membranes and cilia is reversible. The sooner a smoker quits, the sooner this recovery can begin. Also try to avoid exposure to smoke from other people's cigarettes, called sidestream smoke.

Diet and Weight

Diet is very important in maintaining the health of your circulatory system. Recall that red blood cells need iron in order to be able to transport oxygen throughout your body. Refer to Chapter 12 for foods that are good sources of iron. Limit the amount of saturated fats and cholesterol that you eat.

If you maintain a reasonable weight, you avoid straining both the respiratory system and circulatory systems. Remember that the larger the body, the more oxygen that is needed. The respiratory system has to work to get that oxygen into the blood, and the circulatory system has to work to deliver that oxygen to the cells of the body.

Exercise

Aerobic exercise is repetitive, nonstop physical activity that raises the breathing and heart rates. Regular aerobic exercise can increase the efficiency of your heart and lungs. It can also raise your levels of HDL, the lipoprotein carrier that plays a role in eliminating cholesterol. In addition, exercise helps relieve stress, which is a risk factor in heart disease and may contribute to hypertension and asthma. A regular exercise program is an extremely important part of maintaining cardiovascular and respiratory health. You will learn more about the cardiovascular and respiratory benefits from exercise and fitness in Chapter 17.

LESSON 4 REVIEW

1. List three choices you can make that will help keep your circulatory and respiratory systems healthy.
2. Why is it important for smokers to quit smoking sooner rather than later?
3. Explain why excessive body weight puts a strain on both the respiratory and circulatory system.

What Do You Think?

4. Why is diet by itself not the best way to control cholesterol in your blood?

Assessing Cardiovascular Fitness and Determining Target Heart Rate

I n Chapter 15 you assessed your muscular strength, muscular endurance, and flexibility. Here you will test your cardiovascular fitness, which is the ability of your heart, blood vessels, and lungs to deliver nutrients and oxygen to your muscles. When you exercise, your heart and lungs must supply your muscles with more oxygen than they need when you are resting. Your heart, for example, pumps about 5 quarts (about 5 liters) of blood per minute when you are at rest and 20 to 25 quarts (about 19 to 24 liters) when you are exercising vigorously.

Your target heart rate is the heart rate you need to maintain during exercise in order to improve your cardiovascular fitness. Below is a simple test for assessing your cardiovascular fitness and the procedure for determining the range in which your target heart rate should fall. These are followed by some guidelines for improving cardiovascular fitness.

1. Test your cardiovascular fitness

(a) Before you do this test or start an exercise program, have a physical examination to make sure that you do not have any health problems that rule out vigorous exercise. The examination should include a check of your blood pressure and resting heart rate. Do not attempt this test if you are ill or if you have a history of health problems.

(b) To prepare for the test, do the warm-up and stretching exercises described in Building Health Skills for Chapter 17, pages 412–413.

(c) To test your cardiovascular fitness, you must walk and/or run one mile as fast as you can. You can alternate running with walking, but your goal is to cover one mile in as little time as possible. You will need to work with a partner. Your partner should use a watch with a second hand to measure the time, in minutes and seconds, it takes you to complete the distance of one mile.

Mile Walk/Run Times in Minutes and Seconds		
Age	Girls	Boys
14	10:30	7:45
15-18	10:30	7:30

2. Compare your results to recommended results

Compare your score to the scores listed in the table above. To be at a good fitness level, your time should be no greater than the minimum times listed in the table.

3. Take your resting pulse and determine your target heart range

(a) To determine your resting heart rate, you will need a watch or clock with a second hand. Use your index finger or middle finger to find your pulse, either in your wrist or in your neck, as shown in the illustrations. Then count the number of pulse beats during one minute.

(b) Subtract your resting heart rate from 200, which is approximately your maximum heart rate. Then multiply the resulting number first by 0.6 and then by 0.8.

(c) Add your resting heart rate to each of the two numbers you obtained in the previous step. The two sums give you the range in which your target heart rate should be.

4. Choose an exercise program to improve or maintain your cardiovascular fitness

(a) Ask your physical education teacher to help you select appropriate activities for building cardiovascular fitness, such as those in the table. Select moderate intensity activities first, then switch to activities of higher intensity as your fitness improves. Chapter 17 has additional guidelines for choosing a fitness program.

(b) Do these activities three to four times a week. Take your pulse rate immediately after you stop exercising to see if you are exercising in your target heart range. (Since your heart rate begins to decrease as soon as you stop exercising, count the beats in 6 seconds and multiply this number by

10 to get the total number of beats for 60 seconds.)

(c) After you have been exercising regularly for a while, repeat the cardiovascular walk/run fitness test to monitor your progress.

Apply the Skill

1. Complete the timed one mile walk/run to determine your cardiovascular fitness level. Record your results. Be sure to do warm-up stretches before you begin.

2. Determine the range in which your target heart rate falls.

3. After a physical checkup by a qualified health-care professional, design a cardiovascular fitness program that will improve your fitness level.

Cardiovascular Activities
Moderate Intensity
• backpacking
• badminton
• canoeing
• football (tag/touch)
• tennis
• vollyball
• walking
High Intensity
• basketball
• bicycling
• dance (aerobic)
• handball/racquetball
• jogging
• rope jumping
• skiing (cross country)
• soccer
• swimming

CHAPTER 16 REVIEW

KEY IDEAS

LESSON 1

- The function of the respiratory system is to bring oxygen into the body and to remove carbon dioxide from it.
- Disorders of the respiratory system include infections, asthma, bronchitis, and emphysema.

LESSON 2

- The function of blood is to transport materials such as food and oxygen to all parts of the body and to remove wastes.
- The organs of the circulatory system include the heart, arteries, arterioles, capillaries, venules, and veins.
- Blood consists of a liquid part—plasma—and three types of cells—red blood cells, white blood cells, and platelets.

LESSON 3

- Coronary heart disease is caused by a buildup of cholesterol in arteries.
- Hypertension, or high blood pressure, is a serious circulatory system disorder that can lead to atherosclerosis, kidney damage, and stroke.

LESSON 4

- A person can make choices to reduce the risk of developing cardiovascular and respiratory disorders.
- Behaviors that help maintain circulatory and respiratory health include avoiding smoking, limiting dietary fat, maintaining a reasonable weight, and getting adequate exercise.

KEY TERMS

LESSON 1		LESSON 3
allergy	mucous membranes	capillaries	anemia
alveoli	trachea	coronary arteries	atherosclerosis
asthma	tuberculosis	pacemaker	coronary heart
bronchi	LESSON 2	plasma	disease
bronchioles	arteries	platelets	hypertension
bronchitis	atrium	red blood cells	sickle-cell disease
diaphragm	blood group	veins	LESSON 4
emphysema	blood pressure	ventricle	aerobic exercise
	blood transfusion	white blood cells	

Listed above are some of the important terms in this chapter. Choose the term from the list that best matches each phrase below.

1. a respiratory disorder in which alveoli are gradually destroyed

2. a disorder in which blood vessels become clogged with cholesterol

3. the smaller heart chamber that receives blood entering the heart

4. pieces of cells in the blood that start the process of blood clotting

5. the larger heart chamber that pumps blood out of the heart

6. the muscle involved in breathing in and out

7. the windpipe, or pathway through which air moves into the chest

8. high blood pressure

9. thick-walled, elastic vessels that carry blood away from the heart

10. the blood cells that help protect the body against diseases

11. the liquid part of the blood

WHAT HAVE YOU LEARNED?

Choose the letter of the answer that best completes each statement.

12. The systemic circulation involves the flow of blood to all of the following except the

a. kidneys **c.** lungs
b. brain **d.** liver

13. Tiny, hairlike structures that line the air passages are called

a. capillaries **c.** alveoli
b. cilia **d.** bronchi

14. Which of the following can cause asthma attacks?

a. dust **c.** mold
b. pollen **d.** all of the above

15. Which of the following is NOT a symptom of bronchitis?

a. coughing **c.** hoarseness
b. muscle aches **d.** thick mucus

16. The function of hemoglobin is to

a. carry oxygen **c.** fight infection
b. cause blood to clot **d.** eliminate wastes

17. Which of the following is the main risk factor for emphysema?

a. being overweight **c.** too little exercise
b. smoking **d.** atherosclerosis

Answer each of the following with complete sentences.

18. Compare the structure of arteries and veins.

19. How are angina pectoris and a heart attack similar? How are they different?

20. Why is hypertension dangerous?

21. Contrast the processes of inhalation and exhalation.

22. Explain what an allergy is.

23. Identify three effects that air pollution and smoking can have on your lungs.

WHAT DO YOU THINK?

24. Explain why oxygen is sometimes given to victims of sickle-cell disease whose capillaries become blocked by sickled red blood cells.

25. Explain why heavy smokers cough.

26. Your cousin tells you that, even though she does not exercise, she is in no danger of developing coronary artery disease. "After all," she says, "I'm not overweight." Do you think that she is right to be so certain that she will never develop coronary heart disease?

27. You cheered for your team at the basketball game last night. This morning your voice seems very hoarse and you also have a sore throat. You know that many students in your school have come down with flu. What other symptoms would you look for to decide whether you have flu or just an irritation resulting from yelling and cheering?

WHAT WOULD YOU DO?

28. How would you convince someone you know to donate blood?

29. You are going out to lunch with some friends. The restaurant you have chosen has a nonsmoking section, but it is full. Would you take a table in the smoking section, even though none of you smokes? Would you wait for a table in the nonsmoking section? Explain your answer.

Getting Involved

30. Medical equipment called life support systems is sometimes used to keep people alive whose respiratory or cardiovascular systems cannot function on their own. Read about the laws regulating the use of life support systems in your state and the ethical issues involved. Prepare a booklet on this subject and leave a copy in the school library.

EXERCISE, REST, AND RECREATION

Do you realize that physical fitness can be a lot of fun? Your exercise program can include recreational activities, such as hiking and dancing. Variety and enjoyment are the keys to a successful program of lifelong fitness.

CHAPTER PREVIEW

17-1 The Importance of Fitness

- Identify the four components of fitness.

17-2 Finding the Right Exercise Program

- Identify the factors that contribute to a good exercise program.

17-3 Fitness Throughout Life

- Explain how recreation can be an important aspect of fitness and describe activities that can help maintain fitness throughout life.

17-4 Sleep and Feeling Fit

- Describe what happens during sleep and explain the importance of sleep to fitness.

BUILDING HEALTH SKILLS

- Demonstrate appropriate warm-up, cool-down, and stretching activities as part of an exercise routine.

CHECK YOUR WELLNESS

Do you get enough exercise to be physically fit? See how many *yes* answers you give.

- Do you usually have enough energy to do the things you want to do?
- Do you have the strength and endurance necessary for activities such as rowing or shoveling snow?
- Do you exercise three or four times a week for 20 minutes or more?
- Do you warm up, stretch, and cool down when you participate in an athletic activity?
- Do you allow yourself enough time for restful sleep?

KEEPING A JOURNAL

You may be surprised at how much time you already spend on fitness-related activities. For a week, record your different types of physical activity, including such things as sports, washing windows, and walking to school. Also record the time each activity takes.

Take it to the Net
www.phschool.com

THE IMPORTANCE OF FITNESS

GUIDE FOR READING

Focus on these questions as you read this lesson.

- What are the four components of fitness?
- How is aerobic exercise different from anaerobic exercise?

SKILLS

- Activity: Exercise and Carbon Dioxide

Do you think you are physically fit? **Physical fitness** is the ability of the heart, blood vessels, lungs, and muscles to work together to meet the body's needs. When you are physically fit, your body's systems work as a team, allowing you to breathe easily and making your muscles contract in coordinated movement.

Your body is made for activity. Stimulating your muscles, bones, heart, lungs, and blood vessels with regular exercise helps you gain or maintain physical fitness. A program of vigorous exercise, however, is not the only important factor in fitness and a healthy lifestyle. Rest, sleep, and good nutrition are just as important.

Components of Fitness

Each individual has his or her own potential of fitness. For example, you may not have the capability of becoming an Olympic weightlifter or a professional gymnast. Yet you can reach your own personal best. **Physical fitness can be broken down into four health-related parts—cardiorespiratory endurance, muscular strength and endurance, flexibility, and body composition.** Each component is a necessary part of fitness.

CARDIORESPIRATORY ENDURANCE The first component, **cardiorespiratory endurance**, is the ability of your heart, blood vessels, and lungs to distribute nutrients and oxygen and to remove wastes. When you exercise, your heart and lungs must supply more oxygen to your muscles than they need when you are resting. When you are at rest, for example, your heart pumps about 5 to 6 quarts (5 to 6 liters) of blood per minute, but it pumps about 20 to 25 quarts (19 to 24 liters) when you are exercising.

If your heart and lungs function easily during hard exercise and recover quickly afterward, you probably have good cardiorespiratory endurance. People with poor cardiorespiratory endurance might be left short of breath and have a very high heart rate after light exercise. Their lungs and heart are unable to keep up with the muscles' demand for oxygen. Building Health Skills for Chapter 16 describes a way of evaluating your cardiorespiratory endurance.

Figure 17-1 *Physical fitness is necessary for performing many tasks, such as moving furniture.*

MUSCULAR STRENGTH AND ENDURANCE The capacity of a muscle or a group of muscles to exert or resist a force is called **muscular strength.** In contrast, **muscular endurance** is the ability of muscles to keep working for an extended time. For example, the amount of weight you can lift is one measure of your muscular strength. How long you can hold that weight—or how many times you can lift it—is a measure of your muscular endurance. You need muscular strength for all sports and most everyday activities. Acts of muscular endurance include repeated actions, such as raking leaves, shoveling snow, or doing sit-ups. Tests of muscular strength and endurance are given in Building Health Skills for Chapter 15.

FLEXIBILITY The ability to use a muscle throughout its entire range of motion is called **flexibility.** This means that you can bend, stretch, and twist your joints easily. Recall the sit-and-reach test described in Building Health Skills for Chapter 15. This test measures the flexibility of specific groups of muscles in the back and legs, but it is also used to indicate overall flexibility. However, flexibility can vary in different joints. Some people may show poor flexibility in the sit-and-reach test, for example, yet have excellent flexibility in the shoulders and arms. Stretching exercises, if done correctly, can increase flexibility and may reduce the risk of injury during exercise.

BODY COMPOSITION The fourth component of physical fitness, **body composition,** is the amount of body fat compared to lean tissue, such as muscle and bone. Skinfold measurement, which you read about in Chapter 13, is one method for assessing body fat. Excessive body fat has been linked with heart disease, diabetes, arthritis, cancer, and other harmful health conditions.

HISTORY CONNECTION

Great emphasis was placed on physical fitness in the schools of ancient Greece. Students received instruction in exercise and sports such as wrestling, running, and jumping. In fact, the word *gymnasium* comes from the ancient Greek word *gymnasion,* meaning "school."

Figure 17-3 *Regular exercise helps both physical and mental health.*

The Benefits of Exercise

What happens inside you when you run, swim, dance, play hockey, or enjoy some other form of exercise? As the muscles in your arms, shoulders, or legs alternately contract and relax, they use energy that comes from chemical reactions in which oxygen combines with nutrients. Because of the increased needs of your muscles, your heart beats faster, and you breathe more rapidly and deeply. The flow of blood to your heart, lungs, and skeletal muscles increases as your blood vessels dilate, or widen. Your blood pressure and body temperature rise, and you begin to sweat. How do these responses benefit your body?

PHYSICAL BENEFITS Because blood circulates more rapidly through vessels during exercise, the rate at which it brings oxygen and nutrients to, and removes wastes from, your tissues is increased. This increased circulation rate is one reason why you feel refreshed and energetic after a hard workout. In addition, over time, regular exercise may increase the number of capillaries in your body. These additional capillaries provide muscles with a greater supply of blood—not just when you are exercising, but at all times.

Cardiorespiratory endurance is significantly improved by an exercise program. Your heart becomes stronger and pumps blood more efficiently. Regular exercise can also lower your blood pressure and can improve the function of your lungs. Recall from Chapter 16 that an exercise program can help prevent atherosclerosis and coronary heart disease.

Some Benefits of Regular Exercise

Physical Benefits
• Increases muscle strength and endurance
• Increases efficiency of heart and lungs
• Increases physical stamina
• Increases bone strength
• Increases flexibility
• Increases resistance to muscle and bone injury
• Improves posture and appearance
• Reduces blood pressure
• Reduces risk of cardiovascular disease
• Helps reduce excess body fat
• Helps to control appetite
• Aids digestion and helps prevent constipation
• Increases resistance to disease

Psychological and Social Benefits
• Improves mental alertness
• Increases ability to concentrate
• Increases resistance to mental fatigue
• Improves self-image
• Improves self-confidence
• Helps to relieve stress and to improve relaxation
• Helps to control anxiety and depression
• Improves quality of sleep
• Increases social involvement

EXERCISE AND CARBON DIOXIDE

In this activity, you will determine when your lungs release more carbon dioxide—during rest or after exercise.

Materials

bromthymol blue solution, diluted

2 small flasks

6 drinking straws

clock or watch with second hand

Procedure

1. Bromthymol blue, or BTB, is a chemical that turns pale green in the presence of carbon dioxide. Fill the two flasks half-full of dilute BTB solution.
2. Put all six straws in one flask. As you sit relaxed in a chair, exhale normally through all six straws into the BTB solution. **Caution: Do not suck the solution back through the straws; use the straws only for exhaling.** Count the number of times that you must exhale through the straws before the solution turns a pale green color.
3. Now put the six straws in the second flask. Run hard in place for one minute. Then exhale through the straws into the flask. Count the number of times you must exhale before the solution turns pale green.

Discussion

1. Under which condition—rest or after exercise—did fewer breaths turn the BTB solution pale green?
2. Does your body produce more carbon dioxide during rest or during vigorous exercise? Explain.

As you stretch your muscles when you exercise, you can improve your flexibility by loosening stiff muscles and joints. When you run, swim, or do other endurance exercises on a regular basis, your muscles become stronger and are able to work longer. Regular exercise also strengthens your bones, making them thicker and denser. Strong bones and muscles are less likely to be injured than are weak ones.

Exercise can also improve or maintain body composition. A regular workout is important in keeping body fat within recommended levels. As you know from Chapter 13, a program of regular exercise is an important factor in successful weight loss or weight maintenance.

PSYCHOLOGICAL BENEFITS People who exercise regularly are likely to sleep better, feel more self-confident, and focus more productively on their work. Exercise may also increase creativity by releasing body chemicals that stimulate the brain's centers of creativity.

One of the most important psychological benefits of exercise is the reduction of emotional stress. Simple stretching exercises, for example, can help you relax tense muscles and allow you to sleep better. If you are feeling depressed, exercise can generally help make you feel better. In fact, many health professionals consider exercise an important part of a complete treatment for depression, whether the depression is mild or serious.

Have you ever experienced a sense of physical and emotional exhilaration after a hard workout? This feeling is at least partly the result of certain substances called endorphins. **Endorphins** (en DAWR finz), which are chemicals produced in your brain, help to give you a sense of satisfaction and pleasure. During vigorous exercise, cells within your brain produce greater amounts of endorphins.

Fitness Ratings of Physical Activities

Activity	Cardiorespiratory Endurance	Muscular Strength	Muscular Endurance	Flexibility
Aerobic dancing	3-4	2	2	3
Ballet	3	2	2	4
Baseball/Softball	1	1	1	2
Basketball	3-4	1	2	2
Bicycling (at least 10 mph)	3-4	2	3-4	1
Bowling	1	1	1	2
Calisthenics	3	3-4	3-4	3-4
Canoeing	2-3	3	3	2
Football	2-3	2	2	2
Golf	1	1	1	2
Gymnastics	1	4	3	4
Handball/Squash	3	2	3	2
Hiking (uphill)	3	1	2	2
Hockey	2-3	2	2	2
Jogging/Running (at least 6 mph)	3-4	1	3	2
Judo/Karate	1	2	1	3
Jumping Rope	3-4	1	3	2
Racquetball	3-4	1	3	2
Rowing	3-4	3	3	2
Skating (ice, roller)	2-3	1	2-3	2
Skiing (cross-country)	4	2	3-4	2
Skiing (downhill)	3	2	2-3	2
Soccer	3	2	2	2
Swimming	4	2	3	2
Tennis/Badminton (singles)	2-3	1	2-3	2
Volleyball	2	1	2	2
Walking (brisk)	3	1	3	2
Weight training	1-2	4	3	2
Wrestling	3-4	2	3	3

Rating Scale: 1 = Low, 2 = Moderate, 3 = High, 4 = Very high

Figure 17-5 *Swimming is an excellent all-around exercise that is especially good for developing cardiorespiratory and muscular endurance.*

Types of Exercise

No one kind of exercise is a perfect way of improving or maintaining all four components of physical fitness. Figure 17-4 compares the fitness benefits you can receive from many activities. Notice, for example, that recreational activities such as basketball and rowing provide many health benefits.

Exercises can be classified into types, depending on what their performance involves. Included among these are aerobic, anaerobic, isotonic, isometric, and isokinetic exercise.

AEROBIC EXERCISE   Nonstop, repetitive, strenuous physical activity that raises the breathing and heart rates is called **aerobic exercise** (eh ROH bic). Aerobic exercises increase the amount of oxygen that is taken in and used by the body. Swimming, riding a bike, running, brisk walking, and cross-country skiing are all forms of aerobic exercise.

If aerobic exercises last for at least 20 minutes at a time and are done frequently, on a regular, ongoing basis, they will improve cardiovascular endurance. Aerobic exercises are therefore especially important in maintaining the health of your circulatory and respiratory systems. As the information in Figure 17-4 indicates, activities that provide good aerobic exercise do not always improve muscular strength. They do, however, generally improve your muscular endurance.

ANAEROBIC EXERCISE   Imagine that for 20 minutes you exercise like the weight lifter in Figure 17-2. Although your overall exercise time is 20 minutes, the periods of intense physical activity come only when you actually lift the weight. **Anaerobic exercise** (an uh ROH bik) is intense physical activity that lasts only from a few seconds to a few minutes, during which muscles use up more oxygen than the blood can supply. Anaerobic exercise usually improves the flexibility, strength, and sometimes speed, at which muscles work.

However, it does not specifically condition the cardiovascular and respiratory systems. Most anaerobic exercises are designed to develop specific skills, agility, flexibility, or strength. Lifting weights, sprinting, push-ups, and some forms of gymnastics, for example, are usually considered anaerobic activities.

ISOTONIC, ISOMETRIC, AND ISOKINETIC EXERCISE

Three types of exercise—isotonic, isometric, and isokinetic—can increase the strength and endurance of specific groups of muscles. **Isotonic** (eye suh TAHN ik) **exercise** involves the contraction and relaxation of muscles through the full range of their motion. Bending and straightening your arm is an example of an isotonic exercise. You can perform isotonic exercises with or without weights. Through repetition of isotonic exercises, you can develop muscle strength.

Place your palms together and push them against each other. You are performing an **isometric exercise** (eye suh MET rik), in which muscles contract but very little body movement takes place. Pushing against a wall is another example of isometric exercise. Even though this activity involves little movement, your muscles are contracting and thus working. If you continue isometric exercises over a long period, the muscles you use will become stronger.

Perhaps you have seen an accident victim or injured athlete use a special machine in order to recover the use of specific muscle groups. They are performing isokinetic exercises. **Isokinetic exercises** (eye soh kih NET ik) are exercises that involve moving a muscle through a range of motion against a resistance, or weight, that changes. Unlike isotonic exercises, isokinetic exercises always use special machinery to provide the resistance. Many exercise machines in gymnasiums and fitness centers provide isokinetic exercise.

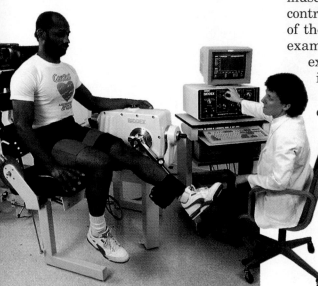

Figure 17-6 *Physical therapists help people perform isokinetic exercises in order to recover the use of muscles.*

LESSON 1 REVIEW

1. Identify the four components of fitness.
2. What changes occur in your body when you engage in vigorous exercise?
3. List three physical benefits of regular exercise. Then list three psychological benefits.
4. How does aerobic exercise differ from anaerobic exercise? Give an example of each.

What Do You Think?

5. How would you convince a friend that starting an exercise program is a wise and healthy decision?

DIFFERENT VOICES SPEAKING

Fifteen-year-old Sylvester Ferguson, who lives in New Jersey, is a member of Special Olympics, which promotes competitive spirit and physical fitness among the disabled. "Sly," who is mentally retarded, won a gold medal at the International Special Olympics in Minneapolis.

Q. Sly, what was it like being in the International Special Olympics?

A. It was very exciting. I had never gone to Minneapolis before. It was my first time being on an airplane and staying in a hotel. Both were a little scary. They were also fun. I went to Minneapolis with my soccer team and with Mr. Endee. Mr. Endee is our coach. He helped get me started in Special Olympics.

Q. Do you have a favorite memory of your trip to Minneapolis?

A. There were two parts I liked a lot. One was meeting [former professional football star] Lynn Swann. He was there on the soccer field. He came to watch us play. I got to shake his hand. I also liked winning a gold medal. I got it for shooting, passing, and dribbling. It felt good to win. It was like all the hard work paid off.

Q. So you have to work hard, then, to be a Special Olympian?

A. Yes. Being in good shape is important. You have to put in extra time. You have to take time warming up before a game.

Q. How do you warm up?

A. We stretch a lot. We do jumping jacks and toe touches. Before soccer, we also dribble the ball 25 yards and back. Sometimes we jog to get ready.

Sylvester Ferguson

Q. How do you keep in shape?

A. I do exercises like push-ups, and I work out with weights. I bench-press 100 pounds, curl 50, and do leg extensions. I also have team practice almost every day. I am in four different sports in Special Olympics. I'm on the soccer team and softball team. I also do track and field and downhill skiing.

Q. Which sport is your favorite?

A. I like skiing a lot because you can go fast. I like to feel the wind on my face. It makes me feel free. Mostly, though, I think I like being part of a team. The other kids on the team are my friends. In soccer in Minneapolis, we didn't get a team medal. We were fourth out of eight teams. Even though I got a medal myself, I felt bad my team didn't win. I cried about it.

Journal Activity

Think about a physical fitness program that appeals to you. Then draw a chart with three columns. In the first column, write the different activities that your program might involve. In the second column, list any obstacles or disadvantages that each activity might present—for example, lack of time. Then, in the third column, write ways that you might overcome these obstacles.

2 FINDING THE RIGHT EXERCISE PROGRAM

Focus on these questions as you read this lesson.

- On what factors does the success of your exercise program depend?
- What are the phases of exercise, and why are they important?

SKILLS

- Setting Goals

Your exercise program should be based on your current fitness ratings and your own interests, needs, and abilities. Even if you think you are perfectly healthy, it makes good sense to check with a physician or other health-care professional to be sure your new activities will not put you at risk. Once you have a physician-approved exercise plan, an exercise specialist, such as your physical education teacher, can help you select the best exercises. Moreover, he or she can give you specific pointers on the techniques that will make the activities safe and effective.

Defining Your Goals

Do you want to obtain total fitness, increase your stamina, have a trimmer body, achieve better coordination, or just feel more alert? Your goals help to determine the best exercise program for you. Re-examine Figure 17-4 on page 392, which lists different types of exercises and their benefits. If your goal is to strengthen muscles, for example, your program might include anaerobic exercises such as lifting weights. If you want to improve your cardiorespiratory endurance, you may develop a program of aerobic exercise. Basketball, jumping rope, or brisk walking will fit into this type of program. Most likely, you have a combination of goals in mind. For example, you may want to increase both your cardiorespiratory endurance and your flexibility.

As you create your exercise program, remember that your fitness program should be fun! Choose activities or a sport that you enjoy and will look forward to. Combine exercise with social activities; for example, take a hike with a group of your friends.

Figure 17-7 *Before planning an exercise program, get a checkup. The health-care professional will ask you questions such as those listed on the right.*

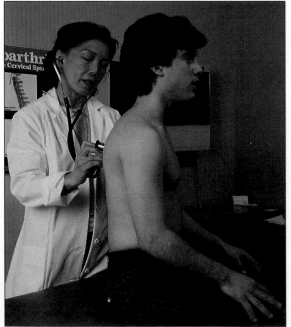

Questions Your Physician Will Ask:

- Do you get out of breath after mild physical activity?
- Do you have a heart condition, such as a heart murmur?
- Do you have pain during or after exercise?
- Do you often feel faint or dizzy?
- Do you have a family history of heart disease, high blood pressure, diabetes, or high levels of blood cholesterol?
- Do you take any medications?
- Do you have any medical condition that may be cause for modifying your physical activity?

A Weekly Exercise Program	
Sunday • Slow, 20-minute run around the pond • Two flights of stairs taken three times	**Wednesday** • Bike to school • Gym class • 40-minute basketball practice
Monday • 20-minute brisk walk to school • Gym class at school • 20-minute walk home	**Thursday** • 20-minute walk to school • Basketball game
	Friday • Gym class • 30-minute aerobics class • 20-minute walk home
Tuesday • Walk to school • 30-minute swim after school • Walk home	**Saturday** • Leaf raking for 40 minutes • Slow 20-minute run

Figure 17-8 *What changes would you make in this weekly exercise program to suit your own needs and interests?*

You can often develop an enjoyable fitness program by expanding on the activities that are already a part of your life, as shown by the weekly exercise record in Figure 17-8.

The FIT Principle

The effectiveness of your exercise depends on three factors: how often you exercise, how hard you exercise, and how long you exercise at each workout session. These ingredients make up the FIT principle, which stands for **F**requency, **I**ntensity, and **T**ime. To achieve fitness, you need to meet minimum standards for each FIT factor.

FREQUENCY OF EXERCISE To stay physically fit, you should exercise frequently, preferably three or more times a week. As you become more fit, some studies suggest that if the intensity of your exercise is moderate, four times a week is most effective in increasing cardiorespiratory endurance and weight loss. If you exercise vigorously, however, do not do so more than five times a week—otherwise, injuries can result.

No matter what your goal is, you should spread your exercise out over the week. Being inactive during the week does not prepare your body for an intense weekend workout. Weekend athletes are more likely to injure themselves than those who exercise regularly throughout the week.

INTENSITY OF EXERCISE If your goal is increased cardiorespiratory endurance, you must work your cardiovascular and respiratory systems with greater-than-normal effort through aerobic exercise. The intensity of a workout is indicated by the number of times your heart beats per minute. The more intense the exercise, the faster your heart rate.

Figure 17-9 *Basketball is one of many fitness-building activities that you can do along with friends.*

Figure 17-10 *Cross-country skiing is good aerobic exercise. The faster you ski, the more intense the exercise becomes.*

Your **maximum heart rate** is your heart's top speed, or your heart rate when you have exercised to the point of exhaustion. For teenagers, this rate is about 200 beats per minute. You should not try to work out at your maximum heart rate, since exercise at that intensity puts a strain on your heart. Your **target heart rate,** which is lower than your maximum heart rate, is the approximate heart rate you need to maintain during aerobic exercise in order to benefit from the workout. Your target heart rate depends on your age, your current level of fitness, your resting heart rate, and your maximum heart rate. It is often expressed as a range—for example, 145 to 170 beats per minute. Building Health Skills for Chapter 16 explains how to determine the range in which your target heart rate should fall.

During exercise, you need to check your heart rate regularly to determine whether it is within your target heart range. To check your heart rate, you need to stop exercising briefly and count your pulse. Your heart rate slows down quickly, so take your pulse for only six seconds and multiply by ten to get an accurate count of the number of heartbeats per minute.

The "talk test" is an easy way to check your exercise intensity. If you are so out of breath while exercising that you cannot talk, your exercise level is too intense. If you can sing while you exercise, however, you probably are not working hard enough. You are working at the proper intensity if you can talk comfortably.

EXERCISE TIME Finally, the amount of time spent exercising affects your level of fitness. If you are just beginning an exercise program, start out with only a short period of exercise—about 10 or 15 minutes. Then increase the exercise time gradually, by no more than 10 percent a week. Once your workout program is well established, most research suggests that 20 to 30 minutes of vigorous exercise four times a week will lead to greater fitness. If your goal is cardiorespiratory improvement, you must exercise within your target heart range for 20 to 30 minutes each session. If your goal is to reduce body fat, your exercise period should be a minimum of 30 minutes, which is longer than the 20-minute minimum required for a cardiorespiratory workout. You should, however, exercise only at a moderate level of intensity—about 60 percent of your maximum heart rate. This is because, at a moderate level of intensity, your muscles tend to use body fat as an energy source, rather than the glucose that is used to provide energy for high-intensity exercise. In order to burn a significant amount of fat, you need to exercise for at least 30 minutes.

Phases of Exercise

A complete fitness workout should be preceded by warming up and followed by cooling down. Although skipping these preliminary and follow-up procedures does not always result in injury, the safest and most healthy exercises include these two phases. Suggestions for warm-up and cool-down procedures—including stretching—appear in Building Health Skills at the end of this chapter.

WARMING UP AND STRETCHING   Before doing any type of exercise you must warm up. A **warm-up** is a five- to ten-minute period of mild exercise that prepares your body for vigorous exercise. During a warm-up, your body temperature begins to rise, your heart rate picks up, blood flow to your muscles increases, and your muscles become more elastic and less likely to become injured.

Some people suggest that you go through the motions of your planned activity when you warm up. But rather than doing these movements at full intensity, do them at a slower

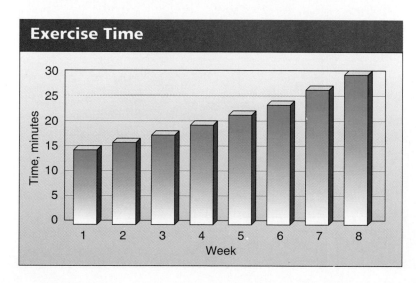

Exercise Time

Figure 17-11 *If you want to increase the time of your workout, do it gradually, at a rate of about 10 percent a week.*

pace. If you are planning to run, for example, start out by walking. Then gradually increase your speed until reaching your usual pace.

Your warm-up should include five to ten minutes of stretching. As you know, stretching increases your flexibility, and proper stretching may decrease your chance of injury. However, it is very important to know your limits and stretch according to safe guidelines, such as those given in Building Health Skills. Don't overstretch, as that can damage ligaments and weaken joints. Stretching should be a constant, even pull on the muscles on both sides of your body. Because muscles work in pairs, you need to stretch both muscles in a pair. As you stretch each muscle group, you should feel tension but not pain. Do not bounce when you stretch, since bouncing can tear muscle fibers.

THE WORKOUT   The goal of this phase of exercise is to improve one or more of the components of physical fitness. Figure 17-13 summarizes the parts of a total fitness workout that includes strength/endurance exercises as well as those designed to improve cardiovascular fitness. Depending on your goals, you may not plan on doing both cardiovascular and strength/endurance exercises. Alternatively, you might switch between cardiorespiratory and strength/endurance workouts in successive exercise sessions. If you do both in the same session, however, the cardiorespiratory workout should be done first.

It is important to do strengthening exercises on alternating days. That is because a full day is needed for your muscles to recover from such a workout. Also, when doing muscle-strengthening exercises, you should plan on short periods or sets of physical activity followed by rest periods during which the muscles can recover.

Figure 17-12 *Walking is a good way to warm up for running.*

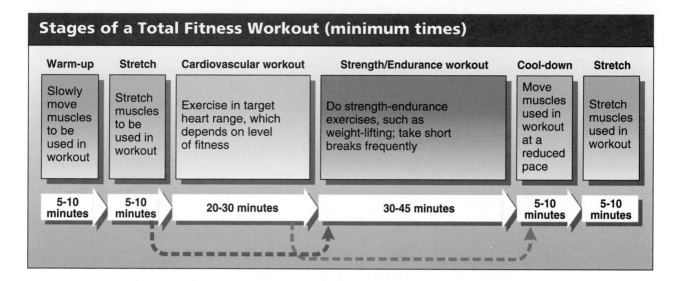

Stages of a Total Fitness Workout (minimum times)

Warm-up	Stretch	Cardiovascular workout	Strength/Endurance workout	Cool-down	Stretch
Slowly move muscles to be used in workout	Stretch muscles to be used in workout	Exercise in target heart range, which depends on level of fitness	Do strength-endurance exercises, such as weight-lifting; take short breaks frequently	Move muscles used in workout at a reduced pace	Stretch muscles used in workout
5-10 minutes	5-10 minutes	20-30 minutes	30-45 minutes	5-10 minutes	5-10 minutes

COOLING DOWN AND STRETCHING A slow warm-up period brings you safely from minimal to maximal activity. The **cool-down** is a period of milder exercise that allows your body and your heart rate to return slowly and safely to their resting states. Your cool-down should be at least as long as your warm-up. If you stop exercising abruptly, blood can collect in the muscles you were using. When this happens, blood may not return fast enough to your heart and brain. As a result, you may become dizzy and faint. Walking is a common method of cooling down.

Stretching after your cool-down loosens muscles that have tightened from exercise and prevents muscle and joint soreness. Spend at least five minutes repeating the stretches you did before your workout.

Figure 17-13 *An exercise session may have up to six parts. Why do you need to warm up and cool down?*

Checking Your Progress

One of the most exciting and gratifying aspects of sticking with a fitness program is seeing your progress. Your fitness will improve only gradually, so wait three or four weeks before retesting your fitness. In most exercise programs, you will begin to notice significant changes within 12 weeks. You may find that you look better, sleep better, or feel more alive. Perhaps you will notice that you have gained muscle strength, lost weight, or lowered your resting heart rate.

YOUR RESTING HEART RATE Someone with average cardiovascular fitness has a resting heart rate between 72 and 84 beats per minute. In general, girls and women have higher resting heart rates than boys and men. In either sex a resting heart rate below 72 beats per minute usually indicates a good fitness level. A young athlete in top competitive condition may have a resting heart rate as low as 40 beats per minute. The athlete's heart is so strong and efficient that it doesn't need to beat more rapidly to meet the body's needs.

Progress Record

Week	Weight	Upper Arm Measurement	Resting Heart Rate	Appetite	Sleep Pattern
0					
3					
6					
9					

Figure 17-14 *A record of your progress might take the form of the table shown above.*

Your resting heart rate will probably not drop that low, but you may notice a drop of five to ten beats per minute after three to four weeks of exercise.

YOUR CHANGING SHAPE   If one of your goals is to lose body fat, you need to combine your exercise program with changes in your eating habits. In Chapter 13, you can find suggestions for how to do this sensibly. As you track your progress, keep in mind that to be healthy, your body must store some fat—you cannot expect to lose all your body fat. In addition, remember that it is possible to lose fat tissue without losing weight. If you lose fat and gain muscle, you may even find that you weigh more than when you began your program. This is because muscle tissue is heavier than fat.

You will, however, have a trimmer body. To get an idea of whether you are losing body fat, you might measure and record the circumference of your upper arm at the start of your exercise program. Then measure your arm again every three to four weeks to track any changes.

To keep track of your overall progress in your workout program, you might keep a record in a table such as that shown in Figure 17-14. About every three or four weeks, write your fitness data in the table. Then, as the weeks go by, you can compare early data with later test results.

A Safe Workout

Anyone who exercises faces the risk of injury. While some injuries may be unavoidable, most can be prevented by following some common-sense practices.

EQUIPPING FOR SAFETY   You do not need expensive equipment in order to be safe—depending on the activity you choose, you may need nothing more than sneakers. The key point is to choose the right equipment for your particular kind of exercise. Proper clothing, footwear, and protective gear help you to avoid discomfort and injury.

Clothing should be comfortable and allow unrestricted movement. Avoid clothing that inhibits your body's ability to cool itself through the evaporation of sweat. Also avoid any

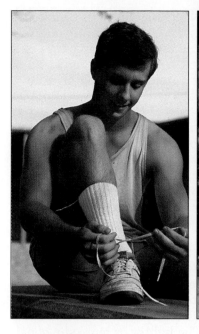

Figure 17-15 *Proper safety equipment can help prevent injuries.*

clothing that can trip you or get caught. For example, do not wear loose-fitting long pants or skirts when bicycling. Long pants and long sleeves are appropriate in sports such as skating, where falls and skin scrapes are a risk.

To protect your feet from injury, footwear must fit properly, be in good condition, and provide support and protection. While athletic footwear is highly specialized, you probably do not need to buy expensive shoes. For example, do not waste your money on shoes meant for professional runners if your main activities are walking and bicycling.

Shoulder pads, helmets, mouthguards, and other protective gear are designed to prevent injuries in contact sports such as football and hockey. Hard-shell helmets worn by football players, hockey players, and baseball players at bat are designed to protect the head from a direct blow. Of course, you would not play a contact sport without a helmet, but did you know that you should regard a helmet as standard operating equipment anytime you get on wheeled sports equipment? A helmet should be worn each time you bike, skateboard, or roller skate. Knee and elbow pads are important equipment for skateboarders and roller skaters.

FLUIDS AND FOOD   Your body can require water even when you are not thirsty. If you exercise for more than 45 minutes, you should take fluids during your exercise period. This is especially important in hot weather. To help prevent dehydration on warm days, you should have a cup of fluid a few minutes before you exercise and every 15 minutes during your exercise.

You need energy for exercising, and you get that energy from the food you eat. Chapter 13 contains information about the kinds of food that help athletic performance.

Figure 17-16 *When you exercise during hot weather, wear lightweight clothing that will allow perspiration to evaporate.*

AVOIDING OVEREXERTION   You may feel unusually tired during the session or even a few hours after if you exercise too intensely, too long, or too often. This tiredness is a signal that you have overworked your body. Other signs of overexertion include nausea or vomiting during or after a workout, and muscle or joint aches and pains that do not go away quickly. If you experience any of these symptoms, you need to cut back the intensity and length of your exercise. Avoid overexertion by sticking to a consistent exercise schedule, rather than occasional bursts of activity followed by periods of inactivity. In addition, always keep your exercise within your comfort level. Do not make the mistake of pushing yourself too hard in order to reach your fitness goal quickly.

WEATHER CONSIDERATIONS   Make sure your clothing is appropriate for the weather. Regardless of the air temperature, you should feel slightly cool at the beginning of your workout. When you exercise outdoors on warm, sunny days, wear light-colored clothing to reflect the sun's rays, and dress lightly to prevent overheating. The lighter or more sun-sensitive your skin is, the more you will need to protect yourself from sunburn with a sunscreen lotion.

When it is cold, your clothing should protect you from frostbite. Cover your hands and head, since you lose a lot of heat from these parts of your body. You may need a sweatsuit for warmth, but do not overdo it. Clothing that is too thick or heavy can inhibit the evaporation of sweat and possibly cause overheating. If you wear layers of clothing, you can regulate your temperature by taking off or adding layers as necessary.

LESSON *2* REVIEW

1. On what factors should you base your personal exercise program?
2. Explain how your target heart rate affects the level of intensity of the exercise you perform to improve your cardiorespiratory endurance.
3. List two ways to reduce your risk of injury when you exercise.
4. As fitness improves, how does a person's resting heart rate usually change?

What Do You Think?

5. Even though Susan rarely exercises during winter, she thinks that she is physically fit because she swims a lot every summer. Do you think she is right? Give reasons for your answer.

3 FITNESS THROUGHOUT LIFE

One of the most important and challenging things you can do for yourself is to start exercising now and continue your program for your entire life. If you begin and continue an exercise program when you are young, it will help you stay healthy and fit as you age. Some people are discouraged from achieving this goal, because they think that exercise is too difficult or time-consuming. They do not realize that many activities that they already perform may actually be forms of exercise. In addition, fitness activities can actually be a lot of fun.

Fitness and Recreation

Do you have fun riding your bike to visit a friend? Is a brisk walk on a cool morning something that you enjoy? At school dances, do you love to jump and turn enthusiastically in time to fast music? Do you and your friends ever get together for a hike, a quick game of basketball, or a swim at a local lake or pool? If you answered *yes* to any of those questions, you already perform activities that contribute to your physical fitness. **Recreational activities that involve exercise, such as walking, biking, dancing, and swimming, are an important part of a fitness program.**

For many people, variety is a key to making a fitness program enjoyable. A fitness program does not have to consist of an unchanging set of exercises. You might take a walk on Monday, play a tennis game on Wednesday afternoon, go to a dance on Friday night, and rake leaves for a couple of hours on Saturday.

GUIDE FOR READING

Focus on these questions as you read this lesson.

- How can recreation be a part of your fitness program?
- What are some ways to make exercise enjoyable?

SKILLS

- Working in Groups

Figure 17-17 *Both aerobic dance classes (left) and recreational dancing (right) can help you become physically fit.*

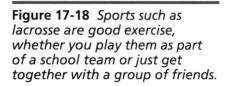

SHARPEN YOUR **SKILLS**

Working in Groups

Plan an exercise activity with a group of friends. Some possibilities include a hike, a soccer game, or a swim party. You and the other group members should cooperate in deciding what you will do and when the activity will take place. If supplies or transportation must be provided, the group members should also cooperate in making those arrangements.

Organized team sports, such as soccer and hockey, are a good form of exercise. However, people who do not enjoy team sports can be physically fit too. If you think that fitness is only for athletes, you are mistaken.

One of the easiest, cheapest, and most effective ways you can exercise is to walk. At any intensity, walking benefits bones and muscles. At high intensity, walking can be a good workout within your target heart range. You can walk by yourself or in a group. You may walk along roads, through a residential neighborhood, at a mall, in a park, across fields, or even indoors on a treadmill. Walking is less stressful on your body and less likely to result in injury than more vigorous activities.

To benefit from walking you should walk at least three times a week, preferably five or six times a week if your pace is slow. For an easy start, walk half a mile every day or every other day to settle into the habit. Then gradually increase to a rate of about 20 minutes per mile. A strenuous walk of three to five miles within 60 minutes is good for those working toward weight loss. Walking can improve your cardiovascular fitness so long as you reach your target heart rate and maintain it for at least 20 minutes.

Aerobic dance programs, in which people perform a set of exercises in time to music, are offered by many community centers, YMCAs, YWCAs, and health clubs. However, recreational dance of almost any kind can be substituted for aerobic dance. In order to increase your cardiorespiratory endurance, you must dance vigorously enough to reach your target heart rate for a minimum of 20 minutes.

Figure 17-18 *Sports such as lacrosse are good exercise, whether you play them as part of a school team or just get together with a group of friends.*

Exercise

1. **MYTH:** "No pain, no gain"—exercise to the point of feeling pain—is the only way to improve your abilities.

   ● **FACT: Pain is a danger signal, a signal that you are causing harm. Sharp or sudden pain should be a signal to stop immediately.**

2. **MYTH:** Sit-ups and other abdominal exercises will decrease fat in the stomach area.

   ● **FACT: You cannot "spot reduce," or lose fat just in one area.**

3. **MYTH:** Drinking fluids before exercising can cause stomach cramps.

   ● **FACT: Plain water will not cause cramps. Without adequate water, you can become dehydrated, which can lead to muscle cramps and other more serious problems.**

4. **MYTH:** Being thin is a sign of fitness.

   ● **FACT: Thin people who do not exercise are likely to have poor heart, lung, and muscular fitness. Cardiovascular fitness is a better indication of overall fitness than your appearance.**

5. **MYTH:** If women lift weights, they will develop large muscles.

   ● **FACT: Women actually have less muscle tissue and more fat tissue than men. They also have a balance of hormones that is different from men and that prevents the development of large muscle mass.**

6. **MYTH:** Exercise is unsafe for older people.

   ● **FACT: The health of elderly people can benefit greatly from moderate exercise.**

Do you still think you just cannot bring yourself to plan and carry out a fitness program? Then at least try to increase your daily level of activity. Make a game out of trying to add just a little more exercise each day. If you travel mostly by car or bus, bicycle or walk instead. Use stairs instead of an elevator. If you already walk quite a bit, pick up your pace or jog for a short distance. A small amount of exercise is better than none at all. People who get even a little bit of exercise have less risk of cardiovascular disease than those who are totally inactive.

Fitness and Aging

You learned in Chapter 11 that as people age, they undergo physical changes. Their bodies become less flexible, and their bones tend to fracture more easily. Those changes do not, however, have to prevent older people from being physically fit. Studies have shown that moderate exercise can help reduce the effects of, and sometimes eliminate, many physical problems associated with old age, such as cardiovascular disease and arthritis. This is true even if exercise begins late in life.

Some older people mistakenly think that they need to avoid exercise in order to protect themselves from injury. In fact, bones and muscles are more likely to stay strong and function well if they are exercised regularly. Exercise can significantly reduce the risk of osteoporosis, a condition in which the bones of elderly people—particularly elderly

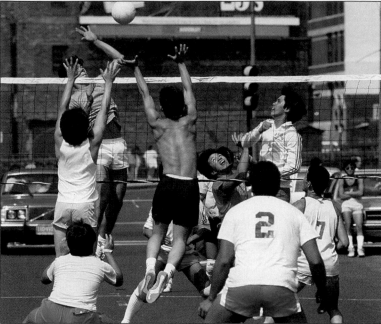

Figure 17-19 *Regardless of age, people can enjoy vigorous activities that help them stay fit.*

women—become fragile. Older people who get little exercise are generally less healthy than those who remain active.

Moderation is especially important in a fitness program for older adults. Older people may not be able to exercise at as high an intensity as they once did. Older people are more likely than younger people to develop circulatory-system problems, and the target heart rate for exercise decreases as a person ages. Elderly people also need to be especially careful not to put too much stress on bones and muscles. If older people exercise carefully and moderately, however, they can continue to benefit from regular exercise.

LESSON *3* REVIEW

1. List some recreational activities that are good forms of exercise.
2. Why is walking such a good way to exercise?
3. In what ways can you increase your fitness without having a scheduled exercise program?
4. Why is moderation an important consideration when elderly people exercise?

What Do You Think?

5. How active are you each day? In what ways do you think you could change your activity level to improve your fitness as you become older?

4 SLEEP AND FEELING FIT

GUIDE FOR READING

Focus on these questions as you read this lesson.

- What happens to your body during sleep?
- How does sleep affect your health?

SKILLS

- Time Management

Sleep, like nutrition and exercise, affects your level of fitness. Your time asleep is your body's recovery period. Your body releases pent-up tension and replaces and repairs damaged tissues during sleep. In fact, much of your body's growth takes place while you are asleep.

What Is Sleep?

Sleep is the deep relaxation of the body and mind during which the eyes are usually closed and there is little conscious thought or movement. **During sleep, your muscles relax, your breathing and heart rates decrease, and your body temperature drops slightly.**

Your temperature, mood, and alertness tend to rise and fall at roughly the same time every day. Such changes are part of a circadian rhythm. A **circadian rhythm** (sur KAY dee un) is a 24-hour cycle of behavior patterns that some living things, including humans, exhibit. During the most active period of the circadian rhythm, your mind is alert and your physical dexterity is at its peak. The several hours that you spend in sleep each day are the least active part of the circadian rhythm. For most people, the sleep period occurs at night.

While a person tends to follow about the same cycle of sleep and wakefulness day after day, different people have different sleeping habits, and these patterns are learned. Although you probably sleep for one long stretch during the night, people who live in countries with hot climates may

Figure 17-20 *Alertness and the ability to concentrate are two benefits of sound sleep.*

have a different pattern. They may wake before dawn to begin work, rest or nap in the afternoon when it is hottest, and then return to work in the cool of the early evening.

THE SLEEP CYCLE   As you sleep, your body and brain undergo changes that make up a sleep cycle. The typical sleep cycle consists of two different types of sleep—nonrapid eye movement sleep and rapid eye movement sleep. During **nonrapid eye movement (NREM) sleep**, your eyes move very little and your body gradually reaches its state of deepest relaxation. NREM sleep has four stages. The first stage consists of a gradual period of falling asleep. During stages two, three, and four, your sleep becomes deeper and your muscles more relaxed. It appears that these stages of deep sleep help restore the body and renew its energy. People who exercise regularly spend more time in third- and fourth-stage NREM sleep than people who do not exercise.

Two things are characteristic of **rapid eye movement (REM) sleep**—rapid flickering of your eyes behind closed eyelids and a high level of brain activity. This is the stage of sleep in which you dream. REM sleep makes up about 25 percent of your sleeping time. Figure 17-21 shows that sleep begins with NREM sleep, progresses to REM sleep, and then cycles back and forth between the two types.

SLEEP DISORDERS   A number of sleep disorders can affect your health. At some point, almost everyone experiences **insomnia**, difficulty in falling asleep or staying asleep. Insomnia can be caused by stress, anxiety, or physical problems. If you are bothered by insomnia, getting more exercise during your waking hours may ease the problem.

Being pleasantly tired when you go to bed is the best way to get a good night's sleep. Avoid heavy exertion like aerobic exercise just before bedtime, since it can increase your alertness, making it harder to fall asleep. Also, if you cannot fall

Figure 17-21 *In the graph showing the sleep cycle during one eight-hour period, notice how sleep cycles back and forth between NREM and REM sleep.*

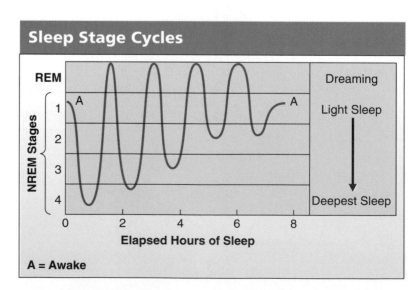

asleep within 15 minutes, or if you find yourself lying awake during the night, do not increase your stress by trying to force yourself to sleep. Get up and do something relaxing, such as reading.

Sleep apnea (AP nee uh) is a disorder in which breathing stops for short periods during sleep and then resumes suddenly. This may happen 300 to 500 times a night without the individual being aware of it. However, he or she may be extremely tired the next day.

People who fall asleep suddenly without warning for short periods of time may suffer from **narcolepsy** (NAHR kuh lep see). Narcolepsy is a disorder of REM sleep that can develop during adolescence or in the early twenties. Sleep specialists think that narcoleptic people frequently enter REM sleep without passing through NREM sleep.

How Much Sleep Is Enough?

No two individuals have exactly the same sleep needs. Healthy adults average seven and a half hours of sleep out of every 24 hours. People who are sick or depressed sometimes need more sleep than those who are feeling well. Because of the rapid changes occurring in their bodies, infants and adolescents need more sleep than other people.

You are probably getting enough sleep if you fall asleep without trouble and wake up feeling refreshed. The quality of your sleep is as important as the amount of time you sleep. Establish a nighttime routine before you go to bed. A routine often helps you relax. Try to stick to a regular bedtime as well, to prepare your body for sleep the way a warm-up cues it for exercise. Avoid going to bed late and getting up late on weekends, a habit that disrupts your circadian rhythm. Keep your bedroom quiet, dark, and ventilated at night. Music or lights may prevent you from reaching the deepest stages of sleep and deny your body the complete rest it needs.

SHARPEN YOUR SKILLS

Time Management

Stephanie is not getting enough sleep. She has a small part in the school play, and she does not start her homework until she gets home after play practice. Then she works until midnight or later. Write a plan showing how Stephanie might do part of her homework before she gets home.

LESSON 4 REVIEW

1. What is a circadian rhythm?
2. Describe what happens to your body as you sleep. Include the kinds of sleep and the stages involved.
3. List and describe three sleep disorders.
4. What are some things you can do to help yourself get a good night's sleep?

What Do You Think?

5. Why do victims of sleep apnea often feel tired even after sleeping for eight hours?

Warming Up, Cooling Down, and Stretching

Imagine that you are about to go on a five-mile bicycle ride or play your favorite sport. You know that these are strenuous activities that put stress on your bones, muscles, and tendons. How should you prepare your body for these activities? After the activity, what should you do to minimize the effects of the stress your body has just undergone?

Before a workout, use slow movements to warm up the muscles that you will use. When the muscles are warmed up, stretch them. Stretching "cold" muscles is not effective and can cause injury. After your workout, cool down by slowly moving the muscles you used. Then stretch these muscles as you did before the workout.

Although no single stretching routine is appropriate for every activity, the stretching exercises that follow provide a base for you to build on. It is important not to rush when you perform these movements. A pulled muscle can hold you up much longer than the few minutes of warming up/stretching and cooling down/stretching needed with each workout.

When you perform stretching exercises, do not bounce. Bouncing can tear muscle fibers, and scar tissue can form as a result.

1. Warming up/cooling down

Before your workout, either walk, jog slowly, or do the activity that you are about to participate in at a reduced pace. This warms up your muscles, preparing them for the more intense activity of the workout itself. Similarly, right after the workout, you need to continue moving your muscles at a reduced pace for five to ten minutes, as you did in the warm-up. This cool-down period helps ease the body back to normal levels of muscular activity.

2. Side stretch

Stand with feet apart, knees bent, and one hand on your hip. Extend the opposite arm overhead and stretch to the side, as shown in the illustration. Hold 15 seconds. Repeat in the other direction. Do five times in each direction.

3. Hand grasp

Grasp your hands behind your back and hold. Stand with your feet apart and knees slightly bent, and lean over at the waist. Pull up your arms behind you as shown in the illustration, and hold 15 seconds.

To warm up for bike riding, begin by pedaling slowly and gradually increase your speed.

4. Lower back curl

Lie on your back with legs extended. Bring one knee up to your chest. Grasp the leg behind the knee and pull the knee closer to your chest. Next, curl your shoulders toward your knee. The illustration shows how this is done. Hold this position for 15 seconds. Switch to the opposite leg and repeat.

5. Calf stretch

Stand in a stride position with your right leg forward and hands on your hips. Lean your upper body forward. Simultaneously bend your right leg and extend your left leg back in a continuous line with your upper body. Push your left heel to the ground. The illustration shows this position. Hold for 15 seconds. Repeat with the other leg. Do this five times on each side.

6. Hamstring stretch

Sit on the floor and extend one leg, toes facing up, as you can see in the photograph on the previous page. Tuck your other foot against your extended thigh. Reach forward over your extended leg and slide your hands down your leg until you feel a stretch. Hold for 15 seconds. Switch to the other leg. Repeat with each leg twice.

Apply the Skill

1. Take five minutes to practice these stretching exercises.

2. Each day for a week, do the stretching routine and record how you felt before and after the routine, including any soreness or stiffness. At the end of the week, evaluate the stretching routine and your reactions to it. What are its benefits?

3. Select a favorite sport or other physical activity, and then ask your physical education teacher or coach to suggest an appropriate warm-up routine for that activity, including stretching exercises.

CHAPTER 17 REVIEW

KEY IDEAS

LESSON 1

- The four basic components of fitness include cardiorespiratory endurance, muscular strength and endurance, flexibility, and body composition.
- Aerobic exercise is continuous physical activity that raises the breathing and heart rates. Anaerobic exercise is intense physical activity that lasts only from a few seconds to a few minutes.

LESSON 2

- The effectiveness of an exercise program depends on the frequency, intensity, and duration of the exercise.
- To avoid injury, you need to follow proper procedures for warming up before exercise and cooling down afterward.

LESSON 3

- Recreational activities, such as walking, biking, and dancing, can be an important part of an exercise program.
- Moderate exercise helps elderly people remain physically fit and can help reduce many physical problems associated with old age.

LESSON 4

- During sleep, your muscles relax, your breathing and heart rates decrease, and your body temperature drops slightly.
- Regular sleeping habits allow the body time to rest, grow, and repair itself. Individual sleeping needs vary, but normal sleep occurs as part of a circadian cycle.

KEY TERMS

LESSON 1

aerobic exercise

anaerobic exercise

body composition

cardiorespiratory endurance

endorphins

flexibility

isokinetic exercise

isometric exercise

isotonic exercise

muscular endurance

muscular strength

physical fitness

LESSON 2

cool-down

maximum heart rate

target heart rate

warm-up

LESSON 4

circadian rhythm

insomnia

narcolepsy

nonrapid eye movement sleep (NREM)

rapid eye movement sleep (REM)

sleep apnea

Listed above are some of the important terms in this chapter. Choose the term from the list that best matches each phrase below.

1. ability to use a muscle throughout its entire range of motion

2. period of mild exercise that gradually prepares the body for vigorous exercise

3. type of sleep in which dreaming occurs

4. type of exercise that involves the use of special machines and may be used for physical therapy

5. difficulty in falling asleep or staying asleep

6. natural painkillers produced in the brain

7. exercise that improves the cardiovascular and respiratory systems

8. type of exercise in which the demand for oxygen exceeds the supply of oxygen

9. ability of the heart, muscles, blood vessels, and lungs to meet the body's needs

10. the amount of fat in your body compared to the amount of lean tissue

11. type of sleep during which your body reaches its deepest relaxation

WHAT HAVE YOU LEARNED?

On a separate sheet of paper, write the word or words that best complete each statement.

12. People should not exercise at their _____ heart rates, since that level of exercise puts a strain on the heart.

13. Pushing your palms together is an example of _____ exercise.

14. Your pattern of sleep and wakefulness probably follows a cycle known as a _____.

15. The four components of fitness are flexibility, cardiorespiratory endurance, muscular strength and endurance, and _____.

16. Symptoms of _____ can include extreme tiredness, nausea, vomiting, and long-lasting aches and pains.

17. A _____ heart rate below 72 beats per minute usually indicates a good fitness level.

18. Most healthy adults need about _____ hours of sleep every 24 hours.

19. FIT stands for frequency, intensity, and _____ of exercise.

Answer each of the following with complete sentences.

20. In what ways does vigorous exercise improve cardiovascular fitness?

21. How can you tell if your heart is more fit as a result of an exercise program?

22. Why is it important for older adults to get regular exercise?

23. Why should you avoid vigorous exercise just before bedtime?

24. What are some forms of recreation that you can do as part of a group?

25. Why should you avoid wearing tightly fitting clothing when you exercise?

26. What types of exercise require a helmet?

27. What are the three stages of an exercise session and what is the goal or function of each stage?

WHAT DO YOU THINK?

28. Imagine that you want to increase the strength and endurance of your arms. What type of exercise—aerobic or anaerobic—would you use? Why?

29. Studies have shown that workers who work nights and sleep days have a higher injury rate on the job than workers who have regular daytime shifts. What do you think might account for the higher rate?

30. Why do you think that true anaerobic exercises can be performed only for short periods of time?

31. Steve has started a program of walking three times a week. He is worried because he cannot afford expensive athletic shoes. Is his concern valid? Explain.

WHAT WOULD YOU DO?

32. Your friend Lee believes exercise takes too much energy, causes pain, and requires several hours each day. How would you convince her that these ideas are false?

33. Your soccer coach insists that the team stretch for 10 minutes after every practice session. Your friend gets angry, says it is a waste of time, and tries to get you to skip it. What would you say? Why?

34. Your elderly uncle says that he does not need to exercise. He claims that he keeps in shape by eating the right foods, watching his weight, and avoiding alcohol and tobacco. What would you tell him?

Getting Involved

35. Research the free or inexpensive exercise or sports facilities and programs that are available in your community, and the hours and days they are available. For example, does your community have public bicycle paths, tennis courts, or swimming pools? What free or inexpensive exercise programs, such as aerobics, are available? To let other people know what you find out, create a brochure, make a poster, or write an article for the school newspaper.

PERSONAL CARE

For many teenagers, their vision of what it means to be "attractive" starts with healthy skin. As a result, a daily routine of face care is often their first step in developing good personal care habits. In this chapter, you find information that will help you make good choices about your skin, hair, nails, eyes, and ears.

CHAPTER PREVIEW

18-1 Your Skin, Hair, and Nails

- Describe the function of your skin and ways in which you can keep your skin, hair, and nails healthy.

18-2 Your Eyes

- Explain how your eyes function and what you can do to protect them.

18-3 Your Ears

- Explain how your ear processes sound vibrations and list some measures for keeping your ears healthy.

BUILDING HEALTH SKILLS

- Recognize misleading claims in advertisements for personal-care products.

CHECK YOUR WELLNESS

What behaviors do you practice to take care of your skin, hair, nails, eyes, and ears? To each of the following questions, answer *usually*, *sometimes*, or *never*.

- Do you protect your skin from overexposure to the sun?

- Do you bathe or shower frequently?

- Do you keep your hair clean?

- Are your fingernails and toenails clean and neatly clipped?

- Do you wear goggles when working with power tools or chemicals, or when playing dangerous sports?

- Do you avoid putting objects, such as cotton-tipped swabs, in your ears?

- Do you minimize your exposure to loud noises?

KEEPING A JOURNAL

Your skin lets you know whether the air is hot, cold, or somewhere in between. Imagine that you suddenly lost this temperature sense. Write a paragraph describing what might happen.

Take it to the Net
www.phschool.com

GUIDE FOR READING

Focus on these questions as you read this lesson.

- What are the characteristics of each layer of your skin?

- What can you do to keep your skin healthy?

- What are some problems that can occur with your hair and nails?

SKILLS

- Activity: What Affects Sweating?

- Filing a Consumer Complaint

Before you leave for school in the morning, you probably glance at your face in a mirror as you comb your hair. After all, your face and hair are the first things people see when they look at you. Healthy skin, hair, and nails will help you look and feel your best.

Skin Structure

Your skin is the largest organ in your body. If it were stretched out flat, how big an area do you think it would cover? The average person's skin has an area of approximately 2 square yards (1.6 square meters).

The skin is made up of two main layers, the epidermis and the dermis. Beneath the skin itself is a third layer of fatty tissue that holds the skin in place. These layers are illustrated in Figure 18-1.

THE EPIDERMIS   The outermost layer of skin is called the **epidermis** (ep ih DUR mis). It is the layer of skin that you see when you look at someone. The epidermis itself has two layers. The outside of the epidermis—the part that comes into direct contact with the external environment—is made up of many dead cells. These dead cells contain a substance called

Figure 18-1 *The skin has a complex structure. In which layer are the nerves located?*

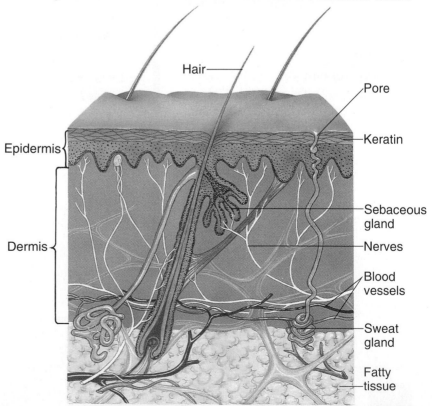

Hair
Pore
Keratin
Epidermis
Sebaceous gland
Nerves
Dermis
Blood vessels
Sweat gland
Fatty tissue

keratin that toughens the skin and makes it waterproof. You are constantly shedding these dead cells. They fall off when you brush against something, bathe, or rub your skin.

Unlike the outside of the epidermis, the inner layer is made up of living cells. These living cells divide over and over, continually producing new skin cells. As new cells are produced here, the older cells above them are pushed upwards toward the skin's surface. Eventually these older cells die and become part of the outside layer.

Special cells in the living part of the epidermis produce a brown substance known as **melanin** (MEL uh nin). Melanin is a major factor in determining the color of your skin—the more melanin in your skin, the darker it is. Sunlight can stimulate melanin production, causing the skin to tan.

THE DERMIS   The **dermis** (DUR mis) is the inner layer of skin that lies below the epidermis. It is tough and elastic, and in most areas of your body, the dermis is much thicker than the epidermis. If you look carefully at Figure 18-1, you will notice that the dermis, unlike the epidermis, contains nerves and blood vessels. The blood that flows through these vessels brings nutrients to the skin and carries waste products away.

Hairs and pores extend downward from the epidermis into the dermis. A **pore** is the opening of a narrow channel, or duct, that leads to a gland. A gland is a structure that produces one or more substances. A sweat gland, for example, produces sweat, or perspiration, which flows out through the pores onto the skin's surface. Another type of gland, called a **sebaceous gland** (sih BAY shus), produces oil. This oil helps waterproof the skin and keep it soft and flexible. It also moisturizes hair.

SOCIAL STUDIES CONNECTION

Fingerprints are created by raised ridges on the skin of the fingers. No two people have fingerprints that are exactly alike. Police began to use fingerprinting as a means of identification in the late nineteenth century.

WHAT AFFECTS SWEATING?

In this activity, you will examine your skin with a magnifying glass and analyze a factor that affects sweating.

Materials

magnifying glass	plastic glove

Procedure

1. Use a magnifying glass to examine the skin on your hand. Look at the palm, the back of your hand, and your fingers. Look for pores and hairs.

2. Put a plastic glove on one hand. Leave it on for five minutes.

3. After five minutes, remove the glove. Compare your two hands for the presence of sweat. Also see which part of your hand—palm, back, or fingers—produced the most sweat.

Discussion

1. What skin structures could you observe with the magnifying glass?

2. Which hand—gloved or ungloved—produced more sweat? Why do you think this happened?

3. What part of your hand appears to sweat most?

Skin Functions

The skin forms a strong and effective barrier between the inside of your body and the environment outside your body. Your skin shields and protects the delicate organs and tissues that lie beneath it, helping to prevent injury and to keep harmful germs out of your body. The nerves in the dermis help you sense your environment. They tell you whether something is hot, cold, rough, or smooth. They also transmit pain messages that warn you of possible danger or injury.

The skin also helps your body maintain a constant temperature. The perspiration produced by your sweat glands is one temperature regulator. Sweat cools your body when it evaporates from your skin. In addition, when your body temperature rises, the blood vessels in your dermis become wider. This widening allows heat to escape from your blood into the environment. If your body temperature becomes lower, the blood vessels in your dermis become narrower. Because less heat can escape from narrower blood vessels, your body temperature then rises.

Finally, skin prevents body fluids from evaporating, in much the same way that plastic wrap keeps foods from drying out. Fluids surround and bathe all of the cells in your body. Without this watery environment, your cells could not function. Thus the skin preserves the environment that your cells need to survive.

Skin Problems

The skin is tough and strong, but sometimes irritations and other problems can develop. Some of these disorders happen because the skin is exposed to environmental hazards. For example, freezing temperatures can cause frostbite, especially on your toes, fingers, ears, and nose. People with black or brown skin are often more sensitive to the effects of cold than are people with lighter skin. Burns, including sunburn, damage the skin and reduce the protection it offers to other tissues and organs. You will learn how to care for frostbite, cuts, and burns in Chapter 29.

Other skin conditions, such as boils and warts, are caused by germs. And some problems, such as acne, can result from changes in the body that occur during adolescence.

ACNE One of the most common skin problems is **acne,** a condition in which the oil glands become blocked, infected, and swollen. Acne frequently develops during adolescence, because at that time the oil glands in the skin begin to produce more oil than before. Excess oil may combine with dead skin cells of the epidermis to form a plug that blocks a pore. When this happens in a pore exposed to the air, a blackhead forms. Whiteheads are blocked pores that are not exposed to air because they are covered by a very thin, transparent layer of epidermis. Bacteria can infect a blocked pore and cause a pimple to form, as shown in Figure 18-4.

The best defense against acne is clean skin. If your skin is oily, you should wash it with mild soap two or three times a day. More frequent washings only stimulate your oil glands to produce more oil. Products that contain benzoyl peroxide, a chemical that dries out pimples and kills bacteria, can help mild cases of acne. Because your fingers and nails can carry bacteria, it is best not to scratch or squeeze pimples, blackheads, or whiteheads. A **dermatologist,** a physician who deals with skin disorders, should treat severe cases of acne to avoid complications.

Figure 18-3 *Perspiration absorbs heat as it evaporates. This process helps cool the body.*

Figure 18-4 *If a pore becomes blocked, bacteria can infect it. A pimple then forms.*

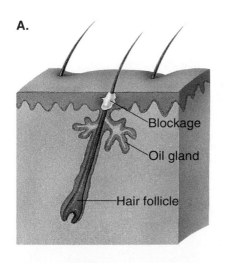

A.

Blockage
Oil gland
Hair follicle

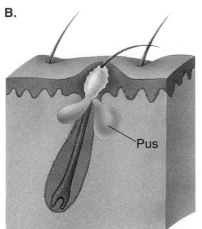

B.

Pus

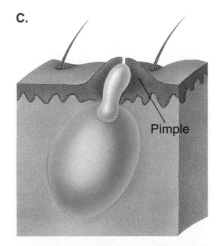

C.

Pimple

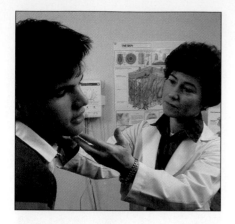

Figure 18-5 *A dermatologist specializes in the care and treatment of skin disorders.*

DERMATITIS Another skin disorder is **dermatitis** (dur muh TY tis), a condition in which an area of skin becomes red, swollen, hot, and itchy. Sometimes the area blisters and oozes. Substances that irritate the skin, such as chemicals, soaps, or poison ivy, can cause dermatitis. Certain medicines and foods may also cause this skin irritation. In most cases, dermatitis can be treated with a medication applied to the skin. You can prevent dermatitis from recurring if you can identify and avoid the substances that irritate your skin.

SKIN INFECTIONS Different types of germs can harm the skin. Boils, which are swollen, painful infections of hair follicles, are caused by bacteria. A virus is a simple kind of germ, and several common skin problems are caused by viruses. One type of virus, **herpes simplex I** (HUR peez), causes clusters of watery blisters, or cold sores. These sores, which usually occur around the mouth, generally heal in seven to ten days. To prevent herpes simplex from spreading to other parts of the body, wash your hands thoroughly after touching affected areas.

Warts, which are hardened growths on the skin, are also caused by viruses. Usually warts go away without any treatment, but sometimes they last a long time. Since warts can grow deep into the skin, they should be removed only by a physician.

Some skin infections are caused by a fungus, a simple type of organism related to molds. Fungal infections usually occur in warm, moist areas of the skin. Ringworm is one fungal infection—in spite of its name, it has nothing whatever to do with worms. The ringworm fungus, which is highly contagious, produces red, scaly patches of skin. After a time, these patches may become ring-shaped. Ringworm is treated with medications prescribed by a physician.

Athlete's foot is a common fungal infection that causes burning, itching, cracking, and peeling of the skin on the bottom of the foot and between the toes. To prevent athlete's foot, keep your feet dry and wear absorbent cotton socks. Avoid sharing towels and washcloths. If you do get athlete's foot, there are nonprescription medications that usually control this infection. However, if you develop a severe infection

Figure 18-6 *Poison ivy and poison sumac both contain chemicals that can cause dermatitis in some people.*

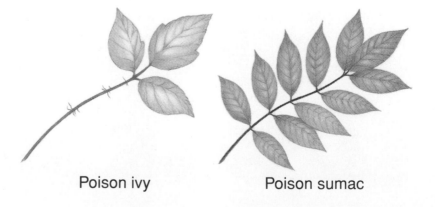

Poison ivy   Poison sumac

Figure 18-7 *You can enjoy the sun and still protect your skin with a sunscreen.*

that does not respond to nonprescription medications, you should see a physician.

SKIN CANCER   A **cancer** is an area of uncontrolled cell growth that invades the surrounding tissue and destroys it. The most common types of skin cancer generally occur in people over 40 years old and are rarely fatal.

Melanoma (mel uh NOH muh) is the most serious form of skin cancer; fortunately, although it can occur in young as well as older people, it is also the rarest type. Melanoma usually starts with an irregularly shaped mole, or brown spot, that suddenly increases in size. The mole may become blue-black or have blackish spots. Unlike other skin cancers, melanoma spreads rapidly to other organs. If you notice any change in a wart or mole—or any skin growth that appears abnormal—you should consult a physician. Most skin cancers, including melanoma, are curable if they are diagnosed and treated early enough.

THE SUN AND YOUR SKIN   Most cases of skin cancer are caused by overexposure to the sun's ultraviolet rays. Tanning lamps also produce this damaging ultraviolet radiation. Besides cancer, long-term exposure to ultraviolet radiation can cause skin to become leathery, wrinkled, and discolored. However, different people are affected by the sun in different ways. In general, the darker the skin, the less sensitive it is to ultraviolet radiation. Dark-skinned people are less likely than light-skinned people to develop skin cancer and wrinkling.

If you have light-colored or sensitive skin, try to cover it with clothing when you are out in the sunlight. To protect exposed areas of your skin, apply a sunscreen, which is a substance that blocks ultraviolet rays. Sunscreens are numbered with a sun protection factor (SPF). The higher the SPF of a sunscreen, the more protection it provides. People with skin that sunburns easily should use a sunscreen with an SPF of 15 or higher and reapply it frequently, especially if they have been swimming or sweating.

Figure 18-8 *Mittens, ear muffs, and scarves can protect your skin from the cold.*

Skin Care

Usually, your skin only needs basic care to stay healthy. Basic skin care includes keeping it clean and preventing overexposure to the sun. You also need to protect your skin from extreme heat or cold, and prevent infection in cuts and scrapes. A balanced diet, regular exercise, and sleep are also essential for healthy skin.

Although manufacturers may claim that the perfumes, deodorants, lotions, extra fats, and vitamins added to their products improve them, the fact is that any soap will get you clean. Deodorants do help to destroy the bacteria that cause odors, but deodorants and perfumes also can irritate the skin and cause a rash. To keep your skin clean, you need to wash away dirt, body oil, perspiration, and cosmetics. The best substance to use is a mild soap.

Your Hair and Nails

Your hair and nails are both outgrowths of your skin. The visible part is made up of nonliving material. That is why it does not hurt when you get a haircut or file your nails.

HAIR PROBLEMS　Head lice are small insects that live on the scalp and lay their eggs on hair. Several special shampoos are available to kill lice. After shampooing, a fine-toothed comb should be used to remove the eggs, or nits, from the hair. The best way to prevent head-lice infections is to avoid sharing combs, brushes, or hats with others.

Figure 18-9 *Shampooing is an important part of keeping your hair healthy and attractive.*

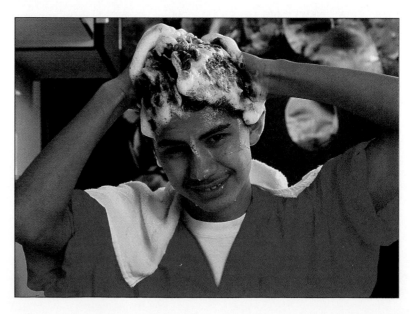

Dandruff is actually a scalp problem. It occurs when dry flakes of skin from the scalp come off as the hair is combed or brushed. Dandruff shampoos can help control the problem if regular shampoos and brushing do not help.

NAIL PROBLEMS If your hands are in water frequently, your nails may become brittle and split. Wearing rubber gloves when you are washing dishes will help protect your nails from becoming brittle. No specific food, mineral, or vitamin will make your nails stronger—not even gelatin.

An ingrown toenail results when the sides of the nail grow into the skin. If not treated properly, ingrown nails can become infected and cause serious problems. To prevent ingrown toenails, clip your toenails straight across.

Although most nail problems are not a sign of illness, your nails can be an indicator of your health. Any dramatic changes in their texture, shape, color, or growth rate may be a signal to seek medical advice.

CARE OF THE HAIR AND NAILS Attractive hair is clean hair. Frequent, gentle brushing helps to remove dirt and makes your hair shine. Shampooing washes away built-up oil and keeps your hair clean and fresh smelling. When used correctly, products that straighten or curl your hair will not damage it. However, these products contain strong chemicals that must be used carefully.

Some people are bothered by unwanted hair on the face and body. There are several ways that unwanted hair can be removed, at least temporarily. The easiest way is shaving. Some people pluck unwanted hairs out one by one, but this can be painful and may lead to infection. Depilatories are creams or lotion that dissolve hair. Since these products can irritate the skin, they should be used carefully and the instructions should be followed exactly.

Clean, well-cared-for nails add to your appearance. A fingernail brush, used regularly, will keep the area under your nails clean. Clip or file your fingernails and toenails so that their edges are smooth and cannot catch on your clothes or scratch your skin.

Figure 18-10 *Regular use of fingernail clippers improves your appearance.*

LESSON 1 REVIEW

1. Name and describe the two main layers of your skin.
2. What are two functions of the skin?
3. Why should depilatories be used carefully?
4. What is one way of preventing brittle nails?

What Do You Think?
5. What would you do to improve your skin?

Focus on these questions as you read this lesson.

- How does your eye work with your brain to enable you to see?

- What are some typical eye problems, and how can they be prevented or corrected?

SKILLS

- Locating Community Resources

2 YOUR EYES

Because of your eyes, you can enjoy the beauty of spring flowers and colorful sunsets. Your eyes warn you when a car is approaching, and they let you recognize the faces of family and friends. Since much of the information you gather about your environment reaches your brain through your eyes, it is important that they function well.

Your eyes are sensitive, but they are protected in several ways. The bones of your eye sockets protect and support your eyes. Your eyelashes and eyebrows help keep dust, dirt, and sweat out. Your eyelids also prevent foreign objects from entering your eyes. When anything, even a gentle puff of air, touches your eyes, your eyelids close. Even your tears help to protect your eyes. The fluids produced by your tear glands, which are located above each eye, keep your eyes moist. Tears wash away foreign particles that can injure the eyes, and they contain a substance that kills bacteria. This substance helps to protect your eyes from infection.

Eye Structure

You can think of your eyes as having three layers. As you see in Figure 18-11, the outside layer, which is white, is the **sclera** (SKLIHR uh), commonly called the white of the eye. Muscles attached to the sclera allow the eye to move within its socket.

Figure 18-11 *Look at this diagram of the eye. Through which structures does light pass before it reaches the retina?*

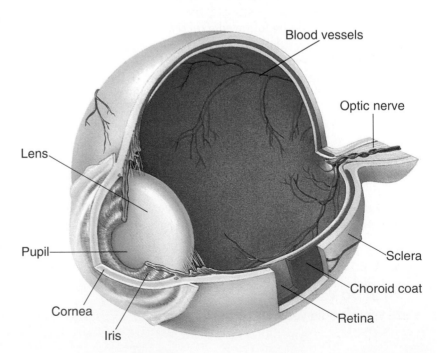

Blood vessels

Optic nerve

Lens

Pupil

Cornea

Iris

Sclera

Choroid coat

Retina

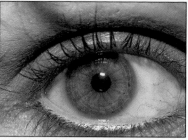

Figure 18-12 *In dim light, the pupil is large. In contrast, the pupil is smaller in bright light, allowing less light into the eye.*

At the back of the sclera is an opening for the **optic nerve,** the nerve that transmits visual information to the brain. The front of the sclera curves outward to form the **cornea** (KAWR nee uh). Because the cornea is transparent, it permits light to enter the eyes. A thin, moist membrane called the **conjunctiva** (kahn jungk TY vuh) covers the front part of the sclera and the inside of the eyelid.

A dark-colored membrane called the **choroid** (KAWR oyd) makes up most of the middle layer of the eye. The choroid, which is filled with blood vessels, lies just inside the sclera. At the front of the eye, the choroid forms the iris. The **iris,** which gives the eye its color, is a disk with an opening in its center. This opening, called the **pupil,** allows light to pass through the cornea to the interior of your eye. The size of the pupil determines how much light enters the eye. In bright light, muscle fibers in the iris contract, causing the pupil to become smaller and let in less light. In dim light, the muscle fibers relax, and the pupil becomes larger, letting in more light.

The **lens,** which lies just behind the iris, is a transparent structure that focuses light on the inner, back side of the eye. Small muscles change the shape of the lens. This change in lens shape enables your eyes to focus on objects at different distances from you.

After passing through the lens, light travels through the interior of the eye, which is filled with a colorless, jellylike substance. Then the light reaches the innermost layer of the eye—a thin, delicate membrane. This membrane, known as the **retina** (RET n uh), is the light-sensing part of the eye. Light produces an image on the retina, much the way a camera creates an image on photographic film. Because of the way that the lens bends light, the image on the retina is upside down.

The retina consists of thousands of special light-receptor, or light-receiving, cells. There are two kinds of light receptor cells—rods and cones. The **rods** only respond to dim light and allow you to see black, white, and gray. The **cones** are only stimulated by bright light and enable you to see color. There are three types of cones—one type for blue light, one for green light, and one for violet light. When at least two types of cones are stimulated at the same time, you see other colors.

CHEMISTRY CONNECTION

Rods and cones both contain light-sensitive substances. When light strikes these substances, it starts a rapid chain of chemical reactions that eventually create an impulse in a nerve cell.

How Vision Occurs

Each rod and cone in the retina is connected to a nerve cell. **The rods and cones convert images focused on the retina to nerve signals, which are transmitted to the brain by the optic nerve.** The brain then interprets these signals, and you see. Because of the way that the brain processes the nerve signals, you see the object right side up, even though the image on the retina is upside down.

Each of your two eyes sees things from a slightly different angle, and therefore your brain actually receives somewhat different signals from each eye. The process by which your eyes see—and your brain interprets—these two different images is called **stereoscopic vision** (stehr ee uh SKAHP ik). Stereoscopic vision helps you see in three dimensions. It also helps you interpret the height, width, and depth of an object, as well as its distance from you.

Have you ever noticed that you can see things on either side of what you are looking at directly? The ability to see things to the side of the object you are looking at is known as **peripheral vision** (puh RIF ur ul). Peripheral vision is especially important in driving, because it allows you to avoid hazards that are not directly in your line of sight. It lets you see a wide area at any one instant.

Eye Problems

Many people have vision problems caused by the inability to focus light correctly. People with **nearsightedness** can see nearby objects clearly but have trouble seeing objects that are far away. Nearsightedness is caused by an eyeball that is too long. As you can see in Figure 18-14, light rays are brought into focus in front of the retina, rather than on it.

The opposite of nearsightedness is **farsightedness.** A person who is farsighted can see faraway objects clearly but cannot see nearby objects well. Farsightedness is caused by an eyeball that is too short, focusing light rays behind the retina.

When the curvature of the cornea or the lens is uneven, light rays entering the eye cannot be focused at a single point on the retina. This causes **astigmatism** (uh STIG muh tiz um), or distorted vision. Eyeglasses or contact lenses can correct nearsightedness, farsightedness, and astigmatism.

The inability to distinguish certain colors is called **color blindness.** Color blindness is usually inherited. A person who is colorblind was born without one or more sets of cones, or with cones that are weak.

Night blindness is the inability to see well in dim light. It results when the rods are not functioning properly. Night blindness can be inherited, or it can be caused by a lack of vitamin A. Sometimes night blindness can be an early sign of other diseases of the retina.

Figure 18-13 *Many vision problems can be corrected after they are detected in an eye examination.*

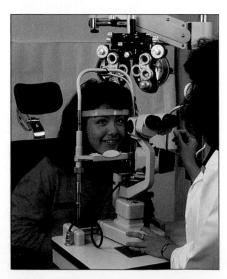

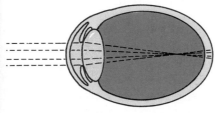

Nearsightedness

Figure 18-14 *In nearsightedness, the eyeball is too long, and distant objects are out of focus. In farsightedness, the eyeball is too short—a farsighted person sees distant objects clearly. How do nearby objects look to a farsighted person?*

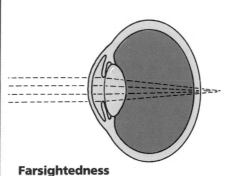

Farsightedness

The space between the cornea and the lens is filled with fluid. If the pressure of this fluid increases beyond its normal level, a condition called **glaucoma** (glaw KOH muh) may develop. This condition primarily occurs in people over 40 years of age. Untreated glaucoma can eventually cause blindness. If the condition is identified early enough, blindness can be prevented.

The clouding of the eye's lens is known as a **cataract** (KAT uh rakt). This condition most commonly occurs in older adults and is treated by surgical removal of the clouded lens. The surgeon may implant an artificial lens, or special glasses or contact lenses may be prescribed to compensate for the lost lens. Since overexposure to bright sunlight may, over the years, contribute to cataract formation, it is important to protect your eyes by wearing sunglasses.

In the condition known as a detached retina, the retina becomes detached from the choroid. If the choroid and the retina are not surgically reattached, blindness can result. Other causes of blindness include injuries to the eye or optic nerve or infections of the eye. Diabetes mellitus can also cause vision problems that, in some cases, lead to blindness.

SHARPEN YOUR *SKILLS*

Locating Community Resources

Find out where you can have your eyes and vision checked in your community. For each place you locate, determine what the examination involves—for example, whether it includes a test for glaucoma as well as nearsightedness and farsightedness. Organize your findings in the form of a chart.

Figure 18-15 *Safety goggles can protect your eyes from injury.*

Sometimes an oil gland at the base of an eyelash becomes infected, resulting in a **sty,** which is a red, painful swelling. **Conjunctivitis** (kun jungk tuh VY tis) is an inflammation of the conjunctiva. The eye may ooze a yellowish fluid, and the white of the eye may become red and itchy. Allergic reactions to pollen, molds, dust, and animals are responsible for some cases. Bacterial or viral infections cause other types, which are extremely contagious. To help prevent the disease from spreading, infected people should avoid touching their eyes or sharing towels or washcloths. Conjunctivitis and sties can be treated with prescription medications.

Eye Care

You can do many things to protect your eyes and keep them healthy. If you work with dangerous substances that could splash into your eyes, or if you work around machinery, you should wear protective glasses or goggles. If you play a sport in which you could be hit in the eye by a ball or some other fast-moving object, you should also wear protective glasses or goggles. Wearing swimming goggles when you swim will protect your eyes from chlorine and other substances that can irritate them. Goggles will also give you better underwater vision. Another way to protect your eyes is to avoid looking directly into the sun or any bright light. Sunglasses, visors, and hats with brims can protect your eyes from the rays of the sun.

Avoiding eyestrain is still another way to keep your eyes healthy. When you read or study, be sure you have adequate light and look up occasionally from your work to relax your eyes and change their focus. If glasses or contact lenses have been prescribed for you, be sure to wear them.

Regular eye examinations can help to detect, prevent, or control many eye problems. In fact, regular eye examinations can reveal much about your health. For example, by looking through your pupils with a special instrument, an eye doctor can see the blood vessels of the retina. Changes in the blood vessels can offer early warnings of illnesses.

LESSON *2* REVIEW

1. How does visual information get from the eye to the brain?
2. What causes astigmatism?
3. Why are regular eye examinations so important?

What Do You Think?

4. What are some good habits that could help protect the health of your eyes?

DIFFERENT VOICES SPEAKING

Katie Roberts, who is 16, has been deaf since birth. She is enrolled at the Model Secondary School for deaf students in Washington, D.C. She communicates by means of American Sign Language.

Q. Katie, what is it like being a deaf person in a hearing world?
A. There are obstacles that I face that hearing people never think twice about. I can't hear the telephone or doorbell ring. If I'm at the mall alone, I can't just pick up a phone and call for a ride home. My biggest problem is the attitudes of hearing people. They simply don't have time or patience for the deaf. When I go into a store, the sales help sometimes acts as if I'm not there.

Katie Roberts

Q. What do you do when that happens?
A. I make my needs known. I get a piece of paper and write down what I want. Then I tap the person on the shoulder. You might say I am teaching them how to deal with people who are different.

Q. What sorts of things do you think hearing people need to be made aware of?
A. They need to understand that deaf people have feelings. They also need to appreciate that, while there are many things we can't do, there are many that we can. I can use a telephone if it has a TDD, or Telecommunications Device for the Deaf, installed. I can also dance.

Q. How do you dance if you can't hear the music?
A. I feel the beat. I also watch the dancers on music videos and study their movements.

Q. It sounds as though you've faced and met some real challenges. Who has helped you the most in meeting these challenges?
A. My family mostly. My parents, brothers, and sister all have been very supportive. I'm very close to them. Sometimes, my mother is strict, but I know she's on my side—that she'll fight for me if she has to. In my family, there's always more than enough love to go around. Another thing that has kept me going is that I'm a fighter. I feel it's important for people like me to stand up for their rights rather than be bitter. One thing I plan to do as an adult is counsel deaf teens. I also support the Americans with Disabilities Act, which ensures that people with disabilities can't be discriminated against when they apply for jobs.

Journal Activity

Katie mentions that her family has been a great source of support. Whom can you count on when you face a problem? Do different people provide different types of support? Divide a page into three columns. At the top of each column, write the name of a person you look to for support. In the space beneath each name, give examples of the kind of support the person provides.

GUIDE FOR READING

Focus on these questions as you read this lesson.

- What are the two main functions of your ears?
- How can loud noises affect your ears?

SKILLS

- Expressing Feelings in a Positive Way

3 YOUR EARS

You know that you hear with your ears, but do you realize that they also help you keep your balance? **The ear converts sound waves into nerve signals that your brain can understand; in addition, the ear senses the position and movement of your head.** By sensing movement and position, your ears enable you to stand upright, walk smoothly, and adjust your body's position.

Structure and Function of the Ear

It is helpful to think of the ear as being divided into three sections—the outer ear, middle ear, and inner ear. The outer and middle parts of the ear transfer sound waves to the inner ear. In the inner ear, these sound waves reach an organ that sends messages to the brain. The inner ear also contains structures that contribute to your sense of balance.

THE OUTER EAR When you look in a mirror, you can see a part of the outer ear. This part, which is covered with a thin layer of skin, acts as a collecting funnel for sound waves. It channels the sound waves into the **ear canal,** a narrow cavity that leads to the middle ear. Find the ear canal in Figure 18-16. Glands in the skin lining the ear canal release a wax that helps trap dust and germs. At the end of the ear canal is a thin membrane called the **eardrum.** The eardrum vibrates when sound waves strike it.

Figure 18-16 *In the diagram of the ear, which middle-ear bone presses against the oval window?*

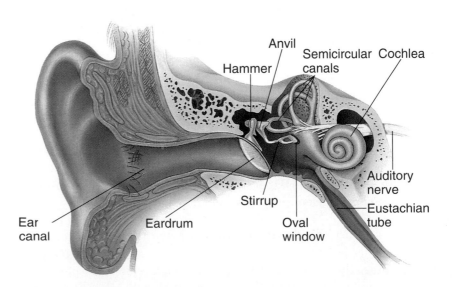

THE MIDDLE EAR   The eardrum marks the beginning of the middle ear, which contains three small bones—the hammer, the anvil, and the stirrup. The hammer receives the vibrations from the eardrum and pushes the anvil, which then moves the stirrup.

Notice the **eustachian tube** (yoo STAY shun) in Figure 18-16. The eustachian tube connects the middle ear with the back of the throat. Most of the time the eustachian tube is closed. When you cough, swallow, or yawn, however, it opens, allowing the air pressure in the middle ear to become the same as the air pressure in the outer ear. Have you ever felt your ears pop as you go up in an elevator? This happens when the air pressure in the outer ear is different from that in the middle ear. Swallowing usually relieves ear popping, because the eustachian tube opens when you swallow. If the eustachian tubes did not help to maintain equal air pressure, your eardrums could burst, or rupture.

THE INNER EAR   The stirrup touches a small membrane-covered opening called the **oval window,** which separates the middle ear from the inner ear. The oval window is actually a part of the wall of the **cochlea** (KAWK lee uh), a hollow, coiled tube that is filled with fluid. When the stirrup vibrates, it pushes on the oval window. This movement then transfers the vibrations to the fluid in the cochlea.

Special vibration-sensing cells line the inside of the cochlea. The movement of the cochlear fluid stimulates some of these cells. These cells connect to nerves that send out nerve impulses. The impulses travel through the **auditory nerve** (AW dih tawr ee) to the brain, where they are interpreted as sound.

The **semicircular canals** are the main inner-ear structures that help give you a sense of balance. These three fluid-filled tubes are lined with tiny hairs and positioned at right angles to one another. When you move your body, the fluid inside the semicircular canals causes the tiny hairs to move. The movement of the hairs then stimulates nerve cells, which in turn send impulses to your brain. Your brain interprets these impulses to determine motion and the position of your body. In response, it sends signals to your muscles that help you maintain your balance.

Hearing Disorders

The term **hearing impairment** usually refers to a partial loss of hearing, while **deafness** indicates a total inability to hear. Hearing impairment and deafness are caused by a variety of factors. Infections of the middle ear sometimes cause hearing impairment—especially if the infections occur frequently and are not treated. Middle-ear infections are especially common in young children. An infected ear usually

Figure 18-17 *Balance is a complex skill that that depends on the functioning of the inner ear.*

aches, feels warm, and may feel as if fluid is running in it. If you have an earache, you should see a physician. Doctors usually prescribe antibiotics, which are medicines that kill the bacteria that have caused the condition.

Middle-ear infections can cause hearing damage by making the eardrum break, or rupture. Although the eardrum will heal, it will be scarred. Scar tissue can make the eardrum less flexible and less able to transmit sound. Infections are not the only cause of eardrum damage. Sharp objects inserted into the ear canal can tear the eardrum and result in scarring.

A buildup of wax in the ear can cause hearing loss because it blocks the passage of sound waves. A doctor can correct this condition by removing the wax or prescribing a wax softener. Abnormal growth of bone tissue in the ear, which prevents movement of the hammer, anvil, and stirrup, can also interfere with the movement of sound waves. Surgery can sometimes correct this condition.

Hearing impairment or deafness can also result from damage to nerves or the vibration-sensitive cells in the cochlea. This type of hearing damage is generally permanent. It can be caused by some diseases and large doses of certain medications. If a pregnant woman gets rubella, or German measles, her baby may suffer hearing damage. However, loud noise, such as rock music, gunshots, and the sounds made by some kinds of machinery, is the most common cause of nerve damage in the ear. The longer and more often a person is exposed to loud noise, the more likely it is that hearing damage will occur.

A hearing aid makes sounds louder. Hearing aids can often help hearing-impaired people, but generally do not work for those who are totally deaf. However, if the deafness is caused by a defect in the cochlea, a relatively new device,

Figure 18-18 *The graph shows the decibel levels of some sounds. The blue bars are sounds that are safe to hear. Prolonged exposure to sounds indicated by yellow bars can damage your hearing. For those sounds indicated by red bars, even short exposure can cause hearing loss.*

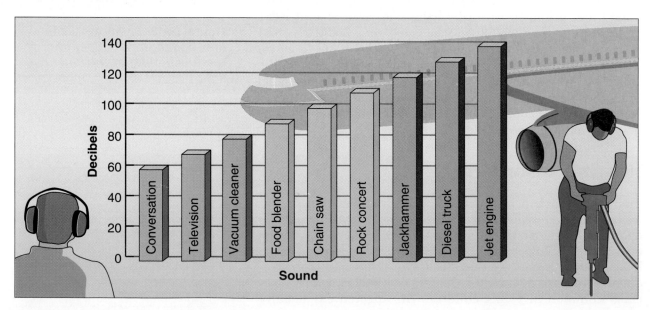

known as a cochlear implant, may help. The device, which is surgically placed in the ear, electrically stimulates the cochlea.

Ear Care

Proper ear care is not difficult. You can use a wet washcloth to clean your outer ear and the front part of your ear canal. Dry your ears thoroughly after you wash them. Never insert a cotton-tipped swab or any other object into your ear canal to clean it. The swab can damage your eardrum. It can also compress the earwax, which prevents the wax from draining away naturally.

Earplugs keep water out of your ears when you are swimming, and this safety measure will help to prevent ear infections. It is especially important to wear earplugs if you have had repeated ear infections or a puncture of the eardrum.

The intensity, or loudness, of sound is measured in units called **decibels** (DES uh bulz). As shown in Figure 18-18, sound above 80 decibels can cause hearing loss. Because loud noises can damage your hearing, wear foam-rubber earplugs or earmuff-type devices when you are using or working near loud equipment, such as lawn mowers, electric saws, and motorcycles.

Televisions, radios, and stereos can also generate sound levels damaging to your hearing. If you wear headphones when you listen to music, keep the volume to a level at which you can enjoy the music but not damage your ears. A noise is too loud if it makes it difficult to hold a conversation with a person 3 feet (about 1 meter) away. After listening to some sounds, if you have trouble hearing normal conversation, if the conversation sounds muffled, or if you experience a ringing in your ears, the sound was too loud.

If you think you have been exposed to too much noise or cannot hear as well as you once could, see a physician. Your physician may then refer you to an **audiologist** (aw dee AHL uh jist), who is trained to check hearing and evaluate hearing loss.

LESSON 3 REVIEW

1. Name the three bones of the middle ear.
2. What is the vibration-sensing organ of the inner ear?
3. What is the function of the semicircular canals?
4. Why should you protect your ears from loud noises?

What Do You Think?

5. In what ways can you take better care of your ears?

Recognizing Misleading Claims

Roger has changed a lot in the past year. He has gotten really tall and muscular. But one change he is not happy about is his complexion—his face keeps breaking out in acne. He looks at the ad shown here for Acne-B-Gone, a skin product that promises to clear up his blemishes. Should he believe what he reads?

Advertisements are designed to sell products or services, and they try to make the product or service as appealing as possible. To do this, ads appeal to people's emotions, and they may also mislead people into believing things about the product that aren't really true. In addition, ads avoid mentioning negative things about the product, such as possible side effects or the fact that it may be more expensive than alternative products. The following guidelines will help you recognize misleading claims in advertisements.

1. Identify the techniques used to sell the product

A variety of techniques are used to sell products. The following are some typical advertising techniques:

• use of **humor,** so you will associate the product with fun or feeling good

• **testimonials,** which are recommendations from famous people who try to convince you to use the product

• mention of **scientific studies** that imply that the product has been proven to be effective, but little specific information about how the studies were performed

• use of the **bandwagon approach,** which tells you that everyone else is using the product, so that you'll want to "jump on the bandwagon" too

• **appeals to the senses,** using beautiful or exciting scenery, colors, or music

• **comparison to other products** to show that the advertised product is supposedly better

• use of **attractive models** to communicate the idea that attractive, successful people use the product

2. Analyze the ad to determine which information is incomplete, misleading, or possibly false

Look carefully at what the ad says. Do any of its claims seem unlikely or exaggerated? Does it imply something about the product without actually saying it? Count the number of claims the ad makes and see how many of them are unlikely or misleading. (For example, many ads imply that if you use the product, it will magically make you happy, successful, or beautiful. Ads may also imply that the product provides a quick, easy solution to a complex problem.)

Acne B–Gone Fights Acne!

Have clear, glowing, beautiful skin! Use *Acne B–Gone* twice a day.

ACNE B–GONE has a special, secret ingredient that prevents pimples from forming. Scientists have proved that *Acne B–Gone* works better than any other product.

The most popular kids at River Street High use *Acne B–Gone* for perfect, blemish-free skin.

---

3. Try to check any claims the ad makes and to find additional information

Read the information on the product's package. Determine whether any of this information makes the product less effective or suitable than the ad implies. You can also write to the product's manufacturer to request further information about any claims that seem suspicious.

Apply the Skill

1. Analyze the ad for Acne-B-Gone. What advertising techniques does it use? Do any of the ad's claims make you suspicious? Why? Is there anything else that you would like to know about Acne-B-Gone?

2. Find four other advertisements for personal-care products, such as shampoos and deodorants, in magazines and on TV. Identify the advertising techniques used and analyze the ads to determine whether they include misleading or false information.

3. Find an ad that claims that a scientific study supports the product's effectiveness. Write to the manufacturer of the product and request a copy of the study or a specific explanation of what it involved. Use the following questions to help you evaluate the information you receive:

- Do the data in the study or experiment really support the claim being made? Are there other ways of interpreting the data?

- Was the product tested extensively, or was the investigation very limited? A conclusion based on an investigation that tests a product hundreds of times will probably be more valid than one that only tested a product a few times.

- Who actually did the testing? Was it done by impartial scientists who did not work directly for the company that manufactures the product, or was the testing done by company employees?

CHAPTER 18 REVIEW

KEY IDEAS

LESSON 1

- The skin is made up of two main layers, the epidermis and the dermis, which protect underlying tissues and help regulate body temperature and moisture.

- Common skin problems include acne, herpes simplex I, athlete's foot, and dermatitis. Skin cancers are caused by overexposure to the sun.

LESSON 2

- In the eye, the rods and cones convert images focused on the retina to nerve signals, which are transmitted to the brain by the optic nerve.

- People can protect their eyes by wearing goggles when they are exposed to hazardous materials.

- Regular eye examinations can detect and often correct conditions such as nearsightedness, farsightedness, glaucoma, and cataracts.

LESSON 3

- The ear converts sound waves into nerve signals that your brain can understand; in addition, the ear senses the position and movement of your head.

- Exposure to loud noise is a major cause of hearing impairment.

KEY TERMS

LESSON 1	LESSON 2	retina
acne	cataract	rods
dermatitis	cones	LESSON 3
dermatologist	conjunctivitis	audiologist
dermis	cornea	auditory nerve
epidermis	farsightedness	cochlea
herpes simplex I	glaucoma	decibels
melanin	iris	eardrum
melanoma	nearsightedness	eustachian tube
pore	optic nerve	semicircular canals
sebaceous gland	pupil	

Listed above are some of the important terms in this chapter. Choose the term from the list that best matches each phrase below.

1. virus that causes cold sores

2. pigment produced by special cells in the upper layer of the skin

3. the light-sensing layer of the eye

4. type of skin cancer that can spread to other tissues

5. structure that equalizes air pressure on the eardrum

6. curved tubes in the inner ear that are involved in the sense of balance

7. units for measuring the loudness of sound

8. a health-care professional who is trained to test hearing

9. gland that produces oil

10. the layer of skin that contains blood vessels and nerve endings

WHAT HAVE YOU LEARNED?

If the statement is true, write "true." If it is false, change the underlined word or words to make the statement true.

11. <u>Acne</u> is a skin irritation that may be caused by poison ivy and certain chemicals.

12. Rods and <u>irises</u> are the two kinds of light-receptor cells.

13. The <u>optic nerve</u> conveys messages from the inner ear to the brain.

14. <u>Astigmatism</u> can be detected by an eye examination.

15. The more melanin in the skin, the <u>lighter</u> the skin will be.

16. To avoid spreading <u>ringworm</u>, it is best not to share combs or hats.

17. Excessive fluid pressure within the eye may cause <u>glaucoma</u>.

18. Products that contain benzoyl peroxide are effective against <u>warts</u>.

Answer each of the following with complete sentences.

19. How does your skin help maintain a constant body temperature?

20. Why is it important for some people to use a sunscreen while they are in the sun?

21. What changes in a mole indicate that it might be cancerous?

22. What is the relationship between the iris and the pupil?

23. Define nearsightedness and farsightedness and contrast their causes.

24. Name the three bones of the middle ear. Identify the bone that is set in motion by the eardrum, and the bone that pushes against the cochlea.

25. Why should you avoid using cotton swabs to clean your ears?

26. Why is peripheral vision so important when a person is driving a car?

27. How would you explain the brief period of dizziness that you experience when you spin around and then suddenly stop?

WHAT DO YOU THINK?

28. Many people think that a deep, dark suntan makes a person look healthy. Do you agree or disagree?

29. Why do you think it is important to test the hearing and vision of school-aged children on a regular basis?

30. Why do you think a very loud noise can result in temporary or permanent hearing loss?

31. How would covering one eye with a patch affect your vision?

32. Victims of serious burns often suffer from infection and loss of body fluids. Explain why this happens.

33. You have been given tickets to a rock concert. What precautions could you take to limit your exposure to the loud noise?

34. Cataracts more commonly occur in older, rather than younger, adults. Why do you think this is so?

WHAT WOULD YOU DO?

35. During your first week as a camp counselor, an all-day trip to the beach is planned. Many children could become sunburned. What will you do?

36. A friend with acne has been washing the affected areas with a strong detergent. Is your friend improving his skin? What would you advise your friend?

37. Your friend just got eyeglasses but will not wear them. How could you encourage your friend to wear the glasses?

Getting Involved

38. Create a poster that shows how to enjoy the outdoors while protecting your skin from overexposure to sun.

ALCOHOL

Drinking and driving remains the number one cause of death among 15- to 19-year-olds. Alcohol abuse is a threat to everyone, and groups of all ages can work in the fight against it. Are you developing healthy habits and attitudes toward alcohol? In this chapter you will learn how alcohol affects the body and mind and how alcoholism causes an emotional ordeal for everyone involved.

CHAPTER PREVIEW

19-1 Alcohol Is a Drug

- State reasons why alcohol is a drug and explain reasons for laws regulating alcohol use.

19-2 Alcohol's Effects on the Body

- Discuss the short-term and long-term effects of alcohol.

19-3 Alcoholism

- Explain the impact of alcohol on alcoholics, their families, and society.

19-4 Choosing Not to Drink

- Identify ways of refusing alcohol when it is offered.

BUILDING HEALTH SKILLS

- Demonstrate ways to refuse when people pressure you against your will.

CHECK YOUR WELLNESS

Are you aware of how alcohol affects people? See if you can answer *yes* to the questions that follow.

- Do you understand how alcohol affects the body and behavior?
- Do you cope with your feelings in healthy ways?
- Do you avoid riding with a driver who has been drinking?
- Will you say no to friends who pressure you to drink?
- Can you recognize the warning signs of alcoholism?
- Would you encourage a friend or family member to seek help for a drinking problem?
- Do you know where to get help for alcohol problems?

KEEPING A JOURNAL

Remember a time when you experienced a personal problem and received help from a friend. Write a list of statements your friend made that you felt were helpful.

Take it to the Net
www.phschool.com

Focus on these questions as you read this lesson.

- What is alcohol, and why is it considered a drug?
- What are the legal risks that may accompany alcohol consumption?

SKILLS

- Recognizing Misleading Claims

In much of American society, drugs are a part of everyday life. Many people rely on drugs to prevent or cure disease, to relieve anxious feelings, or to alter their mental state. A **drug** is any chemical that causes changes in a person's body or behavior. For example, aspirin is a drug that reduces the sensation of pain by changing the way some nerves send pain impulses to the brain. Drugs, such as aspirin, that are used for helping the body fight pain, illness, and disease are called medicines.

Medicines are legal drugs that help people maintain their health. However, **illegal drugs** are chemicals that are forbidden by law because their dangerous and often unpredictable effects outweigh any useful purposes the drugs may have. When people intentionally misuse drugs of any kind for nonmedical purposes, they are engaging in **drug abuse**. For many individuals, drug abuse is an attempt to escape the pressures of life.

Alcohol as a Drug

You may not think of alcohol as a drug. Yet alcohol, like other drugs, is a chemical that causes changes in a person's body or behavior. Did you know that alcohol is the most widely abused drug among high school students?

The alcohol found in beverages such as beer, wine, and liquor is **ethanol** (ETH uh nawl). Ethanol is produced when yeast changes sugar into carbon dioxide and alcohol. Grapes, berries, and malted grains can be used as a source of sugar for yeast.

Figure 19-1 *Yeast changes the sugar in grapes to alcohol, forming wine.*

Figure 19-2 *Rum is made from distilled molasses or sugar cane. It contains a greater percentage of alcohol than does beer or wine.*

Not all alcoholic beverages contain the same amount of ethanol. The alcohol content of most alcoholic beverages is between 6 percent and 50 percent. Beers and wines carry labels indicating the percentage of their alcohol content. Beverages with a greater percentage of alcohol than beer or wine, such as whiskey, gin, and rum, have the proof listed on the label. The **proof** of an alcoholic drink is a measure of the percentage of alcohol in the beverage. The proof is twice the percentage of alcohol by volume. Thus 100-proof vodka is 50 percent alcohol.

Alcohol has powerful effects on the body. **Alcohol is a drug that acts as a powerful depressant.** A **depressant** (dih PRES unt) is a drug that slows the activity of the body's central nervous system. The alcohol in beer, wine, and liquor slows the body's normal reactions. Alcohol may cause confusion, decreased alertness, poor coordination, blurred vision, and drowsiness. The depressant effects of alcohol are very strong. If a person drinks large amounts of alcohol, vital functions such as heartbeat and breathing can be seriously affected, resulting in death.

Who Uses Alcohol?

It is estimated that well over 100 million Americans use alcohol. Alcohol consumption in the United States varies from one group to another. In the past, men usually drank more frequently than women. Today, women's drinking has begun to match men's. Rural areas have a lower percentage of drinkers than do metropolitan areas.

Figure 19-3 *These different quantities of beer, liquor, and wine contain equal amounts of ethanol.*

People often think of a person who has a serious drinking problem as someone who sleeps on park benches and wears shabby clothes. Only a small percentage of heavy drinkers fit this description. In reality, heavy drinkers come from all kinds of cultures, backgrounds, and levels of education. They are all ages and both sexes, and work in all kinds of jobs.

Why People Drink

The reasons why people drink are as varied as people themselves. Many young people first discover alcohol use in their families. Adult family members may drink to celebrate religious events and other special occasions. For example, wine is used in religious observations such as the Jewish Passover dinner and some types of Christian communion. Wine toasts at weddings, births, graduations, holidays, and other family gatherings accompany an expression of congratulations and good wishes.

Alcohol's wide availability makes it easy to obtain the drug. Companies that sell alcohol bombard the public with advertisements for beer, wine, liquor, and other beverages. Television commercials and magazine advertisements often show drinkers in beautiful outdoor settings or at fun-filled parties. Usually the message accompanying an alcohol ad says nothing about the product. Instead, the ads promote an image of drinkers as attractive, healthy, and successful. The ads falsely give the impression that drinking will increase the drinker's sex appeal and popularity.

Legal Risks

Selling alcohol to someone under the age of 21 is a criminal offense for the seller. In some states, it is against the law to serve alcohol to people under the legal drinking age, even at a private party. Laws prohibiting minors (people under the age of 21) from buying or possessing alcohol are enforced with heavy fines and lawful seizure of property. For example,

Figure 19-4 *Wine is an important part of the Jewish Sabbath.*

Figure 19-5 *Drinking alcohol affects a driver's coordination.*

law-enforcement officers in some states can seize a car in which a minor is in possession of alcohol. This may seem harsh, but the dangers associated with teenage drinking and driving are serious enough to justify tough punishments.

In all 50 states, a person must be 21 years old to buy alcohol legally. Laws prohibit drinking in public places such as shopping malls, amusement parks, and beaches. Laws also apply to places with approved liquor licenses, such as restaurants, bars, and liquor stores. These businesses can be held responsible for accidents caused by serving or selling alcohol to someone who is drunk.

The law requires people who are old enough to drink alcohol legally to behave responsibly. The National Highway Traffic Safety Administration estimates that about 40 percent of all fatal automobile crashes are alcohol related. The risk of having an automobile accident increases as the amount of alcohol in the body increases. People found to be driving under the influence of alcohol may have their driver's licenses suspended. They may face other stiff penalties as well. In some states, those found guilty of repeated drunk driving charges can be sent to prison.

LESSON 1 REVIEW

1. What does the term *drug abuse* mean?
2. Describe the depressant drug effects of alcohol.
3. Give two reasons why people may drink.
4. What are the legal risks of possessing alcohol as a minor?

What Do You Think?

5. Some people argue that alcohol should not be considered a drug. After all, it is legal. What do you think?

When a person drinks alcohol, it follows the same pathway as food through the digestive system. However, unlike food, alcohol does not have to be digested by the stomach in order to be absorbed into the blood. **Once alcohol reaches the blood, it is circulated throughout the body and affects every part, including the brain and the rest of the nervous system.**

Short-Term Physical Effects

Alcohol can be toxic, or poisonous. In fact, the term *intoxication* is derived from the word *toxic*. **Intoxication** (in tahk sih KAY shun) refers to the many negative effects alcohol has on a drinker's body and behavior. The short-term effects of alcohol include those that happen within minutes, and sometimes within days, of drinking alcohol. Use Figure 19-6 to identify the short-term effects of alcohol on the body.

BLOODSTREAM When alcohol enters the blood, it causes the blood vessels to widen. More blood flows to the skin's surface. The drinker feels warm for a short time as the skin flushes. However, the drinker's body temperature drops as the increased blood flow to the surface allows body heat to escape. People who drink alcohol in cold weather to get warm actually accomplish the opposite.

Figure 19-6 *How does the body react to the toxic effects of too much alcohol in the stomach?*

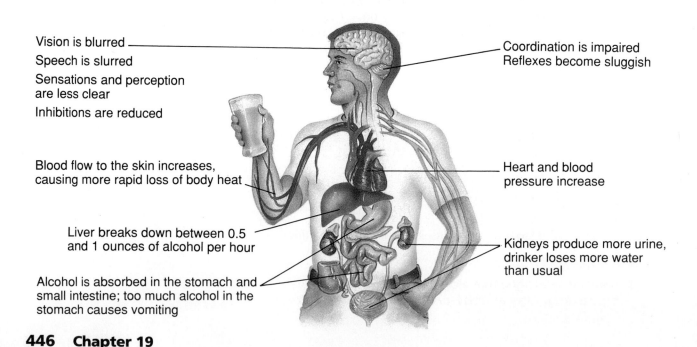

Vision is blurred
Speech is slurred
Sensations and perception are less clear
Inhibitions are reduced

Coordination is impaired
Reflexes become sluggish

Blood flow to the skin increases, causing more rapid loss of body heat

Heart and blood pressure increase

Liver breaks down between 0.5 and 1 ounces of alcohol per hour

Kidneys produce more urine, drinker loses more water than usual

Alcohol is absorbed in the stomach and small intestine; too much alcohol in the stomach causes vomiting

446 Chapter 19

BRAIN Upon reaching the brain, alcohol immediately has a depressant effect. As shown in Figure 19-7, alcohol slows the speed of some brain activities. People who drink alcohol may describe the change as relaxing. What they actually experience are physical changes such as a loss of sensation and a decrease in sharpness of vision, hearing, and other senses. Alcohol also affects the parts of the brain that control muscle coordination, which is why drinkers may lose their balance or stumble.

If drinking continues, alcohol depresses the part of the brain that controls breathing and heartbeat. Breathing rates, pulse rates, and blood pressure, which initially increased, now decrease. A drinker may lose consciousness, slip into a coma, or die from alcohol poisoning.

Heavy drinkers and many first-time drinkers may suffer blackouts. **Blackouts** are periods of time that the drinker cannot recall. Other people recall seeing the drinker talking, walking, and in control. The following day, however, the drinker has no memory of some events from the day before.

LIVER Once in the bloodstream, alcohol is carried to the liver. The liver chemically breaks down alcohol into energy and the waste products carbon dioxide and water. The carbon dioxide is released from the body in the lungs. The water passes out of the body as breath vapor, perspiration, or urine. When people drink alcohol faster than the liver can break it down, they become intoxicated.

KIDNEYS Alcohol prevents the release of body chemicals that regulate how much urine the kidneys make. The kidneys produce more urine than usual, and the drinker loses more water than usual. The drinker becomes very thirsty. In extreme cases, a drinker may lose water needed for the body to function properly.

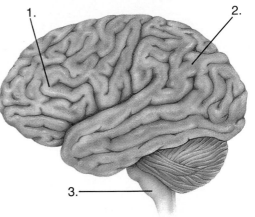

Figure 19-7 *Alcohol abuse may result in decreased brain size and loss of some reasoning ability.*

KEY
1. Alcohol affects areas of the cerebrum that control memory, judgment, senses, and behavior.
2. Alcohol may depress motor centers, slowing the body's response to pain and danger.
3. Severe intoxication depresses those areas of the brain stem that control heartbeat and breathing. Coma and death may result.

Blood Alcohol Concentration

The amount of ethanol in a person's blood is expressed by a percentage called the **blood alcohol concentration** (BAC). BAC measures the number of milligrams of ethanol per 100 milliliters of blood. A BAC of 0.1 percent means that 1/10 of 1 percent of the fluid in the blood is ethanol. A BAC of 0.1 percent reduces a person's muscle coordination, perception, and judgment.

A variety of factors can affect a person's BAC:
- gender
- age, weight, and height
- amount of food in the stomach
- concentration of alcohol in beverages consumed
- volume of alcohol consumed
- rate of consumption and absorption

The rate at which a person's liver can break down alcohol is fairly constant. In one hour, the liver can break down the amount of ethanol in a can of beer, a shot of liquor, or a glass of wine. Thus, someone who has three cans of beer in the last 45 minutes of a three-hour party will become more intoxicated than someone who drinks those three cans of beer over the three-hour period.

Provided the person does not continue to drink, the BAC decreases. The intoxicating effects of alcohol slowly diminish. As reflexes and coordination return to normal, a person gradually becomes steadier. Many people refer to this process as "becoming sober" or "sobering up."

You may have heard that cold showers, exercise, fresh air, or coffee will help a person sober up more quickly. But this is not true. Nothing can speed the liver's ability to break down alcohol. Coffee or fresh air may keep a person awake, but they do not eliminate the intoxicating effects of alcohol.

Drinking heavily usually causes a person to wake up with a hangover. A **hangover** is a term for the physical symptoms, such as nausea, upset stomach, headache, and a sensitivity to noise, that are aftereffects of drinking too much alcohol. It is not clear why some drinkers get a hangover and others do not. The only way a person can be sure to prevent one is to avoid alcohol altogether.

Figure 19-8 *In some states, a person with a BAC of 0.1 percent is legally drunk. Other states have lowered the legal BAC to 0.08 percent.*

Behavioral Effects

In addition to the physical effects of alcohol, certain behavioral, or learned, effects are connected to drinking. A person's mood and reason for drinking can alter the effects of alcohol.

Blood Alcohol Concentration: Effects on the Body

Number of Drinks	Effects	BAC Range*	Approximate Time to Eliminate Alcohol
	Inhibitions, reflexes, and alertness diminished. Judgment and reasoning affected.	.02–.03%	1 1/2 hours
	Drinker gets the mistaken idea that his or her skills and abilities have improved. Self-control declines.	.04–.06%	3 hours
	Unable to think clearly. Judgment, reasoning and muscular coordination is impaired.	.06–.09%	4 to 5 hours
	Most behaviors, including hearing, speech, vision, and balance, are affected.	.08–.12%	5 to 7 hours

*The BAC will vary depending on the alcohol content of the drinks and rate of consumption.

Drinking and Driving?

Janelle attended a party with some of her friends. She planned to get a ride home with Dave, but she had seen him drink four beers since he arrived. Dave was showing some signs of intoxication, and Janelle was not sure if he should drive. Unfortunately, she did not know anyone else at the party who could give her a ride, and Janelle knew that her parents had gone out with friends for the evening. Besides, three of her friends were getting a ride from Dave. "I'm probably getting worried for nothing," thought Janelle. "What could happen in the few miles to my house?"

1. Use the DECIDE process described on page 18 to decide what you would do if you were in Janelle's position. Explain your decision.

2. What role might peer pressure play in influencing Janelle's decision?

3. Suggest a realistic plan that you and your friends could use to avoid situations like the one described above.

Sometimes the person's mood and reason for drinking make the effects stronger; sometimes they make the effects weaker. The environment in which alcohol is consumed may influence its effects as well.

At a quiet family dinner, family members may consume wine with no negative effects. The calm nature of the event and the fact that both parents and children expect each other to behave politely creates an environment in which people drink responsibly.

At a party in which "getting drunk" is the main theme, alcohol consumption often leads to negative behaviors. The loss of coordination may be exaggerated for comic effect. People who have been drinking may insist that they are still perfectly able to drive. They may not want to admit that they cannot drink as much as others.

As alcohol takes effect, drinkers begin to lose judgment and self-control. At the same time, alcohol decreases drinkers' natural fears. When these two effects are combined, the person's inhibitions are reduced. **Inhibitions** (in huh BISH unz) are the controls that people put on their emotions and behavior in order to behave in socially acceptable ways.

Once they lose their inhibitions, drinkers may behave in ways they normally would never consider. For example, a person under the influence of alcohol may express anger in violent or destructive ways. Shy people may behave in outgoing ways, and serious people may act foolishly.

Life-Threatening Short-Term Effects

The short-term effects of intoxication put a drinker at risk. Unintentional death may occur in the following ways.

MOTOR-VEHICLE CRASHES   Almost half of the fatal crashes and about two-thirds of all crashes involving personal injury in the United States are related to alcohol use. In addition, more than one-third of pedestrians who are struck and killed by motor vehicles are drunk.

Driving while intoxicated is illegal in all of the 50 states. **Driving while intoxicated** means a driver exceeds the level of blood alcohol concentration allowed by law in a state. Drivers who cause motor-vehicle crashes usually undergo blood, urine, breath, or saliva tests to determine their BAC. If their BAC is above the legal limit, drunk drivers can have their driver's license taken away and can be prosecuted.

SYNERGISM   Some drugs can interact to produce effects that are many times greater than either drug would produce by itself. When drugs increase each other's effects when taken together, the interaction is called **synergism** (SIN ur jiz um).

Alcohol, you remember, is generally a depressant drug. When a person drinks alcohol and takes another depressant, such as sleeping pills, the combination can cause drastic changes in the body. Together the depressants' effects are more than doubled and can cause a dangerous slowing of breathing and heart rates. In extreme cases, synergism of alcohol and other depressants can lead to coma or death.

OVERDOSE   Taking an excessive amount of a drug that leads to coma or death is called an **overdose.** Severe intoxication causes the heart and breathing to stop, resulting in death from alcohol overdose. Many drinkers assume that they will pass out before drinking a fatal amount. This is not necessarily true. Alcohol continues to be absorbed into the blood for 30 to 90 minutes after the last drink. The drinker's BAC can increase even if the drinker becomes unconscious. First-time drinkers who participate in a drinking contest may die from alcohol poisoning.

Long-Term Health Risks

Adults who use alcohol occasionally and in moderation usually are not at risk of developing the long-term health problems related to alcohol. But when a person drinks heavily over time, every system in the body is affected.

TOLERANCE   When the body becomes accustomed to or builds up a resistance to a drug, the body has developed **tolerance** (TAHL ur uns) to the drug. Tolerance causes a drinker's body to need increasingly larger amounts of alcohol to achieve the effect that was originally produced.

Figure 19-9 *Government warning labels caution people about the dangers of alcohol.*

GOVERNMENT WARNING:
(1) According to the Surgeon General, women should not drink alcoholic beverages during pregnancy because of the risk of birth defects.
(2) Consumption of alcoholic beverages impairs your ability to drive a car or operate machinery, and may cause health problems.

DEPENDENCE   When the body develops a resistance to a drug and requires the drug to function normally, **dependence** occurs. The drinker's body develops a chemical need for alcohol. Dependence occurs as tolerance builds. Dependence is also called **addiction** (uh DIK shun).

A dependent person who stops taking a drug will suffer from **withdrawal.** Signs of alcohol withdrawal include shakiness, sleep problems, irritability, rapid heartbeat, and sweating. The drinker also may see, smell, or feel imaginary objects.

The major psychological symptom of dependence is a strong desire or emotional need to continue using a drug. This need is often associated with specific routines and events. For example, some people drink whenever they face a difficult task or when they feel angry about something.

BRAIN DAMAGE   Long-term alcohol abuse destroys nerve cells in the brain. Destroyed nerve cells usually cannot grow again. The loss of many nerve cells causes forgetfulness, an inability to concentrate, and poor judgment. These losses interfere with normal everyday functions.

DIGESTIVE PROBLEMS   Ongoing drinking irritates the tissues lining the mouth, throat, esophagus, and stomach. The irritation can cause the tissues to swell and become inflamed. Repeated irritation increases the risk of cancers of the mouth, tongue, esophagus, and stomach. Alcohol also affects the intestines and can cause recurring diarrhea. Large amounts of alcohol cause the stomach to produce too much stomach acid. The overproduction of acid may lead to indigestion, heartburn, or ulcers.

LIVER DAMAGE   Alcohol interferes with the liver's ability to break down fats. As a result of heavy drinking, the liver begins to fill with fat. The excess fat blocks the flow of blood in the liver, and the fat-filled liver cells die. **Cirrhosis** (sih ROH sis) of the liver is a disease in which useless scar tissue

Figure 19-10 *A healthy liver (left) contains smooth tissue. The liver of a heavy drinker may be fatty (center) or contain useless scar tissue (right).*

replaces normal liver tissue. Since there is no blood flow in the scarred area, the liver begins to fail. Heavy drinkers suffering from cirrhosis may have high blood pressure, get infections easily, have swelling of the abdomen, and show a yellowing of the skin and eyes. Cirrhosis is the last stage of liver disease and can result in death.

Heavy drinkers often develop **alcoholic hepatitis** (hep uh TY tis), or inflammation of the liver, caused by the toxic effects of alcohol. Hepatitis causes weakness, fever, yellowing of the skin, and enlargement of the liver. Recovery may take weeks. Sometimes hepatitis can lead to liver failure and even death.

HEART DISEASE Excessive drinking contributes to increased blood pressure and heart rate, and irregular heartbeat. These problems can cause disruption in blood flow and possible heart damage. Also, alcohol causes fat to be deposited in heart muscle. Fatty heart muscle, in turn, causes the heart to pump blood through the body less efficiently. Alcohol abuse leads to heart disease, the leading cause of death in the United States.

Fetal Alcohol Syndrome

Pregnant women who drink put the health of their child at risk. A disorder called **fetal alcohol syndrome,** or FAS, refers to the group of birth defects caused by the effects of alcohol on the unborn child. FAS occurs when alcohol in the mother's blood passes into the fetal, or unborn baby's, blood. Babies born with FAS often suffer from heart defects, malformed faces, delayed growth, and poor motor development. Alcohol prevents FAS babies from ever developing the reasoning abilities of healthy babies. Tragically, it is the leading preventable cause of mental retardation in America.

If a woman who is pregnant does not drink, her baby will not be born with FAS. Any woman who is pregnant or planning to become pregnant should not drink alcohol at all.

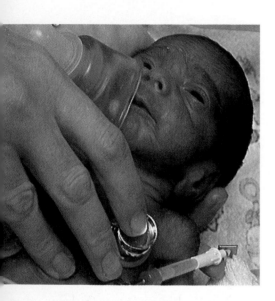

Figure 19-11 *One bout of heavy drinking during the early stages of fetal development can cause fetal alcohol syndrome.*

LESSON 2 REVIEW

1. List the short-term effects of alcohol intoxication.
2. Explain BAC and list six factors that affect a drinker's BAC.
3. Identify six long-term effects of alcohol abuse.

What Do You Think?

4. What information about alcohol will most influence your future decisions about drinking? Why is this information important to you?

3 ALCOHOLISM

Some drinkers cannot control their drinking. Their major goal in drinking is to get drunk. People who have an addiction to alcohol suffer from the disease of **alcoholism**. Psychologically, alcoholics consider drinking a regular, essential part of coping with daily life. Physically, an alcoholic's body requires alcohol to function. An alcoholic's drinking patterns eventually control every aspect of life.

No one is sure why some drinkers become alcoholics. But anyone who drinks—even one drink—is at risk of becoming an alcoholic. Because alcoholism tends to run in families, there appears to be some genetic basis. On the other hand, the attitudes in the home in which a person grows up may play a role in whether or not a person develops a drinking problem.

Stages of Alcoholism

Alcoholics progress through several stages, each of which can last weeks, months, or years. Teenage alcoholics tend to go through the stages faster than adult alcoholics.

EARLY STAGE OF ALCOHOLISM Social drinkers, people who drink small amounts of alcohol with meals and on special occasions, may consume alcohol to try to relieve stress. Gradually the social drinker begins to drink more often, tends to be preoccupied with drinking, and may drink excessive amounts of alcohol. This type of drinking is known as problem drinking.

GUIDE FOR READING

Focus on these questions as you read this lesson.

- What is alcoholism?
- How does an alcoholic's behavior affect other people?
- What are steps in the treatment of alcoholism?

SKILLS

- Intervening to Help a Friend

Figure 19-12 *Teenage alcoholics may never develop emotional control or healthy relationships.*

Figure 19-13 *One or two yes answers to these questions may indicate a drinking problem.*

Problem drinking occurs when drinking alcohol becomes a person's routine way of dealing with stress, or when drinking is used as an escape from problems at home, at school, or at work. Problem drinking is so named because of the many problems associated with excessive alcohol consumption. Problem drinkers often use alcohol as a "crutch." They often drink alone as they become dependent on alcohol, and drink solely to get drunk. Problem drinkers frequently make excuses for their drinking behavior.

Problem drinkers are often involved in motor-vehicle crashes. They are more prone to unintentional injuries such as falls, drownings, fires, and burns. Alcohol consumption also contributes to many violent crimes such as fights, spousal and child abuse, rape, suicide, and murder.

MIDDLE STAGE OF ALCOHOLISM During the middle stage of alcoholism, the alcoholic's dependence on alcohol becomes absolute. The alcoholic generally cannot stop after one drink. The need to drink separates the alcoholic from other heavy drinkers. In this stage, alcoholics may refuse to acknowledge their drinking problem. Some alcoholics are able to hide their problem, and thus outwardly appear normal. Others show signs of the effects of excessive alcohol consumption. These signs may include absence from work or school and strained family, social, and business relationships. Alcohol dominates the drinker's life.

LATE STAGE OF ALCOHOLISM During the late stage of alcoholism, alcoholics rapidly deteriorate mentally, emotionally, and physically. Their entire lives revolve around drinking, and they experience reverse tolerance for alcohol. **Reverse tolerance** is a condition in which less and less alcohol causes intoxication. Chronic alcoholics become isolated from society because all their mental and physical energy is focused on drinking alcohol. Serious health problems, including malnutrition, liver and brain damage, cancer, lung disease, and heart disease are common in this stage. Without psychological and medical help, the chronic alcoholic may die.

When alcoholics are denied alcohol, they suffer severe withdrawal symptoms. About 5 percent of alcoholics experience delirium tremens, also called DTs, when they stop using alcohol. **Delirium tremens** (dih LIHR ee um TREE munz) is a reaction of the central nervous system to the absence of alcohol. DTs are characterized by uncontrollable shaking of the entire body, nightmares, seizures, fear of animals and people, and insomnia. Delirium tremens can be fatal.

Alcoholism and Others

The disease of alcoholism affects people other than the alcoholic. **Alcoholism causes costly problems for society and causes an emotional ordeal for everyone involved—family members, friends, and co-workers.**

COSTS TO SOCIETY Everyone suffers the consequences of alcohol abuse. Alcohol is a factor in about 40 percent of all traffic fatalities. Alcohol-related crimes, medical expenses, injuries, lost productivity on the job, and treatment programs cost the United States between 100 and 200 billion dollars annually. Alcohol is involved in 100,000 premature deaths per year. Most of these deaths are due to violence committed under the influence of alcohol and to automobile crashes involving drunk drivers. Alcohol abuse plays a role in those injuries and violent behaviors highlighted in Figure 19-14. Notice that three-fourths of all injuries that occur on the job are related to alcohol abuse.

ALCOHOLISM AND THE FAMILY About one in every eight Americans grows up in an alcoholic family. Spouses and children of alcoholics live in homes filled with stress arising from uncertainty and embarrassment. In some cases, the alcoholic verbally or physically abuses family members. Family life centers around the drinking member as the needs of other family members are ignored.

Laura knows how alcoholism can affect a family. Her father is an alcoholic. In the past, he sometimes spent the grocery money on alcohol. He often missed work, and once he was fired because of drinking on the job. Her family lost its health insurance and could not pay the medical bills when her younger sister was sick.

Whenever Laura or her mother tried to talk to her father about getting help, he became defensive and angry. Laura's father reacted by drinking more heavily and yelling at them. He refused to admit he had a drinking problem. Laura never asked friends over to her house because she was ashamed of

ENGLISH CONNECTION

Many works of literature deal with the negative effects alcohol has on drinkers and their families. Listed below are a few examples:

- "My Papa's Waltz," by Theodore Roethke
- *The Mayor of Casterbridge,* by Thomas Hardy
- *A Yellow Raft in Blue Water,* by Michael Dorris

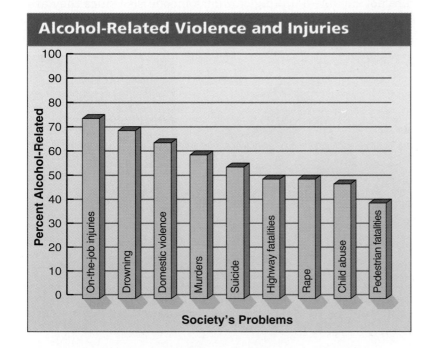

Alcohol-Related Violence and Injuries

Percent Alcohol-Related (y-axis: 0–100)

Society's Problems (x-axis categories): On-the-job injuries, Drowning, Domestic violence, Murders, Suicide, Highway fatalities, Rape, Child abuse, Pedestrian fatalities

Figure 19-14 *What percentage of all drownings are alcohol-related?*

her father and afraid he would embarrass her. The situation in Laura's family became worse and worse as her father's alcoholism worsened. Eventually, Laura's mother decided to end her marriage to save herself and her children from further emotional damage. Laura and her sister now live with their mother while their parents proceed with a divorce.

Although all families faced with alcoholism are not exactly like Laura's, many of the problems Laura faced are common. When a parent is drinking, the money intended for living expenses may be spent on alcohol. Family members are embarrassed when an alcoholic family member displays inappropriate or unpredictable behavior in public. Family members often live in fear of the alcoholic's changes in mood and possibly violent outbursts.

If an alcoholic's family splits up because of divorce, family members may feel they could have done more to help the alcoholic and save the family. They may even blame each other for allowing the alcoholic to break up the family. Whatever the outcome of the family's experience with alcoholism, the process of dealing with an alcoholic is an emotional ordeal for everyone involved.

Codependency

Sometimes people close to an alcoholic let that person's drinking problem change their own daily activities and attitudes. People who assume responsibility for an alcoholic's needs, feelings, and happiness are called **codependents** (koh dih PEN dunts). They do not acknowledge having needs of their own. Codependents focus on taking care of others, losing the sense of their own identity. However, codependents are not capable of taking care of someone else since they are unsuccessful at taking care of themselves.

Figure 19-15 *Making excuses for an alcoholic is an example of codependent behavior.*

Codependents are the primary enablers of their addicted loved ones. **Enablers** are people who unintentionally protect addicts from the consequences of their behavior. Without consequences, addicts are unaware of their dangerous behavior and therefore continue it. Codependents can help the addict to avoid seeking needed help.

Treatment of Alcoholism

With appropriate treatment, the progress of alcoholism can be stopped. Alcoholics can lead productive, happy lives if they stop drinking completely. In the first step of recovery, alcoholics must acknowledge their problem and ask for help. For some, it takes the shock of losing a job or being arrested. For others, it may take the shock of being separated from their families to motivate alcoholics to enter treatment programs.

DETOXIFICATION The physical damage of alcohol must be treated before the alcoholic can restore his or her mental health. The next step in recovery is **detoxification,** which involves removing all alcohol from a person's body. During detoxification, the alcoholic experiences withdrawal symptoms that last from three to seven days. Severe withdrawal symptoms can be extremely dangerous, and the alcoholic requires medical care and perhaps hospitalization.

REHABILITATION As recovery continues, care is given for malnutrition and any other health problems that drinking caused. After detoxification, alcoholics move to places of treatment for care and counseling. The alcoholic achieves a sober state and begins **rehabilitation** (ree huh bil ih TAY shun), which is the process of learning to cope with the stress of everyday living without alcohol. During rehabilitation, alcoholics receive counseling to help them understand their

Figure 19-16 *Through therapy, an alcoholic learns to use positive coping skills instead of drinking.*

Figure 19-17 *Alateen members use understanding and education in their efforts to cope with alcoholics.*

disease and behavior. Alcoholics also receive counseling to help them build healthy relationships.

SUPPORT GROUPS Community, religious, and health organizations often sponsor support groups for alcoholics. One of the most successful groups, **Alcoholics Anonymous** (AA), is composed of recovering alcoholics who give encouragement and support to help other alcoholics stop drinking. Founded in 1935 by two alcoholics who decided to help one another quit drinking, AA now has over a million members, and branches worldwide. Members meet weekly and share their struggles with one another.

Two other groups, Al-Anon and Alateen, are based on the AA self-help process and are designed to help friends and family members of alcoholics. **Al-Anon** helps adult friends and family of alcoholics learn how they can contribute to the recovery process. Also, Al-Anon encourages codependents to seek help for themselves and not wait until the alcoholic decides to get well.

Alateen provides help for teenagers who live with alcoholics. Teenagers meet to discuss how the alcoholic's addiction has affected their lives. Teenagers learn skills to develop self-esteem so that they can overcome guilt feelings and regain emotional and social health. You can find the phone numbers for AA, Al-Anon, and Alateen in your local phone book.

All three support groups encourage friends and family members to help alcoholics confront their disease through intervention. An **intervention** (in tur VEN shun) is a planned confrontation with the alcoholic, family members, a member of a support group, and an alcohol counselor. The group presents the alcoholic with a treatment plan and tells the alcoholic what steps they will take if the alcoholic refuses help. For example, a boss might say "I will fire you if you drink on the job again." Such ultimatums tell alcoholics that enabling will stop and they must take responsibility for their behavior.

LESSON 3 REVIEW

1. Describe the three stages of alcoholism.
2. How does alcoholism affect other people?
3. List three steps in the treatment of alcoholism.
4. Compare the goals of Alcoholics Anonymous, Al-Anon, and Alateen.

What Do You Think?

5. What kinds of school or community programs do you think would help teenagers who have drinking problems?

4 CHOOSING NOT TO DRINK

As you become old enough to make your own decisions, you must begin to accept responsibility for the outcomes of those decisions. When you reach legal drinking age, you will need to decide whether or not to drink and whether to socialize with people who drink. These are among the most important decisions you will make in your life. **Deciding not to drink is a healthy choice because it eliminates the chance that alcohol will become a problem.**

Why People Choose Not to Drink

So far, this chapter has focused on drinkers. Yet one in every three American adults **abstains** from, or chooses not to drink, alcohol. Some people abstain from alcohol for religious beliefs or social customs. Others dislike the taste of alcoholic beverages or react unfavorably to them during or after drinking. Individuals who have certain medical conditions and those taking certain medicines cannot drink alcohol. Recall the deadly synergistic effects of mixing alcohol with other drugs.

Some people look forward to maturing socially and emotionally without depending on a drug. Others may avoid using alcohol or may never use alcohol because its harmful effects far outweigh any positive effects. More and more teenagers are choosing to abstain from alcohol and illegal drugs. Among high-achieving teenage students, two-thirds say they never drink alcohol.

GUIDE FOR READING

Focus on these questions as you read this lesson.

- What are the advantages of not drinking?
- How can you use refusal skills to avoid riding with a drunk driver?
- What are some healthy alternatives to drinking?

SKILLS

- Activity: Resisting Peer Pressure
- Working in Groups

Figure 19-18 *People who are responsible for the safety of others, such as air traffic controllers, could cause injury to others if they drank on the job.*

RESISTING PEER PRESSURE

In this activity you will role-play and practice refusal skills.

Materials

bag of jelly beans

set of five role-playing cards per group

Procedure

1. Work in a group with four other students.

2. Your teacher will distribute a different role-playing card to each group member.

3. Do not discuss your role with other group members.

4. Imagine that you are at a party with friends. Spend five minutes thinking about your assigned role and how you will act during the imagined party.

5. As a group, go to the classroom area designated by your teacher. Each member acts out his or her role.

Discussion

1. Describe your role, and explain how you felt playing that role during the imagined party.

2. How do you think player 4 felt about being pressured to eat the jelly beans when he or she refused?

3. How do you think player 3 felt when he or she first resisted taking the jelly beans? How do you think player 3 felt about giving in?

4. How do you think player 3 felt when player 2 accepted the jelly beans immediately and then pressured player 3 to take them?

5. How do you think player 1 felt about pressuring all the other players?

6. What refusal skills will you use to resist pressure from friends and make your own decisions?

Refusing Alcohol

Alcohol use is always inappropriate when a person must stay alert and think clearly. No one should drink on the job. Choosing not to drink means that you must be able to say *no* confidently in situations where other people are drinking. The skills needed to say *no* are sometimes referred to as refusal skills. **Refusal skills** involve refusing to do something that others may pressure you to do against your will.

By practicing saying *no* in role-playing situations, you can develop the refusal skills you can use in actual social situations. To prepare yourself for the pressure you may face, ask yourself the following questions:

- What are my reasons for not drinking alcohol at this time in my life?
- Are my friends pressuring me into drinking?
- Do I feel pressure to drink to impress others?
- What might happen if I get drunk?

You may find that some people will not accept your decision not to drink. Many people who drink want to see others around them drink so that they can feel accepted. Always remember that you never need to apologize for not drinking.

You need only say *no*. Most people will respect your decision, especially if you are positive in your response. If someone asks, "Would you like a beer?" you can say:

- "No, I don't like the taste of beer. But I'll take a soft drink if you have one."
- "No thanks, I don't drink."
- "I'm not old enough to drink. I'll just have a glass of orange juice, thanks."

Dealing with Drinkers and Driving

Even if you don't drink alcohol, you will probably have to deal with people who have had too much to drink. Remember that intoxicated people must not be allowed to drive. The driver may be a friend, a relative, or the parent of a child for whom you were babysitting. You should not get into a car with anyone who has been drinking.

If you go places where people are drinking, make arrangements for your ride home before you go. Consider taking a taxi, bus, or finding a driver who has not been drinking to take you home. If you find yourself dependent on a drunk person for a ride home, ask someone for help. Do not risk riding with the intoxicated driver.

Alternatives to Alcohol Use

Many teenagers find the time they spend pursuing their personal interests very rewarding. Teenagers who abstain from alcohol are likely to participate in healthy alternatives. Think about the kinds of activities that interest you. You may be interested in sports, hobbies, playing an instrument, helping an organization raise money, or organizing a school activity. You might also consider getting a part-time job to meet people and to make money to spend on social activities or college.

SHARPEN YOUR SKILLS

Working in Groups

Choose one of the risks associated with alcohol abuse. Working with a group of your classmates, design a poster to educate the public about the risk you select.

LESSON 4 REVIEW

1. Give five reasons for abstaining from alcohol.
2. List some positive ways to refuse alcohol when offered an alcoholic beverage.
3. How might you avoid riding with a drunk driver?
4. Describe healthy alternatives to alcohol consumption.

What Do You Think?

5. Do you think postponing the decision about drinking until you are of legal age is a healthy choice? Explain your reasons.

Developing Refusal Skills

Two of the teenagers below are trying to coax their friend into drinking alcohol with them. The friend, however, does not believe in using drugs of any kind. Even so, she worries about what her friends will think if she refuses. Perhaps you have felt this way about saying *no* to your friends. Maybe you worried that if you refused alcohol, your friends would be disappointed or think you were "un-cool." You might even have decided to go along with your friends just to avoid the discomfort of saying *no*.

Refusing your friends is never easy. Nevertheless, being true to yourself and honest with friends are two values that help you develop a sense of your own identity.

To refuse an offer convincingly, you must do more than say *no*. The following guidelines can help you learn to say *no* in a way that tells others you mean it.

The answer you give is up to you. Deciding now and practicing what you want to say when the time comes will make your response easier. Avoiding situations where alcohol is served will make it easier still.

1. Give a reason for your refusal

Don't say *no* without presenting your personal reason(s) for not going along with the suggestion. Be honest; don't supply phony reasons. Honest answers are more easily accepted by other people. Some answers might be:

- *No thanks... I don't want to start a bad habit.*

- *I don't need it to have a good time.*

- *I want to keep a clear head.*

- *My parents would be upset if they knew.*

- *I could get suspended from the team.*

- *I don't use alcohol or other drugs.*

2. Show your concern for others

Express your concern for those trying to persuade you. You might say things like:

- *I couldn't stand it if you hurt yourself doing that.*

- *Your parents would ground you for months if they ever found out.*

- *Some people have died from drinking alcohol or taking other drugs.*

- Call for help rather than ride with a drunk driver.
- Get up and leave a party.
- Start a new activity.
- As soon as possible, start widening your circle of friends.

Apply the Skill

1. Imagine that you are studying for a test with one of your friends when he or she asks you to sit close by during the test and share your answers. Describe how this request would make you feel and some possible ways in which you might respond to the request. If you were to refuse, what honest reason could you give and how would you express it? What do you think would be some of the possible consequences of your saying *no*? What would be some of the possible consequences of saying *yes*?

2. Describe two situations from your past in which you said *no* to others who were trying to convince you to do something you did not want to do. Explain how you felt in each situation. List the things that allowed you to refuse in each of these cases. In which situation was it more difficult to say *no*? Why? Did you use any of the steps presented in this skill when you refused? If so, describe the steps and how effective they were.

- *I'm worried about the amount you drink.*
- *You're only hurting yourself by drinking alcohol.*

3. Provide alternatives

Try to persuade your friends to do something safer or more comfortable. Here are some suggestions:

- *Let's leave this party and go back to my house.*
- *This is boring. Let's watch a movie at my place.*
- *Doesn't anybody feel like going to the gym instead of doing this?*

4. Use body language to reinforce what you say

Your body language can either strengthen or weaken your message. To make it clear that you mean *no* when you say it, you should look your friends in the eyes when presenting your feelings. Try to avoid staring at the ground or glancing away. Also avoid mannerisms that indicate anxiety and nervousness. Do not give power to your persuader by looking away.

5. Take a definite action

If your friends persist in trying to persuade you after you have made your feelings clear to them, it is wise not to continue repeating the point. Instead, try to take a definite action that removes you from the situation and makes it clear that you cannot be persuaded to change your mind.

Here are some examples of specific actions that you can take to remove yourself from potentially harmful situations:

CHAPTER 19 REVIEW

KEY IDEAS

LESSON 1

- Ethanol acts as a powerful depressant to change the activity of brain cells. A person must be 21 years old to buy alcohol legally in all 50 states.

LESSON 2

- The short-term effects of intoxication slow various brain activities, reduce inhibitions, and may depress heart and breathing rates to cause death. Long-term alcohol health risks include dependence, brain and liver damage, digestive problems, heart disease, and cancer.

LESSON 3

- Alcoholism is a disease in which the alcoholic progresses through stages. Treatment for alcoholism involves detoxification, rehabilitation, and membership in support groups.
- Alcoholism causes costly problems for society and an emotional ordeal for everyone involved.

LESSON 4

- Nondrinkers abstain from alcohol for religious beliefs or social customs, and because its harmful effects outweigh helpful effects.

KEY TERMS

LESSON 1
alcohol
depressant
ethanol
proof

LESSON 2
blood alcohol concentration (BAC)
cirrhosis
dependence
driving while intoxicated

fetal alcohol syndrome
hangover
inhibition
intoxication
overdose
synergism
tolerance
withdrawal

LESSON 3
Alateen
Alcoholics Anonymous

alcoholism
codependent
delirium tremens
detoxification
enabler
intervention
rehabilitation
reverse tolerance

LESSON 4
abstain
refusal skill

Listed above are some of the important terms in this chapter. Choose the term from the list that best matches each phrase below.

1. a condition in which the body becomes accustomed to a drug and requires the drug to function normally

2. a disease in which scar tissue replaces healthy liver tissue

3. the controls that people naturally put on their emotions and behavior

4. a support group for teenagers who live with alcoholics

5. a group of birth defects caused by the effects of alcohol on an unborn child

6. a drug that acts as a powerful depressant

7. the disease of uncontrolled drinking

8. a measure of alcohol in the blood

9. to not drink alcohol because of a personal choice to be a nondrinker

10. a person who assumes responsibility for meeting an alcoholic's needs

11. all the negative effects alcohol has on a drinker's body and behavior

12. learning to cope with the stresses of everyday living without alcohol

WHAT HAVE YOU LEARNED?

On a separate sheet of paper, write the word or words that best complete each statement.

13. A condition in which less and less alcohol causes intoxication is called _____ .

14. The _____ of an alcoholic drink is a measure of the percentage of alcohol in the beverage.

15. _____ are periods of time that the drinker cannot recall.

16. When drugs increase each other's effects when taken together, the interaction is called _____ .

17. _____ develops when the body builds up a resistance to a drug.

18. Heavy drinkers often develop _____ or inflammation of the liver caused by alcohol toxins.

19. _____ unintentionally protect addicts from the consequences of their behavior.

20. An _____ is a planned confrontation with the alcoholic, family members, a support group member, and an alcohol counselor.

21. A _____ is a term for the physical symptoms that result from drinking too much alcohol.

Answer each of the following with complete sentences.

22. What organ breaks down alcohol?

23. What factors affect the level of alcohol intoxication?

24. What legal risks are associated with driving while intoxicated?

25. How would you determine whether someone is a social drinker or a problem drinker?

26. What is delirium tremens?

27. Name three of society's alcohol-related problems.

28. What is detoxification? Why may hospitalization be required during detoxification?

29. Name two support groups for victims of alcoholism.

WHAT DO YOU THINK?

30. Do you feel that restrictions should be placed on the sale of alcoholic beverages? If so, what type of restrictions? If not, why not?

31. Do you think the warning labels placed on alcoholic beverage bottles affect who drinks and how they drink? Do you think the labels are harsh enough?

32. Studies show that students who use alcohol regularly are more likely than nondrinking students to get lower grades, drop out of school, and use other drugs. How would you explain this?

33. Why do teenagers drink? How are their reasons different from those of adults?

WHAT WOULD YOU DO?

34. What advice would you give someone whose parents are alcoholics? Be specific.

35. Three members of the football team were suspended from playing for the rest of the season because they were caught at a drinking party. Write a letter to the editor of the school newspaper giving your personal opinion about this situation.

36. Your 18-year-old sister has a date with her boyfriend. He is driving. When he arrives you notice that he is obviously intoxicated. What would you do?

37. What kind of program would you develop to prevent alcohol use by local teens?

Getting Involved

38. What are the laws that regulate alcohol consumption in your state? In your community? Do the laws treat minors differently from adults? Why do you think this is so?

39. What services exist in your community to help problem drinkers or alcoholics and their families? Are these services known and available to students in your school? Develop a database of these services.

Chapter 20

TOBACCO

Many activities, such as playing the saxophone, require healthy lungs. The best way to preserve the health of your lungs is to avoid smoking tobacco. In this chapter you will learn how smoking contributes to serious illnesses and how you can commit to a tobacco-free lifestyle.

CHAPTER PREVIEW

20-1 People and Tobacco

- List the major reasons why people either abstain from or use tobacco.

20-2 Tobacco and Its Chemicals

- Identify the chemicals in tobacco smoke and in smokeless tobacco.

20-3 Health and Tobacco

- Describe the long-term effects of tobacco use and the dangers of passive smoking.

20-4 Choosing a Healthy Lifestyle

- Describe ways to quit smoking and the benefits of quitting.

BUILDING HEALTH SKILLS

- Analyze advertising appeal in tobacco advertisements.

CHECK YOUR WELLNESS

If you abstain from tobacco, see if you can answer *yes* to the questions that follow.

- Do you know how the use of tobacco increases your risk for developing diseases?
- Is it easy for you to refuse tobacco?
- Do you let friends and family know that you mind if they smoke?

If you use tobacco, would you answer *yes* to the questions that follow?

- Do you want to light up whenever you feel upset, tense, or uncomfortable?
- Do you feel more at ease with a cigarette?
- Do you use tobacco without being aware of it?
- If you wanted to stop using tobacco, do you know where to get help?

KEEPING A JOURNAL

If you are a nonsmoker, describe the thoughts that go through your mind when you are in a smoke-filled area. If you are a smoker, describe how you feel when someone asks you not to smoke.

Take it to the Net
www.phschool.com

Focus on these questions as you read this lesson.

- What are some reasons people abstain from tobacco?

- What are some of the factors that may influence people to start using tobacco?

SKILLS

- DECIDE

- Supporting a Friend

1 PEOPLE AND TOBACCO

Can you remember the first time you saw someone use tobacco? How about the most recent time? You probably answered *no* to both of these questions. This is because tobacco use has long been a popular and socially accepted practice in the United States. Tobacco companies glamorize tobacco use in magazines, newspapers, and billboards.

Today, however, people understand more about the dangers of tobacco use than ever before. Because they do, people are avoiding tobacco use in ever-increasing numbers, as shown in Figure 20-1. Over the past ten years, how much has tobacco use decreased?

Given the well-publicized dangers of tobacco use, why do you think tobacco use is still so common today? Do you think it is possible to have a tobacco-free society? Keep these questions in mind as you read this chapter.

Why People Abstain from Tobacco

Most people abstain from tobacco for one simple reason—their health. Many students in elementary school learn about the damage tobacco does to the body. Since childhood

Figure 20-1 *Among people aged 20 and older, the prevalence of cigarette smoking has been declining.*

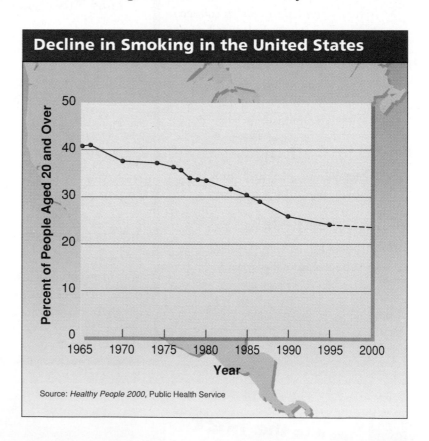

Decline in Smoking in the United States

Percent of People Aged 20 and Over

Year

Source: *Healthy People 2000*, Public Health Service

you have probably heard how easy it is to become dependent on tobacco. These reasons alone may prompt you to stay away from it. You may participate in athletics, play a musical instrument, or be involved in other activities with which tobacco use would interfere. In addition, you may dislike some of tobacco's other effects:

- bad breath
- bad odor on clothes and in hair
- poor complexion
- discolored teeth, fingers, and fingernails
- wrinkled skin
- bone loss around the teeth, more tooth decay, receded gums
- sore throat
- watery eyes
- impaired sense of smell
- impaired sense of taste

Social pressures—from family, friends, and the media—also may have influenced your decision not to use tobacco.

FAMILY AND FRIENDS   Your parents, whether they use tobacco or not, may have made you aware of tobacco's health effects. They may have offered advice on how to avoid tobacco use. Other relatives, such as older brothers or sisters, may serve as role models for you.

If your friends do not use tobacco, it is likely that you have helped one another in the decision not to use tobacco. Most people who become addicted to tobacco start during their teens, so a teenager's friends are an important influence. Have you ever been in a position where you were tempted to use tobacco? Many teenagers who have been tempted credit their friends with helping them to resist the temptation.

ANTITOBACCO ADVERTISING   Advertisements in newspapers, television, and other media also may have influenced your decision. You probably have read or heard much about tobacco through the media. You may have seen antitobacco advertisements like the one shown in Figure 20-2. Many of these advertisements are aimed at teenagers.

Why People Start Tobacco Use

If you do use tobacco, take a minute to think about the factors that influenced you to start. Like many tobacco users, it may be difficult for you to pinpoint the reason you started. You may be surprised to learn that some of the factors tobacco users mention are the same ones that nonusers say led them to the opposite decision. **The strongest factors that influence tobacco users to start are usually social pressures—family members, friends, and the media.**

Figure 20-2 *Antitobacco posters warn people of the health hazards involved in using tobacco.*

Historically, there have been many antismoking advocates. For example, in England in the early 1600s King James I was so opposed to the use of tobacco that he increased the taxes on tobacco by 4,000 percent. In 1683 Chinese law stated that anyone possessing tobacco would be beheaded. In 1790 Frederick the Great, King of Prussia, prevented his mother, the Dowager Queen, from using snuff during his coronation.

For tobacco users, the social pressures seem to outweigh the dangers of tobacco use. When asked why they ignored the health hazards and started smoking, some tobacco users said the dangers did not seem real to them. They did not see any evidence of poor health in friends and relatives who use tobacco. Other tobacco users said their curiosity to try tobacco was too strong. These people tried tobacco despite its dangers. Still others thought that they would not become addicted to tobacco. Yet, 80 percent of adult smokers who began smoking as teenagers are still addicted to tobacco use.

FAMILY MEMBERS Studies have shown that children of smokers are much more likely to develop the habit than are children of nonsmokers. In fact, one study showed that a youngster with one smoking parent was 90 percent more likely to smoke than a child with nonsmoking parents. When both parents use tobacco, the chances are even greater that the child will, even if the parents try to discourage the use of tobacco.

Why are the children of smokers more likely to smoke? They may simply assume that they will use tobacco just as their parents did. Tobacco use is a familiar behavior to them and one that the adults they know seem to enjoy. These children may think of tobacco use as a behavior that signals adulthood and maturity. While growing up, they may have imitated this adult behavior by "smoking" candy cigarettes or

DECIDE

DEFINE
the problem

EXPLORE
alternatives

CONSIDER
the consequences

IDENTIFY
values

DECIDE
and act

EVALUATE
results

A Smoky Vacation?

Julio's vacation is finally here! For months, he has been looking forward to going on a vacation with Greg and his family. But when they arrive to pick Julio up, he finds out that Greg's aunt is going with them. Greg's aunt smokes three packs of cigarettes a day, one right after another.

Julio can't stand breathing cigarette smoke, especially in cars or other enclosed places. The smoke makes his eyes tear, his throat sore, and his nose run. Julio can't bear the thought of an eight-hour car ride under these smoky conditions.

1. Use the DECIDE process described on page 18 to decide what you would do in this situation. Explain the reasons for your decision.

2. How would you put your decision into action? Write out what you would say or do.

pretzels. Also, children may have imitated adult use of smokeless tobacco by chewing bubble gum and candy smokeless products. These factors make children of tobacco users more likely to use tobacco than children of non-users.

FRIENDS WHO USE TOBACCO   If your friends use tobacco, it is more likely that you will. Using tobacco when friends are using it makes a person feel like part of the group. It is difficult to refuse friends who ask you to join in.

Furthermore, if your friends use tobacco, tobacco products are available to you. The government estimates that one billion packs of cigarettes are sold to people under the age of 18 annually, even though the sale of cigarettes to underage smokers is illegal in 45 states. More than half of adult smokers started smoking before they were 18. Nearly 90 percent started smoking before they were 21.

TOBACCO ADVERTISING   Advertising cigarettes on radio or television has been illegal for almost 30 years. Tobacco companies, however, still spend billions on advertising; they spend more to promote smoking than the nation spends to stop smoking. The vast majority of their advertising is designed to attract teens as "replacements" for smokers who have died.

In the mid-1990s the FDA (Food and Drug Administration) declared that cigarettes were an "addictive drug." The focus quickly became to stop children from taking the first "puff." New regulations, such as banning advertisements near schools and prohibiting free samples of cigarettes, were passed. In addition, tobacco companies were required to help pay for the anti-smoking education of the nation's youth.

As the anti-tobacco forces grew stronger, lawsuits against the tobacco industry became more common. Soon, over 30 percent of the states had sued the tobacco industry for damaging the health of their citizens. Individuals sued, too. In 1999, a group of Florida smokers won the first multi-billion dollar lawsuit against the tobacco companies. Five tobacco companies were found guilty of selling a "defective" product that caused cancer, heart disease, and stroke.

Figure 20-3 *Young people may copy film stars or sports heroes who use tobacco.*

LESSON 1 REVIEW

1. Why is tobacco use less socially accepted than it used to be?

2. Give two reasons why people abstain from tobacco.

3. List two reasons why people start to use tobacco.

What Do You Think?

4. What factors do you think influenced your decision about tobacco use?

- How do the chemicals in tobacco smoke affect the body?

- Why is using smokeless tobacco harmful to the body?

SKILLS

- Activity: Making a Smoking Machine

Figure 20-4 *Which of these chemicals in tobacco smoke did you know are poisonous?*

Harmful Chemicals in Tobacco Smoke

acetaldehyde	hydrocyanic acid
acetone	hydrogen cyanide
acetonitrile	
acrolein`	hydrogen sulfide
acrylonitrile	methacrolein
ammonia	methyl alcohol
aniline	methylamine
benzene	methylfuran
benzopyrene	methylnaph- thalene
2,3 butadione	nicotine
butylamine	nitric oxide
carbon monoxide	nitrogen dioxide
dimethylamine	phenol
dimethyl- nitrosamine	pyridine
ethylamine	toluene
formaldehyde	vinyl chloride

2 TOBACCO AND ITS CHEMICALS

Many first-time tobacco users, especially those who inhale tobacco smoke, experience uncomfortable physical reactions. **The physical reactions to tobacco smoke include a racing heart, dizziness, watery eyes, coughing spells, and nausea.** For some, these effects are enough to convince them to avoid tobacco use. For others, they are not.

The Chemicals in Tobacco Smoke

With each puff on a cigarette, cigar, or pipe, a smoker inhales over 4,000 different chemicals. Of these 4,000 chemicals, at least 1,000 are known to be dangerous. Figure 20-4 lists some of the harmful chemicals found in cigarette smoke. Among all the dangerous substances, nicotine, tar, and carbon monoxide can be identified as the most deadly ones found in tobacco smoke.

NICOTINE AND ADDICTION   The drug in tobacco that may act as a stimulant and cause addiction is **nicotine.** A **stimulan**t is a drug that speeds up the activities of the central nervous system, the heart, and other organs. In its pure form, nicotine is one of the strongest poisons known. Taken in large amounts, nicotine can kill people by paralyzing their breathing muscles. Smokers usually take in small amounts of nicotine. However, over several years the effects on the body of much smaller amounts are numerous and severe.

Figure 20-5 shows how nicotine affects the whole body. When tobacco is smoked, nicotine enters the lungs, where it is immediately absorbed into the bloodstream. Seconds later, the nicotine reaches the brain. Chemical changes begin to take place. Nicotine causes the heart to beat faster, skin temperature to drop, and blood pressure to rise. Nicotine constricts blood vessels, which cuts down on the blood flow to hands and feet. Beginning smokers usually feel the effects of nicotine poisoning with their first inhalation. These effects include rapid pulse, clammy skin, nausea, dizziness, and tingling in the hands and feet.

The degree of reaction varies from person to person, depending on the person's tolerance to nicotine. The effects of nicotine poisoning stop as soon as tolerance to nicotine develops. Tolerance can develop in new smokers after the second or third cigarette. The smoker begins to experience a "lift," a physical reaction to the chemicals in nicotine. As tolerance builds, however, the user may need more and more tobacco to produce the same feeling. The Surgeon General, the country's highest medical authority, has called nicotine an addicting drug, just like heroin and cocaine.

Central Nervous System
- Changes brain-wave patterns

Respiratory System
- Allows harmful gases and particles to settle in air passages
- Causes hacking cough
- Causes shortness of breath

Other Effects
- Decreases release of fluid from pancreas
- Increases levels of sugar, lactic acid, and fat-derived substances in blood

Cardiovascular System
- Increases heart rate
- Increases blood pressure
- Increases volume of blood pumped per beat
- Increases force of heart contractions
- Increases coronary blood flow
- Increases blood flow to skeletal muscles
- Narrows blood vessels in skin
- Narrows veins

Peripheral Nervous System
- Activates sympathetic nervous system
- Decreases response level of some reflexes

Endocrine System
- Stimulates release of several hormones from adrenal glands
- Decreases levels of hormone involved in preventing blood clotting

Figure 20-5 *Nicotine and cigarettes affect many body systems.*

In a short time, tobacco users develop an addiction to nicotine. A tobacco addict who goes without tobacco for a short time may experience nicotine withdrawal. **Nicotine withdrawal** is a reaction to the lack of nicotine in the body, which causes symptoms such as headache, irritability, restlessness, increased coughing, nausea, vomiting, a general feeling of illness, and intense cravings for tobacco. Withdrawal effects may begin as soon as two hours after the last cigarette. Physical craving for a cigarette reaches a peak in the first 24 hours.

Tobacco users also suffer psychological withdrawal symptoms when they stop smoking. They feel emotionally and mentally uncomfortable without tobacco. By using tobacco at certain times—when under stress, for example—tobacco users actually condition themselves to rely on tobacco whenever a stressful situation arises. When tobacco users go without tobacco, they may feel unable to handle stress. Many tobacco users begin to depend on tobacco at particular times of the day, such as when they awaken or after they finish a meal. Others begin to depend on tobacco in social or work situations, such as parties or meetings.

TAR The dark, sticky mixture of chemicals that is formed when tobacco burns is known as **tar.** Smokers can see evidence of this substance on their fingers and teeth, which turn brown when tar sticks to them. The tar also sticks to the cells of the respiratory system, where it damages the delicate cells that line the respiratory tract. The cells have tiny hairlike structures, or cilia. The cilia, shown in Figure 20-6, beat back and forth and sweep dust and other foreign particles away from the lungs. If the cilia are damaged, foreign particles can enter the lungs, leading to disease.

Figure 20-6 *Healthy cilia capture and sweep away foreign particles from the air passages.*

MAKING A SMOKING MACHINE

ACTIVITY

In this activity, you will construct a simple smoking machine that demonstrates the effects of smoking.

Materials

1-L clear plastic soft drink bottle with cap (rinsed and dried)

5–10 cm tubing (about the diameter of a cigarette)

cotton ball

clay

cigarette

nail

safety matches

ash tray

twist tie

Procedure

1. Make a hole in the bottle cap the size of the tubing.

2. Put tubing into the hole, and seal with clay.

3. With the twist tie, attach the cotton ball to the end of the tubing on the underside of the cap. Put the cigarette into the other end of the tubing.

4. Screw the cap on the bottle.

5. Using the nail, poke a hole into the side of the bottle. Be careful never to point the nail toward yourself or others.

6. Force the air out of the bottle by pressing on it firmly. Cover the hole with your thumb.

7. Light the cigarette and pump the bottle slowly and steadily to draw air in through the cigarette.

8. When the bottle fills with air, uncover the hole and force the air out. Cover the hole again before pulling air in through the cigarette.

Discussion

1. What does the cotton ball look like after the smoking test?

2. What does the bottle look like?

3. What do you think cigarette smoke does to a smoker's lungs? Teeth? Throat?

The tar in tobacco smoke contains hundreds of chemical **carcinogens** (kahr SIN uh junz), or cancer-causing agents. Cancer of the lungs, throat, and mouth are caused by the inhalation of tar in tobacco smoke.

CARBON MONOXIDE   A poisonous, colorless, odorless gas that is found in cigarette smoke is **carbon monoxide.** You may be familiar with the dangers of carbon monoxide. Deaths that result from leaving a car engine running in a closed area are caused by carbon monoxide poisoning.

Carbon monoxide has a greater attraction for the oxygen-carrying molecules (hemoglobin) in the red blood cells than oxygen does. When carbon monoxide is inhaled, it takes the place of, or displaces, large amounts of oxygen from hemoglobin. The more carbon monoxide present in the blood, the less oxygen in the blood. Carbon monoxide also makes it hard for the oxygen that is left in the blood to get to the muscles and organs. When a person smokes, the heart works harder but accomplishes less. Because their blood contains too little oxygen to function properly, smokers often experience shortness of breath when they are active.

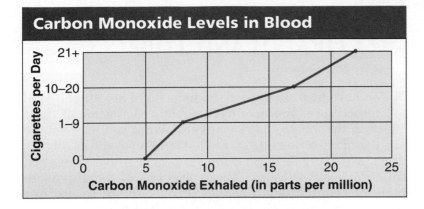

Figure 20-7 *The level of carbon monoxide in the body increases greatly as more cigarettes are smoked.*

Chemicals in Smokeless Tobacco

Most tobacco users smoke cigarettes, cigars, or pipes. And yet there has been an increase, especially among teenage boys, in the use of smokeless tobacco. **Smokeless tobacco** is tobacco that is chewed or sniffed through the nose. Some people who use smokeless tobacco think that the products are safe because no smoke is produced or inhaled. What they may not realize is that smokeless tobacco contains many of the same harmful chemicals found in tobacco smoke, including the highly addictive drug nicotine.

There are two different kinds of smokeless tobacco products. **Chewing tobacco** is poor-quality tobacco leaves mixed with molasses or honey and placed between the cheek and gums. **Snuff** is finely ground tobacco that may be held between the lower lip and teeth or sniffed through the nose. One can of snuff delivers as much nicotine as 60 cigarettes. The nicotine in chewing tobacco enters the bloodstream through the membranes of the mouth. The nicotine in snuff gets into the body through the membranes of either the mouth or the nose. Once it has entered the body, nicotine from smokeless tobacco has the same effects as nicotine from cigarettes.

LESSON 2 REVIEW

1. Name the substance in tobacco that contains cancer-causing chemicals.
2. What are some immediate effects that nicotine has on the body?
3. Describe nicotine withdrawal.
4. Why is smokeless tobacco harmful?

What Do You Think?

5. What facts about tobacco would you use to convince a friend that tobacco use is harmful?

GUIDE FOR READING

Focus on these questions as you read this lesson.

- What are some of the long-term health effects of tobacco use?
- What are some of the dangers of passive smoking?

SKILLS

- Being Assertive

You have just read about the immediate health effects of tobacco use. You may have already seen some of these effects in the tobacco users you know. What you may not see are the more serious diseases that are developing. Tobacco users, especially teenagers, may appear healthy. **However, tobacco users increase their chances of cardiovascular and respiratory diseases, lung cancer, and other forms of cancer each time they use tobacco.**

The Long-Term Effects of Tobacco

Did you know that tobacco products are directly responsible for the deaths of 400,000 Americans each year, or more than 1,000 people a day? Worldwide, smoking-related health problems will kill one in five people. Tobacco use continues despite laws that prohibit television and radio advertisements and the warning labels that all tobacco products are required to carry by the government. The warnings shown in Figure 20-8 list some of the serious diseases that may be caused by tobacco use.

CARDIOVASCULAR DISEASES Cardiovascular diseases, diseases of the heart and blood vessels, kill over 115,000 tobacco users in the United States each year. The following statistics will give you an idea of the cardiovascular problems tobacco users face:

- A smoker is three times more likely to suffer a heart attack than is a nonsmoker.
- A heart attack is five to ten times more likely to kill a smoker than a nonsmoker.

These statistics really are not surprising when you consider the damage that nicotine, tar, and carbon monoxide do

Figure 20-8 *The Surgeon General's warnings on tobacco products caution people about the dangers of tobacco use.*

to the cardiovascular system. These chemicals force the heart to work harder to deliver oxygen to the cells of the body. Blood vessels weaken due to the increased force of the blood pushing against the blood vessels' walls. These conditions lead to high blood pressure. Studies have shown that nicotine promotes the buildup of fatty material on the walls of blood vessels. This buildup increases the chances that a blood vessel near the heart will break or become blocked, resulting in a heart attack. If a blood vessel in the brain breaks or becomes blocked, a stroke may result.

RESPIRATORY DISEASES Many smokers suffer from a dry or hacking cough, one sign of serious damage to the respiratory system. What causes this cough? As tars destroy the cilia that line the respiratory tract, dust, foreign particles, and mucus accumulate in the air passages. Coughing is the body's attempt to clear air passages of this material.

As a person continues to smoke, coughing can no longer keep the air passages clear. Mucus fills the smoker's bronchial tubes, which are the tubes leading from the trachea, or windpipe, to the lungs. In time, chronic bronchitis may develop. **Chronic bronchitis** (brahng KY tis) is a condition in which the bronchial tubes become swollen and clogged with mucus. People with chronic bronchitis find it difficult to fill their lungs with air. Simple activities, such as climbing stairs, may leave people gasping for breath, and they are unable to participate in many sports. There is no cure for chronic bronchitis, but prescription medicines can temporarily open the bronchial tubes to make breathing easier.

Smoking can lead to a more serious disease of the respiratory system called emphysema. **Emphysema** (em fuh SEE muh) is a breathing disorder in which the small air sacs in the lungs lose their ability to expand and contract. Oxygen passes through the air sacs into the bloodstream, while carbon

Figure 20-9 *A person who smokes will become easily winded during strenuous activity.*

Figure 20-10 *A normal lung (left); lung tissue damaged by emphysema (center); lung tissue attacked by cancer (right).*

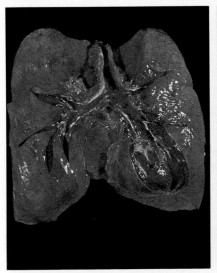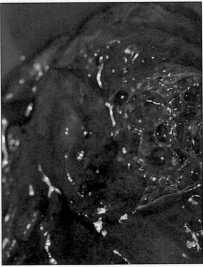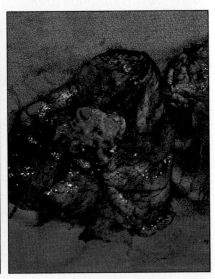

dioxide passes through the air sacs out of the body. When people have emphysema, the air sacs resemble tiny balloons that no amount of puffing will blow up. People with emphysema cannot get enough oxygen into the body or rid the body of carbon dioxide. They are always short of breath. For some, even blowing out a match is difficult. Unfortunately, the damage done to the lungs by emphysema cannot be reversed. Even if an emphysema victim quits smoking, the condition does not improve. Figure 20-10 illustrates how smoking damages the lungs.

CANCER   Tobacco use is also a major factor in the development of certain cancers. Cancer is an area of uncontrolled cell growth that invades the surrounding tissue and destroys it. Cancers can begin anywhere in the body and travel to other parts of the body. In the United States today, lung cancer is the most deadly form of cancer. Scientists estimate that 87 percent of the deaths caused by lung cancer are related to smoking.

Unfortunately, lung cancer is difficult to detect early, when treatment would be most effective. By the time most cases of lung cancer have been detected, successful treatment is impossible. For this reason, lung cancers are often fatal. Yet if no one smoked, there would be few cases of lung cancer.

Lung cancer is now the leading cause of cancer deaths among women in the United States. It is also one of the leading causes of death from cancer among men. As shown in Figure 20-11, cigarette consumption in the United States has started to decline. However, the rate of lung cancer deaths continues to rise. This is because lung cancer caused by smoking takes at least 15 to 20 years to develop.

Tobacco use is also associated with **oral cancers**, or cancers of the mouth, throat, and tongue. At first, hard, white, leathery patches or sores, known as **leukoplakia** (loo koh PLAY kee uh) form on the inside of the mouth. In time, leukoplakia may develop into cancer. Cancers of the mouth and

Figure 20-11 *Despite a decrease in cigarette consumption, lung cancer deaths continue to rise.*

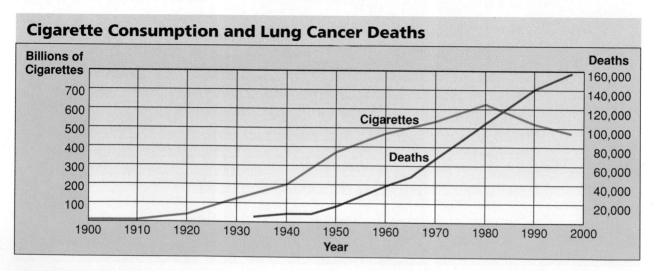

Cigarette Consumption and Lung Cancer Deaths

throat are common in smokers, especially among cigar and pipe users. If a smoker also uses alcohol, the risk of these cancers increases.

Individuals who use smokeless tobacco are at risk of developing oral cancers. Tobacco juices irritate the sensitive tissues of the mouth, lips, and throat, causing sores and leukoplakia. Snuff users and tobacco chewers are three times more likely than smokers to develop mouth sores. Long-term users of smokeless tobacco have a 50 percent greater risk of developing oral cancer than do nonusers.

TOBACCO USE AND PREGNANCY   You may have heard the saying that pregnant women are "eating for two." It also can be said that pregnant women are "breathing for two." Many of the harmful chemicals in tobacco smoke pass directly from the mother to the developing baby. This is why doctors recommend that pregnant women do not smoke. The antitobacco poster in Figure 20-12 is an attempt to discourage pregnant women from smoking.

Tobacco smoke increases the baby's heart rate, reduces its oxygen supply, and slows cell growth. Babies born to mothers who smoke weigh, on average, about six ounces (200 grams) less than the babies of nonsmokers. Women who smoke have higher rates of premature births, miscarriages, and stillbirths than women who do not. The dangers of tobacco smoke continue after the baby is born. When nursing mothers smoke, the nicotine from their cigarettes can pass into their milk and then to the infant.

OTHER PHYSICAL EFFECTS   In general, people who use tobacco are in poorer health than those who do not. Illnesses such as colds, allergies, gum disease, influenza, and pneumonia are more common in tobacco users. Some tobacco users have constant runny noses, sore throats, and headaches. Additional dangers are associated with smokeless tobacco use. Some smokeless tobacco products contain high levels of sodium (salt), which can contribute to high blood pressure. Most smokeless tobacco products contain particles of sand and grit that destroy the surface of the teeth. They also contain sugars, which lead to dental cavities and tooth loss.

Smoking increases an individual's chance of developing an ulcer, or an open sore, in the lining of the stomach or nearby part of the digestive system. Ulcers are difficult to treat in smokers because smoke continually irritates the sores. The use of smokeless tobacco may also aggravate ulcers of the stomach or small intestine.

Fire is another health hazard posed by smoking. Fires caused by careless smokers kill about 3,000 people and injure many thousands of people, both smokers and nonsmokers, each year.

Figure 20-12 *Smoking exposes both the pregnant mother and her developing baby to harmful chemicals.*

Figure 20-13 *Careless smoking causes over 20 percent of the fatal fires in the United States.*

Sidestream Smoke: The Grim Statistics

- As many as 3,000 lung cancer deaths annually are caused by sidestream smoke.
- The concentration of carbon monoxide is 2.5 times higher in sidestream smoke than it is in mainstream smoke.
- Nonsmokers exposed to 20 or more cigarettes a day at home are twice as likely to develop lung cancer as other nonsmokers.
- Nonsmokers married to heavy smokers are two to three times more likely to develop lung cancer than those married to nonsmokers.
- Up to one million existing cases of childhood asthma get worse each year due to passive smoking.
- Passive smoking increases the risk of heart disorders, triggering 35,000 deaths a year.

Figure 20-14 *The effects of sidestream smoke.*

Financial Costs to Society

Estimates of the financial costs of smoking to society range from $50 to $100 billion per year. These costs include smokers and nonsmokers who involuntarily breathe tobacco smoke. Consider these expenses:

- treating tobacco-related diseases
- the loss of earnings from disease and early death
- absenteeism caused by smoking-related illnesses
- fire damage, injury, and death caused by careless smokers
- increased cost of health and fire insurance
- installing special air filters or new air conditioning systems
- lawsuits involving the tobacco industry

Figure 20-15 *Children of smokers have increased risk of colds, coughs, and ear infections.*

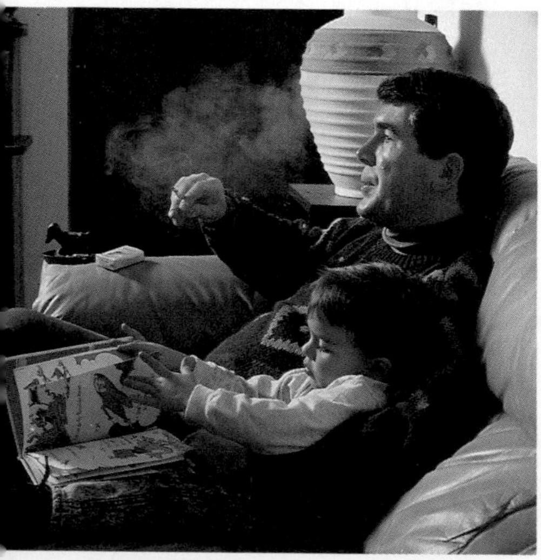

Passive Smoking

Every time a smoker lights up, smoke enters the air from two sources. The first is **mainstream smoke**, which smokers inhale into their lungs and then exhale into the air. The smoker's lungs and the cigarette filter trap much of the matter and chemicals in mainstream smoke. The second is sidestream smoke. **Sidestream smoke** goes directly into the air from burning tobacco. Sidestream smoke has not passed through a smoker's lungs or been changed by a cigarette filter. So, sidestream smoke contains higher concentrations of some harmful chemicals and is more harmful to the passive smoker than is mainstream smoke.

The nonsmokers who involuntarily breathe this sidestream smoke become **passive smokers**. You are a passive smoker whenever you breathe the smoke in the air from other people's cigars, pipes, or cigarettes. Passive smoking can irritate the nose and throat and cause the eyes to burn, itch, and water. What is more significant, however, is that passive smoking is harmful to your health.

DANGERS OF PASSIVE SMOKING   Some studies show that there is twice as much tar and nicotine in sidestream smoke as in mainstream smoke. Studies also show that sidestream smoke contains three times as much carbon monoxide as mainstream smoke. Inhaled sidestream smoke robs the blood of oxygen. Each year, passive smoking contributes to 150,000 to 300,000 cases of bronchitis and pneumonia in babies and triggers 8,000 to 26,000 new cases of asthma in previously unaffected children. In addition, asthma and other allergies are often made worse in the presence of tobacco smoke. In fact, long-term exposure to other people's smoke increases your risk of heart disease and lung cancer. See Figure 20-14 for some statistics on the effects of sidestream smoke. If you are a nonsmoker, how could you be more assertive in telling smokers that you mind when they smoke near you?

AVOIDING PASSIVE SMOKING   Although passive smoking is still a serious problem, great progress is being made to eliminate it. Federal, state, and local laws now prohibit or restrict smoking in public places and public workplaces. Car rental agencies, hotels, and motels continue to reserve more vehicles and rooms for nonsmokers. Smoking is prohibited or restricted in hospitals, other health-care facilities, buses, planes, and trains. Many employers have discovered that prohibiting smoking in the workplace leads to better health among their employees. Most restaurants now have nonsmoking areas. Many health organizations, such as the American Lung Association and the American Cancer Society, as well as private citizens' groups, are continuing to press for more restrictions. As smoking becomes less socially acceptable, smoking in public will become less common. Being able to breathe clean air is a serious issue for everyone.

LESSON 3 REVIEW

1. What are five long-term effects of tobacco?
2. How can smoking lead to a heart attack?
3. Name two respiratory diseases caused by smoking.
4. List three health hazards of passive smoking.

What Do You Think?

5. What would you do if you were a nonsmoker who worked in a smoke-filled area?

Focus on Issues

Can Smokers Be Denied a Job?

Smoking costs the United States about $65 billion dollars each year in health-care costs and lost productivity. That's $262 per American per year!

Employers at some companies are taking steps to prevent or cut costs created by smokers. Some employers screen job applicants and will not hire applicants who smoke.

Employers who support not hiring smokers contend that smokers cost more money to employ than nonsmokers. These employers are unwilling to pay higher rates for smokers' health-care benefits, pay higher health insurance premiums, or absorb a loss in profits from smokers' illness, disease, and early death.

Other people think that what smokers do on their own time is their private business. How can an employer determine that a prospective employee's smoking will prevent him or her from performing on the job? Besides, any employee who is 18 years of age or older uses tobacco legally. Smokers assert that employers violate the basic freedom of right to privacy guaranteed them under the United States Constitution.

☞ **Do you think people should be denied a job if they smoke outside the workplace?**

DIFFERENT VOICES SPEAKING

Barbara Maxcy, 15, lives on the Pauma Reservation, one hour outside San Diego, California. Harold Diaz, also 15, lives nearby on the Pala Reservation. For the past year, the teens have been working as peer counselors, telling other Native American teens about the dangers of tobacco.

Q. Harold, how did you and Barbara get involved in your fight against tobacco?

A. My mom works here at the Indian Health Council. She got me interested in working as a peer counselor. Barbara and I went through orientation together. We naturally became a team because we each have different strengths in reaching young audiences.

Q. What kinds of strengths do you mean?

A. At our presentations, I deal mostly with the hard facts about tobacco, about the diseases that tobacco use can cause, for example. Barbara is more into talking about tobacco's history, about the role it has played in past generations of Native Americans.

Q. Barbara, can you explain a little more about this historical side of tobacco?

A. Yes. Smoking goes back a long way in Native American culture. Our ancestors treated tobacco as a symbol. They smoked the Pipe, you know? The Pipe continues to this day to be used at tribal offerings. This role of tobacco in our culture and history has confused many Native Americans. It has made them fail to understand the health risks involved in lighting up.

Q. Harold, what do you do at your presentations to get the point across about tobacco?

Barbara Maxcy and Harold Diaz

A. Our presentations last anywhere from 45 minutes to an hour. In that time, we show a working model of the mouth, to illustrate how tobacco affects the teeth, tongue, and gums. We give information from the American Cancer Society on lung cancer and other tobacco-related diseases, plus statistics on the number of deaths. Then we show them a video. We also spend time on smokeless tobacco, a big problem for young Native Americans. It starts as early as age eight!

Q. Barbara, do you think you're succeeding in reaching your audience?

A. The older ones—the 18-year-olds—seem to think like the grownups on our reservations, who say, "Hey, I'm going to die anyway." The younger ones, though—the 12-year-olds—do seem to get the message pretty well. I guess that's maybe where our hope for the future is—in the little ones.

Journal Activity

Harold and Barbara ask the listeners at their peer presentations to sign an anti-smoking pledge. In your health journal, write a pledge that contains facts from the chapter to persuade people to quit or never start using tobacco. See how many people you can get to sign your pledge.

4 CHOOSING A HEALTHY LIFESTYLE

GUIDE FOR READING

Focus on these questions as you read this lesson.

- What physical changes occur in the body when a tobacco user quits?
- Describe some steps for quitting smoking.

SKILLS

- Locating Community Resources

Despite the dangers of tobacco use, many people believe that "low tar" and "low nicotine" cigarettes are safer than regular cigarettes. Others believe that flavored bidis, pipes, and cigars are safer than cigarettes, that smokeless tobacco is safe to use, or that herbal cigarettes are a safe alternative to tobacco. An **herbal cigarette** is any cigarette made from plant materials other than tobacco. All of these beliefs are myths, or misconceptions.

Myths can be dangerous when they lead people to behaviors that are harmful. Understanding why myths about tobacco products are untrue can help to prevent a nonuser from trying tobacco. It can also help a tobacco user give up his or her tobacco addiction. Listed below are some of the myths and facts about tobacco use. Can you add other myths and facts to the list?

MYTHS & FACTS

Tobacco

1. **MYTH:** Low tar, low nicotine cigarettes are safer than regular cigarettes.

   ● **FACT:** Smokers of low tar, low nicotine cigarettes inhale the same harmful chemicals as smokers of regular cigarettes. These cigarettes may contain less nicotine and produce less tar than regular cigarettes, but the levels of many chemicals, such as carbon monoxide, are not reduced. In fact, some smokers inhale more deeply or smoke more frequently to reach the nicotine levels to which they are accustomed.

2. **MYTH:** Cigarettes with filters are safe.

   ● **FACT:** Cigarette filters reduce the amount of nicotine inhaled through tobacco smoke. However, the chemicals that are inhaled are the same ones that kill thousands of people a year.

3. **MYTH:** Smoking pipes or cigars is safer than smoking any type of cigarette.

   ● **FACT:** Cigars and pipes produce more tar and other harmful chemicals than cigarettes produce. As a result, pipe and cigar smokers have a high incidence of cancer of the lip, mouth, and throat. Former cigarette smokers who switch to cigars or pipes tend to inhale smoke more deeply than pipe and cigar smokers do; they run the serious risk of developing lung cancer.

4. **MYTH:** Smokeless tobacco is a safe form of tobacco.

   ● **FACT:** Smokeless tobacco contains many of the same harmful chemicals that regular tobacco contains. Studies have shown a definite connection between smokeless tobacco use and a high incidence of diseases, including cancer of the nose, mouth, throat, voice box, and esophagus.

5. **MYTH:** Bidis, the flavored Indian cigarettes, are safer than tobacco cigarettes.

   ● **FACT:** These little cigarettes may taste good, but they're NOT candy. They're made of flaked tobacco and produce more tar and nicotine and three times more carbon monoxide than traditional cigarettes. They're also addictive.

Quitting Tobacco Use

In this country more than 50 million people smoke. But surveys show that as many as nine out of ten want to quit. Quitting tobacco use is not easy; it involves breaking the addiction to nicotine that a user has developed. It also involves breaking many habits associated with smoking. Knowing what the benefits of quitting will be, however, can make the process easier.

BENEFITS The tobacco user who quits can expect many immediate, as well as long-term, benefits. **Immediate benefits of quitting tobacco use include a reduction in blood pressure and a decrease in pulse rate.** In addition, as carbon monoxide levels drop off, oxygen levels in the blood quickly return to normal.

Gradually, the cilia that line air passages begin to grow back and resume their normal functions. Breathing becomes easier as the lungs and air passages begin to clear themselves. The smoker's raspy voice and cough eventually disappear, along with the frequent colds and congestion. The senses of taste and smell become stronger again, and the complexion improves. As the time without tobacco lengthens, the risk of developing some tobacco-related diseases decreases. Figure 20-16 summarizes the changes that occur in a smoker's body after quitting.

Quitting tobacco use also results in psychological benefits. People who have quit usually feel increased confidence in

Figure 20-16 *The health benefits of quitting smoking begin immediately and continue throughout life.*

Changes in a Smoker's Body After Quitting

Within 20 minutes of last cigarette:
- Blood pressure and pulse rate return to normal levels.
- Body temperature of hands and feet increases to normal.

8 hours:
- Carbon monoxide level in blood drops to normal.
- Oxygen level in blood increases to normal.

1 day:
- Chance of heart attack decreases.

2 days:
- Ability to smell and taste improves.

3 days:
- Bronchial tubes relax.
- Lung capacity increases.

2 weeks to 3 months:
- Circulation improves.
- Walking becomes easier.
- Lung function increases up to 30%.

1 to 9 months:
- Coughing, sinus congestion, fatigue, shortness of breath decrease.
- Cilia regrow, increasing ability to handle mucus, thus reducing risk of infection.
- Body's overall energy level increases.

5 years:
- Risk of developing lung cancer or coronary heart disease decreases dramatically.

10 years:
- Precancerous cells are replaced.
- Risk of developing lung cancer is nearly the same as for a nonsmoker.

themselves. They feel that they have gained control over the use of tobacco in their lives rather than allowing the tobacco to control them.

Many people, especially teenage girls, do not give up tobacco because they fear they will gain weight or become irritable when they stop. Although many smokers do have a slight weight gain after they quit, the health benefits of quitting far exceed the problems of a minor weight gain. Exercise helps many former tobacco users to control weight changes after giving up tobacco.

TIPS FOR QUITTING Breaking an addiction to tobacco is not easy, but millions of people have done it. Most people quit on their own. Others attend classes or seek other professional help. Many people who have quit found that quitting abruptly, or going "cold turkey," worked for them. Others quit by gradually reducing their use of tobacco over an extended period of time. No single method works best for everyone. However, smokers who stop using tobacco abruptly experience a shorter nicotine withdrawal period than gradual quitters. Regardless of method, the most important element in successfully quitting is a strong personal commitment to quitting.

If you are a smoker and have tried to quit but have not been successful, do not get discouraged. It only means you did not use a method that works for you. Each time you try, you gain more experience in how to quit, and you improve your chances of success. You will be free of many physical

Figure 20-17 *Substituting positive, healthy behaviors for tobacco use is one way to quit.*

Tips for Quitting Tobacco Use

- Try to quit together with a friend or friends.

- Solicit support from family and friends.

- Remind yourself of the benefits of quitting—physical, mental, financial.

- During the first week, drink milk or water instead of coffee or tea; avoid chocolate.

- Take a warm, not a hot, shower or bath in the morning and at night for the first 4 to 5 days.

- Try doing vigorous exercise to reduce the craving for tobacco.

- Substitute other activities for tobacco. Eat carrot or celery sticks; go for a walk.

- Avoid being around people who are smoking.

- Change the routine associated with the times you use tobacco.

- Use positive coping techniques to relieve stress—exercise, meditation, stretching, deep breathing.

- Put aside money or reward yourself when you do not use tobacco.

- Tell yourself that the sooner you quit the sooner you will feel better.

Figure 20-18 *Much literature is available to help people give up tobacco use.*

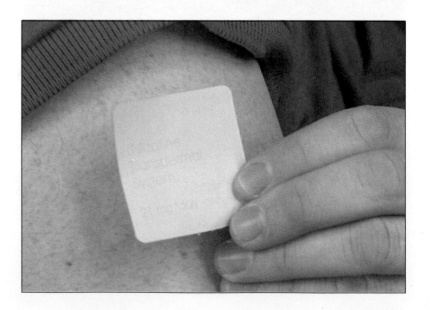

SHARPEN YOUR *SKILLS*

Locating Community Resources

What resources are available to help people in your area stop tobacco use? Compare the services or programs they offer. Which do you think would be most helpful to people your own age who are interested in quitting tobacco use? Suggest ways to share the information with others.

symptoms after three or four days, the length of time nicotine takes to leave your body. Psychological symptoms may continue. Quitting is most difficult within a week or two after the last cigarette. Figure 20-17 offers some basic tips to help you in stopping your use of tobacco. Can you think of other tips that would be helpful?

GETTING HELP Many resources are available to tobacco users who are trying to quit. If you want to quit on your own, you can obtain booklets and pamphlets containing tips and other helpful information from various health organizations. Groups such as the American Lung Association and the American Cancer Society provide written information and speakers for those interested in learning more about quitting tobacco use. If you feel you need professional help, you may want to attend local workshops, classes, or support groups. These groups are often advertised on the radio, in local newspapers, and on community bulletin boards. Local hospitals and other health-care facilities frequently offer programs for helping tobacco users. A doctor also can help you to set up a program or advise you where to get help.

Some tobacco smokers have such a strong physical dependence on nicotine that they seem unable to give up smoking. Two products—nicotine gum and the nicotine patch—may be able to help these tobacco users to quit.

Nicotine gum is a chewing gum containing nicotine that allows a person to quit smoking tobacco without experiencing withdrawal symptoms. Although users of the gum are not smoking, they are still exposed to the harmful effects of nicotine. Nicotine gum is available only with a physician's written prescription.

The **nicotine patch** is also designed to reduce a smoker's craving for cigarettes. Each nicotine patch provides a 24-hour supply of nicotine, which is absorbed through the skin. The

Figure 20-19 *The nicotine patch helps to reduce a person's craving for cigarettes.*

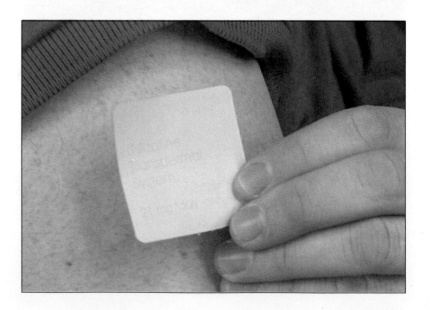

recommended treatment lasts up to three months, during which time the dosage of nicotine is gradually reduced. Some smokers who had not been able to overcome nicotine dependence using other methods have been successful with the nicotine patch. But many physicians warn that users of the patch are trading one addiction for another. Remember that nicotine acts as a stimulant to speed up the heart, increase blood pressure, and promote a fatty buildup on the walls of blood vessels. Early studies show that smokers who continue to smoke while wearing a nicotine patch may be at an even higher risk for heart attacks than smokers who do not use the patch.

Both the gum and the patch are meant to be used as only the first of several steps in a program to break the nicotine addiction completely. Both products carry warning labels that are similar to those on other tobacco products, and neither is recommended for use by pregnant women.

Tobacco-Free Lifestyle

Tobacco is the single most preventable cause of death and illness in the United States. If you have chosen to abstain from tobacco, your decision is reinforced daily by your awareness of how avoiding tobacco enhances the quality of your life. In fact, your example might encourage others to avoid using tobacco. As a nonuser, you are part of the growing majority of teenagers and adults who do not use tobacco.

If you have started using tobacco, you have two options. You can decide to quit, or you can continue to use tobacco and live with the consequences. Deciding to quit tobacco use does not limit your choices—it expands them. Living without tobacco frees you to enjoy the full potential of a healthy body.

Do you think it is possible to have a tobacco-free society? The answer depends on your personal decisions about tobacco and on how strongly you encourage others not to use tobacco.

Figure 20-20 *Teenagers have many healthy alternatives to smoking.*

LESSON **4** REVIEW

1. Why are low tar, low nicotine cigarettes unsafe?
2. What are the risks of smoking pipes or cigars?
3. What are four benefits of quitting the use of tobacco?
4. How can exercise help someone quit using tobacco?
5. How does using nicotine gum and the nicotine patch help smokers to break their dependence on tobacco?

What Do You Think?

6. What would you do to help a friend who is trying to quit using tobacco?

Analyzing Advertising Appeal

In just one year, 1996, tobacco companies spent more than 6 billion dollars on cigarette advertising and promotion. That means they spent the equivalent of almost 18 million dollars every day for an entire year. Why do companies spend so much money on advertising? The purposes of advertising, in general, are to recruit new users for a product, to increase buyers' consumption of a product, and to get buyers to switch brands. In short, advertising increases profits.

The following guidelines will help you to identify the appeal or central message of an advertisement and be better able to resist the pressure of advertising.

Melissa Antonow submitted this poster in a contest among New York City school students for the best smoke-free ad. Melissa's poster has been displayed in subway cars throughout New York City.

Come to where the Cancer is.

Smoking kills more Americans each year than alcohol, cocaine, crack, heroin, homicide, suicide, car accidents, fires, and AIDS combined.

1. Describe the advertising techniques used to sell the product

A variety of techniques are used to attract your attention and to sell products. The techniques include:

- **humor**, so you'll associate the product with fun or feeling good

- **attractive models** that imply that you will be more attractive if you use their product

- a **positive image** that shows strength or independence or success and implies that you need the product to have these attributes

- a **bandwagon approach** that tells you that everybody else is using it so you'll want to "jump on the bandwagon" too

- **appeals to the senses** using beautiful images or colors that associate the product with good feelings

- **slogans, jingles, and catchy phrases** that help you remember the product

- **endorsements or testimonials** made by entertainers, athletes, or other celebrities that make claims about the product's effectiveness

- **price appeals** that imply the product gives you more for your money

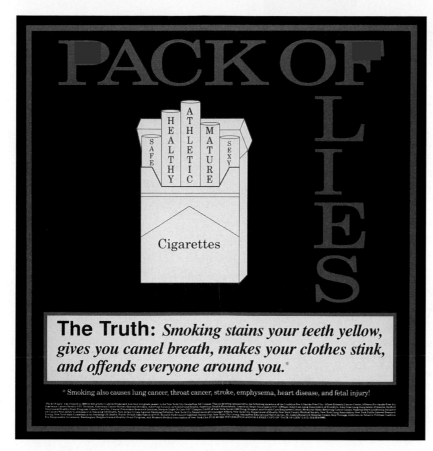

"Pack of Lies" poster is one of the winners in the Smokefree Educational Services counteradvertising poster contest.

1. Look in different kinds of magazines that are aimed at different groups of people. For example, look in women's magazines, men's magazines, general magazines, and magazines for young people or college students.

Collect at least five different cigarette ads from these magazines. Choose three ads that are most different from one another to analyze for their appeal. For each ad, describe the audience, setting, techniques, messages, and information given as well as what is not being said in the ads. Choose the ad that most appeals to you and determine why.

2. Work in a small group and compare ads. Identify the most common themes or messages in cigarette ads. Determine if there are different themes for different target audiences.

3. Use one or more of the advertising techniques described here to create an antitobacco poster.

2. Identify the message of the ad

• Does the ad promise that using the product makes you more successful?

• Does the ad emphasize that using the product will make you more independent and stand out from the crowd?

• Does the ad imply that using the product will make you more attractive and bring you friends, and possibly romance?

• Or does the ad imply that using the product makes other activities more fun?

3. Identify which ads appeal to you most, and why

• Identify the audience for which the ads are targeted. Notice what kind of people are shown in the ads.

• Describe the setting in which the ad's action takes place. Is it at a sporting event or by a waterfall? What are the people in the ad doing?

• Describe the specific information given about the product's features or benefits.

• Identify what is not being said about the product that might be important in making a decision to try it or not.

CHAPTER 20 REVIEW

KEY IDEAS

LESSON 1

- People are influenced not to use tobacco by knowing about the dangers of tobacco use and by family members, friends, and the media.
- People start to use tobacco because of pressure from family members, friends, and the media.

LESSON 2

- Nicotine, tar, and carbon monoxide are the most deadly substances found in tobacco smoke.
- Smokeless tobacco contains many of the same harmful chemicals found in regular tobacco, including nicotine.

LESSON 3

- Long-term effects of tobacco use include cardiovascular diseases, respiratory diseases, cancer, ulcers, and tooth loss.
- Passive smokers face the same health risks as smokers.

LESSON 4

- Quitting the use of tobacco requires a strong personal desire to quit. Support from family, friends, and programs offered by professionals assist users who are trying to quit.
- Those who quit using tobacco can expect to look and feel better and to reduce dramatically their chances of developing a tobacco-related disease.

KEY TERMS

LESSON 2
carbon monoxide
carcinogen
chewing tobacco
nicotine
nicotine withdrawal
smokeless tobacco
snuff
stimulant
tar

LESSON 3
chronic bronchitis
emphysema
leukoplakia
mainstream smoke
oral cancer
passive smokers
sidestream smoke

LESSON 4
herbal cigarette
nicotine gum
nicotine patch

Listed above are some of the important terms in this chapter. Choose the term from the list that best matches each phrase below.

1. anything that causes cancer

2. the drug in tobacco that acts as a stimulant and causes addiction

3. a cigarette made from plant material other than tobacco

4. chewing tobacco and snuff

5. a condition in which the bronchi swell and clog with mucus

6. involuntary smokers

7. the leathery white patches or sores caused by the use of chewing tobacco

8. the dark, sticky mixture of chemicals formed by burning tobacco

9. smoke that goes directly into the air from burning tobacco

10. tobacco substitute worn on the skin

11. a breathing disorder in which the air sacs lose their ability to expand and contract

WHAT HAVE YOU LEARNED?

Choose the letter of the answer that best completes each statement.

12. When a person's body becomes dependent on nicotine to function normally, the person experiences

a. tolerance **c.** nicotine poisoning
b. addiction **d.** withdrawal

13. The poisonous, colorless, odorless gas in cigarette smoke is

a. oxygen **c.** carbon monoxide
b. carbon dioxide **d.** nitric oxide

14. A tobacco product made from poor-quality tobacco leaves is

a. snuff **c.** cigarettes
b. chewing tobacco **d.** cigars

15. Uncontrolled cell growth that invades tissues and destroys them is called

a. emphysema **c.** an ulcer
b. chronic bronchitis **d.** cancer

16. Smoke that a smoker inhales, then exhales, into the air is called

a. smog **c.** mainstream smoke
b. passive smoke **d.** sidestream smoke

17. A product that may help smokers quit tobacco use without nicotine withdrawal is

a. herbal cigarette **c.** chewing gum
b. nicotine patch **d.** snuff

Answer each of the following with complete sentences.

18. Why does smoking during pregnancy affect a developing baby?

19. What is the most important factor for a person trying to quit smoking?

20. What problems are caused by the use of smokeless tobacco?

21. How does cigarette smoke affect a smoker's air passages?

22. Name the symptoms of nicotine poisoning. Why does it occur?

23. Describe the kinds of cancer that have been linked to tobacco use.

WHAT DO YOU THINK?

24. Why do you think some baseball players use chewing tobacco? How might an athlete's use of chewing tobacco influence young baseball fans?

25. Do you think there should be more or fewer restrictions on the advertising and sale of tobacco products? Explain.

26. Why do you think the number of female smokers has increased over the past decade?

27. What do you think are the most effective ways to protect nonsmokers from the effects of sidestream smoke? Explain.

28. What would you suggest to an ex-smoker to help him or her not resume smoking?

WHAT WOULD YOU DO?

29. You and two smoking friends have just arrived at a restaurant for dinner. Your friends want to sit in the smoking section. You are a nonsmoker and prefer to sit in a nonsmoking section. How do you handle the situation?

30. Your community is considering a law that bans smoking in public buildings. What arguments could be used for or against such laws?

31. You are selling advertisements for a school paper, and a tobacco shop wants to buy space for an ad. Would you accept the ad? Why or why not?

Getting Involved

32. Interview some people who have quit smoking. Ask them how they stopped smoking, how difficult it was, and how their lives have changed. Write a report on your findings.

33. Calculate the cost of smoking one pack of cigarettes a day for one week, one month, and one year. Share your findings with your class.

PREVENTING DRUG ABUSE

After 30 hours of training as a peer leader, this teenager is sharing facts about the dangers of drug abuse with her classmates. Being informed about the dangers of drugs makes it easier to refuse them. In this chapter, you will learn how drugs affect the body and how you can live a drug-free life.

CHAPTER PREVIEW

21-1 Legal and Illegal Drugs

- Differentiate between legal and illegal drugs and explain how psychoactive drugs affect the body.

21-2 Risk Factors and Drug Abuse

- Identify various factors that contribute to the risk of drug abuse among teenagers.

21-3 Commonly Abused Drugs

- Describe how drugs work, what their side effects are, and how they are commonly abused.

21-4 Choosing to Be Drug Free

- Explain how to treat drug abuse and addiction and describe healthy alternatives to drug abuse.

BUILDING HEALTH SKILLS

- Develop strategies to intervene to help a drug-dependent friend.

CHECK YOUR WELLNESS

See if you can answer *yes* to the following questions about drug use.

- Do you avoid using drugs, such as steroids or diet pills, instead of changing your eating and exercise habits?

- Do you avoid situations where you think illegal drugs might be used?

- Do you exercise or use other techniques to reduce stress in your life?

- Do you try to solve your problems in healthy, constructive ways?

- Have you thought about or practiced refusing an offer of illegal drugs?

- Would you recognize the signs of drug dependency in a friend and know where to get help?

KEEPING A JOURNAL

Daily, you receive information from television, radio, or newspapers about refusing drugs. For one week, keep a journal in which you describe the information that you see or hear about the dangers of drug abuse.

LEGAL AND ILLEGAL DRUGS

GUIDE FOR READING

Focus on these questions as you read this lesson.

- How do prescription, over-the-counter, and illegal drugs differ?

- How do psychoactive drugs affect the body and why is their abuse dangerous?

SKILLS

- Finding the Facts

Figure 21-1 *Most drugs are manufactured for medical purposes.*

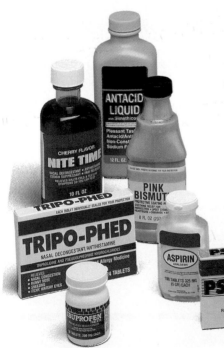

D rug use is part of life in the United States. Every year, physicians write countless prescriptions and consumers spend millions of dollars on nonprescription drugs. When taken as directed, prescription and nonprescription drugs treat many illnesses effectively. However, if drugs are not used as directed, health problems can result. The improper use of drugs is called **drug misuse**. Examples of drug misuse include taking more than the prescribed amount, taking drugs with the wrong foods or at the wrong time of day, and not taking them for the correct period of time.

Types of Drugs

Medicines are legal drugs that help the body fight injury, illness, and disease. Medicines can be classified into two groups of legal drugs: over-the-counter drugs and prescription drugs. **Over-the-counter drugs** may be purchased legally in pharmacies and other stores that sell medicines without a physician's prescription. Over-the-counter drugs include pain relievers such as aspirin, cold and cough remedies, and sleep aids. Any over-the-counter drug has the potential of being harmful if the label instructions are not followed.

Prescription drugs must be obtained through a written prescription from a physician and can be purchased only at a pharmacy. Prescription drugs require more government control than over-the-counter drugs because of their potential harm. A physician determines the correct amount for an individual patient at the time a prescription is written. Taking someone else's prescription can be dangerous and illegal.

Drug abuse occurs when people intentionally misuse any kind of drugs for nonmedical purposes. **Prescription and over-the-counter drugs are legal; however, illegal drugs are chemicals that are unlawful because their dangerous and often unpredictable effects outweigh any useful purposes the drugs may have.** The use, misuse, and abuse of legal and illegal drugs will be discussed in this chapter.

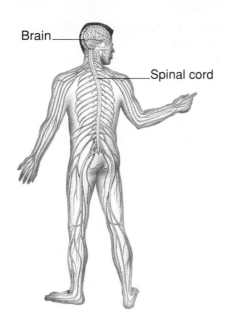

Brain

Spinal cord

Psychoactive Drugs

Recall from Chapter 19 that a drug is any chemical that causes changes in a person's body or behavior. As you can see in Figure 21-2, the central nervous system consists of the brain and spinal cord. This system coordinates all of your thoughts, actions, and body functions. **Psychoactive drugs** (sy koh AK tiv) are chemicals that affect the activity of brain cells to alter perception, thought, and mood, and possibly to create illusions in the mind of the user.

Psychoactive drugs include stimulants, depressants, hallucinogens, inhalants, alcohol, and chemical compounds from the marijuana plant. People who wish to alter their feelings or moods often abuse psychoactive drugs. For this reason, psychoactive drugs are also called mood-altering drugs. Some psychoactive drugs have positive medical benefits when used in controlled situations. For example, physicians use morphine to control severe pain caused by injury and illness.

Dangers of Drug Abuse

Psychoactive drugs can produce powerful changes in the body. Although a few of these changes are medically useful, most are harmful. Abusing drugs subjects the user to these harmful changes. For this reason, drug abuse is dangerous.

SIDE EFFECTS   What a drug does to your body is called the **drug's action**. What you feel is the **drug's effect,** or the physical and mental response to the drug's actions. When use is controlled, the effects of most drugs are predictable or known. Whereas a drug's effect may help you feel better, drugs can also produce side effects. **Side effects** are unwanted, even dangerous, physical and mental effects caused by a drug, such as nausea, dizziness, or drowsiness. Since each person's body is unique, side effects can occur with any drug. This is particularly true of psychoactive drugs that are unregulated or self-administered.

Psychoactive drugs can produce various side effects that range from uncomfortable to dangerous to life-threatening. For example, some athletes abuse stimulants to improve their athletic performance. However, stimulants can also produce side effects such as headaches, dizziness, tremors, and irregular heartbeat.

When a drug is repeatedly used, the body may develop resistance, or tolerance, to the drug. The tolerance causes the user to need increasingly larger amounts of the drug to achieve the desired effect. Abusers of psychoactive drugs can also develop tolerance. As an abuser takes more and more of some psychoactive drugs, the risk for overdose increases. **Overdose** is a serious reaction to an excessive amount of a drug. An overdose can result in coma or death.

ADDICTION AND WITHDRAWAL Abuse of psychoactive drugs often results in dependence or addiction. An addicted person's body becomes adjusted to the drug and requires that drug to function normally. If a person who is addicted to a psychoactive drug stops taking the drug, that person will experience withdrawal symptoms. These symptoms are the body's way of reacting to not having the drug. Withdrawal symptoms include nausea, vomiting, fever, headaches, dizziness, body aches, cramps, and seizures. During treatment for drug addiction, the drug must be withdrawn slowly. In this way, the addicted person's body is not shocked by the abrupt absence of the drug.

The major psychological symptom of addiction is a strong emotional desire or need to continue using a drug. A person

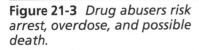

Figure 21-3 *Drug abusers risk arrest, overdose, and possible death.*

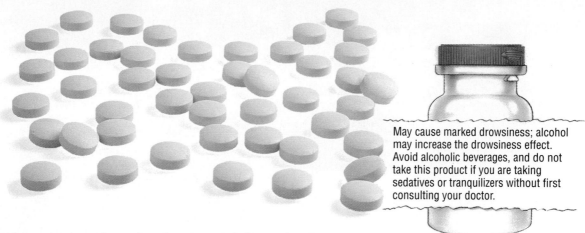

May cause marked drowsiness; alcohol may increase the drowsiness effect. Avoid alcoholic beverages, and do not take this product if you are taking sedatives or tranquilizers without first consulting your doctor.

Figure 21-4 *Drug labels warn of possible side effects and precautions you need to take.*

addicted to some psychoactive drugs may believe that he or she can stop using the drug at any time. However, stopping drug abuse is not easy once a person has become dependent. Even though the person may not experience physical withdrawal symptoms, he or she will have a strong, continued need to experience the drug's effect.

DRUG INTERACTIONS   Many psychoactive drug abusers take more than one drug at a time. Sometimes this is accidental; the abuser forgets about taking one of the drugs. Often, however, abusers intentionally combine drugs to either increase or decrease the effects of the drugs.

Drugs can interact, or change each other's effect, when they are taken together. When drugs are combined, a number of interactions may occur. An **antagonistic interaction** (an tag uh NIS tik) occurs when each drug's effect is canceled out by the other or the action of each drug is reduced. Neither drug has the predicted effect. For example, people taking drugs to lower their blood pressure are warned not to use tobacco, because the nicotine will have an antagonistic interaction with their medication. The nicotine may cancel out the beneficial effect of the blood-pressure medication because nicotine causes a rise in blood pressure.

Another type of interaction occurs when certain drugs taken together combine their actions. If the drugs interact to produce effects greater than those that each drug would produce alone, a **synergistic interaction** (sin ur JIS tik) occurs. A synergistic interaction can be life-threatening when it causes drastic changes in the body. For example, people may take sleeping pills, which depress the central nervous system. If they drink alcohol and take high doses of sleeping pills, the effects of both drugs are more than doubled and can lead to coma or death.

Drug interactions are common when people use illegal drugs. Individuals who sell illegal drugs often mix them with less expensive substances. In many cases, the user does not know what other substances have been added. These substances can be harmful in themselves, or they might interact with other drugs taken, causing harmful effects.

Preventing Drug Abuse   **497**

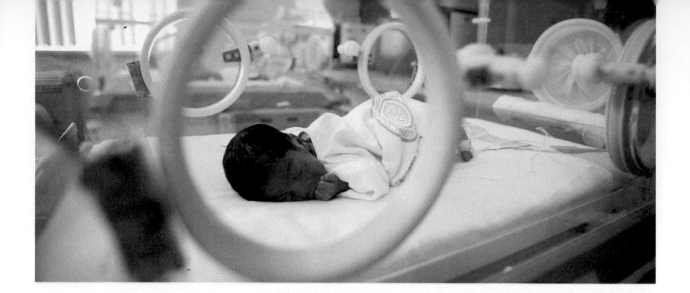

Figure 21-5 *This baby's mother was addicted to "crack" cocaine, so the baby was born addicted also.*

Figure 21-6 *Pregnant women should avoid taking any drug unless prescribed or recommended by a physician.*

AIDS AND HEPATITIS   Anyone who shares needles to inject drugs is at risk for contracting hepatitis B, hepatitis C, and HIV infection, the virus that causes AIDS. Hepatitis infects the liver. About 10 percent of drug users develop chronic hepatitis, a serious infection that causes severe and often fatal damage to the liver. HIV negatively affects the body's immune system. Persons with AIDS cannot fight off illnesses that usually are not a threat to persons with healthy immune systems.

HIV and hepatitis B and C can be transmitted through the exchange of body fluids, including blood. When intravenous drug abusers share needles, small amounts of blood contaminated with hepatitis or HIV left in the needle can carry the viruses from user to user. These infections can also be transmitted from infected intravenous drug users to their sexual partners. Pregnant women may pass them to their children before or during childbirth.

RISKS TO UNBORN CHILDREN AND NEWBORNS
Medical research has proven that the use of psychoactive drugs by a pregnant woman places her baby at high risk for developing physical and mental problems. Psychoactive drugs cross the membrane separating the baby's blood and the mother's blood. So when a pregnant woman uses psychoactive drugs, her unborn child is also exposed to the drugs.

Psychoactive drugs can also pass into a mother's breast milk. When the baby nurses, it is exposed to the drugs. Therefore, to safeguard the health of her baby, a nursing mother must abstain from psychoactive drug use.

EFFECTS ON FAMILY AND FRIENDS   When a family member abuses drugs, the entire family suffers. Relationships within the family become strained as the behavior and personality of the abuser change. An abuser often behaves unpredictably. He or she may have wild mood swings or become withdrawn and uninterested in family relationships and responsibilities. Other family members may experience anger, fear, resentment, or frustration, particularly when they are not aware that drugs are the cause of the abuser's abnormal behavior. If the drug abuse continues, the family can reach a crisis as members struggle to cope with the building stress. Friends also experience the effects of the abuser's changed behavior and personality. These changes can place a strain on the friendship. The interests and activities that the friends once shared may no longer exist. Often, friends drift apart.

LEGAL RISKS Federal and state governments and most local governments have laws dealing with drug abuse. The penalties for individuals who produce, possess, transport, or sell illegal drugs include long prison terms and heavy fines. Even when a fine or jail term is not imposed, the individual is put on record as a drug violator. Such a criminal record makes it difficult to get a job or to be admitted into schools and the military. In addition, many drug abusers commit other crimes, such as shoplifting and robbery, to support their drug addiction. The legal penalties for these drug-related crimes include fines and imprisonment.

COSTS TO SOCIETY Since the early 1980s, the United States government has spent billions of dollars in efforts to stop illegal drug manufacture, sale, and abuse. Many of these efforts have been unsuccessful because the profits to be made in illegal drug manufacture and sale encourage risk taking.

Significant financial resources also go toward drug prevention, education, treatment, and rehabilitation programs. These programs provide hope for many drug abusers. However, the demand for these programs often exceeds the supply. More financial resources are needed to meet the demand for such programs.

SHARPEN YOUR SKILLS

Finding the Facts

What are some of the penalties for illegal drug-associated activities in your state? You may be able to find out by calling or writing the local law-enforcement public relations office. Prepare a chart that summarizes your findings.

LESSON 1 REVIEW

1. What is the difference between an illegal drug and a prescription drug?
2. What is a psychoactive drug?
3. How is a drug's side effect different from the drug's effect?
4. List five dangers of drug abuse.

What Do You Think?

5. Do you think that spending large numbers of tax dollars on drug prevention, education, treatment, and rehabilitation programs is worthwhile? Why or why not?

Focus on this question as you read this lesson.

• What are some of the risk factors that contribute to teenage drug abuse?

SKILLS

• Coping with Change

2 RISK FACTORS AND DRUG ABUSE

Why do some people abuse drugs? Some people turn to drugs as a way of coping with life's problems and stresses. Other people attempt to improve their mental or physical abilities with drugs. Still others use drugs to try to feel good or get "high." Unfortunately, a drug's desired effects are often followed by its unpleasant, harmful side effects.

Risk Factors

Some teenagers who have difficulty coping turn to drugs. **Three major types of factors contribute to the risk of drug abuse among teenagers: family factors, social factors, and personal factors.** You will learn some healthy alternatives to drug abuse in Lesson 4.

FAMILY FACTORS   One of the risk factors for teenage drug abuse is poor family relationships. If teenagers have good relationships with their families, they can learn to deal with life's problems and stresses. In a close, supportive relationship, the teen will be able to confide in parents or siblings and find the guidance needed to cope.

However, if family relationships are not close and supportive, the teenager may not get needed guidance. The teen may feel alienated from the family. This alienation may cause the teen to feel closer to peers, and therefore more vulnerable to the influence of peers who abuse drugs.

Figure 21-7 *Family attitudes and behaviors influence how teens solve problems or relieve stress.*

Figure 21-8 *One way of avoiding drug use is choosing friends who choose healthy activities instead of drugs.*

SOCIAL FACTORS   Peer pressure is one of the factors that contributes to drug abuse in teenagers. Most teens who have tried drugs were introduced to them by their friends or peers. They may have initially tried drugs because they were curious. Some continue to abuse drugs because they want to be "part of the crowd" or be accepted by friends who abuse drugs.

Mike is a 15-year-old high school student who has smoked marijuana almost every day for two years. Mike was introduced to marijuana by some of his friends and continues to use it in order to be accepted by them. Mike says that he can stop using marijuana at any time, although he has yet to try. Mike may not realize that regular use of marijuana often results in a strong emotional need to continue smoking it.

PERSONAL FACTORS   Stress, low self-esteem, and lack of confidence are personal factors that can place a teen at risk for drug abuse. From time to time, most teenagers experience stress. Stress may occur as a result of a death of a friend or family member, a change in an important relationship, an illness, or an academic or social problem. Some of the symptoms of stress are nervousness, inability to concentrate or sleep, irritability, and depression.

Sometimes teenagers turn to drugs to decrease or avoid the negative feelings and symptoms associated with stress. However, abusing drugs will not decrease the underlying causes of stress. Drug abuse ultimately makes life more stressful. Stress and negative feelings are a normal part of life. With the proper guidance and advice from positive adult or peer role models, teens can learn techniques for managing stress and negative feelings.

Talia broke up with Chad after they had dated for two years. Chad kept to himself and pretended the breakup with Talia did not bother him. Chad never really dealt with the sadness over the loss of his girlfriend. Eventually, Chad began to feel depressed; he couldn't sleep very well. Several of his classmates encouraged Chad to get "high" so that he would get out of his slump.

SHARPEN YOUR *SKILLS*

Coping with Change

Often changes such as a long-distance move, a death, or a divorce in the family cause stress. Devise some healthy coping strategies to use if these changes occur. Make a list that describes your coping strategies; then share your list with classmates.

Perhaps if Chad had been able to talk about his sadness and deal with the breakup of his relationship with Talia, he would not have felt a need to deal with his negative feelings by getting high. Strong social ties and supports can act as powerful buffers, cushioning the negative effects of stress.

Another risk factor for drug abuse is the desire by some teenagers to change their body image or to excel at school athletics. These teens often think that their popularity will increase if they are outstanding athletes. Some athletes abuse anabolic steroids, synthetic drugs that build up protein tissue in the body. Abusers use steroids to boost muscle size and make their bodies stronger.

Other athletes believe that the use of psychoactive drugs such as amphetamines, or "speed," will help them concentrate on the game. They may hope that amphetamines will give them extra energy. Still other athletes think that using narcotics, or "pain pills," will enable them to continue performing even after they have been injured.

Peggy is a 16-year-old high school athlete who sprained her ankle before the volleyball team try-outs. She wanted to try out, but her ankle hurt a lot. A friend offered Peggy some "pain pills" and told her that professional athletes take painkillers all the time.

Peggy's friend is wrong. Although most professional and amateur athletes consult their physicians or trainers about aching muscles, sprains, or other complaints, only a few athletes use drugs unwisely. Athletes who use painkillers during competition are likely to sustain more serious injuries that can end their careers. Those who abuse drugs to increase their abilities may face lifelong or life-threatening disorders. For these reasons, organizers of athletic events forbid athletes to use drugs before or during competition.

LESSON 2 REVIEW

1. What three types of risk factors are related to drug abuse?
2. Explain how peer pressure contributes to teenage drug abuse.
3. How do good family relationships help teens avoid drug abuse?
4. Name three personal factors that can place a teenager at risk for drug abuse.

What Do You Think?

5. What advice would you give a friend who is using illegal drugs to help cope with negative feelings?

DIFFERENT VOICES SPEAKING

Melissa Saunders, 17, is a senior at Oldham County High School, Kentucky, which has been named a drug-free school by the U.S. Department of Education. Melissa lives with her mother, stepfather and sister.

Q. Melissa, how did your school become drug free?

A. The solution for us was that everyone in the community became involved. It wasn't just a few teachers or counselors looking over the kids' shoulders. Instead it was everyone—teachers, parents, students—agreeing that there was a problem and joining forces to tackle it.

Q. Did you play a role in your school's drug-free image?

A. To an extent, I think I did. For a long time we had a chapter of an organization that urges young people not to drink and drive. I felt that gave a mixed message—that it implied it was OK for teens to drink as long as they didn't drive. I wanted to change that message. So, I got the support of the principal and student affairs coordinator to organize a chapter of an organization that's similar but that takes a hard "no-use" stance. Then I enlisted the help of 15 other students and together we began recruiting people.

Q. It appears, then, that you don't believe a person needs drugs to have a good time.

A. Absolutely not! My friends and I all share a common bond, and that is that we don't feel any temptation to "party hardy" with things like crack or marijuana or beer. Instead we get a lot of people together and go to the movies or golfing. Sometimes we go to the park and play volleyball or basketball.

Melissa Saunders

Q. Do you have any other school involvement?

A. Yes. As Senior Class President, I'm in charge of planning and delegating responsibilities for different school events. Right now, for example, we're working on homecoming, which is a week-long celebration.

Q. With such a busy schedule, do you feel stress?

A. Occasionally I do, but I've found ways of handling it. I find that just writing about my feelings helps. Talking through what I'm feeling with a friend or one of my parents also works for me.

Q. What advice do you have for other teens?

A. I have two pieces of advice. The first is to go after what you want, not to sit back and wait for it to happen. Second, I've come to realize that people who use drugs are in search of something. My advice would be to search in other areas. You won't find what you're looking for in drugs.

Journal Activity

Divide a page of your health journal into two columns. In one column identify different moods and occasions, such as *happiness, loneliness,* and *need to celebrate.* In the second column write three alternatives to using drugs for each mood or occasion.

Drugs are categorized according to their actions and effects. **Depending on the category, drugs may depress or stimulate body processes, or they may alter perception, mood, and thought.** Many commonly abused psychoactive drugs have little, if any, medical value. Figure 21-14 on pages 508–509 lists some psychoactive drugs and their effects.

Depressants

Psychoactive drugs that slow brain and body reactions are called **depressants.** Depressants slow down heart and breathing rates, lower blood pressure, relax muscles, and relieve tension. Sedatives, anti-anxiety drugs, and narcotics are types of depressants. Physicians sometimes prescribe depressants to relieve stress and pain and to treat sleep disturbances. However, depressants also have mood-altering effects. Depressant abusers experience various short-term and long-term side effects and withdrawal symptoms.

SEDATIVES AND ANTI-ANXIETY DRUGS   Sedative-hypnotics are depressants that relax a person and induce sleep. **Barbiturates** (bahr BICH ur its) are a type of sedative-hypnotic. In small doses, barbiturates are sedatives—they relax a person. In high doses, barbiturates are hypnotics—they induce sleep. Today, physicians rarely prescribe barbiturates for people suffering from sleep disturbances. Physicians may prescribe barbiturates for treating seizures and preparing people for some types of surgery.

Figure 21-9 *Many drug abusers start to take drugs to escape from problems. However, drugs do not solve problems and usually lead to worse problems.*

Barbiturate abuse produces dependence. Abusers often develop tolerance to barbiturates quickly. They need to take larger and larger doses to get the desired sedative or hypnotic effect. As tolerance increases, an abuser's body begins to slow down. Barbiturate abusers walk slowly, slur their speech, and react more slowly to their environment.

Tranquilizers (TRANG kwuh lyz urz), also known as anti-anxiety drugs, slow nerve activity, relax muscle tension, lower alertness, and cause drowsiness. Physicians commonly prescribe tranquilizers to treat anxiety, sleeping disorders, muscle spasms, and convulsions. For medical use, tranquilizers have generally replaced barbiturates, which have a greater potential for abuse. However, when tranquilizers are abused, dependence and tolerance can occur.

NARCOTICS   A **narcotic** is any depressant drug made from or chemically similar to opium. **Opium** is a drug obtained from the seed pod of a poppy plant. **Morphine** (MAWR feen) and **codeine** (KOH deen) are natural narcotic compounds that are contained in opium.

Narcotics in small doses act to dull the senses, relieve pain, and induce sleep. Morphine and codeine, for example, are used in prescription medications to help reduce severe pain. Some prescription cough medicines contain codeine, which acts to suppress coughing. Both morphine and codeine can produce tolerance and lead to dependence. Although morphine is the stronger of the two, both drugs cause the user to lose appetite and feel drowsy. Figure 21-14 lists some other short-term effects of narcotics.

One of the most frequently abused narcotics in the United States is heroin. **Heroin,** which is usually injected, is a narcotic made from morphine in a laboratory. Heroin use creates a sense of well-being by dulling the senses. Abusers can ignore pain and fear; they may appear dazed. Dependence develops quickly, sometimes after only days of regular use. Withdrawal symptoms include sweating, shaking, chills, nausea, and cramps. Heroin abusers who share needles can become infected with HIV and hepatitis B and C.

Heroin addicts are always at risk of overdose. If they combine heroin with other depressants, the risk increases. An overdose can cause loss of consciousness, coma, and death. Dealers often "cut," or dilute, the drugs by adding other substances, so the purity of the drug is different each time. Some common additives are other mood-altering drugs, powdered laxatives, sugar, quinine, cleansing powder, or rat poison. The cutting substance may contribute to an overdose.

Stimulants

Drugs that speed up activities of the central nervous system are called **stimulants**. These drugs increase heart rate, blood pressure, and breathing rate. Stimulants make the

Figure 21-10 *The seed pod of the opium poppy plant is the source of many narcotics.*

Figure 21-11 *Cocaine is derived from the leaves of the South American coca shrub.*

and alert. Physicians sometimes prescribe stimulants to treat sleep disorders and childhood behavioral disorders.

With most stimulants, an abuser develops dependence as well as tolerance. Short-term and long-term side effects and withdrawal symptoms of stimulant abuse are provided in Figure 21-14.

AMPHETAMINES   A powerful prescription drug that is made artificially is **amphetamine** (am FET uh meen). This stimulant produces feelings of well being and high energy. However, the effect wears off, quickly leaving the user depressed. The "down" often leads to taking another—and another—dose. The result may be drug dependence.

A related, but even more powerful drug is methamphetamine, which has many names: "meth," "speed," "crank," "ice," "glass," or "crystal." "Meth" can make the user feel great, or it can make the user confused, shaky, anxious, irritable, or violent. It can also cause strokes and deadly convulsions.

COCAINE   A powerful but short-acting stimulant that affects the central nervous system is **cocaine.** Physicians sometimes prescribe cocaine as a local pain medication. However, cocaine is often sold illegally to those who abuse it for its stimulant effects. Cocaine abusers sniff the drug into the nose or inject it into their bloodstream.

Cocaine is highly addictive. Tolerance develops rapidly, causing abusers to need larger and larger amounts. When the effects wear off, the abuser often experiences a severe depression, also known as a "crash."

An overdose of cocaine, which can be caused by even a small amount, may produce seizures, heart failure, or respiratory failure. A cocaine overdose can be fatal.

A process called "free-basing" changes cocaine into a concentrated, smokable form known as crack. **Crack,** also called "rock," is the most potent form of cocaine. Because of its strength, the short but powerful effects produced by crack occur within eight seconds after it is smoked. These effects lead many people to believe, mistakenly, that crack is purer

Figure 21-12 *People in many communities are speaking out about the dangers of cocaine abuse.*

Figure 21-13 *Mescaline comes from the buttons of the peyote cactus.*

than other forms of cocaine. However, the effects are a result of the free-basing process, not of the drug's purity.

Hallucinogens

Psychoactive drugs that alter perception, thought, and mood are called **hallucinogens** (huh LOO suh nuh junz). Hallucinogens are illegal and have no medical use. Sometimes abusers of hallucinogens cannot tell what is real. Hallucinogens can produce frightening and unpredictable mood swings. Abusers may experience memory loss and personality changes, be unable to perform normal activities, or lose track of time and their surroundings. Tolerance to the mind-altering effects of hallucinogens develops after several doses.

LSD   The strongest known hallucinogen is lysergic acid diethylamide, or **LSD.** LSD's effects are unpredictable—they can either stimulate or depress the central nervous system. Abusers experience hallucinations in which they may see colorful visions and mistakenly feel they have superhuman powers. The drug may also shorten a person's attention span, causing the mind to wander.

LSD can cause unpleasant side effects, such as shaking, nausea, and chills. Also, LSD use can lead to frightening episodes known as "bad trips." Some abusers become so frightened that they fear they are in real danger. LSD has another unpredictable effect called a "flashback." A flashback is an unexpected return to a bad trip that may occur long after the LSD was taken. Flashbacks can happen at any time without warning.

MESCALINE   The psychoactive component of the peyote cactus is called **mescaline** (MES kuh leen). The peyote cactus grows in the southwestern United States and in Mexico. Users of mescaline, like LSD users, see imaginary shapes and colors. These users may experience unpleasant effects as well, including vomiting and stomach cramps.

Some Effects of Psychoactive Drugs

Psychoactive Drug	Short-term Side Effects	Long-term Side Effects	Withdrawal Symptoms
Alcohol	Depression, nausea, decreased alertness	Malnutrition, fetal alcohol syndrome, mental disorders, liver damage, brain damage	Hallucinations, irregular heart rates, disorientation, anxiety, shaking or tremors, nausea, diarrhea, seizures, heart failure
Barbiturates	Poor coordination, slurred speech, decreased alertness	Sleepiness, irritability, confusion	Convulsions, nausea, breathing difficulty, insomnia, hallucinations, tremors, possible death
Tranquilizers	Blurred vision, dizziness, slurred speech, drowsiness, headache, skin rash	Blood and liver disease	Anxiety, nausea, cramps, diarrhea
Narcotics (including opium, codeine, morphine, and heroin)	Nausea, hallucinations, decreased alertness, drowsiness	Constipation, temporary sterility and impotence, convulsions, coma, death	Watery eyes, runny nose, yawning, loss of appetite, irritability, tremors, panic, chills and sweating, cramps, nausea
Marijuana (including hashish)	Panic, anxiety, vomiting	Lung cancer, bronchitis, irritation of respiratory tract, possible fetal damage	Irritability, restlessness, sleep disturbances, weight loss, loss of appetite

Depressants — rows: Alcohol, Barbiturates, Tranquilizers, Narcotics

Marijuana — row: Marijuana

Category	Drug	Short-term effects	Serious or life-threatening effects	Withdrawal symptoms
Hallucinogens	Hallucinogens (including LSD, psilocybin, mescaline, and PCP)	Anxiety, vomiting, panic, impaired memory, irrational thought patterns, hallucinations	Delusions, increased panic, severe changes in behavior, sometimes violent	None
Stimulants	Amphetamines	Restlessness, rapid speech, blurred vision, dizziness	Hyperactivity, irritability, irregular heart rate, liver damage, paranoia	Depression, fatigue, increased appetite, thirst
Stimulants	Cocaine	Loss of appetite, sleep disorders, stillborn births, premature births, birth defects	Depression, paranoia, damage to lining of nose, irritability, weight loss, irregular heart rate, convulsions, respiratory failure, cardiovascular failure, liver damage	Depression, paranoia
Stimulants	Nicotine	Nausea, loss of appetite, headache	Heart and lung disease, difficulty breathing, heavy coughing	Nervousness, irritability, drowsiness, depression, headache, digestive problems
Inhalants	Inhalants	Depression, drowsiness, headaches, nausea, blurred vision	Damage to liver, kidneys, bone marrow, and brain; hallucinations, unconsciousness, fetal defects	Insomnia, decreased appetite, depression, irritability, headache

Figure 21-14 *Psychoactive drug abuse leads to many serious or even life-threatening side effects and withdrawal symptoms. Which drugs cause long-term side effects in a developing fetus?*

PSILOCYBIN   Another hallucinogen, called **psilocybin** (sil uh SY bin), is obtained from certain South American mushrooms. The effects of using psilocybin are much like those of LSD. However, LSD is more than a hundred times stronger than psilocybin. Tolerance to psilocybin develops quickly.

PCP   Another psychoactive drug that can act as a stimulant, a depressant, or a hallucinogen is phencyclidine, or **PCP.** PCP was originally used as an anesthetic for large animals. Today, PCP, or "angel dust," is only available illegally.

PCP abusers sprinkle the drug on tobacco or marijuana cigarettes and inject, sniff, or eat it. Abusers have been known to engage in violent acts and even commit suicide. Some PCP abusers develop signs of mental illness. PCP's effects remain long after drug use ends, and a flashback may occur at a later time.

Marijuana

The leaves, stems, and flowering tops of the hemp plant *Cannabis sativa,* shown in Figure 21-15, contain several psychoactive substances. The main psychoactive ingredient is a chemical called THC. Most people know the illegal psychoactive drug obtained from the hemp plant as **marijuana** (mar uh WAH nuh). Today marijuana is one of the most frequently abused psychoactive drugs.

Marijuana, also known as "pot" or "grass," is a depressant and stimulant, as well as a mild hallucinogenic drug. Generally, marijuana leaves and stems are smoked in a pipe or in a handmade cigarette called a "joint." Active ingredients pass through the lungs, into the blood, and are carried to the brain. Researchers have found that THC changes the way sensory information reaches and is acted upon by the brain.

Smoking marijuana can depress the user's body functions and cause confusion, sudden mood changes, memory problems, and loss of coordination. Some abusers become withdrawn. Because marijuana can act as a depressant, users often feel sleepy or drowsy. Driving a car is especially dangerous when under the influence of marijuana.

Many of the long-term effects of smoking marijuana are similar to those of smoking tobacco. However, marijuana smoke contains more cancer-causing agents than tobacco smoke. A single joint has the same amount of tar and other harmful substances as approximately 14 or 15 tobacco cigarettes.

The hemp plant is also the source of the illegal drug called **hashish** (HASH eesh). Hashish, or "hash," is often sold as tiny brown chunks that are smoked. Some abusers boil hashish to make an even stronger drug called hashish oil, which is mixed with tobacco and smoked. Both forms of hashish produce the same short-term and long-term effects as marijuana. However, they are more likely than marijuana to cause an altered mental state.

Figure 21-15 *Marijuana is considered a gateway drug, meaning that people who use marijuana often go on to use other drugs.*

Inhalants

Drugs that are inhaled, or breathed in through the nose, to produce a desired effect are called **inhalants** (in HAYL unts). Most inhalants belong to a group of chemicals called volatile organic solvents. A volatile solvent rapidly changes from a liquid to a vapor. Inhalants affect the body quickly because they are able to enter the bloodstream directly through the lungs, and from there they are carried to the brain.

Some people unknowingly misuse or abuse commercial volatile solvents. Products such as paint thinner, cleaning fluid, nail polish remover, and spray paints all give off dangerous fumes. One way to prevent inhalant misuse is to learn how to use these products properly. You should use volatile chemicals only in large, airy spaces, preferably with the windows open. Containers should be kept closed at all times to prevent the escape of fumes and accidental inhalation.

Some people abuse inhalants to achieve brief feelings of excitement or giddiness. Actually, inhalant abusers replace the oxygen in their inhaled breath with another substance, which can either depress brain functions or stimulate heart functions. One type of inhalant abuse is purposefully inhaling glue fumes, or glue sniffing. Some of the short-term and long-term effects of inhalant abuse include headaches, blurred vision, and damage to the kidneys, liver, bone marrow, and brain.

Anabolic Steroids

Synthetic drugs that resemble the male hormone testosterone are called **anabolic steroids** (an uh BAH lik STIHR oydz). The name of these drugs comes from the Greek word, *an abold,* meaning to "build up." Physicians prescribe anabolic steroids for patients with skeletal and growth disorders.

....

SHARPEN YOUR *SKILLS*

Working in Groups

Work in groups of four or five to organize a health fair to provide other students with information about drugs. The fair could include games that test participants' drug I.Q. as well as posters, brochures, and buttons.

Figure 21-16 *Athletes who turn to steroids risk permanent damage to their bodies.*

Drug use can affect a person's job performance. Some employers think that employee drug testing is necessary, especially when the safety and security of others is at stake.

One method of drug testing called urinalysis involves identifying drug residues in a person's urine. Traces of most drugs show up in the urine for up to two to three days after being taken. After that time, most drugs are not detectable in the urine.

A method of drug testing called radioimmunoassay of hair (RIAH) also detects drug use. Like urine, hair carries traces of the drugs a person takes. The advantage of RIAH is that each strand of hair records long-term drug use. That is, it records drug use for as long as the hair was in the person's scalp. RIAH requires about 60 strands of hair. Washing the hair does not affect the test. Drug residues farthest from the hair root represent drugs taken longest ago.

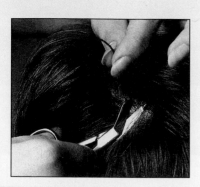

Anabolic steroids also are used to treat certain types of anemia and to offset the negative effects of cancer therapy. Though steroids are not psychoactive drugs, they are often abused by athletes who want bigger and stronger bodies.

Steroid abuse has harmful consequences, such as liver and heart damage and increased blood pressure. Steroid abuse can also alter appearance by stimulating overgrowth of skull and facial bones. Because anabolic steroids are chemically related to testosterone, female abusers can develop masculine traits such as facial hair and a low voice. In addition, steroids can be injected, so abusers risk HIV infection and hepatitis B and C when they share needles.

Steroid use is especially dangerous for teenagers, whose growing bodies can be permanently damaged. Studies have shown that teens who use steroids risk stunted growth, infertility, aggressive behavior, and violent mood swings.

Designer and Look-Alike Drugs

Most commonly abused drugs are **controlled substances,** or substances whose manufacture, possession, or sale is controlled by law. Less common are the so-called designer drugs. A **designer drug** is a new chemical substance that has been designed to be chemically similar to a controlled substance. However, the designer drug is not always controlled by law because its chemical structure is different from the controlled substance it imitates.

Sometimes the change in a designer drug's chemical structure results in fatal toxic effects. Also, the user of a designer drug does not know just how strong the drug is and can easily experience unpleasant side effects or even overdose. The use of designer drugs can lead to dependence.

Drugs that are sold on the street and made to look like commonly abused drugs are called **look-alike drugs.** These drugs may contain any kind of substance. A drug abuser expecting to buy an amphetamine may be buying a cold remedy instead. Other look-alike drugs contain more dangerous, unknown substances, and may be life-threatening.

LESSON 3 REVIEW

1. What are some medical uses of depressants?
2. How do stimulants affect the body?
3. What is a controlled substance?
4. Why do some people abuse anabolic steroids?

What Do You Think?

5. Do you think that all volatile organic solvents should be controlled substances? Why or why not?

4 CHOOSING TO BE DRUG FREE

GUIDE FOR READING

Focus on these questions as you read this lesson.

- How can drug abuse be treated?
- What are some alternatives to drug abuse?

SKILLS

- Activity: Making a Public Service Television Commercial
- Locating Community Resources

You may already know about the pressures to experiment with psychoactive drugs. How can you help yourself and others stay away from drug abuse? What can you do to help someone who is abusing drugs?

Treating Drug Abuse and Addiction

Before drug abusers can be helped, they need to recognize their problem. Unfortunately, this may be difficult for them. Many abusers deny their behavior; others deny the problems that led them to drug abuse. Figure 21-17 lists some of the signs of drug abuse. This list may help you recognize a drug abuse problem in a friend or classmate and allow you to convince the abuser that he or she has a drug problem.

Once drug abusers recognize their problem, many options are available to them. **Options for drug abusers include programs in which people withdraw from the drug under medical care and treatment centers in which abusers learn to live drug-free lives.** Programs to help abusers and their families are available. Understanding the underlying cause for the drug abuse and involving family members can restore and reinforce the family's stability.

Many organizations counsel people about drug problems. Community hospitals have clinics or programs that provide low-cost or volunteer counseling for teenagers and adults. Local schools and governments also schedule parent meetings, peer group counseling, and drug-free programs.

DETOXIFICATION PROGRAMS   One type of drug abuse treatment is a **detoxification program** (dee tahk suh fih KAY shun). A detoxification program involves gradual but complete

Signs of Drug Abuse

- Major changes in behavior
- Lying, cheating
- Sudden changes in mood
- Forgetfulness, withdrawn attitude
- New friends who are suspected of abusing drugs
- Loss of memory
- Poor school performance
- Poor coordination
- Changes in appearance
- Slurred speech
- Irresponsible decision-making
- Attention-getting behavior
- Aggressiveness
- Denial of any problems

Figure 21-17 *Learning to recognize the signs of drug abuse can make a difference.*

Drug Counselor

A person trying to overcome a drug abuse problem may need assistance from someone outside of his or her circle of family and friends. A drug counselor can help. **Drug counselors** are trained to help abusers overcome the difficult problem of drug abuse. These counselors also often work with the abuser's family.

Drug counselors work in one-on-one situations, in group situations, in special drug abuse clinics, in hospitals, or for companies with employee drug programs. They also work for telephone hotlines or run private counseling services.

No certification or license is needed for this career. However, a drug counselor must have compassion and an ability to gain a client's trust. A high school diploma and training are sufficient to become a drug counselor. However, college and master's degree programs are available.

Figure 21-18 *Family support is an important part of recovery from drug abuse.*

withdrawal from the abused drug. People who enter detoxification programs usually receive medical treatment and supervision in a hospital. Drug abusers may stop taking the drug all at once, or physicians may reduce the drug dosage slowly to avoid painful withdrawal symptoms. Detoxification programs always include counseling to help program participants deal with their abuse and to cope constructively with the problems that led to it and were caused by it.

THERAPEUTIC COMMUNITIES   Another type of drug abuse treatment is therapeutic communities. A **therapeutic community** (thehr uh PYOO tik) is a residential treatment center where drug abusers live and learn to adjust to drug-free lives. Members of therapeutic communities lend support and friendship to each other. Often drug abusers are required to undergo detoxification before becoming a part of the community. Therapeutic communities provide medical advice and counseling to help abusers develop a sense of personal and social worth. The staff of therapeutic communities usually consists of health-care professionals and former drug abusers.

METHADONE MAINTENANCE PROGRAMS   A third type of drug abuse treatment, called methadone maintenance, helps heroin abusers. **Methadone** (METH uh dohn) is a drug that produces many effects similar to heroin, but does not produce the same "high" that causes heroin addicts to crave the drug. This type of treatment involves substituting methadone for heroin. Small, regular doses of methadone prevent withdrawal symptoms. Methadone treatment is intended to eliminate the desire for heroin.

Methadone can cause dependency. Therefore, a trained professional must carefully monitor treatment and slowly lower the dosage. Long-term methadone use causes side

MAKING A PUBLIC SERVICE TELEVISION COMMERCIAL

In this activity, you will plan a 30-second commercial to help teens cope with the peer pressure to try drugs.

Materials

6 pieces of poster-board	colored markers or pencils

Procedure

1. Work in groups of four to brainstorm ideas, characters, and a theme for a 30-second television commercial. The commercial should give advice to teenagers about coping with peer pressure to take drugs. The theme could be something like "Teen Decisions" or "Wise Choice."

2. Two group members should prepare the visual part of the commercial by illustrating six storyboards. The storyboards will show what will appear on the television screen every five seconds.

3. The other two group members should prepare the audio part of the commercial by writing the script. The script, when read aloud, should be about 30 seconds long.

4. When the visual and audio parts of your commercial are complete, work together to develop music or sound effects to accompany the commercial.

5. Combine the visual, audio, and sound effects and present your commercial to your classmates. Ask for their reactions.

Discussion

1. What was the theme of your commercial? Why did you choose this theme?

2. Who were the characters in your script? What was their message?

3. Did your classmates think your public service commercial was effective for teenagers? Why or why not?

effects such as liver damage. Methadone is not a cure for heroin addiction, but it can be a first step.

Avoiding Drug Use

You make decisions every day. You decide what to eat, which clothes to wear, and how much to exercise. You may also make decisions about drugs.

REFUSING DRUGS Deciding not to take drugs can be a difficult decision when you are faced with pressure to take them. There are ways to avoid drugs in your life. One way is to refuse when someone offers you drugs. To be effective, you can present your personal reasons for not wanting to take drugs. Be honest—do not supply phony reasons. For example, you could say, "No thanks… I want to keep a clear head," or "I don't want to become addicted," or simply "I don't use drugs." To make it clear that you mean what you say, look the person in the eyes when presenting your thoughts about drug abuse.

Methods for Managing Stress

- Run, swim, ride a bike, or engage in some other form of vigorous exercise
- Take a hot shower or bath
- Consciously relax all the muscles in your body
- Do deep-breathing exercises
- Learn to manage your time effectively

If the person who is offering you drugs continues to try to persuade you, make a definite action that removes you from the situation. This action should make it clear that you cannot be persuaded to change your mind. For example, you can simply get up and leave or enjoy activities with another group of nonabusing friends.

MANAGING STRESS   Another way to avoid drugs is to manage the stress in your life. There are many methods that you can use to help manage stress. Several are suggested in Figure 21-19.

GETTING HELP   If you decide that the stresses and problems in your life are too much to manage, find someone to help you. Many people are willing to help, but first you must let them know that you need help. Parents, teachers, friends, brothers, sisters, school counselors, school nurses, and members of the clergy are usually available for guidance and support. A second option is to call one of the national hotlines that tell you where to call for drug information and treatment referral in your area. For these numbers, call 1-800-662-HELP.

Alternatives to Drug Use

Turning to drugs to try to feel good or deal with problems is a risky choice. You can get involved in many healthy and constructive activities to lift your mood, feel better about yourself, and deal with the pressures in your life.

Engaging in physical activity is one way to help yourself feel better. Physical activity not only helps improve your mood, but it also relieves the negative effects of stress. Getting enough exercise and getting involved in sports can help you feel energetic, positive, and self-confident.

Helping other people can give you a good feeling about yourself, too. Many social service agencies need volunteers. You could volunteer to read to someone with a visual handicap, make a social visit to an elderly person in a nursing facility, or teach a hobby or sport to a youngster.

Participating in youth groups can help you feel a sense of belonging and connection to others. The members of these

Figure 21-20 *Helping others can boost your self-esteem and build friendships with other people.*

groups support one another as each person strives to find his or her place in the world. Youth groups also volunteer to help others in need.

Working at a part-time job not only provides you with spending money, but can also give you a sense of accomplishment and increased self-esteem. Not only can you learn a new skill, but you can meet new friends. Your family, friends, or school counselor may be able to help you find such a job.

Remember that abusing drugs cannot relieve the pressures and problems in life. It can only postpone decision-making and create more problems. Imagine how you would feel if you had to tell lies, hide your physical condition, worry about police, and deal with drug side effects. People who become dependent on drugs spend almost all of their time thinking about drugs, taking drugs, getting the money for drugs, and looking for drugs. Drugs end up controlling their lives. By deciding not to use drugs, you are acting to take control of your life.

LESSON **4** REVIEW

1. What are four clues that might warn you that someone you know is abusing drugs?

2. What are two types of drug abuse treatment programs? How do these programs work?

3. Why is methadone used as a treatment for heroin addiction? Are there drawbacks to its use?

4. List two alternatives to drug use. Explain how they work.

What Do You Think?

5. Suppose you were at a party where drugs were being used. What would you do?

Intervening to Help a Friend

Jen had been concerned about her friend Christina's use of marijuana for some time, but last night was the final straw. Jen and Christina were to meet at a friend's party, but Christina showed up two hours late and was "high." Christina was feeling drowsy and acting uncoordinated. So Jen drove her home. The next day, Christina told Jen that she was perfectly fine at the party and could have driven herself home. Christina also declared that she could quit smoking marijuana easily at any time.

Other friends have started to give up on Christina. But Jen still cares about Christina and fears her friend may be in trouble with drugs. She wants to help, but how can she when Christina is so out of touch with reality?

Intervening to help a friend who abuses drugs is difficult. You fear you may lose the friend. But your friend's behavior may cause that loss through a fatal accident. Use these guidelines to help save your friendship and your friend.

A friend may need your help to overcome a drug problem.

1. Stop enabling behaviors

Enabling behaviors are actions you take that allow, or enable, someone to continue to behave dangerously without facing the consequences. By making it more difficult for people to behave dangerously, you may make them rethink what they are doing.

You will help your friend most if you stop:

- **Covering up**—such as saying your friend is at your house when he or she is not.

- **Giving second chances**—such as repeatedly lending money when your friend has not paid back previous loans.

- **Making excuses**—such as, "That's OK, everyone's late sometimes."

2. Talk to your friend

Talking to your friend about his or her behavior will not be easy, but it is worthwhile if you:

- **Express your concern**—say you are intervening because you are worried about his or her well-being.

- **Help your friend face the facts about his or her destructive behavior**—present specific evidence of the problem.

Describe behaviors accurately and simply, using dates and times when possible.

● **Describe your feelings**—tell how your friend's behavior affects you. For example, Jen might say to Christina, "I was worried something had happened to you when you were late. And when you showed up so 'high' that you were drowsy and uncoordinated, it hurt me."

● **Don't criticize or argue**—resist the temptation to be judgmental. You are objecting to the behavior, not the person. Do not get drawn into "no-I-didn't, yes-you-did" arguments. Expect your friend to deny drug dependency or other destructive patterns of behavior. If your friend argues, say "I just want you to know how I feel," and leave.

● **Offer specific help and support**—prepare a list of resources that your friend can go to for help. Include names, addresses, and phone numbers. Offer to go with your friend to the school counselor, a social service center, a member of the clergy, a health professional, or other resource.

3. Ask another friend to help

The more people speaking the truth and offering support, the better. Be sure to discuss your concerns and guidelines for intervening with the second friend. Work together.

4. Follow through

Do what you said you would do, and stop doing what you said you would not do anymore. Be sure your friend knows that your determination to stop enabling is firm and that your offers of support can be counted on.

5. Seek adult or professional help

If you think your friend is in a life-threatening or similarly serious situation, find a more experienced person to intervene directly.

Remember, you can only be responsible for yourself. You cannot *make* another person get help or change behavior. If you have done the above, you have done all you can, and you are a good friend.

Apply the Skill

1. Review Jen's situation.

(a) What were Jen's enabling behaviors? Explain.

(b) Write a dialogue between Jen and Christina reflecting the guidelines presented in step 2.

(c) Under what circumstances do you think Jen should consider asking for adult or professional help? Explain.

2. Give two specific examples of enabling behaviors often used by (a) parents, (b) teachers, and (c) friends of a drug-dependent person. For each, explain how the enabling behaviors made the situation worse.

3. Prepare a list of local resources for alcoholism, drug dependency, eating disorders, and depression. Include addresses, phone numbers, and hours the resources are available.

CHAPTER 21 REVIEW

KEY IDEAS

LESSON 1

- When used as directed, legal drugs help the body fight injury and disease. The effects of illegal drugs outweigh any useful purposes. Both legal and illegal drugs can be misused and abused.

- Although some psychoactive drugs are medically useful, many subject abusers to dangerous consequences.

LESSON 2

- The three major types of risk factors for drug abuse are family factors, social factors, and personal factors.

- The more these risk factors dominate a teenager's life, the more likely it is that a teenager may turn to drugs.

LESSON 3

- Commonly abused drugs include depressants, stimulants, alcohol, hallucinogens, marijuana, inhalants, anabolic steroids, designer drugs, and look-alike drugs.

- The abuse of psychoactive drugs and anabolic steroids can result in short-term and long-term side effects.

LESSON 4

- You can avoid drug abuse by using refusal skills, learning to manage stress and solve problems, getting help, or finding healthy activities.

- Treatment for drug abuse includes detoxification, therapeutic communities, and methadone maintenance programs.

KEY TERMS

LESSON 1

antagonistic interaction

drug abuse

medicines

overdose

psychoactive drug

side effects

synergistic interaction

LESSON 3

amphetamines

anabolic steroids

barbiturates

cocaine

controlled substances

depressants

designer drug

hallucinogens

hashish

heroin

inhalant

LSD

marijuana

narcotic

stimulants

tranquilizers

LESSON 4

detoxification program

methadone

therapeutic community

Listed above are some of the important terms in this chapter. Choose the term from the list that best matches each phrase below.

1. a category of drugs that slow brain and body reactions

2. a serious reaction to a large amount of a drug that can result in death

3. drugs used for helping the body fight injury, illness, and disease

4. unwanted physical and mental effects caused by a drug

5. program that involves gradual but complete withdrawal from an abused drug

6. anti-anxiety drugs

7. drug interaction that produces greater effects than what two drugs would produce alone

8. drugs that can alter perception, thought, and mood

9. a substance that is breathed in through the nose to produce a desired effect

10. substances whose manufacture, possession, and sale are controlled by law

WHAT HAVE YOU LEARNED?

On a separate sheet of paper, write the word or words that best complete each statement.

11. A category of drugs that speed up activities of the central nervous system is called _____.

12. Psychoactive drugs can pass from a mother to her newborn through _____.

13. Three factors that contribute to the risk of drug abuse among teenagers include _____.

14. _____ occurs when a person addicted to a psychoactive drug stops taking it.

15. Two types of psychoactive hallucinogens are _____.

16. Intravenous drug abusers who share needles are at risk for contracting _____.

17. _____ are natural narcotics that are contained in opium.

18. Methadone maintenance involves substituting methadone for _____.

Answer each of the following with complete sentences.

19. What are the immediate and long-term effects of smoking marijuana?

20. Why do drug abusers sometimes take more than one drug at a time?

21. How does drug abuse affect the abuser's family and friends?

22. Why is drug dilution harmful?

23. How can anabolic steroids be harmful to an individual's health?

24. What is the goal of a detoxification program?

25. Why are designer drugs dangerous?

26. What is a flashback and with which drug does it occur?

27. Name and briefly describe three types of drug interactions.

28. What causes withdrawal symptoms to occur in the drug abuser?

WHAT DO YOU THINK?

29. Recently a new mother who had abused psychoactive drugs while she was pregnant was convicted of "drug delivery" to her newborn infant and was sentenced to 14 years on probation. Some people think that an infant's right to be born drug free is more important than a mother's freedom of choice. What do you think? Explain your position.

30. In what ways are drug abuse and criminal acts linked together?

31. Studies show that students who regularly abuse illegal drugs tend to get lower grades in school, do not participate in organized sports activities, and are more likely to lie or steal. Why do you think this is true?

32. Some people do not approve of methadone treatment programs because they say that they substitute one drug dependence for another. Do you agree? Explain your answer.

WHAT WOULD YOU DO?

33. Your younger sister has been invited to a party. She has heard there will be drugs there, and she is curious. What advice would you give your sister to discourage her from experimenting with drugs?

34. How might you tell a friend that you suspect he or she is abusing drugs?

35. If you were a newspaper editor, would you print a story about a movie star who overdoses on illegal drugs? Explain your answer.

Getting Involved

36. Invite a local law-enforcement official to your school to talk about illegal drug activity in your area. What particular problems and dangers do officers face in the course of their investigations?

INFECTIOUS DISEASES

Staying home and resting is important when you are suffering from an infectious disease. It helps you to recover quickly, and it prevents you from spreading the disease to other people. In this chapter, you will learn about infectious diseases—their causes, how they spread, your body's defenses against them, what you should do when you are ill, and the ways to help reduce the risk of infection.

CHAPTER PREVIEW

22–1 The Nature of Infectious Diseases

- Discuss the causes of infectious diseases and the ways in which diseases are spread.

22–2 The Body's Defenses Against Infection

- Explain how your body defends itself against infectious diseases.

22–3 Development of Infectious Diseases

- Identify the stages of an infectious disease and the factors involved in treating and preventing infectious diseases.

22–4 Common Infectious Diseases

- Describe the symptoms and treatment of some common infectious diseases.

BUILDING HEALTH SKILLS

- Describe how to use medicines safely and effectively.

CHECK YOUR WELLNESS

Do you protect yourself from infectious diseases? See if you can answer *yes* to the following questions.

- Do you keep your hands, hair, and skin clean?
- Are you careful to use only your own eating utensils, towels, toothbrush, and grooming items?
- Do you eat a balanced diet, get enough sleep, and exercise regularly?
- Have you checked to make sure your immunizations are current?
- Do you know how often you should receive a tetanus booster shot?
- Do you know the conditions under which you should seek medical care?

KEEPING A JOURNAL

Which of your behaviors do you feel you should change to reduce your chances of acquiring an infectious disease? Write down your ideas and some specific goals in your journal.

Take it to the Net

GUIDE FOR READING

Focus on these questions as you read this lesson.

- What are the causes of infectious diseases?

- How are infectious diseases spread?

SKILLS

- DECIDE

For as long as there have been humans, there have been infectious diseases. Also known as communicable diseases, **infectious diseases** (in FEK shus) are caused by organisms that enter, live in, and multiply within the human body. Most disease-causing organisms are so small that they can be seen only through a microscope. When organisms are this small, they are called **microorganisms** (my kroh AWR guh niz ums).

Causes of Infectious Diseases

Not all microorganisms that enter and live in your body cause disease. In fact, many microorganisms are present in your body all the time and cause no problems. They are found in your mouth, on your skin, and in your digestive tract. Most of them are harmless as long as they stay where they belong. Many of them actually help with normal bodily functions and protect against invasion by pathogens.

Organisms that cause disease are called **pathogens** (PATH uh junz). Pathogens do not belong in your body. If they enter your body and multiply, they create an infection and you develop a disease. There are many kinds of pathogens.

BACTERIA Simple, single-celled microorganisms that can live almost anywhere are called **bacteria** (bak TEER ee uh). Bacteria live in air, soil, food, and in and on the bodies of plants and animals, including your own body. Bacteria even live in the freezing waters at the North and South poles and in the boiling waters of hot springs. Most bacteria are not pathogens. Several different types of bacteria are shown in Figure 22-1.

Some bacteria cause disease by entering cells and damaging them. Other bacteria injure cells by giving off poisons called **toxins** (TAHK sinz). Food poisoning, for example, can be caused by toxins given off by certain kinds of bacteria that

Figure 22-1 *Bacteria are either spherical, rod-shaped, or spiral-shaped.*

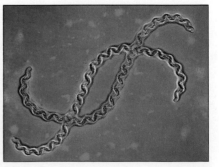

grow on food. Another type of bacteria found in soil and on objects produces a toxin that causes **tetanus** (TET n us). This type of bacteria grows inside a deep wound, especially one that does not drain. Tetanus toxin damages the nervous system, causing uncontrollable muscle contractions, paralysis, and often death.

VIRUSES   The smallest pathogens are **viruses.** They are about 100 times smaller than most bacteria. Viruses can multiply only by entering living cells and taking over the cells' reproductive mechanisms, resulting in cell damage or death. An example of a human virus is shown in Figure 22-2.

Different types of viruses invade different types of cells. Some viruses, such as those that cause the common cold, invade the cells of the respiratory tract. Other viruses invade other regions of the body. A virus that invades the liver, for example, causes liver disease. One that infects the salivary glands around the mouth causes mumps.

FUNGI   Small, simple organisms related to molds are known as **fungi** (FUN jy). Fungi, which include such things as yeasts and mushrooms, grow best in warm, dark, moist areas. Two examples of fungal disease are athlete's foot and ringworm, a skin infection that forms a reddish circle just under the skin's surface.

PROTOZOANS   Single-celled organisms that are hundreds of times larger and have a more complex structure than bacteria are known as **protozoans** (proh tuh ZOH unz). Protozoans have the ability to move through fluids in search of food. Diseases caused by protozoans include malaria, African sleeping sickness, and amebic dysentery.

OTHER PATHOGENS   Some diseases are caused by animals such as mites, lice, and parasitic worms. For example, the trichina worm is a parasitic worm that can live in the muscle tissue of certain animals, such as pigs. If the meat of

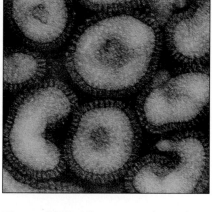

Figure 22-2 *Viruses, such as the ones shown here, cause many human diseases.*

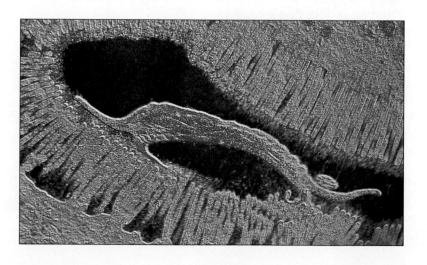

Figure 22-3 *Water contaminated with the protozoan giardia causes diarrhea. Here, a single giardia is shown inside the intestine of an animal.*

an infected animal is not thoroughly cooked, a person who eats the meat can become infected.

Spread of Infectious Diseases

How does a person come in contact with pathogens? **People come in contact with pathogens through contact with an infected person, a contaminated object, an infected animal, or a contaminated substance.** Some pathogens are breathed in with air, and some are swallowed. Others enter the body through large or small breaks in the skin or in the moist linings of the eyes, ears, nose, mouth, or other openings of the body.

CONTACT WITH AN INFECTED PERSON   Many infectious diseases are spread through some form of contact with a person who has the disease. The contact may be direct physical contact, such as hand-to-hand contact or kissing. Often areas of infection, such as sores on an infected person's skin, contain pathogens. Sexually transmitted diseases are transmitted through direct physical contact.

Indirect contact with an infected person can occur in a number of ways. One way occurs when you inhale the tiny droplets of moisture sneezed or coughed into the air by an infected person. Influenza, colds, mumps, and chicken pox, for example, can be spread by droplet infection. Contact with an infected person's blood, such as when needles are

D DEFINE the problem	

D DEFINE the problem

E EXPLORE alternatives

C CONSIDER the consequences

I IDENTIFY values

D DECIDE and act

E EVALUATE results

An Unsanitary Restaurant

Derek works as a waiter at the neighborhood's most popular restaurant. At work yesterday, he noticed several mice chewing through a loaf of bread in the kitchen. This was not the first time Derek had seen evidence of mice in the restaurant. When he informed the manager, however, she told him there were no mice in the restaurant. The manager also told Derek that he should stop spreading false rumors about the restaurant if he wanted to keep his job.

Derek realized that the restaurant was breaking state health codes, but he also knew that a good job like his was hard to find.

1. Use the DECIDE process on page 18 to decide what you would do if you were Derek. Explain your reasons for making this decision.

2. List the steps you would take to put your decision into effect.

shared to inject illegal drugs, is another form of indirect contact with a person that can spread a disease.

CONTACT WITH A CONTAMINATED OBJECT   Some pathogens can survive outside a person's body. These pathogens can be spread from one person to another on objects, such as doorknobs, eating and drinking utensils, and needles used for body piercing and tattoos. Drinking from a cup used by an infected person, for example, can spread pathogens. If you handle objects that have been sneezed on, coughed on, or in some other way contaminated by an infected person, you can transfer the pathogen to yourself when you touch your mouth or your food. This is why it is always a good idea to wash your hands before eating.

Water and food contaminated with pathogens from an infected person are additional sources of infection. Drinking water contaminated by human sewage is a common source of disease in many areas of the world.

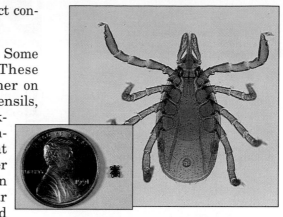

Figure 22-4 *The deer tick transmits the bacteria that cause Lyme disease. Shown here are a highly magnified view of a deer tick and a view comparing it in size to a penny.*

CONTACT WITH AN ANIMAL   Some serious infectious diseases are transmitted to humans through the bites of animals. For example, rabies, a deadly disease of the nervous system, can be transmitted by the bite of an infected animal, such as a dog or raccoon. Malaria, a disease that is common in the tropics, is spread from person to person through mosquito bites. Tick bites can transmit Lyme disease and Rocky Mountain spotted fever.

CONTACT WITH ENVIRONMENTAL SOURCES   Some pathogens may be naturally present in food, water, and soil, or on the surfaces of objects, without having come from an infected person. These are environmental sources of infection. Tetanus and food poisoning are two examples. One common type of food poisoning is caused by salmonella bacteria, which are often present in poultry, eggs, and meat. Another type of bacterium that grows in improperly processed canned foods causes **botulism** (BAHCH uh liz im), a very serious and often deadly kind of food poisoning.

LESSON **1** REVIEW

1. What is an infectious disease?
2. What are the various types of pathogens?
3. How do viruses multiply?
4. Name four ways that infectious diseases are spread.

What Do You Think?

5. How do you think a disease such as malaria could be controlled?

Focus on these questions as you read this lesson.

- How does the body protect itself from infection?
- How does your immune system function?

SKILLS

- Being Assertive

2 THE BODY'S DEFENSES AGAINST INFECTION

If pathogens are everywhere, and your body comes in contact with them every day, why are you not always sick? When you do get sick, what keeps the pathogens from multiplying until they take over your body? The answer to both of these questions is that your body has a number of different defenses against infection. **Your body protects itself from infection with physical and chemical defenses, inflammation, and the immune system.**

Physical and Chemical Defenses

Your body's first line of defense is its protective coverings. Your skin, for example, is a physical barrier to pathogens. The surface cells of your skin are hard and have no gaps between them. Your skin also has chemical barriers, such as sweat. Sweat contains acids that kill many bacteria. Finally, your skin constantly sheds old cells, and the pathogens on these cells are shed, too. In fact, your skin is such an effective barrier that microorganisms usually cannot get through unless the skin has a cut, scrape, burn, or other injury.

The openings into your body, such as your mouth, eyes, and nose, have their own physical and chemical barriers. These openings have moist, protective linings called **mucous membranes** (MYOO kus). Mucous membranes secrete a sticky liquid called **mucus** that covers the surface of the membranes. The mucus traps many pathogens and washes them away. Your saliva and tears also trap and wash away pathogens. In addition, chemicals and specialized cells in mucus, saliva, and tears attack pathogens. Some of the pathogens are killed, while others are kept from reproducing or getting food. These attacks can keep pathogens from getting into your body to cause disease.

If a pathogen gets beyond your body's entrance points, other defenses are present to block its way. Surface membranes, chemicals, and the cells that line your air passages, digestive tract, and urinary tract prevent entry into your body. These barriers also can physically remove pathogens. For example, inhaled pathogens that reach your windpipe may be trapped by mucus. **Cilia** (SIL ee uh), tiny hairlike structures that line your air passages, beat rhythmically, moving the mucus upward toward your mouth. When you cough or blow your nose, the pathogens are removed along with the mucus. Alternatively, the pathogens can be attacked by the chemicals in saliva and swallowed.

Acids in your stomach and other chemicals in your digestive tract kill many pathogens. In addition, the normal

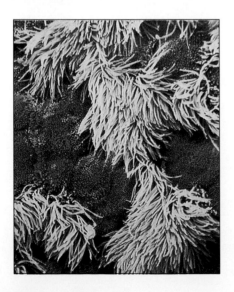

Figure 22-5 *Cilia that line the respiratory tract continuously move mucus toward the mouth and nose.*

motions of the digestive tract not only move food through your system but also move pathogens out. Bacteria living in the digestive tract compete with pathogens for food and space. These resident bacteria also give off substances that harm or kill invading bacteria. In your urinary tract, the acid of urine can kill some pathogens.

Inflammation

If a pathogen is able to get through the physical and chemical barriers of your body and begins to injure cells, your body is ready with its second line of defense—inflammation. **Inflammation** (in fluh MAY shun) is your body's response to all kinds of injury, from cuts and scrapes to internal damage caused by infectious diseases. Inflammation fights infection and promotes healing.

When your body is damaged in any way—by a burn, a cut or scrape, a splinter, or a pathogen—the inflammation process begins within seconds. Damaged cells release chemicals that cause several responses. Tiny blood vessels in the injured area enlarge, allowing more blood to flow to the area. Fluids leak out of the blood vessels along with cells called phagocytes. **Phagocytes** (FAG uh syts) are white blood cells that "eat up" foreign cells.

The phagocytes begin to eat up any pathogens that may be present. At the same time, other phagocytes are attracted to the injury from nearby tissues. While this is happening, the infected area becomes red, swollen, and sore; in other words, inflamed. The phagocytes and the chemicals released in the area continue to kill pathogens. The phagocytes digest not only pathogens, but also any dead cells. They also give off substances that cause healing to begin. The fluids, phagocytes, and dead cells that accumulate at the site often result in the formation of a thick, white liquid, or **pus.** Eventually, the inflammation process heals the damage, and the inflammation subsides.

Figure 22-6 *A phagocyte kills a pathogen by engulfing and then digesting it.*

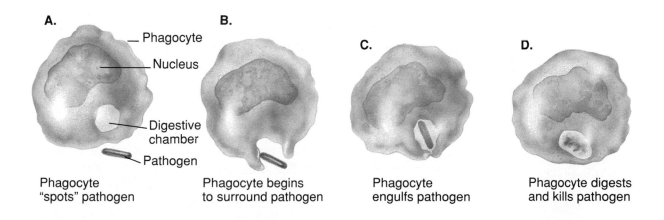

A.
Phagocyte
Nucleus
Digestive chamber
Pathogen

Phagocyte "spots" pathogen

B.
Phagocyte begins to surround pathogen

C.
Phagocyte engulfs pathogen

D.
Phagocyte digests and kills pathogen

The Immune System

Your body's last and most sophisticated line of defense against pathogens is your **immune system** (ih MYOON). Your immune system produces a separate set of weapons for each kind of pathogen that it encounters. The immune system is made up of cells in your blood, lymph, bone marrow, and other tissues. Unlike the phagocytes and chemicals that attack all kinds of pathogens, certain cells in the immune system are "tailor-made" for each pathogen. As a result, the immune system can recognize, seek out, and destroy specific pathogens throughout your body.

WHAT DOES THE IMMUNE SYSTEM DO? Pathogens that enter your body for the first time often cause disease. If your immune system is functioning, why does this happen? The explanation is that your immune system must not only recognize a new pathogen, but must also build up its arsenal of weapons against that pathogen. This process takes time, during which a pathogen can be multiplying in your body and causing disease. Once the immune system's arsenal is built up, the immune system kills the pathogens, and your body gradually recovers from the infection. At the same time, inflammation is working to heal injured tissues.

What happens when your immune system encounters pathogens that have previously invaded your body? If a pathogen that has previously entered your body enters your body again, your immune system will quickly recognize it and launch an immediate attack. The attack is so quick and effective that it can usually prevent an infection from developing. When this happens, you are said to be immune to the disease. **Immunity** (ih MYOON ih tee) is your body's ability to destroy pathogens that it has previously encountered before the pathogens are able to cause disease.

THE LYMPHATIC SYSTEM Much of your immune system is contained within your lymphatic system. Your **lymphatic system** (lim FAT ik) is a network of vessels that collects fluid from the tissues of your body and returns it to the bloodstream. The fluid that flows through the lymphatic system is called **lymph** (LIMF).

As shown in Figure 22-7, the lymphatic vessels have hundreds of small stations, called lymph nodes. Each lymph node acts as a sort of filter. Phagocytes and cells called lymphocytes are present in the lymph nodes and attack pathogens as they pass through.

LYMPHOCYTES The cells that carry out most of the immune system's functions are a type of white blood cell called **lymphocytes** (LIM fuh syts). There are two types of lymphocytes—B lymphocytes and T lymphocytes.

The B lymphocytes, or **B cells,** produce substances called antibodies. **Antibodies** (AN tih bahd eez) are proteins that

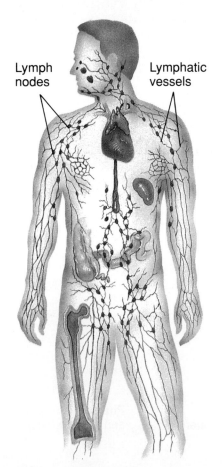

Figure 22-7 *Your lymphatic system is made up of a complex network of vessels and nodes.*

Lymph nodes

Lymphatic vessels

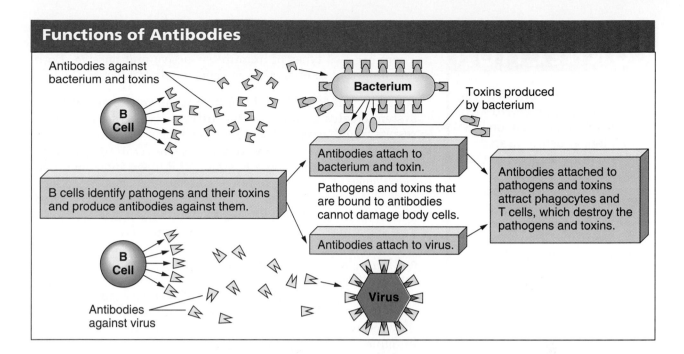

Functions of Antibodies

Antibodies against bacterium and toxins

B Cell

Bacterium

Toxins produced by bacterium

B cells identify pathogens and their toxins and produce antibodies against them.

Antibodies attach to bacterium and toxin.

Pathogens and toxins that are bound to antibodies cannot damage body cells.

Antibodies attached to pathogens and toxins attract phagocytes and T cells, which destroy the pathogens and toxins.

Antibodies attach to virus.

B Cell

Antibodies against virus

Virus

attach to the surface of pathogens or to the toxins produced by pathogens, as shown in Figure 22-8. This binding action keeps the pathogen or toxin from harming the body. It also helps phagocytes find and consume the pathogens. Each type of B cell produces antibodies that can attack a particular kind of pathogen or toxin.

Once an infection is overcome, your B cells stop producing antibodies, but they do not "forget" how to produce them. The B cells continue to circulate in your bloodstream and lymph for years, ready to produce antibodies quickly if the same pathogen reenters your body. This memory property of B cells is part of what can make you immune to a disease that you already have had.

Like B cells, T lymphocytes, or **T cells**, live in the blood and lymphatic system of your body. Unlike B cells, T cells do not produce antibodies. Instead, they have a variety of functions. Some T cells, called killer T cells, kill pathogens directly. Others, called helper T cells and suppressor T cells, produce substances that regulate the activities of other cells of the immune system.

One of the regulatory substances that T cells produce is called **interferon** (in tur FEER ahn). Interferon stimulates phagocytes and other cells, including B cells, to fight off infection. When an infection has been brought under control, some of the T cells then "turn off" the activated cells with other chemicals. T cells also help your immune system "remember" pathogens in case they ever reenter your body. This memory capacity of T cells, along with the memory capacity of B cells, is what maintains the immunity of your body to pathogens.

Figure 22-8 *Different B cells produce different antibodies, each specific to a particular pathogen.*

HISTORY CONNECTION

Edward Jenner, a British physician, is generally credited with discovering immunization in 1796. Jenner demonstrated that exposing a person to the disease cowpox made that person immune to smallpox, a closely related disease. However, centuries earlier the Chinese were practicing a form of immunization for smallpox.

Types of Immunity

There are two types of immunity—active and passive. Both are important in protecting the body against infections.

ACTIVE IMMUNITY Immunity that your own immune system creates is called **active immunity.** Active immunity results from having a disease or receiving a vaccine.

When you were a baby, you may have received injections to protect you from some common childhood infectious diseases, such as measles, mumps, and rubella. These injections that cause you to become immune to a disease are called **immunizations** (im yuh nih ZAY shunz), or vaccinations. The substance that is injected is a **vaccine** (vak SEEN). Vaccines contain small amounts of dead or modified pathogens or their toxins. A vaccine causes your immune system to make antibodies to the pathogen or the toxin, as if you were actually infected with the pathogen. This gives you immunity without having to experience disease. After a few years, you may receive a booster dose of some vaccines to "remind" your immune system to maintain your immunity.

Many people need additional immunizations because of the work they do, the places to which they travel, or accidental exposure to an unusual pathogen. Other people may need to be immunized because of risk factors such as old age or poor health. Influenza vaccines, for example, are given to elderly people to protect them from the flu. During influenza

Figure 22-9 *Children should be immunized according to the schedule shown here.*

Recommended Immunization Schedule

<table>
<tr><th>Vaccine</th><th>Birth</th><th>2 mos.</th><th>4 mos.</th><th>6 mos.</th><th>12 mos.</th><th>15 mos.</th><th>18 mos.</th><th>4-6 yrs.</th><th>11-12 yrs.</th><th>14-16 yrs.</th></tr>
<tr><td rowspan="2">Hepatitis B</td><td colspan="2">inoculation 1</td><td></td><td></td><td></td><td></td><td></td><td></td><td></td><td></td></tr>
<tr><td></td><td colspan="2">2</td><td colspan="4">3</td><td></td><td>*</td><td></td></tr>
<tr><td>Diphtheria, Tetanus, Pertussis</td><td></td><td>1</td><td>2</td><td>3</td><td></td><td colspan="2">4</td><td>5</td><td colspan="2">Tetanus, diphtheria only</td></tr>
<tr><td>Haemophilus influenzae type b</td><td></td><td>1</td><td>2</td><td>3</td><td colspan="2">4</td><td></td><td></td><td></td><td></td></tr>
<tr><td>Polio</td><td></td><td>1</td><td>2</td><td></td><td colspan="3">3</td><td>4</td><td></td><td></td></tr>
<tr><td>Measles, Mumps, Rubella</td><td></td><td></td><td></td><td></td><td colspan="2">1</td><td></td><td>2 or</td><td>2</td><td></td></tr>
<tr><td>Varicella Zoster (chicken pox)</td><td></td><td></td><td></td><td></td><td colspan="3">1</td><td></td><td>*</td><td></td></tr>
</table>

* Recommended for children not previously vaccinated.

Source: Centers for Disease Control

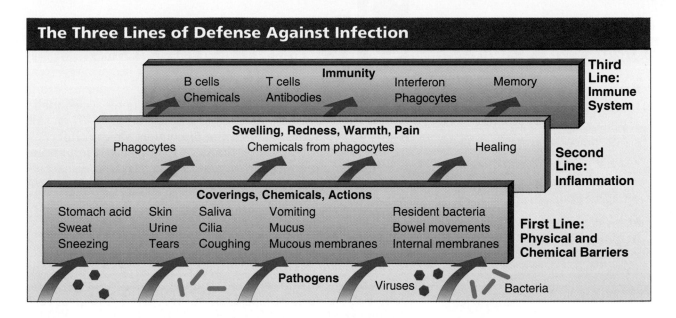

The Three Lines of Defense Against Infection

Third Line: Immune System
Immunity
B cells   T cells   Interferon   Memory
Chemicals Antibodies   Phagocytes

Second Line: Inflammation
Swelling, Redness, Warmth, Pain
Phagocytes   Chemicals from phagocytes   Healing

First Line: Physical and Chemical Barriers
Coverings, Chemicals, Actions
Stomach acid   Skin   Saliva   Vomiting   Resident bacteria
Sweat   Urine   Cilia   Mucus   Bowel movements
Sneezing   Tears   Coughing   Mucous membranes   Internal membranes

Pathogens   Viruses   Bacteria

epidemics, immunization is recommended for everyone who is at increased risk of serious disease.

PASSIVE IMMUNITY   Immunity that is acquired by receiving antibodies from another immune system is called **passive immunity**. This type of immunity is temporary, not lifelong. It occurs naturally in babies, who receive antibodies from their mothers before birth. After birth, antibodies also pass to an infant in the mother's breast milk. These antibodies protect newborns before their own immune systems have developed active immunity.

Passive immunity also can be artificially acquired. For example, suppose you were bitten by a dog with rabies. Antibodies to rabies can be obtained from the blood of horses that have been exposed to the rabies virus. A physician would give you injections of the rabies antibodies to help prevent you from developing the disease. Eventually these antibodies would disappear from your body.

Figure 22-10 *Can you explain how the body's three lines of defense work against infection?*

LESSON *2* REVIEW

1. What are the three lines of defense against infection?
2. Where does inflammation occur?
3. What are antibodies?
4. How does a vaccine cause immunity?

What Do You Think?

5. Children usually have more infectious diseases per year than adults. Why do you think this is so?

Focus on these questions as you read this lesson.

- What are the stages of an infectious disease?
- What behaviors help protect a person from getting infectious diseases?

SKILLS

- Activity: Bacterial Multiplication

3 DEVELOPMENT OF INFECTIOUS DISEASES

Despite all your body's defenses, pathogens occasionally are able to enter your body and cause disease. When this happens, you suffer through the discomfort that an infection usually causes. Gradually, thanks to your body's inflammation and immune responses, you recover from the disease. A quick recovery, however, depends on getting rest and eating a well-balanced diet.

Stages of Infectious Disease

Suppose you have been exposed to a virus that causes **influenza,** a viral infection of the upper respiratory system. Your body would respond to the infection and progress through the five stages of disease, as shown in Figure 22-11.

THE INCUBATION STAGE   Before you begin to feel ill, the influenza virus has entered your body, invaded cells in your respiratory system, and multiplied. The time between entry of the virus and the time when you begin to feel ill is called the **incubation stage** (in kyuh BAY shun). You feel fine during the incubation stage, even though the pathogen is multiplying inside your body.

THE PRODROMAL STAGE   After a few days, your throat may feel sore, or you may feel hot and feverish. Taking your temperature confirms that you have a mild fever, and looking in the mirror confirms that your throat is inflamed. These feelings caused by the disease are the **symptoms** (SIMP tumz) of the disease. When the first symptoms occur, you have entered the **prodromal stage** (proh DROH mul) of

Figure 22-11 *Many infectious diseases, such as influenza, develop in stages.*

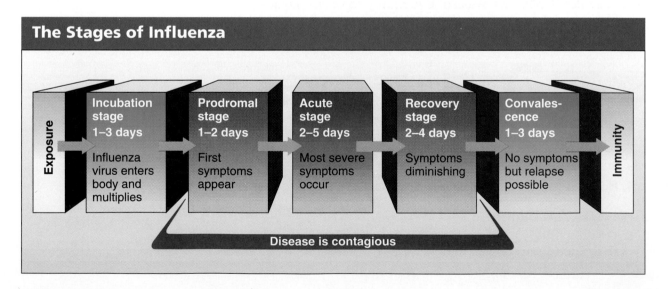

The Stages of Influenza

Exposure → Incubation stage 1–3 days — Influenza virus enters body and multiplies → Prodromal stage 1–2 days — First symptoms appear → Acute stage 2–5 days — Most severe symptoms occur → Recovery stage 2–4 days — Symptoms diminishing → Convales-cence 1–3 days — No symptoms but relapse possible → Immunity

Disease is contagious

BACTERIAL MULTIPLICATION

In this activity, you will demonstrate how rapidly a bacterial population can grow.

Materials

128 paper clips	paper and pencil

Procedure

1. Place a paper clip in front of you. Imagine that it represents a single disease-causing bacterium. Under ideal conditions, a bacterium grows and divides to form two new bacteria about every 30 minutes.

2. Imagine that 30 minutes pass and the bacterium represented by the one paper clip divides, producing two new bacteria. Add one paper clip to the first so there are two paper clips to represent the two new bacteria of the second generation.

3. Suppose that another 30 minutes pass and each of the two bacteria divides to produce two new bacteria each. Represent this third generation by adding two more paper clips to the population.

4. Continue to repeat this process until you have used up all the paper clips.

Discussion

1. How many generations, or rounds of reproduction, did it take to produce 128 bacteria?

2. If each generation takes 30 minutes, how long does it take to produce 128 bacteria starting from one bacterium?

3. If the bacteria continued to divide every 30 minutes, how many bacteria do you think would be present after 24 hours?

4. How does this activity relate to infectious diseases and your health?

---

illness. During this stage, you may be contagious; that is, you can pass the flu virus to others. Your immune system has discovered that a pathogen has entered your body, but it is a long way from destroying it.

THE ACUTE STAGE　Soon your head aches, your muscles feel sore, and you are sneezing and coughing. You take your temperature and discover you have a fever of 102°F. **Fever**, a body temperature above 98.6°F, is a common sign of most infectious diseases. It occurs because infection causes the release of chemicals in your body that signal your brain to raise body temperature. No one is quite sure what purpose a fever serves in infection. It is possible that higher body temperatures harm some pathogens.

At this stage you may go to bed early and stay home from school for the next two days. This stage of your illness, when your symptoms are most severe, is the **acute stage** (uh KYOOT). Your tissues are inflamed, and your immune system is working overtime to fight off the infection.

RECOVERY STAGE　Two days later, you wake up feeling a little better. Your fever is down to 99.8°F, and you decide to get up for breakfast. You have begun the **recovery stage.** You may stay home for the rest of the week, but your immune system is winning!

Figure 22-12 *Recovery from disease requires rest.*

CONVALESCENCE By the end of the week, your aches and pains have disappeared and your temperature is normal. Your immune system has won, but you do not feel as energetic as usual. This period, between the end of infection and feeling really well, is called **convalescence** (kahn vuh LES uns). If you do not take care of yourself during this stage, you may have a relapse. A **relapse** is the return of disease during or soon after convalescence.

Treating Infectious Diseases

If you do get an infectious disease, you can help your body to recover by going to bed and resting. This treatment and well-balanced meals are all that you need to recover from most mild infections. However, what if you have an infection that is not mild? How ill should you feel before you seek professional medical care?

WHEN TO SEEK MEDICAL CARE You need to seek professional medical care if you have any of the conditions listed in Figure 22-13. In addition, if you are worried about your health for any reason, see a physician and discuss your concerns with him or her.

USING MEDICINES A physician may prescribe medicines to treat a disease. A medicine that is available only with a written order from a physician or dentist is called a prescription medicine. **Antibiotics** (an tih by AHT iks), drugs that inhibit or kill bacteria, are prescribed to cure bacterial infections. They do not cure viral infections. At the moment, there is no cure for most viral infections. The best treatment for viral infections includes rest, a well-balanced diet, and plenty of fluids.

Hundreds of over-the-counter medicines—those available without a prescription—are also used to treat diseases. Many over-the-counter medicines treat the symptoms of viral infections. They may make you feel better while you have a viral infection, but they do not cure the infection. Taking over-the-

Figure 22-13 *Knowing when to seek medical care for an infectious disease can help you recover and avoid complications.*

When To Seek Medical Care

Seek medical care if you have any of the following conditions:

- An extremely sore throat, earache, vomiting, diarrhea, or a temperature of 101°F that lasts more than two days

- Mucus from your nose or throat that is thick and yellowish green

- Difficulty in breathing

- Severe pain anywhere

- A cut, scrape, or sore that does not seem to be healing as it should

- An illness that lasts longer than usual

counter medicines can cause problems if they make you feel well enough to go about your usual routine when you should be resting. Over-the-counter medicines also can hide symptoms that would normally cause you to seek medical care.

Whether you use over-the-counter or prescription medicines, follow the instructions on the container. Never take a drug prescribed for someone else or give yours to another person. To avoid giving a new "mutant" bacterium a chance to develop, use antibiotics EXACTY as they are prescribed.

Preventing Infectious Diseases

You can protect yourself from infectious diseases in three ways: by avoiding contact with pathogens, being immunized with a vaccine, and choosing healthful behaviors. It is difficult to avoid some pathogens, and immunizations are not available for all infectious diseases. However, choosing healthful behaviors—the best long-term strategy for preventing disease—is something you can always do.

Here are some healthful behaviors you can practice.

- Eat well-balanced meals and do not skip meals.
- Get at least eight hours of sleep each night, and spend some time every day relaxing.
- Exercise regularly, at least three or more times a week.
- Avoid stress if you can. If you cannot avoid stress, get the help you need so that you can cope with it.
- Avoid unhealthful substances, such as tobacco, alcohol, and illegal drugs.
- Do not share items that can transfer pathogens, such as a toothbrush, hairbrush, or drink container.
- Keep your body clean, and wash your hands several times a day, especially before eating.
- Check that your immunizations are current.

LESSON 3 REVIEW

1. What are the stages of a typical infectious disease?
2. What is a fever?
3. Under what conditions should you seek medical care?
4. Name at least five behaviors that can help prevent infectious disease.

What Do You Think?

5. If you had the flu, how would you try to reduce the chances of spreading it to other members of your family?

EXPLORING

CAREERS

Pharmacologists and Pharmacists

Physicians can prescribe hundreds of medicines. These medicines represent years of hard work by pharmacologists. **Pharmacologists** work in research laboratories to develop new drugs to treat or prevent diseases. Their work progresses slowly, since the drugs they develop must be tested carefully for effectiveness and safety.

To become a pharmacologist, a person must earn a Ph.D. degree in pharmacology or a related medical field. Sometimes a person who has earned a medical degree goes on to specialize in pharmacology.

A **pharmacist** dispenses medicines that have been prescribed by physicians and other health care providers. Pharmacists also advise people on the use of nonprescription medicines. To become a pharmacist, a person must earn a degree in pharmacy, usually from a five-year college program, and obtain a state license.

Infectious Diseases **537**

COMMON INFECTIOUS DISEASES

GUIDE FOR READING

Focus on these questions as you read this lesson.

- What are some common infectious diseases?
- What are the common infectious diseases against which people can be immunized?

SKILLS

- Evaluating Health Information

Infectious diseases affect everyone. **There are thousands of kinds of infectious diseases; some are common in one part of the world but rare or absent in other places.** Over 40 kinds of infectious diseases commonly occur in the United States. Some are described below and in Figure 22-16.

The Common Cold

The common cold is really a group of symptoms caused by a variety of viruses. One or two days after exposure to a cold virus, infected people develop sneezing, sore throats, runny noses, coughing, chest congestion, fever, headaches, and muscle aches. Most colds last three to seven days. A person with a cold is most contagious during the first day or two of symptoms. Colds spread when a person touches contaminated objects or inhales droplets from sneezes and coughs.

Unfortunately, there is no cure for the common cold. Even so, many products—over $500 million worth every year—are sold to reduce cold symptoms. Some of these products may hide the symptoms of more serious diseases. The best way to treat a cold is to stay home, rest, eat well-balanced meals, and drink plenty of fluids. You should stay home to avoid giving your cold to others. If severe symptoms last more than two to three days, you should seek medical care.

Influenza and Pneumonia

Influenza, also known as the flu, is a common viral infection of the upper respiratory system. Like the common cold, influenza is spread by airborne droplets and contact with

Figure 22-14 *Flu vaccines can prevent the spread of influenza.*

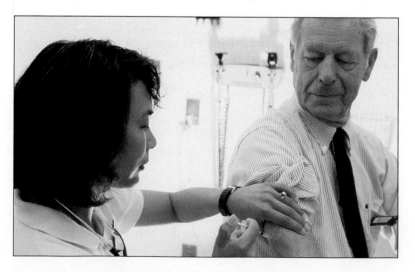

contaminated objects. High fever, sore throat, headache, and a cough are its usual symptoms. Influenza viruses can cause more serious illness than cold viruses, especially in infants, the elderly, and people with heart and lung diseases. In an average year, twenty thousand Americans die of the flu. Some types of influenza can be prevented by immunization.

In people who are elderly or who have heart disease or breathing problems, flu may develop into **pneumonia** (noo MOHN yuh), a serious infection of the lungs. Many people die each year from pneumonia, which can be caused by viruses, bacteria, or even fungi.

Rubella

German measles, or **rubella** (roo BEL uh), is caused by a virus. The symptoms include a mild fever, rash, coughing, sneezing, sore throat, swollen glands in the back of the neck, and chest congestion. In adults, rubella usually has no long-term effects. However, if a woman who is in the first few months of pregnancy contracts rubella, her child may be born with birth defects. Fortunately, a rubella vaccine is available.

Hepatitis

Inflammation of the liver, or **hepatitis** (hep uh TY tis), is caused by a group of viruses that infect the liver. Because the liver is important to so many bodily functions, hepatitis is a serious disease. Symptoms of hepatitis include fever, nausea, pain in the abdomen, tiredness, **jaundice** (JAWN dis), or yellowing of the skin, and sometimes, brown urine. People who have hepatitis need medical care.

Hepatitis types are identified by letter. The most common are hepatitis A, B, and C. Hepatitis A, formerly called infectious hepatitis, is transmitted in human wastes, contaminated water, and contaminated food, especially shellfish. Illness begins from three to six weeks after exposure,

Figure 22-15 *Raw shellfish harvested from contaminated waters can be a source of hepatitis.*

Some Common Infectious Diseases

Disease	Pathogen	Symptoms	How Spread	Treatment	Prevention
Chicken pox	Virus	Fever and weakness, red itchy rash	Contact with rash, droplet inhalation	Antiviral drug (for adults)	Vaccine
Cholera	Bacterium	Vomiting, severe diarrhea	Contaminated water or food	Bed rest, fluid replacement	Vaccine
Diphtheria	Bacterium	Fever, sore throat, nasal discharge, rapid pulse	Droplet inhalation	Bed rest, liquid/ soft diet, antibiotic	Vaccine
Haemophilus influenza type b (Hib)	Bacterium	Irritability, vomiting, fever, loss of appetite	Droplet inhalation	Bed rest, fluid replacement	Vaccine
Lyme disease	Bacterium	Red rash at site of tick bite, chills, fever, body aches, joint inflammation	Bite of infected deer tick	Antibiotic	Pants tucked into socks, long-sleeved shirt; vaccine
Measles (rubeola)	Virus	High fever, sore throat, cough, rash, sneezing, swollen eyelids, white spots on cheek lining	Droplet inhalation	Bed rest, cough medicine	Vaccine
Meningitis	Bacterium or virus	Fever, drowsiness, headache, vomiting, stiff neck	Droplet inhalation	Antibiotic for bacterial form	Vaccine for one bacterial form
Mumps	Virus	Fever, headache, weakness, swollen salivary glands	Droplet inhalation	Bed rest	Vaccine
Pertussis (whooping cough)	Bacterium	Hacking cough, tearing, sneezing, nasal congestion	Droplet inhalation	Fluids, antibiotics	Vaccine
Poliomyelitis (polio)	Virus	Fever, headache, muscle weakness, difficulty swallowing	Droplet inhalation	Bed rest	Vaccine
Rabies	Virus	Drooling, difficulty swallowing, skin sensitivity, alternating periods of rage/calm	Animal bite	Antibody and vaccine	Vaccine
Scarlet fever	Bacterium	Fever, sore throat, vomiting, rash on neck and chest	Contact with rash or discharge	Bed rest, liquids, antibiotic	
Tetanus (lockjaw)	Bacterium	Jaw, neck muscle stiffness/spasms, difficulty swallowing	Deep wound	Antibiotic, opening and cleaning of wound	Vaccine
Typhoid fever	Bacterium	Fever, sore throat, cough, diarrhea	Contaminated food or water	Antibiotic	Vaccine

Figure 22-16 *Which diseases are spread by animals?*

and recovery takes several weeks. A new vaccine for hepatitis A has succeeded in preventing the disease.

Hepatitis B and C are more severe than type A. These viruses are transmitted in blood or during sexual contact. Over a million Americans carry hepatitis B, for which there is an effective vaccine. Almost four million carry hepatitis C, for which there are few treatment options at this time.

Tuberculosis

A highly contagious bacterial infection that most often affects the lungs is **tuberculosis** (too bur kyuh LOH sis), or TB. Throughout the world, three million people die of tuberculosis each year. It is transmitted when droplets from the cough or sneeze of an infected person are inhaled. Symptoms, which include fatigue, weight loss, a mild fever, night sweats, and a chronic cough, may not show up for many years after the initial infection. Tuberculosis has always been a major health problem in developing countries. In the United States, however, TB was almost eliminated. Then HIV soared to epidemic levels and the incidence of HIV-related TB soared with it. Now, the number of TB cases is once again declining.

Most cases of TB can be cured with a combination of medicines that need to be taken for up to a year. Unfortunately, recently some strains of TB have become resistant to medicines and are more difficult to treat.

Infectious Mononucleosis

"Mono," or **infectious mononucleosis** (mahn oh noo klee OH sis), is a viral infection that causes the lymph nodes, tonsils, and spleen to become swollen and tender. Symptoms include fever, chills, a sore throat, and extreme fatigue. Many people develop mononucleosis during their teenage years. Usually, the infection disappears in three to six weeks. Treatment consists of bed rest and eating well-balanced meals.

Figure 22-17 *X rays of the lungs can reveal the presence of tuberculosis.*

LESSON 4 REVIEW

1. Name five common infectious diseases and the type of pathogen that causes each.
2. Why is rubella a serious disease for a pregnant woman?
3. Which organ is affected in hepatitis?
4. What disease is transmitted by a deer tick?

What Do You Think?

5. Why do you think tuberculosis is increasing in the United States?

Using Medicines Correctly

Felicia got home from her after-school job, ate dinner, and sat down to read her favorite magazine. All of a sudden, she realized she had forgotten to take an antibiotic tablet while at work. The antibiotic had been prescribed by a physician for her arm infection. She grabbed the bottle and tried to decide what to do. Should she take two tablets now to make up for the one she missed, or take one now and then one every six hours from then on? She asked her mother, who suggested that Felicia call and ask the pharmacist. The pharmacist told Felicia she should take just one tablet now and then continue taking the tablets according to her original schedule.

To be safe and effective, medicines must be used according to directions that are specific to each medicine. When should you use a medicine, and how can you make sure that you use it correctly? The guidelines below will help you decide.

1. Seek medical care when you are ill

Tell your physician what medicines, if any, you are taking. When prescribing a medicine, a physician needs to know this information because certain medicines can interact to produce unfavorable effects. Also, tell the physician if you have had any negative reactions to medicines in the past.

2. Ask how the medicine should affect you

Ask your physician about the medicine's desired and undesirable, or side, effects. Also ask about how soon the medicine should take effect. Your pharmacist also can answer these questions.

3. Read all the information on the label

Medicine labels indicate how much medicine you should take (the dosage) and how often you should take it. The label also may state special instructions or precautions. Labels for over-the-counter medicines also indicate what conditions the medicine will treat.

4. Follow the directions on the label

Be sure to take your medicine in the amount prescribed and according to the schedule indicated on the label. Keep a record of the times when you take your medicine. Many drugs need to be taken on a regular schedule to build up and maintain an effective amount of medicine in your body. If you forget to take a medicine at a scheduled time, do not take a double dose to try to make up the time. Take a single dose and get back on the original schedule. If you miss more than one

dose, consult with your pharmacist or physician. With an antibiotic, continue taking it until you
have used all of it. If you do not
finish the entire prescription,
your infection may return.

● ● ● ● ● ● ● ● ● ● ● ● ● ● ● ● ● ● ●

5. Take medicines pre-scribed only for yourself

Medicines are prescribed
according to factors that are
specific to each person, such as
age, weight, pregnancy, other
health conditions, other medicines being taken, and previous
reactions to drugs. It is dangerous to use medicines prescribed
for another person.

● ● ● ● ● ● ● ● ● ● ● ● ● ● ● ● ● ● ●

6. Call your physician if a medicine causes serious side effects

All medicines have side effects,
some more serious than others.
Side effects might include such
things as headache, dizziness,
drowsiness, excitability, and
nausea. Common allergic reactions to medicines include a skin
rash, runny nose, difficulty in
breathing, and rapid heartbeat.
If you develop serious side
effects to any medicine, contact
your physician or a hospital
emergency room immediately.

● ● ● ● ● ● ● ● ● ● ● ● ● ● ● ● ● ● ●

7. Never combine medi-cines without checking with your physician

Sometimes it is necessary to use
different medicines at the same
time to treat a single problem
or to treat several problems.
Not all medicines, however, can
be used in combination with

each other. Before you start
using more than one medicine
at a time, check with your physician or a pharmacist.

● ● ● ● ● ● ● ● ● ● ● ● ● ● ● ● ● ● ●

8. Never drink alcohol when taking medicines

Alcohol and medicines can be a
dangerous and even deadly
combination. Anyone taking
medicines should avoid any
form of alcohol.

● ● ● ● ● ● ● ● ● ● ● ● ● ● ● ● ● ● ●

9. Store medicines according to the label's instructions

Keep medicines in their original
containers so that their directions for use, precautions, and
expiration dates are always with
the medicines. Keep medicines
out of the reach of children.

● ● ● ● ● ● ● ● ● ● ● ● ● ● ● ● ● ● ●

10. Throw away a medi-cine that is beyond its expiration date

Many medicines lose their effectiveness over time and should
not be used. Dispose of medicines so they are kept away
from children and animals.

Esparza's Pharmacy
180 Woodward Drive
St. Charles, MO.
Tel. 555-3528

Date: 11/15/01
No. 1185423
Thomas Washington

Dr. C. Chin

*Take one capsule four times daily
until all are taken.*

Tetracycline
EXP. 11/15/02

Tabs. 250 mg
Qty. 28

 Take medication on an empty stomach three hours
before or two to three hours after a meal unless
otherwise directed by your doctor.

 Do not take
with dairy
products

 IMPORTANT
FINISH ALL THIS MEDICATION
UNLESS OTHERWISE DIRECTED
BY PRESCRIBER

Apply the Skill

1. Study the prescription medicine label above. What medicine has been prescribed? For
whom is the medicine intended? What is the dosage? How
often should the person take
the medicine? What physician
wrote the prescription?

2. Refer to the label again.
Should this medicine be taken
with meals? Are there specific
foods or fluids that should not
be taken with this medicine?
Should the person stop taking
the medicine as soon as symptoms of the illness disappear?

3. At your local drugstore, read
the label of an over-the-
counter medicine, such as
aspirin or a cold-relief medicine. What is the medicine used
for? What warnings or cautions
are on the label? What is the
recommended dosage? How
often should the medicine be
taken? Under what conditions
should you consult a physician?

CHAPTER 22 REVIEW

KEY IDEAS

LESSON 1

- Infectious diseases are caused by pathogens such as bacteria, viruses, and fungi, that enter, live in, and multiply within the human body.
- People come in contact with pathogens through contact with an infected person or animal, a contaminated object, or a contaminated substance.

LESSON 2

- Your body protects itself from infection with physical and chemical barriers, inflammation, and the immune system.
- Immunity is the ability to produce antibodies to pathogens before they are able to cause disease.

LESSON 3

- Antibiotics are effective against bacterial, but not viral, infections.
- You can protect yourself from infectious diseases in three ways: by avoiding contact with pathogens, being immunized with a vaccine if available, and choosing healthful behaviors.

LESSON 4

- There are thousands of kinds of infectious diseases; some are common in one part of the world but rare or absent in other parts.
- The cold, influenza, rubella, tuberculosis, infectious mononucleosis, and hepatitis are some common infectious diseases in the United States.

KEY TERMS

LESSON 1
bacteria

infectious disease

pathogen

toxin

virus

LESSON 2
active immunity

antibodies

B cells

cilia

immunity

immunization

inflammation

lymphocytes

mucous membranes

mucus

passive immunity

phagocytes

T cells

vaccine

LESSON 3
antibiotic

acute stage

convalescence

fever

incubation stage

influenza

prodromal stage

recovery stage

symptom

LESSON 4
hepatitis

jaundice

pneumonia

tuberculosis

Listed above are some of the important terms in this chapter. Choose the term from the list that best matches each phrase below.

1. cells that eat up foreign cells

2. inflammation of the liver

3. cells that produce antibodies

4. tiny hairlike structures that beat mucus upward through the air passages

5. feelings caused by a disease

6. moist, protective linings

7. a body temperature above 98.6°F

8. type of immunity present after a disease

9. the body's response to injury

10. harmful chemical substance that is produced by bacteria

WHAT HAVE YOU LEARNED?

On a separate sheet of paper, write the word or words that best complete each statement.

11. The sticky fluid that covers the linings of body surfaces and traps pathogens is _____ .

12. White blood cells that carry out most of the immune system's functions are _____ .

13. Receiving a _____ is one way of acquiring active immunity.

14. Hepatitis may result in _____ , a condition in which the skin becomes yellow.

15. During the _____ of a disease, the first symptoms of a disease are experienced.

16. _____ is the body's ability to destroy pathogens that it has previously encountered before they are able to cause disease.

17. Antibiotics are effective against bacteria but not against _____ .

18. _____ occurs in babies who receive antibodies from their mothers.

Answer each of the following with complete sentences.

19. List the four ways that pathogens can come in contact with your body.

20. How do bacteria injure the body's cells? How do viruses injure the body's cells?

21. How is your skin a barrier to pathogens?

22. How do your mucous membranes protect your body from pathogens?

23. What do phagocytes do?

24. Name two ways that lymphocytes protect your body.

25. Define the five stages that are typical of an infectious disease.

26. Explain how a vaccine creates immunity in your body.

27. What is the fastest way to get over a viral infection, such as the common cold?

WHAT DO YOU THINK?

28. You are not sure whether you have been immunized for rubella. Is it important to find out? Why or why not?

29. Why do you think some infectious diseases are more common in young people than in older people?

30. There has been a flood in your region. Why has the department of public health advised people to boil tap water for five minutes before using it for drinking?

31. You are taking a trip to India. Do you think you will need more immunizations? Why or why not?

32. More people get flu during the winter months than at any other time of year. Why do you think this is true?

WHAT WOULD YOU DO?

33. It is Saturday, and you are looking forward to going to the basketball game. But you are getting a headache, and your throat is starting to feel a little sore. Would you go to the game, or stay home and rest? What is likely to happen as a result of your choice?

34. Someone at school asks to borrow your hairbrush. Would you say yes or no? Why?

35. Your dog gets into a fight with another dog and one of them bites you. Will you tell anyone about the bite? Why?

36. You left a chicken casserole from last night's dinner on the counter all night. What will you do with the chicken casserole now? Explain your answer.

Getting Involved

37. Contact your town or city health department and ask about its immunization programs. What programs exist for school-age people and for other age groups? How are the immunization programs publicized?

AIDS AND SEXUALLY TRANSMITTED DISEASES

Over the last twenty years, AIDS has killed hundreds of thousands of Americans. The AIDS Quilt is a memorial to those who have died. Unfortunately, there is still no sure cure for AIDS. The best defense is to avoid behaviors that put a person at risk. In this chapter you will learn about AIDS and other sexually transmitted diseases. More importantly, you will learn how these diseases can be prevented.

CHAPTER PREVIEW

23-1 The Silent Epidemic

- Explain how the spread of sexually transmitted diseases can be prevented.

23-2 Kinds of STDs

- Describe the symptoms and treatment of common sexually transmitted diseases.

23-3 HIV and AIDS

- Describe the symptoms, mode of transmission, testing, and treatment of HIV infection and AIDS.

23-4 Preventing HIV Infection

- Identify behaviors that put a person at risk for contracting HIV and behaviors that can help to prevent the spread of HIV.

BUILDING HEALTH SKILLS

- Describe ways to find reliable information on a health topic.

CHECK YOUR WELLNESS

Test your knowledge by deciding whether each of these statements is true or false.

- It is possible to have a healthy, caring relationship without the risk of sexually transmitted diseases.

- It takes only one sexual contact with an infected person to get a sexually transmitted disease.

- No one has immunity to sexually transmitted disease.

- Many sexually transmitted diseases can be passed from an infected woman to her child during birth.

- The AIDS virus cannot be transmitted through ordinary casual contact, such as coughing or hugging.

- Sexual abstinence is the surest way to avoid AIDS.

KEEPING A JOURNAL

If you were to design a memorial for the people who have died from AIDS, what would you choose? Possibilities may include a park, scholarship fund, or work of art. Describe or draw your memorial in your journal.

Take it to the Net
www.phschool.com

GUIDE FOR READING

Focus on these questions as you read this lesson.

- What is causing the current epidemic of sexually transmitted diseases (STDs)?
- What behaviors can prevent the spread of STDs?

SKILLS

- Developing Refusal Skills

L orene is 25 and has been happily married for three years. Two years ago she and her husband decided that they wanted to start a family. They repainted the small bedroom in the back of their apartment in anticipation of the happy event, but Lorene never became pregnant. Frustrated, she and her husband went for checkups at a local health clinic. Lorene's physician told her that she was unlikely to become pregnant because her fallopian tubes were badly scarred.

Several years before, Lorene had contracted gonorrhea, a common sexually transmitted disease. Any disease that spreads from one person to another during sexual intercourse is a **sexually transmitted disease,** or STD. Unfortunately, Lorene never suspected that she had an STD. She believed many of the myths about STDs that are listed on the next page. How well-informed about STDs are you?

Concern About STDs

By all standards, the occurrence of STDs in the United States today represents an epidemic. An **epidemic** (ep uh DEM ik) is an unusually high occurrence of a disease in a certain place during a certain time period. About 12 million new cases are reported each year in the United States. Of those cases, two-thirds occur in adolescents and young adults.

The STD epidemic is a serious concern for several reasons. When ignored, STDs can be very damaging. Untreated infections increase the risk of infertility in both men and women. **Infertility** (in fur TIL ih tee) is the reduced ability to have children. Some STDs are also associated with an increased risk of cancer. In addition, infants born to mothers with certain STDs risk infection, blindness, and even death.

Unlike many other infectious diseases, people cannot develop immunity to STDs. A person can be cured and then reinfected with the same STD again. Moreover, some STDs are incurable. If untreated, several STDs are fatal.

Finally, STDs are costly, not only in terms of physical and emotional suffering, but financially as well. Yearly health-care expenses related to STDs are well over a billion dollars.

Reasons for the STD Epidemic

There are several reasons for the current STD epidemic. First, many people begin to have sexual intercourse at a young age, and they tend to have multiple sexual partners during their lifetimes. The more sexual partners a person has, the greater the chance of contracting an STD.

Figure 23-1 *Getting the facts about STDs is the first step in fighting the epidemic.*

MYTHS & FACTS

Sexually Transmitted Diseases

1. **MYTH:** Teenagers seldom get STDs.
   - **FACT: Hundreds of thousands of teenagers get STDs each year.**

2. **MYTH:** Birth control pills prevent STDs.
   - **FACT: Birth control pills provide no protection against STDs.**

3. **MYTH:** A person cannot get an STD by having sex only once.
   - **FACT: It takes only one sexual encounter with an infected person to get an STD.**

4. **MYTH:** Anyone who has an STD will show signs of it.
   - **FACT: Many STDs have no symptoms early in the infection. Others have symptoms that come and go. Symptoms of AIDS may not show up for ten years or more.**

5. **MYTH:** A person cannot get more than one STD at a time.
   - **FACT: It is possible to have several STDs at the same time. STDs that cause open sores increase the risk of infection by other STDs, particularly AIDS.**

6. **MYTH:** There are vaccines to prevent STDs.
   - **FACT: The only STD for which there is a vaccine is hepatitis B.**

7. **MYTH:** If a person gets an STD once, he or she cannot get it again.
   - **FACT: There is no effective immunity against STDs. People can get STDs again and again with equal severity.**

8. **MYTH:** If the symptoms of an STD go away, a person does not need to see a doctor.
   - **FACT: The disappearance of the symptoms of an STD does not mean that the disease is over. Only a doctor can tell whether or not a person is still infected.**

9. **MYTH:** STDs can enter the body only through the genitals.
   - **FACT: The pathogens that cause STDs can enter the body through openings of the body or cuts or sores in the skin.**

10. **MYTH:** All STDs can be cured by antibiotics.
    - **FACT: Viral STDs, such as genital herpes, genital warts, and AIDS, are incurable.**

Second, many people who are sexually active do not take precautions against infection. They often do not realize the risks of contracting STDs or they choose to ignore the risks. Adolescents in particular tend to ignore the risks, thinking "It can't happen to me." The tragedy is that it can and it does.

Third, some people who become infected do not seek immediate medical treatment. Sometimes people are too embarrassed to seek treatment. Other times people do not know that they have an STD because they do not recognize the symptoms. In some cases STDs have no symptoms and can only be detected by laboratory tests. Sometimes the symptoms go away temporarily, making the person think the disease has been cured when in reality it has not. In all of these situations, the disease goes untreated, increasing the chances that the person will spread the disease to others.

Avoiding STDs

The good news about STDs is that most are preventable. But you need to know the facts about STDs and then apply that knowledge in making healthy choices. As indicated by their

Figure 23-2 *Sexual fidelity eliminates the risk of contracting an STD through sexual contact.*

name, STDs are transmitted mainly through sexual intercourse. A few STDs are also transmitted through contact with the blood of an infected person.

ABSTINENCE   Because STDs are spread mainly by sexual intercourse, the most certain way to avoid STDs is to practice sexual abstinence. **Sexual abstinence** means not having sexual intercourse until you are ready to commit yourself to a long-term, caring relationship, such as marriage. By choosing abstinence, a person chooses to remain sexually healthy. **As the former Surgeon General of the United States has said, "...abstinence is the only sure way to protect oneself from acquiring an STD."**

SEXUAL FIDELITY   For people who are involved in a sexual relationship, the most certain way to avoid most STDs is for both partners to practice sexual fidelity. **Sexual fidelity** is practiced when both partners in a caring, committed relationship, such as marriage, agree to have sexual intercourse only with one another. If both partners are uninfected, sexual fidelity eliminates the risk of getting an STD through sexual intercourse. However, the only way to be sure that both partners are not infected is to have a medical checkup.

PRECAUTIONS   How can individuals who are sexually active prevent STDs? For people in this category, there is only one way to significantly reduce the risk of STDs. The male should always use a latex condom during sexual intercourse. A condom is a sheath that covers the penis and serves as a physical barrier to most—but not all—of the micro-organisms that cause STDs.

It can take only one sexual contact with an infected person to become infected. Therefore, to be effective, a condom must be used each time a person has sexual intercourse, and it must be used from start to finish. The condom must be free of tears and it must be used in accordance with directions on the package. The condom should be made of latex rubber, because viruses can pass through condoms made of natural materials, such as sheep intestine. A condom should never be tested before use and should never be reused.

Although a condom can reduce the risk of contracting an STD, it does not entirely eliminate the risk. Because condoms can break, there is always a small chance of failure.

AVOIDING DRUG ABUSE   Some STDs can be transmitted by blood-to-blood contact between an uninfected person and an infected person. People who use illegal drugs run a high risk of contracting certain STDs when they share needles that have been contaminated with the blood of an infected person. Individuals who share needles when they inject steroids are also at risk. To reduce the risk of STDs, people should not inject illegal drugs.

Drugs such as alcohol play an indirect role in the STD epidemic. People who drink alcohol may not think clearly and may make choices that they later regret. For example, they may engage in sexual behaviors that place them at risk for infection with STDs.

Healthy Choices

Each person has a responsibility to act in ways that prevent STDs. The safest behaviors are abstinence or mutual sexual fidelity and avoidance of drugs. Individuals who are sexually active should use condoms during every sexual encounter.

People who participate in high-risk behaviors should get medical checkups every six months. Many states have clinics that test for STDs. The results of these tests are confidential. Information about clinics can be obtained by calling a state's department of public health or the national toll-free STD hotline. The number for the hotline can be obtained from the information operator at 1-800-555-1212.

A person who suspects an STD infection should take measures that will prevent further spread of the disease. These measures include refraining from sexual intercourse and seeing a physician for a diagnosis. If an infection is present, the person needs to start treatment immediately. The person should also notify any sexual partners, so they may seek treatment as well. After completing the prescribed treatment, the person should be checked again by a physician to be sure the infection is gone. The person should refrain from sexual intercourse until the disease is cured. If the STD is not curable, the physician can give advice about how to live with the disease and how to prevent passing it to others.

You will find more information about STDs in the remaining part of this chapter, but it may not answer all your questions. To get more information, you should ask adults at home, a physician, a nurse, a teacher, or a counselor. Information is also available at your local library or by calling your state's public health department or the national STD hotline.

SHARPEN YOUR *SKILLS*

Developing Refusal Skills

Two of your classmates have asked you to a party where illegal drugs will be available. How would you say *no* to their invitation? With two other classmates, prepare a skit to show how you would respond.

LESSON **1** REVIEW

1. Why should teenagers be concerned about STDs?
2. What are three main reasons for the STD epidemic?
3. What behaviors help prevent the spread of STDs?
4. Where can a person get information on preventing the spread of STDs?

What Do You Think?

5. Why do you think there are so many myths about STDs?

Focus on these questions as you read this lesson.

- What are the common STDs?
- What are the symptoms of and treatments for STDs?

SKILLS

- Locating Community Resources

2 KINDS OF STDs

Early diagnosis and treatment of STDs are essential in preventing long-term ill effects. Although a few STDs are characterized by a lack of symptoms, most have distinct symptoms. This lesson describes the transmission, symptoms, potential dangers, and treatments for some of the more common STDs. **Two of the most serious STDs are syphilis and hepatitis C; other common STDs include chlamydia, trichomoniasis, gonorrhea, genital warts, genital herpes, chancroid, candidiasis, pubic lice, and scabies.** The most serious of all STDs is AIDS, which is discussed in Lessons 3 and 4.

Chlamydia

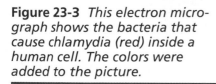

The most common bacterial STD in the United States is **chlamydia** (kluh MID ee uh). Researchers estimate that this STD infects about 4 million people each year. Half of those are women aged 15 to 19. All people who are sexually active should be checked regularly for chlamydia. The infection can be cured with antibiotics.

In females, chlamydia often has no symptoms other than a yellowish vaginal discharge. However, an untreated case of chlamydia can cause **pelvic inflammatory disease,** or PID, which is a serious infection of the reproductive organs. PID can lead to infertility and a potentially fatal tubal pregnancy. In addition, a pregnant woman can pass chlamydia to her baby during birth. If an infected infant survives, it may suffer damage to the lungs or eyes.

Infected males often experience a painful, frequent urination and discharge from the penis. If untreated, they may suffer from **nongonococcal urethritis** (nahn gahn uh KAHK ul yoor ih THRY tis) or NGU. Urethritis is an inflammation of the lining of the urethra.

Figure 23-3 *This electron micrograph shows the bacteria that cause chlamydia (red) inside a human cell. The colors were added to the picture.*

Trichomoniasis

Figure 23-4 *The protozoans that cause trichomoniasis, photographed through a scanning electron microscope.*

A sexually transmitted protozoan infection of the urinary tract or vagina is **trichomoniasis** (trik uh muh NY uh sis). Symptoms of trichomoniasis in males include some itching in the penis and clear discharge or painful urination. Symptoms in females include itching and burning in the vagina, smelly, greenish-yellow discharge, and pain when urinating.

If untreated, trichomoniasis can lead to urethritis in males and vaginitis in females. **Vaginitis** (vaj uh NY tis) is a vaginal infection or irritation. A physician can prescribe medicine to cure a trichomoniasis infection.

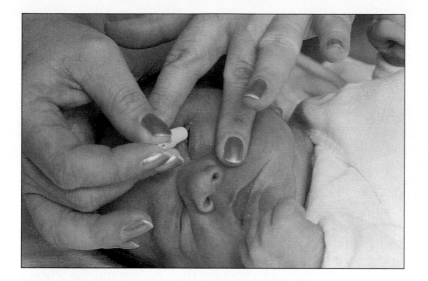

Gonorrhea

One serious bacterial STD is **gonorrhea** (gahn uh REE uh), an infection of the urinary tract of males and females and the reproductive organs of females. Males usually have a thick, puslike discharge from the penis and painful urination. Females sometimes experience painful urination and puslike discharge from the vagina or urinary tract. More often, however, symptoms in a woman are very mild and may not be noticed. If left untreated in males, gonorrhea can lead to urethritis and sterility. In females it may lead to PID and infertility.

An infected woman can transmit gonorrhea to her baby during birth. In the United States babies are given medicated eyedrops at birth to prevent infection of the eyes.

Because gonorrhea often has no noticeable symptoms, people participating in high-risk behaviors should get regular medical checkups. Treatment for gonorrhea requires antibiotics, usually penicillin. Strains of gonorrhea that are resistant to penicillin must be treated with other antibiotics.

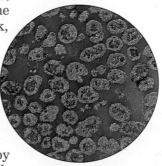

Figure 23-6 *A color-enhanced electron micrograph of the bacteria that cause gonorrhea.*

Genital Warts

The most common viral STD in the United States is **genital warts,** or HPV. The cause is the **human papilloma virus** (pap uh LOH muh). Once a person is infected, the virus stays for life. One or more months after infection, warts may appear around the genitals. The warts may itch or burn. A physician can remove the warts, but the virus remains, so the warts may reappear. HPV can remain in the body for years without any symptoms, so it is difficult to identify the source of an infection. Some people may never know they carry HPV. A few types of HPV are linked to cervical cancer. Women with those types of HPV should have an annual physical.

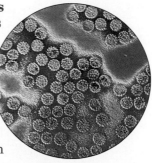

Figure 23-7 *An electron micrograph of human papilloma virus—the virus that causes genital warts.*

Genital Herpes

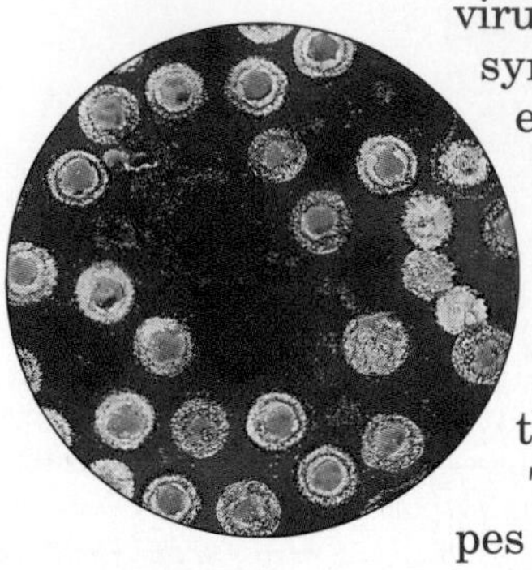

Another incurable viral STD is **genital herpes** (HUR peez), which produces painful blisters around the genital area. The virus that causes genital herpes is herpes simplex. The first symptoms of infection usually appear 2 to 10 days after exposure. These symptoms may be hardly noticeable, or they may include a flulike feeling and a tingling sensation at the site of infection. Later the infected person will experience periodic outbreaks of blisters. A physician can prescribe medicine that helps relieve the discomfort and dry up the blisters, but there is no cure for the disease.

To prevent spreading the disease, people with genital herpes should refrain from sexual intercourse during an outbreak of blisters and shortly after the blisters disappear. An infected person should also keep the area around the blisters clean and dry.

A woman with genital herpes can infect her infant during birth, causing blindness and possibly death. In some cases, a physician may recommend that an infected woman's baby be delivered by cesarean section. **Cesarean section** (sih ZAIR ee un) is a surgical method of birth.

Figure 23-8 *A color-enhanced micrograph of the virus that causes genital herpes.*

Syphilis

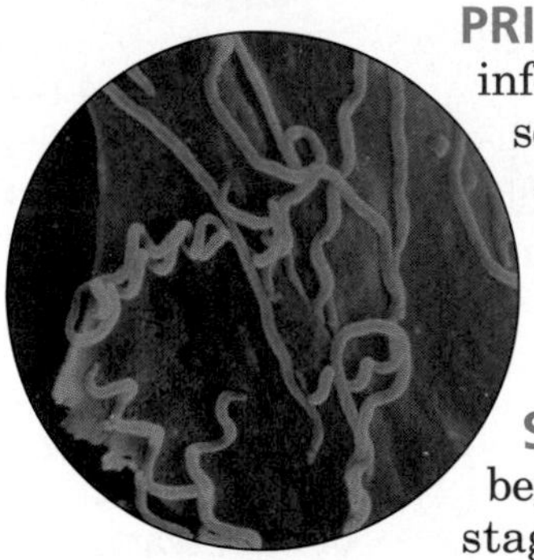

A serious bacterial STD that progresses through several distinct stages is **syphilis** (SIF uh lis). The stages of the disease are as follows.

Figure 23-9 *A scanning electron micrograph of the bacteria that cause syphilis.*

PRIMARY SYPHILIS Between one and 12 weeks after infection with the bacteria that cause syphilis, a painless sore called a **chancre** (SHANG kur) appears. The chancre occurs at the site of exposure, which may be in a place where it is not noticeable. In a few weeks, the sore goes away, leaving a small scar. The bacteria, however, remain and spread to different parts of the body.

SECONDARY SYPHILIS The second stage of syphilis begins from two to eight weeks after the first stage. This stage is characterized by sores in the mouth and flulike symptoms—fever, headache, swollen lymph glands, and loss of appetite. A nonitchy skin rash appears on different parts of the body, often on the hands and feet. If the infected person does not seek treatment, the disease moves to the latent stage.

LATENT SYPHILIS In the latent stage of syphilis, symptoms may disappear for years. During this time the bacteria attack internal parts of the body, such as the brain and heart. Damage that occurs in this stage is permanent and can eventually lead to death. The only way to diagnose syphilis during this stage is by a blood test.

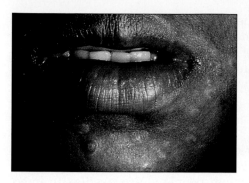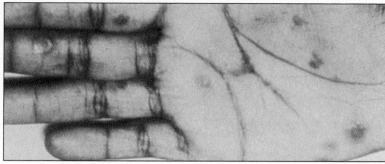

LATE (TERTIARY) SYPHILIS Untreated syphilis in an adult causes brain damage, paralysis, and heart disease. By the late stage, the damage that has occurred becomes evident. This stage can lead to death.

The first two stages of syphilis are the most infectious. Any direct contact with a chancre or the blood of an infected person can spread the disease. At any stage of the disease, a pregnant woman will pass the disease to her developing baby. A baby born with syphilis is said to have **congenital syphilis.** Congenital syphilis damages the skin, bones, eyes, teeth, and liver of the baby.

Syphilis can be treated and cured with antibiotics in its early stages. Once it progresses beyond the second stage, the bacteria can be killed, but any damage that has already occurred is permanent. If an infected mother receives treatment during pregnancy, congenital syphilis can be prevented.

Figure 23-10 *The sign of primary syphilis is a small, painless sore. During secondary syphilis an itchless rash appears on the skin.*

Chancroid

A bacterial STD with symptoms similar to primary syphilis is called **chancroid** (SHANG kroyd). In this disease painful sores appear around the genitals. The sores are deeper than the chancre associated with syphilis and may have a gray coating. The sores are very infectious and provide openings through which other pathogens can infect the person. Chancroid can be treated with antibiotics.

Candidiasis

An infection in the vagina caused by the fungus *Candida* is known as **candidiasis** (kan dih DY uh sis), or moniliasis. Although it usually is not caused by sexual contact, candidiasis can be passed to a partner during sexual intercourse. In women the symptoms are a white, cheesy discharge and itching. Men may have no symptoms.

Candidiasis is the most common type of the so-called vaginal yeast infections. These infections most often occur as a result of a change in the conditions of the vagina. The bacteria that normally live in the vagina prevent fungi from growing there. If these bacteria are destroyed, the fungi may then

SHARPEN YOUR SKILLS

Locating Community Resources

Suppose that a friend confided to you that she thought she had an STD, but did not know where to go to get treatment. Where in your community could your friend get tested for STDs? Report your findings to your class.

be able to multiply. When a woman takes an antibiotic, the bacteria in the vagina may be destroyed, resulting in candidiasis. The frequent use of douches may also increase the possibility of fungal infections. Candidiasis and other fungal infections can be cured with medication.

Hepatitis

Hepatitis B and hepatitis C are sexually transmitted diseases that attack the liver. They are also spread by blood-to-blood contact, such as when people share needles to inject drugs or pierce body parts. The medical community tends to use the term *HBV* for hepatitis B and *HCV* for hepatitis C. Street names for the diseases are "hep B" and "hep C."

People who are infected with hepatitis B or C are often unaware of their infection. HBV symptoms do not appear until two to six months after infection. An HCV victim can go for years without realizing that a virus is slowly destroying his or her liver. The most common symptoms for either HBV or HCV are fatigue, abdominal pain, loss of appetite, nausea, and vomiting. Victims may also have jaundice, a condition in which the skin and eyes become yellowish. As the disease progresses, the chance of developing **cirrhosis** (sih ROH sis), in which scar tissue replaces normal liver tissue, increases. In other cases, the HBV or HCV may lead to liver cancer.

Hepatitis B or C can be diagnosed by a blood test. Medications may be prescribed to relieve the disease symptoms, but there is no cure for either HBV or HCV. Bed rest and a controlled diet are the usual treatment.

An HBV vaccine is available, and children are now routinely vaccinated. Those who missed a childhood vaccination should see a doctor for a "catch-up" vaccine.

HCV is a bigger problem. Health officials expect HCV to be a public health threat for many years because the virus is difficult to study and because the disease is already widespread. There is currently no vaccine for HCV.

Figure 23-11 *A scanning electron micrograph of a pubic louse.*

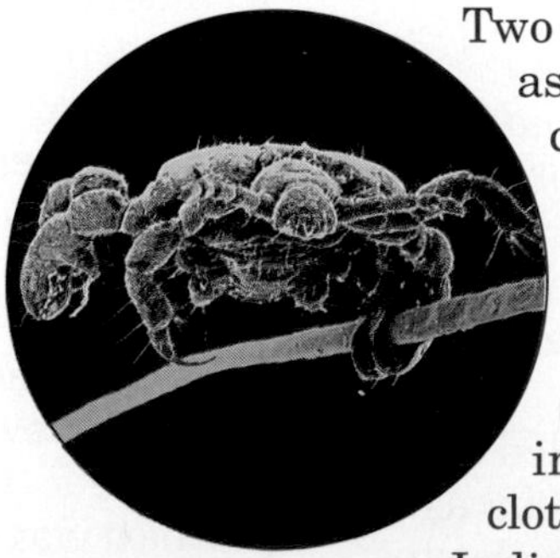

Pubic Lice and Scabies

Two conditions involving infestations of tiny animal parasites can be sexually transmitted. One condition is caused by **pubic lice** (PYOO bik), or crab lice, tiny insects that infest the hair around the genitals. The other condition, known as **scabies** (SKAY beez), results from an infestation of mites. Both conditions cause itching and sometimes a rash. They can be spread through direct physical contact with an infested person and by contact with contaminated clothing or bedding.

Individuals who are infested with pubic lice or scabies need to get medical treatment in the form of shampoos or ointments that kill the animals and their eggs. All bedding

Figure 23-12 *It is important to seek treatment at the first sign of an STD.*

and clothing should be washed in very hot water, dried in a hot dryer, and ironed to kill any remaining eggs.

From Information to Action

Knowing the facts about STDs helps prevent the spread of these diseases. As you know, the most healthy choices are to practice abstinence and to avoid using illegal drugs. Individuals who choose these behaviors almost totally eliminate their risk of exposure to STDs.

Individuals who suspect they may be infected should seek prompt medical treatment. They also should notify sexual partners so they can be treated as well. Information about clinics that test for STDs is available from state and local public health departments or from the national toll-free STD hotline.

LESSON 2 REVIEW

1. What is the most common bacterial STD in this country? Why is it important to get early treatment for this infection?
2. Which STDs can be treated but not cured?
3. What is congenital syphilis?
4. Why is it risky to share a toothbrush or eating utensil with someone who is infected with hepatitis B?

What Do You Think?

5. When should a couple discuss their concerns about sexual health?

3 HIV AND AIDS

Paul is an honors student who has completed his first year of college. Paul is just like any other boy his age—except that he is infected with the AIDS virus. Paul contracted the virus from a girl he met at a party. No one could be more surprised and angry than Paul is. He never thought his behavior could put him at risk for AIDS. Now he is learning to live with a disease for which there is no sure cure. To help others, he spends time each week talking to teens at local youth centers. "AIDS shouldn't be happening to me or anyone else," he says.

AIDS—acquired immunodeficiency syndrome—is an often fatal disease of the immune system that is caused by a virus. In the United States the first documented cases of AIDS were reported in 1981. Since then the number of cases has increased so rapidly that the incidence of AIDS is considered an epidemic. Teenagers are particularly at risk, because, like Paul, they don't think AIDS can happen to them. Before you read further, see how much you know about AIDS by reading the myths and facts on page 559.

HIV Infection

When AIDS was first discovered, scientists knew very little about the disease. Now it is known that AIDS is the last and most severe stage of a sexually transmitted disease caused by **HIV**—the **human immunodeficiency virus.** To understand the relationship between HIV infection and AIDS, you need to know about the characteristics of the virus.

HIV cannot live very long outside of human tissues. Transmission usually occurs during sexual contact with an infected person or through contact with certain body fluids of an infected person.

Inside the body, HIV attacks an important part of the immune system, the T lymphocytes, or T cells. You may recall from the previous chapter that lymphocytes signal the immune system to produce antibodies, the proteins that help destroy viruses and bacteria. The immune system of a newly infected person tries to fight off HIV by producing antibodies. Unfortunately for most HIV-infected people, these antibodies are not effective in stopping the progression of the disease.

Despite the production of antibodies, HIV soon outstrips the body's defenses and destroys ever-increasing numbers of T cells, crippling the immune system. HIV infects T cells, reproduces, and then moves on to destroy other T cells. By counting the number of certain T cells that remain active in the body, the progression of HIV infection can be monitored. The fewer of these T cells, the more advanced the disease.

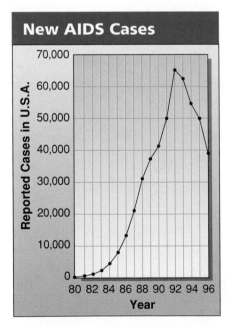

New AIDS Cases

Figure 23-13 *The number of new AIDS cases rose dramatically during the 1980s and early 1990s, then began to decline. During the later 1990s, the number of new cases hovered around 40,000 per year.*

HIV and AIDS

1. **Myth:** Teenagers cannot get AIDS.

   ● **Fact: Anyone who is sexually active or who shares needles to inject drugs is at risk for getting AIDS.**

2. **Myth:** A person can be infected with HIV through the bite of a mosquito.

   ● **Fact: There are no cases of HIV transmission through the bite of any insect, including mosquitoes.**

3. **Myth:** Only male homosexuals get AIDS.

   ● **Fact: Anyone who engages in high-risk behavior is at risk of contracting HIV. Men, women, and children get AIDS.**

4. **Myth:** It is not a good idea to eat in restaurants, because the people handling the food might be infected with HIV.

   ● **Fact: There are no cases of HIV being transmitted through air, water, or food, or by any objects such as eating or cooking utensils.**

5. **Myth:** You can tell if a person is infected with HIV just by the way he or she looks.

   ● **Fact: People can harbor HIV in their bodies for many years without showing any signs of illness.**

6. **Myth:** A person infected with HIV cannot infect another person until he or she develops symptoms of AIDS.

   ● **Fact: Any time after being infected with HIV, a person can transmit the virus to another person through body fluids, such as blood, semen, or vaginal secretions.**

7. **Myth:** If you want to be safe, you should not get near a person infected with HIV.

   ● **Fact: HIV cannot be transmitted through normal, everyday contact such as talking with, touching, or being in the same classroom with an HIV-infected person.**

8. **Myth:** You are likely to get infected with HIV from blood used in a transfusion during an operation in a hospital.

   ● **Fact: Since 1985, when a blood test for HIV was put into use, the chances of getting HIV from blood transfusions have become extremely small in this country.**

9. **Myth:** You can get infected with HIV by donating blood.

   ● **Fact: The sterile procedures used to collect blood prevent any risk of infection to a donor.**

Symptoms of HIV and AIDS

How do people know if they are infected with HIV? Often within three to four weeks of exposure to HIV, an infected person experiences several symptoms: fever, swollen lymph glands, and tiredness. At the same time the infected person's immune system has started to produce antibodies against HIV. At this early stage of infection, the only way the person can know for sure if he or she has HIV is by being tested for HIV antibodies. It usually takes between 6 and 12 weeks for the body to produce detectable levels of HIV antibodies.

The first symptoms of infection usually go away after a few weeks and generally are followed by a period of many months or years during which the person shows no outward signs of disease. Many infected persons look and feel fine and may have no idea they have HIV. For others the only sign of infection may be lymph glands that remain swollen for many months. A person may be infected with HIV for many years

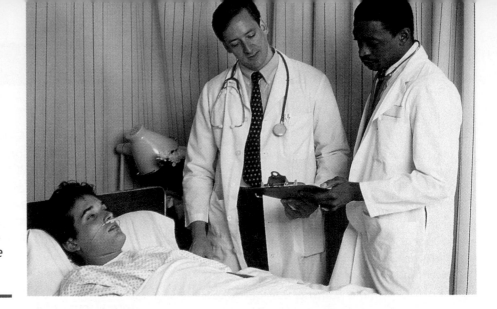

Figure 23-14 *As HIV attacks the immune system, individuals become more susceptible to opportunistic diseases.*

Figure 23-15 *This electron micrograph shows human immunodeficiency viruses (blue) coming out of a human T cell. The T cell will die, and the viruses will attack other T cells.*

before the onset of AIDS. Without treatment, it may take between 7 and 10 years from the time of infection until AIDS develops. But a person with no symptoms can still pass the infection to others through sexual contact.

Although there may be no symptoms, the virus steadily increases in number and spreads to different parts of the body. Following a long period of few or no symptoms, individuals infected with HIV may begin to lose weight, experience a constant tired feeling, and develop a persistent fever and diarrhea. These symptoms generally mark the onset of AIDS, which is signaled by very low levels of certain T cells.

As the number of T cells falls, the body becomes more and more susceptible to other diseases. The diseases that attack a person with a weakened immune system are called **opportunistic diseases.** AIDS is characterized by the appearance of one or more opportunistic diseases. These opportunistic diseases include tuberculosis, recurrent pneumonia, a lung disease called **pneumocystis carinii pneumonia** (noo muh SIS tis kahr IN ee ee), cancer of the cervix, and a kind of skin cancer called **Kaposi's sarcoma** (kuh POH seez sahr KOH muh).

Other conditions that affect persons with AIDS include severe weight loss and fungal infections. As the disease progresses, the virus may attack the brain and nervous system, causing blindness, depression, and mental deterioration. Death is usually caused by an opportunistic disease.

Transmission of HIV

Individuals who are infected with HIV have the potential to pass the virus on to someone else through the exchange of blood, semen, vaginal secretions, or breast milk. People with HIV are infectious whether or not they have symptoms of disease.

MODELING THE SPREAD OF HIV

In this activity, you will learn why abstinence is the only sure way to prevent the transmission of HIV.

Materials

safety goggles

plastic cups containing liquid, one per student

eyedroppers, one per student

Procedure

1. Put on your safety goggles.

2. According to your teacher's instructions, obtain one plastic cup half filled with a clear liquid. Do not taste, smell, or directly touch the liquid at any time.

3. At your teacher's signal, begin to talk with your classmates. Your conversation can be as simple as introducing yourself. Try to talk with at least three classmates. Each time you talk to a different classmate, add half a drop-perful of liquid from your cup to the cup of your classmate.

4. At the end of the conversation period, your teacher will add several drops of a pH indicator solution to each person's cup. If the indicator turns pink, the solution is alkaline.

Discussion

1. Assume that any solution that turns pink represents HIV-infected fluid. Is the liquid in your cup "infected"? How many students in your class have infected solutions in their cups?

2. Only one of your classmates started out with an alkaline, or "infected," solution. The identity of that person is known only to your teacher. Can you figure out which classmate started out with the "infected" solution?

3. How would the results of the activity have been different if each person had been allowed to talk with more people?

4. How does this activity mimic the way that a sexually transmitted disease is spread?

There are four main ways that HIV can be passed from person to person:

- through any form of sexual intercourse with an infected person
- through shared needles or syringes that are contaminated with the blood of an infected person
- through contact with blood or blood parts of an infected person
- from an infected mother to child, either during pregnancy, during birth, or by breast-feeding

As will be discussed in more detail in the next lesson, people can almost eliminate their risk of HIV infection by refraining from sexual intercourse outside of marriage and by not injecting illegal drugs. Mothers with HIV should not breast-feed their babies.

You may be wondering if it is risky to get a blood transfusion. The answer is that the risk of getting HIV from blood transfusions is extremely small. Since 1985 all of the blood that is collected in the United States has been tested for the

Figure 23-16 *Children of women who are infected with HIV may be born with the infection. Here a volunteer holds a baby who is HIV-positive.*

presence of HIV. Blood that tests positive for HIV antibodies is discarded. Potential donors are interviewed and are not allowed to give blood if they have been engaging in behaviors that place them at risk for HIV infection. Sometimes, however, a person who is HIV infected may have no reason to suspect that he or she is infected. If this person also has not yet developed antibodies for HIV, it is possible that the blood would not be identified as contaminated. The risk is extremely small but not totally absent. For this reason, people who may need a blood transfusion because of a surgical procedure are advised to donate their own blood before the operation.

Donating blood does not put you at risk for HIV infection. The equipment used to collect blood is sterile and uncontaminated. It is used only on the individual donating blood, and then it is discarded. Therefore it is safe to give blood. Of course, individuals who think they may be at risk for HIV infection should not donate blood.

Small amounts of HIV occur in saliva, tears, and perspiration. However, the amounts are so small that infection from contact with these fluids is unlikely.

An important point to remember is that HIV is not transmitted by casual contact with an infected person. You cannot get HIV by holding hands or hugging an infected person. You cannot get HIV by going to classes or eating lunch with an infected person, or by visiting someone in the hospital. Families who live with an infected person are not at risk of contracting HIV unless they engage in high-risk behaviors.

Testing for HIV

How does a person get tested for HIV? People who think that they may be infected with HIV should have their blood tested at a clinic or by a private physician. The blood is tested for HIV antibodies. If antibodies are detected, further tests are done to verify the result. A person who is diagnosed as being infected with HIV is said to be **HIV-positive.**

It is almost always difficult to cope with positive results of the test. For this reason, it is recommended that individuals receive counseling before taking the test. People who are diagnosed as HIV-positive should receive additional counseling to help them live with the infection and prevent transmission to others.

If no antibodies are detected, but the person is engaging in behaviors that expose him or her to HIV, the person should return for regular checkups. The person could be newly infected with HIV, and his or her body has not yet had time to develop antibodies for HIV. Early diagnosis of HIV infection is important to prevent the spread of the disease to others and to facilitate effective treatment.

Treatment for HIV

Although HIV infection and AIDS cannot be completely cured, some treatments can add many years to the patient's life. The preferred treatment, known as HAART for Highly Active AntiRetroviral Therapy, uses a combination of drugs to reduce the amount of HIV in the blood. In some cases, HIV drops to undetectable levels. Unfortunately, HAART treatment is complex and expensive; it involves side effects; and drug resistance can develop quickly if too many doses are missed. Another drug, AZT, reduces HIV transmission to newborns.

As with any fatal disease, persons with HIV infection and their loved ones need a lot of support to help them deal with their distress and anxiety. Support includes counseling, health-care services, and financial assistance. HIV-positive persons need to be treated with compassion. They also need to be allowed to live out their lives with dignity. Because HIV cannot be transmitted by casual contact, such as hugging or shaking hands, no one needs to be fearful of working or going to school with someone who is HIV-positive.

LESSON **3** REVIEW

1. What is the relationship between HIV infection and AIDS?
2. How does HIV weaken the immune system?
3. What are the four main ways that HIV can be transmitted from one person to another?
4. How is HIV treated?

What Do You Think?

5. The armed forces test soldiers for HIV infection. Do you think this is a good idea? Why or why not?

DIFFERENT VOICES SPEAKING

For the past year and a half, Joyell Hayes has volunteered her time as a peer counselor on a national AIDS hotline for teens. Joyell, who hopes to become an environmental engineer, lives in Missouri.

Q. *Joyell, what got you interested in volunteering?*

A. It's a habit I picked up from my parents, who are very civic-minded people. They've always been active in our church, and when I was ten, I began volunteering my time, too, going out and visiting with old people in the community. I've also done a lot of peer tutoring with kids in my neighborhood, and I donate time to a local home for children with behavioral problems.

Q. *How did you get involved in the AIDS hotline?*

A. I saw a poster for it at school. It said that they were looking for teens who felt they could relate to other young people. Since my personal motto is "Make a difference," I saw this as a perfect opportunity—a chance to listen to other people and help them deal with a problem.

Q. *What was training like?*

A. It took the form of an overnight retreat. They told us about the types of calls we would be receiving and how to deal with them. They also gave us a lot of information on AIDS and how HIV is spread. Judging from the misconceptions I hear in a four-hour phone shift, this is information too few people have.

Q. *What kinds of questions do callers ask?*

A. They want to know things such as whether they can get infected with HIV by hugging or touching another person. They are usually

Joyell Hayes

relieved to find out that you can't become infected through casual contact.

Q. *Do you ever get any frantic calls?*

A. Sometimes I do. People will call in because they have flu-like symptoms, and they are scared. Luckily, we have phone numbers and locations of places in different cities where people can be tested. I always advise people to get tested if they admit to having been involved in one of the behaviors that can lead to infection.

Q. *Are your efforts in educating people about AIDS limited to the hotline?*

A. No, I also go out and talk to young children in school settings about AIDS. Basically, the information is the same but in a form that's easier to understand. The one thing we stress, both to school kids and callers to the hotline, is that there's only one way to avoid HIV infection and that is through abstinence. That's a lesson I wish more people would learn.

Journal Activity

Imagine that you are a hotline volunteer. Write a fictionalized conversation between yourself and a caller who is seeking information on AIDS or another STD. Be sure to include at least five facts from the chapter.

4 PREVENTING HIV INFECTION

GUIDE FOR READING

Focus on this question as you read this lesson.

- What behaviors help prevent HIV infection?

SKILLS

- Choosing Abstinence

Although at present there is no sure cure for AIDS, the good news is that HIV infection is largely preventable. Fortunately you can choose behaviors that will help you avoid actions that put you at risk for becoming infected with HIV.

Low-Risk Behaviors

The only no-risk sexual behavior with respect to HIV and AIDS is abstinence. Within a committed sexual relationship such as marriage, sexual fidelity between two uninfected partners presents the least risk of getting HIV. The key here is to know for sure that both partners are uninfected. The past behaviors of either partner may have exposed him or her to HIV. Remember, a person who is HIV-positive can look and feel as healthy as anyone else for months, or even years, before the onset of AIDS. If either partner has practiced risky behaviors in the past, he or she should be tested for HIV. If an HIV infection is recent, a test may not be accurate. There is a lapse between the time of infection and the time antibodies show up in the test.

Avoiding drug use is also extremely important for reducing the risk of HIV infection. People who share contaminated needles to inject themselves with drugs are at a high risk for contracting HIV. People who have sex with drug abusers are also at high risk. Do not inject illegal drugs and avoid sexual contact with anyone who uses illegal drugs.

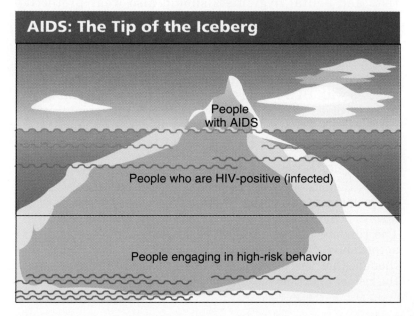

AIDS: The Tip of the Iceberg

People with AIDS

People who are HIV-positive (infected)

People engaging in high-risk behavior

Figure 23-17 *The number of people with AIDS is only a small proportion of those who are infected with HIV or are engaging in high-risk behavior.*

Preventive Behaviors

Some people may be at greater risk for HIV infection because of their lifestyle choices. For these people, certain behaviors can help reduce the risks of contracting HIV.

AVOIDING CONTACT WITH BLOOD OR BODY FLUIDS

Since it is impossible to tell by looking whether or not someone is HIV-positive, people should not share any personal items that may have blood or other body fluids on them. For example, toothbrushes, razors, medical syringes, and piercing and tattoo needles should not be shared with others.

Health-care providers often come into contact with the blood of patients. To reduce the risk of transmission of HIV, physicians, nurses, and other health-care workers should wear gowns that prevent them from coming into direct contact with the blood or other body fluids of their patients. Dentists and dental hygienists should also wear protective clothing such as latex gloves and masks.

KNOWING PERSONAL HISTORIES

Find out the history of another person before becoming sexually involved. If a person has ever practiced high-risk behaviors, he or she may be infected with HIV. It is also important to avoid becoming sexually involved with someone who has had sexual intercourse with many partners. Individuals who engage in prostitution are often infected with HIV.

HAVING PROTECTED SEX

For people who are sexually active, the only way to reduce the risk of HIV-infection is to use a latex condom. To be effective, a latex condom must always be used during sexual intercourse from start to finish. The condom must be free of tears, and it must be used in accordance with the directions on the package. Remember though, that the condom must be latex, and it only reduces the risk of infection—it does not make sex completely safe.

AVOIDING DRUGS Using alcohol or other drugs can impair a person's judgment. People with impaired judgment are more likely to engage in behaviors that place them at risk. To guard against infection, people need to be able to think clearly so that they can make healthy decisions.

GETTING CHECKUPS People at risk for HIV infection should get regular checkups at a clinic or by a private physician. Persons who think they may have been exposed to HIV should abstain from sexual intercourse and should be tested for HIV. The names, locations, and telephone numbers of clinics that test for HIV are available from each state's department of public health or from the national toll-free AIDS hotline. The AIDS hotline number can be obtained from the information operator at 1-800-555-1212.

ACTING RESPONSIBLY If a person is diagnosed as HIV-positive, then he or she needs to notify all previous sexual partners so that they also can be tested for the infection. In addition, a person who is HIV-positive needs to take care not to transmit the disease to anyone else. Anyone who is HIV-positive should seek a program of treatment and counseling. The sooner treatment is given, the more effective it is in slowing the progress of the disease.

Attitudes About AIDS

The early years of the AIDS epidemic were accompanied by a secondary epidemic referred to as "AFRAIDS." People became hysterical from fear of the unknown. This fear created many of the myths that are listed on page 559. It also

Figure 23-19 *AIDS rallies help to raise public awareness of HIV infection.*

Figure 23-20 *Ryan White dedicated his life to teaching others about HIV infection.*

generated anxiety about people who are HIV-positive. For example, students who were HIV-positive were sometimes denied the right to attend public schools. Other people lost their jobs or were denied health insurance. Only through education have these attitudes begun to change.

One person who suffered from other's attitudes about AIDS was Ryan White. Ryan was a hemophiliac who, at age 13, was diagnosed as having AIDS. Ryan had become infected with HIV through infected blood products used to treat his hemophilia. Ryan met with discrimination in his hometown, so eventually he and his family moved to another town. Fortunately, the citizens in his new home of Kokomo, Indiana, prepared a massive community education program. As a result, Ryan was welcomed into his new school. Until his death in 1990, Ryan devoted his life to teaching others about AIDS. As a result, the U.S. Congress enacted the Ryan White Comprehensive AIDS Resources Emergency Act, which provides funding for AIDS testing and treatment.

One law that helps protect the rights of individuals who are HIV-positive is the Americans with Disabilities Act. This law requires that individuals who are HIV-positive be given the same employment opportunities and public services as are given to everyone else. As the number of persons infected with HIV increases, more and more community support will be needed. People with HIV need compassion as they struggle to live with this deadly disease.

The information on HIV changes rapidly as scientists and health-care providers make new discoveries. It will be up to you to keep informed by reading reports in newspapers and government publications, asking questions via the AIDS hotline, or talking to health-care professionals. As you learn, help educate others. Share the facts and help others prevent the spread of HIV.

LESSON 4 REVIEW

1. What is the only no-risk sexual behavior with respect to HIV infection?
2. Why is it important to know the history of a person's behavior before becoming sexually involved?
3. What precautions should health-care providers take to prevent contact with HIV-infected blood?
4. Why should someone who is practicing risky behaviors get tested regularly for HIV infection?

What Do You Think?

5. Suppose an HIV-positive student enrolls in your school. What would you say to your fellow classmates to reassure them that they are not at risk for infection?

Finding the Facts

Joanne has just learned that a classmate at school has tested positive for HIV. She is concerned and wants to find out everything she can about HIV and AIDS. Some of the questions Joanne would like to answer include: Will her classmate definitely develop AIDS if she has HIV? Is there an effective treatment for AIDS? Can anyone else catch HIV from her? Everyone in her class has an opinion, but no one knows the facts.

Where could Joanne go to find up-to-date facts about HIV and AIDS? Use the following steps to help find the facts on any subject you may want to know about.

1. Identify the topic you want to research

• Make a list of the key words that relate to this topic. For example, Joanne could list the terms *AIDS, HIV,* and *sexually transmitted diseases.*

2. Check the library catalog for books on the subject

• Check under the subject headings in your library's computerized on-line catalog or in the card catalog. If you need assistance in using either catalog, ask a librarian or media specialist.

• In the catalog, look at the copyright dates of the books on your subject. Choose the most current books. In an area such as health, where information changes rapidly, choose only books published within the last two to three years.

3. Search for current information

• Check your subject area in *Info Track,* a computerized listing of magazines that includes the past three years. Ask a librarian or media specialist for assistance if you are not familiar with *Info Track.*

• Look for magazine articles in the *Reader's Guide to Periodical Literature.* Instructions on using the *Guide* are in the front of bound volumes.

• Use the *Health Reference Center,* a computerized database of health and medical information that includes the text of magazine articles.

• Choose a WWW search engine, such as askjeeves.com or dogpile.com. Enter a term from the list you made in (1). Click on several of the search results to learn more.

4. Use the 800 number telephone directory

• Look for hotlines and information centers on your topic. Call and ask for information that can be given over the telephone or that can be mailed to you.

5. Call a health clinic

• Make a list of specific questions to ask a health-care provider and arrange a time to speak with him or her. Ask for any pamphlets about your topic.

Apply the Skill

Make a list of health-related decisions that you and other people your age may have to make. Choose two of these decisions and find the facts that would help you make a responsible decision.

CHAPTER 23 REVIEW

KEY IDEAS

LESSON 1

• The most effective way to prevent the transmission of STDs is to choose sexual abstinence and to avoid the use of illegal drugs.

LESSON 2

• The most serious STDs in this country are chlamydia, gonorrhea, syphilis, genital herpes, hepatitis B, and AIDS. Other STDs include trichomoniasis, candidiasis, genital warts, pubic lice, and scabies.

• STDs that are caused by bacteria can be cured with antibiotics, if treated early. STDs that are caused by viruses usually cannot be cured.

LESSON 3

• The human immunodeficiency virus (HIV) causes AIDS. HIV gradually destroys the immune system.

• There are four main ways in which HIV is transmitted: sexual intercourse with an infected person; using a needle that is contaminated with blood of an infected person; contact with blood of an infected person; from an infected mother to her unborn child or nursing infant.

LESSON 4

• Everyone has a responsibility to prevent STDs, including AIDS, by behaving responsibly, keeping informed, and helping to educate others.

KEY TERMS

LESSON 1
epidemic
infertility
sexually transmitted
  disease

LESSON 2
candidiasis
chancre
chancroid
chlamydia

genital herpes
genital warts
gonorrhea
hepatitis B
human papilloma virus
nongonococcal urethritis
pelvic inflammatory
  disease
pubic lice
scabies

syphilis
trichomoniasis
vaginitis

LESSON 3
AIDS
HIV-positive
human immunodeficiency
  virus
opportunistic disease

Listed above are some of the important terms in this chapter. Choose the term from the list that best matches each phrase below.

1. a disease that attacks a person whose immune system is weakened by HIV

2. the reduced ability to have children

3. an incurable STD characterized by painful blisters around the genital area

4. the painless sore that is the first sign of a syphilis infection

5. the most common bacterial STD in this country

6. a serious infection of the female reproductive organs that can cause infertility

7. a bacterial STD with symptoms similar to primary syphilis

8. an STD caused by a protozoan that infects the vagina or urinary tract

9. the virus that causes genital warts

10. an itchy condition caused by tiny mites that infest the hair around the genitals

WHAT HAVE YOU LEARNED?

Choose the letter of the answer that best completes each statement.

11. If left untreated, gonorrhea can lead to
a. jaundice   **c.** nongonococcal urethritis
b. infertility   **d.** opportunistic infection

12. An STD that CANNOT be treated by antibiotics is
a. gonorrhea   **c.** genital herpes
b. chancroid   **d.** syphilis

13. An STD that attacks the liver is
a. vaginitis   **c.** scabies
b. trichomoniasis   **d.** hepatitis B

14. The stage of syphilis in which it is hardest to detect infection is
a. primary syphilis   **c.** secondary syphilis
b. latent syphilis   **d.** late syphilis

15. The virus that causes AIDS is
a. NGU   **c.** PID
b. STD   **d.** HIV

16. AIDS can be transmitted by
a. hugging   **c.** sharing needles
b. shaking hands   **d.** donating blood

Answer each of the following with complete sentences.

17. List two myths about STDs. Then list two facts that correct these myths.

18. Give three reasons why there are so many cases of STDs in this country.

19. Why is it important to get prompt medical attention for STDs?

20. What steps should be taken by a person who suspects that he or she is infected with an STD?

21. How can STDs affect a newborn?

22. Name three curable STDs other than gonorrhea, syphilis, and chlamydia.

23. Describe four ways that HIV is spread.

24. How does the abuse of drugs increase the risk of contracting an STD?

25. What single behavior is the best prevention for STDs and AIDS?

WHAT DO YOU THINK?

26. The Centers for Disease Control and Prevention considers education critical in preventing STDs. What do you think? Why?

27. Certain groups, such as the military and JOB Corps, require testing for HIV. What are your thoughts on mandatory testing?

28. Many states require couples to be screened for some STDs before getting a marriage license. Is this a good idea? Explain.

29. Why do pregnant women who have been exposed to STDs need medical counseling?

30. Do the media (television, radio, newspapers, magazines) do a good job in educating people about STDs and HIV? Give examples to support your answer.

31. Abstinence is the best protection against AIDS for teens. What could students do to make this an easier choice for their peers?

WHAT WOULD YOU DO?

32. How would you discuss the subject of STDs or AIDS at home? Try writing a script of the conversation.

33. Social service agencies are looking for foster homes for children with HIV. How would you feel about having an HIV-positive foster child in your home?

34. If you found out that the person you were dating had experimented with intravenous drugs in the past, how would you discuss it, and how might it change your relationship?

Getting Involved

35. Some schools introduce STD and HIV prevention education in grades six to eight. Find out if you or a group of classmates could prepare a program to help educate these younger students on how to protect themselves from these diseases.

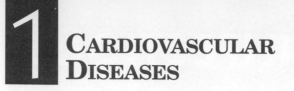

1 CARDIOVASCULAR DISEASES

GUIDE FOR READING

Focus on these questions as you read this lesson.

- What are the types of cardiovascular disease, and how do they affect a person's health?
- What behaviors can help prevent cardiovascular disease?

SKILLS

- DECIDE
- Working in Groups

Figure 24-1 *Blood pressure is higher during physical activity than when the person is at rest.*

This chapter focuses on the major types of noninfectious diseases. **Noninfectious diseases** are diseases that are not caused by pathogens. They cannot be transmitted by contact with a person, object, animal, or substance. They are not communicable or contagious. Rather, noninfectious diseases are caused by a variety of risk factors that may be behavioral, environmental, or hereditary.

The most common noninfectious disease is cardiovascular disease. **Cardiovascular disease** (kahr dee oh VAS kyuh lur) are diseases of the heart *(cardio)* and blood vessels *(vascular)*. More than one in four Americans suffers from some form of cardiovascular disease. Almost 40 percent of all deaths each year are from cardiovascular diseases. Whenever any part of the cardiovascular system develops a problem, the entire system is at risk of becoming diseased. One of the most common forms of cardiovascular disease is high blood pressure.

Many people think of cardiovascular disease as a problem for older people. Unfortunately, more and more young people—even teens—are suffering from cardiovascular disease.

High Blood Pressure

As blood circulates throughout the body, it exerts pressure against the walls of the blood vessels. Normal blood pressure varies. It is usually low when you sleep, but higher when you are nervous, excited, or physically active. If blood pressure increases above normal limits and remains high, the result is **high blood pressure, hypertension,** or HBP.

Blood pressure readings are in the form of two numbers, such as 120/80, stated as "120 over 80." The first and larger number is the blood pressure while the heart is contracting. The second and smaller number is the pressure between heart beats. Pressures above 140 for the higher reading or 90 for the lower reading are too high. For example, readings of 130/95, 145/80, and 148/95 all indicate high blood pressure.

Nearly one out of four American adults has high blood pressure, but half of them do not know it. High blood pressure is especially prevalent among African Americans. In fact, after age 60, sixty percent of African American males and 80 percent of African American females will have high blood pressure.

Over time, high blood pressure causes the artery walls to thicken, narrowing the passageways in the vessels through which the blood must flow. Because the heart must work

Concern for a Friend's Health

Your friend Dave has high blood pressure. He was keeping it under control by being careful about his diet. But lately he seems to be using more salt and eating more fatty foods than he should, especially when he is with his friends. Instead of considering his special condition, he orders what everyone else does. When you spoke to Dave about cutting down on salt and fat, he got angry and said that a real friend wouldn't nag him. You are concerned, however, that he could be seriously damaging his health.

1. Use the DECIDE process on page 18 to decide what you would do in this situation. Explain your reasons for making this decision.

2. Suppose the action you chose did not bring the desired results. What would you do next?

3. List some ways that a person can show support for a friend who has a particular physical illness or restriction.

harder to pump blood through the narrower blood vessels, heart disease may result. Since it has no obvious symptoms and frequently goes undetected, high blood pressure is called the "silent killer."

Many people can help reduce their risk of developing high blood pressure by following healthful behaviors such as exercising regularly and maintaining weight at a healthy level. For those who are salt sensitive, have high blood pressure, or have inherited a risk of HBP, using salt and sodium only in moderation can help control the severity of hypertension.

High blood pressure cannot be cured, but it can be controlled with medications. Some of these medications promote the excretion of urine. This decreases blood pressure by decreasing the volume of fluid in the blood vessels. Other medications lower blood pressure by causing blood vessels to relax. Untreated high blood pressure can lead to serious complications such as kidney failure and heart disease.

Atherosclerosis

Atherosclerosis (ath uh roh skluh ROH sis), illustrated in Figure 24-2, is a disease in which the fatlike substance **cholesterol** (kuh LES tur awl) is deposited on the inside wall of the arteries. These deposits, called **plaque** (plak), narrow or block the arteries. The greater resistance to blood flow resulting from the narrowed blood vessels raises blood pressure, causing the heart to pump harder.

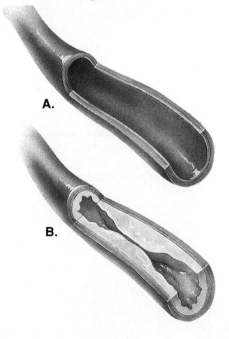

Figure 24-2 *An artery with atherosclerosis (B) offers more resistance to blood flow than a normal artery (A).*

A.

B.

Noninfectious Diseases and Disabilities **575**

In 1867, the Swedish chemist Alfred Nobel invented dynamite—the explosive formed by combining the chemical nitroglycerine with porous sand. The fortune that Nobel made from this invention allowed him to establish a fund that today supports the Nobel Prizes—awards made for outstanding contributions in science, literature, economics, and peace.

Ironically, Nobel might never have had the opportunity to establish the fund if it were not for a drug that he used to relieve his severe angina. That drug was nitroglycerine—the same chemical used in dynamite! Even today, nitroglycerine remains an effective drug in controlling angina.

Eating food high in saturated fat can increase the risk of getting atherosclerosis because saturated fats tend to increase cholesterol levels in the blood. Other major risk factors for developing atherosclerosis are smoking, diabetes, obesity, a family history of the disease, and lack of exercise.

The condition in which the arteries lose their elasticity and become stiff is called **arteriosclerosis** (ahr teer ee oh skluh ROH sis), or hardening of the arteries. People who suffer from atherosclerosis often have arteriosclerosis as well. High blood pressure is a major factor in the development of arteriosclerosis.

Coronary Heart Disease

Many heart problems are caused by coronary heart disease. **Coronary heart disease** occurs when the coronary arteries become blocked as a result of atherosclerosis. The coronary arteries are those arteries that supply the muscle tissues of the heart with blood. As the coronary arteries become narrower, blood flow to the heart muscle decreases. This leads to the conditions known as angina pectoris and heart attack.

ANGINA PECTORIS   The chest pain associated with coronary heart disease is called **angina pectoris** (an JY nuh PEK tur is), or angina. It occurs when an area of tissue in the heart does not get enough blood because of a narrowed or blocked artery. The decreased blood flow reduces the amount of oxygen reaching the heart muscle. Angina often occurs during periods of physical activity or emotional stress, when the heart rate and blood pressure increase and the heart muscle needs more oxygen than usual. The pain, which usually lasts for a few minutes, eventually disappears with rest. Medications are available that relax blood vessels, allowing more blood to flow through the coronary arteries. If the oxygen supply to the heart continues to be inadequate, however, a heart attack is likely to occur.

HEART ATTACK   Each year, over a million people in the United States suffer a heart attack; 500,000 die. A **heart**

Figure 24-3 *Recognizing these warning signs and acting on them can help save a life.*

Warning Signs of Heart Attack

- Uncomfortable pressure or pain in the center of the chest lasting for two minutes or longer

- Pain spreading to the shoulder, neck, or arms

- One or more of the following: severe pain, dizziness, fainting, sweating, extreme anxiety, nausea, or shortness of breath

A person experiencing the warning signs of an attack should be kept calm and taken immediately to a hospital, even if the pain seems to go away or the person denies a problem.

attack occurs when some of the heart tissue is prevented from receiving its normal blood supply and dies. The blockage is usually due to the formation of a blood clot in a coronary artery that has been narrowed by atherosclerosis. Five major risk factors for coronary heart disease and heart attack are high blood pressure, high levels of cholesterol in the blood, physical inactivity, smoking, and bacterial infections. Figure 24-3 lists the warning signs of a heart attack.

Depending on the amount of tissue death in the heart, a heart attack can be life-threatening or it may result in some lessening of heart function. The more heart tissue that dies, the more severe the heart attack. If the area of tissue supplied by the blocked artery is large, for example, many heart cells die. The result is that the individual suffers a major heart attack, or "coronary," which often results in death.

A heart attack may cause the heart to stop beating entirely, a condition known as cardiac arrest. In case of cardiac arrest, a person trained in basic life support must administer **cardiopulmonary resuscitation** (kahr dee oh PUL muh nehr ee rih sus ih TAY shun), or CPR. CPR combines mouth-to-mouth breathing with chest compression. These actions maintain a flow of oxygen-rich blood to the brain while the heart is not working. Have you been trained to perform CPR in case of an emergency?

Irregular Heartbeat

Irregular heartbeats, called **arrhythmias** (uh RITH mee uhs), are another form of heart disease. The heart may beat too slowly, too quickly, or with an uneven rhythm. Arrhythmias may result from damage caused by a heart attack, or they may develop spontaneously. **Fibrillation** (fib ruh LAY shun) is a life-threatening type of arrhythmia in which the heart twitches in an uncoordinated fashion instead of contracting in a regular rhythm.

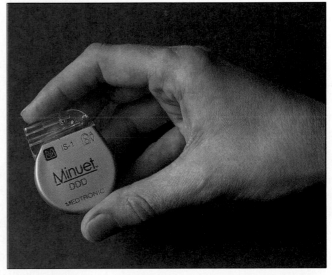

Figure 24-4 *An artificial pacemaker provides electrical impulses that keep a heart beating regularly.*

Some abnormal heartbeats can be controlled by medications or by artificial pacemakers. An **artificial pacemaker,** shown in Figure 24-4, is a small, battery-operated unit that is connected to the heart by means of a surgical procedure. The unit produces electrical impulses that make the heart beat rhythmically.

Congestive Heart Failure

Unlike a heart attack, **congestive heart failure** is not a single event but a condition in which the heart slowly weakens. Usually years of arteriosclerosis and high blood pressure contribute to congestive heart failure. These conditions make the heart work harder than it should.

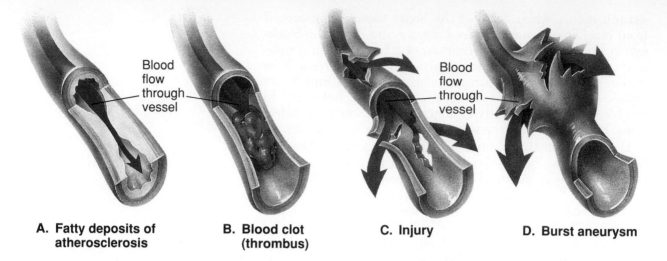

A. Fatty deposits of atherosclerosis

B. Blood clot (thrombus)

C. Injury

D. Burst aneurysm

Figure 24-5 *A blockage (A, B) or break (C, D) in an artery in the brain causes a stroke.*

As the heart becomes weaker, it is unable to pump as much blood as it once did. Swelling of the feet and lower legs is one of the symptoms of congestive heart failure. Drugs that relax blood vessels and thus decrease the strain on the heart are used to treat people with congestive heart failure.

Stroke

A sudden disruption of blood flow to part of the brain is known as a **stroke.** Without a supply of blood, brain cells soon die from lack of oxygen. The effects of a stroke on a person can vary widely, depending on the type of stroke and the area of the brain affected. Brain damage from a stroke can affect the senses, speech, comprehension, behavior, thought patterns, and memory. Paralysis on one side of the body is common. If the patient survives, sometimes normal function can be regained with therapy. This happens when an undamaged part of the brain "relearns" what was lost in a part damaged by the stroke.

One type of stroke occurs when an artery supplying blood to one area of the brain is blocked. The blockage may be caused by atherosclerosis or by a blood clot, as shown in Figure 24-5. A second type of stroke occurs when a weakened artery in the brain bursts, flooding the surrounding tissue with blood. If the bleeding comes from an artery in the cerebrum, the main portion of the brain, the stroke is called a **cerebral hemorrhage** (suh REE brul HEM ur ij).

Cerebral hemorrhage may also be caused by a head injury or by an aneurysm that bursts. An **aneurysm** (AN yuh riz um) is a blood-filled weak spot that balloons out from the artery wall. The weak spot is usually caused by high blood pressure. Aneurysms do not always cause trouble, but when one bursts in the brain, a stroke results. The warning signs of stroke are shown in Figure 24-6.

Each year in the United States, about 500,000 people experience a stroke. Nearly 150,000 of these cases result in death.

The Warning Signs of Stroke

- Sudden, severe headache with no apparent cause

- Sudden weakness or numbness of the face, arm, and leg on one side of the body

- Loss of speech, trouble talking, or trouble understanding speech

- Dimness or loss of vision, particularly in one eye

- Unexplained dizziness, nausea, unsteadiness, or sudden falls

- Strokes may be preceded by "little strokes." Little strokes are warnings that a major stroke may occur if blood pressure and stress are not reduced.

Figure 24-6 *A person who experiences any of the warning signs of stroke, whether mild or severe, should receive prompt medical attention.*

Many people who survive a stroke become severely disabled. Risk factors for stroke include high blood pressure, high blood cholesterol, smoking, excessive use of alcohol, physical inactivity, and obesity.

Other Cardiovascular Diseases

As you learned in Chapter 16, the heart has valves that help to keep the blood flowing in one direction. If the valves are damaged or malformed in some way, they do not open and close as they should. This condition is called heart valve disease. Some heart valve disorders are the result of abnormal development of the heart valves before birth. Such congenital heart defects are usually discovered in infancy and often may be corrected by surgery.

Rheumatic heart disease results from the infectious disease rheumatic fever. In rheumatic fever, the same bacteria that cause strep throat attack and damage the heart's valves. This is why a strep throat infection should be treated by a physician—before the bacteria can cause infection in other areas of the body.

Detecting and Treating Cardiovascular Disease

Cardiovascular disease cannot be cured, but it can often be controlled or prevented from getting worse. For this reason, early detection and treatment are important. Several tests are used to detect cardiovascular disease.

TESTS FOR CARDIOVASCULAR DISEASE Abnormalities in heart rhythm or other heart trouble can be shown on an **electrocardiogram** (ih lek troh KAHR dee uh gram), or ECG. An ECG is a recording of the heart's electrical activity. The electrical impulses that cause the heart to beat are detected by electrodes attached to the patient's skin. The impulses are recorded as a pattern on graph paper, as Figure 24-7 illustrates. Variations from a standard pattern may indicate heart disease or damage from a heart attack. An ECG can be obtained when the patient is at rest or during exercise. If it is obtained while exercising, the procedure is called a cardiac stress test.

Figure 24-7 *Compare the normal electrocardiogram on the left with the abnormal one on the right.*

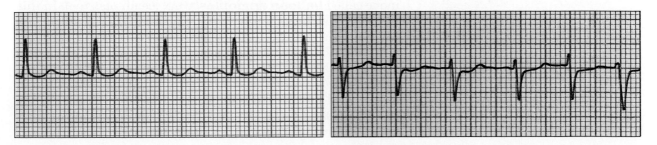

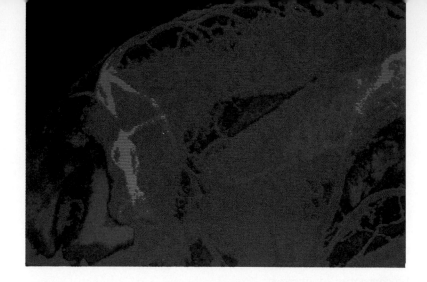

Figure 24-8 *This coronary angiograph shows arteries in the heart that are blocked by atherosclerosis.*

Blocked coronary arteries can be detected by an X-ray technique called **coronary angiography** (KAWR uh nehr ee an jee AHG ruh fee). Because blood vessels do not show up well in conventional X-rays, a special X-ray-absorbing dye must be released into the coronary arteries. To do this, a flexible tube is threaded through an artery in an arm or leg until it reaches the heart. The dye is released from the tube into the coronary arteries, and X-rays are taken. From the appearance of the dye in the coronary arteries, physicians can tell if blockage or narrowing of the arteries has occurred. A coronary angiograph is shown in Figure 24-8.

Several techniques use sound to diagnose heart conditions. In one technique, microphones placed on the chest detect sounds made by the heart beating. A printout of the sounds can reveal certain heart disorders. Another technique uses sound waves generated by a device placed against the chest. The sound waves reflect off the heart and are used to create an image that can show heart problems.

TREATMENT OF CARDIOVASCULAR DISEASE Treatment of a cardiovascular disease depends on the specific condition. In the case of coronary heart disease, surgery is commonly used to improve the blood supply to the heart muscle. Surgeons use a vein—usually taken from the patient's leg—or an artificial blood vessel to construct a detour around a blocked coronary artery. This procedure is called **coronary bypass surgery.**

Coronary heart disease also can be treated using a technique called **balloon angioplasty** (AN jee uh plas tee). In this technique, a thin tube with an expandable tip (balloon) is inserted in a patient's arm or leg and guided into a coronary artery. At the point of blockage, the balloon is inflated. The expanding balloon flattens the cholesterol deposits against the artery wall, widening the inside of the artery. The result is better blood flow through the artery. Since the blockage may re-form, however, balloon angioplasty may provide only temporary improvement.

Sometimes a person's heart is so diseased or overworked that it cannot function adequately. In such cases, the diseased heart may be replaced with the heart of an organ donor who has died. Although this surgical procedure has saved many lives, it is risky because the immune system attacks and rejects the new heart. To lower rejection rates, physicians use drugs to suppress the immune system.

Preventing Cardiovascular Disease

Obviously, preventing cardiovascular disease is better than going through the pain and expense of the procedures just described. **Prevention of cardiovascular disease involves avoiding or treating risk factors that cause the heart to become weakened and unhealthy.** The primary risk factors are smoking, physical inactivity, high cholesterol, and high blood pressure. Bacterial infections are an additional risk factor. Some behaviors to help you prevent cardiovascular disease are listed below.

- Do not start smoking. Smokers have a higher risk of heart attack and stroke than nonsmokers.
- If you smoke, quit. Risks of heart disease are greatly reduced within two years after quitting and are about the same as for a nonsmoker after ten years.
- Exercise regularly. Regular exercise strengthens the cardiovascular system and can lower blood pressure.
- Choose a diet high in plant products and low in fat, especially saturated fat, and cholesterol. Have your blood cholesterol levels checked regularly at a clinic.
- Avoid obesity. If you are overweight, your heart has to work harder than it should.
- Control your blood pressure. It should be checked regularly by a physician or nurse.
- Control bacterial infections with antibiotics. Avoid infections by keeping your hands and mouth clean.

LESSON 1 REVIEW

1. What are four behaviors that can contribute to high blood pressure?

2. What is atherosclerosis, and what causes it?

3. What is coronary heart disease?

4. Distinguish between a stroke and a heart attack.

What Do You Think?

5. What behaviors would you practice if you were in a high-risk group for heart disease?

Focus on these questions as you read this lesson.

- What is cancer and what are its causes?
- What are the warning signs of cancer?
- What behaviors can reduce the risk of getting cancer?

SKILLS

- Activity: Save Your Skin
- Breast and Testicular Self-Exams

2 CANCER

A variety of different diseases that involve the rapid, uncontrolled growth and spread of abnormal cells are known as **cancer.** In the United States, one in every four deaths is due to cancer, making it the second leading cause of death in adults.

Cancer cells form a mass of tissue called a **malignant tumor** (muh LIG nunt). The cells of a malignant tumor grow out into and destroy surrounding tissues. In addition, some cancer cells break away from the original tumor and travel through blood and lymph vessels to other parts of the body. There the cancer cells start new tumors. The spread of cancer from where it first develops to other parts of the body is called **metastasis** (muh TAS tuh sis).

Malignant tumors should not be confused with benign, or noncancerous, tumors. **Benign tumors** (bih NYN) form from cells that grow more rapidly than normal cells but more slowly than most cancer cells. In addition, a benign tumor has a surrounding membrane or sheath. The cells of a benign tumor remain within the membrane and do not spread to other areas of the body.

Many cancers can be cured if they are detected early and treated promptly. Because cancer cells eventually replace normal, functioning cells, death results if the spread of cancer is not stopped.

What Causes Cancer?

There is no single cause for all forms of cancer. In fact, many experts believe that the development of most cancers depends on a combination of factors—some hereditary and others environmental or behavioral. For example, a person may inherit a tendency to develop a certain form of cancer. The cancer may never develop, however, unless the person is also exposed to one or more specific cancer-causing agents called **carcinogens** (kahr SIN uh junz).

Carcinogens may be chemical, physical, or biological. Chemical carcinogens include numerous substances, such as asbestos, arsenic, certain types of solvents, and pesticides. Many carcinogens are present in combustion products, including tobacco smoke. Physical carcinogens include ultraviolet and high-energy radiation, such as X-rays and the radioactive gas radon. Prolonged exposure to ultraviolet radiation—from the sun or sun lamps—can cause skin cancer. Biological carcinogens include some types of viruses.

All human cells contain hereditary factors, or genes, that control normal cellular reproduction. Research suggests that exposure to certain carcinogens can transform some of these

Figure 24-9 *Removal of asbestos, a known carcinogen, requires the use of protective gear.*

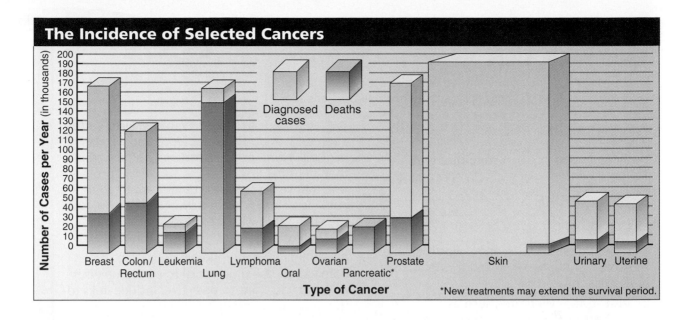

The Incidence of Selected Cancers

Number of Cases per Year (in thousands)

200 190 180 170 160 150 140 130 120 110 100 90 80 70 60 50 40 30 20 10 0

Diagnosed cases   Deaths

Breast Colon/Rectum Leukemia Lung Lymphoma Oral Ovarian Pancreatic* Prostate Skin Urinary Uterine

Type of Cancer

*New treatments may extend the survival period.

normal genes into cancer-causing genes, or **oncogenes** (AHN kuh jeenz). Oncogenes allow cells to reproduce in a rapid, uncontrolled manner.

Types of Cancer

Cancer can occur in almost any part of the body. As you can see in Figure 24-10, some cancers occur only rarely while others are common. Many cancers grow slowly; others spread rapidly. A cancer is named according to the part of the body where it first develops.

SKIN CANCER   The ultraviolet rays of sunlight are the principal cause of skin cancer, the most common of cancers. There are three types of skin cancer. The two most common types are very slow growing and almost always curable. The least common type, called **melanoma** (mel uh NOH muh), is the most serious. It usually begins in a mole or other dark area on the skin and spreads very rapidly. Warning signs of melanoma include a change in size of a mole or dark area, tenderness, itchiness, and pain.

The amount of pigment in your skin affects how vulnerable you may be to the damaging effects of sunlight. People with light skin are more likely to develop skin cancer than dark-skinned people. No matter what your skin color, however, always try to minimize your exposure to the sun. If you need to be in the sun, use sunscreen and wear protective clothing.

LUNG CANCER   Lung cancer is the most common type of life-threatening cancer. It is the leading cause of cancer deaths among American men and women. Cigarette smoking is the leading cause of lung cancer.

Figure 24-10 *The incidence of cancer varies greatly according to type.*

Noninfectious Diseases and Disabilities   **583**

SAVE YOUR SKIN

In this activity, you will design a Web site for schoolchildren that explains how they can protect themselves from the sun.

Materials

unlined paper
colored pencils

computer with
WWW access

Procedure

1. Write down three "search" words, such as *sunscreen*, that are connected to the topic of skin cancer protection.

2. Visit several Web sites, such as **www.bess.net, www.cyberkids.com,** and **www.yahooligans.com,** that are designed for children. Use the search words to find age-appropriate information on skin protection. Write down the address to three or more sites that you think are especially good.

3. Design your own kid's Web site. First, write a sentence about your audience and what it might like and dislike. Next, write a paragraph that identifies key concepts about skin protection that you want to communicate to your audience. Finally, write a sentence describing the "bait" that will get kids to visit your site. Will you offer games? graphics? funny jokes?

4. On unlined paper, sketch your Web site's home page. Use blue pencil to underline each link that you want to be active. Include links to the sites you found in 2.

Discussion

What do you think will be the hardest sun/skin cancer information to explain to schoolchildren? Why?

Lung cancer is often difficult to detect because symptoms do not appear until the disease is quite advanced. Symptoms include a persistent cough, chest pain, and repeated attacks of pneumonia or bronchitis. Surgery is the most common form of treatment. It may be combined with other treatments using radiation and chemicals.

ORAL CANCER Cancer of the mouth can affect any part of the oral cavity—the lips, tongue, mouth, or throat. It is usually detected in the early stages by a physician or a dentist. Oral cancer is found most frequently in men over 40 and occurs more often in men than in women. Recently, oral cancer has been occurring more often in younger people, particularly those who use smokeless tobacco products.

Early warning signs of oral cancer include lumps, a sore that bleeds easily, and a red or white patch of tissue in the mouth. Later symptoms of oral cancer include difficulty in chewing, swallowing, or moving the tongue or jaws. Cigarette, cigar, and pipe smoking; smokeless, or chewing, tobacco; and excessive use of alcohol are risk factors for developing oral cancer.

COLON AND RECTAL CANCER Cancers of the colon and rectum are the second most common types of fatal cancer, after lung cancer. Warning signs include bleeding from the rectum, blood in the feces, and changes in bowel habits. Evidence suggests that bowel cancer may be linked to diets that are high in fat and low in fiber.

BREAST CANCER   In women, breast cancer is the second most common cancer and the second leading cause of cancer death. Women with increased risk include those who are obese, have had few or no children, were first pregnant when they were older than 35, or whose mothers had breast cancer.

Effective treatment of breast cancer depends on early diagnosis. This is why a monthly breast self-examination should be a lifelong habit from the teenage years on. The breast self-examination is described in Building Health Skills for Chapter 8.

An X-ray picture of the breast called a **mammogram** (MAM uh gram) can detect cancer before other methods. Women should consult with their physicians to determine when they should have their first mammogram and how often after that they should have subsequent mammograms.

Mammogram results can be unclear. Being asked to return for a second test does not mean that you have cancer.

REPRODUCTIVE CANCERS   In women, the reproductive organs that most commonly develop cancer are the cervix, uterus, and ovaries. Cervical cancer is detected by means of the Pap test. In the **Pap test,** a physician removes a tiny amount of tissue from the area around the cervix, the opening to the uterus. Examination under a microscope reveals even the earliest cell changes associated with cancer. When it is detected early, cervical cancer is curable.

Uterine cancer is almost always curable if it is detected early. Ovarian cancer is considerably less common than uterine cancer, but causes more than twice as many deaths. Often there are no early symptoms of this disease. Women whose mothers had ovarian cancer, who have never had children, who have had breast cancer, or who are over 60 are at higher risk for this type of cancer. Regular and thorough pelvic exams can detect ovarian cancer.

In men, cancer of the prostate gland is second only to skin cancer as the most common form of cancer. Warning signs include painful or burning urination, blood in the urine, and pain in the lower back or pelvis. A regular rectal examination by a physician, especially for men over 40, helps detect prostate cancer.

Cancer of the testes is one of the most common cancers in men between 15 and 34 years of age. Young men with testes that have not descended into the scrotum are at a higher risk. Testicular cancer can be detected with the self-examination described in Building Health Skills for Chapter 8.

LEUKEMIA AND LYMPHOMA   **Leukemia** (loo KEE mee uh) is a cancer of the blood-forming tissues in the bone marrow. In leukemia, abnormal, immature, white blood cells are

SHARPEN YOUR SKILLS

Breast and Testicular Self-Exams

Knowing the self-exams for breast or testicular cancer could help save your life. If you are not familiar with these procedures, refer to Building Health Skills for Chapter 8.

Figure 24-11 *A physical exam can detect signs of cancer and other diseases.*

released into the bloodstream in great numbers. These non-functioning cells reduce the effectiveness of the body's normal blood cells. Warning signs of leukemia include weight loss, repeated infections, fatigue, and swollen lymph nodes. Some types of leukemia respond well to drug treatment. In some cases, bone marrow transplants have been used successfully to cure leukemia.

Lymphoma, a cancer in which the lymph cells multiply uncontrollably, comes in two main types: Hodgkin's and non-Hodgkin's. Scientists have recently found the cell that causes Hodgkin's disease, and vaccine studies are underway. There are about 30 non-Hodgkin's lymphomas that differ mainly by the kind of cell that is affected. Since the early 1970s, the incidence of non-Hodgkin's lymphoma has almost doubled.

Detecting and Treating Cancer

The key to curing cancer is early detection and treatment. The American Cancer Society lists seven common warning signs of cancer, as shown in Figure 24-13. Early detection depends on each person being alert to these warning signs and to other unusual symptoms.

Notice that the first letters of the warning signs spell "caution," not "panic." Because your body is always undergoing change, most changes are not signs of cancer. However, if you experience any of the warning signs of cancer or other unusual changes, it is always advisable to seek medical care.

Tests for early detection of disease are known as screening tests. Mammograms and chest X-rays are screening tests. If the result of a screening test indicates that cancer may be present, it must be confirmed by another test. Surgeons often remove a small piece of the tissue in question to examine it under a microscope for signs of cancer. This procedure is called a **biopsy** (BY ahp see).

Treatment of cancer depends on the type of cancer, its location, and its stage of development. Surgery may be performed to remove a malignant tumor. **Radiation therapy,** the use of high-energy radiation to kill cancer cells, can slow or stop the spread of cancer. It may be used alone or in combination with surgery. Once cancer has spread, however, surgery and radiation are less useful. Another method, **chemotherapy** (kee moh THEHR uh pee), uses drugs to attack cancers, reducing the rate at which cancer cells reproduce. Over time, chemotherapy can eventually destroy all cancerous cells. In another type of treatment called **immunotherapy** (im yuh noh THEHR uh pee), drugs are used to stimulate the body's own immune system to attack cancer cells.

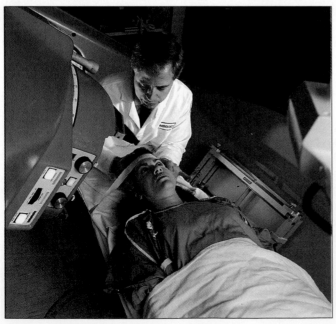

Figure 24-12 *High-energy radiation is used to kill cancerous tumors.*

Most cancers are considered cured if the patient exhibits no signs of the disease for five years or more after treatment is stopped. The cancer is then said to be in complete remission. Unfortunately for many patients, remission may last only a few years. If the cancer returns after remission, it is usually more difficult to treat than the original cancer.

Preventing Cancer

Although the specific cause of most cancers is unknown, certain behaviors have been shown to decrease the risk of cancer. Here are a few suggestions to help you reduce your risk of developing cancer.

- Do not use any form of tobacco. Tobacco and tobacco smoke contain carcinogens, and smoking is the most preventable cancer risk factor of all. Smokeless tobacco, or snuff, can cause oral cancer.

- Avoid drinking alcohol. Drinking, especially along with smoking, greatly increases the risks of oral cancer and liver cancer.

- Respect the sun's ultraviolet rays. Wear protective clothing and use a sunscreen especially between the hours of 10 A.M. and 4 P.M.

- Choose a diet that is low in saturated fat and cholesterol.

- Choose a diet with plenty of whole-grain products, vegetables, and fruits. Such a diet is rich in vitamins and fiber, which may reduce the risks of some cancers.

- Exercise regularly to maintain a healthy weight.

- Avoid unnecessary X-rays and radiation, especially during pregnancy.

- Avoid known carcinogens and cancer-causing chemicals. If you cannot avoid them, wear protective clothing or equipment.

Early detection of cancer cannot prevent the disease, but it may prevent your death. Regularly examine your skin and breasts or testicles for abnormal lumps or growth. Periodically, visit a doctor for a physical examination.

The Seven Warning Signs of Cancer

- **C**hange in bowel or bladder habits, such as constipation, diarrhea, or incomplete emptying of the bowel
- **A** sore that does not heal
- **U**nusual bleeding or discharge, particularly from the rectum or vagina
- **T**hickening or lump in the breast or elsewhere
- **I**ndigestion or difficulty in swallowing
- **O**bvious change in a wart or mole, such as growth, discharge, or unusual appearance
- **N**agging cough or hoarseness

Figure 24-13 *Any of these warning signs can alert you to a possible problem that should be checked by a physician.*

LESSON 2 REVIEW

1. Distinguish between the two types of tumors.
2. How does cancer spread?
3. What is a carcinogen?
4. Name four ways of reducing the risk of cancer.

What Do You Think?

5. What would you tell a friend who is reluctant to perform a self-exam for cancer?

3 DIABETES AND ARTHRITIS

Diabetes and arthritis are two common and serious noninfectious diseases. Neither disease has a cure yet, but both can be treated. Diabetes, if not strictly controlled, can be life-threatening. Arthritis is not life-threatening, but can be extremely painful and disabling.

Diabetes

Any disease in which the body's ability to use blood sugar (glucose) is impaired is known as **diabetes** (dy uh BEE tis). Diabetes involves **insulin** (IN suh lin), a hormone produced by the pancreas that stimulates body cells to take up and use blood sugar. Diabetes occurs if too little insulin is produced by the body, or if the body's cells do not respond normally to insulin. Diabetes affects about 1 in every 20 persons in the United States—nearly 16 million people. Nearly one third of those affected do not know that they have the disease.

About 150,000 people in the United States die each year from diabetes, making it the fourth leading cause of death from a disease. People with diabetes are also at risk for developing blindness, heart disease, stroke, kidney disease, and infections requiring amputation. In women, diabetes reduces the chances of becoming pregnant or of completing pregnancy, and increases the chances of birth defects.

TYPE I DIABETES   There are two common types of diabetes, type I and type II. **Type I diabetes** is the more serious and makes up 5 to 10 percent of all diabetes cases. A person with type I diabetes, which is also known as insulin-

Figure 24-14 *Regular exercise is important to everyone's health, including people with diabetes.*

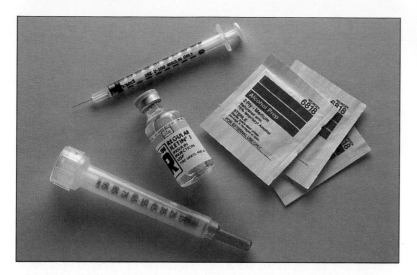

Figure 24-15 *The materials in an insulin kit allow people with type I diabetes to give themselves insulin injections.*

dependent diabetes, produces little or no insulin. Without insulin, the body's cells cannot use the glucose that is supplied in the bloodstream. As a result, glucose levels in the blood remain high. Symptoms, which usually appear suddenly, include thirst, frequent urination, nausea, hunger, fatigue, irritability, and weight loss.

Although it can strike at any age, type I diabetes usually first appears in children and so is often called juvenile-onset diabetes. Before insulin was discovered in 1921 and became available as a medication, people with type I diabetes did not live much beyond the age when they developed the disease. Today, people who have the disease give themselves insulin injections according to a strict schedule. In addition, they need to eat on a regular schedule and have the proper amount of carbohydrates and other nutrients in each meal. Regular exercise also helps to control their blood sugar level.

With type I diabetes, taking too much insulin, missing a meal, or exercising too much can result in low blood sugar levels. The symptoms of low blood sugar are trembling, nausea, and confusion. In most cases, eating some sugary foods can correct the situation. If nothing is done, the person may lapse into **insulin shock**, which is unconsciousness caused by too little sugar and too much insulin in the blood.

The opposite condition—high blood sugar—occurs when too little insulin is taken or too much food is eaten. Symptoms develop slowly and include nausea, vomiting, weakness, and increased breathing rate. If not treated promptly with insulin, this condition, called **diabetic coma** (dy uh BET ik), can also be life-threatening.

TYPE II DIABETES People who produce sufficient insulin but whose body cells do not respond normally to insulin have **type II diabetes,** or noninsulin-dependent, diabetes. As in type I diabetes, the result is a high level of glucose in the blood. This form of diabetes, which occurs most often in people over the age of 30, is also called adult-onset diabetes.

Type II diabetes usually develops slowly and often goes undetected until symptoms become severe. Symptoms are the same as for type I diabetes, but also include frequent, hard-to-heal infections, drowsiness, itching, blurred vision, and numbness in hands or feet. **Risk factors for type II diabetes include a family history of diabetes, being overweight, and lack of physical activity.**

Fortunately, many people can prevent type II diabetes by maintaining a desirable body weight and by exercising regularly. Some people who develop the disease can control it if they follow a weight-loss and exercise program. In other cases, medications may be used. Excessive sugar consumption is not thought to be a direct cause of type II diabetes. However, eating a high-sugar diet can cause excess weight which, in turn, can increase the chances of a person developing type II diabetes.

Arthritis

Inflammation or irritation of a joint is known as **arthritis** (ahr THRY tis). Arthritis is one of the most common noninfectious diseases, affecting nearly one in every seven people in the United States. Arthritis can be severe or mild. It can affect children as well as adults. There is no cure for most types of arthritis. However, treatments can reduce the severity of the symptoms. The symptoms of arthritis include swelling in one or more joints, early morning stiffness, recurring pain or tenderness in any joint, redness and warmth in a joint, weight loss, fever or weakness combined with joint pain, and inability to move a joint normally. Two of the more common types of arthritis are osteoarthritis and rheumatoid arthritis.

Figure 24-16 *Compare the structure of a normal joint (left) with that of a joint with osteoarthritis (middle) and a joint with rheumatoid arthritis (right).*

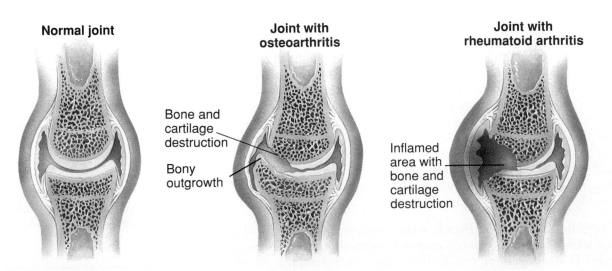

Normal joint

Joint with osteoarthritis

Joint with rheumatoid arthritis

Bone and cartilage destruction

Bony outgrowth

Inflamed area with bone and cartilage destruction

OSTEOARTHRITIS The most common type of arthritis is **osteoarthritis** (ahs tee oh ahr THRY tis). This form of arthritis is caused by wear and tear on a joint after many years of use or because of repeated injuries to a joint. The symptoms develop slowly, usually as a mild ache or soreness when a joint is moved.

Osteoarthritis can occur in almost any joint, but the most common are hips, knees, spine, and fingers. When it occurs at the finger joints, bony growths often appear. A high incidence of osteoarthritis is found in the elderly. In fact, most people who live past 60 will have some form of osteoarthritis.

Treatment for osteoarthritis may involve drugs, heat and cold treatments, exercise, and rest. Exercise is important to maintain joint flexibility. In some cases, weight reduction is recommended to ease the stress on the joints. In severe cases of osteoarthritis, surgery may be required to repair or replace affected joints.

RHEUMATOID ARTHRITIS In **rheumatoid arthritis** (ROO muh toyd), the membrane surrounding a joint becomes inflamed, and the inflammation spreads to other areas of the joint. An affected joint becomes hot, red, and swollen. Areas of the body other than joints also may become inflamed. The cause of rheumatoid arthritis is not known. Some evidence suggests that a malfunction in the immune system causes it to attack some of the body's own cells. About three times as many women as men have the disease.

Any joint may be affected, but joints in the wrist and knuckles are most often involved. If not treated, rheumatoid arthritis can cause joints to stiffen in deformed positions. The damage can be so severe that it changes the shape of the joint. Treatment includes aspirin or other anti-inflammatory drugs, exercise, and rest. Early diagnosis and a physician-directed treatment program are the best means of reducing the severity of the disease.

LESSON 3 REVIEW

1. What is the role of insulin in diabetes?
2. Name two risk factors for type II diabetes.
3. What is the most common form of arthritis, and what is its cause?
4. What treatment is available for rheumatoid arthritis?

What Do You Think?

5. Suppose an older relative is concerned about getting type II diabetes. What would you explain to your relative regarding ways to help prevent the disease?

4 DISABILITIES

Focus on these questions as you
read this lesson.

- What are some guidelines for
  interacting with people who
  have physical disabilities?

- How are the needs of disabled
  Americans addressed by the
  Americans with Disabilities
  Act?

SKILLS

- Locating Community
  Resources

A **disability** is any physical or mental impairment that limits or reduces normal activities, such as attending school, working, talking, walking, seeing, hearing, or caring for oneself. Disabilities include poor vision or blindness, poor hearing or deafness, and restricted, or lack of, mobility. People with disabilities have the same life goals as people who do not have disabilities. These goals require that they be integrated into school, the workplace, and the community.

Within any disability, there is a wide range in the extent to which the disability limits a person's activities. Some disabilities cause only minor or insignificant limitations on a person's activities. Other disabilities may cause severe limitations. Whatever the disability or its severity, there are usually devices and ways of modifying the physical environment that can help reduce and, in some instances, even eliminate the limitations.

Types of Physical Disabilities

The three most common types of physical disabilities are impaired sight, impaired hearing, and impaired mobility.

IMPAIRED SIGHT About 5 percent of the population, or 1 out of 20 people in the United States, suffers from some form of impaired, or restricted, sight. Most of these people can see to some extent with the aid of contact lenses or eyeglasses. Even with glasses, however, about 1 out of every 60 people cannot see well enough to read, and about 1 out of 200 people are blind. Some causes of sight impairment include congenital defects in the eye, cataracts (cloudiness in the lens) in elderly people, glaucoma (pressure buildup in the eyeball), diabetes, and physical injury to the eye.

Figure 24-17 *Performing artists such as Ray Charles illustrate the level of achievement that people with disabilities can attain.*

Guidelines for Interacting with a Sight-Impaired Person

- Speak right away so that the person will know you are present. Ask if you can help.
- If the person asks to be guided, extend your arm and place the person's hand on it. Do not grab the person by the arm.
- Remember that a guide dog is a worker, not a pet. Ask the person's permission before you touch or talk to the dog.
- Help the person to become oriented to a new environment by describing where things are and who is present.

Figure 24-18 *How could you familiarize a sight-impaired person with a new place?*

People with severe sight impairment usually depend on sound as a primary means of gathering information. Information is available from sound recordings of printed material and voice media, such as radio. Material written in braille, a system that uses characters made up of raised dots, is also available as an information source. Specially marked canes, which signal others of a person's sight impairment, are used to detect obstacles, such as curbs. Trained guide dogs allow mobility for many sight-impaired people. A list of guidelines for interacting with a sight-impaired person is provided in Figure 24-18.

IMPAIRED HEARING About 22 million people in the United States have some degree of hearing impairment. Of this number, nearly 2 million are profoundly (completely) deaf. Some causes of hearing impairment include congenital ear defects, exposure to excessive noise, and ear infections.

People with hearing impairment can use a variety of devices and techniques to aid them in hearing or communicating by other means. Hearing aids, for example, can help some people by increasing the loudness of sounds. Special telephones can amplify sound for the hearing-impaired, and systems of lights can replace telephone rings and doorbells. Those who have profound hearing loss may learn to communicate by using sign language or by speech reading. Signing, for example, is a language consisting of hand positions and movements.

Of course, people who are deaf frequently communicate by writing. One way of writing is by means of a telecommunications device for the deaf, or TDD. A TDD consists of a typewriter-style keyboard and a video monitor that connect to a telephone. Messages typed on the keyboard can be sent through the telephone to the TDD monitor of another person. For guidelines on communicating with hearing-impaired persons, see Figure 24-19.

Figure 24-19 *Why should a hearing-impaired person be able to see your mouth?*

Guidelines for Interacting with a Hearing-Impaired Person

- First, touch the person gently to gain attention and make the person look directly at you.
- Find out whether the person hears better on one side and position yourself on the person's "good" side.
- Speak slowly and clearly and be sure your mouth is visible to the person.
- Do not shout, but remember that some people with hearing aids can hear you better if you speak more loudly than usual.

IMPAIRED MOBILITY The ability of the body to move depends on having nervous, muscular, and skeletal systems

Guidelines for Interacting with a Mobility-Impaired Person

- Be patient.
- Move only as quickly as the person can keep pace.
- Be ready to give assistance if asked, or ask the person if he or she would like assistance.
- Seat yourself if the person is seated; do not stand and "talk down" to the person.

Figure 24-20 *What courtesies should you show a mobility-impaired person?*

that function together in a well-coordinated fashion. Disease in, or injury to, any of these body systems may result in some kind of impaired mobility.

In children, impaired mobility can be caused by diseases such as cerebral palsy and muscular dystrophy. In the elderly, arthritis as well as conditions such as Alzheimer's disease, Parkinson's disease, and heart disease are common causes of impaired mobility.

Paralysis of arms or legs resulting from injuries to the brain or spinal cord is a major cause of impaired mobility in many age groups. Unfortunately, these kinds of injuries are frequently the result of unnecessary risk-taking, substance abuse, or violent behavior.

The loss of arms or legs is another major cause of impaired mobility. This condition can result from injury as well as diseases such as diabetes and cancer, where limbs are surgically removed to save the life of the affected individual.

Individuals with impaired mobility can use devices such as canes, walkers, wheelchairs, crutches, braces, and artificial limbs to be mobile. Elevators, curb cuts, and ramps at the entrances to buildings allow people in wheelchairs access to places and services. For people who are paralyzed, research on nerve cell function holds some promise. Scientists are exploring ways to make damaged nerves grow and repair themselves. Figure 24-20 gives guidelines for interacting with mobility-impaired people.

Living with Physical Disabilities

Do you have a disability, or do you know someone who does? If you do, you know that the key to living with a disability is adaptation. People adapt to physical disabilities in different ways, depending on the type and extent of the disability, their feelings about it, the amount of support they receive from others, and the success of therapy and helping devices. Many organizations exist to help people adapt to disabilities by providing equipment, education, and emotional support.

Figure 24-21 *People with disabilities contribute in all areas of the work force.*

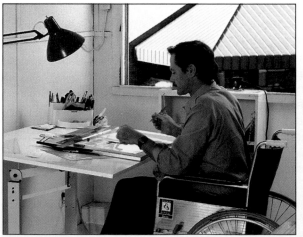

In the past, the ability of people with physical impairments to adapt has often been limited by outside factors. These factors included the negative attitudes of other people toward people with disabilities and the lack of access to many services, such as public transportation. To address these problems, the Americans with Disabilities Act (ADA) was signed into law in 1990. The ADA guarantees the civil rights of an estimated 43 million Americans who have physical or mental disabilities. This includes people who are physically impaired, blind, deaf, or mentally retarded, as well as those who have cancer, epilepsy, and AIDS, or who are HIV-positive. It also protects people who are undergoing or have completed rehabilitation for alcoholism or drug abuse. **The law guarantees that people with disabilities have access to the same employment opportunities, public services, public transportation, public accommodations, and telephone communications capabilities as everyone else.**

Interacting with People Who Have Disabilities

When and how should you help a person who has a physical disability? The best way is to let the person take the lead. You can do this by waiting for the person to perform the activity independently or to ask for your assistance. Most people with physical disabilities want to function independently. Your role is to help them do things for themselves and to respect their independence.

A second guideline is not to assume that a person with a physical disability has a mental disability as well. This should be obvious, but it is often overlooked. People with impaired muscular coordination, such as that caused by most forms of cerebral palsy, have normal intelligence, hearing, and sight. People in wheelchairs are not out of hearing range just because you are standing and they are sitting. People who cannot see usually can hear well, and those who cannot hear are sensitive to attitudes expressed by a person's face and body language.

The first two guidelines can be summed up by a third one: Do not underestimate a person who has a disability. More than anything else, a person with a disability wants to be involved and included in activities just as other people do. This can mean offering help when it is needed and wanted, or not offering help—as a way of recognizing the person's capabilities and independence.

LESSON 4 REVIEW

1. What is a disability?
2. What devices are available to help mobility-impaired individuals be more mobile?
3. State two guidelines to practice when you are with a person with a physical disability.
4. What needs of people with disabilities are addressed by the Americans with Disabilities Act?

What Do You Think?

5. How would you want to be treated by others if you had a physical disability, such as impaired mobility? If you had impaired hearing?

Evaluating Health Information

Imagine that just two days ago you were overjoyed about getting a summer job lifeguarding at a local beach. This was a job you had been hoping to get ever since last year. Now you are reading a magazine article stating that people who spend a lot of time in the sun risk getting skin cancer and premature wrinkling. All of a sudden, the lifeguard position does not seem to be the healthy job you thought it would be.

Now what do you do? Should you give up the lifeguard position, or take the risk of being overexposed to the sun? Before making any decision, you should attempt to verify the information in the article. In the rapidly changing fields of health and medicine, new studies sometimes contradict old studies, and experts often disagree about the significance of new results. This makes it difficult to report research findings. Thus news stories may contain misleading or even false information. You need to determine when information is or is not accurate.

How can you sort all this out? When reviewing new health information, keep an open, yet critical, mind. Use the following questions to evaluate health reports.

1. Who is the author?

If possible, determine who wrote the article and what the person's credentials are. Usually, health professionals (physicians and medical researchers) are the best qualified authors. Health information experts (writers trained to interpret health information) are also well qualified, but they lack the specialized training of health professionals. General reporters and people who write advertisements may not be well qualified to interpret health and medical information.

2. Is the source trustworthy?

Reliability depends on more than just the author. Where the information appears is also important to consider. The most reliable sources are medical and scientific journals. These journals accept articles only from reputable professionals and after thorough review by experts. The least reliable sources are advertisements and publications funded by firms with financial interests in the field—for example, a booklet or brochure funded by a vitamin manufacturer. Sources such as these are likely to be weighted in favor of one viewpoint.

3. Is the evidence convincing?

It is important to assess the quality of the evidence upon which the news is based. Some signs of weak evidence are

- the use of vague statements that lack supporting information, such as "doctors recommend" or "according to the latest reports"

- statements based on people's opinions rather than experimental results

- phrases like "in animals," "of that age group," or "in laboratory tests." These indicate that the findings are based on studies done on a limited basis.

- lack of information about a key aspect of the topic

4. Has the information been verified?

The most reliable information is based on evidence that has been tested. When different researchers arrive at similar results by independent means, the results are more likely to be accurate. Thus, the best way to assess new health information is to compare it with other reliable sources.

Unfortunately, verifying information is not always simple or foolproof. Often experts disagree about the conclusions that can be drawn from research findings. By becoming familiar with all the views on an issue, however, you can be confident of making a decision that is based on the best available information.

Apply the Skill

1. Read the Breakthrough article "Diabetes Research" on page 589. Do you believe it is accurate? Why? Make a list of facts you need in order to assess its accuracy.

2. Suppose this vaccine is available. Write an advertisement for the vaccine .

3. Suppose you have type I diabetes and you have just read an advertisement for a diabetes vaccine. List the information you would need about the product before deciding if it will offer any health benefits to you.

4. Choose a health news item from an Internet site or from a recent newspaper or magazine. Using the guidelines outlined above, write a report evaluating the article.

CHAPTER **24** REVIEW

KEY IDEAS

LESSON 1

- Prevention of cardiovascular disease involves avoiding or treating risk factors that cause the heart to become weakened and unhealthy.

- People can reduce the risk of developing cardiovascular disease by exercising regularly, eating a diet low in saturated fat and high in plant products, maintaining normal body weight, reducing stress, and not smoking.

LESSON 2

- Although the specific cause of most cancers is unknown, certain behaviors, such as tobacco use and overexposure to the sun, have been shown to increase the risk of certain cancers.

- Many cancers can be cured if they are detected early and treated promptly by medical professionals.

LESSON 3

- Risk factors for type II diabetes include a family history of diabetes, being overweight, and lack of physical activity.

- Arthritis is not curable, but is treatable with drugs, exercise, and rest.

LESSON 4

- The law guarantees that people with disabilities have access to the same employment opportunities, public services, public transportation, public accommodations, and telephone communications capabilities as everyone else.

KEY TERMS

LESSON 1
angina pectoris
arrhythmia
arteriosclerosis
artificial pacemaker
atherosclerosis
cerebral hemorrhage
cholesterol
congestive heart failure
coronary angiography
coronary heart disease
heart attack
high blood pressure

plaque
stroke

LESSON 2
biopsy
cancer
carcinogen
chemotherapy
immunotherapy
malignant tumor
mammogram
metastasis
oncogene
Pap test

radiation therapy

LESSON 3
arthritis
diabetes
diabetic coma
insulin
insulin shock
osteoarthritis
rheumatoid arthritis
type I diabetes
type II diabetes

LESSON 4
disability

Listed above are some of the important terms in this chapter. Choose the term from the list that best matches each phrase below.

1. regulates uptake of blood sugar
2. detects cervical cancer
3. hardening of the arteries
4. chest pain of coronary heart disease
5. a mass of cancerous cells

6. detects breast cancer
7. death of some of the heart tissue
8. irregular heartbeat
9. bleeding in the brain
10. a cancer-causing substance

WHAT HAVE YOU LEARNED?

If the statement is true, write "true." If it is false, change the underlined word or words to make the statement true.

11. Reducing the intake of salt will help to reduce <u>atherosclerosis</u>.

12. Deposits of <u>saturated fat</u> build up on the inner walls of blood vessels, causing blockage of blood flow.

13. <u>Congestive heart failure</u> can be controlled by means of an artificial pacemaker.

14. A biopsy is the removal and testing of a piece of tissue for the presence of <u>cancer</u>.

15. For a person with type I diabetes, overeating or injecting too little insulin can lead to <u>high</u> blood sugar levels.

16. Melanoma is a dangerous type of <u>lung cancer</u>.

17. Long-term wear and tear on a joint may result in <u>osteoarthritis</u>.

18. Hodgkin's disease is one type of cancer of the <u>skin.</u>

19. A TDD allows people who are <u>blind</u> to communicate with other people through a telephone line.

20. The Americans with Disabilities Act protects the rights of people who <u>hire people with disabilities</u>.

Answer each of the following with complete sentences.

21. Why is high blood pressure, or hypertension, sometimes called the "silent killer"?

22. What is the difference between a heart attack and congestive heart failure?

23. How are a heart attack and a stroke similar to each other?

24. What is the cause of cancer?

25. Identify the seven warning signs of cancer.

26. What are the two types of diabetes and how do they differ?

27. How can you best help a person who has a physical disability?

28. What is the key approach to living with a physical disability?

WHAT DO YOU THINK?

29. Why do you think noninfectious diseases have replaced infectious diseases as the leading causes of death in developed countries?

30. Many buildings and businesses now ban smoking. Do you think that the health benefits to society justify this restriction? What about the rights of people who smoke?

31. What kinds of health programs would you want the government to support to help reduce the incidence of cardiovascular diseases? Would such programs save money? Explain.

32. What would you recommend to provide greater job and community-involvement opportunities for people in your community with disabilities?

WHAT WOULD YOU DO?

33. Your elderly next-door neighbor is shoveling snow. Suddenly he sits down, clutching his chest. What should you do?

34. An overweight relative has been exhibiting symptoms of type II diabetes. What would you do?

35. You will be out in the sun all day. What will you do to protect yourself?

36. What would you do if you learned that a local supermarket where your family buys its food has asbestos insulation in its ceilings? Asbestos causes cancer.

Getting Involved

37. Many communities have services to assist people with disabilities. Use a telephone directory to find out what services are available in your community for helping people with disabilities. Then make a report to your class on your findings.

1 THE ENVIRONMENT— YOUR HOME

GUIDE FOR READING

Focus on these questions as you read this lesson.

- How does the health of people depend on the health of the environment?
- How is the health of the environment affected by the activities of people?

SKILLS

- Finding the Facts

Figure 25-1 *Raw materials such as carbon dioxide and oxygen are continuously being cycled in the environment.*

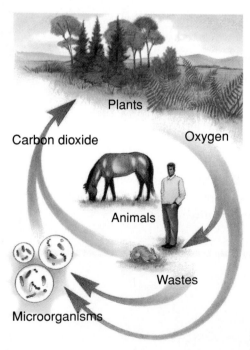

Carbon dioxide

Plants

Oxygen

Animals

Wastes

Microorganisms

Have you ever thought about how dependent you are on the environment? The **environment** (en VY run munt) is everything that makes up your surroundings—air, water, soil, rocks, plants, animals, and microorganisms. All living things are part of the environment and depend on it for all their needs. The air you breathe, the water you drink, and the food you eat come from the environment.

You, in turn, contribute to the environment in many ways. For example, as shown in Figure 25-1, as you breathe in oxygen, eat and use food, and drink water, you produce carbon dioxide and other body wastes, which enter the environment. Bacteria and other microorganisms use the wastes as food, breaking them down and releasing minerals and more carbon dioxide. Plants use the minerals and carbon dioxide to make their own food, and, in the process, release oxygen. You and other organisms use the plants as food and also use the oxygen they produce. Thus, materials in the environment are continually being used and reused in a never-ending cycle.

The Balance of Nature

The cycling of materials helps to keep conditions relatively constant in the environment. This steady state, known as **homeostasis** (hoh mee oh STAY sis), is maintained as long as all the parts of the environment are healthy. When any part of the environment is harmed or destroyed, the environment's homeostasis, or the "balance of nature," is changed.

Environmental Damage

The environment is constantly being disturbed—by natural events and by human activities. Natural events such as volcanoes, earthquakes, and floods can be devastating, but the environment eventually recovers from them. In fact, these events are part of cycles of renewal in the environment, as, for example, when ash from a volcano creates new soil. In contrast, many human activities such as clearing rain forests or polluting a lake cause harm that may permanently damage the balance of nature.

HABITAT DESTRUCTION   Humans have been altering the environment for thousands of years—for farming, settlement, and harvesting resources such as lumber. In modern times, however, the demand for land—on which to grow crops and live and for water and other resources—is accelerating as the human population rapidly expands.

Increasingly, more natural areas are being destroyed. When this happens, the survival of many types of organisms is threatened. As a result, the environment as a whole becomes less stable.

POLLUTION   All living things depend on the environment. **Pollution**—the accumulation of harmful wastes or other harmful substances in the environment—harms you and all other living things. **When the environment becomes polluted, the air you breathe, the water you drink, and the food you eat become polluted.** Substances that cause pollution are known as **pollutants.**

As part of the normal processes of life, all organisms produce wastes. These wastes usually do not cause pollution. Why? Because, as you see in Figure 25-1, they are broken down by microorganisms and reused by other living things. Wastes that can be broken down by microorganisms are called **biodegradable wastes**. Pollution from biodegradable wastes occurs only if the wastes are released into the environment more rapidly than they can be decomposed. This happens, for example, when raw, or untreated, sewage is released into a river.

In addition to biodegradable body wastes, humans create wastes that are not, or are only partially, biodegradable. Wastes of this type include motor oil, pesticides, solvents, mercury, arsenic, and lead. Many of these wastes are poisonous or cause cancer. Such wastes are serious pollutants because they accumulate in the environment and contaminate organisms.

The environmental damage resulting from human activities is serious, but there are solutions. Land use can be controlled, and many forms of pollution can be eliminated through new technologies. Even simple actions can bring about enormous improvements. People are beginning to recycle materials, for example. **Recycling,** the use over and over again of materials such as metal and glass, is one practical way to help keep the environment healthy.

SHARPEN YOUR SKILLS

Finding the Facts

The single greatest source of air pollution from human activities is the burning of fossil fuels. Alternative sources of energy include solar, wind, water, and nuclear power. Choose one of these energy sources and research its advantages and disadvantages.

LESSON 1 REVIEW

1. What is the environment?
2. What is pollution?
3. How does the environment's health affect your health?
4. How is the balance of nature affected by pollution?

What Do You Think?

5. What could you do to help reduce pollution in your immediate environment?

A Healthy Environment   **603**

GUIDE FOR READING

Focus on these questions as you read this lesson.

- What is the major source of air pollution?
- What can be done to reduce air pollution?

SKILLS

- Recognizing Misleading Claims

2 AIR POLLUTION AND HEALTH

You breathe in air and any pollutants that are present in the air. Some of these pollutants may damage the delicate tissues of your respiratory system. Others may enter your bloodstream and harm other parts of your body. The same air pollutants that are harmful to you also harm plants and animals in the environment.

Gases That Pollute

Air is a mixture of gases and small particles. The one gas you need—oxygen—makes up about 20 percent of the air. The remaining 80 percent of the air consists mainly of nitrogen plus small amounts of other naturally occurring gases, including carbon dioxide and argon.

When harmful gases and particles enter the air, the air becomes polluted. **Burning is the greatest source of air pollution.** Whenever substances such as coal, oil, natural gas, gasoline, wood, paper, and trash are burned, particles and harmful waste gases are produced. Harmful gases also are released into the air when liquids such as gasoline or paint thinner evaporate or when gases are released from natural sources such as volcanoes.

CARBON DIOXIDE The primary waste given off during burning is the nonpoisonous gas **carbon dioxide**. Carbon dioxide is normally present in the atmosphere, and, as you know from Figure 25-1, is essential for living things. Why do some people consider it a pollutant? The answer is that the widespread burning of coal, petroleum, and other fossil fuels has caused a substantial increase in the level of carbon dioxide in the atmosphere. Carbon dioxide absorbs heat. When Earth is warmed by the sun, the heat that would normally escape into outer space is absorbed by the carbon dioxide in the atmosphere. As a result, the atmosphere is warmed more than it would be if carbon dioxide levels were lower. Many scientists think that this warming effect, called the **greenhouse effect,** will lead to harmful changes in global weather patterns.

CARBON MONOXIDE A poisonous waste produced when most substances are burned is **carbon monoxide**, a colorless, odorless gas. Carbon monoxide is dangerous because it combines with **hemoglobin** (HEE muh gloh bin), the substance in your red blood cells that carries oxygen to all the cells of your body. Carbon

Figure 25-2 *Motor vehicles are the major source of air pollution in most cities.*

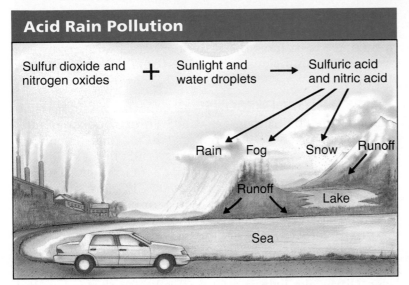

Acid Rain Pollution

Sulfur dioxide and nitrogen oxides $+$ Sunlight and water droplets $\rightarrow$ Sulfuric acid and nitric acid

Rain   Fog   Snow   Runoff

Runoff   Lake

Sea

Figure 25-3 *Acid rain, which results from the burning of fossil fuels, is damaging forests in many parts of the world.*

monoxide binds to hemoglobin, preventing it from carrying oxygen. As a result, your body does not receive enough oxygen. Tobacco smoke and the exhaust gases from motor vehicles are sources of carbon monoxide.

OXIDES OF NITROGEN AND SULFUR   Other gases that form when fossil fuels are burned include nitrogen oxides and sulfur oxides. These gases may cause your eyes to burn and tear. They also can damage lung tissues and worsen existing respiratory problems. As you can see in Figure 25-3, when these gases mix with water in the air, **nitric acid** (NY trik) and **sulfuric acid** (sul FYOOR ik) are formed. Rain that contains one or both of these acids is called **acid rain**. Snow, sleet, and fog also can contain these acids, which dissolve stone, corrode metals, and damage plants. Acid rain and snow increase the acidity of lakes, ponds, and streams, preventing the growth of many water-dwelling organisms. When acid rain enters the soil, it releases certain toxic minerals, which are then taken up by plants. In many parts of the world, acid rain has caused severe damage to trees, as you can see in Figure 25-3.

HYDROCARBONS   Liquid fuels and solvents that evaporate, natural gas that escapes into the air, and incompletely burned fossil fuels are sources of airborne hydrocarbons. **Hydrocarbons** (hy druh KAHR bunz) are substances made up of hydrogen and carbon. Many hydrocarbons are poisonous, and some can cause cancers. Motor vehicles are a major source of hydrocarbons. When hydrocarbons react with nitric oxide in the presence of sunlight, a brownish haze called **smog** forms. Substances in smog are harmful to plants as well as animals.

OZONE   In the presence of sunlight, nitrogen oxides and hydrocarbons from sources such as motor vehicles react to produce ozone. **Ozone** is a form of oxygen that chemically reacts with many things. It causes severe damage to plants. In humans, it irritates the respiratory tract and aggravates respiratory conditions such as asthma, bronchitis, and emphysema.

CHLOROFLUOROCARBONS Chemicals containing chlorine, fluorine, and carbon are called **chlorofluorocarbons** (klawr oh floor oh KAHR bunz), or CFCs. These chemicals have been widely used as the cooling fluids in air conditioners and refrigeration units, as propellants in aerosol spray cans, and in foam insulating materials. CFCs are serious air pollutants because they destroy the **ozone layer**, a region of the atmosphere with a high concentration of ozone.

In contrast to its role as a pollutant near Earth's surface, the ozone in the ozone layer has a protective role. Most of the ultraviolet light from the sun is absorbed by Earth's ozone layer. Ultraviolet light is a form of radiation that is harmful to all living things. In humans, it causes skin cancer and cataracts (cloudiness of the eye's lens) and may damage the immune system. Scientists are concerned that increasing levels of ultraviolet radiation will damage plants, reducing food supplies on land and in oceans as well. Since CFCs are destroying the ozone layer, more ultraviolet light than ever before is reaching Earth's surface.

Particle Forms of Air Pollution

Particles in the air—such as dust, soot, and mold spores—are another type of air pollution. You see evidence of this if you wipe a windowsill with a clean, white cloth. The dirt on the cloth is mostly particles, or **particulates** (pahr TIK yuh lits), that settled out of the air. Particle pollution enters your breathing system with the air you breathe. The tiny hairlike structures, or **cilia** (SIL ee uh), that line your breathing passages trap many of these particles before they reach your lungs, but they can still damage your body.

LEAD One type of particle pollutant that can cause serious harm is lead. Lead can poison the liver, kidneys, and nervous system. Lead poisoning in babies and young children can result in slow mental development.

For many years, lead was added to gasoline to improve the performance of engines. When the gasoline was burned, tiny particles of lead were released into the air from the exhaust gases of engines. People inhaled the lead particles as they breathed. When leaded gasoline was phased out and unleaded gasoline came into use, the levels of lead in people dropped dramatically.

Tiny particles of lead continue to enter the air from another source—lead paint. Lead used to be

Figure 25-4 *The use of unleaded gasoline in the United States has reduced lead air pollution.*

an ingredient in most paints. As old lead paint flakes off or is removed, particles of paint are released into the air. People in areas where lead paint is being removed should wear breathing filters to avoid inhaling paint dust. Most serious cases of lead poisoning occur in children who eat bits of lead paint.

ASBESTOS   Another particle-type air pollutant is asbestos. **Asbestos** (as BES tus) is a mineral that occurs in the form of fibers. Because it does not burn, asbestos was widely used in shingles, floor coverings, ceiling materials, insulation, and brake linings. Unfortunately, bits of asbestos flake off easily. When asbestos fibers are inhaled into the lungs, they damage the cells of the lungs, causing a disease called **asbestosis** (as bes TOH sis). Asbestos also may cause lung cancer, especially in people who also smoke.

Weather and Air Pollution

Although the weather does not cause air pollution, it can affect it. When the air close to Earth's surface is warmer than air at higher elevations, which is usually the case, the warm air rises, carrying air pollutants upward. This prevents pollutant levels from building up near the ground. When a **temperature inversion** occurs, however, a layer of cool air near the ground is trapped under a layer of warm air, as shown in Figure 25-5. As a result, pollutants are not carried away and may accumulate to dangerously high levels.

Weather reports for cities and other areas with air pollution problems often include government air quality ratings. The ratings, which are based on air quality standards, range from "good" to "unhealthy" to "very hazardous." People who have respiratory problems should stay indoors and avoid physical activity during periods of severe air pollution.

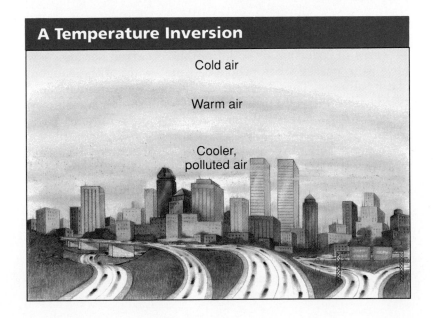

A Temperature Inversion

Cold air

Warm air

Cooler, polluted air

Figure 25-5 *A temperature inversion results in a buildup of air pollutants in a cool layer of air near Earth's surface.*

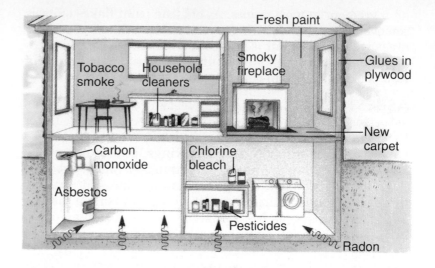

Figure 25-6 *A variety of sources may contribute to indoor air pollution.*

Fresh paint

Tobacco smoke

Household cleaners

Smoky fireplace

Glues in plywood

Carbon monoxide

Chlorine bleach

New carpet

Asbestos

Pesticides

Radon

Indoor Air Pollution

Most people think that air pollution occurs only outdoors. Yet studies have shown that levels of air pollutants indoors can be higher than those outdoors. Indoor air pollution is most severe in homes and other buildings that have been sealed against air leaks, usually as a way to prevent energy loss. A building with few air leaks uses less energy for heating and cooling. Unfortunately, inside such energy-efficient buildings, pollutants can build up to high levels.

Indoor air pollutants include such things as asbestos and the gases, vapors, or particles given off by carpets, paints, pesticides, glues in plywood, foam insulation, gas stoves, fuel-burning indoor heaters, air fresheners, and burning tobacco. Another indoor air pollutant, to be discussed later in this chapter, is the naturally occurring radioactive gas radon.

What Can Be Done?

Progress in reducing air pollution has occurred because new laws were passed when people became aware of the dangers of air pollution. The Clean Air Act of 1970, for example, identified major air pollutants and set standards for air quality. Since 1970, Congress has made changes and additions to the Clean Air Act every few years. To comply with federal laws, some factories and power plants use scrubbers, or filters, on smokestacks to remove some pollutants. More efficient ways of burning oil, coal, and gas also have helped reduce the amount of pollution from these sources.

Congress has also passed separate laws to regulate pollution from automobiles. Catalytic converters on automobiles have dramatically reduced hydrocarbons and carbon monoxide in automobile exhausts. Also, many states now require that motor vehicles pass annual inspections that include a check of exhaust pollutants.

Other measures to reduce air pollution include the development of cleaner-burning fuels and alternative energy sources. Fuels such as natural gas, methanol, and hydrogen burn more cleanly than gasoline. Adapting automobile engines to burn these fuels will reduce air pollution. Electric-powered automobiles also are being developed. In addition, progress is being made to improve the efficiencies of nonpolluting energy sources such as wind and solar power.

Other sources of air pollution are also being addressed. Some countries, including the United States, have banned CFCs in aerosol cans. Scientists have already developed alternatives to CFCs that will not damage the ozone layer. The use of asbestos now is severely limited and banned entirely in construction. Asbestos removal programs for buildings such as schools have helped reduce exposure to this pollutant. Reducing indoor air pollution even extends to the design of buildings. Now, some houses are being designed to allow for adequate year-round ventilation.

Reducing air pollution depends on the actions of individuals as well as government and industry. You can help reduce air pollution by practicing some of the following:

- Whenever you can, walk or ride a bicycle instead of using a motor vehicle.
- Use public transportation instead of an automobile.
- Recycle materials such as glass, metal, plastic, and paper. Making goods from recycled materials requires less energy (fuel) than making them from raw materials.
- If you drive, avoid unnecessary trips. Also, be sure the vehicle is well-tuned so it produces the least pollution.
- Turn off lights and appliances that are not being used. Saving energy saves fuel, which reduces air pollution.
- Clean the cooling fans or coils on refrigerators and air conditioners so they will work more efficiently.
- In winter, set the thermostat lower and wear extra clothes indoors. In the summer, if you have an air conditioner, set it at the highest comfortable temperature.

SHARPEN YOUR *SKILLS*

Recognizing Misleading Claims

An advertisement for a new household air filter claims that it "…will remove all forms of air pollution from a house or apartment." Would you believe the advertisement? Why or why not? How would you go about finding out if the claim is true?

LESSON 2 REVIEW

1. What is the source of most air pollution?
2. How do chlorofluorocarbons harm the environment?
3. How does asbestos endanger human health?
4. How do temperature inversions affect air pollution?

What Do You Think?

5. Would you favor increasing taxes on gasoline? Why or why not?

GUIDE FOR READING

Focus on these questions as you read this lesson.

- What are sources of water pollution?
- What are ways of reducing water pollution?

SKILLS

- Activity: Nontoxic House-cleaning

Clean, available, fresh water is something most of us take for granted until there is a crisis—for example, pollution of water supplies by toxic chemicals. More and more people are becoming concerned about our water resources. **In the United States and all over the world, wastes from household, industrial, and agricultural sources cause pollution of water resources.** Laws now help prevent some kinds of water pollution that occurred in the past. However, individuals also need to be aware of how their actions can help protect water resources.

Sources of Water Pollution

Bodies of water such as lakes, rivers, and oceans have always been used to dispose of wastes. If the wastes are biodegradable and in small enough volumes, microorganisms can break down the wastes. However, as both the volume and types of wastes increase, pollution of water becomes more and more of a problem. To understand the scope and nature of water pollution, you need to understand its sources.

SEWAGE The waste material carried from toilets and drains is referred to as **sewage.** Most wastes in sewage are human body wastes. If released into the environment too rapidly, sewage can make water foul-smelling and unable to support life. Sewage also can contain bacteria and viruses that cause disease. For example, in coastal areas, shellfish such as clams or oysters may become contaminated with the hepatitis A virus from human sewage. People who eat the shellfish raw may develop hepatitis A.

As recently as the 1970s, many communities in the United States discharged raw, or untreated, sewage directly into rivers or the ocean. In 1972, the Clean Water Act required communities to treat their raw sewage before releasing it into the environment.

Sewage treatment makes use of microorganisms to break down the wastes in the water. Septic tanks, cesspools, and municipal sewage treatment plants are all forms of sewage treatment facilities. Each provides conditions that allow microorganisms to break down wastes before they are released into the environment.

INDUSTRIAL WASTES Wastes produced from industrial operations, such as mining and manufacturing, can produce some of the most dangerous types of water pollution. Many industrial wastes are extremely toxic or not biodegradable, or both. Industrial wastes include such things as dyes, acids,

Figure 25-7 *Clean, unpolluted water is something no one should take for granted.*

NONTOXIC HOUSECLEANING

In this activity, you will demonstrate the effectiveness of cleaners made from nontoxic materials.

Materials

bucket	cornstarch
water	white vinegar
baking soda	stirrer
soap flakes	sponge
	rags or paper towels

Procedure

1. In a bucket, make a nontoxic, all-purpose cleaner by adding 1/2 tablespoon of baking soda and 1/8 cup of soap flakes to 1/2 gallon of hot water. Stir until all ingredients are completely dissolved.

2. With a sponge, use the cleaning solution to clean your desktop or another surface that your teacher selects. Note how easily and effectively the cleaner works.

3. Make a nontoxic glass cleaner by adding 1 tablespoon of cornstarch and 1/4 cup of white vinegar to 1/2 gallon of warm water. Stir well.

4. Moisten a rag or paper towel with the glass cleaner. According to your teacher's instructions, try cleaning a window or mirror.

Discussion

1. How well did the cleaners work? How do they compare with commercially prepared products you have used?

2. How do you think most people dispose of cleaning products? What effect do you think disposing of cleaning products would have on the environment?

3. What are the benefits and drawbacks of making your own nontoxic cleaners?

solvents, and heavy metals such as mercury, lead, and cadmium. In the past, it was common for industrial wastes to be discharged into ground and surface waters, contaminating organisms that lived in or drank the water.

RUNOFF The water that drains from land into streams is called **runoff.** Runoff can carry with it many kinds of substances that pollute water supplies. Runoff from agricultural land, for example, often contains pesticides, herbicides, and fertilizers. **Pesticides** are chemicals that kill crop pests. **Herbicides** are chemicals that kill weeds. Many pesticides and herbicides are toxic and do not decompose, or decompose slowly. People who drink water contaminated with these chemicals can suffer harm. Even if the water is not used by humans, fish in the water pass the contamination on to people who eat the fish.

Fertilizers are chemicals that contain minerals needed by plants. Some of the minerals, such as nitrates and phosphates, are carried by runoff into streams, rivers, and lakes. There these minerals cause small water plants, or **algae** (AL jee), to grow rapidly. When the algae die, they serve as food for huge populations of microorganisms. The microorganisms, which require oxygen to live, grow so rapidly that they

Figure 25-8 *Pesticides in agricultural runoff can pollute water resources.*

Figure 25-9 *Oil spills are devastating to animal and plant life.*

use up all the oxygen in the water. Without oxygen, most of the water-dwelling organisms die, and the water becomes foul-smelling and unfit for use. This process of excessive algae growth followed by decay and lack of oxygen is called **eutrophication** (yoo troh fih KAY shun).

OIL SPILLS   Oil spills are major sources of water pollution, especially in the world's oceans. The dependence of the world on petroleum means that millions of gallons of oil and petroleum products are being transported every day throughout the world. This level of activity makes it likely that oil spills will occur, and, in fact, they do. Most oil spills are not large. No matter what their size, however, the pollution that results is very damaging to the environment. The 11-million-gallon oil spill in 1989 from the *Exxon Valdez* in Alaska was but one of many oil spills that have seriously polluted large areas.

HOUSEHOLD CLEANERS   Household cleaners can be a source of pollution if they contain harsh chemicals such as chlorine, or plant nutrients such as phosphates. Chlorine is toxic to all forms of life. Chlorine also can react with certain substances dissolved in water, forming cancer-causing substances. Phosphates, which are plant nutrients, may cause excessive algae growth, leading to eutrophication.

What Can Be Done?

As you know, federal laws require communities to treat their sewage. However, sewage treatment can do nothing to decompose many kinds of pollutants that are poured into drains. Everyone can help prevent water pollution by not dumping toxic materials such as oil, solvents, paints, or pesticides into a drain. Most communities have waste collection centers to which these chemicals can be taken for safe disposal. If you have a question about how to dispose of chemicals safely, call your local health department or state agency for environmental protection.

LESSON *3* REVIEW

1. What pollutants are present in agricultural runoff?
2. How are microorganisms involved in sewage treatment?
3. Why are industrial wastes usually so damaging to the environment?
4. How have laws helped to prevent water pollution?

What Do You Think?

5. What would you suggest to reduce the chances of oil spills?

DIFFERENT VOICES SPEAKING

New Jersey native Chris Allieri is pursuing a career as an environmentalist at the University of Colorado. He has received numerous awards for his work in helping to protect the environment.

Q. Chris, how did you first become interested in protecting the environment?

A. My parents motivated me initially by their own example. They have long been nature enthusiasts, and they always taught my brothers, sisters, and me never to take what we have for granted. My big involvement as an environmental activist, however, came on the twentieth anniversary of Earth Day. I was in Central Park in New York as a volunteer, and there were speakers. I was moved by the experience and by the magnitude of the problem facing the planet. I felt that the time had come for me to spread my awareness. It was soon afterward that I founded SAFE.

Q. What is SAFE?

A. It's an environmental club that I started at my high school. The name SAFE is an acronym for Student Activists for the Environment. Initially people I discussed the idea with were skeptical, but I was persistent. Luckily, I won the support of a biology teacher I really admire. The club started with 15 members. Today the enrollment is around 80, and another chapter has formed at a junior high school in my home community.

Q. What are some of the activities SAFE has carried out?

A. One of our major tasks was storm drain stenciling. We stenciled a blue fish on storm

Chris Allieri

drains all over town and then followed up with a community-wide educational program. We called it "the fish connection." We were trying to make people aware that what they put down the drain ends up in the ocean. The response from the community was great. We also initiated cleanups around the high school, the community, and area beaches. In our efforts to educate the public, we also arranged for guest speakers on recycling and set up an alumni forum for those interested in environmental careers.

Q. What do you hope to accomplish in your life goals as an environmentalist?

A. I hope to get people to embrace environmental awareness on a global scale—to wake up to the dangers that face us. We need to do that if the planet is to survive. A first step in that direction is education, so I guess you might say I plan to be an educator.

Journal Activity

Chris stresses the importance of education in saving the planet. In your health journal, write an open letter to the citizens of Planet Earth. In your letter, mention at least six steps that you feel must be taken to clean up Earth and keep it safe for future generations.

GUIDE FOR READING

Focus on these questions as you read this lesson.

- How do wastes buried on land pose a health problem?
- What are some strategies to solve the problem of solid waste disposal?

SKILLS

- Analyzing Risks and Benefits

The amount of waste material produced in the United States every year is staggering—over 300 million tons. Much of the waste material is buried in landfills. A **landfill** is an area where trash, garbage, and other wastes are deposited and covered with soil. **Many of the wastes buried in landfills are toxic or cancer-causing and are potential sources of air and water pollution.**

Land Disposal of Wastes

Landfills have been widely used around the world for disposal of solid and liquid wastes. One problem with landfills is that space for them is running out. Many landfills across the country are at or near full capacity.

Another more serious problem is that many landfills contain hazardous wastes that may be leaking into water supplies. The Environmental Protection Agency (EPA), the federal agency in charge of enforcing environmental laws, calls substances **hazardous wastes** if they are flammable, explosive, corrosive, or toxic to human or other life. Each year, millions of tons of hazardous wastes are produced in the United States alone. According to the federal government, many of these wastes have been disposed of in landfills in unsafe ways. At thousands of landfills across the country, hazardous wastes are threatening to pollute underground and surface water supplies.

Fortunately, newer landfills, like the secure landfill illustrated in Figure 25-10, are designed to prevent leakage of liquid wastes into the surrounding soil. Many experts agree, however, that even these landfills may not be 100 percent

Figure 25-10 *Landfills can be designed to prevent pollution.*

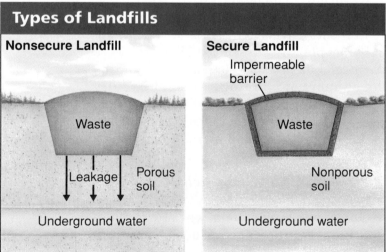

Types of Landfills

Nonsecure Landfill

Waste

Leakage   Porous soil

Underground water

Secure Landfill

Impermeable barrier

Waste

Nonporous soil

Underground water

safe and that alternative waste disposal methods need to be developed.

Most hazardous wastes that are dumped in landfills or elsewhere are produced by industries. Many of the wastes were dumped before their dangers were known. One instance of this took place between 1946 and 1958 when one chemical company dumped toxic chemical wastes into the ground around the Love Canal in upstate New York. Later, many homes and a school were constructed in the area. The chemical wastes received national attention in 1978, when heavy rains flooded basements in the Love Canal area. Oily liquids entered the basements with the rainwater. These oily liquids were leaking out of the dump site. Studies in the area showed an increase of disease, which was linked to the chemicals underneath the homes and school. Because of this evidence, the state government evacuated people from their homes. Today, the area is unpopulated because of the toxic materials in the soil.

The chemicals dumped in landfills or other hazardous waste sites may be extremely harmful. People who clean up these sites are never sure what they may encounter. They wear protective gear that prevents them from coming into direct contact with any of the waste materials. Some of the wastes are poisons that damage parts of the body such as the nervous system, lungs, liver, or kidneys. Other wastes may be cancer-causing substances, called **carcinogens** (kahr SIN uh junz). Still others may be **mutagens** (MYOO tuh junz)—chemicals that cause changes in a cell's hereditary material. The children of people exposed to mutagens have an increased risk of birth defects.

What Can Be Done?

Many sites where hazardous wastes have been dumped legally or illegally have been identified and are scheduled for cleanup. The EPA has identified over 20,000 dumps in the

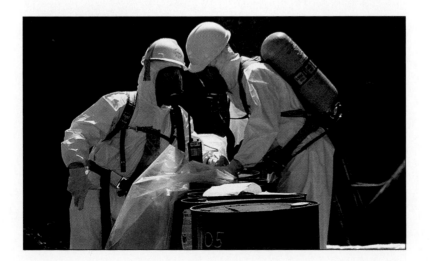

Figure 25-11 *The cleanup of hazardous waste sites requires strict safety precautions.*

Medical Writer and Biological Photographer

Issues involving health and the environment are complex. **Medical writers** help make these issues easy to understand. They may prepare articles for newspapers and magazines, or write books or scripts for radio and TV. Many medical writers are self-employed, while others work on the staffs of newspapers, magazines, research institutions, and hospitals.

Medical writers must have a knack for writing plainly about technical subjects. This career requires a bachelor's degree and a background in journalism, English, or science.

Biological photographers communicate information through visual images. They photograph things as varied as surgical procedures, bacteria under a microscope, or the effects of acid rain on a lake. Some 2- and 4-year colleges offer training in biological photography.

United States that contain hazardous substances. Many dump sites have been identified only after citizens have notified authorities. Other sites have not been identified. If you suspect hazardous chemicals have been dumped at a site, you should notify your local health department or state agency for environmental protection.

Legislation now makes it difficult for industries to dump wastes illegally. Legal dump sites for hazardous chemicals are designed to prevent the escape of wastes into the environment. Many companies are taking measures to reduce the amount of wastes they generate or to recycle their wastes. New technologies for destroying hazardous chemicals, such as high-temperature incineration, may provide a way of destroying large amounts of hazardous wastes. Many communities have special collection centers where residents can turn in hazardous wastes for proper disposal. Also, many states and communities now require residents to recycle materials such as newspapers, metals, plastics, and glass.

You can help reduce the problems associated with land disposal of wastes by doing the following:

- Recycle as much material as you can. Glass, metal, plastics, newspaper, and car batteries can be recycled.
- Avoid using disposable, nonbiodegradable products such as plastic razors and styrofoam cups.
- Use cloth bags or reuse paper bags for grocery shopping.
- Purchase products in recycled or recyclable packages.
- Buy products that are biodegradable or that are made from recycled material.
- Use only as much of a product or material as you need.
- Do not put hazardous wastes such as pesticides, oil, and batteries into your trash. Save these for hazardous waste collection centers. If you have questions about hazardous wastes, check with your local health department or state agency for environmental protection.

LESSON 4 REVIEW

1. What is a landfill?
2. What are hazardous wastes?
3. Why are landfills potential sources of water pollution?
4. What is a way you can reduce the volume of solid waste?

What Do You Think?

5. Suppose you had to develop new packaging for a fast-food restaurant. What type of packaging would you use to protect the food yet not harm the environment?

5 RADIATION AND NOISE POLLUTION

High-energy radiation and noise are two types of pollution that seem to be getting worse rather than better. **High-energy radiation** is a form of energy that damages living things. High-energy radiation includes ultraviolet light, X-rays, cosmic rays, and the energy that is given off by certain substances, such as uranium. Substances that give off radiation are said to be **radioactive**.

Sounds tell you something about your surroundings, but loud sound, or **noise**, is a nuisance that can harm your health. Airplanes, trains, motor vehicles, appliances, television, radio, stereo equipment, and machinery are some of the sources of noise to which you are exposed.

Radiation and Health

There are many natural sources of high-energy radiation, such as ultraviolet light from the sun, cosmic rays from space, and radiation from naturally occurring radioactive substances in the air, water, and soil. These natural sources of radiation make up what is called **background radiation**. Background radiation, along with routine exposure to X-rays for medical and dental care, are the normal sources of radiation exposure for most people.

EFFECTS OF RADIATION Under certain conditions, people may be exposed to radiation above background levels. For example, people who receive radiation therapy for cancer, who mine radioactive materials such as uranium, or who work in the nuclear weapons or nuclear power industries are exposed to doses of radiation higher than those of the average population.

Exposure to radiation may cause cancer. The greater the exposure, the greater is the risk of developing cancer. In some cases, however, even a small amount of radiation may be all that is necessary to cause cancer. To prevent radiation injury, people who work with radiation wear protective clothing and undergo periodic tests to monitor their exposure levels. Exposure to large doses of radiation results in **radiation sickness.** The symptoms of radiation sickness are nausea, diarrhea, fatigue, and hair loss. Severe radiation sickness can lead to death.

SOURCES OF RADIATION POLLUTION In the past, radioactive substances were released into the atmosphere when nuclear weapons were tested above ground. Winds carried this airborne radioactivity

GUIDE FOR READING

Focus on these questions as you read this lesson.

- What are some natural sources of high-energy radiation?
- What is the danger of exposure to loud noise?

SKILLS

- Supporting a Friend

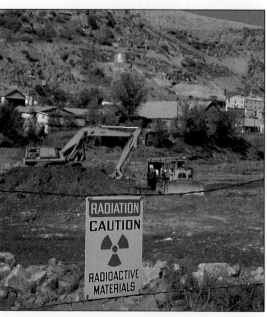

Figure 25-12 *Nuclear wastes are a serious environmental hazard.*

throughout the atmosphere. Eventually, the radioactive material settled to the ground in rain or snow or as dust particles. Radioactivity that falls to the ground in this manner is called **fallout.**

Nuclear power plants use radioactive materials to generate power. Because of their potential danger, nuclear power plants are highly regulated and have many safety systems built into their operation. Nonetheless, it is possible for a nuclear power plant to malfunction and release radioactive material. In 1986, tons of radioactive materials were released from a nuclear reactor at Chernobyl in the former Soviet Union. Radioactivity from this accident was spread by winds, contaminating areas in many countries of Europe. This was the worst accident to date of this type.

Other radioactive materials in the environment are the result of wastes produced by the medical uses of radioactive materials, nuclear weapons manufacturing and testing, nuclear power plants, and the mining of radioactive minerals. Since these wastes will give off radiation for thousands and even hundreds of thousands of years, they present a long-term danger to people.

The radioactive gas **radon** is estimated to cause 5,000 to 20,000 deaths from lung cancer each year. Radon is produced by radium, a radioactive substance found naturally in certain rocks. Radon becomes a serious indoor air pollutant when it leaks from the ground into the foundations of buildings and builds up to dangerous levels.

Noise and Health

Prolonged exposure to loud noise causes permanent hearing loss. The louder the noise and the longer the period of exposure, the greater the risk of hearing loss. Hearing loss in teens who listen to loud music is a growing problem.

Figure 25-13 *Noise from many sources can be harmful.*

The loudness of sound is measured in units known as **decibels.** Leaves rustling create a sound of about 10 decibels. Fifty decibels of sound can interfere with sleep. Normal conversation is about 60 decibels. Hearing loss begins to occur around 80 decibels, which is approximately the loudness of a vacuum cleaner.

Except for hearing loss, a firm connection between noise and disease has not been established. However, many experts believe that noise contributes to stress.

What Can Be Done?

Radiation and noise pollution cannot be avoided completely. They are part of our daily lives. However, you can take some preventive measures. Remember, the effects of exposure to all forms of radiation add up. Physicians recommend that you limit your exposure to the sun. If you are in the sun, wear protective clothing and sunglasses and use sunscreen. Physicians also suggest that you limit your exposure to X-rays. The risk involved in a single X-ray exposure is small, and the medical benefits of a correct diagnosis are great, but you should limit X-rays to those that are medically neccessary.

In some parts of the country, experts recommend that people test their living quarters for radon. Testing kits can be purchased at hardware and other stores. Some state environmental agencies provide these tests. If a radon problem exists, improving ventilation and sealing cracks in foundation walls and floors are recommended as corrrective actions.

Limit your exposure to loud noises. Loud music, especially when using headphones, is a major cause of permanent hearing loss in teenagers. Avoid areas where noise levels are high. If you cannot avoid loud noises, wear ear covers or plugs when you are in a noisy environment.

LESSON **5** REVIEW

1. How is radiation a danger to human health?
2. What are some natural sources of radiation?
3. What is the natural source of radon, and how can exposure to radon be reduced?
4. What are sources of noise in your life? How do these noises affect your health?

What Do You Think?

5. What would you suggest to reduce the amount of noise in people's lives?

>> BREAKTHROUGH >>

Bioremediation

Cleaning up sites contaminated with radioactive uranium is not a simple task. If recent research is successful, however, the job may be made much easier with a process that uses bacteria that normally live more than 650 feet below Earth's surface.

In the process of bioremediation, water contaminated with dissolved uranium is pumped into a reaction tank containing the bacteria. When they are supplied with a food source, the bacteria convert the uranium from its water-soluble form to a water-insoluble form. The water-insoluble uranium settles to the bottom of the tank. It is still radioactive, of course, but because it is insoluble, it is much easier to separate and remove.

If the process works as well as expected, the bacteria may be used to help clean up uranium-contaminated sites.

BUILDING HEALTH *SKILLS*

Being Assertive

While Joe and some of his friends were eating lunch in the no-smoking section of a local restaurant, cigarette smoke began drifting over from the next booth. At first Joe tried to ignore the smoke, but he soon decided that the "No Smoking" sign entitled him to a smoke-free meal. Joe politely asked the person to observe the no-smoking rule.

Joe behaved assertively when he stood up for his rights as a nonsmoker. Could you be assertive in a similar situation? If not, you are not alone. Assertiveness is a skill that many people find difficult to master, but one that is very necessary in order to function well in society.

Being assertive means expressing your feelings honestly in a way that respects your rights and the rights of others. Acting assertively can help you feel more self-confident and more in control of factors that affect your life. You will feel good that you can express your needs and stand up for yourself without hurting others.

The step-by-step process that follows will help you master the skill of assertiveness. The process is especially helpful in situations where you would like to act assertively but find it difficult to do so.

1. Evaluate your current behavior

To understand what kept you from acting assertively in a particular situation, ask yourself these questions:

- What outcome did I desire?
- What outcome did I get?
- What negative thoughts kept me from acting assertively in this situation?
- What was I afraid might have happened if I had acted assertively?

2. Observe a role model in action

Identify a person who is able to act assertively in difficult situations. Observe the person as he or she handles a situation in an assertive manner. Pay attention to the words, tone of voice, and body language the person uses. Afterwards, think about other ways in which you could act assertively in the same situation. What else could you say? How else could you say it?

3. Conduct a mental rehearsal

Conducting a mental rehearsal is like running a movie in your mind. Try to imagine yourself being assertive in a situation you expect to be involved in. Mental rehearsal helps you think in detail about how you will look, act, and feel in the actual situation. It also helps you plan for any difficulties you might encounter.

4. Take action

Now you are ready to act assertively. When the situation you have rehearsed actually presents itself, put your plan into action. Keep the following pointers in mind:

Verbal Behavior

• Ask for what you want by using "I" messages. For example, begin statements by saying "I feel" or "I want." Do not try to blame or demand things of others by saying "You should …" or "You did…."

• Be specific about what you want to say. Try not to speak in terms that are too general.

• Be direct and unapologetic when speaking to the other person. For example, say "I believe I was ahead of you." Do not assume that the other person did something on purpose; it may have been accidental.

• Talk calmly and clearly. Take time to think things through. When listening, pay full attention to the other person.

Nonverbal Behavior

• Pay attention to your body language. Be sure to use gestures and facial expressions that match what you are saying.

• Look directly at the other person when speaking. Make direct eye contact.

• Stand a comfortable distance from the person to whom you are speaking. Standing too close may seem uncomfortable or threatening to some people.

5. Evaluate yourself

After the encounter, ask yourself these questions:

• Did I say what I intended to say?

• Was I direct and unapologetic, yet considerate?

• Did I stand up for myself without becoming defensive or infringing on the other person's rights?

• Was my body language assertive?

• Did I feel good about myself after the encounter?

• Do I think the other person felt comfortable with my interaction?

Questions to which you answered *no* indicate areas you should work to improve for future encounters.

CHAPTER 25 REVIEW

KEY IDEAS

LESSON 1

- When the environment becomes polluted, the air you breathe, the water you drink, and the food you eat become polluted.

- Wastes broken down by microorganisms are called biodegradable wastes.

LESSON 2

- The burning of materials is the single greatest source of air pollution.

- Major air pollutants include carbon dioxide, carbon monoxide, oxides of nitrogen and sulfur, ozone, hydrocarbons, chlorofluorocarbons, lead, and asbestos.

LESSON 3

- Water pollution is caused by household and industrial wastes and agricultural chemicals.

- The Clean Water Act requires communities to treat their raw sewage before releasing it into the environment.

LESSON 4

- Many of the wastes in landfills are potential sources of air and water pollution.

- Some hazardous chemicals are poisonous; others act as carcinogens or mutagens.

- Individuals can help reduce land pollution by recycling wastes and by properly disposing of hazardous chemicals.

LESSON 5

- Ultraviolet light from the sun, cosmic rays from space, and radioactive substances are sources of high-energy radiation.

- Prolonged exposure to loud noise causes permanent hearing loss.

KEY TERMS

LESSON 1
biodegradable wastes
environment
pollutant
pollution
recycling

LESSON 2
acid rain
asbestos
carbon dioxide

carbon monoxide
chlorofluorocarbons
greenhouse effect
hydrocarbon
ozone
ozone layer
smog
sulfuric acid
temperature inversion

LESSON 3
eutrophication
fertilizer
herbicide
pesticides
runoff

LESSON 4
carcinogen
hazardous waste
landfill

LESSON 5
background radiation
decibels
fallout
high-energy radiation
noise
radioactive
radon

Listed above are some of the important terms in this chapter. Choose the term from the list that best matches each phrase below.

1. a site where wastes are covered with soil

2. a part of the atmosphere that absorbs ultraviolet light

3. formed when sulfur oxides react with water

4. the physical world and the living things that inhabit it

5. chemicals that destroy the ozone layer

6. a substance that causes pollution

7. when cold air is trapped below warm air

8. a gas that causes the greenhouse effect

9. a radioactive gas

10. a pollutant that binds to hemoglobin

WHAT HAVE YOU LEARNED?

On a separate sheet of paper, write the word or words that best complete each statement.

11. Water that drains from land into streams is called ____.

12. ____ results when fertilizers drain into ponds, lakes, or streams.

13. Reactions of nitric acid and hydrocarbons in the presence of light produce ____.

14. X-rays, ultraviolet light, and cosmic rays are forms of ____.

15. ____ is a form of oxygen that absorbs ultraviolet light.

16. ____ is the process by which materials are used over and over again.

17. A substance known to cause cancer is a ____.

18. A substance formerly used in building materials that is an air pollutant is ____.

Answer each of the following with complete sentences.

19. How are living things dependent on the physical environment?

20. What happens to natural wastes in the environment?

21. Why is the level of carbon dioxide in the atmosphere increasing?

22. Why are chlorofluorocarbons considered a problem in the environment?

23. What are two common particle forms of air pollution?

24. Name three sources of water pollution.

25. How can a landfill cause water pollution?

26. When is a substance considered to be hazardous to life?

27. Name an artificial source of radiation.

28. Why is loud noise harmful?

WHAT DO YOU THINK?

29. How do toxic substances dumped into the oceans affect people?

30. How do you think technology has helped to make people aware of pollution?

31. Some people say that nuclear power plants are a clean source of energy. What do you think they mean by this, and why might other people disagree with this view? What is your opinion?

32. What do you think are the advantages and disadvantages of burning trash?

33. What has caused people to be more concerned about pollution now than they were 50 years ago?

WHAT WOULD YOU DO?

34. Suppose you are offered two jobs after graduation. One job pays well, but the office you will work in is noisy and unattractive. The other job pays less, but the office is attractive and quiet. Which job would you choose? Why?

35. You recently learned that a friend has been changing her own oil and dumping the used engine oil into the town sewer system. What would you do to discourage her from this activity?

36. A friend of yours suggests that the actions of one person have little effect on the environment. What arguments could you use that might change his or her view?

Getting Involved

37. Find out what kinds of treatment facilities are available to deal with wastes in your town or city. You might be able to arrange a visit to a waste treatment facility near you. If you can, write a report that includes pictures of your visit.

38. Organize and develop support for a community volunteer clean-up project. Select a lake, stream, road, park, or other area in your community to clean up. Make a report to your class about the experience.

chapter 26

CHOOSING HEALTH CARE

When you are injured, you may have to seek medical care immediately. However, it is best not to wait until a problem arises to develop a comfortable relationship with a physician you trust. In this chapter, you will learn about the kinds of health-care services that are available and the information you need to be a wise consumer of those services.

CHAPTER PREVIEW

26-1 The Health-Care System

- Identify the kinds of health-care services that are available to the consumer.

26-2 Participating in Your Health Care

- Describe what you can expect during a medical examination.

26-3 Paying for Health Care

- Explain the difference between conventional health insurance and managed-care health insurance.

26-4 Being a Wise Consumer

- Tell how to evaluate health-care products and services.

BUILDING HEALTH SKILLS

- List the steps to follow in filing a consumer complaint.

CHECK YOUR WELLNESS

How wise a consumer of health-care services and products are you? See if you can answer *yes* to these questions.

- Do you know what types of health-care professionals can help you with your medical needs?

- Do you know where to go for medical care?

- Do you know what health insurance provides?

- Are you aware of your rights as a patient?

- Do you ask your physician to explain things you do not completely understand?

- Do you try to obtain reliable information about products and services before you purchase them?

- Do you resist attempts by advertisers and salespeople to sell you products you do not need or want?

- Do you follow the instructions on medicine labels?

KEEPING A JOURNAL

Most people need to consult a physician some time in their lives. In your journal, describe the qualities you would like your physician to have.

Take it to the Net
www.phschool.com

GUIDE FOR READING

Focus on these questions as you read this lesson.

- Who are the professionals that provide health-care services?
- What facilities provide health care?

SKILLS

- Setting Goals

As you grow older, you will make more and more choices as a consumer of health-care products and services. A **consumer** is anyone who buys goods and services. To make wise health-care choices, you need to know about health-care products and services and consumer issues in general. Being a wise consumer of health-care products and services is an important part of staying healthy.

When your grandparents were growing up, physicians were trained to do everything from delivering babies to performing surgery and setting broken bones. Since then, health care has become highly specialized. Today, many kinds of health professionals—from dietitians to laboratory technicians to surgeons—are available to provide health care.

Health-Care Providers

The basic health-care providers are medical doctors, or physicians. **Physicians work with many other health-care professionals to bring patients the care they need.** Other health-care professionals include nurses, dietitians, physical therapists, dental hygienists, social workers, and psychologists.

PHYSICIANS The health-care professionals who take care of most people's routine medical needs are **primary-care physicians.** Most primary-care physicians are medical doctors who have specialized in one of three areas of medicine—family practice, pediatrics (children's medical care), or internal medicine. A medical doctor, or **physician**, is a person who has spent four years in a medical school and earned a medical degree—either a Doctor of Medicine (M.D.) degree or a Doctor of Osteopathy (D.O.) degree. **Osteopathy** (ahs tee AHP uh thee) is a branch of medicine that emphasizes the relationship of the body's muscular and skeletal systems to general health.

To practice medicine, a physician must spend at least one year after medical school as an intern in a hospital. At the end of the training period, an intern must pass the medical licensing test of the state in which he or she intends to practice. Once licensed, a physician can make a diagnosis, provide treatment, and write a prescription for medication. A **diagnosis** (dy ug NOH sis) is a physician's opinion of the nature or cause of a medical condition. A **prescription** is a written order from a physician or dentist to a pharmacist authorizing that a patient be given a particular medicine.

Figure 26-1 *Medical students receive training in hospitals.*

When you have a condition that requires specialized treatment, a primary-care physician will refer you to a medical specialist. A **medical specialist** is a physician who has received additional training in a particular branch of medicine and has passed a test that certifies him or her to practice in that specialty.

NURSES   A **nurse** is a licensed health-care professional who works in collaboration with physicians to provide direct care to patients. Depending on the level of training and experience, a nurse may work closely with a physician or may function more independently.

Licensed practical nurses (LPNs) and licensed vocational nurses (LVNs) usually must complete one to two years of training in a program of practical nursing and pass a state licensing test. Registered nurses (RNs) must complete a two- to four-year nursing program and pass a state licensing examination. RNs observe and assess patient symptoms, plan the best approach to promoting recovery, and evaluate progress. They also counsel people of all ages about ways to stay healthy, prevent injury, and live to their fullest capacity.

Registered nurses who have received additional training in a specialized program may become registered nurse practitioners. **Nurse practitioners** are trained to do many of the tasks that only physicians used to perform. For example, they take medical histories, perform physical exams, order diagnostic tests, treat routine medical problems, and advise patients on how to prevent disease. Nurse practitioners are fairly independent. They usually work with, but not under the supervision of, a physician.

Figure 26-2 *A physician usually concentrates in one area.*

Medical Specialists

Allergist: Diagnoses and treats allergies and other immune disorders

Dermatologist: Diagnoses and treats skin diseases

Family physician: Provides primary care for all age groups

Gynecologist: Diagnoses and treats disorders of the female reproductive system

Internist: Diagnoses and treats internal disorders

Neurologist: Diagnoses and treats nervous system disorders

Oncologist: Diagnoses and treats cancers

Ophthalmologist: Diagnoses and treats eye disease

Orthopedic surgeon: Diagnoses and treats bone and joint disorders

Pediatrician: Provides primary care for children

Psychiatrist: Diagnoses and treats mental disorders

Urologist: Diagnoses and treats urinary tract disorders

Figure 26-3 *Nurses are among the many kinds of health-care professionals who attend to the needs of patients.*

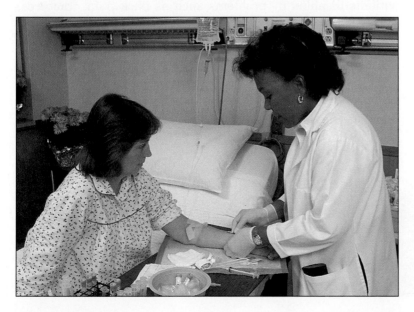

Dental hygienist: Cleans and X-rays teeth and assists dentists in various procedures

Emergency medical technician (EMT): Provides immediate care to ill or injured patients in an emergency situation

Laboratory technician: Performs laboratory tests, such as blood tests

Nurse's aide: Performs basic tasks in hospitals, such as feeding and washing patients and making beds

Occupational therapist: Evaluates and trains disabled people to adapt to daily activities and develop job skills

Optometrist: Tests vision and prescribes eyeglasses

Pharmacist: Prepares and dispenses medicines prescribed by physicians and dentists

Physical therapist: Uses exercise, massage, heat, and ultrasound to relieve pain and restore flexibility and muscle strength

Physician's assistant: Examines patients, performs some diagnoses, and suggests treatment under a physician's supervision

Psychologist: Uses counseling and therapy to treat people with mental-health problems

Radiology technician: Takes and develops X-rays

Registered dietitian: Plans menus according to specific health needs of patients; provides nutritional counseling

Respiratory therapist: Treats respiratory problems under a physician's order

Social worker: Provides counseling to people and their families to help resolve health-related problems; facilitates access to health services

Speech therapist: Helps people overcome speech impairments

Figure 26-4 *Many areas of health care are represented by health-care professionals.*

Figure 26-5 *Physical therapists help patients regain muscular strength and mobility.*

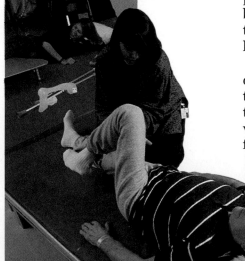

Other Health-Care Professionals

A variety of health-care professionals provide services that complement the work of physicians and nurses. For example, physicians are sometimes helped by physician's assistants. These are individuals who have received specialized training to perform certain tasks previously done by physicians. These tasks may include taking medical histories and performing physical exams. Unlike nurse practitioners, physician's assistants always work under the close supervision of a physician.

Physical therapists are persons trained to rehabilitate patients disabled by problems such as back pain, fractures, burns, strokes, sports injuries, and nerve injury. A physical therapist uses various physical agents, such as exercises and heat, to relieve pain and improve strength and mobility.

A registered dietitian is someone who has completed a degree program in foods and nutrition. This training enables the dietitian to set up and supervise food services for institutions such as hospitals. Registered dietitians may also provide nutritional counseling to patients in a health-care facility or in private practice.

Health-Care Facilities

During your life you will probably have different kinds of medical needs. Depending on what those needs are, you may seek medical care at a private physician's office, clinic, hospital, or specialized health center.

PHYSICIANS' OFFICES   Perhaps the most frequently used health-care facility is the physician's private office, which may be in a hospital or in a private building. Here physicians, nurse practitioners, or physician's assistants do routine examinations and tests to diagnose and treat minor illnesses and injuries. Minor surgery, such as removing a wart, may also be done in a physician's office. Routine health care provided in a physician's office is called **primary health care.**

CLINICS   When a medical test or procedure cannot be performed in a physician's office, a person may be tested or treated in an outpatient clinic. A **clinic** is a facility in which primary health care is provided by one or more physicians and other health-care workers. An **outpatient** is a person admitted to a clinic or hospital for tests or treatments that do not require an overnight stay.

A variety of tests and certain surgical procedures are performed at clinics. For example, cataract surgery, which involves removing a cloudy lens from an eye, can be performed on an outpatient basis. Outpatient care is less costly than a hospital stay because there is less expense for a hospital room, meals, and nursing services.

There are many types of clinics. Most treat all types of medical problems, but some specialize in certain types of illnesses. Mental-health clinics, for example, provide counseling and other treatments for people with mental illness.

HOSPITALS   Diagnosis and treatment of serious disorders such as heart attack or stroke require the services of a hospital. A **hospital** is a facility that is equipped and staffed to provide comprehensive health-care services, especially those requiring complicated or advanced procedures. Hospitals provide overnight accommodations for patients. A patient who is required to stay in a hospital for overnight or longer is called an **inpatient.** Health care given to a patient in a hospital is known as **secondary health care.** The patient's primary-care physician and specialist physician, such as a surgeon, visit the patient every day to note progress and make any necessary adjustments in the patient's care.

A hospital may be a general hospital or a specialty hospital. A **general hospital** treats patients of all ages and with all kinds of illnesses and injuries. A **specialty hospital,** such as a children's hospital, specializes in treating one age group or one type of disorder. Some hospitals are called **teaching hospitals.** They are located near medical schools whose faculty members are on the hospital staff. Medical students, physicians, and other health-care workers train at these hospitals. They visit patients and review cases with doctors. Because many doctors at teaching hospitals carry out medical research, these hospitals often offer advanced and experimental medical care.

Figure 26-6 *Clinics provide primary health care in many communities.*

Choosing Health Care   **629**

Should Experimental Medicines Be Available to Terminally Ill People?

The testing period for new drugs is lengthy. This ensures that only drugs that are safe and effective will become available to the public. Many people feel, however, that patients who are dying should have access to experimental drugs. They argue that experimental drugs should be available to dying patients with no other options who might benefit from the drug.

Other people feel that the effects of an experimental drug might be worse than the disease being treated. Some people also argue that if dying patients are allowed to use experimental drugs, further testing will be more difficult. This is because few people with a disease will volunteer for studies that require some of them—the control group—not to receive the new drug. If such studies cannot be carried out, dangerous side effects of drugs may never be detected.

Another argument against early approval of experimental drugs is that there is no fair way to decide who should receive the drugs. Experimental drugs are in short supply, and the number of patients wanting to try the drugs usually exceeds the supply.

☞ **Should experimental medicines be made available to terminally ill people?**

LONG-TERM CARE FACILITIES   Some patients need basic nursing care over a long period of time without the costly services of a hospital. Facilities providing this type of care are rehabilitation or convalescent homes and nursing homes.

A **convalescent home** (kahn vuh LES unt) provides care for people who are recovering from surgery, illness, or injury. These people eventually return to their homes. A **nursing home** is a facility that provides long-term care for elderly or chronically ill people who are incapable of caring for themselves. Some patients needing long-term care can also receive medical care in their own homes. Home-health care provided by nurses who visit a private home is usually less expensive than nursing-home care.

A special kind of nursing care is available for patients who are terminally ill. This care can be given in the home or in a live-in facility called a **hospice** (HAHS pis). Hospice care is usually short-term and focuses on helping a dying patient live as comfortably as possible.

OTHER HEALTH-CARE SERVICES   A variety of private and governmental agencies provide services to people in need of medical care. The American Red Cross, for example, provides free medical care, housing, and food during emergencies. The American Cancer Society offers free transportation to local cancer-treatment centers and lends equipment such as walkers and wheelchairs.

Local and state health departments also provide services at little or no cost. In many communities, public-health nurses visit local schools to give free hearing and vision tests or give immunization injections. Local and state health departments also provide dental care, mental-health care, visiting nursing services, and care to pregnant women. Local and state health departments are listed in the telephone directory.

LESSON 1 REVIEW

1. Explain the role of a primary-care physician.
2. What is the difference between an inpatient and an outpatient?
3. How does secondary health care compare with primary health care?
4. How do convalescent homes and hospices differ?

What Do You Think?

5. What kind of facility would you choose to obtain a routine physical examination?

2 PARTICIPATING IN YOUR HEALTH CARE

GUIDE FOR READING

Focus on these questions as you read this lesson.

- Where can you go for health-care services?
- What should you expect from a complete medical exam?
- What are your rights and responsibilities as a patient?

SKILLS

- DECIDE

Up to now, adults have probably made most of the decisions about your health care. As you grow older, however, you will take on these responsibilities for yourself. Knowing some basics about your health-care choices can help you choose what is best for you.

Choosing Health Care

Deciding where to go or what physician to see for routine health care deserves careful consideration. After all, you want health care delivered by qualified people with whom you feel comfortable.

Many people prefer to see a physician in a clinic. At some clinics you can arrange to see the physician of your choice. At others, you may see the first available physician. Some clinics also give you the option of seeing a nurse practitioner.

Rather than seeing a physician at a clinic, some people prefer to see a physician who is in **private practice,** working for himself or herself. Often several physicians in private practice have their offices together in the same building and work together in a **group practice.** Although it may be more expensive to see a physician in private practice than in a clinic, you can usually expect to see the same physician every time you make an appointment.

Whether you choose a physician at a clinic or in private practice, you will want one who is suited to your needs. The best way to begin your search is to ask for recommendations from family members and friends. Also, you can ask the opinion of other health-care professionals you know, such as your school nurse.

When you have the names of some recommended physicians, you might check the *American Medical Directory* in your local library. This directory lists the names of physicians, the year they received their medical degrees, their areas of specialization, and whether or not they are board-certified. A board-certified physician has completed three or more years of additional training in a medical specialty and has passed an exam certifying his or her knowledge in the area of specialization.

Once you have this basic information, begin to think about your own preferences. Do you want a young physician, or would you prefer an older one? Would you be more comfortable with a male physician or a female physician? Do you want a physician with an outgoing personality, or one who is more reserved?

Figure 26-7 *Take time to research information about physicians.*

Figure 26-8 *Ask yourself these questions when you want to evaluate your physician.*

Evaluating a Physician

- Does the physician listen and respond thoughtfully to what you say?

- Does the physician discuss your concerns in a way that makes you feel comfortable?

- Does the physician answer your questions in a way that you can understand?

- Does the physician explain the reasons for medical tests?

- Does the physician clearly explain the results of tests?

- Does the physician explain the reasons for medicines and the effects you should expect from them?

- Does the physician perform examinations carefully and thoroughly?

- Is the physician willing to refer you to other physicians for special health problems?

The best time to make your first visit to a physician is while you are well. Then, when you need a physician, you will know whom to see. Figure 26-8 lists some questions you might ask yourself when choosing a physician.

The Medical Examination

Have you ever put off seeing a physician because you were afraid of getting a shot or dreaded getting undressed in the examining room? If so, you are like many other people. You might find it helpful, however, to look upon a visit to a physician as an opportunity to find out more about your body and to get some answers to important questions you may have.

A complete medical examination has three parts: a medical history, a time to talk with the physician about your health concerns, and a physical examination. A record of your present and past health as well as the health of members of your family is your **medical history.** You may have to fill out a medical history form, which the physician will review with you. The physician will ask you questions about your family's medical history and your previous illnesses, immunizations, and lifestyle.

Your medical examination should also include time for you to ask questions and talk about any health concerns and health-related issues in your life. It is a good idea to bring a list of questions to make sure that you cover everything you want to discuss.

After you have talked to the physician, you will have a **physical examination,** a head-to-toe check of your body to identify any medical problems you may have. It usually begins with measurements of your height and weight, and blood pressure and body temperature readings. The physician may examine your skin, eyes, ears, nose, throat, and

Figure 26-9 *Part of a complete physical exam includes a check of reflexes.*

D	DEFINE the problem
E	EXPLORE alternatives
C	CONSIDER the consequences
I	IDENTIFY values
D	DECIDE and act
E	EVALUATE results

A Patient's Dilemma

You have been suffering from a severe earache all week long. Finally you decide to see a physician at your local clinic. When you arrive for your appointment, you find out that the only physician available is the one you saw once last year. At that time, the physician spent only a few minutes with you. She did not ask you many questions and seemed unconcerned about your condition. When you asked her questions, she did not seem willing to take the time to fully answer your concerns. You suspect that you will have the same difficulty communicating with her again.

1. Use the DECIDE process on page 18 to decide what you would do under these circumstances. Explain your reasons for making this decision.

2. How would having confidence and being an assertive person affect the type of decision you make?

teeth. He or she may also test your hearing and vision. During the examination of your upper body, the physician will listen to your lungs and heart. As the examination continues, the physician will check your abdominal organs and look for any signs of unusual tissue growth.

An examination of the reproductive organs usually follows. For boys this includes the external reproductive organs. For girls the physician examines the internal reproductive organs for disease or structural problems.

The physician may decide to have your blood and urine tested. Usually samples are sent to a separate testing facility. The physician will contact you later with the results.

Finally, the physician checks your muscles, bones, and nervous system. This includes your arms, legs, hands, and feet for signs of joint swelling or bone problems. The physician also will check your spine for abnormal curvature and your reflexes, balance, and coordination.

If the physician finds a medical condition requiring attention, he or she will discuss it with you. The physician should explain what the condition means in terms of treatment, testing, and possible short-term and long-term effects. It helps to keep in mind that you and your physician are a team working together. Good communication is important. Regardless of how foolish you think your questions are, keep asking them. Getting answers to questions about your body will help you participate more fully in your own health care.

A Patient's Rights

- The right to competent, considerate, and respectful care
- The right to a second opinion
- The right to refuse or withdraw from care and be informed of the medical consequences of such action
- The right to all information concerning your diagnosis and treatment
- The right to have your medical information kept confidential
- The right to review your medical records
- The right to know if the hospital performs experimentation that could affect your treatment or care

Figure 26-10 *Which rights do you feel most strongly about?*

Your Rights and Responsibilities as a Patient

It is important to realize you have certain rights as a patient. If, for example, your physician recommends you have your tonsils removed, it is your right to have each step of the procedure explained to you. You also have the right to know why you need the procedure, what risks are involved, and what the cost will be. If there is something you still do not understand or feel comfortable about, you have the right to a second opinion. A **second opinion** is a diagnosis and advice from another physician. A second opinion is especially advisable for voluntary procedures. You also have the right to refuse the suggested treatment, tests, examinations, and medicines.

As a patient you also have certain responsibilities. One of your responsibilities is to ask your physician about anything that concerns your health. Most physicians expect questions. Asking questions, even ones that seem awkward, can help you understand your body and whatever treatment you may receive. If a physician seems annoyed by your questions, it would be wise to look for another physician.

It is also your responsibility to answer your physician's questions honestly. A physician needs accurate information from you to make a correct diagnosis. Information about symptoms, medications you are taking, and any activities or behaviors that may affect your health or treatment are important for your physician to know. The more information you can provide, the more likely it is that the physician will give a correct diagnosis.

Physicians and other health-care professionals vary in their attitudes, professional styles, and how they relate to people. If you are not satisfied with the services provided by a clinic or physician, you do not have to return. Receiving good health care means being satisfied with the medical as well as the personal treatment you receive. Remember, you owe it to yourself to select what is best for you.

LESSON 2 REVIEW

1. How would you obtain the information you need to select a physician?
2. When is a second opinion especially important?
3. Briefly describe the parts of a medical examination.
4. List your rights and responsibilities as a medical patient.

What Do You Think?

5. What patient right is most important to you? Explain.

3 PAYING FOR HEALTH CARE

GUIDE FOR READING

Focus on these questions as you read this lesson.

- How does conventional health insurance work?
- What are the features of a managed-care insurance plan?

SKILLS

- Finding the Facts

At some point in the future, you will be paying for your health care. Knowing what choices are available can help you select the method of paying that is best for you. One way is to pay directly for all of your own medical expenses. This is called out-of-pocket payment. However, most people do not have the financial resources to pay for major medical expenses. Another way of paying for medical care is through health insurance. **Health insurance is a payment plan that pays for a major part of an individual's medical expenses.** People who can buy health insurance do so because it covers large medical bills that otherwise would be difficult or impossible to pay.

Conventional Health Insurance

Conventional private health insurance may be offered as individual or group plans. In an individual plan, an individual who wants insurance pays an insurance company an annual fee called a **premium.** For the premium, the insurance company guarantees to pay the person's medical expenses for the year within the limits set in the insurance plan.

A group insurance plan works the same as an individual plan except that the premiums are usually lower because a person joins as a member of some group or organization. A common group insurance plan is one covering the employees of a company. The company often pays part of the premium as a job benefit.

Most insurance plans require each member to pay the first part of his or her medical expenses for each year. This fixed amount, called the **deductible,** is the portion of a person's yearly medical expenses that he or she must pay before the insurance company begins paying. For example, suppose an insurance plan has a $300 deductible. Each year, a person covered by this plan has to pay the first $300 of his or her medical expenses for the year. Once the person's medical expenses exceed the deductible amount, the insurance company starts to pay its portion of the medical bills.

Insurance plans usually pay only a certain percentage of a person's medical expenses, for example, 80 percent. The remaining amount, which the individual must pay, is called the **copayment.** Suppose, for example, that the charges for a medical service were $200. The insurance company might pay 80 percent, or $160. The patient would have to pay the remaining $40.

Figure 26-11 *Major surgery is one of the most costly medical services.*

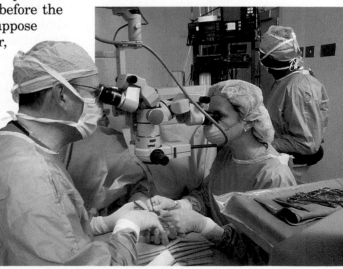

Medical Insurance Statement

Patient: John Duncan
Provider: M.C. Garcia, M.D.

Benefit Year: 2001

Service Dates	Codes	Charges
10/01	03	58.00
10/08	06	122.00
		180.00

Covered Expenses: $180.00 Payable at 80% equals $144.00 You pay: $ 36.00
Date of Payment: 10/28/01

See reverse for explanation of codes.

Figure 26-12 *How much of the medical bill must be paid by the patient?*

Insurance plans have limits on the amount they will allow for medical procedures. If the bill for a procedure exceeds the amount allowed by the plan, the insurance pays only the allowable amount. If the bill is for a procedure that the policy does not cover, no payment is provided. The patient must pay the total amount of the bill. Some serious diseases that require long-term or major medical expenses also may not be covered by health insurance.

Managed-Care Health Insurance

One alternative to conventional health insurance is a plan known as **managed care.** In this form of health insurance plan, each member chooses a primary-care physician from a group of physicians who participate in the plan. The primary-care physician "manages" each member's care by providing routine medical care directly to members and making referrals to specialists within the plan when necessary.

HEALTH MAINTENANCE ORGANIZATIONS The most common managed-care plans are called health maintenance organizations. A **health maintenance organization**, or HMO, is a group of physicians and other health-care workers that provides complete medical services to members of the HMO. Members of an HMO pay a set fee every month. In return, the HMO covers the cost of all or nearly all needed health services.

HMOs emphasize preventive health practices, such as annual physical exams, weight-reduction and smoking cessation classes, routine immunizations, prenatal care, and health education. These services rarely are covered by conventional insurance plans. A disadvantage of an HMO is that it covers the costs of health services provided only by the HMO staff and affiliated hospitals. If you see a physician outside of the HMO without being referred by your primary-care physician, you must pay for the full cost of the service.

SHARPEN YOUR SKILLS

Finding the Facts

Find out whether any HMOs or PPOs exist in your area. Create a poster that compares their services and fees.

PREFERRED PROVIDER ORGANIZATIONS Another, more recent form of managed care is the **preferred provider organization,** or PPO. In this type of insurance plan, participating physicians and hospitals—the preferred providers—agree to charge reduced fees to plan members. As in an HMO, members choose a primary-care physician. Unlike an HMO, however, the plan pays for services by out-of-plan physicians, but at a lower rate. For example, a PPO member may have to pay 5 percent of a fee from a plan physician, but 30 percent of the fee from an out-of-plan physician.

Government-Supported Health Insurance

Elderly people, people with severe disabilities, and people with low incomes may not be able to afford private health insurance. These people may be eligible for government health insurance programs.

MEDICARE   The federally financed insurance program for elderly people is **Medicare.** Medicare is also available to younger people who are disabled or who have chronic kidney disease. Medicare comes in two parts. Medicare Part A, which is free, covers most people 65 years old or older who are eligible for Social Security or Railroad Retirement benefits. It has a deductible and provides coverage for 60 days of hospitalization per year. It does not cover physicians' bills. Medicare Part B, which can be purchased for a small monthly fee, helps pay physicians' bills, outpatient hospital services, and the costs of some medical services and supplies. Anyone 65 years old or older can purchase Medicare Part B.

MEDICAID   Another program, **Medicaid,** is a state and federal program that pays for the health care of people whose incomes are below an established level, regardless of their age. Medicaid benefits vary from state to state. A person can obtain information about Medicaid from the local state welfare office or other social service agency.

Figure 26-13 *Do the advantages of HMOs outweigh their disadvantages?*

Advantages and Disadvantages of HMOs

Advantages

- Lower out-of-pocket cost for health care
- No need to submit claims and wait for reimbursement
- In some HMOs, one-stop shopping for health care, i.e., full range of doctors, testing, and laboratory and pharmacy facilities available at HMO site
- Less time spent in hospital
- Preventive health-care coverage
- More complete coverage

Disadvantages

- Less choice of health-care providers, such as doctors and hospitals
- For policy coverage, patient must have permission of primary-care physician for each visit to a specialist
- Provider may not have facilities in every state
- Notification of HMO required when emergency out-of-plan medical care delivered

LESSON 3 REVIEW

1. Why do people buy health insurance?
2. What is a major difference between a PPO and an HMO?
3. What is meant by the term *deductible?*
4. Who is eligible for Medicare? For Medicaid?

What Do You Think?

5. If the costs of joining an HMO and a conventional insurance plan are the same, which would you choose? Why?

4 BEING A WISE CONSUMER

Focus on these questions as you read this lesson.

- What are the different ways advertisers make products appealing to consumers?

- What are the rights of consumers when they purchase medicines or medical services?

SKILLS

- Activity: Comparing Antacids

Eventually you will be making decisions about health-care services and products. Knowing all you can about these services and products will help you obtain what you need at a reasonable cost.

Consumers and Advertising

Businesses spend millions of dollars on advertising because advertising attracts customers. Everyone is influenced to some extent by advertising. While advertising can let you know what products are available, it seldom provides the information you need to make wise choices. **As a consumer you need to base your choices on facts, not on what advertisements attempt to tell you.**

Recognizing advertising methods such as those listed in Figure 26-14 can help you be a wise consumer. An advertisement might say, for example, that scientific studies have shown one product to be three times as effective as another product. Since it provides no specific information about how the studies were done or what their outcomes actually were, the statement may be misleading. In another example, a medicine may be advertised as containing the ingredient most physicians recommend. This might make you think it is the only product containing that ingredient. Chances are that many other products contain the same ingredient. For more information on advertising, refer to the Building

Figure 26-14 *Which of these advertising techniques have you seen or heard before?*

Advertising Methods

Technique	Message	Example
Scientific studies	Scientific tests prove the product is more effective than the competition.	"Tests prove that Brand X is three times as effective as the leading brand."
Bandwagon approach	Everyone is using the product. You should, too.	"Don't be left behind—use Product X."
Testimonial	The product is effective because trustworthy people recommend it.	"The medicine recommended by doctors and their families."
Comparison to other products	The product is more effective than any others.	"Brand X now has 20% more painkiller than Brand Y."
Emotional appeal	The product is safest for you and your family.	"Choose Brand X—because your family's health depends on it."
Price appeal	The product gives you more for your money.	"Brand X—the most for the least."

Health Skills entitled "Recognizing Misleading Claims" on pages 436–437.

To choose health-care products wisely, ask for recommendations from health professionals such as a physician or pharmacist. Read product labels. Compare products for ingredients and cost. Often products used for the same purpose contain the same ingredients.

Choosing Medicines

Many health-care products you will choose are medicines. A **medicine** is any substance used to treat a disease, disorder, or injury. Medicines are either prescribed by a physician or dentist—**prescription medicines**—or available without a prescription—**over-the-counter** (OTC) **medicines**. Prescription medicines can be obtained only with a prescription. Over-the-counter medicines, also called nonprescription medicines, can be purchased by anyone, anytime.

Often a prescription medicine has a standard name, or **generic name** (jih NEHR ik), under which it is sold. Several different manufacturers might make this medicine. Another manufacturer, usually the one that originally developed the

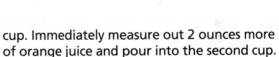

COMPARING ANTACIDS

In this activity you will compare the effectiveness of two antacids in reducing the acidity of orange juice.

Materials

two kinds of antacid tablets	2 metal spoons
	measuring cup
two cups or bowls	orange juice
masking tape	pH paper
	pencil and paper

Procedure

1. Put each antacid tablet into a different cup. Use tape to label each cup with the kind of antacid it contains.

2. Using a separate spoon for each tablet, finely crush each antacid tablet against the side and bottom of the cup.

3. Measure 2 ounces of orange juice in a measuring cup. Test the pH of the orange juice with a strip of pH paper and record the pH.

4. Pour the 2 ounces of orange juice into one cup. Immediately measure out 2 ounces more of orange juice and pour into the second cup. Mix each solution once with its own spoon.

5. After 5 minutes, measure and record the pH of the juice in each cup. Repeat testing and recording the pH every 5 minutes until 20 minutes have passed.

Discussion

1. How did the antacid tablets affect the pH of the orange juice in each cup?

2. How did the pH values of the orange juice solutions compare over 20 minutes? Did one antacid work faster than the other?

3. How much antacid (calcium carbonate or sodium bicarbonate) does each tablet contain?

4. How is this experiment related to the effect of antacids in a person's stomach?

Figure 26-15 *A wide variety of over-the-counter medicines are available to consumers.*

medicine, will make the identical medicine but give it a company, or brand, name. "Erythromycin stearate," for example, is the generic name of a prescription medicine used to treat respiratory infections. The same medicine is also sold under a brand name given to it by the manufacturer.

A brand-name medicine is usually more expensive than the same medicine sold under its generic name. Buying generic medicines, therefore, can save you money. In a brand-name medicine, however, the inactive ingredients, such as coloring, flavoring, fillers, or a protective coating, may differ from those in the generic form. If your physician prescribes a medicine, ask if the generic form is available.

Over-the-counter medicines such as many antiseptics and painkillers are sold under company or brand names and under generic names. Different brands of OTC medicines that are sold for the same purpose often have the same active ingredients. Get the most for your money by reading the ingredient labels and comparing prices.

Using Medicines Wisely

If you are using a prescription or an OTC medicine, always read the label and any package leaflet information. Use medicines only as instructed and take note of any warnings or precautions. Never drink alcohol when taking medicines.

Some medicines cause **side effects**—unpleasant responses of your body to the medicine. Although side effects are usually mild, such as a headache or skin rash, they can be severe or life-threatening. Always ask your physician about potential side effects of a medicine. Stop using a medicine that produces side effects until you check with your physician. In case of severe side effects, go to the nearest hospital emergency room for treatment. If you have questions about a medicine, ask your pharmacist. To make sure you do not misuse any medicines, refer to the Building Health Skills entitled "Using Medicines Correctly" on pages 542–543.

Quackery

Figure 26-16 *Promises of impossible cures are a sure sign of quackery.*

Selling useless medical treatments or products is known as **quackery** (KWAK ur ee). People involved in this kind of fraud are known as quacks. Quacks promise treatments or products that will bring about miracle cures or revitalize a person's health. They depend on people's lack of knowledge and often desperate desire to be rid of some chronic disease. Quackery is often involved with products that are supposed to treat conditions such as arthritis, cancer, and overweight. People can avoid quackery by carefully evaluating claims made for a treatment or product. Quackery is likely to be involved when any of the following conditions exist:

- The product or treatment is said to be the only possible answer to a medical problem.
- The promised results seem too good to be true.
- The product or treatment is claimed to be a cure for a number of different ailments.
- The product has special, secret ingredients that promise a miracle cure.

If you have doubts about any product or treatment, ask a physician or pharmacist. The danger of quackery is that it can delay or prevent someone from receiving proper medical care. As long as a person believes a quack remedy is working or might work, he or she will postpone seeing a physician.

The government agencies listed in Figure 26-17 will take action against quack products and practices. In addition, if you should purchase a deceptive or fraudulent item through the mail, notify your local postmaster. Also notify your state's attorney general's office about fraudulent practices within your state. If a local business is involved, you should notify your local Better Business Bureau as well.

Your Rights as a Consumer

Regardless of the services or products you buy, you have certain rights as a consumer. First and foremost is your right to choose any product you want. You also have the right to information. You should be able to learn enough about a service or product to make an informed judgment about it. You also have the right to safety. Any service or product should be reasonably safe.

If you believe a product has not helped you or was misrepresented, you should complain to the manufacturer and ask for a refund. If you are still not satisfied, you should complain to a consumer protection agency. Refer to the Building Health Skills entitled "Filing a Consumer Complaint" on the following pages for additional information.

Help for the Consumer

The Food and Drug Administration
5600 Fishers Lane
Rockville, MD 20857
- Protects public from sale of unsafe foods, drugs, and cosmetics

The Federal Trade Commission
6th St. and Pennsylvania Ave. NW
Washington, DC 20580
- Prevents unfair or deceptive advertising

The Consumer Product Safety Commission
5401 Westbard Avenue
Bethesda, Maryland
(mailing address: Washington, DC 20207)
- Establishes safety standards for consumer goods and takes dangerous products off the market

Figure 26-17 *Which federal agency would you notify if you were a victim of false advertising?*

LESSON 4 REVIEW

1. Describe four ways advertisers try to influence consumers.
2. How are generic and brand-name forms of a medicine different?
3. When should you suspect quackery?
4. What are the rights of a consumer?

What Do You Think?

5. How would you decide between a brand-name first-aid spray and a less-well-known spray?

Filing a Consumer Complaint

Paula saved her money to buy an exercise cycle so she could stay in good physical condition all year round. A week after she bought it, a pedal broke off. She went back to the store and was given a replacement part. Two months later, the speedometer stopped working. She went back to the store again, but the salesperson told her the exercise cycle had only a 30-day warranty, and the store was no longer responsible. Paula was upset and not sure what her rights were as a consumer. She wondered where she could go to resolve the problem.

When you are dissatisfied with a product, how can you make an effective consumer complaint that gives you the results you want? The guidelines below will help you resolve consumer complaints, large and small.

1. Identify the problem

Be clear in your mind what it is about the product or service that is unsatisfactory. Be as specific as possible.

2. Decide how you want the problem resolved

Decide what you think is a fair way to resolve your complaint. Do you want a refund, replacement, repair, or credit?

3. Collect the documents you need to support your complaint

Gather sales receipts, warranties, canceled checks, contracts, or repair records to back up your complaint.

4. Return to where you purchased the service or product

State the specific problem to the appropriate person—the salesperson, a customer service person, or a supervisor or manager. Explain why the product or service is unsatisfactory. Show your supporting documentation, and describe the way you would like your complaint resolved. If your complaint is not immediately resolved, continue with step 5.

If a product was purchased by mail order, or from a business distant from where you now live, write a letter to the store or company. Include in the letter the information described in step 5, which is shown in the sample complaint letter.

5. Put your complaint in writing

If you do not receive an immediate resolution to your problem, follow up with a letter. (A sample letter is provided on the following page.) The letter should summarize the specifics of your complaint and suggest ways to resolve it. A letter is especially important in case the product has a time-limited warranty. It is also an important record if you later need to show when and how you filed your complaint.

Your letter should be typed or written neatly. Include the following information:

• the product's model and serial number and the location and date of purchase

- your name, address, and phone number and the best times to reach you
- the specifics of your complaint
- a description of any conversations you have had with sales representatives
- copies of all documents supporting your complaint; do not send original documents
- a reasonable date by which you expect action to be taken

The letter should be written in a calm, respectful tone. Be firm, but avoid writing an angry or threatening letter. Keep a copy of your letter for your records.

• • • • • • • • • • • • • • • • • • • •

6. Follow up until you are satisfied

If you do not receive a response or are dissatisfied with the response:

- Contact the national headquarters of the company. If you do not know the company's address, you can find it listed in the *Thomas Register*. You can find names and addresses of directors of consumer relations departments and company presidents in *Standard and Poor's Register of Corporations, Directors, and Executives*. Both of these references can be found at any local library reference desk.
- Write a letter to the Better Business Bureau or your local or state consumer protection agency. You can find the addresses of these agencies in the telephone book or in the reference section of any library.

Sample Complaint Letter

Your address
Date

Appropriate Person
Company Name
Address
City, State, Zip Code

Dear Appropriate Name:
On Date I purchased (or had repaired) Name of Product with Model and Serial Number from Store Name and Location. I have had trouble with it (or not been satisfied with it) because Describe Problem. I would like Specific Action You Want. Enclosed are copies of my records. (Include sales receipts, warranties, guarantees, contracts, canceled checks, etc.)

I am looking forward to your reply within the next 30 days explaining what you will do about my problem. If you need any further information, I can be contacted at the above address or by phone. (Give phone number and times you can be reached.) Thank you.

Sincerely,
Your name

Include a summary explaining what you have already done up to that point to get your complaint resolved.

- If all else fails to resolve the problem, file a complaint in small claims court. These court proceedings usually do not require a lawyer and are relatively simple, quick, and inexpensive. For information on filing a small claims complaint, call your local small claims court or legal services department. Ask the information operator for the number.

Apply the Skill

1. Think of a time you bought a product that was not satisfactory. How did you complain? Did you get the results you wanted? What else would you do now, knowing the steps for filing a complaint?

2. Write an effective complaint letter for any product or service with which you have been dissatisfied.

CHAPTER 26 REVIEW

KEY IDEAS

LESSON 1

- Physicians work with many other health-care professionals to bring patients the care they need.

- Medical care can be obtained in private offices, clinics, hospitals, and specialized health centers.

LESSON 2

- A complete medical examination consists of a medical history, time to talk with the physician about your health concerns, and a physical examination.

- As a patient, you have certain rights and responsibilities.

LESSON 3

- Health insurance is a health-care payment plan that pays for a major part of an individual's medical expenses.

- Consumers can choose from among conventional or managed-care types of health insurance plans.

LESSON 4

- As a consumer, you need to base your consumer choices on facts and reliable information, not on advertisements.

- For safety and effectiveness, use medicines only according to directions.

KEY TERMS

LESSON 1
clinic
convalescent home
diagnosis
hospice
inpatient
medical specialist
nurse
nurse practitioner
nursing home
outpatient

physician
primary-care physician
primary health care
secondary health care

LESSON 2
medical history
second opinion

LESSON 3
copayment
deductible
health insurance

Medicaid
Medicare
premium

LESSON 4
generic name
medicine
over-the-counter medicine
prescription medicine
quackery
side effect

Listed above are some of the important terms in this chapter. Choose the term from the list that best matches each phrase below.

1. the portion of each year's medical bills paid by the patient

2. facility where tests and procedures are performed on an outpatient basis

3. a physician with several years of additional training in a particular branch of medicine

4. facility that focuses on helping dying patients live as comfortably as possible

5. record of health in a person's family

6. person who receives treatment at a hospital but does not stay overnight

7. an unpleasant response to a medicine

8. health-care payment plan that pays for a major part of an individual's medical costs

9. the annual fee paid to an insurance company for insurance protection

10. the promotion of useless medical products or treatments

WHAT HAVE YOU LEARNED?

If the statement is true, write "true." If it is false, change the underlined word or words to make the statement true.

11. A <u>nurse practitioner</u> is trained to perform many of the same tasks as a physician.

12. A medical doctor who takes care of most people's routine medical needs is a <u>primary-care physician</u>.

13. A drug sold under its generic name is usually <u>less</u> expensive than when sold under its brand name.

14. The government health insurance plan that pays the medical expenses of persons 65 years old and older is <u>Medicaid</u>.

15. Health care received in a hospital is known as <u>primary</u> health care.

16. An unpleasant reaction to a drug is known as a <u>diagnosis</u>.

17. The premium is usually <u>less</u> for a group health insurance plan than for an individual insurance plan.

18. A copayment is the portion of a medical bill that <u>a patient</u> pays.

19. <u>Over-the-counter</u> medicines can be obtained only with a physician's prescription.

20. A <u>nursing home</u> is a facility that cares for people recovering from major surgery or a severe illness or injury.

Answer each of the following with complete sentences.

21. What are three things that a physician is licensed to perform?

22. How do LPNs and RNs differ?

23. Describe two medical specialties.

24. What is a board-certified physician?

25. What are some ways you can get information about physicians in your area?

26. Explain two responsibilities of a patient.

27. Name the three parts of a complete medical examination and explain what is involved in each part.

28. How does advertising attempt to influence you?

29. What is quackery?

30. What is one advantage of buying a medicine under its generic name?

WHAT DO YOU THINK?

31. Explain why a patient might receive more advanced care at a teaching hospital than at another type of hospital.

32. What are some advantages to getting a second medical opinion?

33. Why do you think that advertising for health-care products might appeal to your emotions rather than your ability to reason?

34. Why do some people buy useless medical products?

WHAT WOULD YOU DO?

35. You have a choice of two health-insurance plans that have the same benefits. Plan A has an annual deductible of $100; Plan B has an annual deductible of $1,000. Your employer will pay the premium for Plan B; Plan A will cost you $50 per month. Which would you choose? What must you consider in addition to cost?

36. A small mole on your arm has become larger and changed texture. You hear of a new skin cream that costs little and produces miraculous results. Would you try the cream before seeing your physician? Why?

37. You are told to take a prescription medicine for a week. However, after three days you feel fine. What would you do?

Getting Involved

38. Make a directory of the health-care facilities in your community. List their special features, such as cardiac fitness clinics or trauma centers. Then list the name, address, and phone number of each facility.

GUIDE FOR READING

Focus on these questions as you read this lesson.

- What historical conditions led to the creation of public health services?
- What kinds of health problems are addressed by the modern public health system?

SKILLS

- Intervening to Help a Friend

Imagine if you could find no clean drinking water, or if there were no place to dispose of garbage. What if restaurants and grocery stores were not required to be clean and pest-free? What if people were not immunized against serious diseases such as polio? These are all matters that affect public health. **Public health** involves the study and practice of protecting and improving the health of people in a group or community.

Fortunately, these examples of health-threatening conditions rarely exist in the United States. A public health system is in place to prevent them. A **public health system** includes all the government and private organizations that work with the public to prevent disease and promote positive health behaviors.

The History of Public Health

The causes of diseases were unknown to early peoples. Nevertheless, many of them associated disease with unclean or unsanitary conditions and took measures to promote cleanliness. The ancient Hebrews, for example, established rules for the sanitary preparation of foods. The Arabs also had excellent standards for food preparation. The ancient Romans built efficient systems to supply people with clean water and to remove wastes. They also set up strict health codes and encouraged physicians to tend to the needs of all people, not just the wealthy.

During the Middle Ages, the ideas of public health were largely forgotten in Europe. Cities were crowded with people, animals, and their wastes. Epidemics swept across the continents of Africa, Asia and Europe. The only effective way people knew to combat the epidemics was through disinfection procedures and quarantine. **Quarantine** (KWAWR un teen) is a period of isolation imposed on people who may have been exposed to an infectious disease. Quarantine prevents people who may be infected from spreading the disease. In addition, hospitals were established to treat the sick and dying. Despite these advances in public health, the causes of disease remained largely unknown. Many people still believed that diseases were caused by demons or evil spirits.

In 1850 a London physician, John Snow, studied an outbreak of cholera. **Cholera** (KAHL ur uh) is an infectious disease of the small intestine that causes severe diarrhea and vomiting. Dr. Snow found that the victims of this cholera outbreak all drank water from the

Figure 27-1 *A healthy and productive society depends on an effective public health system.*

same well. He was able to show that this well was contaminated with cholera-causing bacteria. Dr. Snow's method for identifying the source of an infectious disease became a model for modern public health studies.

The publication of the Shattuck report in Massachusetts in 1850 marked the beginnings of a formal public health policy in the United States. The report recommended disposal systems for sewage, sanitary drinking water supplies, and better health statistics and health education.

At first, public health regulations were made and enforced almost entirely by state and local governments. As the nation grew, however, the need for a national public health policy became evident. In response, the federal government started to fund public health programs.

During the latter half of the 1800s, scientists began finding that many diseases were caused by microorganisms. In the 1880s, the French chemist Louis Pasteur proved the value of vaccination. Starting in the early 1900s, vaccines and drugs against a variety of serious diseases became available. As a result, the federal government launched nationwide programs to immunize people. The effects of the immunization programs were dramatic. The incidence of many infectious diseases, such as measles, was greatly reduced.

The Changing Needs of Modern Public Health

As the United States has grown and changed, so have its public health needs. Public health now addresses many more problems than ever before. **The public health system continues to combat infectious diseases but also seeks to prevent a broad range of other health problems, many of them related to people's behaviors.** For example,

Figure 27-2 *People once thought that diseases were spread by demons.*

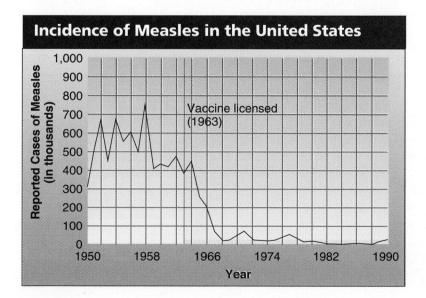

Incidence of Measles in the United States

(Graph: y-axis "Reported Cases of Measles (in thousands)" from 0 to 1,000; x-axis "Year" from 1950 to 1990. Label: "Vaccine licensed (1963)")

Figure 27-3 *The incidence of measles declined rapidly shortly after introduction of a measles vaccine. Recently, the Centers for Disease Control and Prevention announced that just about the only measles left in the US are imports.*

problems such as drug and alcohol abuse, teen pregnancy, sexually transmitted diseases, infant death, and child abuse are public health problems that result from human behavior. Both Public Health Service plans—*Healthy People 2000* and *Healthy People 2010*—identify prevention as the key to improving the health and quality of life of all Americans.

FIGHTING NONINFECTIOUS DISEASES In most countries with high standards of living, deaths from noninfectious diseases exceed those from infectious diseases, as shown in Figure 27-4. As you may recall, noninfectious diseases are associated with a variety of risk factors, which include unhealthy behaviors. The onset of high blood pressure and heart disease, for example, are associated with stress, smoking, lack of exercise, and a high-fat, low-fiber diet. Similarly, smoking is the single greatest risk factor for lung cancer.

Today, many public health education programs are aimed at reducing the incidence of noninfectious diseases. They emphasize the importance of practicing behaviors such as regular exercise and proper nutrition that help reduce the risks of many noninfectious diseases.

HELPING POPULATIONS AT RISK One of public health's greatest challenges is providing services to high-risk populations. **High-risk populations** are groups of people who, because of age, behavior, or some other factor, are likely to contract a serious disease or disorder. Teenage mothers and their children, people who abuse alcohol and drugs, people with emotional problems, elderly and disabled people, and people with low incomes are examples of high-risk populations. The need for basic health services in these groups is growing.

The federal government funds programs aimed at helping high-risk populations. One type of program, for example, provides prenatal care to pregnant women from low-income

Figure 27-4 *In developed countries, noninfectious diseases cause more deaths than infectious diseases.*

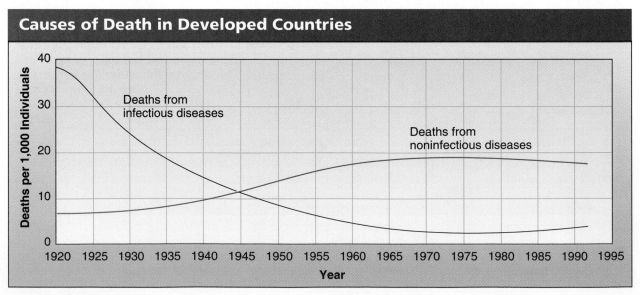

Causes of Death in Developed Countries

Deaths from infectious diseases

Deaths from noninfectious diseases

Deaths per 1,000 Individuals

Year

Figure 27-5 *Older people benefit from a variety of public health programs, including nutritional counseling.*

families. **Prenatal care** is medical care given to a woman during pregnancy. Such care ensures the health of a pregnant woman and her unborn baby. Prenatal-care programs serve women who otherwise would not seek or could not afford such services. Prenatal care dramatically increases a baby's chances of being born healthy. Related to the need for prenatal-care programs is another public health problem—the high incidence of teenage pregnancies in the United States. Education and counseling programs aimed at reducing teenage pregnancy inform and advise teenagers about the problems associated with pregnancy and parenting.

Another high-risk population, the elderly, also benefits from public health programs. Immunizations, disease screening, exercise and fitness programs, and nutritional counseling are examples of public health services for the elderly.

SAFETY AND ENVIRONMENTAL HEALTH   Public health concerns itself with safety issues in all areas of society. Safety standards, for example, are required in the workplace, in the design and construction of buildings, in the transportation industry, and in the safety and effectiveness of many household and medical products.

The public health system also addresses environmental concerns. Laws regulate pollution from industries and motor vehicles. Federal and state agencies monitor levels of toxic and cancer-causing substances in the environment. In addition, there are programs that fund removal of hazardous materials such as lead paint and asbestos.

Public Health in Action

Outbreaks of infectious diseases occur frequently throughout the world. If an outbreak is judged to be dangerous, health-care workers specially trained in epidemiology investigate the disease. **Epidemiology** (ep ih dee mee AHL uh jee) is the

SHARPEN YOUR SKILLS

Intervening to Help a Friend

Suppose you realize a friend has a drug dependency problem. How would you go about convincing your friend to seek help in a drug rehabilitation center?

Figure 27-6 *Epidemiology requires careful laboratory analysis of specimens and samples.*

study of disease among populations and the ways to prevent or control disease.

A recent case of an outbreak of cholera shows how the public health system responds to the threat of a disease. The outbreak came to the attention of the public health system when hospitals in Los Angeles reported four cases of cholera to the Los Angeles County Department of Health Services. County health service workers soon discovered that all four people had been on the same airplane flight from Argentina to Los Angeles.

The county health department notified the airline, the state health services department, and the Centers for Disease Control and Prevention (CDC), the federal agency that investigates disease outbreaks. Since a cholera epidemic had been sweeping through Argentina at the time, the Food and Drug Administration (FDA), another federal agency, also became involved. One of the FDA's duties is to prevent diseases from entering the United States in imported food.

Health workers began locating the passengers and crew members. The investigators interviewed 173 of the 356 people on the flight. Of the 173 people, 75 had experienced some vomiting and diarrhea, and another passenger later died. The health workers knew that cholera is often transmitted through food or water contaminated by human wastes that contain the cholera bacteria. Workers immediately tried to locate food samples and to check that leftover airline food was disposed of in a way that would prevent further spread of the disease.

No food samples remained for testing, and many of the passengers could not remember what they had eaten during the flight. However, investigators gathered enough information to conclude that the shrimp salad served on the flight had been contaminated with cholera bacteria. As with the thousands of other cases that occur each year, the action of many kinds of public health workers was effective in ensuring the public's health.

LESSON 1 REVIEW

1. What problems does the public health system address?
2. During the past century, what measures have reduced the incidence of some serious infectious diseases?
3. What is the importance of prenatal care?
4. Name four high-risk populations.

What Do You Think?

5. Which major public health challenges do you feel should be given the highest priority? Why?

2 PUBLIC HEALTH IN THE UNITED STATES

GUIDE FOR READING

Focus on these questions as you read this lesson.

- How is the public health system organized at the federal, state, and local levels?
- How are federal public health policies carried out?

SKILLS

- Locating Community Resources

Public health in the United States is primarily a governmental responsibility that is managed at the federal, state, and local levels. A variety of private organizations also contribute significantly to the advancement of public health.

The Federal Government

The federal agency with the widest range of responsibilities for public health is the **Department of Health and Human Services**. It sponsors health research and education, compiles and analyzes health information, sets health and safety standards, supports state and local health departments, and funds programs for people in need of public health services.

The Department of Health and Human Services is made up of four divisions. The Health Care Financing Administration supervises Medicare and Medicaid. **Medicare** is the health-care insurance program for elderly and disabled people. **Medicaid** is a health insurance program for low-income families. The Social Security Administration provides income to people who are retired or disabled. The Administration for Children and Families administers programs that improve the lives of children from low-income families and people with disabilities. Finally, the **Public Health Service** sets and implements national health policy, conducts medical research, promotes disease prevention, and enforces health and safety standards.

THE PUBLIC HEALTH SERVICE The United States Public Health Service has expanded its functions to meet the growing public health needs of the nation. It has a broad range of functions, as you can see from the following descriptions of the roles of its agencies.

Figure 27-7 *Each of the agencies within the Department of Health and Human Services is responsible for different areas of public health.*

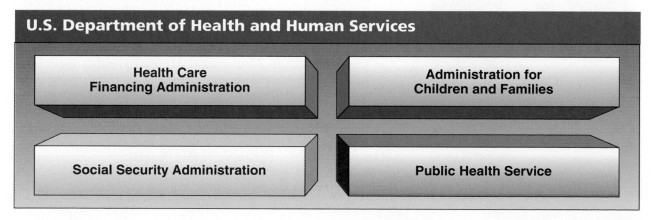

U.S. Department of Health and Human Services

Health Care Financing Administration	**Administration for Children and Families**
Social Security Administration	**Public Health Service**

Figure 27-8 *FDA investigators inspect products from foreign countries to ensure the products meet U.S. health and safety standards.*

- The **Agency for Health Care Policy and Research** promotes improvements in the practice of medicine, the organization and financing of health care, and access to quality care.

- The **Agency for Toxic Substances and Disease Registry** investigates and assesses risks to human health from hazardous materials.

- The **Centers for Disease Control and Prevention** (CDC) collects data and conducts research on nearly all types of diseases, disorders, and disabilities.

- The **Food and Drug Administration** (FDA) inspects, tests, and assesses the safety of food, drugs, and a variety of consumer goods.

- The **Health Resources and Services Administration** funds health services and resources for underserved populations such as migrant workers, people with AIDS, and homeless people.

- The **Indian Health Service** (IHS) provides comprehensive health care for Native Americans.

- The **National Institutes of Health** (NIH) is the primary biomedical research facility of the federal government. NIH conducts research in all areas of human health. It also provides grants to support medical research at institutions throughout the country.

- The **Substance Abuse and Mental Health Services Administration** supports programs that prevent and treat mental illness and substance abuse. It assists states, communities, and health-care facilities in substance-abuse and mental-health services.

OTHER FEDERAL PUBLIC HEALTH AGENCIES A number of agencies outside the Department of Health and Human Services provide public health services. Several of these are described here.

Figure 27-9 *Many Native Americans receive health care through programs sponsored by the Indian Health Service.*

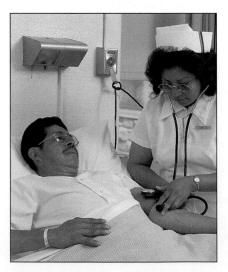

- The **Occupational Safety and Health Administration** (OSHA), in the Department of Labor, identifies occupational hazards and enforces laws requiring minimum safety standards in the workplace.
- The **Department of Agriculture** (USDA) is responsible for inspecting and grading meat, poultry, and other agricultural products. It also manages nutrition programs such as school-lunch programs and food stamps. People with financial resources below a certain level can purchase food with USDA food stamps.
- The **Environmental Protection Agency** (EPA) protects the public from environmental hazards. It enforces laws that regulate pollution and sets standards for safe exposure levels for toxic substances and radiation.
- **Volunteers in Service to America** (VISTA) is one of several volunteer service organizations sponsored by the federal government. VISTA volunteers work full time for one year in a federal, state, or private nonprofit agency.

Figure 27-10 *The USDA stamp on meat and poultry products indicates that the food meets standards set by the USDA.*

State Government

Although the federal government establishes broad public health objectives, it depends on the states to carry out programs to meet the objectives. The federal government accomplishes this by making funds available to the states for special health programs. State health departments apply for these federal funds. If a state receives funds, it distributes the money to its local health departments or to private health-service providers. These agencies then carry out specific health programs, such as drug rehabilitation and prenatal care.

Most states have several departments or agencies involved in public health functions. State departments of public health, mental health, rehabilitation, environmental health, and social services are some common examples. In addition, some states have separate departments for children, elderly people, and people with disabilities.

State health departments are also responsible for other services needed to maintain public health within the state. For example, they inspect health-care and food-handling facilities; test water, food, and medical samples; compile health statistics; plan for future health needs; and monitor the environment.

Local Government

In most states, public health services are provided directly by **local health departments.** Local health departments provide a full range of public health services to the people in the

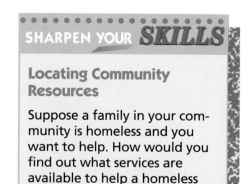

SHARPEN YOUR SKILLS

Locating Community Resources

Suppose a family in your community is homeless and you want to help. How would you find out what services are available to help a homeless family?

- Counseling and therapy for people with family problems, or with drug- or alcohol-abuse problems
- Testing for and treatment of sexually transmitted diseases
- Health education
- Prenatal care
- Immunizations
- Screening for tuberculosis, high blood pressure, cholesterol, and diabetes
- Home health services for people confined to their homes

Figure 27-11 *Local health departments provide many health services directly to members of the community.*

communities they serve. Their services are available to anyone. Some are free. Others have a fee based on a person's income. For teenagers, services are usually free. Among the services provided by many local health departments are those listed in Figure 27-11.

Local health departments are also responsible for enforcing state health codes. **Health codes** are standards established by the state for certain factors that affect health, such as water quality, sanitation in restaurants, and sewage treatment facilities. Local health departments also collect **vital statistics**—the numbers of births and deaths and the numbers and kinds of diseases within a population.

You can call your local health department to find out what services it provides. For the telephone number, check the self-help guide in the front of your telephone directory or call the local information operator.

Private Organizations

Many private organizations play important roles in supporting and providing public health services. Some of these are national organizations. Others exist only at the local level, in the communities they serve.

A number of national organizations raise funds to support specific health causes. Some you may be familiar with are the American Heart Association, American Cancer Society, and Muscular Dystrophy Association. Funds raised by these and other organizations are used to support medical research, health services, and educational programs.

In most communities, churches and other community-based organizations offer public health services. These organizations set up food banks; provide counseling, education, and training programs; sponsor soup kitchens and shelters for the homeless; and offer other support services. Do you know of organizations in your community where you can volunteer to help others?

LESSON *2* REVIEW

1. How does the Food and Drug Administration affect you?
2. What is the function of the National Institutes of Health?
3. What is the relationship between state and federal governments regarding public health?
4. Name five services of a typical local health department.

What Do You Think?

5. Should all high school students be required to perform some public health service?

DIFFERENT VOICES SPEAKING

At age 5, Christine Pham moved with her family from Vietnam to Oregon. Now 22 and a graduate of Northwestern University, Christine is spending a year as a VISTA volunteer.

Q. Christine, what prompted you to be a VISTA volunteer?

A. My specific motivation for joining VISTA came when I read a position paper published by VISTA that spelled out its commitment to public health. This is an area that has interested me for some time.

Q. What interests you about public health?

A. It is tied into a personal awareness I developed when I was away at college. I began to see that there are so many things going on in the world that need attention; I realized how sheltered I had been. I now believe that every person has a responsibility to do his or her part for society—to get involved. That's what public health is all about—getting involved. It's an area where you can have an impact on a lot of people, and not just by making policy, but by intervening in their lives and educating them about health choices. It's a direction I see all of medicine moving in.

Q. Can you give an example of this kind of intervention in action?

A. Yes, it's in operation in Healthy Start, the clinic program I volunteer in. Healthy Start is geared at helping low-income pregnant women get the maternity care they need. A first step in the process is community outreach. We try to go out into the community and raise women's awareness of prenatal care and the difference it can make in the health of the

Christine Pham

developing baby. By getting pregnant women to come into the clinic, we can reduce such problems as underweight babies.

Q. How do you go about reaching your audience?

A. We do this in a variety of ways. Since a major target of our clinic's outreach effort is teenagers, we turn to the schools. We try to find the right person there to talk to, and arrange to do a presentation.

Q. What do you think is the single biggest health problem that our society is facing today?

A. Runaway insurance costs is certainly up there. About two-thirds of the clients who come into our clinic work but have no health insurance because their employers can't afford it. I think an equally serious problem, however, is a failure of individuals to take responsibility for their health. If people would sit up and accept the control they have over their lives and health, we'd be a much healthier nation.

Journal Activity

Christine talks about the importance of getting involved. In your health journal, write a one-page essay addressing three public health problems that you feel could be solved through public intervention.

3 INTERNATIONAL PUBLIC HEALTH

Focus on these questions as you read this lesson.

- What are some major, world-wide public health problems?

- How do organizations work to help solve international public health problems?

SKILLS

- Activity: Food for Thought

About 75 percent of the world's people live in developing nations. Developing nations are countries with poor economies and low standards of living. In many of these countries it is difficult, if not impossible, for most people to meet their basic needs for food, water, and shelter. As a result, they suffer from serious health problems. **International health organizations work in developing countries to overcome public health problems such as malnutrition, lack of basic medical care, poor sanitation, and lack of clean water resources.**

International Health Organizations

International health organizations work to improve health conditions in countries that cannot support their own public health systems. Some health organizations are sponsored by the United Nations, some by individual governments, and others by private donations. Most of the efforts of these organizations are directed at improving people's lives by preventing malnutrition and infectious diseases.

AGENCIES OF THE UNITED NATIONS   A number of United Nations agencies are directly involved in improving the living conditions of people in developing countries. The **World Health Organization** (WHO) provides countries in need with people trained in medicine, agriculture, water quality, engineering, and other health-related skills. WHO workers seek to help boost food production and prevent diseases through education and immunization programs. WHO

Figure 27-12 *World Health Organization personnel, like this medical worker in Honduras, help provide medical care for people in developing countries.*

FOOD FOR THOUGHT

In this activity, you will experience how the availability of food depends on where you live in the world.

Materials

numbered tags	water
cooked rice	paper plates
fruit juice	paper cups

Procedure

1. Randomly choose a tag from the bag your teacher has prepared.

2. People with number 1 tags represent the 10 percent of the world's population in the richest countries.

3. People with number 2 tags represent the 15 percent of the world's population in middle-income countries.

4. People with number 3 tags represent the 75 percent of the world's population in the poorest countries.

5. Your teacher will seat each group in a designated area and serve a "meal" of rice and a beverage. The amount of food you receive will depend on the income level of the country you are in.

6. As you eat your "meal," observe the other groups.

Discussion

1. What was the mood among the members of your group during the "meal"?

2. What seemed to be the mood among the members of the other two groups?

3. During the "meal," what action, if any, did you want to take?

4. What would you expect to be the health of the people in each group?

5. How did this activity affect your understanding of the problem of world hunger?

---

also collects worldwide health statistics to evaluate and predict health threats. The most spectacular success of WHO's immunization programs was the worldwide elimination of smallpox, which was completed in 1980. This success has led to similar efforts to eradicate measles and polio worldwide. Since the mid-1980s, WHO has been involved in a global educational effort to prevent the spread of HIV infection, the virus that causes AIDS. This deadly disease continues to be at epidemic levels in all areas of the world. AIDS is discussed in detail in Chapter 23.

WHO works closely with another United Nations agency, the **United Nations International Children's Emergency Fund** (UNICEF). UNICEF aids children through immunization programs, day-care and health centers, school food programs, and the training of nurses and teachers.

Another United Nations agency, the **Food and Agriculture Organization** (FAO), works to improve food production and distribution in developing countries.

AGENCY FOR INTERNATIONAL DEVELOPMENT The **United States Agency for International Development** (USAID) was established to provide support for developing

Figure 27-13 *Peace Corps volunteers work with people in developing countries to improve all aspects of public health.*

countries. A major focus of this support is the distribution of food to countries stricken with famine. **Famine** is a widespread lack of food. USAID also funds programs for immunizations, medicines, sanitation, health-care training, and oral-rehydration therapy. **Oral-rehydration therapy** is the gradual reintroduction of fluids to someone who has suffered severe water loss. Severe water loss resulting from diarrhea is the major cause of death among young children in developing countries.

THE PEACE CORPS The **Peace Corps** is a United States government organization that trains volunteers for public health work in developing countries. The work of the volunteers depends on their background and training and the needs of the countries that invite them. Volunteers may help by improving agricultural techniques, teaching and providing health care, constructing shelters, and improving sanitation facilities and water supply systems.

In addition to health programs, some Peace Corps volunteers serve as advisors in the areas of education, technology, business, and industry. They also may work in conjunction with workers from USAID to carry out new programs.

INTERNATIONAL COMMITTEE OF THE RED CROSS The world's largest private international public health organization is the **International Committee of the Red Cross,** known in Moslem countries as the Red Crescent. This privately funded organization began in 1859, originally to aid victims on the battlefield. It still provides aid to soldiers, but its services have greatly expanded. The International Committee of the Red Cross organizes assistance anywhere in the world for victims of disasters, providing medical care, food, clothing, and temporary shelter.

OTHER AGENCIES   In addition to the United States government, the governments of a number of other countries sponsor agencies that provide assistance to developing countries. Also, a number of privately supported organizations provide health care or health-related services worldwide. OXFAM is best known for its food-relief efforts in areas of famine. CARE, the Cooperative for American Relief Everywhere, provides health care, food, water, and emergency assistance to refugees and disaster victims. Many churches and missionary groups provide hospital, disease-prevention, and relief services. A few examples are Church World Services, the Salvation Army, World Vision, the American Friends Service Committee, Save the Children Foundation, and Catholic Relief Services. Are there others that you have heard about that are helping people around the world?

LESSON 3 REVIEW

1. Name two major health problems in developing countries.
2. Name three United Nations agencies concerned with public health.
3. Explain the role of USAID in international public health.
4. Describe the functions of the Peace Corps.

What Do You Think?

5. If you had the opportunity to join the Peace Corps, in what part of the world would you want to serve, and why?

Working in Groups

Sumiko sat listening as the other student council members argued about how they should raise money for the March of Dimes.

"We should have a walk-a-thon," said Sam.

"No, that's a bad idea," said Sylvia. "Let's have a…"

"I say we have a car wash," Tom interrupted.

Finally, Sumiko stood up and pointed out that no one was listening to anyone else's ideas. "If we're going to get anything accomplished," said Sumiko, "we have to start working together as a group."

Have you ever wondered why some groups get a lot done and others do not? Group success often depends on group dynamics, how members work together. Since you participate in many groups—your family, friends, a sports team, this class—learning about group dynamics can be helpful. The following guidelines will help you learn to understand and work successfully in groups.

1. Set goals and priorities

The first task of a group is to set clear and realistic goals. If there are several purposes, decide which ones are most important. All members should be involved in setting the group's priorities.

2. Choose a leader

Groups work best when members select a leader. A good leader has the time, interest, and patience to see that things run smoothly. The respect of the other group members is also important.

3. Make a schedule

As a group, decide what steps are necessary to reach your goals. Which members have special skills or resources for these tasks? Divide activities so that everyone is involved. Finally, work together to set up a realistic schedule for all tasks.

4. Monitor group dynamics

People play different roles in groups. Use the examples below to help you identify the roles that people have taken in the groups you have been in. You can improve group dynamics by encouraging helpful behaviors and discouraging disruptive ones.

Starter: Often begins discussions, introduces new ideas.

Clarifier: Requests additional information. Restates points so they are clear to all.

Peacemaker: Suggests common ground and compromise when people disagree. Encourages positive group feelings.

Supporter: Is friendly and responsive to others and their ideas. Encourages shy members to join in.

Clown: Uses jokes to attract attention. Disrupts group.

Blocker: Always disagrees with others' ideas or focuses on trivial issues.

Dominator: Tries to control group. Bullies others.

Urge everyone to adopt a positive role. Choose a comfortable meeting place where all group members can be seen and heard.

• • • • • • • • • • • • • • • • •

5. Evaluate group progress

Are members working together productively? Are tasks being completed on time? If not, the group should discuss why. Ask: Were the goals or schedule unrealistic? Were a few people doing all the work? Are there conflicts, and are they being handled well? Was there a communication problem within the group? Remember that a group functions best when all members share in the process of helping the group meet its goals.

Apply the Skill

1. Choose a group you belong to, such as a school club, a sports team, a class group, or even some friends getting together with a specific purpose in mind. Watch the group in action. Use the following questions to analyze how well the group works. Refer to the preceding guidelines for extra help.

2. What are the goals of the group? List them in order of importance. How were the group's priorities decided?

3. Who is the leader? How was that person selected? Does the leader guide the group well, or is the leadership too strong or too weak? Explain.

4. Does the group have a schedule for accomplishing its goals? How was it decided? Is it realistic? Do all members have tasks that are suited to their own

strengths? Does every member feel that he or she is contributing to the goals of the group?

5. Identify the roles members play in the group. Who plays positive roles? Negative roles? What roles do you play? Do all members do their share? Are any left out because of "in groups" within the group?

6. Does your meeting place encourage everyone to participate? Is it free of distractions? Is it comfortable?

7. Is your group accomplishing its goals? Do members communicate well and meet deadlines? Is working with your group enjoyable? Why or why not?

8. Look over your answers to the questions above. For each of the questions give your group an overall grade. Where does it do best? Worst? List some suggestions for improving the dynamics and productivity of your group.

CHAPTER 27 REVIEW

KEY IDEAS

LESSON 1

- Public health is the study and practice of protecting and improving the health of people in a group or community.

- A public health system is all the government and private organizations that work to prevent disease and promote positive health behaviors in the general public.

- Public health combats infectious diseases and seeks to prevent a broad range of other health problems, many of them related to people's behaviors.

LESSON 2

- Public health in the United States is managed at the federal, state, and community levels.

- The federal government establishes broad public health objectives but depends on the states to carry out the programs to fulfill the objectives.

- The local health department provides a variety of public health services directly to the people in the community.

LESSON 3

- International health organizations work to overcome malnutrition, lack of basic medical care, poor sanitation, and lack of clean water supplies.

- International health organizations are supported by the United Nations, individual countries, or private donations.

KEY TERMS

LESSON 1
cholera
epidemiology
high-risk population
prenatal care
public health
public health system
quarantine

LESSON 2
Centers for Disease Control and Prevention

Department of Health and Human Services
health codes
local health department
National Institutes of Health
Occupational Safety and Health Administration
Public Health Service
vital statistics
Volunteers in Service to America (VISTA)

LESSON 3
famine
International Committee of the Red Cross
oral-rehydration therapy
Peace Corps
United Nations International Children's Emergency Fund (UNICEF)
World Health Organization

Listed above are some of the terms in this chapter. Choose the term from the list that best matches each phrase below.

1. isolation of a person who may be infected from people who are not infected

2. the study of disease occurrence and control

3. a widespread lack of food

4. an infectious disease of the small intestine that causes severe diarrhea and vomiting

5. a group of people who are likely to develop a serious disease or disorder

6. the number of births, deaths, and diseases in a population

7. standards for factors that affect health

8. a technique for restoring lost body fluids

9. the federal agency that sets and implements national health policy

10. the study and practice of protecting and improving the health of people in a community

WHAT HAVE YOU LEARNED?

Choose the letter of the answer that best completes each statement.

11. The type of care needed by a woman during pregnancy is

a. prenatal care   **c.** immunization
b. oral-rehydration therapy   **d.** quarantine

12. Which of the following describes a scientist who studies outbreaks of disease?

a. orthodontist   **c.** epidemiologist
b. pediatrician   **d.** gynecologist

13. Which agency sends volunteers abroad to help people in developing nations?

a. CDC   **c.** Peace Corps
b. Public Health Service   **d.** NIH

14. The government agency whose volunteers work within the United States is

a. Peace Corps   **c.** USAID
b. VISTA   **d.** CARE

15. The federal agency that inspects meat, poultry, and other agricultural products is

a. OSHA   **c.** IHS
b. FDA   **d.** USDA

16. The major biomedical research facility of the federal government is

a. NIH   **c.** USAID
b. CDC   **d.** EPA

Answer each of the following with complete sentences.

17. Why did some people believe that epidemics were caused by demons?

18. Why is there a need for a public health system?

19. How can quarantine help prevent the spread of a disease?

20. How does the public health system control infectious disease?

21. What federal government agency has the major responsibility for public health?

22. What kinds of public health services do local health departments provide?

23. Describe two types of public health programs sponsored by private or volunteer organizations.

24. What is the role of WHO?

WHAT DO YOU THINK?

25. Some lawmakers in the U.S. believe that people entering the U.S. for the first time should be tested for a variety of infectious diseases. What do you think?

26. Should funding for private health organizations be provided by voluntary donations or by the federal or state government?

27. Suppose the FDA recently approved a new synthetic dye for use as a food coloring. Would you feel safe eating food with this coloring? Why or why not?

28. Should children in the U.S. be required to have immunizations against diseases that rarely occur today? Why or why not?

WHAT WOULD YOU DO?

29. You notice the water in your school water fountains has an unpleasant smell and taste. You are concerned about the possible cause. What would you do?

30. How would you propose to solve the problem of homeless people in this country?

Getting Involved

31. Work with other students in your class to identify the local public and private health agencies that offer services to teens. Compile your findings into a resource guide that will be available to students in your school.

Include addresses, phone numbers, a brief description of the services, and any costs such as transportation services.

32. Organize a public health fair at your school. Invite exhibitors from local agencies and organizations to talk about and display information about their services to teens. You can also include information on public health career opportunities.

1 SAFETY AT HOME AND IN YOUR COMMUNITY

GUIDE FOR READING

Focus on these questions as you read this lesson.

- What are four factors that can prevent unintentional injury?
- What are the leading hazards in the home?
- What are some examples of disasters that affect the community?

SKILLS

- Activity: Looking Out for Safety

To many people, the word *accident* refers to an event that cannot be predicted or prevented. Most events that are considered accidents, however, can be prevented. This chapter uses the term *unintentional injury* instead of *accident* to help make everyone aware of the need to prevent injuries.

How can you prevent unintentional injuries or reduce their severity? One way is to recognize risks to your safety and practice behaviors that promote your safety. A **risk behavior** is a behavior that increases a person's chances of a harmful outcome. A **safe behavior** protects a person from danger and lessens the effects of a harmful situation. **Four factors that can help prevent unintentional injuries or lessen the damage they cause are knowledge, ability, state of mind, and environmental conditions.**

- **Knowledge and awareness:** Recognize risks to your safety, and know what actions to take to reduce the risk of unintentional injury. You should know, for example, that it is risky to operate an electric hairdryer when you are wet or near water.

- **Ability:** Be realistic when you judge your ability and that of others. A child who has just learned to walk, for example, cannot safely walk down a flight of stairs without help.

- **State of mind:** Be aware of your own condition and that of others. A person who is tired, rushed, distressed, or under the influence of drugs or alcohol is more likely to be injured or to cause injury to others.

- **Environmental conditions:** Consider the hazards in your environment that might cause an accident. For example, if the floor has just been washed, do not run across it when the telephone rings.

Hazards in Your Home

According to Figure 28-2, the leading cause of death due to unintentional injuries is motor-vehicle crashes. However, one-third of all unintentional injuries occur in the home.

FALLS   Young children are especially likely to be injured in falls. Whenever you put a baby into a crib, make sure that the sides of the crib are in the highest position and are locked into place. Cribs should have no more than 2 3/8 inches of space between the slats. Never leave a baby alone on a table or other raised surface. Use safety gates at the bottom and top of stairs to keep young children from falling downstairs. Do not allow children to sit on windowsills or lean against

Figure 28-1 *Make sure you operate electrical appliances, such as hairdryers, safely.*

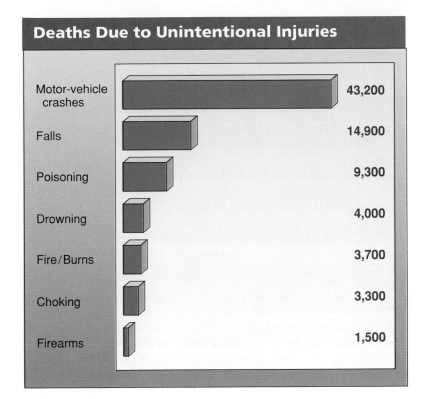

Deaths Due to Unintentional Injuries

Motor-vehicle crashes	43,200
Falls	14,900
Poisoning	9,300
Drowning	4,000
Fire/Burns	3,700
Choking	3,300
Firearms	1,500

Figure 28-2 *This graph shows data for a recent year. What is the second leading cause of death due to unintentional injuries?*

screens. Keep children away from decks or porches without railings. Do not allow a toddler to climb into a highchair alone. Discourage children from playing roughly indoors.

Hazards in the home can result in a fall for anyone. The main factor in avoiding falls is to consider environmental conditions. To keep falls to a minimum:

- Make sure that all stairways are in good repair and have nonslip treads and strong railings.
- Keep stairs and walkways uncluttered and well lighted.
- Anchor all carpets and rugs firmly.
- Make sure floors are not slippery, and clear them of small objects.
- Keep stepladders in good repair.
- Equip bathtubs and showers with handrails and non-skid rubber mats or decals.
- Keep outdoor steps and sidewalks in good repair and free of ice, leaves, toys, and other obstacles.

FIRES AND BURNS The six most common causes of household fires are careless smoking, faulty or overloaded electrical wiring, unsafe heating units, faulty or improperly used fireplaces, children playing with matches, and improper storage of flammable materials. **Flammable materials** catch fire easily or burn quickly. If your area does not have 911 emergency calling, keep the number of your fire department near the telephone.

Reducing Fire Risks

- Have working smoke detectors on each floor of your home and outside of all bedrooms.
- Practice a fire escape plan and keep the route clear.
- Have fire extinguishers in the kitchen, garage, and on each floor of your home.
- Make sure electrical plugs are not overloaded.
- Make sure electrical appliances are installed properly and in good repair.
- Replace frayed or cracked appliance cords.
- Use the proper fuses.
- Remove extension cords from under rugs or furniture.
- Discourage smokers from smoking in bed.
- Keep matches and lighters out of reach of small children.
- Make sure the pilot lights of gas stoves are working.
- Use a cover when cooking with oil at high temperatures.
- Keep flammable materials away from heat sources.
- Avoid storing flammable materials in your home or garage, or store them in fireproof, labeled containers.

Figure 28-3 *How could you reduce the risk of fire in your home?*

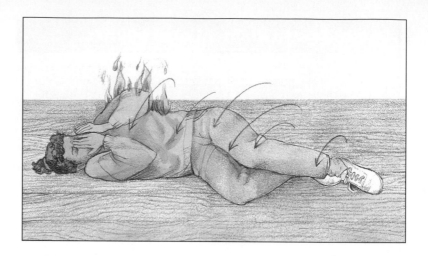

Preventing Poisoning at Home

- Do not leave any medications or poisonous substances such as household cleansers, cosmetics, alcohol, or gasoline products within a child's reach.

- Avoid chewing, swallowing, or rubbing the skin against houseplants, especially philodendron and diffenbachia.

- Make sure that all poisonous substances are clearly labeled.

- Never place poisonous substances in food containers.

- Keep hazardous substances in a cabinet that is locked or has a childproof latch.

- Always carefully follow the directions for taking or giving medications.

- Post the telephone number to call for poisoning emergencies (Poison Control Center, or 911, or 0) next to your telephone.

- Keep a remedy for accidental poisoning (such as syrup of ipecac) in your medicine cabinet, but do NOT use it until you have consulted with the Poison Control Center or other medical authority.

Figure 28-5 *What is the telephone number of the Poison Control Center in your area?*

If a small fire starts on the stove, put it out using a kitchen fire extinguisher. Never use water on a grease fire, since this will cause the fire to spread. If a small fire begins to get out of control, leave immediately and alert other residents to the danger. If your home is on fire, leave immediately. If there is a lot of smoke, cover your face and nose with a wet cloth and crawl along the floor to the nearest exit. Do not pause to telephone anyone or to collect belongings. Once you are outside, do not go back in. Go to a neighbor's or to the nearest fire-alarm box, and alert the fire department.

If a person catches fire, follow the procedure shown in Figure 28-4. By rolling the person on the ground, in a rug, or in a heavy coat, you cut off the air the fire needs.

POISONING   Most incidents of poisoning take place in the home. They usually involve children under the age of five who eat or drink poisonous substances left within their reach. Almost every room of a home contains substances that can poison a child. If you have a local **Poison Control Center,** it can provide information about what household substances are poisonous and can tell you what to do in the event of poisoning. Figure 28-5 indicates some safety guidelines you can follow to prevent unintentional poisoning.

SUFFOCATION AND DROWNING   When a person's supply of air is cut off, the result is **suffocation.** Suffocation can be caused by choking when an object gets caught in the breathing passages, by smothering, or by being trapped in an enclosed space. Suffocation can result in death.

If you are caring for small children, remember the following safety rules. Do not let children put small toys or other objects in their mouths. Cut food into small pieces. Never prop a bottle in a baby's mouth and then leave the baby alone. Keep plastic bags away from children. Make sure bed pillows, blankets, sheets, and clothing do not interfere with a child's breathing. Teach children not to wind ropes or long scarves around their necks.

LOOKING OUT FOR SAFETY

In this activity you will conduct a survey to determine the percentage of homes equipped with safety equipment and then create a public service announcement to address the safety problems you found.

Procedure

1. Check to see if your home is equipped for safety.

- Do you have a working smoke detector on each floor and outside the bedrooms?

- Is there a fire extinguisher available in the kitchen and on each floor?

- Do you have a first-aid kit available?

2. Survey five other people (who live in different homes) to see if their homes are equipped for safety with working smoke detectors, fire extinguishers, and a first-aid kit.

3. Compile your survey results with your class and determine the percentage of homes that are not equipped for safety.

4. Create a one-minute public service announcement (PSA) for radio that would address the safety problems you found and convince people to equip their homes for safety. Practice giving your PSA to other classes or a parent group.

Discussion

1. Which was the biggest safety problem you found in your survey?

2. How would you measure the effectiveness of your PSA?

3. What other strategies would convince people to equip their homes for safety with smoke detectors, fire extinguishers, and first-aid kits?

To prevent drowning, never leave young children alone in the bathroom or in or near a pool. Closely watch children who are using flotation devices in a pool. Never allow anyone who has been using drugs or alcohol in a home pool.

FIREARMS Each year more than 1,000 people are unintentionally killed by firearms in their homes. Most of the deaths occur among young people between the ages of 15 and 24. To keep this from happening to you or someone you know, keep firearms unloaded and locked in a place where children cannot reach them. Lock ammunition in a separate place. Always point a firearm away from yourself and others when you are cleaning or showing it. Do not handle firearms if you have not been trained in their use.

OTHER HOME HAZARDS Electricity and faulty or misused equipment pose other risks. Make sure that your home is properly wired. Keep all home appliances in good repair, and know how to use them safely. Never try to repair an electric appliance when it is plugged in.

Death from direct contact with electricity is called **electrocution** (ih lek truh KYOO shun). To prevent electrocution, keep young children away from electrical outlets. Place safety covers over unused electrical outlets. Never use appliances when you are wet or near water.

Figure 28-6 *More tornadoes form in the United States than in any other country.*

Disasters

Hurricanes, tornadoes, blizzards, floods, earthquakes, and forest fires are all examples of natural disasters. **Disasters** are sudden, catastrophic events that affect many people. Disasters may be natural or the result of technology or human error. Nuclear power plant accidents, hazardous material spills, illegal dumping of toxic wastes, and some forest and brush fires are examples of disasters caused by humans.

What can you do to prepare for disasters or lessen the effects of disasters on you and your family? Emergency management authorities, such as civil defense personnel, work to prevent or lessen the effects of disasters and help communities recover. If a disaster occurs in your area, follow the instructions given over the emergency broadcast system on your radio or television.

HURRICANES   A **hurricane** is a powerful tropical storm characterized by heavy rains and winds over 74 miles per hour. If you hear that a hurricane is coming, place tape across window glass and then board up the windows if possible. Anchor or bring inside any furniture or other items outside your home. Hurricane-force winds can knock down power lines. Avoid contact with downed power lines.

TORNADOES   Another kind of natural disaster is the tornado. A **tornado** is a rapidly rotating column of air whirling at speeds of up to 500 miles per hour. Tornadoes are frequent occurrences in parts of the central and southern United States. If you are caught outdoors during a tornado, move

away from the tornado at right angles to its path. If the tornado is too close for you to escape, find shelter or lie flat in the nearest ditch or low place in the ground. If you are at home, go to the lowest floor of your home. Keep some windows open to equalize pressure, but stay away from them. If you live in a mobile home, go to a tornado shelter.

BLIZZARDS   A heavy snowstorm with winds over 34 miles per hour is called a **blizzard.** Generally, the safest place to be during a blizzard is inside your home or other warm shelter. If you have a problem requiring special treatment, alert local authorities so that you can be evacuated safely from your home. Do not try to go out on your own.

FLOODS   Most floods can be predicted, but a **flash flood** can occur suddenly, without warning, after a heavy rainfall or snow melt. Check the history of your area to find out if there is a risk of flash flooding. If your area is at risk, find out where you should go if evacuation is ordered. In the event of any flood, turn off the water, gas, and electricity and move your belongings to the highest floor before leaving home. When you are able to return home, discard any liquids or foods touched by flood waters. Drink bottled water until local authorities tell you that the tap water is safe.

EARTHQUAKES   An **earthquake** is a sudden shaking of the ground caused by the release of stress accumulated along geologic faults or by volcanic activity. So far, scientists have had little success in predicting major earthquakes. If you are indoors during an earthquake, stand under the frame of an interior door or crawl under a table or desk. Stay away from windows, glass doors, heavy hanging objects, or furniture that might tip over. If you are outside, stay in the open, away from buildings, walls, and electrical wires. If you are driving, pull over and stop. After a major earthquake, turn off the gas and electricity in your home to prevent a gas leak or fire.

How to Be Prepared for a Disaster

- Know where your family's first-aid kit is kept.
- Have flashlights and a supply of fresh batteries on hand.
- Keep a battery-powered radio for listening to emergency broadcasts.
- Store a two-week supply of bottled water.
- Maintain a supply of pre-cooked canned foods.
- Find out how to turn off the main switches to the gas, the electricity, and the water in your home.
- Be sure your vehicle's gas tank is kept at least half full at all times.

Figure 28-7 *Would your family be prepared if a disaster struck?*

LESSON 1 REVIEW

1. List the four factors that can help prevent unintentional injuries.
2. Name the six leading causes of unintentional death in the home.
3. What are four ways of keeping falls to a minimum?
4. How would you prepare for a major disaster?

What Do You Think?

5. What changes would you make in your home to assure a 1-year-old's safety during a visit?

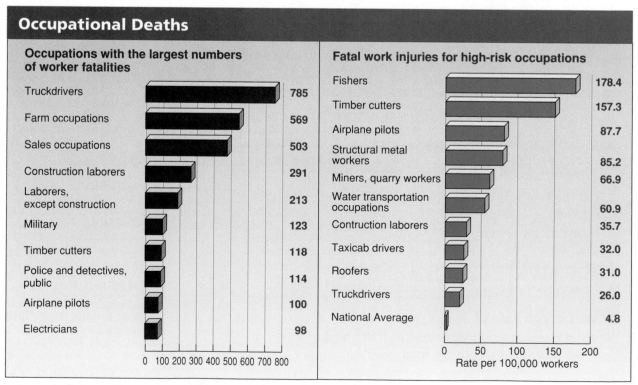
GUIDE FOR READING

Focus on these questions as you read this lesson.

- How can occupational injuries and illnesses be prevented or made less serious?
- What are the basic safety guidelines for recreational activities?

SKILLS

- Locating Community Resources

Many unintentional injuries occur either at work or while people are participating in recreational activities. Although you are not working full time yet, you probably will be someday. In preparation for that time, you should know about the possible hazards of the workplace and what to do about them. You should also be aware of the hazards of any leisure-time activities you are involved in.

Occupational Safety

Each year more than one-and-a-half million workers suffer disabling injuries on the job. Another 10,000 are killed, and 250,000 workers develop work-related illnesses.

The **Occupational Safety and Health Administration** (OSHA) is the U.S. government agency that identifies occupational hazards and sets standards for safety. OSHA defines an **occupational injury** as any injury that results from a work accident or from exposure to a hazard in the work environment. OSHA defines an **occupational illness** as any abnormal condition or disorder, excluding injuries, caused by exposure to the workplace environment. Certain cancers, for example, are classified as occupational illnesses.

Figure 28-8 *These graphs show data for a recent year. Which occupation had the greatest number of injuries?*

Occupational Deaths

Occupations with the largest numbers of worker fatalities

Truckdrivers	785
Farm occupations	569
Sales occupations	503
Construction laborers	291
Laborers, except construction	213
Military	123
Timber cutters	118
Police and detectives, public	114
Airplane pilots	100
Electricians	98

0 100 200 300 400 500 600 700 800

Fatal work injuries for high-risk occupations

Occupation	Rate
Fishers	178.4
Timber cutters	157.3
Airplane pilots	87.7
Structural metal workers	85.2
Miners, quarry workers	66.9
Water transportation occupations	60.9
Contruction laborers	35.7
Taxicab drivers	32.0
Roofers	31.0
Truckdrivers	26.0
National Average	4.8

0   50   100   150   200
Rate per 100,000 workers

Figure 28-9 *Studies are under way to determine whether there are hazards associated with working at video display terminals.*

Which jobs are most hazardous to your health? Figure 28-8 gives information about occupational deaths and injuries in various industries. Overall, however, the rates of death, injury, and illness have been declining steadily.

One major way in which many occupational injuries and illnesses can be prevented or made less serious is by the removal of potential hazards from the work environment. It is the responsibility of your employer to keep the workplace as healthy as possible and to inform you of any on-the-job hazards. It is your responsibility to be well rested and alert, to be sober and drug-free, to wear appropriate clothing, and to follow safety procedures.

Whatever job you choose, you should know the health risks involved. Be informed about how these risks can be prevented or reduced. You may need to change jobs if a job proves to be dangerous.

Recreational Safety

Almost everyone in this country enjoys some kind of recreational activity. What leisure-time activities do you like? Swimming? Boating? Basketball? Jogging? Camping? Whatever activities you enjoy, there are four basic safety guidelines you should follow.

- Learn and apply the proper skills.
- Have appropriate, well-maintained equipment.
- Know the safety rules specific to the activity.
- Prepare adequately for the activity.

As you read about various recreational activities, keep these four guidelines in mind.

● ● ● ● ● ● ● ● ● ● ● ● ●
SHARPEN YOUR *SKILLS*

Locating Community Resources

Research and present to your class a list of local facilities that offer swimming instruction. Describe the different types of classes available, including classes for people who are afraid of the water.

Using Your Clothing to Help You Float

1. Tuck in and button shirt or blouse. Unbutton a middle button; blow into opening.

2. The air bubble in the shoulders will help you float.

Survival Floating

1. Take a breath and hold it. Put face in water; let arms and legs dangle. Rest.

2. Tilt head back so your mouth clears the water. Exhale. Press down with your arms and bring legs together. Repeat step #1.

Figure 28-10 *Survival swimming techniques allow a nonswimmer to stay afloat until help arrives.*

WATER SAFETY Drowning is the fourth leading cause of unintentional death in the United States. Most of these drownings are associated with swimming and boating. The highest number of drownings occurs among young people between the ages of 15 and 24.

Most drownings can be prevented if the person can swim 20 yards. Even if you never learn how to swim, however, you should know how to protect yourself from drowning. Figure 28-10 shows **survival floating,** a lifesaving water safety technique that allows you to float and breathe without using much energy. You also should be aware of the water safety tips given in Figure 28-11.

Local Coast Guard auxiliaries, community boating facilities, and the American Red Cross offer boating safety classes. Before you go out in a boat, check the weather conditions, and make sure the boat is in good repair. Each person on the boat should have an approved flotation device, such as a life preserver or life jacket. Nonswimmers and young children should wear flotation devices at all times. Signal lights should be kept on between dusk and dawn, and you should have a whistle or horn to signal with when visibility is poor. No alcohol or drug use should be allowed on board a boat.

The overturning of a boat is called **capsizing.** Capsizing is the most frequent cause of death among people who use small boats. Usually capsizing results from improper loading and unloading of the boat, but it can also occur when a boat has a motor that is too powerful or during stormy weather. If you are in a boat when it capsizes, grab your flotation device and stay with the boat until you are rescued.

If someone falls overboard, immediately toss a flotation device and a towline to the person. Shut off the motor, and help the person into the boat. If the person is injured, have a strong swimmer, wearing a flotation device with a line attached, slip into the water to rescue the injured person.

SPORTS SAFETY   Sports injuries usually occur when you do not warm up properly before vigorous activity or cool down properly afterward. Injuries also occur when you have faulty or inappropriate equipment. For example, if you are roller-skating or skateboarding you should wear protective equipment, such as a helmet, wrist guards, elbow and knee pads, and light gloves.

Injuries can occur too if you engage in a sport in hazardous situations. Do not skate or skateboard on heavily trafficked roads. Be alert to your surroundings—do not wear headphones. You should never engage in a sport when you are ill or if you have used alcohol or drugs.

When you are exercising vigorously, your body uses up fluids rapidly. Whenever you are exercising, you should drink lots of water, even in cold weather.

Camping or hunting outdoors presents special safety risks. To avoid hazards, camp or hunt only in approved areas. Always let someone know where you are and when you expect to return. Before you go, find out about potential dangers, such as bears, ticks, or poisonous snakes and plants. Take along a first-aid kit, and know how to respond to hazardous situations, such as snakebites or skin infections. Be

Figure 28-11 *Which of these tips do you already practice?*

Water Safety Tips

- Always swim with at least one other person.
- Do not swim immediately after eating.
- Always swim in a known, supervised area.
- Know your swimming ability. Make sure that you can return to shore easily.
- Do not use underwater equipment unless you have received proper training and instructions.
- Wear a flotation device when required; do not rely on a float or rubber tube.
- Never dive in an area where the water may not be deep enough for diving or where there may be rocks, swimmers, or other obstacles.
- Never swim or dive after drinking alcoholic beverages or taking drugs.
- Do not walk on the ice over a lake, river, or pond unless local recreation authorities state that it is safe.
- If you are on an ice-covered body of water and the ice begins to crack, immediately lie down and crawl to shore.

Figure 28-12 *Always wear the protective gear that is appropriate for your sport or activity.*

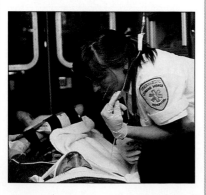

Figure 28-13 *Wearing brightly colored clothing is a safety precaution observed by hunters.*

sure to take plenty of food and water. In your camp area, stow food and garbage so as not to attract animals. Cook in a protected area so that sparks will not start a brush or forest fire. Check the weather conditions, and be prepared. Dress appropriately for the weather, and follow all posted campsite rules.

If you are hunting, wear a bright-colored vest or hat so that you will not be mistaken for prey by another hunter. While you are hunting, keep the safety on your gun until you are ready to shoot. Keep your trigger finger outside the trigger guard. Unload your gun as soon as you have finished hunting.

LESSON 2 REVIEW

1. From what government agency can you obtain information about occupational hazards and safety regulations?
2. Name one major way in which many occupational injuries and illnesses can be made less serious.
3. What are the four basic safety guidelines for recreational activities?
4. Select one recreational activity and describe what you can do to prevent unintentional injuries when you are participating in this activity.

What Do You Think?

5. Suppose a friend tries to persuade you to go diving with him in a water-filled quarry at night. How would you talk your friend into doing something less hazardous?

3 VEHICLE SAFETY

GUIDE FOR READING

Focus on these questions as you read this lesson.

- What is the main factor contributing to vehicle crashes?
- What are some rules for safe bicycle operation?

SKILLS

- Setting Goals

Each year more than 40,000 deaths and millions of injuries occur as a result of motor-vehicle crashes. On average, one out of every two Americans will be involved in a motor- vehicle crash during his or her lifetime.

Motor-Vehicle Safety

The main factor contributing to vehicle crashes is the human factor, especially among young drivers. The human factor includes a driver's knowledge and awareness, experience, ability, and state of mind. Drivers between the ages of 15 and 24 are involved in more crashes than any other age group. Males have a higher rate of reckless driving than females. Because of their higher rate of crashes, young drivers pay high insurance premiums.

The use of alcohol and drugs is a major factor in motor-vehicle crashes and injuries. Over 40 percent of all fatal crashes involving motor vehicles are linked to alcohol use. As you read in Chapter 19, alcohol inhibits good judgment and self-control, slows reaction time, blurs vision, and reduces coordination. Drivers between the ages of 20 and 24 have more drunk-driving convictions and alcohol-related crashes than any other group.

Other factors contributing to motor-vehicle crashes are the condition of the vehicle and environmental conditions. Defective brakes, lights, tires, and windshield wipers contribute to many motor-vehicle crashes. Poor environmental conditions, such as defects in the road, bad weather, and low visibility, increase the likelihood of motor-vehicle crashes. The risks of

Figure 28-14 *Safety belts have saved many lives.*

Motorcycle and Moped Safety

- Always wear a helmet. Have an extra helmet for a passenger to wear.

- Learn how to operate your vehicle safely before taking it on the open road.

- Follow the traffic rules that apply to larger vehicles.

- Never ride your vehicle when using alcohol or drugs.

- Do not listen to headphones while riding.

- Avoid carrying anything that will interfere with your ability to drive.

- Only carry an additional passenger if your vehicle has an attached second seat and foot rests.

- Never grab on to another moving vehicle.

- If your vehicle lacks a windscreen, wear eye protection, such as goggles.

- Make sure your vehicle has a working headlight, taillight, stoplight, reflectors, and rear-view mirror.

- Signal stops, turns, or changes in direction.

- Watch for possible hazards, such as a car door opening or a rope or wire across your driving path.

- Get your vehicle inspected periodically to make sure it is in good repair.

- Wear bright-colored, sturdy clothing that will not catch on the moving parts of your motorcycle or moped.

Figure 28-16 *Motorcyclists and moped riders need to take special safety precautions.*

Safe Driving Tips

- Never let a person who is using alcohol or drugs drive.

- Always wear a safety belt and sit 10 inches away from the steering wheel. Insist that everyone wear a safety belt, even in cars with air bags.

- If young children or babies are in the car, make sure that they are fastened securely into an approved car safety seat.

- Allow enough distance between you and the car in front of you so that you can stop suddenly without hitting it.

- On slippery roads, rather than using the brake, shift to a lower gear and let the engine slow the car.

- Practice defensive driving, which means anticipating the worst from other drivers and being alert to possible road hazards.

- Do not let passengers ride in the back of an open truck.

- Never carry a flammable substance, such as extra gasoline, in the trunk of your car.

- Eliminate distractions, such as loud music, hot liquids that might spill, and animals inside the car.

Figure 28-15 *Which of these tips are especially important?*

serious injury and death are compounded by excessive speed and by not using safety belts. Always wear a safety belt when you are in a motor vehicle, even if the car is equipped with air bags.

FOUR-WHEEL MOTOR VEHICLES   There are steps you can take to reduce your chances of being involved in a motor-vehicle crash or being seriously injured in one. To start with, take a course in driver education, keep your vehicle in good repair, and avoid driving when you are tired, angry, or depressed. Figure 28-15 provides more safe driving tips.

TWO-WHEEL MOTOR VEHICLES   Human error is the main contributing factor to most crashes with two-wheel motor vehicles, such as motorcycles and mopeds. It is therefore up to riders to enhance their own safety. Figure 28-16 lists some suggestions for motorcycle and moped riders.

Bicycles and Recreational Vehicles

Many people, especially young people, are killed or injured each year in incidents involving bicycles or recreational vehicles, such as snowmobiles or all-terrain vehicles (ATVs). These incidents usually are the result of mechanical problems, poor judgment, and ignorance of basic safety rules.

BICYCLES Before you buy or ride a bike, inspect it thoroughly to make sure it is the right size for you and that it is safe and properly equipped. You should be able to touch the ground with the toes of both feet when you are seated on the bicycle. Figure 28-17 shows you how to decide whether or not a bicycle is in good repair and adequately equipped. About one-fifth of all bicycle crashes are the result of mechanical problems with the bicycle. Before riding your bicycle a long distance, make sure cycling conditions are safe. Check the weather report. Avoid taking a long ride on a hot day. Take along some water to drink. Never ride when you are ill or on medication. Do not ride immediately after eating.

The most dangerous bicycle accidents are collisions with motor vehicles. Fifty percent of all collisions occur at intersections, and 70 percent occur during the daylight hours. In most cases, the bicyclist was disobeying traffic laws at the time of the accident. Follow these rules to be sure you are operating your bicycle safely.

- Always wear a bicycle safety helmet.
- Do not listen to headphones while riding.
- Ride single file on the right, with the flow of traffic.
- Obey all traffic rules and laws.
- Signal your intentions with hand signals before turning or stopping.
- Always use crosswalks to walk your bicycle across busy intersections.

Figure 28-17 *Before riding a bicycle, be sure it is in good repair.*

Bicycle Maintenance

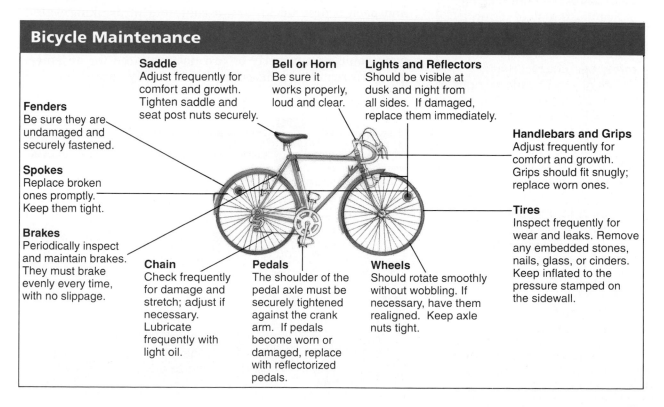

Saddle
Adjust frequently for comfort and growth. Tighten saddle and seat post nuts securely.

Bell or Horn
Be sure it works properly, loud and clear.

Lights and Reflectors
Should be visible at dusk and night from all sides. If damaged, replace them immediately.

Fenders
Be sure they are undamaged and securely fastened.

Spokes
Replace broken ones promptly. Keep them tight.

Brakes
Periodically inspect and maintain brakes. They must brake evenly every time, with no slippage.

Chain
Check frequently for damage and stretch; adjust if necessary. Lubricate frequently with light oil.

Pedals
The shoulder of the pedal axle must be securely tightened against the crank arm. If pedals become worn or damaged, replace with reflectorized pedals.

Wheels
Should rotate smoothly without wobbling. If necessary, have them realigned. Keep axle nuts tight.

Handlebars and Grips
Adjust frequently for comfort and growth. Grips should fit snugly; replace worn ones.

Tires
Inspect frequently for wear and leaks. Remove any embedded stones, nails, glass, or cinders. Keep inflated to the pressure stamped on the sidewall.

Should We Be Required to Use Safety Belts?

Cars being manufactured today have automatic safety belts. However, there are still many people who refuse to use them. As a result, many states have passed or are considering laws requiring their use.

People in favor of a safety-belt law claim that safety belts protect against injury and death in automobile crashes. They say that a properly worn safety belt almost guarantees that injuries will be less severe. They also point out that automobile injuries cost our society millions of dollars each year in medical costs, worker's compensation, welfare, and related expenses. Thus, safety-belt laws protect not only the individual, but all of society as well.

People who are against a safety-belt law feel that it denies our constitutional right to freedom of choice. They also claim that safety belt use actually makes injuries in some cases worse by causing internal bleeding. Safety belts might also prevent a person from escaping from a car if it were to plunge into a body of water or catch fire. For these reasons, they feel that people should be left to decide for themselves whether or not to use safety belts.

☞ Do you feel that safety-belt use should be required by law? Why or why not?

- For riding in traffic, use a rear-view mirror attached either to your bicycle or to your helmet.
- If a mechanical emergency occurs, get your bike well off the road before making repairs.
- Attach reflective tape to your bicycle and your clothing.
- Equip your bike with lights and reflectors if you ride it at dusk, at dawn, or after dark.
- Always be alert for hazards, such as oil spills, gravel, ice, ruts, potholes, railroad tracks, or opening car doors.
- Whenever possible, avoid riding on roadways where traffic is heavy or where cars maintain high speeds.
- Use specially designated bicycle paths if available.
- Never grab on to another moving vehicle.
- Do not carry riders on your bicycle.

RECREATIONAL VEHICLES   Snowmobiles and all-terrain vehicles (ATVs) are two popular kinds of recreational vehicles. Both kinds of vehicles should be used with caution. Rough terrain and uneven surfaces can flip the machine over. Speeding can cause you to be thrown out of the vehicle.

To prevent crashes, know the terrain, do not speed, avoid roadways, and never venture out onto an ice-covered body of water. Be sure recreational vehicles are permitted in the area where you plan to go. Do not wear loose scarves or clothing that can become tangled in the machinery. Wear a safety helmet. Always go with a friend when traveling any distance, and pack a first-aid kit and a container of drinking water. Take enough emergency food and equipment to enable you to survive and signal for help if you should need it. If you use your vehicle improperly or are not prepared for an emergency, recreational vehicles can be extremely hazardous.

LESSON 3 REVIEW

1. Name the factor that plays a major role in all kinds of vehicle accidents.
2. What is meant by defensive driving?
3. Describe some safety guidelines for operating a motorcycle or moped and tell how they prevent accidents.
4. List six of the rules to follow for safe bicycle operation.

What Do You Think?

5. A good friend of yours is, in your view, an unsafe driver. He drives at high speeds, disobeys traffic rules, and frequently takes his eyes off the road. What could you say to your friend to encourage him to drive more safely?

DIFFERENT VOICES SPEAKING

Seventeen-year-old John Chan of Brooklyn, New York, put his knowledge of first aid to good use several summers back, when he rescued a person suffering from heat exhaustion.

Q. John, how did you happen to rescue someone?

A. It was a very hot day. We were standing on a subway platform; the train was slow to come. As I was waiting, I noticed a woman who was kind of wobbly on her feet. She must have been there a long time and obviously didn't recognize what was happening to her. By the time I noticed her, she was pretty incoherent.

Q. What did you do?

A. I went to her and tried to take her to the nearest cool place. I knew I needed to get her cooled off as fast as possible. Otherwise there was a risk of heat stroke, which is more serious since the body systems begin to fail. Luckily an air-conditioned train pulled into the station, and I managed to get her on and seated. After a while, she began to return to normal. Several stations later, she was on her feet.

Q. Do you remember how you felt during the rescue?

A. I wasn't really paying too much attention to my own feelings. I was focused on what was going on at the moment—on getting the job done.

Q. How did you know what action to take?

A. It was one of a number of lifesaving techniques I learned through the Red Cross. I took a course there. In fact, last year I received my certification as a first-aid instructor.

John Chan

Q. What caused you to become involved with the Red Cross?

A. I was exposed to CPR in a health class in junior high school. Because I have an elderly grandmother living in my home, I thought it would be a good skill to have. So I signed up for a basic lifesaving course.

Q. You mentioned that you teach. Are your students mostly other teens?

A. No, the age range actually begins as early as preschool. We teach a program called YIP—short for Youth Injury Prevention. It includes such things as fire safety. I feel strongly that there is no age group too young to start learning preparedness. If you learn to be careful and aware of your surroundings and circumstances, you can avoid disaster. Certainly the woman I saved could have benefited by being better prepared. That's why my motto is, "Safety first—and last."

Journal Activity

Unlike the majority of people who learn life-saving techniques, John had to apply his skills in a real-life emergency. In your health journal, write a fictionalized first-person account of a rescue you made. You may choose any of the emergency situations covered in the chapter.

4 AVOIDING VIOLENCE

Focus on these questions as you read this lesson.

- How can you protect yourself from assault or reduce the likelihood of injury?
- What are some myths and facts about rape?

SKILLS

- Finding the Facts

Unfortunately, some injury is the result of crime. You may be unable to stop crime, but you can avoid some situations that put you at risk. How can you reduce your risks?

Self-Protection

An **assault** is an unlawful attempt or threat to harm someone. **You can prevent assault or reduce the likelihood of injury by following certain safety guidelines, especially the most basic one—avoid risky situations.**

AT HOME If you are at home alone or babysitting in someone's home, lock all doors and windows. If a stranger knocks at the door, do not allow him or her inside. If the person asks for help, tell him or her to stay outside while you telephone for help. Never let a caller know you are by yourself or give your name, address, or telephone number to a person who has called the wrong number. If you hear someone breaking in, leave immediately and call the police from a neighbor's house or public phone. Do not keep keys to your home in an obvious hiding place, such as under a doormat.

AWAY FROM HOME Avoid deserted places, such as dark streets, parks, and garages. Make sure you are with a friend if you must enter or walk through a deserted or dangerous area. Always walk purposefully and quickly. Stay away from dark doorways and hedges where an attacker might be hiding. If someone starts to follow you, step into a nearby store or restaurant, or walk up to the door of a house and ring the bell.

When driving, keep the car doors locked and the windows rolled up far enough so that no one can reach inside. If a menacing person tries to get into your car, honk your horn. Do not hitchhike or pick up hitchhikers. If your car breaks down, pull over to the side of the road, raise your hood, and turn on your emergency flashers. If a stranger stops to help, do not open your car door; just ask the person to call the police.

When you go to a place where you will be leaving your car, be sure to park in a well-lit place, close all the windows, and lock all the doors. Before getting back into your car, always check to make sure no one is hiding in the back seat or on the floor. Lock the doors as soon as you get into your car, to avoid the possibility of "carjacking."

Figure 28-18 *When walking through a deserted area, always walk with someone and be aware of your surroundings.*

Rape

1. **MYTH:** Only young, attractive women are raped.

   ● **FACT: Both males and females of all ages are potential victims of rape.**

2. **MYTH:** Rapists are always strangers.

   ● **FACT: A rapist can be a date or another person who is known to the rape victim, as well as a stranger.**

3. **MYTH:** Rapists are driven by the urge to have sex.

   ● **FACT: Rape is more an act of violence than an act of sex; rapists are usually angry and are trying to humiliate or demonstrate their power over another person.**

4. **MYTH:** Rape is usually an unplanned assault.

   ● **FACT: Rapists generally select a vulnerable person and then plan their attack.**

5. **MYTH:** Some victims "ask for it" by the way they dress and act.

   ● **FACT: Studies show that rapists look for people who appear weak and vulnerable, not people who dress or act in a certain way.**

6. **MYTH:** Rapes usually occur in unfamiliar, deserted places.

   ● **FACT: Rapes are most likely to occur in a familiar place, such as a person's home or apartment building.**

7. **MYTH:** Most rapists are poor, uneducated, and emotionally disturbed.

   ● **FACT: Most rapists appear to be normal and can come from any kind of background—rich, middle-class, poor, educated, or uneducated.**

IF YOU ARE ATTACKED Your possessions are not as important as your survival. If someone tries to rob you, give them what they want. Do not resist, or you may be physically harmed or killed. Report the attack to the police as soon as it is safe to do so.

WITNESSING A CRIME If you see a crime in progress, call the police immediately. Do not try to intervene by yourself, especially if weapons could be involved. Give the police as much detailed information as you can: location; license plate and type of car; description of the suspect; your name, address, and telephone number. Do not hang up until you have given all the necessary information and have answered any questions the police may have.

Rape Prevention

One type of assault that is both physically and psychologically painful is rape. **Rape** means that one person forces another to have sexual relations. Study the myths and facts about rape on this page. Which facts are new to you?

Contrary to the myths, rapes usually are carried out by someone the victim knows, in a place that is familiar to either the victim or the rapist. Date rape occurs when a rape is carried out by someone the victim is going out with; acquaintance rape is a rape carried out by someone known to

Finding the Facts

Sexual harassment is a problem that has received increased attention in recent years. Find out what sexual harassment is and what laws and regulations have been established to protect people from sexual harassment. Prepare a written report of your findings.

the victim. It is hard to tell if a person is a potential rapist, but it is important to trust your own judgment. If you feel that you might be in danger, you probably are. However, it does not always work the other way around. Feeling "safe" with someone does not mean that you are safe. Always let someone know where you are and when you will return home. Stay away from a person who

- acts strangely to you and makes you uncomfortable
- pays no attention to you when you say *no* or *stop*
- tries to touch you when you do not want to be touched or says suggestive things to you
- pushes you to do sexual things you do not want to do

Some drugs, known as "date rape" drugs, can make you an easy victim. Don't swallow any unknown substance, and watch your drink at parties and clubs.

If someone tries to rape you, do whatever you need to do to protect your life. Each situation is different; use your common sense to decide what to do. Escape as soon as you can and don't believe what a rapist tells you.

All rape victims should seek medical treatment immediately. Reporting a rape is not easy. Recalling the event can be extremely painful. Most police departments, however, have police officers who specialize in helping rape victims. Many communities have hotlines and **rape crisis centers**, agencies that provide counseling and support for rape victims.

A **stalker** is someone who repeatedly calls, writes letters to, or otherwise harasses the victim and may threaten to kill or injure the person. If you are stalked, notify the police. New laws can help protect you from a stalker.

Figure 28-19 *Rape crisis centers provide support for rape victims.*

Crime Prevention Programs

You can help reduce crime in general by taking part in organized crime-prevention programs in your community. In some communities, volunteers have formed **Neighborhood Crime Watch** groups who report any suspicious activities they see to the police. Some communities also have block parents, who provide a safe place for children who feel threatened on the street.

Operation Identification is a nationwide program to encourage marking personal property. Your local police department can provide you with marking materials and a decal to post in your window, which may prevent a burglary. Many police departments have special crime prevention officers who can advise you.

LESSON 4 REVIEW

1. What is the basic safety guideline you should follow to prevent assault or reduce the likelihood of serious injury?
2. List four steps you can take to prevent assault when you are home by yourself.
3. How can you reduce your chances of being assaulted when you are away from home?
4. How can a person reduce the chances of being raped in a dating situation?

What Do You Think?

5. Suppose you had a weekend job working until midnight at a restaurant about a mile from your house. How would you get home each night? What safety precautions would you take?

Analyzing Risks and Benefits

LaToya's friends invited her to go skating with them in the city park. She had never done it before, but everyone said it was fun and that she would catch on quickly. LaToya wanted to go, but she worried about getting hurt just before basketball season started. Should she take the risk?

The risk may be worth taking if LaToya decides that there is a benefit greater than the possible harm. For example, skiing is another activity that involves some risk of injury. Many people decide that skiing is worth the risk, however, because it is enjoyable and healthy. They also realize that there are ways they can reduce the risks involved.

Making responsible decisions about behaviors is a sign of maturity. It shows that you are beginning to take control of your own well-being. Learning to think about the possible effects of your actions may be difficult, but it is an important thing to do. How can you analyze the risks and benefits of an action you might take? The guidelines that follow will help you.

1. Identify the possible risks involved in taking this action

A risk is a possible harmful outcome or consequence of taking a certain action. These negative consequences may be physical, emotional, legal, or social.

• Identify all the possible negative consequences of taking this action. Write them on a chart like the one on the next page.

• Determine if any of these negative consequences are likely to cause a serious injury.

• Rate the likelihood of these negative consequences happening, from 1 for highly likely to 5 for very unlikely.

2. Identify the possible benefits of taking this action

• Identify all the possible positive consequences of taking this action.

• Rate the importance of these benefits to you, from 1 for very important to 5 for not very important.

3. Determine what you could do to reduce the risk of injury

• Consider how certain factors might reduce the degree of risk

including the likelihood of risks occurring, the importance of the benefits to you, and strategies for reducing the risk of injury.

- Ask yourself if the benefits outweigh the risks for you.
- Decide whether or not to take the action.

Apply the Skill

1. Review LaToya's situation. What are all the possible risks involved in going skating? What are the possible benefits? What are some other strategies she could use to reduce the risks and increase the benefits of doing this activity? What decision would you make after weighing the risks and benefits in this situation?

2. Consider a recent action you have taken and analyze it for risks and benefits using the steps described here. What things could you have done to minimize the possible risks and increase the benefits?

involved and maximize the benefits. For example:

Knowledge and awareness: LaToya could find out if the place where they are planning to rent the equipment rents protective equipment like wrist, elbow, and knee guards. She could find out what skating route has the fewest hills or pedestrians.

Ability: LaToya could take a lesson in in-line skating before she goes off with her friends.

State of mind: LaToya could make sure she is well rested and not under the influence of alcohol or any other drugs when she tries skating.

Environmental conditions: LaToya could agree to go only if it had not been raining, so the paths wouldn't be slippery, or if her friends would stop skating before it got dark.

- Design a strategy you could follow to reduce the risks involved in taking the action.

• • • • • • • • • • • • • • • • • • •

4. Determine if the benefits outweigh the risks

- Compare and analyze your chart of risks and benefits,

Action	Risks— Possible Negative Consequences	Likelihood of Event Happening Rate 1–5 1 = high 5 = low	Strategies for Reducing Risks	Benefits— Possible Positive Consequences	Importance of Benefits to You Rate 1–5 1 = high 5 = low
Go in-line skating with friends	• Injure a bone, muscle, or joint • Can't play basketball • Look foolish	• 3 • 3 • 4	• Wear padding • Take a lesson • Be well rested • Don't involve alcohol or drugs	• Learn a new skill • Have fun with friends	• 3 • 1
Decision:					

CHAPTER 28 REVIEW

KEY IDEAS

LESSON 1

- Knowledge and awareness, ability, state of mind, and environmental conditions are the four main factors to consider when trying to prevent or lessen the effects of unintentional injuries.
- The leading causes of unintentional death in the home are falls, fire, poisoning, suffocation, firearms, and drowning.

LESSON 2

- The Occupational Safety and Health Administration is the U.S. government agency that identifies hazards in the workplace and sets standards for safety.
- The four basic safety guidelines for recreational activities are to learn and apply proper skills; to have appropriate, well-maintained equipment; to know the safety rules; and to prepare adequately.

LESSON 3

- The human factor, the use of alcohol and other drugs, the condition of the vehicle, and driving conditions are the main elements contributing to motor-vehicle crashes.
- When riding a bicycle, always wear a helmet and ride with the flow of traffic. Be sure to keep the bicycle in good repair.

LESSON 4

- To lessen the chances of being assaulted, keep doors and windows locked at home, and do not let strangers in. Outside, avoid deserted places, and walk with someone.
- To avoid rape, do not allow yourself to be alone with anyone who shows little respect for you. In a rape situation, do not put your life at risk.

KEY TERMS

LESSON 1
blizzard
disaster
earthquake
electrocution
flammable material
flash flood
hurricane
Poison Control Center

risk behavior
safe behavior
suffocation
tornado

LESSON 2
capsizing
occupational illness
occupational injury
survival floating

LESSON 4
assault
Neighborhood Crime Watch
Operation Identification
rape
rape crisis center
stalker

Listed above are some of the important terms in this chapter. Choose the term from the list that best matches each phrase below.

1. place where a person can obtain information about how to treat a poisoning victim

2. any abnormal condition or disorder, excluding injuries, caused by exposure to environmental factors in the workplace

3. action that protects a person from danger or lessens the effects of a harmful situation

4. unlawful attempt to harm someone

5. place that helps sexual assault victims

6. lifesaving water safety technique

7. death from exposure to electricity

8. substance that can catch fire easily or burn quickly

9. program of observing and reporting suspicious activities to the police

10. obstruction of a person's breathing

WHAT HAVE YOU LEARNED?

Choose the letter of the answer that best completes each statement.

11. A storm with heavy rains and winds over 74 miles per hour is a(n)
a. tornado   **c.** earthquake
b. blizzard   **d.** hurricane

12. A storm with heavy snow and strong winds is a(n)
a. hurricane   **c.** earthquake
b. tornado   **d.** blizzard

13. The overturning of a boat is called
a. drowning   **c.** capsizing
b. survival floating   **d.** flotation

14. The group of drivers who are involved in the greatest number of car crashes is
a. males 15–24   **c.** males 24–35
b. females 15–24   **d.** females 24–35

15. If your home is on fire, you should first
a. gather your belongings
b. leave immediately
c. telephone the fire department
d. go back in to help

16. A young child who plays with a plastic bag could
a. be suffocated   **c.** drown
b. be electrocuted   **d.** be poisoned

17. The major factor that contributes to accidents with two-wheeled motor vehicles is
a. mechanical breakdown
b. not using safety belts
c. human error
d. mental and physical health

Answer each of the following with complete sentences.

18. Why can all-terrain vehicles be dangerous?

19. What safety behaviors can you practice in your home to prevent injuries due to falling?

20. Where can a rape victim go for help?

21. How do emergency management authorities notify people during a disaster?

22. Give one example each of occupational injury and occupational illness.

23. What safety precautions would you take before riding a motorcycle or a moped?

24. What should you do if you see a crime?

25. How can you discourage burglars?

WHAT DO YOU THINK?

26. Which safe behaviors are the most important ones when caring for an infant?

27. Explain how alcohol or drug use on board a boat can endanger everyone on the boat and in the surrounding waters.

28. The sale of three-wheel ATVs has been banned in the United States because of the high rates of death and injury associated with their use. Do you think that the three-wheel ATVs already sold should be recalled? Why or why not?

29. Suppose you have just bought a new electric saw. You have been using electric saws for years. Should you read the instruction manual before you use it? Why or why not?

WHAT WOULD YOU DO?

30. Falls are especially hazardous for older adults. Suppose your grandmother was going to move into your home. What changes would you make to ensure her safety?

31. If a friend invited you to go on a day-long bicycle trip, how would you prepare for it?

32. List the kind of information your class would need to plan a safe camping trip.

Getting Involved

33. Develop a series of public safety service announcements for use in your school that discuss some of the safety issues addressed in this chapter.

34. Contact your local fire department and find out how your household can plan a fire escape route. Following these guidelines, plan the escape route with your family and practice it so that all family members understand what to do.

THE IMPORTANCE OF FIRST AID

GUIDE FOR READING

Focus on these questions as you read this lesson.

- What is first aid?
- Why is it important to learn first-aid techniques?

SKILLS

- Locating Community Resources

In an emergency, you may have only seconds to save a life. The only person you may have to depend on is yourself. **First aid** is the immediate care given to a victim of injury or sudden illness before professional medical help arrives. **Properly administered first aid can prevent or reduce pain and the long-term effects of an injury—in some cases it can mean the difference between life and death.** Many of the people killed or injured in accidents each year could have been helped if someone had recognized that an emergency existed and given first aid.

Guidelines for First Aid

There are many different types of emergencies. A car skids off an icy road, hitting a tree, and someone is injured; the result is an emergency. You are eating in a busy restaurant, and a person at the next table begins to choke. This, too, is an emergency. Other emergency situations may not be as obvious. For instance, the signals of a heart attack or stroke are not always clear. It may be difficult to tell if someone is behaving strangely, especially if you do not know the person.

Whatever the emergency, there are certain procedures you should follow when you react to the situation.

CHECK THE SCENE AND THE VICTIM

- Assess the situation and the immediate environment for possible dangers to you and the victim. Never put your own safety at risk when you are trying to rescue a person or perform first aid.

- Determine whether or not the individual is conscious by tapping him or her on the shoulder and shouting, "Are you OK?" If the individual does not respond, send someone to call the local emergency number immediately. If you are alone, position the person on his or her side and make the call yourself. Return quickly to care for the person until the ambulance arrives.

- Check whether or not the person is breathing and has a pulse. You will learn these procedures later in this chapter. If there are no signs of breathing or a pulse, or if there is severe bleeding, care for these conditions first because they are life-threatening.

- Examine the individual's body from head to toe. Do not stop after finding one injury. Look for a Medic Alert tag around the neck, wrist, or ankle. This tag, which is shown in Figure 29-1, provides information about medical problems.

Figure 29-1 *A Medic Alert tag provides useful medical information about the person wearing it.*

Figure 29-2 *Emergency personnel are trained to help victims of all types of injuries.*

CALL THE EMERGENCY NUMBER   Call or send someone to call for an ambulance. Calling your emergency number is often the most important thing you can do in an emergency. It is often critical to get professional medical help on the scene as soon as possible. In many communities, you can dial 911 for help in any type of emergency. Otherwise, dial your local seven-digit phone number for medical emergencies or dial 0, the operator, for assistance. Be prepared to follow the steps given below.

- Speak slowly and clearly.
- Identify yourself and the phone number from which you are calling.
- Give the exact location of the accident. Give the town, street name, and number. If you are calling at night, describe the building.
- Describe what has happened. Give essential details about the victim(s), the situation, and any treatments you have given.
- Ask for advice. Let the person on the other end ask you questions and tell you what to do until help arrives. Take notes, if necessary.
- Hang up last. The person on the other end may have more questions or advice for you. Let the other person hang up first.

When to Call 911 or Your Local Emergency Number

Call for an ambulance if the victim

- Is or becomes unconscious
- Has trouble breathing
- Has persistent chest pain or pressure
- Is bleeding severely
- Has persistent pain or pressure in the abdomen
- Is vomiting
- Has seizures, slurred speech, or persistent severe headache
- Appears to have been poisoned
- Has injuries to the head, neck, or back
- Has possible broken bones

Also call if there is

- A fire or explosion
- A downed electrical wire
- Swiftly moving or rapidly rising water
- Poisonous gas present
- A vehicle collision

Figure 29-3 *Do you know when to call your local emergency number?*

Figure 29-4 *You should be prepared to deal with all types of emergencies.*

GIVE CARE

- Monitor the person's condition. Watch for changes in the person's breathing and consciousness. Continue to give care until medical help arrives.
- Do not move the person unless there are nearby dangers, such as fire, poisonous gases, or downed power lines.
- Help the person rest comfortably.
- Keep the person from getting overheated or chilled.

As the first person on the scene of an accident, you need to identify the injuries, give emergency treatment, contact the proper rescue personnel, and prevent further injury. If the victim is conscious, identify yourself as someone who has some first-aid training and ask for permission to give care. If the person is unconscious, or is a small child, you may assume that you have permission.

It is also important to keep an injured or ill person calm. You can reassure an individual through your words and actions. Demonstrate that you are in control of the situation and that you know what you are doing.

The Good Samaritan Law

Sometimes complications occur even when first aid has been administered properly. To protect the rescuer, most states have enacted a **Good Samaritan law.** This law protects

Signals of an Emergency	
Things You See:	**Things You Smell:**
Smoke or fire Broken glass An overturned pot Downed electrical wires	Unrecognizable odors Odors that are particularly strong
Things You Hear:	**Other:**
Screams, moans, or calls for help Crashing metal, breaking glass, screeching tires Sudden, loud noises	Clutching the chest or throat Difficulty breathing Blurred vision Unexplainable confusion or drowsiness Slurred speech Unusual skin color

Figure 29-5 *Be alert to the signals of an emergency.*

people from lawsuits if medical complications arise after they have administered first aid correctly. If someone's life is in danger and you are knowledgeable, you should give first aid. If the person is conscious, always ask for permission to help. Be sure, however, that your help will not harm the individual. Stay with the basics. If you are not sure of a procedure, you probably should not try it.

First-aid courses and regular refresher classes are the best way to become prepared for any emergency. A first-aid class provides you with the opportunity to practice basic skills and build confidence in your knowledge and abilities. Contact the local branch of the American Red Cross or the American Heart Association to find out about the first-aid and CPR classes offered in your area. Often local police departments, fire departments, schools, community colleges, and organizations like the YMCA and YWCA offer classes in first aid.

SHARPEN YOUR *SKILLS*

Locating Community Resources

Make a list of emergency phone numbers your family might need. Find out the numbers and post the list near each telephone in your home. Include numbers for police, fire, ambulance, poison control center, and any others you think are important.

LESSON 1 REVIEW

1. What is first aid? Why is it important to be able to perform first aid?
2. What information should you provide in an emergency phone call?
3. What is the purpose of Good Samaritan laws?

What Do You Think?

4. How would you react if you were the first person on the scene of an accident? What feelings and thoughts would run through your mind?

Focus on these questions as you read this lesson.
- What six life-threatening emergencies must you treat before any other injury?
- How should you respond to these emergencies?

SKILLS

- Using Medicines Correctly

2 FIRST-AID PRIORITIES

One of the basic principles of first aid is that some injuries must be treated before others. **Life-threatening situations—respiratory emergencies, heart attack or cardiac arrest, stroke, severe bleeding, poisoning, and shock—must be treated before any other injury.** After these problems are under control, look for other injuries.

Respiratory Emergencies

When breathing stops, the body's cells quickly run out of oxygen and begin to die. This is especially dangerous to the brain cells. Permanent brain damage usually takes place four to six minutes after breathing has stopped.

BREATHING FAILURE You can recognize total breathing failure by the absence of breathing movements or a bluish color to the lips, tongue, and fingernails. If a person stops breathing, you should perform rescue breathing immediately. **Rescue breathing** is a method of inflating a person's lungs with air from your lungs. It is done by blowing air slowly into the individual's mouth or nose or both. Each breath should last long enough to make the chest rise gently.

Figure 29-6 *The steps of rescue breathing.*

A. Open airway by tipping head back while lifting jaw

B. Look, listen, and feel for breathing

C. With head tipped back, pinch the nose closed

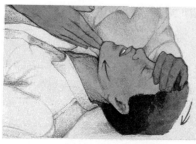

D. Form an airtight seal with your mouth over the victim's mouth and give 2 slow breaths until the chest rises

E. Check for a pulse by placing 2 fingers on the side of the neck and feeling for rhythmic pulsations

F. If there is a pulse, give one breath about every five seconds for adults, 1 breath about every 4 seconds for children, or 1 breath about every 3 seconds for infants

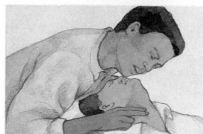

CHOKING   When food or some other object becomes lodged in the throat or airway, it can cause choking. The person may gasp for breath, have violent fits of coughing, or be unable to talk or cough forcefully. The person may become pale, then blue, or even unconscious.

If a choking individual can speak or cough loudly, you should encourage the person to keep coughing. Do not interfere with the person's attempts to dislodge the object. If the person cannot speak and is coughing weakly or not at all, perform the **Heimlich maneuver** (HYM lik). The Heimlich maneuver is a technique that uses abdominal thrusts to dislodge the object blocking an individual's airway. It is such an important procedure that laws in many places require restaurants to display a poster showing how to perform it. Some states require that restaurants have an employee on the premises at all times who knows how to perform the Heimlich maneuver. Building Health Skills on pages 718–719 describes how to apply this technique.

Heart Attack and Stroke

The failure of a person's heart or circulatory system to function properly often causes a life-threatening situation. A common cause is that the heart's normal blood supply is blocked, as in a **heart attack**, or that the heart stops, as in **cardiac arrest**. Other causes include a break in a blood vessel, a drug overdose, poisoning, and electrical shock. When the circulatory system fails, immediate action is necessary to prevent brain damage.

Figure 29-7 *In CPR, alternate rescue breathing with chest compressions.*

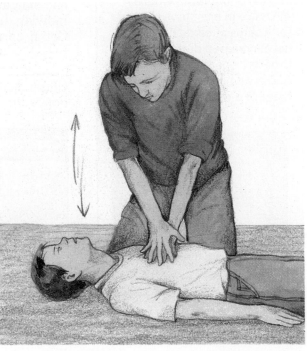

New Hope for Cardiac Arrest Victims

In 1966 an electric-shocking device was introduced to help victims of cardiac arrest. Called a defibrillator, it is used to analyze the heart's rhythm and provide an electric shock to help restore the rhythm.

Defibrillators have saved many lives. Unfortunately, their use requires specialized training. Now a new Automatic External Defibrillator, or AED, is available.

When the older defibrillators are used, an advanced medical professional must analyze the heart rhythm. With the new AED, a computer chip analyzes the heart rhythm and determines whether a shock is needed.

The advantage of the AED is that it requires little training. In communities where AEDs are in use, survival rates for victims of cardiac arrest have increased dramatically. Experts hope that eventually AEDs will be available to all types of emergency personnel.

CARDIAC ARREST   Cardiac arrest, or failure of the heart to beat, can be recognized by the absence of a pulse. When a person's heart stops beating, breathing automatically ceases. **Cardiopulmonary resuscitation** (kahr dee oh PUL muh nehr ee rih suhs uh TAY shun) can keep the individual alive. Cardiopulmonary resuscitation is a procedure that uses both chest compressions and rescue breathing to keep oxygen-rich blood circulating to the brain. As shown in Figure 29-7, a rescuer alternates rescue breathing with a series of chest compressions. CPR is done until professional medical help arrives and can provide more advanced care. The combination of prompt CPR and more advanced care saves thousands of lives every year. If you want to learn CPR, check with your local chapters of the American Red Cross or the American Heart Association. They frequently offer courses in this life-saving technique.

The most common cause of cardiac arrest is a heart attack, which results from a block in an artery that supplies the heart with oxygen-rich blood. Symptoms of a heart attack include persistent chest pain, sweating, shortness of breath, and nausea. In caring for a heart attack, you should follow the guidelines given in Figure 29-8.

STROKE   A **stroke** occurs when a blood vessel in the brain ruptures, or breaks, or when a blood clot forms and blocks the flow of blood in the brain. A person who has suffered a stroke may show some or all of the following signs: paralysis on one side of the body, pupils of unequal size, dizziness, difficulty in breathing, slurred speech, mental confusion, or loss of consciousness.

If a person has had a stroke, gently place the person on one side and cover him or her with a blanket. Monitor the individual's breathing, as rescue breathing may be necessary. Get medical help as soon as possible.

Figure 29-8 *Begin care for a heart attack as soon as you notice the signals.*

Care for a Heart Attack

- Have the victim rest in a comfortable position. Sitting may make it easier for the victim to breathe.

- Call for an ambulance immediately. If possible, contact the victim's physician.

- If the victim takes heart medication, such as nitroglycerin, help administer it. If in doubt and if possible, consult with the victim's physician.

- Monitor the victim's condition. Rescue breathing or CPR may be necessary.

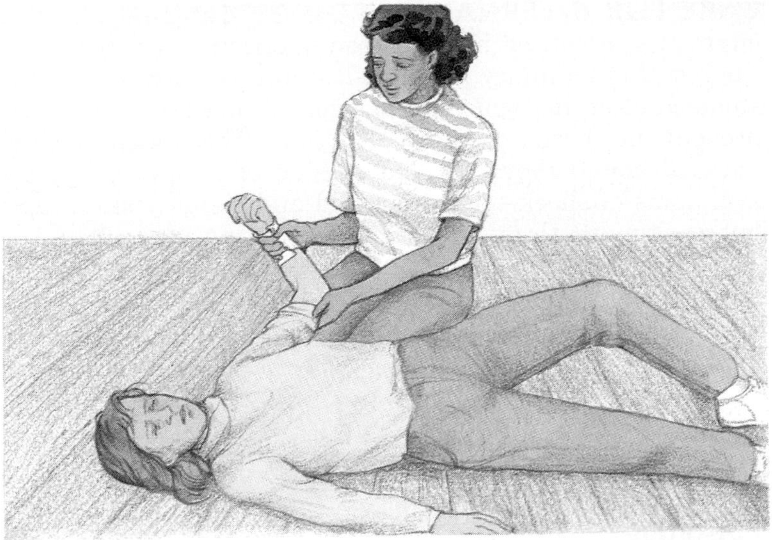

Figure 29-9 *To control bleeding, apply pressure on the wound and raise the injured arm or leg above the heart.*

Severe Bleeding

Severe bleeding, or **hemorrhage** (HEM uh rij), can result in shock and death if not treated promptly. The severity of bleeding depends upon the size of the injured blood vessels. The larger the vessel, the more blood it carries, and the more severe the bleeding will be.

STEPS FOR CONTROLLING BLEEDING   The procedure for controlling severe bleeding is the same no matter what kind of blood vessel is affected. It is a good idea, however, to avoid direct contact with the individual's blood when performing the procedure. This will prevent the transmission of any infectious disease either you or the injured person is carrying. You should wear plastic or latex gloves, a sheet of plastic, or many layers of absorbent cloth when following the steps given below.

1. Apply pressure against the wound with a **dressing**, a clean, absorbent cloth usually made of gauze. If blood begins to soak through a dressing, do not remove it. Apply another dressing on top of it.

2. Apply a bandage snugly, using overlapping turns with a roll of gauze. A bandage applied in this manner is called a **pressure bandage.** Most bleeding, even severe bleeding, can be stopped by applying pressure and raising the injured arm or leg as shown in Figure 29-9.

3. If the bleeding still does not stop, apply pressure to the **pressure point**, the point at which the injured artery lies near the skin surface and passes over a bone above the injury. Figure 29-10 shows the four major pressure points. Apply pressure with the flat parts of your fingers or palm at the appropriate pressure point until the ambulance arrives.

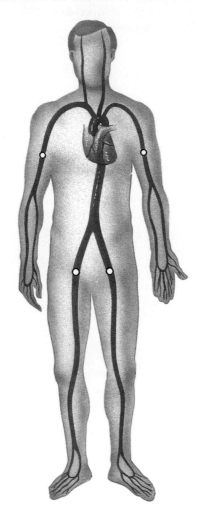

Figure 29-10 *The four major pressure points.*

CARE FOR INTERNAL BLEEDING Internal bleeding often goes unnoticed if the person is unconscious. It may be the result of an injury or a physical illness, such as a severe stomach ulcer. Recognizing the signs of internal bleeding can prevent life-threatening complications. These signs include pain, although there may be no sign of injury, and/or the symptoms of shock—paleness, cold and clammy skin, rapid but weak pulse, thirst, nausea, and vomiting.

If you suspect internal bleeding, keep the person quiet and lying down. If the person is unconscious, is vomiting, or feels nauseous, place him or her on the side with the head turned to one side to prevent choking. Call the emergency number for an ambulance immediately.

Poisoning

Poisoning is the effect of one or more harmful substances on the body. Poisons can be swallowed, inhaled, injected, or absorbed through the skin. Once in the body, a poison may damage or destroy the body's cells and tissues, cause severe discomfort or pain, disrupt normal body functions, and in some cases cause death.

ORAL POISONING Oral poisoning occurs when a harmful substance, such as a household cleaner, a medication, or a poisonous plant, is swallowed. Some common signs of oral poisoning are listed in Figure 29-11. If a person shows signs of oral poisoning, you must act quickly.

First aid for oral poisoning depends on the substance swallowed. Call a poison control center or your local emergency number immediately. Give all the information you have to the poison control expert and follow the instructions that you are given. If the person is unconscious and breathing has stopped, apply rescue breathing through the individual's nose to avoid contact with any poison that may be on the mouth. Get medical help as quickly as possible.

Figure 29-11 *Do you know the signs of oral poisoning?*

Signs of Oral Poisoning

- Sudden, severe abdominal pain
- Nausea or vomiting
- Chemical burns on the lips and mouth
- Drowsiness followed by unconsciousness
- Dilated or constricted pupils
- Chemical odor on the breath
- Presence nearby of a container of a poisonous substance

INHALATION POISONING   Poisoning by gases or fumes causes over 2,000 deaths each year in the United States. Poisonous gases include carbon monoxide, chlorine, and the fumes from certain glues, paints, and petroleum-based fuels and solvents.

Carbon monoxide, a frequent cause of inhalation poisoning, is a tasteless, colorless, odorless gas. It forms when fuels such as gasoline or kerosene are burned incompletely. Carbon monoxide poisoning can occur whenever there is poor ventilation and a source of carbon monoxide, such as the exhaust from an automobile. The poisoning occurs rapidly. Although the person usually experiences dizziness or a headache before becoming unconscious, he or she often does not realize what is happening. Fresh air is vital to the victim of inhalation poisoning, but you, as the rescuer, must protect yourself first. If it is not safe to approach the scene, stay at a safe distance. If you encounter a situation involving inhalation poisoning, follow these steps.

1. Protect your own safety first. If the area is not safe, retreat and call the local emergency number immediately.

2. Once it is safe, quickly remove the victim from the area.

3. If the victim is unconscious, tilt the head back and check for breathing and pulse. Give rescue breathing or CPR if necessary.

4. If the victim is conscious, loosen clothing around the neck and waist. Watch the victim's breathing. If the victim's breathing stops, apply rescue breathing.

CONTACT POISONING   Poisons that come in contact with the skin may affect only the area touched by the poison or the entire body. Solvents, pesticides, and plants, such as poison ivy, poison oak, and poison sumac, are common

Figure 29-12 *Car exhaust is a source of carbon monoxide.*

sources of contact poisons. Learning to recognize poisonous plants is the first step in avoiding contact with them. Study Figure 29-13 to become familiar with the characteristics of poison ivy, poison oak, and poison sumac.

Although some people do not react to these poisonous plants, people who are affected develop a severe rash on areas of the skin touched by the plant. Swelling, blisters, burning, and itching are typical symptoms that usually occur a day or two after contact. In severe cases a person may develop a fever for several days.

To treat any type of contact poisoning, remove any contaminated clothing and flush the affected area with large amounts of water. If a rash develops, apply calamine lotion to reduce itching. In cases of severe irritation, inflammation, and pain, contact a doctor. If the poisoning is from a solvent, pesticide, or other chemical, follow the treatment given for chemical burns on page 709.

Shock

Any serious injury or illness can be accompanied by shock. **Shock** is a condition in which the heart fails to circulate blood adequately to the vital organs. Consequently, the amount of oxygen reaching the body cells becomes less than normal. The more severe the injury, the more likely that shock will develop. Even if the injury or illness itself is not immediately life-threatening, shock can lead to death.

The early signs of shock include restlessness, thirst, pale skin, and a rapid, weak heartbeat. The person going into shock may appear calm and tired. The individual may begin sweating, making the skin feel cool and clammy to the touch. As shock progresses, the individual begins to breathe in small, fast breaths or gasps, even if the airway is clear. He or she may stare vacantly into space and become unresponsive. Eventually, the individual will become unconscious. Giving care for the specific condition and calling for an ambulance is the best care you can give to minimize shock.

LESSON 2 REVIEW

1. List six life-threatening situations.
2. In a respiratory emergency, how do you open a victim's airway?
3. What is the general procedure for controlling bleeding?
4. What are some signs of oral poisoning?

What Do You Think?

5. At what age should people take a course in first aid?

3 COMMON EMERGENCIES

GUIDE FOR READING

Focus on these questions as you read this lesson.

- What are some common injuries that require first aid?
- What kinds of first aid should you give for these injuries?

SKILLS

- Activity: Making a First-Aid Kit

Suppose a friend of yours complained of being dizzy, and then fainted. What would you do? What if you began having a nosebleed? Would you know what to do? **Injuries requiring first aid, including fractures, sprains, burns, nosebleeds, objects in the eye, and others, happen frequently.** Although these injuries are not usually life-threatening, they still require prompt first aid.

Bone, Joint, and Muscle Injuries

Bone, joint, and muscle injuries, although usually not life-threatening, require proper first aid to prevent further injury and increase the chances for a speedy recovery. As you know, these injuries should be treated only after life-threatening conditions have been handled.

FRACTURES   A break or crack in a bone is a **fracture.** There are two types of fractures. In a **closed fracture,** the broken bone does not push through the skin's surface. Although the skin's surface is not broken, the tissue beneath the skin may be damaged. If a fracture involves an open wound, such as when a broken end of a bone pierces the skin, the fracture is called an **open fracture.** An open fracture may bleed heavily and can become infected.

Fractures may or may not be easy to detect, depending on the type and location of the break. An X-ray, like the one in Figure 29-14, is the only sure way to diagnose a fracture. At the scene of an accident, however, you will not have an X-ray, so you should be able to recognize some of the common symptoms of fractures. These include deformity, such as crookedness; swelling; discoloration (black and blue); a grating sound; exposed bone; inability to use or move the part; and severe pain. Sometimes there is a cracking sound at the time of injury.

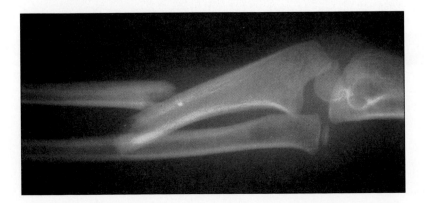

Figure 29-14 *X-rays can detect both open and closed fractures.*

Figure 29-15 *Splints help to immobilize a broken bone and to prevent further injury.*

Figure 29-16 *In treating a strain, when would you use heat?*

To care for a possible fracture, you should follow the steps given below.

1. If the fracture is open, stop the bleeding. Using a dressing, apply pressure around the bone end that is piercing the skin. DO NOT put pressure directly on the bone. DO NOT attempt to push the bone back through the skin.

2. Immobilize the injured area. If you do not have to move the individual, support the fracture site between your two hands and caution the individual not to move it. Keep the region immobilized until medical help arrives. Do not move the individual unless it is essential in order to get medical attention or it is necessary to escape further danger. Not moving the victim is especially important if there is any chance the spine has been injured.

If you must move the individual, apply a splint. A **splint** is any rigid material that is used to keep the injured part from moving. Splints can be rigid, soft, or anatomic. You can make splints from boards, folded newspapers, a pillow, a folded blanket, or a towel. An anatomic splint involves using another part of the body to immobilize an injured part. You are using an anatomic splint when you tape an injured finger to an uninjured one or when you bind an injured arm to the chest with a wide, folded triangular bandage.

Attach the splints so that the joints above and below the broken bone cannot move, as shown in Figure 29-15. Secure the splint at several points above and below the site of injury. Be sure the material used as a tie does not limit circulation and that the knots are on the splint, not on the injured limb. Check circulation by feeling for warmth and color in the fingers or toes.

SPRAINS AND STRAINS   When ligaments or tendons near a joint are torn or stretched, the injury is called a **sprain. Ligaments** are the fibrous bands of tissue that prevent the bones from popping apart at a joint. **Tendons** are thick strands of tissue that connect muscles to bones.

Sprains often result from violently twisting a joint. They frequently affect ankles, wrists, and knees. Sprains present some of the same signs and symptoms as fractures: pain on movement, swelling, and discoloration. If the pain and

Care for Sprains and Strains	
Sprains	**Strains**
1. Apply cold packs to the area.	**1.** Rest the injured part.
2. Elevate the injured part.	**2.** For a back strain, apply moist heat. For other strains, elevate the injured area and apply cold packs.
3. Do not use or walk on the injured part if doing so causes pain.	**3.** Get medical help, especially if pain persists.

MAKING A FIRST-AID KIT

In this activity you will make a basic first-aid kit for your home.

Materials

Container: small tote bag or box with cover

Dressings: adhesive bandages in assorted sizes, butterfly bandages, sterile gauze pads (4″ x 4″), sterile nonstick pads, gauze roller bandages (2″ wide), elastic bandage (3″ wide), surgical adhesive tape (1″), triangular bandage, sterile eyepatches, and sterile cotton balls

Instruments: blunt-tipped scissors, tweezers, bulb syringe, and thermometer

Medicines: antiseptic wipes or antiseptic solution (like hydrogen peroxide), antibiotic ointment, antiseptic spray, calamine/antihistamine lotion, sterile eye wash, and syrup of ipecac

Miscellaneous supplies: cotton-tipped swabs, chemical cold compresses, eye cup or small plastic cup, packet of tissues, soap, safety pins, disposable latex gloves, pad and pencil, candle and matches, space blanket, and first-aid manual

Procedure

1. Look at home for a first-aid kit. If you have one, survey the materials you already have to determine what is missing.

2. Gather all the necessary materials to complete a basic first-aid kit. Purchase any that you do not already have.

3. Put the first-aid kit together in a container and label it.

4. Decide where the first-aid kit will be kept. Let everyone in your family know where it is, and describe what everything in the kit can be used for.

Discussion

1. What common household injuries can be taken care of by your first-aid kit?

2. How would you use your first-aid kit to stop minor bleeding? To dress a minor wound?

3. What other supplies might need to be added to a basic first-aid kit, depending on a family's special needs?

---

swelling remain severe, an X-ray should be taken to rule out the possibility of a fracture.

Overstretching a muscle or tendon often results in a **strain.** Back strains are commonly caused by lifting heavy objects incorrectly. The signals of a strain can include intense pain, slight swelling, and difficulty moving or using the affected part. Since the signs and symptoms of sprains and strains are similar to those for fractures, you should always treat the injury as if it were a fracture. Remember, an X-ray is the only sure way to know whether or not the injury involves a broken bone. Figure 29-16 summarizes the correct procedures to follow when treating sprains and strains.

DISLOCATION   A **dislocation** is a separation of the bone from its joint. People who participate in contact sports, such as football, often suffer dislocations. Common signs and symptoms include deformity, pain, and loss of function.

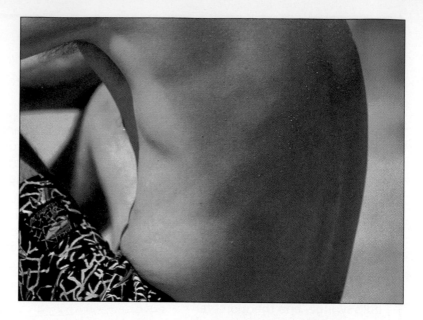

Figure 29-17 *Most sunburns are first-degree burns.*

If you suspect a dislocation, follow these steps.

1. Do not try to set the joint. Immobilize and support the affected part, as in the treatment for a fracture.

2. Apply cold packs to the injury to keep swelling down.

3. Seek immediate medical attention.

Burns

A burn is an injury caused by exposure to hot liquids, chemicals, electricity, fire, or the sun's rays. Burns are classified according to the degree of damage they cause. **First-degree burns** are surface burns in which the outer layer of the skin is reddened and painful. **Second-degree burns** extend through the outer layer of the skin, causing blisters and reddening. **Third-degree burns** damage all the layers of the skin and the tissues underneath. In these burns, the skin may look gray or charred. The three steps of burn care are to stop the burning, cool the burn, and cover the burn to prevent infection.

MINOR BURNS To treat a first-degree burn, such as a sunburn, apply cool water to the burned area until the pain decreases. For a small burn that is blistered, immerse it in cool water and then cover it with a clean dressing to prevent possible infection. Do not break any blisters.

SEVERE BURNS Medical attention is needed for severe burns in which the skin is blistered and charred; any burn affecting more than one body part; any burn affecting the hands, feet, head, or genitals; or any burn other than a very minor one that occurs to an infant or an elderly person. While waiting for medical help to arrive, you should take steps to prevent contamination and infection.

1. Stop the burning.

2. For as long as 15 minutes, cool the burn with lots of cool water.

3. Place a clean, dry dressing over the burned area. A clean sheet may be used if a dressing is not available. If pieces of clothing are stuck to the burn, do not try to remove them. Do not clean the burn in any way or break any blisters. DO NOT put any ointment or medication on the burn.

4. Monitor the person until the ambulance arrives.

CHEMICAL BURNS   When an irritating chemical comes in contact with the skin, it can burn the skin. Many common household products, such as bleach and ammonia, can cause chemical burns. Chemical burns need immediate treatment.

1. Have the victim remove clothing that has had the chemical spilled on it.

2. Flush the skin with cool water for at least 15 minutes, or until the ambulance arrives.

3. Call a poison control center or a doctor for specific instructions on how to treat the burn.

If a chemical has gotten into the eye, flush the eye with water immediately. As Figure 29-18 shows, hold the eyelid open and flood the eye with water from the nose outward for at least 15 minutes. Make sure that the chemical does not wash into the other eye. Cover the eye with a clean, dry dressing, and seek medical attention.

Figure 29-18 *When flooding the eye, be careful the chemical does not get into the other eye.*

Electrical Shock

When an electrical current passes through the body, **electrical shock** results. Even low-voltage currents, including those found in the home, may cause cardiac or respiratory failure. Electrical shock is not the same as shock caused by injury or illness.

Electrical shock can occur indoors or outside. Working or playing outside during an electrical storm can result in a high-voltage electrical shock by lightning. Coming into contact with downed "live" electric power lines can also result in a high-voltage electrical shock. Inside the home, electrical shock may happen when a person does not shut off the electricity before repairing electrical appliances. Using power tools or small appliances in wet areas also may result in electrical shock. Stay at a safe distance and call your emergency number immediately.

DO NOT touch a person who is in contact with an electric current. The current, which is passing through the person's body, will be passed on to you.

1. If the main switch is nearby, turn it off.

2. After you have turned off the current, start rescue breathing or CPR if needed.

3. Cover the burned area with a clean, dry dressing.

Nosebleeds

Nosebleeds can occur as a result of a blow or as the result of a cold, sinus infection, or dry air. During a nosebleed, the nose usually bleeds from one nostril. Minor nosebleeds seldom require medical attention. People who experience frequent nosebleeds should see a doctor. To treat a minor nosebleed, follow the steps given below.

1. Have the person sit in a chair, bend slightly forward as shown in Figure 29-19, pinch the nostrils together, and breathe through the mouth for about five minutes. A cold, wet towel placed across the bridge of the nose for five minutes may help.

2. If these procedures do not stop the bleeding, continue step 1 and seek medical attention.

Figure 29-19 *Most nosebleeds can be stopped by leaning forward and pinching the nostrils together.*

Hyperventilation

Hyperventilation (hy pur ven tl AY shun) is rapid, deep breathing, sometimes accompanied by dizziness, chest pains, and fainting, that lowers the level of carbon dioxide in the blood. Anxiety, emotional disturbance, or poor circulation to the brain are frequent causes of hyperventilation. The treatment for hyperventilation attempts to return the level of carbon dioxide in the blood to normal.

1. Attempt to keep the individual calm. Have the person sit down and lower his or her head.

2. Coach the individual to slow his or her breathing. You may have to breathe with the person. Try to have the person breathe into cupped hands, as shown in Figure 29-20, to help the carbon dioxide level in the blood return to normal.

3. If these efforts fail, seek medical attention.

Fainting

Fainting is a temporary loss of consciousness that is usually caused by too little blood flowing to the brain. Paleness, weakness, cold perspiration, and dizziness usually precede unconsciousness. An individual who faints usually regains consciousness within a few minutes. However, fainting may be caused by a more serious problem.

1. If someone complains of weakness and dizziness, have the individual lie down, sit down, or bend over and lower the head to increase the flow of blood to the brain.

2. If the person does faint, keep him or her lying down.

3. If the person does not recover within five minutes, call the emergency number for an ambulance.

4. While waiting for medical help, monitor the victim's condition in case rescue breathing is necessary.

Figure 29-20 *Breathing into cupped hands helps to restore carbon dioxide in the blood to normal levels.*

Convulsions

Convulsions are alternating periods of severe muscular contraction and relaxation. The jerking, twisting, wrenching movements during a convulsion may be accompanied by a loss of bladder or bowel control, chewing on the tongue and inner cheeks, and drooling. In infants and young children, convulsions sometimes accompany a high fever. Epilepsy, food poisoning, and other diseases, including malnutrition and infection, also can cause convulsions. Follow the steps described in Figure 29-21 in treating a person having convulsions.

Objects in the Eye

An eyelash, dust particle, or other foreign object in the eye can cause pain and irritation. Do not rub the eye, because further injury can result.

1. If the object is under the upper eyelid, grasp the eyelashes of the upper lid and pull the lid up and away until tears flow freely. The tears usually wash out the object.

2. If the particle is not washed out by tears, inspect the eyeball and look under the lower lid. Gently brush the object away with the moist, clean corner of a handkerchief.

3. If the object is not under the lower lid or on the eyeball, inspect the inside of the upper lid. To do this, grasp the eyelashes with the thumb and index finger, and place a small stick or swab over the lid. Pull the lid over the stick, as shown in Figure 29-22. Examine the inside of the lid while the person looks down. Gently remove the particle with the moist, clean corner of a handkerchief. Flood the eye with water.

4. If the pain and irritation continue, place a loose, dry, clean bandage over the eye and seek medical help.

If an object is embedded in the eyeball, DO NOT try to remove the object. Protect the injured eye and prevent it and the object from moving by covering *both* eyes and stabilizing the object with loose bandages. Get medical help as quickly as possible.

Steps For Treating Convulsions

1. Call the emergency number for an ambulance.

2. Protect the victim from further injury by placing a small folded towel beneath the head, removing any objects that may be nearby, loosening tight clothing, and clearing away furniture.

3. Do not restrain the victim. DO NOT put anything into the victim's mouth.

4. Watch the breathing, as rescue breathing may be necessary.

5. If the victim is unconscious after the convulsions have ended, turn on one side. Let the victim rest.

Figure 29-21 *First aid for convulsions is aimed at preventing injury.*

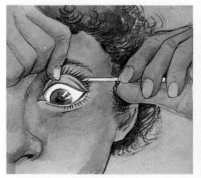 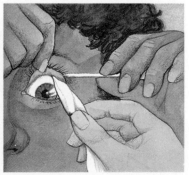

Figure 29-22 *If an object is lodged beneath the upper eyelid, pull the lid over a small stick or swab and remove the object with a moist, clean cloth.*

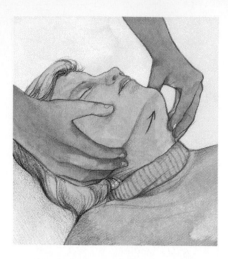

Figure 29-23 *To perform rescue breathing when a spinal injury is suspected, try lifting the jaw without tilting the head.*

Head Injuries

Scalp wounds are injuries to the surface of the head. A scalp wound may affect only the blood vessels supplying the scalp. Sometimes, however, scalp wounds are more serious and are accompanied by severe head injuries, such as skull fractures or brain injuries.

Most scalp wounds, even minor ones, bleed heavily because of the large number of blood vessels in the scalp. The first aid you offer should be directed toward stopping the bleeding as quickly as possible.

1. If there are no signs of a serious head or spine injury, elevate the victim's head and shoulders. Otherwise, leave the victim lying flat.

2. Apply a dressing directly to the wound.

3. Get medical help.

Fortunately, most head injuries are minor. The skull provides the brain with a great deal of protection. However, if the cause of the injury involves a collision or a fall from a height, always suspect a severe head injury. Look for the following signs: loss of consciousness, vomiting, slow breathing, convulsions, slurred speech, pupils of unequal size, memory loss, or blood or other fluid escaping from the nose or ears. If there is paralysis, or if the head or spine is in an unnatural position, the individual may have suffered a neck or spinal injury. If you suspect a neck or spinal injury, do not move the individual unless the person is in immediate danger.

For severe head injuries, care for any life-threatening conditions you find and call for an ambulance immediately. If rescue breathing is necessary, move the individual's head and neck as little as possible. Try to open the airway by pulling the person's jaw forward without tipping the head back, as shown in Figure 29-23. If you can't get air in, tip the head back until you can.

LESSON 3 REVIEW

1. Name six common injuries that may require first aid.
2. What is a splint?
3. On what basis are burns classified?
4. How do you stop a nosebleed?
5. If a spinal injury is suspected, what should you NOT do to the individual?

What Do You Think?

6. What would you say to calm an anxious burn victim while waiting for an ambulance?

4 OUTDOOR EMERGENCIES

In recent years, more and more people have begun to enjoy outdoor activities, such as hiking, camping, bicycle riding, and skiing. If you participate in these exciting and healthy activities, it is important for you to know how to handle any outdoor emergencies that may occur. **Emergencies that may occur outdoors include snakebites and other animal bites, stings, reactions to heat and cold, and water emergencies.** If you feel confident in your ability to handle these emergencies, you will enjoy your outdoor activities even more.

Snakebites

Coral snakes, rattlesnakes, copperheads, and water moccasins (cottonmouths) are poisonous snakes found in the United States. Coral snakes are members of the cobra family; rattlesnakes, copperheads, and water moccasins belong to the family of pit vipers. A person who has been bitten by a poisonous snake will experience swelling and pain soon after being bitten. Breathing difficulties, nausea, twitching, convulsions, and unconsciousness may occur shortly thereafter. If a person has been bitten and you do not know whether or not the snake was poisonous, you should treat the bite as if it were made by a poisonous snake.

1. Keep the individual calm and lying still. If the bite is on an arm or leg, keep the affected area still and below the level of the heart.

2. Wash the wound with soap and water.

3. Seek medical attention immediately. Individuals who have suffered poisonous snakebites must receive medical care promptly.

GUIDE FOR READING

Focus on these questions as you read this lesson.

- What are some injuries that occur outdoors?
- What kinds of first aid should you give for these injuries?

SKILLS

- DECIDE

GEOGRAPHY CONNECTION

Snakes are found virtually everywhere in the world except New Zealand, Ireland, Iceland, and some oceanic islands. Most snakes are harmless. Australia, however, has the most dangerous snake population in the world. Venomous snakes found there include death adders and taipans. Only a few species of snakes that live in Australia are harmless.

Figure 29-24 *Left to right: rattlesnake, copperhead, water moccasin, and coral snake.*

Other Bites and Stings

Although most other types of bites and stings are minor, some can be deadly. For this reason, it is important to know the correct treatment for them.

INSECT STINGS   Some people are allergic to the stings of certain insects, such as bees, hornets, and wasps. These people suffer severe reactions and can die in a short time. For people who are not allergic to insect stings, there will be some pain, redness, and itching.

1. Examine the sting site. If a stinger is embedded in the skin, gently scrape it off with your fingernail or the edge of a credit card. Do not pull the stinger out, as this may force more venom into the individual's body.

2. Wash the sting with soap and warm water. Then cover it with a clean cloth moistened with cold water.

3. Watch the individual for at least 30 minutes for signs of an allergic reaction.

If you know the individual is allergic to insect stings, or if the person has trouble breathing or experiences dizziness, nausea, stomach pains, or wheezing, call the emergency number for an ambulance or your health-care provider immediately. If necessary, begin rescue breathing.

ANIMAL BITES   The major concerns in animal bites are bleeding and infection. The bites of mammals, such as humans, dogs, cats, squirrels, rats, bats, and raccoons, can result in **tetanus**, a bacterial disease that can be fatal. Diseased animals may also carry **rabies**, a serious viral disease that can be passed to people. If possible, have the animal caught so that health authorities can examine it for rabies. Do not risk injury to do this.

1. Control severe bleeding, if necessary.

2. Wash the bite with soap and water.

3. Cover the wound with a dry, clean dressing.

4. Seek medical attention and notify the health department. Treatment for tetanus or rabies may be needed.

Drowning

Each year in this country, about 4,000 people drown. People drown for many reasons, including inability to swim, overestimation of swimming ability, and panicking in the water. Some people drown because they were swimming while under the influence of alcohol or drugs. Sometimes, a person may drown after suffering a heart attack, muscle cramps, or physical injury in the water. Small children can drown in water only a few inches deep, such as in a tub or toilet.

Figure 29-25 *Which of these rescue methods would you use to save a person from drowning?*

Help for Someone in Danger?

Early one morning, Keith went for a jog along the river near his house. As he ran, he noticed a lone boat on the river about half a mile ahead of him. The boat seemed to be having difficulties on the rough water.

As Keith got closer to the boat, he saw a person fall out of the boat into the river. Keith quickly glanced around, but did not see anybody else to help.

1. If you were Keith, what would you do in this situation? Explain your reasoning.

2. Would the DECIDE process on page 18 be helpful if you were really in a situation like this? Why or why not?

3. Would your decision be different if the drowning person was someone you knew? If there were other people around? Explain.

If a swimmer seems to be having trouble, assess the situation quickly. Then call loudly or send someone for help, and determine how you can rescue the person without risking your own safety. Reaching and throwing assists are best. Speed is essential.

1. To reach the victim, use one of the methods shown in Figure 29-25. If needed, begin rescue breathing.

2. If you can't get air into the lungs so that the chest rises, give up to five abdominal thrusts, sweep out the mouth, and attempt rescue breaths again. Repeat the sequence of breaths, thrusts, and a finger sweep until you can get air in. Once air goes in, continue rescue breathing.

3. If necessary, begin CPR.

Frostbite

When a person is exposed to cold temperatures for some period of time, **frostbite,** or the freezing of body tissue, may result. The body parts most easily frostbitten are the cheeks, nose, ears, hands, and feet. Frostbite can involve only the skin or extend deep beneath it. Frostbitten skin appears pale or grayish-yellow in color. It feels cold and numb. The frozen area feels doughy. In deep frostbite, the area is hard and solid. Blisters will appear on the skin within 24 hours.

1. Cover or wrap the frostbitten area with a blanket or clothing. Keep it dry.

Figure 29-26 *To treat frostbite, immerse the area in warm water until the skin becomes flushed.*

2. Bring the person indoors if possible.

3. Do not massage or rub the area. Immerse in warm, NOT hot, water (about 102°F) to heat it gradually, as shown in Figure 29-26. Do not permit the individual to stand or sit near a radiator, stove, or fire.

4. When the area becomes flushed, discontinue warming. Apply dry, clean bandages over and around the frostbitten area or part. As long as the feet are not involved, elevate the part that was frostbitten and have the individual exercise it. If the feet are affected, do not allow the victim to walk.

5. Seek medical attention immediately. This is especially important if deep tissue damage has occurred, as infection may result from it.

Hypothermia

Another hazard associated with exposure to cold temperatures is **hypothermia** (hy poh THUR mee uh). Hypothermia is a serious loss of body heat that causes the body temperature to fall well below normal. It can occur whenever and wherever the temperature is low—outdoors, in a shelter, or in water. Hypothermia is most common when temperatures are between 30°F and 50°F, when it is rainy and windy, and when a person is tired or run down. The signs of hypothermia include shivering, slurred speech, muscular weakness, excessive tiredness, slow breathing and pulse, confusion, drowsiness, and hallucinations. This condition can be fatal.

1. Check the person's breathing and heartbeat. If necessary, begin rescue breathing or CPR.

2. Call for an ambulance or send someone for medical help.

3. Bring the individual into a warm room. Remove wet clothing and dry the individual.

4. Warm the person slowly, using hot-water bottles wrapped in towels or clothing, warm blankets, the warmth of people's bodies, or other sources of heat. If the person is fully conscious, give him or her hot liquids to drink that do not contain caffeine or alcohol. Be careful that the hot liquid does not burn the individual.

5. Continue to monitor the individual's condition until help comes.

Heat Exhaustion

Participating in vigorous outdoor exercise, such as running or basketball, on a hot day may lead to a condition known as heat exhaustion. **Heat exhaustion** occurs when a person is exposed to excessive heat over a period of time. It is caused by the loss of water and salt from the body through excessive

Figure 29-27 *Avoid frostbite or hypothermia by dressing appropriately for outdoor activities in cold weather.*

perspiration. Symptoms can include headache, heavy sweating, weakness, dizziness, and muscle cramps. The skin may become pale and clammy. Heat exhaustion can occur either gradually or suddenly. Heat-related illnesses are progressive and can be life-threatening.

1. Move the individual into a cool, shaded area.

2. Loosen or remove wet clothing.

3. Cool the victim with cool, wet cloths and fanning.

4. If the individual is fully conscious, give a glass of cool water to sip. Should the individual become nauseated, vomit, or lose consciousness, call your emergency number for an ambulance immediately.

Heatstroke

Prolonged exposure to high heat may lead to a condition known as heatstroke. **Heatstroke,** also known as sunstroke, is a life-threatening emergency. When the signals of heat exhaustion are ignored, the result can be heatstroke.

The first sign of heatstroke may be a lack of perspiration. Other signs of heatstroke include high body temperature, reddened skin, and changes in consciousness. Unconsciousness may come suddenly or may be preceded by headache, dizziness, rapid pulse, nausea, vomiting, and mental confusion. A rescuer must take immediate action to cool the person's body.

1. Call the emergency number for an ambulance.

2. Move the person to a shaded area and remove clothing.

3. If possible, place the individual in a tub of cool water or a cool shower. If this is not possible, place ice packs in the groin, under the arms, and along the sides of the neck.

4. Monitor the person's condition. If the skin feels cool and has regained normal color, discontinue cooling.

Figure 29-28 *Heat exhaustion may occur after a person participates in vigorous exercise on a hot day.*

LESSON 4 REVIEW

1. List four emergencies that may occur outdoors.
2. How should you treat a bee sting? What should you do if the person is allergic to insect stings?
3. Under what weather conditions is hypothermia most likely to occur?
4. What are some symptoms of heatstroke? What action should you take to help a victim of heatstroke?

What Do You Think?

5. If you were going on a camping trip, what items would you include in a first-aid kit?

The Heimlich Maneuver

Suppose you were eating lunch with your friends, and someone started to choke on a piece of food. Would you know what was happening? How would you react?

You might be surprised to learn that choking is the sixth leading cause of accidental death in this country. Choking is an emergency situation—there is no time to call an ambulance. A choking person may die or suffer permanent brain damage within four minutes if the object is not dislodged.

In order to prevent a death from choking, you must be prepared to take immediate action. The American Red Cross and the American Heart Association recommend the Heimlich maneuver, also known as abdominal thrusts. The Heimlich maneuver works by using the air trapped in the lungs to force an obstruction out of the airway. If you master the steps of the Heimlich maneuver, given on these two pages, you may save the life of a choking person.

How would you react in a choking emergency?

1. Determine that the person is choking

Ask the person, "Are you choking?" If the person is unable to speak, cough or breathe, he or she may be choking. In addition, a choking person may

- be unable to cough or breathe, or may do so weakly
- turn white, blue, or red
- make the universal choking signal, shown below

2. Position yourself behind the person

Stand or kneel behind the person so that you can easily reach around the waist.

3. Position your hands on the person's abdomen

Make a fist with one hand and place the thumb side of the fist against the person's abdomen, slightly above the navel and below the rib cage.

4. Deliver abdominal thrusts

Grasp the fist with your other hand and press into the abdomen with a quick upward thrust. Repeat the thrust several times, if necessary, until the object is dislodged, or the person can cough or breathe.

5. What to do if the person becomes unconscious

(a) Lay the person down on his or her back.

(b) Check the throat for an obstruction, using the finger sweep. With your thumb in the victim's mouth, lift the jaw to open the mouth. With the index finger of your other hand, sweep across the back of the mouth from one cheek to the other.

(c) Attempt to ventilate (as in rescue breathing, page 698).

(d) If the chest does not rise, deliver up to five abdominal thrusts.

(e) Repeat the finger sweep, ventilations, and thrusts until the object is dislodged.

Special Case: You are alone and choking

1. Perform the Heimlich maneuver on yourself, following steps 3 and 4 outlined above.
2. If this is not successful, position yourself over the edge of

a firm surface, such as the back of a chair. Give thrusts by pushing upward and in against your abdomen.

Apply the Skill

1. Following your teacher's instructions, practice the steps of the Heimlich maneuver with a classmate. DO NOT actually deliver the abdominal thrusts (step 4), as this could result in injury.

2. At home, teach your family members how to perform the Heimlich maneuver. Again, DO NOT deliver the abdominal thrusts when you are demonstrating or practicing the procedure with family members.

3. In addition to the special case presented here, there are variations of the Heimlich maneuver that can be used for pregnant women, obese individuals, and infants. Find out about the recommended procedures in each of these cases and how to apply them. Make a poster describing one of these special cases. Report on your findings to the class.

CHAPTER 29 REVIEW

KEY IDEAS

LESSON 1

- In an emergency, properly applied first aid can mean the difference between life and death.

- A rescuer must be both knowledgeable and confident in his or her ability to perform first aid.

LESSON 2

- A rescuer should treat life-threatening conditions first. These are respiratory emergencies, cardiac arrest, stroke, severe bleeding, poisoning, and shock.

- Respiratory emergencies can lead to brain damage and death in minutes.

- An individual who has suffered any serious injury may also develop shock.

LESSON 3

- Injuries to bones, joints, and muscles, although not life-threatening, require first aid to relieve pain and prevent further injury to the area.

- Burns are classified according to the degree of damage they cause. They must be treated properly to avoid infection and shock.

- A rescuer should be prepared for common emergencies such as nosebleeds, fainting, and eye injuries.

LESSON 4

- Common outdoor emergencies include snakebites and other animal bites, stings, reactions to heat and cold, and water emergencies.

KEY TERMS

LESSON 1
first aid
Good Samaritan law

LESSON 2
cardiac arrest
cardiopulmonary
  resuscitation (CPR)
heart attack
Heimlich maneuver
hemorrhage
pressure point

rescue breathing
shock
stroke

LESSON 3
closed fracture
convulsions
dislocation
fainting
first-degree burn
hyperventilation
ligament

open fracture
second-degree burn
sprain
strain
tendon
third-degree burn

LESSON 4
frostbite
heat exhaustion
heatstroke
hypothermia

1. an injury to a muscle or a tendon

2. a procedure using chest compressions and rescue breathing

3. a condition in which the heart suddenly stops beating

4. a point at which an artery lies near the skin surface and passes over a bone

5. an effective technique for forcing a foreign object out of the throat

6. a condition resulting from the separation of the bone from its joint

7. a life-threatening condition that can accompany any serious injury

8. an injury in which the skin is charred

9. an injury in which the end of a broken bone sticks through the skin

10. a life-threatening condition in which the body's temperature falls well below normal

WHAT HAVE YOU LEARNED?

If the statement is true, write "true." If it is false, change the underlined word or words to make the statement true.

11. The freezing of body tissue is known as <u>hypothermia</u>.

12. <u>Tetanus</u> is a serious viral disease that can be passed from animals to people.

13. Another term for severe bleeding is <u>hemorrhage</u>.

14. The immediate care given in an accident or sudden illness is called <u>rescue breathing</u>.

15. A <u>first-degree</u> burn is generally considered a minor burn.

16. Heat exhaustion is a <u>less</u> serious emergency than heatstroke.

17. <u>Tendons</u> are strands of tissue that connect muscles to bones.

18. Breathing into cupped hands may help a victim of <u>fainting</u>.

Answer each of the following with complete sentences.

19. What are the major responsibilities of the first person on the scene of an emergency?

20. How can you determine if a person has stopped breathing?

21. What should you do if a person is bleeding severely from the leg? How would the procedure differ if you suspect a leg fracture?

22. What steps should you take if someone has swallowed a poisonous substance?

23. Describe the three classifications of burns and the proper treatment for each.

24. Why are insect stings sometimes dangerous? What symptoms should you look for in a person who has been bitten?

25. What are some causes of hyperventilation and how should you treat it?

26. Which parts of the body most commonly suffer from frostbite?

27. How can you distinguish between heat exhaustion and heatstroke?

28. What is a splint, and what is the correct way to apply it?

29. What are some of the common signals of a heart attack?

WHAT DO YOU THINK?

30. Which first-aid procedures do you feel are most important for a babysitter to know?

31. Why do you think it is important to treat for shock before there are any symptoms?

32. Why do you think that breathing automatically ceases when the heart stops?

33. Do you think the Good Samaritan law is a fair law? Why or why not?

34. Should all high school students be required to take a course in first aid? Explain.

WHAT WOULD YOU DO?

35. Suppose you are eating in a restaurant when the person at the table next to yours begins coughing loudly and holding his throat. His dinner companion shouts frantically, "Does anyone know the Heimlich maneuver?" What would you do?

36. How would you attempt to calm an anxious accident victim who is bleeding moderately from the leg?

37. What would you do if, while jogging near your home, you were bitten by a stray dog?

38. Suppose you were playing tennis on a hot day and your partner started complaining of dizziness and weakness. What would you do?

39. What would you do if you came upon an unconscious accident victim, but you were unsure of your ability to perform first aid?

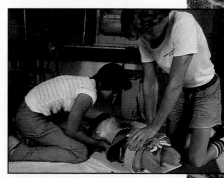

Getting Involved

40. Find out about various first-aid courses offered in your area. Report your findings to your class. Be sure to include the name of the organization offering the course, the type of course, when and where it meets, and the cost.

GLOSSARY

abstain To choose not to take a particular action. (459)

acid rain Rain that contains nitric acid, sulfuric acid, or both. (605)

acne A condition in which the oil glands in the skin become blocked, infected, and swollen. (421)

active immunity Immunity that is created by a person's own immune system as the result of having a disease or receiving a vaccine. (532)

active listening Focusing your full attention on what the other person is saying while at the same time letting that person know you understand and care. (121)

acute stage The stage of an illness during which the symptoms are most severe. (535)

addiction Dependence on a drug. (451)

additive A chemical added to a food to prevent spoiling, to control and improve color and texture, to replace or add nutrients, or to improve flavor. (308)

adolescence The period from about age 12 to 19 during which a child changes into an adult. (223)

adoption The legal process by which parents take another person's child into their family to be raised as their own. (100, 198)

adrenal glands Two small endocrine glands, located one above each kidney, that produce hormones affecting kidney function, metabolism, and response to stress. (171)

adrenaline A hormone produced by the adrenal glands that is released in response to fear or stress; it causes heartbeat, blood pressure, and breathing rate to increase. (54, 171)

aerobic exercise Repetitive, nonstop activity that raises the breathing and heart rates. (381, 393)

afterbirth The placenta, when it is delivered after childbirth. (210)

aggressive Communicating one's opinions and feelings in a way that may seem threatening or disrespectful to others. (25, 122)

AIDS Acquired immunodeficiency syndrome: a fatal disease of the immune system that is caused by human immunodeficiency virus (HIV); it is characterized by very low levels of certain T cells and the appearance of one or more opportunistic diseases. (558)

Al-Anon A support group for adult family and friends of alcoholics. (458)

Alateen A support group for teenagers who live with alcoholics. (458)

alcoholic hepatitis An inflammation of the liver caused by the toxic effects of alcohol. (452)

Alcoholics Anonymous A support group composed of recovering alcoholics who give encouragement and support to help other alcoholics stop drinking. (458)

alcoholism A disease in which the person is addicted to alcohol. (453)

algae Tiny water plants. (611)

allergy A reaction of the body to an irritating substance. (367)

alveoli The balloonlike air sacs at the end of the bronchioles. (365)

Alzheimer's disease A form of dementia caused by degeneration of brain cells. (256)

amalgam A silver-colored mixture of several metals used by dentists to fill teeth. (317)

amino acid One of about 20 different chemical substances that make up proteins. (272)

amnesia The sudden loss of memory. (83)

amniocentesis A procedure in which a small amount of amniotic fluid is removed from the uterus and examined for the presence of substances that may indicate an inherited disorder in the fetus. (207)

amniotic fluid The fluid within the amniotic sac, within which the embryo floats. (203)

amniotic sac The bag of thin tissue that encloses a developing embryo. (203)

amphetamine One of a group of powerful stimulants that are made artificially. (506)

anabolic steroid Any of a group of synthetic drugs that resemble the male hormone testosterone. (511)

anaerobic exercise Intense physical activity that lasts only from a few seconds to a few minutes, during which muscles use up more oxygen than the blood can supply. (393)

anemia A condition in which there are too few red blood cells or too little hemoglobin in the blood. (277, 379)

aneurysm A blood-filled weak spot that balloons out from the wall of an artery. (578)

angina pectoris The chest pain that occurs when the flow of oxygen to the heart is reduced. (376, 576)

anorexia nervosa A serious eating disorder in which a person refuses to eat enough food to maintain normal body weight. (79)

antagonistic interaction An interaction that occurs when drugs are taken together and each drug's effect is canceled out or reduced by the action of the other. (497)

antibiotic A drug that inhibits or kills bacteria. (536)

antibody A protein that attaches to the surface of pathogens or to the toxins produced by them; the binding action may keep the pathogen or toxin from harming the body. (530)

anus The opening of the rectum. (324)

anxiety disorder A mental illness in which anxiety persists and interferes with normal functioning. (77)

anxiety Fear that does not have an identifiable source or that is caused by a danger that no longer exists. (77)

aorta The largest artery in the body, through which blood leaves the left ventricle. (372)

Apgar score A scale that rates a newborn's heart rate, breathing, muscle tone, ability to react to a stimulus, and skin color. (210)

appendicitis An infection of the appendix. (327)

appendicular skeleton Bones of the arms, legs, shoulders, and hips. (338)

appetite A desire for food that is based on emotional factors rather than on nutritional need. (300)

arrhythmia An irregular heartbeat. (577)

arteries Thick-walled, elastic vessels that carry blood away from the heart. (372)

arterioles Smaller blood vessels that branch off from arteries. (372)

arteriosclerosis The condition in which the arteries lose their elasticity and become stiff; hardening of the arteries. (576)

arthritis A disease characterized by painful swelling and inflammation of the joints. (255, 343, 590)

artificial pacemaker A small, battery-operated unit that is connected to the heart and produces electrical impulses that make the heart beat regularly. (577)

asbestos A mineral that occurs in the form of fibers and was formerly used as an insulating material. (607)

asbestosis A disease that results when asbestos fibers are inhaled into the lungs, damaging them. (607)

assailant A person who physically attacks another person. (147)

assault An unlawful attempt or threat to harm someone. (684)

assertive Self-assured; able to stand up for oneself and express feelings in a nonthreatening way. (25, 122)

asthma A respiratory disorder that involves difficulty in breathing, wheezing, and coughing due to narrowed air passages. (58, 367)

astigmatism Distorted vision resulting from unevenness in the curvature of the cornea or lens. (428)

atherosclerosis A condition in which cholesterol and other fatty materials build up on artery walls. (376, 575)

atrium One of the two chambers of the heart that receive blood. (370)

auditory nerve The nerve that transmits sound from the cochlea to the brain. (433)

autonomic nervous system The part of the peripheral nervous system that regulates actions that happen automatically, such as heartbeat, breathing rate, and digestion. (352)

autonomy Independence. (236)

axial skeleton The portion of the skeleton that includes the skull, the breastbone, the ribs, and the vertebrae. (338)

axon A long, thin fiber of a neuron that carries impulses away from the cell body. (349)

B cell A type of lymphocyte that produces antibodies; a B lymphocyte. (530)

background radiation High-energy radiation that comes from natural sources. (617)

bacteria Small, single-celled organisms that can live almost anywhere. (524)

balloon angioplasty A method of treating coronary heart disease in which a balloon is inflated inside a coronary artery at the point of blockage, widening the inside of the artery. (580)

barbiturate A type of depressant, a sedative-hypnotic. (504)

basal metabolic rate The rate at which a person uses energy when the body is at rest. (299)

benign tumor A mass of cells that grow more rapidly than normal cells but more slowly than most cancer cells and do not spread to other areas of the body. (582)

bile A substance produced by the liver that aids in the digestion of fats by breaking large droplets of fat into smaller ones. (323)

biodegradable waste Waste that can be broken down by microorganisms. (603)

biofeedback The technique in which a person learns to control a specific physical function by recognizing his or her body's signals. (66)

biopsy The removal of a small piece of tissue for diagnostic purposes. (586)

birthing room A hospital room that resembles a bedroom, used for childbirth. (208)

blackout A period of time that a person who has been drinking cannot recall. (447)

bladder The muscular sac that stores urine until it is released from the body. (330)

blastocyst A hollow, spherical structure made up of about 500 cells, formed when a zygote divides and grows. (201)

blended family A family that consists of a biological parent, a stepparent, and the children of one or both parents. (101)

blizzard A heavy snowstorm with winds over 34 miles per hour. (673)

blood alcohol concentration A measure of the amount of alcohol in a person's blood, stated as the number of milligrams of ethanol per 100 milliliters of blood. (447)

blood group A classification of blood based on whether certain proteins are present on the surface of the red blood cells; blood type. (374)

blood pressure The force with which blood pushes against the walls of the blood vessels. (373)

blood transfusion The procedure in which blood is taken from one person and then transferred to someone else's bloodstream. (374)

body composition The amount of body fat compared to lean tissue, such as muscle and bone. (389)

body language A way of communicating information or feelings nonverbally, through body movements, posture, gestures, and facial expressions. (122)

botulism A serious and often deadly kind of food poisoning caused by bacteria. (527)

brain A moist, spongy organ, located within the skull, that is made up of billions of neurons; it controls sense experiences, actions, thoughts, and memory. (350)

brainstem The area of the brain below the cerebellum at the base of the

skull; it controls heartbeat, breathing, and blood pressure. (351)

bronchi Two cartilage-ringed tubes that go from the trachea to each lung. (365)

bronchioles Narrower branches off the bronchi. (365)

bronchitis An inflammation and swelling of the mucous membranes that line the bronchi. (368)

bulimia A serious eating disorder in which a person alternates eating binges with purging. (80)

bursitis A painful irritation of the fluid-filled sac that cushions certain joints and tendons. (343)

calculus A material formed when plaque hardens on the teeth; tartar. (318)

calories Units used to measure the amount of energy released when nutrients are burned. (269)

cancer The rapid, uncontrolled growth and spread of abnormal cells. (423, 582)

candidiasis A fungal infection, often of the vagina, caused by the fungus *Candida*. (555)

capillaries The smallest blood vessels in the body. (372)

capsizing The overturning of a boat. (676)

carbohydrate A class of nutrients that includes sugars and starches. (269)

carbohydrate loading The practice by which athletes greatly increase their carbohydrate intake and decrease their levels of exercise in the days immediately before a competition, in an attempt to make extra carbohydrates available to supply energy for the muscles. (306)

carbon dioxide A gas that is the primary waste given off during burning. (604)

carbon monoxide A poisonous, colorless, odorless gas produced when substances are burned. (474, 604)

carcinogen A substance or agent that causes cancer. (474, 582, 615)

cardiac arrest The sudden stoppage of the heart. (699)

cardiac muscle Involuntary muscle found only in the heart. (346)

cardiopulmonary resuscitation A method of combining chest compressions with rescue breathing to maintain a flow of oxygen-rich blood to the brain while the heart is not working. (577, 700)

cardiorespiratory endurance The ability of a person's heart, blood vessels, and lungs to distribute nutrients and oxygen and to remove wastes. (388)

cardiovascular diseases Diseases of the heart and blood vessels. (574)

cardiovascular system The circulatory system. (370)

cartilage A tough supportive tissue that is softer and more flexible than bone. (338)

case history A brief description of a person who suffers from a particular disorder. (77)

cataract A condition in which the eye's lens becomes clouded. (429)

cell The smallest unit of living things. (320)

cementum The outer tissue of a tooth's roots that covers the root dentin. (316)

Centers for Disease Control and Prevention (CDC) The agency within the Public Health Service that collects data and conducts medical research. (654)

central nervous system The brain and spinal cord. (350)

cerebellum The area of the brain beneath the back part of the cerebrum. (351)

cerebral hemorrhage A stroke in which an artery in the cerebrum bursts. (578)

cerebral palsy Nervous system damage that occurs before, during, or shortly after birth, resulting in a lack of full control of body movement. (355)

cerebrospinal fluid A liquid located between the middle and inner meninges and in certain spaces within the brain that helps to cushion and protect the brain and spinal cord. (350)

cerebrum The large upper region of the brain. (351)

cervix The narrow base, or outer end, of the uterus. (179)

cesarean section A surgical method of birth. (211, 554)

chancre A painless sore that appears at the site of exposure to syphilis. (554)

chancroid A bacterial STD with symptoms similar to primary syphilis that causes sores around the genitals. (555)

chemotherapy The use of drugs to attack cancer and reduce the rate at which cancer cells reproduce. (586)

chewing tobacco Leaves of poor-quality tobacco mixed with molasses or honey, placed between the cheek and gums. (475)

chlamydia A common bacterial STD that may have no symptoms and if untreated can cause infections of the urinary tract in men and infections of the reproductive organs in women. (552)

chlorofluorocarbon (CFC) A chemical containing chlorine, fluorine, and carbon. (606)

cholera An infectious disease of the small intestine that causes severe diarrhea and vomiting. (648)

cholesterol A waxy, fatlike substance found in the cells of all animals. (271, 575)

chorion A part of the developing placenta. (207)

chorionic villus sampling A procedure in which a small piece of the developing placenta is removed and examined for signs of inherited disorders in the fetus. (207)

choroid The dark-colored membrane, filled with blood vessels, that lies just inside the sclera and makes up most of the middle layer of the eye. (427)

chromosomes Tiny structures in cells that contain hereditary information. (184)

chronic bronchitis A condition in which the bronchial tubes are swollen and clogged with mucus. (477)

chyme The thick liquid formed in the stomach; a mixture of food and gastric juices. (322)

cilia Tiny hairlike structures that line the air passages and sweep foreign particles away from the lungs. (364, 528, 606)

circadian rhythm A 24-hour cycle of behavior patterns that some living things, including humans, exhibit. (409)

circumcision A surgical procedure in which the foreskin is removed from the penis. (173)

cirrhosis A disease of the liver in which useless scar tissue replaces normal liver tissue. (451, 556)

climacteric The gradual slowing down of hormone production that takes place during middle adulthood. (250)

clinic A facility in which health care is provided by one or more physicians and other health-care workers. (629)

clinical depression A mental disorder in which a person is overwhelmed by sad feelings for months and stops being able to carry out everyday activities. (81)

clinical psychologist A mental-health professional who specializes in recognizing and treating abnormal behavior. (90)

clique A narrow, exclusive group of people with similar backgrounds or interests. (129)

closed fracture A fracture in which the broken bone does not push through the skin's surface. (705)

cluster suicide A situation in which several people in the same community attempt to kill themselves within a short period of time. (88)

cocaine A highly addictive, powerful stimulant drug. (506)

cochlea A hollow, coiled, fluid-filled tube in the inner ear. (433)

codeine A narcotic compound derived from opium. (505)

codependent A person who assumes responsibility for an addict's needs, feelings, and happiness. (456)

color blindness The inability to distinguish certain colors. (428)

coma A prolonged period of deep unconsciousness that may result from a severe brain injury, a disease, or a drug overdose. (354)

commitment The determination to develop a fulfilling relationship. (136)

communication The sharing of information, thoughts, or feelings. (109)

compatibility The ability to exist in harmony with another person. (135)

compromise An agreement in which each party gives up something. (124)

compulsion An unrealistic need to behave in a certain way. (78)

concussion A short loss of consciousness following a severe bump to the head, during which the soft brain tissue comes into contact with the skull. (353)

cones Light-receiving cells on the retina that enable a person to see color. (427)

congenital heart disorder A structural problem of the heart that is present at birth. (377)

congenital syphilis Syphilis passed from a mother to her baby during pregnancy. (555)

congestive heart failure A condition in which the heart slowly weakens from overwork. (577)

conjunctiva The thin, moist membrane that covers the front part of the sclera and the inside of the eyelid. (427)

conjunctivitis An inflammation of the conjunctiva, caused by an allergic reaction or by a bacterial or viral infection. (430)

conscious thoughts Those thoughts of which a person is aware. (28)

consumer Anyone who buys goods and services. (626)

continuum A gradual or continual progression through many stages between one extreme and another. (5)

contraception Any method of preventing pregnancy; birth control. (198)

controlled substance A substance whose manufacture, possession, or sale is controlled by law. (512)

convalescence The stage of an illness between the end of infection and the time the person feels well. (536)

convalescent home A facility that provides care for people who are recovering from surgery, illness, or injury. (630)

convulsions Alternating periods of severe muscular contraction and relaxation. (711)

cool-down A period of milder exercise at the end of an exercise period that allows the body and heart rate to return slowly and safely to their resting states. (401)

cooperation The act of working together for a common goal or purpose. (123)

copayment The amount of a person's medical expenses not paid by the insurance company, for which the individual is responsible. (635)

coping strategy A way of dealing with an uncomfortable or unbearable feeling or situation. (41)

cornea The transparent front of the sclera, through which light enters the eye. (427)

coronary angiography An X-ray technique used to detect blocked coronary arteries. (580)

coronary arteries The arteries that carry blood to the heart muscle. (372)

coronary bypass surgery A surgical procedure in which a vein or artificial blood vessel is used to construct a detour around a blocked coronary artery. (580)

coronary heart disease The condition that occurs when the coronary arteries become blocked as a result of atherosclerosis. (376, 576)

Cowper's glands In males, a pair of glands located at the base of the penis that provide 5 percent of the fluid to semen. (174)

crack A concentrated, smokable form of cocaine. (506)

cranial nerves Twelve pairs of nerves that emerge from the brain. (352)

cranium The thick, hard part of the skull that encloses and protects the brain. (338)

Crohn's disease An ongoing inflammation of the lower part of the small intestine. (327)

crown The part of a tooth that can be seen above the gum. (316)

culture The beliefs and patterns of behavior that are shared by a group of people and passed from generation to generation. (10)

cystic fibrosis A recessive genetic disorder in which the lungs and

pancreas secrete abnormally thick mucus; it occurs mainly among whites. (188)

Daily Value A recommendation, developed by nutrition experts in the United States government, for the amount of a specific nutrient that the average person should obtain each day. (283)

deafness A total inability to hear. (433)

decibel The unit used to measure the loudness or intensity of sound. (435, 619)

deductible The portion of a person's yearly medical expenses that he or she must pay before the insurance company begins paying. (635)

defense mechanism An unconscious coping strategy; a way of defending oneself against difficult feelings. (42)

deficiency A condition in which a person does not obtain enough of a specific nutrient. (275)

dehydration A serious reduction in the body's water content. (278)

delirium tremens A reaction of the central nervous system to the absence of alcohol, characterized by uncontrollable shaking of the entire body, seizures, hallucinations, and insomnia. (454)

delivery The actual birth of the baby, during which the baby is pushed through the cervix and vagina. (209)

dementia A group of symptoms characterized by loss of mental abilities, abnormal behavior, and personality changes; it may be caused by a variety of disorders. (75, 255)

dendrite One of the short, branching fibers of a neuron that carry nerve impulses toward the cell body. (349)

dentin The yellowish bonelike material that makes up most of a tooth. (316)

deoxyribonucleic acid (DNA) The chemical substance within cells of which chromosomes are made. (184)

dependence A state in which a person's body has become resistant to a drug and requires the drug to function normally. (451)

depressant A drug that slows the activity of the central nervous system. (443, 504)

depression An emotional state in which the person feels hopeless and worthless. (40)

dermatitis A condition in which an area of skin becomes red, swollen, hot, and itchy. (422)

dermis The inner layer of skin that lies below the epidermis. (419)

designer drug A new chemical substance that has been designed to

be chemically similar to a controlled substance. (512)

detoxification The process of removing all of an abused substance from a person's body. (457)

detoxification program A drug abuse treatment program that involves gradual but complete withdrawal from an abused substance. (513)

diabetes Any disorder in which the body does not produce or properly use insulin, resulting in high levels of glucose in the blood. (304, 588)

diabetic coma A life-threatening condition that may occur in a person with type I diabetes, resulting from high blood sugar. (589)

diagnosis A physician's opinion of the nature or cause of a medical condition. (626)

diaphragm A dome-shaped muscle that lies just below the lungs and is the main muscle involved in breathing. (366)

diastolic pressure The second and lower blood pressure number, representing the force recorded when the ventricles are relaxed. (373)

digestion The process by which the nutrients in food are broken down into a form the body can absorb and use. (316)

disability Any physical or mental impairment that limits or reduces normal activities. (8, 592)

disaster A sudden, catastrophic event that affects many people. (672)

discrimination The mistreatment of a person or group based on prejudices. (154)

dislocation The separation of a bone from its joint. (342, 707)

dissociative disorder A mental disorder in which a person becomes disconnected from his or her former identity. (83)

distress Stress that produces negative effects. (52)

divorce A legal agreement to end a marriage. (99)

Down syndrome A genetic disorder resulting from an extra chromosome; people with Down syndrome are mentally retarded, may have heart defects, and have a distinctive physical appearance. (189)

dressing A clean, absorbent cloth, usually made of gauze, which is applied to a wound. (701)

driving while intoxicated A criminal offense in which a driver exceeds the level of blood alcohol concentration allowed by law in a state. (450)

drug Any chemical that causes changes in a person's body or behavior. (442)

drug abuse The intentional misuse of any kind of drug for nonmedical purposes. (442, 494)

drug misuse The improper use of drugs. (494)

drug's action What a drug does to the body. (495)

drug's effect The physical and mental response to a drug's action. (495)

Duchenne muscular dystrophy A sex-linked disorder in which the person lacks a protein needed for muscle function; as a result, muscle tissue breaks down and a person loses muscle control. (189)

ear canal The narrow cavity that leads from the outer ear to the middle ear. (432)

eardrum The thin membrane at the end of the ear canal that vibrates when sound waves strike it. (432)

early bloomer An adolescent who develops physically at an early age, before most other adolescents. (225)

earthquake A sudden shaking of the ground caused by the release of stress accumulated along geologic faults or by volcanic activity. (673)

ectopic pregnancy The condition that occurs when a blastocyst becomes implanted in the fallopian tube or elsewhere in the abdomen instead of in the uterus. (210)

ego According to Freud, the thoughtful, decision-making part of the personality. (28)

ejaculation The ejection of semen from the penis. (175)

elasticity For skin, the extent to which it molds to one's body or snaps back into place when pulled. (254)

electrical shock Injury that occurs when electrical current passes through the body. (709)

electrocardiogram A recording of the heart's electrical activity. (579)

electrocution Death from direct contact with electricity. (671)

electrolyte One of the dissolved substances found in water that regulates cell processes. (278)

embryo Name given to the blastocyst after it has attached itself to the wall of the uterus. (201)`

emotion Feeling; a reaction to a situation that involves a person's mind, body, and behavior. (37)

emotional abuse The nonphysical mistreatment of a person. (107)

emotional intimacy The openness, sharing, affection, and trust that can develop in a close relationship. (134, 249)

emotional neglect The situation in which parents fail to give their child love and emotional support. (107)

empathy An ability to understand how another person feels. (126)

emphysema A breathing disorder in which the small air sacs in the lungs lose their ability to expand and contract. (368, 477)

emulsifier A food additive used to keep fats from separating from the other ingredients in a food. (308)

enabler A person who unintentionally protects an addict from the consequences of his or her behavior. (457)

enamel The hard outer layer that covers the crown of a tooth. (316)

endocrine gland One of a group of ductless glands that release hor-mones directly into the bloodstream. (168)

endometriosis A condition in which tissue from the lining of the uterus grows outside the uterus, in the pelvic cavity. (181)

endometrium The lining of the uterus. (179)

endorphins Chemicals produced in the brain that help give a sense of satisfaction and pleasure. (392)

enriched Term used to describe a food to which nutrients have been added to replace those lost during processing. (308)

environment All of the physical and social conditions surrounding a person. (9, 602)

enzyme A substance that helps carry out chemical reactions in the body. (321)

epidemic An unusually high occurrence of a disease in a certain place during a certain period. (548)

epidemiology The study of disease among populations and the ways to prevent or control disease. (651)

epidermis The outermost layer of skin. (418)

epididymis A J-shaped tube located on the back of each testis, in which sperm are stored for two to four days after they are formed. (173)

epiglottis A small flap of tissue that covers the opening to the windpipe during swallowing. (321)

epilepsy A disorder in which the brain's impulses become disturbed and cause seizures. (355)

escalate To grow more intense. (155)

esophagus The muscular tube that connects the mouth and the stomach. (321)

essential amino acid One of the nine amino acids that the body cannot manufacture. (273)

estrogen A hormone produced by the ovaries that regulates the development of female secondary sex characteristics and controls the sex drive. (172)

ethanol The alcohol found in beverages such as beer, wine, and liquor. (442)

eustachian tube A narrow tube that connects the middle ear with the back of the throat. (433)

eustress Stress that produces positive effects. (52)

eutrophication The process of excessive algae growth followed by decay and lack of oxygen. (612)

excretion The process by which the body collects and removes wastes produced by its cells. (329)

extended family A network of close relatives living together or near each other. (100)

extrovert A friendly, outgoing person. (24)

eye contact Direct visual contact with someone's gaze. (122)

fad diet A popular diet that may help a person lose weight but without proper regard for nutrition and other matters of health. (302)

fallopian tube One of two narrow tubes through which eggs pass from the ovaries to the uterus. (178)

fallout Radioactive material that settles to the ground in rain or snow or as dust particles. (618)

famine A widespread lack of food. (660)

farsightedness A vision problem characterized by the inability to focus clearly on nearby objects. (428)

fasting Refraining from eating all foods. (303)

fat The class of nutrients with the highest energy content. (271)

feces Solid waste materials eliminated through the digestive system. (323)

fertilization The joining of a sperm with an egg; conception. (173, 201)

fertilizer A chemical that contains minerals needed by plants. (611)

fetal alcohol syndrome A group of birth defects caused by the effects of alcohol on an unborn child. (206, 452)

fetus Name given to the developing embryo from the end of the second month of pregnancy until birth. (203)

fever A body temperature above 98.6°F. (535)

fiber The indigestible material found in whole grains, vegetables, fruits, and seeds that is necessary for the proper functioning of the digestive system. (270)

fibrillation A life-threatening type of arrhythmia in which the heart twitches in an uncoordinated fashion. (577)

fight or flight response A series of physical changes that prepare the body to react to stress. (55)

first aid The immediate care given to a victim of injury or sudden illness before professional medical help arrives. (694)

first-degree burn A surface burn in which the outer layer of the skin is reddened and painful. (708)

flammable material A material that catches fire easily or burns quickly. (669)

flash flood A flood that occurs suddenly, without warning, after a heavy rainfall or snow melt. (673)

flexibility The ability to use a muscle throughout its entire range of motion. (389)

follicle-stimulating hormone (FSH) A hormone produced by the pituitary gland that acts in females to stimulate estrogen production and the maturation of egg cells, and in males to stimulate sperm production. (172)

Food Guide Pyramid A graph that groups foods according to types and indicates how many servings of each type should be eaten daily. (279)

fortified Term used to describe a food that has had nutrients, such as vitamins, minerals, or proteins, added to it, which it does not normally contain. (308)

foster family A family in which an adult or couple provides care and a temporary home for children whose biological parents are unable to care for them. (101)

foster parents Parents who take care of children whose own parents are unable to do so. (199)

fracture A break or crack in a bone. (342, 705)

fraternal twins Twins who develop from two eggs fertilized by two sperm. (212)

free-floating anger The frustration and hostility that sometimes result when people feel unable to improve their lives. (148)

friendship A give-and-take relationship based on mutual trust, acceptance, and common interests or values. (125)

frostbite The freezing of body tissue. (715)

functional disorder A mental disorder that cannot be traced to a physical cause. (76)

fungus A small, simple type of organism related to molds. (525)

gallbladder A sac attached to the liver, in which bile is stored before being released into the small intestine. (323)

gender roles The behaviors and attitudes that are socially accepted as either masculine or feminine. (127)

gene A section of a chromosome that determines a single trait; the basic unit of heredity. (185)

general hospital A hospital that treats patients of all ages and with all kinds of illnesses and injuries. (629)

generativity According to Erikson, the shift in concern from oneself in the present to the welfare of others in the future. (251)

generic name The standard name of a medicine. (639)

genetic disorder An abnormal, inherited condition. (187)

genital herpes An incurable viral STD that produces painful blisters around the genital area. (554)

genital warts Warts in the genital area that are caused by the human papilloma virus. (553)

gingiva The tissue that surrounds the teeth and covers the bone around the teeth; the gum. (316)

gingivitis A condition in which the gums become red and swollen and bleed easily. (318)

glans The tip of the penis. (173)

glaucoma A condition in which the pressure of the fluid between the cornea and the lens increases beyond its normal level. (429)

glucose A simple sugar that is the major provider of energy for the body's cells. (269)

glycogen A type of starch stored in the body; it can be converted to or from glucose. (270)

goal A result that a person aims for and works hard to reach. (4)

gonorrhea A bacterial STD that infects the urinary tract of males and females and the reproductive organs of females. (553)

Good Samaritan law A law enacted in most states that protects people from lawsuits if medical complications arise after they have administered first aid correctly. (696)

greenhouse effect Warming caused by increasing levels of carbon dioxide in the atmosphere. (604)

grief Deep sorrow. (40)

group practice A working arrangement in which a group of physicians have their offices in the same building and work together. (631)

habit A pattern of behavior that has become automatic and is hard to change. (16)

halitosis Bad breath. (317)

hallucinogen One of a group of psychoactive drugs that alter perception, thought, and mood. (507)

hangover All of the physical symptoms, such as nausea, upset stomach, headache, and a sensitivity to noise, that for many people are the aftereffects of drinking too much alcohol. (448)

hardiness A personality trait of people who possess resistance to stress and do not seem to suffer negative effects from it. (62)

hashish A psychoactive drug obtained from parts of the Indian hemp plant that produces effects similar to those of marijuana but is more likely to cause an altered mental state. (510)

hazardous waste Waste that is flammable, explosive, corrosive, or toxic. (614)

health code A standard set by the state for a factor that affects health, such as water quality, sanitation in restaurants, and sewage treatment facilities. (656)

health literacy A person's ability to gather and understand health information and then use the information to improve his or her health. (17)

health maintenance organization A group of physicians and other health-care workers that provides complete medical services for a set monthly fee. (636)

health The well-being of your body, your mind, and your relationships with other people. (2)

hearing impairment A partial loss of hearing. (433)

heart The muscular organ that pumps blood throughout the body. (370)

heart attack The condition that results when some of the tissue in the heart is prevented from receiving its normal blood supply and dies. (376, 576, 699)

heat exhaustion A condition that occurs when a person is exposed to excessive heat over a period of time, caused by the loss of water and salt from the body through excessive perspiration. (716)

heatstroke A life-threatening condition caused by prolonged exposure to high heat. (717)

Heimlich maneuver A technique that uses abdominal thrusts to dislodge an object blocking a person's airway. (699)

hemoglobin The iron-containing substance found in red blood cells, which carries oxygen from the lungs to all parts of the body. (277, 604)

hemophilia A sex-linked disorder in which the person's blood does not clot properly. (189)

hemorrhage Severe bleeding. (701)

hemorrhoids Enlarged veins in the anal area. (326)

hepatitis B A sexually transmitted disease that attacks the liver. (556)

hepatitis Inflammation of the liver. (539)

herbal cigarette Any cigarette made from plant materials other than tobacco. (483)

herbicide A chemical that kills weeds. (611)

heredity The passing on of biological characteristics from parent to child. (8, 184)

heroin A narcotic drug made from morphine. (505)

herpes simplex I The virus that causes cold sores. (422)

hierarchy of needs According to Maslow, the order in which a person's basic needs must be met. (31)

high blood pressure Blood pressure that is consistently above normal limits. (574)

high-energy radiation A form of energy that damages living things, including ultraviolet light, X-rays, cosmic rays, and the energy given off by radioactive substances. (617)

high-risk population A group of people who, because of age, behavior, or some other factor, are likely to contract a serious disease or disorder. (650)

HIV-positive Term used to describe a person who is diagnosed as being infected with human immuno-deficiency virus. (563)

homeostasis A steady state or balance; the normal, balanced state of the body's internal systems. (54, 278, 602)

homicide The intentional killing of one person by another. (146)

hormone A substance that acts as a chemical messenger in the body. (168)

hospice A live-in facility or program for terminally ill people and their families. (259, 630)

hospital A facility that provides comprehensive health-care services and overnight accommodations for patients. (629)

human chorionic gonadotropin (HCG) The hormone produced by a human embryo at the time of implantation. (202)

human immunodeficiency virus (HIV) The virus that causes AIDS. (558)

human papilloma virus The virus that causes genital warts. (553)

hunger A feeling of physical discomfort that is caused by the body's need for nutrients. (300)

hurricane A powerful tropical storm characterized by heavy rains and winds over 74 miles per hour. (672)

hydrocarbon A substance made up of hydrogen and carbon. (605)

hypertension Blood pressure that is consistently higher than normal. (378, 574)

hyperventilation Rapid, deep breathing, sometimes accompanied by dizziness, chest pains, and fainting, that lowers the level of carbon dioxide in the blood. (710)

hypochondria A somatoform disorder characterized by a constant fear of disease and a preoccupation with one's health. (78)

hypoglycemia A condition in which the body produces too much insulin, resulting in low blood sugar. (171, 305)

hypothalamus A part of the brain that regulates body temperature, sleep, water balance, and blood pressure, as well as regulating the hormones of the endocrine system. (170, 352)

hypothermia A serious loss of body heat that causes the body temperature to fall well below normal. (716)

"I" message A statement of one's feelings and expectations that does not blame or judge the other person. (121)

id According to Freud, the part of the personality that consists of biological urges, such as hunger and thirst. (28)

identical twins Same-sex twins who develop from the same fertilized egg and have identical inherited traits. (212)

identity Who a person is; a person's distinct personality or individuality. (30, 231)

illegal drug A chemical that is forbidden by law because its dangerous and often unpredictable effects outweigh any useful purpose it may have. (442)

Illness-Wellness continuum A model that illustrates the full range of health between the extremes of illness on one end and wellness on the other end. (5)

immune system The internal system that protects the body from disease by recognizing and destroying pathogens. (254, 530)

immunity The body's ability to destroy pathogens that it has previously encountered before they are able to cause disease. (530)

immunization An injection given for the purpose of stimulating immunity to a disease. (532)

immunotherapy The use of drugs that stimulate the body's own immune system to attack cancer cells. (586)

implantation The process by which the blastocyst is attached to the wall of the uterus. (201)

incubation stage The time between entry of a virus and the time when a person begins to feel ill. (534)

incubator A special chamber that protects a premature baby until it is more developed. (212)

infatuation A feeling of intense attraction to another person. (131)

infectious disease A disease caused by organisms that enter, live in, and multiply within the human body. (524)

infectious mononucleosis A viral infection that causes the lymph nodes, tonsils, and spleen to become swollen and tender. (541)

infertile Unable to have biological children. (198)

infertility The reduced ability to have children. (548)

inflammation The body's response to injury; it fights infection and promotes healing. (529)

influenza A viral infection of the upper respiratory system. (366, 534)

inguinal hernia A condition that occurs when part of the intestine pushes into the scrotum. (176)

inhalant Any drug that is breathed in through the nose. (511)

inhibitions The controls people put on their emotions and behavior in order to behave in socially accepted ways. (449)

inpatient A patient who is required to stay in a hospital overnight or longer. (629)

insomnia Difficulty in falling or staying asleep. (410)

instigator A person who encourages fighting between others while staying out of the fight. (154)

insulin A hormone produced by the pancreas that enables glucose to pass from the blood into the body's cells. (304, 588)

insulin shock A life-threatening condition that may occur in a person with type I diabetes, resulting from low blood sugar. (589)

integrity According to Erikson, the stage of feeling complete. (257)

interferon A regulatory substance produced by T cells that stimulates phagocytes and other cells to fight off infection. (531)

interneuron A type of neuron, located only in the brain and spinal cord, that passes impulses from one neuron to another. (350)

intervention A planned confrontation with the alcoholic, family members, a member of a support group, and an alcohol counselor. (458)

intolerance A lack of acceptance of another's opinions, beliefs, or actions. (154)

intoxication The negative effects alcohol has on a person's body and behavior. (446)

introvert A person whose thoughts and feelings are directed inward. (24)

iris The colored disk at the front of the eye, with an opening in its center through which light passes. (427)

isokinetic exercise Exercise that involves moving a muscle through a range of motion against a resistance that changes. (394)

isometric exercise Exercise in which muscles contract but very little body movement takes place. (394)

isotonic exercise Exercise that involves the contraction and relaxation of muscles through the full range of their motion. (394)

jaundice Yellowing of the skin, usually as the result of liver disease. (539)

joint The point at which two bones come together. (340)

Kaposi's sarcoma A rare form of skin cancer that occurs in people with AIDS. (560)

kidney dialysis A process in which a machine is used to filter blood in place of the kidneys. (332)

kidney One of two organs, located on either side of the spine, that filter wastes from the blood. (329)

kidney stone A mass of salts in the kidney or urinary tract. (331)

labor The work of pushing the fetus out of the mother. (208)

lactic acid A waste product that sometimes accumulates in muscles after very intense exercise. (346)

lactose intolerance An inability to digest lactose because the digestive system does not produce enough lactase. (324)

landfill An area where trash and other wastes are deposited and covered with soil. (614)

large intestine A tubelike organ, also known as the colon, that absorbs water and gets rid of waste; it leads from the small intestine to the outside of the body. (323)

larynx The voice box, located at the top of the trachea. (365)

late bloomer An adolescent who develops physically at a late age, after most other adolescents. (225)

leavening agent A food additive that makes baked goods rise. (308)

lens The transparent structure just behind the iris that focuses light on the inner, back side of the eye. (427)

leukemia A cancer of the blood-forming tissues in the bone marrow. (585)

leukoplakia Hard, white leathery patches or sores that form on the inside of the mouth and may develop into cancer; they are often the result of smokeless tobacco use. (478)

ligament A fibrous band of tissue that holds bones together at a joint. (340, 706)

liver A large organ that removes harmful materials from the body and produces bile. (323)

look-alike drug A drug that is made to look like a commonly abused drug but may actually contain any kind of substance. (512)

LSD The strongest known hallucinogen; lysergic acid diethylamide. (507)

lungs The elastic, spongy organs through which the body absorbs oxygen. (365)

luteinizing hormone (LH) A hormone produced by the pituitary gland that acts in females to stimulate ovulation and progesterone production, and in males to stimulate sperm and testosterone production. (172)

lymph The fluid that flows through the lymphatic system. (530)

lymphatic system A network of vessels that collect fluid from the tissues of the body and return it to the bloodstream. (530)

lymphocyte The type of white blood cell that carries out most of the immune system's functions. (530)

mainstream smoke Tobacco smoke that a smoker inhales into the lungs and then exhales into the air. (480)

malignant tumor A mass of cancer cells. (582)

malnutrition Any condition in which a person's nutrient consumption is inadequate or unbalanced, usually as the result of consuming too little of one or more nutrients. (284)

malocclusion The condition that occurs when the upper and lower teeth do not meet properly. (318)

mammogram An X-ray of the breast. (183, 585)

managed care A form of health insurance in which each member chooses a primary-care physician from a group of physicians who participate in the plan. (636)

marijuana An illegal psychoactive drug made from parts of the Indian hemp plant; it is one of the most frequently abused psychoactive drugs. (510)

marital roles The responsibilities that each partner assumes in a marriage. (137)

marrow The soft tissue that fills the spaces inside bones. (341)

maturity The state of being fully grown. (246)

maximum heart rate The heart's top speed; the heart rate when a person has exercised to the point of exhaustion. (398)

mediation A process in which conflicts are resolved with the help of a neutral third party. (160)

Medicaid A state and federal program that pays for the health care of people whose incomes are below an established level. (637, 653)

medical history A record of a person's present and past health as well as the health of members of his or her family. (632)

medical specialist A physician who has received additional training in a particular branch of medicine and has passed a test that certifies him or her to practice in that specialty. (627)

Medicare A federally financed insurance program for elderly people and for younger people who are disabled or have chronic kidney disease. (637, 653)

medicine A legal drug that helps the body fight injury, illness, or disease. (494, 639)

melanin A brown substance found in special cells in the epidermis; melanin is a major factor in determining the color of skin. (419)

melanoma An uncommon but extremely serious form of skin cancer. (423, 583)

meninges Three layers of membranes that cover and protect the brain. (350)

meningitis An inflammation of the meninges of the brain and spinal cord. (354)

menopause The period when menstruation ceases, occurring usually between the ages of 45 and 55. (181)

menstrual cycle The process during which an egg matures and is released, and the uterus prepares to receive it; on average, the menstrual cycle lasts 28 days. (179)

menstruation The discharge of blood and tissue from the uterus. (179)

mental disorder An illness that affects the mind and prevents a person from being productive, adjusting to life situations, or getting along with others. (74)

mental health The state of being comfortable with oneself, with others, and with one's surroundings. (25)

mescaline A hallucinogen obtained from the peyote cactus. (507)

metabolism The chemical process by which the body breaks down food to obtain energy. (268)

metastasis The spread of cancer from where it first develops to other parts of the body. (582)

methadone A drug sometimes used as a substitute for heroin in treatment for drug abuse. (514)

microinsults A term used by psychologists to describe small but frequent episodes of discrimination. (154)

microorganism An organism that can be seen only through a microscope. (524)

migraine headache An especially severe, long-lasting headache that may be caused by swelling of the brain's blood vessels. (355)

mineral One of a class of nutrients that are not made by living things and are required only in small amounts. (275)

miscarriage The expulsion of a dead zygote, blastocyst, embryo, or fetus from the uterus. (210)

modeling Copying the behavior of others. (27)

mood disorder A mental disorder in which a person's moods or emotions become extreme and interfere with daily life. (80)

morning sickness Attacks of nausea that may occur during pregnancy, usually during the first trimester. (204)

morphine A narcotic compound derived from opium. (505)

motor neuron A type of neuron that transmits impulses to the muscles and glands. (350)

mucous membrane The moist, protective lining that covers some of the openings to the body and the air passages. (364, 528)

mucus The sticky liquid that covers the surface of mucous membranes. (528)

multiple birth The delivery of more than one baby. (212)

multiple sclerosis A progressive condition in which patches of myelin are slowly destroyed, resulting in difficulty with muscular control, speech and vision problems, and sometimes paralysis. (356)

muscle tone Slight, constant contraction of a muscle due to the contraction of some of its fibers. (346)

muscular dystrophy An inherited condition in which the muscles gradually become weaker because the muscle fibers are slowly destroyed. (348)

muscular endurance The ability of muscles to keep working for an extended time. (389)

muscular strength The capacity of a muscle or group of muscles to exert or resist a force. (389)

mutagen A substance that causes changes in a cell's hereditary material. (615)

myelin The fatty material with which many axons are coated; it insulates the axon and increases the speed at which an impulse travels. (349)

narcolepsy A disorder of REM sleep in which the person falls asleep suddenly without warning for short periods of time. (411)

narcotic Any depressant drug made from or chemically similar to opium. (505)

nearsightedness A vision problem characterized by the inability to focus clearly on objects that are far away. (428)

Neighborhood Crime Watch A group of volunteers who report suspicious activities in their neighborhood to the police. (687)

nephritis An inflammation or swelling of the nephrons. (331)

nephron The filtering unit of the kidney. (330)

neurologist A physician who specializes in detecting and treating organic disorders of the brain and nervous system. (90)

neuron The basic cell of the nervous system. (349)

nicotine gum Chewing gum containing nicotine that is used to aid smokers in quitting smoking. (486)

nicotine patch An adhesive patch that is attached to the skin and from which nicotine is absorbed, used to aid smokers in slowly overcoming nicotine dependence. (486)

nicotine The drug in tobacco that may act as a stimulant and cause addiction. (472)

nicotine withdrawal A reaction to the lack of nicotine in the body. (473)

nitric acid An acid formed when nitrogen oxides in the air mix with water. (605)

nocturnal emission Erection and ejaculation during sleep; also known as a "wet dream." (175)

noise Loud sound. (617)

nongonococcal urethritis (NGU) In males, an inflammation of the lining of the urethra, usually caused by chlamydia that is left untreated. (552)

noninfectious disease A disease that is not caused by a pathogen. (574)

nonrapid eye movement (NREM) sleep The stage of sleep during which the eyes move very little and the body gradually reaches its state of deepest relaxation. (410)

nuclear family A family that consists of a mother and father and their child or children, living together in one household. (100)

nursing home A facility that provides long-term care for elderly or chronically ill people who are incapable of caring for themselves. (630)

nutrient A substance found in food that the body needs to regulate bodily functions, promote growth, repair body tissues, and obtain energy. (268)

nutrient density The proportion of nutrients in a food compared to the number of calories. (282)

nutrition The process by which the body takes in and uses nutrients. (268)

obesity The condition that occurs when a person's weight is 20 percent or more above an appropriate weight. (300)

obsession An idea or thought that takes over the mind and cannot be forgotten. (78)

Occupational Safety and Health Administration (OSHA) The government agency that identifies occupational hazards and sets standards for safety. (655, 674)

occupational illness Any abnormal condition or disorder, excluding injuries, caused by exposure to the workplace environment. (674)

occupational injury Any injury that results from a work accident or from exposure to a hazard in the work environment. (674)

oncogene A gene that becomes a cancer-causing gene as a result of exposure to a carcinogen. (583)

open fracture A fracture in which the broken end of a bone pierces the skin. (705)

Operation Identification A nationwide crime prevention program that encourages marking personal property. (687)

opium A narcotic drug obtained from the seed pod of a poppy plant. (505)

opportunistic disease A disease that attacks a person with a weakened immune system. (560)

optic nerve The nerve that transmits visual information from the eye to the brain. (427)

optimist A person who focuses on the positive side of things and expects a favorable outcome. (24)

oral cancer Cancer of the mouth, throat, or tongue. (478)

oral-rehydration therapy The gradual reintroduction of fluids to someone who has suffered severe water loss. (660)

organic disorder A mental disorder with a physical cause. (75)

orthodontist A dentist who specializes in correcting the position of teeth. (319)

ossification The process by which cartilage changes to bone. (341)

osteoarthritis Arthritis caused by wear and tear on a joint after many years of use or because of repeated injuries. (591)

osteopathy A branch of medicine that emphasizes the relationship of the body's muscular and skeletal systems to general health. (626)

osteoporosis A condition in which bones become brittle and break easily due to loss of calcium. (256, 344)

outpatient A person admitted to a clinic or hospital for tests or treatments that do not require an overnight stay. (629)

ova (Singular: ovum) The female sex cells, or eggs. (172)

oval window A small, membrane-covered opening that separates the middle ear from the inner ear. (433)

ovaries The two female reproductive glands, located one on each side of the body, a few inches below the waist. (172)

over-the-counter drug A medicine that can be purchased legally without a prescription. (494, 639)

overdose A serious reaction to an excessive amount of a drug that can result in coma or death. (450, 496)

ovulation The release of one or more eggs from an ovary. (178)

oxytocin The hormone that causes the uterus to contract and get smaller and also helps the breast tissue to eject milk. (212)

ozone A form of oxygen that chemically reacts with many substances. (606)

ozone layer A region of the atmosphere with a high concentration of ozone. (606)

pacemaker A group of cells in the wall of the right atrium that helps regulate the rate at which the heart beats. (372)

pancreas A large gland located behind the stomach that is part of two systems. As an endocrine gland, it secretes hormones that control blood-sugar levels. As a digestive organ, it secretes pancreatic juice into the small intestine. (171, 323)

Pap test A procedure in which cells are removed from the cervix and examined for signs of cancer. (183, 585)

paralysis The loss of feeling in and the ability to move some part of the body. (146, 354)

paraplegia Paralysis of the lower body and legs. (354)

parathyroid glands Four tiny endocrine glands attached to the back of the thyroid gland that regulate the levels of calcium and phosphorus in the body. (171)

Parkinson's disease A disease of the nervous system characterized by progressive loss of muscle function. (255)

particulate A tiny pollutant in the air, such as dust, soot, and mold spores. (606)

passive Holding back one's feelings and yielding to others. (25, 122)

passive immunity Immunity acquired by receiving antibodies from another person's immune system. (533)

passive smoker A smoker who involuntarily breathes sidestream smoke. (480)

pathogen An organism that causes disease. (524)

PCP A psychoactive drug that can act as a stimulant, a depressant, or a hallucinogen; phencyclidine. (510)

peer group People who are about the same age and share similar interests. (27)

peer pressure The need to conform to the expectations of friends and classmates. (129, 228)

pelvic inflammatory disease (PID) A serious infection of a woman's reproductive organs that can result in infertility. (552)

penis The male organ through which sperm and urine leave the body. (173)

peptic ulcer An open sore that forms in the lining of the stomach or the upper part of the small intestine. (326)

perfectionist A person who has extremely high standards and accepts nothing less than excellence of himself or herself. (61)

periodontitis An advanced stage of gum disease in which the buildup of plaque and calculus causes the gum to pull away from the teeth and form pockets. (318)

periosteum The tough membrane that covers bones and contains cells that form new bone during growth and repair. (341)

peripheral nervous system All the nerves that connect the brain and spinal cord to other parts of the body. (350)

peripheral vision The ability to see things to the side of what one is looking at. (428)

peristalsis The wavelike muscular action that pushes food through the esophagus and the rest of the digestive system. (322)

personality disorder A condition characterized by behavior that is inflexible and interferes with a person's life. (83)

personality The qualities and traits, including behavior and feelings, that are characteristic of a person. (24)

pessimist A person who focuses on the negative side of things and expects an unfavorable outcome. (24)

pesticide A chemical that kills crop pests. (611)

phagocyte A white blood cell that "eats up" foreign cells. (529)

pharynx The throat. (364)

phenylketonuria (PKU) A recessive genetic disorder in which the body cannot break down phenylalanine; it can cause mental retardation. (188)

phobia Anxiety that is related to a specific situation or object. (77)

physical abuse Punishment that leaves a mark that can be seen the next day. (106)

physical examination A head-to-toe check of a person's body to identify medical problems. (632)

physical fitness The ability of the heart, blood vessels, lungs, and muscles to work together to meet the body's needs. (388)

physical peak The state of having one's physical abilities at their maximum levels. (246)

physician A medical doctor; a person who has earned a medical degree. (626)

pituitary gland A small endocrine gland, located at the base of the brain, that controls activities such as growth rate, metabolism, and reproduction. (169)

placenta The organ that holds the embryo to the wall of the uterus. (202)

plaque A sticky, invisible, bacteria-filled film that covers the teeth (317); deposits of cholesterol that narrow or block arteries. (575)

plasma The liquid part of blood. (373)

platelets A type of structure found in blood that starts the process of blood clotting. (374)

pneumocystis carinii pneumonia An opportunistic disease of the lungs that attacks people with AIDS. (560)

pneumonia A serious infection of the lungs that can be caused by viruses, bacteria, or fungi. (366, 539)

poisoning The effect of one or more harmful substances on the body. (702)

pollutant A substance that causes pollution. (603)

pollution The accumulation of harmful wastes or other harmful substances in the environment. (603)

pore The opening of a narrow channel or duct in the skin, leading to a gland. (419)

postpartum period A period of adjustment for parents and their newborn that begins with delivery and lasts about six weeks. (212)

preferred provider organization A type of insurance plan in which participating physicians and hospitals charge reduced fees to plan members. (637)

prejudice A negative feeling about a certain group of people, based on stereotypes. (130)

premature birth The delivery of a live fetus before it is ready to be born. (211)

premenstrual syndrome A group of symptoms, including nervous tension, mood swings, headaches, bloating, and irritability, that occurs in some women before the menstrual period. (181)

premium The fee that a person pays for insurance. (635)

prenatal care Medical care during pregnancy. (198, 651)

prescription A written order from a physician or dentist to a pharmacist authorizing that a patient be given a particular medicine. (626)

prescription drug A medicine that can be obtained only through a written prescription from a physician and can be purchased only at a pharmacy. (494, 639)

preservative A food additive used to prevent spoilage or to keep foods from losing their natural color or texture. (308)

pressure bandage A snug bandage used to control bleeding. (701)

pressure point A point on the body where a major artery lies near the skin surface and passes over a bone. (701)

prevention The practice of healthy behaviors that keep a person free of disease and other health problems. (14)

primary health care Routine health care provided in a physician's office. (629)

primary-care physician A health-care professional who takes care of most people's routine medical needs. (626)

private practice A working arrangement in which a physician works for himself or herself. (631)

prodromal stage The first stage of an illness, during which the person may be contagious. (534)

product date A date printed on some food packages that is an estimate of how long the product will be usable. (309)

progesterone A hormone produced by the ovaries that controls the development of the endometrium during the menstrual cycle and helps to maintain the uterus during pregnancy. (172)

prolactin The hormone that causes milk to form in the breasts. (212)

proof A measure of the percentage of alcohol in a beverage; the proof is twice the percentage of alcohol by volume. (443)

prostate gland In males, a gland located near the bladder that provides 35 percent of the fluid to semen. (174)

protein The class of nutrients that contain nitrogen as well as carbon, hydrogen, and oxygen; besides being a source of energy, proteins play an important role in the growth and repair of body tissues. (272)

protein-energy malnutrition A serious condition in which the diet does not contain adequate protein and does not supply enough calories to meet the body's energy needs. (284)

protozoan A single-celled organism that is hundreds of times larger and has a more complex structure than bacteria. (525)

psilocybin A hallucinogen obtained from certain mushrooms. (510)

psychiatrist A physician who specializes in diagnosing and treating mental disorders. (89)

psychoactive drug A chemical that affects the activity of brain cells to alter perception, thought, and mood, and possibly to create illusions in the mind of the user. (495)

psychoanalysis A form of therapy developed by Freud, in which memories are brought into the conscious mind so that inner conflicts can be resolved. (29)

psychologist A health professional who studies the human mind and behavior and helps people with emotional problems; psychologists usually have two to six years of training beyond college. (25)

psychosomatic illness A disorder that results from stress or other emotional causes. (57)

psychotherapy A treatment method that involves conversations with a trained professional who helps an individual understand and overcome a mental disorder. (92)

puberty The period of sexual development during which males and females become sexually mature and able to produce children. (173)

pubic lice Tiny insects that infest the hair around the genitals; crab lice. (556)

public health system All the government and private agencies that work with the public to prevent disease and promote positive health behaviors. (648)

public health The study and practice of protecting and improving the health of people in a group or community. (648)

pulmonary circulation The pathway that blood follows from the heart to the lungs. (371)

pupil The opening in the center of the iris that relaxes and contracts to change the amount of light entering the eye. (427)

pus The mixture of fluids, phagocytes, and dead cells that accumulates at the site of an infection. (529)

quackery The sale of useless medical treatments or products. (640)

quadriplegia Paralysis of the body from the neck down, including the arms as well as the legs. (354)

quality of life The degree of overall satisfaction that a person gets from life. (2)

quarantine A period of isolation imposed on people who may have been exposed to an infectious disease. (648)

rabies An infection of the central nervous system transmitted from the bite of an infected animal. (355, 714)

radiation sickness A condition caused by exposure to large doses of radiation. (617)

radiation therapy The use of high-energy radiation to kill cancer cells. (586)

radioactive Term used to describe substances that give off radiation. (617)

radon A naturally occurring radioactive gas. (618)

rape An assault in which one person forces another to have sexual relations. (685)

rape crisis center A local agency that provides counseling and support for rape victims. (686)

rapid eye movement (REM) sleep The stage of sleep during which the eyes flicker rapidly behind closed eyelids and the person dreams. (410)

recovery stage The stage of an illness that follows the acute stage, during which the person begins to feel better. (535)

rectum The last few inches of the large intestine, in which feces are held until they are released from the body. (324)

recycling The use over and over again of materials such as metal and glass. (603)

red blood cells The blood cells that carry oxygen from the lungs to all parts of the body. (373)

reflex An automatic response of the nervous system to the environment. (353)

refusal skills The skills needed to say *no* when others are pressuring a person do to something against his or her will. (460)

rehabilitation The process of learning to cope with the stress of everyday living without using alcohol. (457)

relapse The return of a disease during or soon after convalescence. (536)

relationship A meaningful association between people, such as friends or members of one's family. (98)

reproductive maturity The ability to produce children, signaled by the onset of ovulation in girls and of sperm production in boys. (223)

rescue breathing A method of inflating a person's lungs by blowing air slowly into the individual's mouth or nose or both. (698)

retina The innermost layer of the eye; the light-sensing part of the eye. (427)

reverse tolerance A condition in which less and less alcohol causes intoxication; it occurs during the late stage of alcoholism. (454)

Rh factor A protein found on the surface of some people's red blood cells. (375)

Rh negative Term used to describe blood that does not contain the Rh factor. (211)

Rh positive Term used to describe blood that contains the Rh factor. (211)

rheumatic heart disease Damage to the valves of the heart caused by rheumatic fever. (377)

rheumatoid arthritis Arthritis caused by inflammation of the membrane surrounding a joint. (591)

risk behavior A behavior that increases a person's chance of a harmful outcome. (668)

risk factor Any action or condition that increases the likelihood of injury, disease, or other negative outcome. (7)

rods Light-receiving cells on the retina that enable a person to see black, white, and gray. (427)

root canal The channel in a tooth through which nerves and blood vessels connect with nerves and blood vessels in the jawbone. (316)

rubella A viral disease that causes a rash and can cause birth defects in babies whose mothers have been exposed during the first few months of pregnancy; also known as German measles. (539)

runoff The water that drains from land into streams. (611)

safe behavior A behavior that protects a person from danger and lessens the effects of a harmful situation. (668)

saliva A liquid made by the salivary glands that aids in digestion. (321)

saturated fat A fat that contains as many hydrogen atoms in its structure as is possible chemically. (271)

scabies A condition caused by an infestation of mites in the hair around the genitals. (556)

schizophrenia A serious mental disorder characterized by unpredictable disturbances in thinking, mood, awareness, and behavior. (84)

sclera The outside layer of the eye, commonly called the white of the eye. (426)

scoliosis An abnormal curvature of the spine. (343)

scrotum The external sac of skin in which the testes are located. (173)

sebaceous gland A type of gland found in the dermis that produces oil. (419)

second opinion A diagnosis and advice from a physician other than the one who made the original diagnosis. (634)

second-degree burn A burn that extends through the outer layer of the skin, causing blisters and reddening. (708)

secondary health care Health care given to a patient in a hospital. (629)

secondary sex characteristics Physical changes during puberty that are not directly related to reproduction. (223)

seizure An attack caused by a sudden storm of brain activity, during which the person may lose consciousness, the arms and legs may jerk, and the teeth may lock together. (355)

self-actualization According to Maslow, the process by which each person strives to be all that he or she can be. (31)

self-esteem How much one likes and feels good about oneself; self-respect. (34, 231)

semen A liquid that contains sperm as well as fluids provided by the seminal vesicles, Cowper's glands, and prostate gland. (174)

semicircular canals Three hollow, fluid-filled tubes in the inner ear that help provide a sense of balance. (433)

seminal vesicles In males, a pair of glands located near the bladder that provide 60 percent of the fluid to semen. (174)

sensory neuron A type of neuron that picks up information about a person's internal and external environment and transmits it to interneurons in the brain or spinal cord. (350)

separation An arrangement in which spouses live apart and try to work out their problems. (104)

sewage Waste material carried from toilets and drains. (610)

sex-linked disorder A genetic disorder caused by a gene that is found on a sex chromosome, usually the X chromosome. (189)

sexual abstinence The practice of not having sexual intercourse until a person is ready to commit to a long-term, caring relationship, such as marriage. (550)

sexual abuse A criminal offense in which an adult uses a child or adolescent for sexual purposes. (107)

sexual fidelity The practice by which both partners in a caring, committed relationship, such as marriage, agree to have sexual intercourse only with each other. (550)

sexually transmitted disease Any disease that spreads from one person to another during sexual intercourse. (548)

shock A condition that may accompany any serious injury or illness, in which the heart fails to circulate blood adequately to the vital organs. (704)

siblings Brothers and sisters. (109)

sickle-cell disease A recessive genetic blood disorder characterized by red blood cells with an abnormal sickle shape; it occurs most frequently among people of African descent. (187, 379)

side effect An unwanted or even dangerous physical or mental effect caused by a drug or medicine. (495, 640)

sidestream smoke Smoke that goes directly into the air from burning tobacco. (480)

single-parent family A family in which only one parent lives with the child or children. (100)

sinus One of the hollow spaces above the nose that are lined with mucous membranes. (364)

skeletal muscle Voluntary muscle; muscle attached to the bones of the skeleton. (345)

sleep apnea A disorder in which breathing stops for short periods during sleep and then resumes suddenly. (411)

small intestine The long, tubelike organ in which chemical digestion and the absorption of nutrients take place. (322)

smog A brownish haze that forms when hydrocarbons react with nitric acid in the presence of sunlight. (605)

smokeless tobacco A form of tobacco that is chewed or sniffed. (475)

smooth muscle Involuntary muscle that works automatically to control movements inside the body, such as those involved in breathing and digestion. (345)

snuff Finely ground tobacco that may be either sniffed through the nose or held between the lower lip and teeth. (475)

socialization The process by which children learn from people close to them to behave in a way that is acceptable to the family and to society. (101)

somatic nervous system The part of the peripheral nervous system that is responsible for actions under a person's control. (352)

somatoform disorder A mental disorder in which a person complains of physical symptoms for which no underlying physical cause can be found. (78)

specialty hospital A hospital that specializes in treating one age group or one type of disorder. (629)

sperm The male sex cells, produced in the testes. (172)

spinal cord Part of the central nervous system consisting of nerve tissue that extends from the brain down the back to just below the ribs. (352)

spinal nerves Thirty-one pairs of nerves that branch off from the spinal cord; each pair serves a particular part of the body. (352)

splint Any rigid material used to keep an injured part of the body from moving. (706)

sprain An injury that occurs when ligaments or tendons near a joint are torn or stretched. (343, 706)

stalker A person who repeatedly calls, writes letters to, or otherwise harasses another person and may threaten to kill or injure the person. (686)

stereoscopic vision The process by which the eyes see and the brain interprets two different images; it helps a person see in three dimensions. (428)

stereotype An exaggerated or overgeneralized belief about an entire group of people, such as an ethnic group, religious group, or gender. (130)

sterility The condition in which a person is incapable of producing offspring. (176)

stillbirth The birth of a dead, full-term fetus. (210)

stimulant A drug that speeds up the activities of the central nervous system, the heart, and other organs. (472, 505)

stomach A muscular, saclike organ in the digestive system in which food is stored, churned, mixed, and broken up. (322)

strain An injury caused when a muscle or tendon is overstretched. (707)

stress A reaction of the body and mind to threatening or challenging events in one's life. (50)

stressor Something that causes stress. (50)

stroke A reduction in blood flow to a part of the brain. (378, 578, 700)

sty A condition in which an oil gland at the base of an eyelash becomes infected, resulting in a red, painful swelling. (430)

suffocation The condition that results when a person's supply of air is cut off. (670)

sulfuric acid An acid formed when sulfur oxides in the air mix with water. (605)

superego According to Freud, the part of the personality that judges right and wrong; the conscience. (28)

support group A network of people who help each other cope with a particular problem. (112)

survival floating A lifesaving water safety technique that allows a person to float and breathe without using too much energy. (676)

sympathetic pregnancy A condition in which an expectant father experiences some of the mother's physical discomfort of pregnancy, such as morning sickness or frequent urination. (205)

symptom A feeling caused by a disease. (534)

synapse The space between an axon and the structure with which the neuron communicates. (350)

synergism The interaction of two or more drugs in a way that increases each other's effects. (450)

synergistic interaction An interaction that occurs when drugs that are taken together combine their actions, so that the total effect is greater than either drug would produce alone. (497)

synovial fluid The fluid secreted by membranes around a joint that lubricates the joint and reduces wear on the bones. (340)

syphilis A serious bacterial STD that progresses through several stages. (554)

systemic circulation The route that blood follows from the heart to most of the body and then back to the heart. (371)

systolic pressure The first and higher blood pressure number, representing the force caused by the surge of blood that moves as a result of the contraction of the ventricles. (373)

T cell A type of lymphocyte that kills pathogens or produces substances that regulate the activities of other cells of the immune system. (531)

tar The dark, sticky mixture of chemicals that is formed when tobacco burns. (473)

target heart rate The approximate heart rate a person needs to maintain during aerobic exercise in order to benefit from the workout. (398)

Tay-Sachs disease A recessive genetic disorder characterized by the lack of an important chemical in the brain and resulting in brain damage. (188)

teaching hospital A hospital that provides training for medical students, physicians, and other health-care workers. (629)

temperature inversion The condition that occurs when a layer of cool air near the ground is trapped under a layer of warm air. (607)

tendinitis Painful irritation of a tendon. (347)

tendon A thick strand of connective tissue that attaches muscles to bones. (345, 706)

terminal illness An illness that results in death. (260)

territorial gang A highly organized group of young people whose focus is on protecting the boundaries of their territory, or "turf." (151)

testes (Singular: testis) The two male reproductive glands, located in the scrotum. (172)

testosterone A hormone produced by the testes that affects the production of sperm, the development of male secondary sex characteristics, and the sex drive. (172)

tetanus A bacterial disease that damages the nervous system and can be fatal. (525, 714)

thalamus A small part of the brain that acts as a relay station for the senses, receiving impulses from sense organs and modifying them before they reach the cerebrum. (351)

theory An organized set of ideas used to explain something. (28)

therapeutic community A residential treatment center where drug abusers live and learn to adjust to drug-free lives. (514)

therapy A particular treatment technique. (91)

third-degree burn A burn that damages all the layers of skin and the tissues underneath. (708)

thymus An endocrine gland located in the upper chest, that helps to develop the body's defenses against infection. (171)

thyroid gland An endocrine gland located at the front of the neck, that regulates the rate of metabolism and helps to regulate the amount of calcium in the blood. (171)

tolerance A state in which a person's body becomes resistant to a drug. (450)

torn cartilage Serious damage to the cartilage that covers the ends of bones in a joint. (343)

tornado A rapidly rotating column of air whirling at speeds of up to 500 miles per hour. (672)

toxemia A serious condition during pregnancy characterized by high blood pressure, protein in the urine, and swelling of the body tissues. (210)

toxic shock syndrome A bacterial infection characterized by sudden high fever, rash, vomiting, diarrhea, and dizziness, occurring chiefly among women who use tampons. (182)

toxin A poisonous substance. (524)

trachea The pathway through which air moves from the pharynx into the chest; the windpipe. (364)

tranquilizer A type of depressant that slows nerve activity, relaxes muscle tension, lowers alertness, and causes drowsiness; an anti-anxiety drug. (505)

trauma A painful physical or emotional experience. (83)

trichomoniasis A sexually transmitted protozoan infection of the urinary tract or vagina. (552)

trimester One of three three-month periods into which the nine months of pregnancy are divided. (204)

tuberculosis A bacterial disease that affects the lungs and other parts of the body. (367, 541)

type A personality A behavior pattern characterized by competitiveness and a strong desire to succeed. (60)

type B personality A behavior pattern characterized by calm behavior and noncompetitiveness. (60)

type I diabetes The type of diabetes in which the body produces little or no insulin; also known as insulin-dependent diabetes or juvenile-onset diabetes. (588)

type II diabetes The type of diabetes in which the body produces sufficient insulin but does not respond normally to insulin; also known as noninsulin-dependent diabetes or adult-onset diabetes. (589)

ulcer An open sore, especially one in the lining of the stomach or other part of the digestive tract. (58)

ultrasound High-frequency sound waves used to make an image of a developing fetus. (207)

umbilical cord The cordlike structure that connects the embryo and the placenta. (202)

unconscious thoughts Those thoughts of which a person is not aware. (28)

undescended testes A condition that occurs when one or both of the testes does not descend into the scrotum at birth. (176)

unit price The cost per unit of measurement of a product. (309)

unsaturated fat A fat that contains fewer than the maximum possible number of hydrogen atoms in its structure. (271)

urea The major waste product produced from the breakdown of protein. (329)

uremia A serious disorder in which the body is poisoned by the failure of the kidneys to remove wastes from the bloodstream. (332)

ureter One of two long tubes, each carrying urine from a kidney to the bladder. (330)

urethra The tube that passes from the bladder to the outside of the body, through which urine and, in males, semen, travel. (174, 330)

urine The liquid waste from the kidneys, containing water, urea, and other substances. (330)

uterus A hollow, muscular organ located between the ovaries and behind the urinary bladder, in which a fertilized egg grows and develops. (178)

vaccine A substance that contains small amounts of dead or modified pathogens or their toxins and is used in vaccination. (532)

vagina The passage leading from the cervix to the outside of the body; also known as the birth canal. (179)

vaginitis A vaginal infection or irritation. (181, 552)

validation Reassurance from others that one's feelings, ideas, or decisions are reasonable. (248)

values Standards, beliefs, and ideals that are important to a person and help the person clarify what he or she believes is right or wrong. (16, 231)

vas deferens One of two tubes that carry sperm from the epididymis to the urethra. (174)

vegetarian A person who does not eat meat. (305)

veins Large, thin-walled, slightly elastic vessels that carry blood to the heart. (372)

ventricle One of the two chambers of the heart that pump blood from the heart to the rest of the body. (370)

venules Small blood vessels that join together to form veins. (372)

vertebrae The 33 bones that make up the spinal column. (338)

victim One who is attacked and harmed physically by another. (146)

villi Tiny, fingerlike projections that line the wall of the small intestine and through which nutrients are absorbed into the bloodstream. (323)

violence The use of physical force with the intent to injure or kill. (146)

virus The smallest type of pathogen. (525)

vital statistics The numbers of births and deaths and the numbers and kinds of diseases within a population. (656)

vitamin One of a class of nutrients that are made by living things, are required only in small amounts, and assist many chemical reactions in the body. (273)

warm-up A five- to ten-minute period of mild exercise that prepares the body for vigorous exercise. (399)

wellness A broad concept of health that includes a combination of physical, mental, and social well-being. (4)

white blood cells The blood cells that help protect the body against diseases and foreign substances. (374)

withdrawal A group of symptoms that occur when a dependent person stops taking a drug. (451)

zygote The united egg and sperm. (201)

INDEX

TEXT, continued

pp. 18–19 "DECIDE," adapted from The Stanford DECIDE Drug Education Curriculum, Garfield Company, CA.

p. 51 "Ranking of Stressors by High School Students, Reprinted with permission from *Journal of Psychosomatic Research*, 16 (1972), Pergamon Press Ltd., Oxford, England.

p. 85 from *Vivienne: The Life and Suicide of an Adolescent Girl* by John Mack and Holly Hickler. Copyright © 1981 by David Loomis and Paulette Loomis. By permission of Little, Brown and Company.

p. 122 "Assertive, Passive, and Aggressive Communication," adapted with permission from *Self Discovery*, Gussin & Buxbaum (1984), Management Sciences for Health, Boston.

p. 128 "Making New Friends," adapted with permission from *Self Discovery*, Gussin & Buxbaum (1984), Management Sciences for Health, Boston.

p. 454 "A Problem Drinker's Self-Test," adapted with permission from *A Message to Teenagers*, A.A. World Services, Inc., NY, NY, 1980. *Use of this material does not mean that AA has reviewed or approved the contents of this publication.*

p. 475 "Carbon Monoxide Inhaled per No. of Cigarettes Per Day," adapted with permission from Vogt, Selvin, Widdowson, and Hulley, "Expired air carbon monoxide and serum thiocyanate as objective measure of cigarette exposure," *American Journal of Public Health*, 67: 545–549, June 1977.

p. 649 "Incidence of Measles in the United States," adapted from Maxcy-Rosenau-Last, *Public Health and Preventive Medicine*, John Last and Robert Wallace, editors, 13th edition, with permission of Appleton and Lange, Norwalk, CT, 1992.

p. 650 "Causes of Death in Developed Countries," adapted by permission from Green and Anderson, *Community Health*, 5th edition, St. Louis, The C.V. Mosby Co., 1986.

ILLUSTRATION CREDITS

Boston Graphics: 4, 44, 68, 69, 146, 241, 286, 287, 292, 311, 317T, 317B, 318, 367, 383, 397, 402, 410, 422, 437, 450, 474, 475, 478, 497, 543, 602, 605, 607, 608, 614, 681, 689

Carmella Clifford: 180, 321, 322, 323, 366, 418, 421, 426, 429, 432

Function thru Form: 6, 13, 31, 150, 185, 224, 268, 272, 279, 300, 303, 390, 399, 401, 434, 455, 468, 531, 533, 534, 558, 565, 583, 649, 650, 653, 669, 674

Floyd Hosmer: 349, 353

Keith Kasnot: 169, 202, 203, 206, 209, 320, 329, 330, 365, 372

Fran Milner: 174, 176, 179, 339, 340, 341, 345, 350, 352, 370, 371, 373, 446, 447, 473T, 473B, 495, 529, 530, 575, 578, 590, 702

Susan Spellman: 55, 190, 191, 333, 357, 358, 383, 412, 413, 670, 676, 698, 699, 701, 706, 709, 710, 711, 712, 714, 716, 718, 719

Pearl Weinstein: 636

PHOTO CREDITS

Key to Photo Source Abbreviations The Image Bank=IB; Photo Researchers=PR; PhotoEdit=PE; The Picture Cube=PC; Stock Boston =SB; The Stock Market=SM; Tom Stack & Associates=TSA; Ken Karp=KK; Larry Lawfer=LL; Woodfin Camp & Associates=WC; Tony Stone Worldwide=TSW

Photo Positions Top=T; Bottom=B; Right=R; Middle=M; Left=L

Photo Research Photosearch

Front Cover Scott Foresman

Front Matter iiiL, Bob Daemmrich; iiiM, Courtesy of Kathy Crumpler; iiiR, Stu Rosner; v, Gabe Palmer/SM; vi, Tom McCarthy/Rainbow; vii, Bob Daemmrich/SB; viii, Steven Mays; ix, David Madison; x, Bob Daemmrich; xi, Paul Barton/SM; xii, Richard Pasley/SB.

Chapter One xvi, Michael Keller; 2, David Madison; 3L, Myrleen Ferguson/PE: 3R, Bob Daemmrich/SB; 4L, Tim Davis/PR; 4R, Frank Siteman/SB; 4B, Susan Lapides/WC; 7L, Chris Luneski/PR; 7R, Brian Parker/TSA; 8, Bob Daemmrich/SB; 9L, Robert Winslow/TSA; 9R, Tony Freeman/PE; 10L, Bob Daemmrich/SB; 10R, Benny Tillman/IB; 11, David Madison; 15, KK; 17, Erika Stone; 18, 19, LL; 21, Dan McCoy/Rainbow.

Chapter Two 22, LL; 25L, Alan Marsh/First Light; 25R, Nancy Sheehan; 26, Donald Smetzer/TSW; 27, Lawrence Migdale/SB; 28, Walter Hodges/First Light; 30, Laima Druskis/PR; 32, Miller Francis/Life Magazine © 1963, Time, Inc.; 33, Richard Haynes/RMIP; 34, Richard Hutchings/PE; 35, David Young-Wolff/PE; 37, Suzanne L. Murphy/TSW; 38B, Robert Frerck/Odyssey Productions; 38T, Donna Binder/Impact Visuals; 39, Gabe Palmer/SM; 40, James Whitmer; 43, Leslie Powell; 44, 45, LL; 47, Jessie Parker/First Light.

Chapter Three 48, Index Stock Photography; 50, KK; 52, Bob Daemmrich/SB; 53, David Sams/Daemmrich Associates; 54, Walter Chandoa; 56, Brent Petersen/SM; 57, KK; 59L, Richard Hutchings/PR; 59R, Donald Smetzer/TSW; 60, KK/Ardsley Hardware, Ardsley, NY; 61L, KK; 61R, Renee Lynn/PR; 63, LL; 64L, Roy Morsch/SM; 64R, LL; 66B, Terry Farmer/TSW; 66T, Bob Daemmrich/SB; 68, 69, KK; 71, James Whitmer.

Chapter Four 72, Bob Daemmrich/SB; 74, Frank Siteman/PC; 75L, Harold Sund/IB; 75R, Alan Mercer/SB; 78, Steve Dunwell/IB; 79, Nina Berman/Sipa Press; 80, Gia Barto/IB; 82L, Erik Hill/Anchorage Daily News; 82R, Nancy Sheehan; 83, The Memory Shop; 84, Evelyn Raske; 85, Mike Mazzaschi/SB; 88, KK; 89, Lawrence Migdale; 90L, Mieke Maas/IB; 90M, Andrew Brilliant/Brilliant Palmer; 90R, Mary Kate Denny/PE; 92, Lawrence Migdale; 93, KK; 95, Bob Daemmrich/SB.

Chapter Five 96, Bill Bachmann/PE; 98, Owen Franken/SB; 99L, Mark Sherman/Bruce Coleman; 99R, Lori Adamski-Peek; 100, Lawrence Migdale/SB; 101, Michael Heron; 103, David Rusk; 104, Blair Seitz/PR; 105, Bob Daemmrich; 106, KK; 107, Erika Stone; 108, Bob Daemmrich; 109, David Stoecklein/SM; 110, Erika Stone; 112, Grant Spencer/SB; 113, Bill Bachmann/Southern Stock Photo Agency; 114, 115, LL; 117, Richard Hutchings/PR.

Chapter Six 118, Richard Hutchings/PR; 120L, Sobel/Klonsky/IB; 120R, David M. Grossman/PR; 121, Blair Seitz/PR; 123, Lawrence Migdale/PR; 124, Maria Iacobo/Courtesy of Children's Hospital, Boston; 125, Richard Hutchings/PR; 126L, Melchior DiGiacomo/IB; 126R, Willie Hill, Jr./The Image Works; 127, First Light; 129, Richard Hutchings/PR; 130, Catherine Karnow/WC; 131, Bob Daemmrich/SB; 132, Bob Daemmrich; 133, Paul Barton/SM; 134, Nancy Sheehan; 135, Melanie Carr/Southern Stock Photo Agency; 136, SuperStock; 137, Charles Gupton/SB; 138, Jose Carrillo; 139L, Nancy Sheehan; 139R, KK; 140, 141, KK/Central Park Zoo, NYC; 143, Mark Burnett/PR.

Chapter Seven 144, M. Greenlar/The Image Works; 148, Ray Pfortner/Peter Arnold, Inc.; 150, Yvonne Hemsey/Gamma-Liaison, Inc.; 152, Barbara Burnes/PR; 153, David K. Crow/PE; 154, Paul Brou/Picture Group, Inc.; 155, David Young-Wolff/PE; 156, Bob Daemmrich; 157, 158, KK; 159, Bob Daemmrich; 160, Mitchell Layton/Duomo; 162, 163, KK; 165, Donald Smetzer/TSW.

Chapter Eight 166, Myrleen Ferguson/PE; 168, KK; 171, David Madison; 172, Michael Newman/PE; 175, David Phillips/PR; 177, Bob McKeever/TSA; 181, KK; 182, Frank Siteman/SB; 183, David York/Medichrome; 184, Janet S. Mendes/PC; 186L, Bob Daemmrich/SB; 186R, Owen Franken/SB; 187BL,BR, Bill Longcore/PR; 187TL,TR, Omnikron/Science Source/PR; 188, Simon Fraser/PR; 189, Richard Hutchings/PR; 193, Bill Dobbins/Allsport.

Chapter Nine 194, Anthony A. Boccaccio/IB; 196, Walter Hodges/First Light; 197, Michael Heron; 198, Bob Daemmrich; 200, KK/Baby Boom, Yonkers, NY; 201, David Phillips/Visuals Unlimited; 204, Nestle/PR; 207, KK/The Westchester Birth Center, Yonkers, NY; 208, William Thompson; 211, Herb Snitzer/SB; 212L, Ulrike Welsch/PE; 212R, Mary Kate Denny/PE; 213, Myrleen Ferguson Cate/PE; 214, 215, 217, KK.

Chapter Ten 218, Gale Zucker/SB; 220, KK; 221, Joe Devenney/IB; 222, Bob Daemmrich/SB; 225, KK; 226, Stan Flint/IB; 227, Rhoda Sidney/SB; 228, Mieke Maas/IB; 230, Miro Vintoniv/SB; 231, Robert W. Ginn/PC; 232, Tom McCarthy/Rainbow; 233, 234, KK; 236, Billy E. Barnes/SB; 237, Schmid/Langsfeld/IB; 238, Bob Daemmrich/SB; 239, Michael Heron; 240, 241, KK/Modell's, Yonkers, NY; 243, J. Lotter/TSA.

Chapter Eleven 244, Elyse Lewin/IB; 246, Bryan Yablonsky/Duomo; 248, Owen Franken/SB; 249, B. Bachmann/The Image Works; 250, Ted Cordingley; 251, KK; 252, Don Klumpp/IB; 253, Mark Wise; 254, Alon Reininger/Contact Press Images; 256, Stacy Pick/SB; 257, Spencer Grant/PR; 258, David Young-Wolff/PE; 259, William Thompson; 260, James Whitmer; 262, 263, LL; 265, Richard Hutchings/PR.

Chapter Twelve 266, Jerry Howard/Positive Images; 269-275, Steven Mays; 277T, Roy Morsch/SM; 277B, Steven Mays; 278, Joe McNally/IB; 280T, KK; 280BL, BR, 281T, B, Steven Mays; 282, KK; 283, Steven Mays; 284, Jean-Claude Coutausse/Contact Press Images; 286, 287, KK; 289, David Lissy/PC.

Chapter Thirteen 290, SuperStock; 293, KK; 296, Bob Winsett/TSA; 297, Robert R. Mercer; 298, Craig Hammell/SM; 299, KK; 302, Mark Bray/Unicorn Stock Photos; 304, Susan Lapides/WC; 305L,R, 306, David Dempster/Offshoot Stock; 307, KK/A&P Supermarket, Scarsdale, NY; 308, Steven Mays; 310, KK; 313, David Young-Wolff/PE.

Chapter Fourteen 314, Esbin-Anderson/The Image Works; 319, D.C. Lowe/Medichrome; 322, Ed Reschke/Peter Arnold, Inc.; 324, 325, Steven Mays; 326, KK; 327, Robert Frerck/Odyssey Productions; 328, Tom Wagner; 331T, Roy Morsch/SM; 331B, KK; 332, Courtesy of Candela Laser Corporation; 335, KK.

Chapter Fifteen 336, Dan Helms/Duomo; 338, Bob Daemmrich/The Image Works; 341, Manfred Kage/Peter Arnold, Inc.; 342, Scott Camazine/PR; 343, Mike Valeri/FPG International; 346, KK; 348, Dan McCoy/Rainbow; 351, LL; 354, David Young-Wolff/PE; 355, KK; 356T, Addison Geary/SB; 356M, Dennis Stock/Magnum Photos; 356B, Bob Daemmrich; 357, Jean Marc Barey/PR; 361, Brian Parker/TSA.

Chapter Sixteen 362, Rudi von Briel/PE; 364, Bob Daemmrich/SB; 368, Philip Wallick/SM; 369, Gary Milburn/TSA; 373, Bob Daemmrich; 374, Dr. Dennis Kunkel/Phototake; 375, Nicholas Thomas/Medical Images, Inc.; 376L, Ed Reschke/Peter Arnold, Inc.; 376R, Martin M. Rotker/PR; 377, Tony Freeman/PE; 378, Steve Hansen/SB; 380, Bob Daemmrich/SB; 382, Bob Daemmrich; 385, Bob Daemmrich/SB.

Chapter Seventeen 386, William Johnson/SB; 388, KK; 389, 393, David Madison; 394, Larry Mulvehill/The Image Works; 395, Tom Wagner; 396, LL; 397, Mark Burnett/SB; 398, David Stoecklein/SM; 400L,R, KK; 403L, Melchior DiGiacomo/IB; 403R, Tony Freeman/PE; 405L, Griffin/The Image Works; 405R, Alon Reininger/Contact Press Images; 406, Craig Hammell/SM; 408L, Peter Menzel/SB; 408R, Lou Jones; 409, Miguel/IB; 410, Ted Cordingley; 412, 413, Bob Daemmrich; 415, KK.

Chapter Eighteen 416, Ariel Skelley/SM; 419, George E. Jones, III/PR; 421, David Madison; 422, Bob Daemmrich; 423, David Young-Wolff/PE; 424T, Roy Morsch/SM; 425, Bob Daemmrich; 427L,R, L.V. Bergman & Associates; 428, Bob Daemmrich; 429T,B, Runk/Schoenberger/Grant Heilman; 430, Robert Semeniuk/SM; 431, Goodman/Van Riper Photography; 433, Eli Reed/Magnum Photos; 436, KK; 437, Richard Hutchings/PR; Lawrence Migdale/SB.

Chapter Nineteen 440, George DiSario/SM; 442, Pluriel/Super Stock; 443T, Catherine Karnow/WC; 443B, Ted Cordingley; 444, David Austen/SB; 445, KK; 449, KK; 451, A. Glauberman/PR; 452, Dan McCoy/Rainbow; 453, Vicky Kasala/IB; 456, KK; 457, KK/Julia Dyckman Andrus Memorial, Yonkers, NY; 458, KK; 459, Elaine Harrington/SM; 462, 463, LL; 465, Ted Cordingley.

Chapter Twenty 466, Bob Daemmrich/SB; 469, Courtesy of American Cancer Society; 470, LL; 471, Photofest; 473, CNRI/Science Photo Library/PR; 476, KK; 477T, Bob Daemmrich; 477BL, H.C. Overton/Phototake; 477BM, Javier Domingo/Phototake; 477BR, Dianora Niccolini/Medical Images, Inc.; 479T, Courtesy of American Cancer Society; 479B, Mike Yamashita/WC; 480, Custom Medical Stock Photo; 482, S. Kammerer; 485, Susan Van Etten/PC; 486, Michael Tamborrino/Medichrome; 487, Tom Sobolik/Black Star; 488, Art by Melissa Antonow, reprinted from *Kids Say Don't Smoke* by permission of Workman Publishing © 1991; 489, Courtesy of Caheim Drake 4th Grade, Smokefree Educational Services, Inc.; 491, Ted Cordingley.

Chapter Twenty-One 492, LL; 494, KK; 496, Larry Mulvehill/PR; 497, KK; 498T, Vivian Moos/Sipa Press; 498B, Erika Stone/PR; 500, Choice Photos/IB; 501, First Light; 503, William Strode; 504, G.L. Cryslin/IB; 505, Charles Marden Fitch/Taurus Photos; 506T, Dr. Morley Read/PR; 506B, Sudhir Daea/Picture Group, Inc.; 507, Walter H. Hodge/Peter Arnold, Inc.; 510, Schleikorn/Custom Medical Stock Photo; 511, Jeff Jacobson/Archive; 512, Courtesy of Psychemedic Corporation; 514T, Mieke Maas/IB; 517L,R, Bob Daemmrich; 518, 519, LL; 521, Bob Daemmrich.

Chapter Twenty-Two 522, LL; 524L,M,R, CNRI/Science Photo Library/PR; 525T, K.G. Murti/Visuals Unlimited; 525B, CNRI/Science Photo Library/PR; 526, Bob Daemmrich/SB; 527, CBC/Phototake; 527 inset, Larry Mulvehill/The Image Works; 528, CNRI/Science Photo Library/PR; 536, KK; 537, Stacy Pick/SB; 538, William Thompson; 539, Owen Franken/SB; 541, KK; 542, KK/Greenleaf Pharmacy, Hastings-on-Hudson, NY; 545, KK.

Chapter Twenty-Three 546, Paul Conklin/PE; 548, Bob Daemmrich/SB; 550, Jon Feingersh/SB; 552T, CNRI/Science Photo Library/PR; 552B, David M. Phillips/Visuals Unlimited; 553T, Biomedical Communications/PR; 553M, Moredun Animal Health Ltd./PR; 553B, Institut Pasteur/CNRI/Phototake; 554T, CDC/Science Source/PR; 554B, NIAID/NIH/Peter Arnold, Inc.; 555L, Custom Medical Stock Photo; 555R, Courtesy of Center for Prevention Services; 556, Science Photo Library/PR; 557, KK; 560T, Custom Medical Stock Photo; 560B, Lennart Nilsson/© Boehringer Ingelheim International GmbH; 562, Mike Okonewski/The Image Works; 563, Alexander Tsiaras/SB; 564, Robert Barrett/Barrett Photography; 566, KK; 567, Tom McKitterick/Impact Visuals; 568, Ed Hubbard/Gamma-Liaison, Inc.; 569, KK; 571, Bob Daemmrich.

Chapter Twenty-Four 572, Richard Hutchings/PE; 574, David Madison; 575, Tony Freeman/PE; 577, KK; 579L,R, Mary Ann Fittipaldi; 580, Science Photo Library/PR; 582, Phil Savoie/PC; 585, KK/Scarsdale Medical Group, Scarsdale, NY; 586, Yoav Levy/Phototake; 588, David Madison; 589T, KK; 589B, Biohybrid Technologies Inc.; 592, Adam Scull/Globe Photos; 594, Stephen Frisch/SB; 596, 597T, SuperStock; 597B, Russ Lappa; 599, Bob Daemmrich/The Image Works.

Chapter Twenty-Five 600, Tom & Pat Leeson/PR; 604, Stephanie Maze/WC; 605, Judy Canty/SB; 606, First Light; 610, David Dempster/Offshoot Stock; 611, Frank Fournier/WC; 612, Ken W. Davis/TSA; 613, Greg Schlack; 614, Bob Daemmrich; 615, Holt Confer/The Image Works; 616, Bob Daemmrich; 617, Steven Gottlieb/FPG International; 618L, David Conklin/PC; 618ML, J.D. Sloan/PC; 618MR, John Coletti/PC; 618R, Greg Vaughn/TSA; 619, Martin Bond/PR; 620, 621, LL; 623, Bob Daemmrich.

Chapter Twenty-Six 624, Bob Daemmrich/SB; 626, Richard Pasley/SB; 627, Jebb Dunn/SB; 628, Hank Morgan/Rainbow; 629, Tony Freeman/PE; 631, KK; 632, KK/Dr. Stephen P. Kelly, Dobbs Ferry, NY; 633, KK; 635, Jim Pickerell/SB; 640T, KK/Genovese Store #16, Ardley, NY; 640B, North Wind Picture Archives; 642, 645, KK.

Chapter Twenty-Seven 646, Harvey Finkle/Impact Visuals; 648, R.B. Sanchez/SM; 649, Bettmann Archive; 651, Blair Seitz/PR; 652, Stacy Pick/SB; 654T, Bob Daemmrich/The Image Works; 654B, Michael Heron; 655, Russ Lappa; 657, Robert Graves; 658, Bob Daemmrich/The Image Works; 660, Carolyn Watson/Peace Corps; 661, Wesley Boxce/PR; 662, 663, LL; 665, Bob Daemmrich.

Chapter Twenty-Eight 666, 668, KK; 672, A&J Verkaik/SM; 675, Frank Siteman/Rainbow; 677, Mike Greenlar/The Image Works; 678T, Roy Morsch/SM; 678B, Dorothy Littell/SB; 679, 683, 684, 686, KK; 687, Leslye Borden/PE; 688, 689, KK; 691, Ted Cordingley.

Chapter Twenty-Nine 692, Herman Kokojan/Black Star; 694, Bob Daemmrich/The Image Works; 695, Spencer Grant/PR; 696, Catherine Ursillo/PR; 700, W.B. Spunbarg/PE; 703, Ted Cordingley; 704T, Gil Fahey/PC; 704M, Spencer Grant; 704B, Perry D. Slocum/Earth Scenes; 705, D. Davidson/TSA; 708, Sinclair Stammers/PR; 713L, ML, Z. Leszczynski/Animals Animals; 713MR, Joe McDonald/Animals Animals; 713R, Z. Leszczynski/Animals Animals; 715, Robert Frerck/Odyssey Productions; 716, Paul Mozell/SB; 717, Bob Daemmrich/SB; 718, 719, KK; 721, Frank Siteman/PC.